THE CREATIVE GIFT, DÜRER, DADA AND DESOLATION ROW

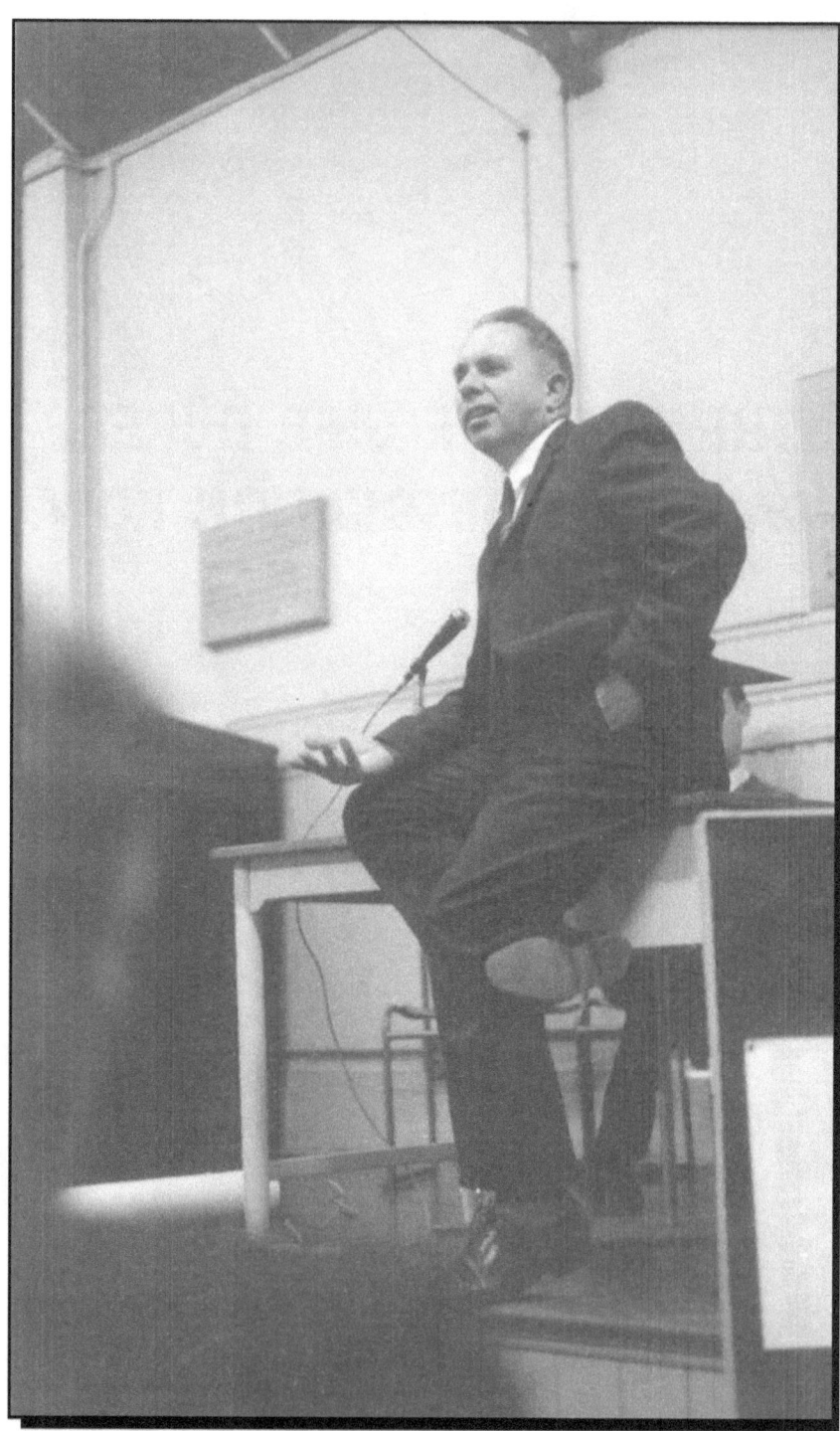

Photograph by Sylvester Jacobs

THE CREATIVE GIFT, DÜRER, DADA AND DESOLATION ROW

The Complete Works of Hans R. Rookmaaker

Volume 3

Edited by
Marleen Hengelaar-Rookmaaker

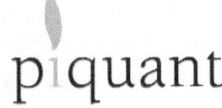

Copyright © 2002 by Marleen Hengelaar-Rookmaaker

This edition copyright © 2021 by Piquant Editions in the UK

Piquant Editions
Website: www.piquanteditions.com

First edition 2002
Paperback edition 2021

ISBN for this volume: 978-1-909281-82-0

The right of Marleen Hengelaar-Rookmaaker to be identified as author of this work has been asserted by her in accordance with the Copyright, Designs and Patents Act, 1988.

All Rights Reserved. No part of this publication may be reproduced, stored in a retrieval system or transmitted, in any form or by any means, electronic, mechanical, photocopying, recording or otherwise, without the prior written permission of the publisher or the Copyright Licensing Agency.

Kunst en Amusement ©1962 by H.R. Rookmaaker (Kampen: J.H.Kok, 1962); copyright © 2000 by Marleen Hengelaar-Rookmaaker (translated into English for this edition by Herbert Donald Morton)
The Creative Gift: The Arts and the Christian Life, copyright © 1981 by Anky Rookmaaker (Leicester: Inter-Varsity Press, 1981 / Westchester, Il: Cornerstone Books, 1981); copyright © 2000 by Marleen Hengelaar-Rookmaaker
Articles on history, faith and culture, lifestyle, and scholarship, and the Westminster discussions: copyright © by H.R. Rookmaaker; copyright © 2000 by Marleen Hengelaar-Rookmaaker
Unless otherwise stated or the author's own paraphrase is used, Scripture quotations are from the HOLY BIBLE, NEW INTERNATIONAL VERSION ® NIV®, copyright © 1973, 1978, 1984 by the International Bible Society.
All rights reserved.

British Library Cataloguing-in-Publication Data
A catalogue record of this book is available in the UK from the British Library.

ISBN 978-1-909281-82-0

Cover art: Marc de Klijn, detail from
Monuments in the (pre)history of modern art (2000)
Cover design: Jonathan Kearney

Piquant Editions actively supports theological dialogue and an author's right to publish but does not necessarily endorse the individual views and opinions set forth here or in works referenced within this publication, nor guarantee technical and grammatical correctness. The publishers do not accept any responsibility or liability to persons or property as a consequence of the reading, use or interpretation of its published content.

Overview Contents for the Six Volumes of the Complete Works of Hans Rookmaaker

The contents of volumes 1 to 6 have been organized partly chronologically and partly thematically. Most of the writings compiled in volumes 1 and 2 date from before 1960, while most of the materials brought together in volumes 3 to 6 were written after 1960. Each of the volumes contains one or more books as well as articles. Two books, previously published in Dutch only, appear in English for the first time: *Jazz, Blues and Spirituals* (1960) and *Art and Entertainment* (1962). In addition, roughly a thousand pages of Dutch articles have been translated into English: exhibition and music reviews; many short articles on art, music, and Christianity and culture written for Christian periodicals; articles that are scholarly and art-historical; and articles that are long and philosophical like the ones for *Philosophia Reformata*. Also included are the lectures given at l'Abri and Westminster Seminary. The two series of lectures, on 'God's Hand in History' and 'Revelation', have been integrated by Colin Duriez into one unit entitled 'God's Hand in History'.

Volume 1: ART, ARTISTS AND GAUGUIN

- Foreword by Jeremy Begbie
- Scholarly introduction by Graham Birtwistle
- Gauguin and Nineteenth-Century Art Theory (*Synthetist Art Theories*)
- Rookmaaker as art critic (1949–1956): exhibition reviews

Volume 2: NEW ORLEANS JAZZ, MAHALIA JACKSON AND THE PHILOSOPHY OF ART

- Philosophy and aesthetics: articles on style, world view, philosophy of art and education
- *Jazz, Blues and Spirituals*
- Music articles: African-American music, blues, spirituals and gospel, jazz, rock, and classical music

Volume 3: THE CREATIVE GIFT, DÜRER, DADA AND DESOLATION ROW

- *Art and Entertainment*
- *The Creative Gift*
- Articles on history, faith and culture, faith and lifestyle, faith and scholarship, and the Westminster discussions on faith, art, culture and lifestyle

Volume 4: WESTERN ART AND THE MEANDERINGS OF A CULTURE

- Articles on Western art from the Middle Ages until the nineteenth century: themes and motifs, general reflections on art, plus an unfinished manuscript
- *Art Needs No Justification*
- The Christian and art: articles and letters
- Miscellaneous articles and exhibition reviews

Volume 5: MODERN ART AND THE DEATH OF A CULTURE

- *Modern Art and the Death of a Culture*
- *Art and the Public Today*
- Articles on twentieth-century artists and streams, modern art, and the question: Do we need to be modern in order to be contemporary?
- Reviews of books on modern art and reviews of expositions of twentieth-century sculpture

Volume 6: OUR CALLING AND GOD'S HAND IN HISTORY

- Biography of Hans Rookmaaker by Laurel Gasque
- Interviews
- 'God's Hand in History' and the l'Abri lectures
- Indexes to all six volumes of the *Complete Works*

Contents of Volume 3

List of Plates   x
Acknowledgments   xi

Part I: Art and Entertainment

Acknowledgments to the Original Edition   3
1 Crisis and the Bible   5
   Crisis in the orthodox Christian world (7); Crisis in contemporary culture (10); Apocalypse (14); The Bible today (15)
2 The Meaning of Art and Entertainment in Human Life   19
   Entertainment (19); Norms in the choice of our entertainment (21) What does our own level depend on? (24) Entertainment? (26); Our wisdom in the discussion with and about art (28); The importance of art for life (29); Works of art in relation to reality (32); A landscape by Jan van Goyen (38); Jan Steen's St Nicholas morning (41)
3 Art and our Life and World View   43
   Art, the spirit of the times and the artist's attitude to life (51); Lifestyle and art (56); Sense of reality and art (58); What does the development in art since the seventeenth century teach us? (60)
4 Norms for Art and Entertainment   75
   Whatever is true ... (78); Whatever is noble ... (87); Whatever is right ... (91); Whatever is pure ... (92); Whatever is lovely ... (100); If there is any virtue and if there is anything praiseworthy ... (104)
5 Norms in our Association with Art   105
   How shall we judge concretely? (105); No prescriptions are given (107); The lesson of Colossians 2 (111); Our life in freedom (114); There is much to enjoy (119); Why we must involve ourselves with art and entertainment (122); Sojourners (123); Our freedom and our effort (124); Conclusion (128)

Part II: The Creative Gift

Introduction to the First Edition: The Centre of History   135
Part One: Being a Christian in a Broken World
1 Our Calling in God's Creation   139

God's hand in history (139); Human work in history (140); Freedom and authority (148); The easy-chair mentality (150); The Christian's task (153)

2 Our Calling in Culture   155

Christianity and culture – a false dichotomy (155); Defining 'culture' (156); The Christian's participation in culture (158)

Part Two: Freedom within a Framework

3 Creativity in Love and Freedom   167

Christ the Creator – made in his image (167); Christ the Redeemer – his restored purpose (170); True humanness in Christ (175)

4 Authority and Permissiveness   181

What has happened to authority? (181); Who solves the problems in a normless society (183); The age of permissiveness (185); The Christian minority (188)

5 Art and Freedom – Buñuel and the Bible   190

A message of absurdity (190); Freedom and art (195)

6. Does Art Need Justification?   204

A new secular religion? (204); A hedonistic pastime? (206); A gift of God? (207)

Appendix: Letter to a Christian Artist   209

Part Three: Creative Sharing of the Gospel

7 Communicating the Gospel to Modern People   215

Our point of contact (215); Some basic questions (223); Principles of personal evangelism (228); The danger of Christian utilitarianism (234); What is an evangelist? (234)

8 Dürer's Apocalypse: An Artist's Message to his Contemporaries   237

Part III: Articles on History, Faith and Culture, Lifestyle, and Scholarship, and the Westminster Discussions

The Constituent Factors of a Historical Deed   247

1 World order (257); 2 The situation (270); 3 The personality (285); 4 World view (292); Epilogue (305) Summary: the constituent factors of a historical deed (308)

Faith and Culture   314

On being salt that salts (314); Faith and culture (319); Christianity and culture: a reply (335); Affluence, the welfare state and culture (337); Some comments on the culture state (360); Youth in revolt, youth in trouble: who's to blame? (368)

Faith and Lifestyle   375
> Art and lifestyle (375); Art and entertainment on radio and television (385); On Art and Entertainment: a response letter (403)

The Westminster Discussions: Faith, Art, Culture and Lifestyle   407
> What is art (407); Learning to see (411); Judging works of art (414); Certainty (415); Can we use modern and abstract forms? (423); Christian art (427); On portraying God and Christ (430); Art and mission (433); Christianity and culture (435); Nudity (444); Television and film (455)

Faith and Scholarship   460
> Gird your minds for action and keep sober in the Spirit (460); Book review: Kalsbeek, Faith and Science (476); The method of art history (479); Depth and breadth of art history (481); Art history at the Free University of Amsterdam (491); Interview by art history students from the Free University (496)

Notes to Volume 3   503

List of Plates

Plate 1
Jan van Goyen, *Approaching storm* (1646). Location unknown.

Plate 2
Jan Steen, *St Nicholas morning* (c. 1670). Rijksmuseum, Amsterdam.

Plate 3
Baptism of Christ. Miniature from *Sacramentaire de Limoges* (c. 1100).

Plate 4
Piero della Francesca, *The Baptism of Christ* (c. 1450). National Gallery, London.

Plate 5
Peter Paul Rubens, *The abduction of the daughters of Leucippus by Castor and Pollux* (1618). Alte Pinakothek, Munich.

Plate 6
Rembrandt van Rijn, *Bathsheba at her bath* (1654). Louvre, Paris.

Plate 7
Francisco de Goya y Lucientes, *Battle of second of May, 1808* (1814). Museo del Prado, Madrid.

Plate 8
A.J.Veldhoen, *Fighter pilot* (1958). Private collection.

Acknowledgments

Alida L. Sewell and Edith M. Reitsema each translated one article in this volume, respectively 'The Constituent Factors of a Historical Deed' and the review of a book by Kalsbeek. Herbert Donald Morton translated the rest. I thank them for their work.

I also want to thank Robb Ludwick and Joël Valk for their willingness to transcribe the Westminster tapes which appear in Part III.

Marleen Hengelaar-Rookmaaker
The Netherlands

Part I

ART AND ENTERTAINMENT

Acknowledgments to the Original Edition[1]

Through the years many people have contributed in various ways to the development of the ideas set forth in this book. It would be impossible to mention them all. An attempt to do so would leave me feeling dissatisfied because, without a doubt, I will forget one or several people. My wife, who assisted me from beginning to end by reading critically, typing, correcting and more, I certainly owe many thanks.

I also would not like to leave unmentioned the small number of friends who contributed very directly to the final result. M. Siesling read the manuscript very critically and suggested many improvements, especially in linguistic matters. His remarks have all been incorporated in the text. C. Priester read the manuscript as it came off the typewriter and with perceptive questions and remarks she elicited many clarifications and revisions. I am very thankful to them both for their self-sacrificial and enthusiastic cooperation.

Finally I want to thank the publisher for his initiative as well as for his willing cooperation in all sorts of matters of detail.

I hope that this work may contribute to that spiritual renewal for which we all pray fervently.

H.R. Rookmaaker

1
Crisis and the Bible

The sixteenth century was the century of Savonarola, Luther, Calvin, Münzer and Ignatius of Loyola, a century in which the breakthrough towards a more worldly culture, begun in the fifteenth century with the Renaissance, was arrested. For those who thought along humanistic lines it was a difficult time, spiritually. Bearing witness to the crisis is also Marlowe's stage version of the story of Dr Faust, a masterpiece in which we see the struggle of an unbeliever: he will not and cannot love the Lord, but desires to be a person who holds sway over the cosmos in full freedom; at the same time he believes in the truths of the Christian religion. It is in that light that one should read the awesome ending, in which Faust just before his death still considers appealing to the blood of Christ but cannot quite bring himself to do it!

Three and a half centuries have passed since then. Humanism has created a world view for itself in the work of Descartes, Leibniz, Hume, the Encyclopedists,[2] Kant, Freud and ever so many others. In the French Revolution the tension between the world picture of the Enlightenment and a reality that failed to measure up to it was released in a lightning bolt of violence; the thunder that followed, however, the resonance of the unchristian ideas – so clearly identified by Groen van Prinsterer in his *Unbelief and Revolution* – continues to resonate even today. The storm has not yet subsided.

Yet for the present Christian generation the roles have been reversed. If it was difficult for sixteenth-century humanists to form a world picture consistent with their own starting point, it has now also become difficult for Christians to think in a truly Christian way. 'Science' and the urge to construct the world according to human measures have a grip on Christians as well, and they find it difficult to doubt the 'truths' and 'discoveries' of science, which for unbelievers have taken the place of God's revelation.

Christians might thereby have become all the more aware of their being strangers in the midst of this earthly race. Instead they are often so powerfully gripped by the 'truths', by the culture, that they have to ask themselves whether Christianity can really still be creatively operative. So powerful is this grip of the spirit of the times that a Christian may seem to be a person with two faces, with two minds: he or she confesses the truths of the Scriptures and wants to see in Christ alone the way, the truth and the life, but by the same token he or she lacks the courage to label as a lie or even call into doubt the way and the truth proclaimed by the world. This is the basis of the crisis that holds sway today in the orthodox Christian milieu.

Calvinism and art. A strange combination? It may be true that Calvin and his entourage were not at all hostile to art – Doumergue and Wencelius are not the only ones who have touched up our image of Calvin in this regard[3] – yet it is also true that Calvinism has stood strongly aloof from artistic life, at least since the middle of the seventeenth century. It has either in a puritan manner neglected almost entirely every creative activity in this field or, more strongly, disqualified art and entertainment altogether. Moreover, little has been written about art in Calvinistic circles. And not only that, there has seldom been any effort to provide a reasonable answer to the questions that arise in our association with works of art or with what is offered us by way of entertainment. I do not mean to overlook what Kuyper and later commentators have had to say about these matters, but for all that, what has been achieved has been limited almost entirely to discussions of literature – and even there the harvest has been slim – or to a formulation of wishes and possibilities to be realized, perhaps, in the future.

But the time to afford the 'luxury' of such a state of affairs is past. In every conceivable manner, particularly through the many, many means of modern communication, 'common people', who today have both money and time, are now confronted with the arts. Where even the rudiments of a proper approach in the spirit of our own [Calvinistic] view of life are missing, is it any wonder that many have been left with perplexing questions? Do not trivialize the problem! The questions are often of vital importance. They show clearly, moreover, that the crisis reaches deep even into Calvinistic, orthodox Christian circles.

This situation, this problem, or to put it more gravely, this crisis, is something at which we must dare to take an honest look. So much so that we may seek a way out and, as we hope and pray, may indeed discover one. Standing on the foundations of Calvinism and recognizing our heritage, we shall have to walk on in this world although we are not of this world. The Scriptures are a lamp to our feet and a light for our path [Psalm 119:105], but in order to proceed safely we shall have to use that light and keep a sharp eye on the path, the culture in which we live. We shall have to test not only the world but also ourselves: it is only as people who know themselves to have been purchased by their Saviour and Lord, and who therefore must wait upon him for all things, that we can learn to walk the path as God would have us walk it. It will be clear that 'we' here alludes to those who call themselves Calvinists (those who have the Synod of Dordt as part of their heritage). Among them may be some who are faithful and some who are 'weak' believers and some who are just connected by tradition, the 'active' and the indifferent, yet in the pure sense 'Reformed' or 'orthodox' refers to that form of Christianity which is faithful to the Bible and, therefore, is reformational.

Crisis in the orthodox Christian world

The word 'crisis', figuratively speaking and literally, describes something broad in scope and grave in content. Its use here certainly seems justifiable to me. It indicates the state of uncertainty in which many from Calvinistic homes find themselves about the path they are on and the path they should take in life, given their sense that the old values have lost their meaning in today's world. They are sceptical about the Christian nature of all sorts of so-called Christian activities that are based on principles which they now doubt are as biblical as an earlier generation believed or experienced them to be. They see the work of their hands destroyed and ask themselves what it may still mean in this present age to believe and trust in God.

Organized 'Christian endeavours', such as the ones that emerged in particular during the second half of the nineteenth century in orthodox Calvinistic circles, were certainly originally motivated by a love for God and one's neighbour, and a living faith was at work in many activities. But gradually faith vanished, quite literally, as biblical belief became more of an implied presupposition. For many these endeavours and the organizations connected with them became purely human affairs. People believed they had to do things themselves. They lost sight of the fact that a Christian will never be able to do Christian work without God's help. Prayer and waiting for the guidance and blessing of the Lord were increasingly relegated to the background in the spiritual mindset of a great host of orthodox Christians.

This decline was certainly keenly sensed by a small minority who pressed for a return, not to the Scriptures, however, but to the former principles. They lauded strongly the attainments of tradition and pleaded for a new love for the old cause. The unintentional result was often that Christian zeal acquired a legalistic emphasis, a mandatory character in the pursuit of human goals. To be sure, every Christian activity that is not directly bound by trust in and dependence upon the living God will end up in this way.

Eventually, as a result of this development, many young people in our day were plunged into crisis and came to feel that they no longer knew the way. They know their 'confession' and certainly want to live in God's way according to the Scriptures, but they no longer see how they can do so concretely. What is the connection, they ask themselves, between these traditional, widely praised Christian activities and organizations and personal belief in God? They are willing to accept that such belief was once the driving force, but they can hardly feel it for themselves. They can see that many Christian organizations are declining in strength and Christian character, and many are truly saddened by this. But how can there be a renewal? What can they themselves contribute? That is what they cannot see.

Thus our young people are confronted with great questions. How can they be constructively active in a biblical, Christian sense? What does it mean, concretely, to live 'in the salvation of Jesus Christ'? And to whom shall they turn for counsel and leadership? All too often young people find that leaders are extremely zealous in typically legalistic debates about Calvinistic principles and orthodox truths but that upon closer acquaintance, gained through deeper discussion, these leaders sometimes exhibit a startling lack of genuine Christian belief – although there are some notable exceptions as well. But our young people have to ask: What are our leaders really fighting for? For their own group or organization? For power or influence? Does the God of the Bible, the Father of our Lord Jesus Christ, really still have anything to do with all this? What has become of piety and belief?

No one has a right to throw the first stone here. We must begin by accepting tradition as a part of reality, and especially not disregard its goodness, as young people are prone to do in reaction. In the Netherlands, by the grace of God, much has been gained through Christian, Calvinistic scholarship and insight. We must endeavour to preserve what is good, and yes, even to extend it. But we must also have the courage to acknowledge the situation that I have sketched above and to ask ourselves how we can again become the beneficiaries of a lifestyle directly attuned to the Bible.

For it is precisely a personal Christian style of living of one's own, based on the Bible and looking to the living God, that is most eagerly sought. At the same time this is exactly where the shortcomings of tradition most clearly take their toll. Orthodox scholarship has been devoted too exclusively to theology and the study of political, social and economic principles. For as scarce as the voices were of those who called for a return to the Bible in order to build upon it – I am thinking here for example of the work of Revd de Graaf and of the sadly less well known A. Janse – so difficult it was for them to gain a wide hearing. That is how it came about that people stood strong as orthodox Christians in matters of theory and principle but less strong in matters of everyday life.

The crisis in the world of the Reformed community arose primarily as a result of the impotence of people to appropriate their knowledge of faith, built up through preaching and catechization, directly and personally as it were, instead of via theoretical elaboration and abstraction, and in this way to come to a living faith that would empower them to find direct solutions in their everyday lives.

Just how much has lain fallow in this regard becomes evident when one sets out to explore the Christian reading materials and literature of the last half century [the early twentieth century], especially those materials that have come to enjoy a certain esteem as the most representative. Sifting through the writings of this time one finds little, precious little for a community numbering in the hundreds of thousands, about the importance of prayer, the work of the Holy Spirit, and the need to walk with a personal trust in the living God as the foundation of daily Christian living.

It is therefore understandable that our young people, who long for the answer to the question 'What does it mean to "walk with God" in this time with its new problems?' have the feeling that they have been abandoned, left to their own devices, not so much with respect to theory but in matters of everyday life. The little that might help them is often hedged around by negative judgments or fails to reach them altogether through lack of familiarity.

I wrote 'new problems' above, and as most important of these I regard the questions asked by today's young people concerning our approach to art and entertainment. These questions were left almost entirely unaddressed by earlier generations, partly because they seemed less urgent at the time, forced into the background by more urgent social and economic concerns, but also partly because such questions were considered inappropriate, in the Anabaptist vein of 'do not touch it, taste it, or meddle with it.'

Because the crisis briefly analysed above presents itself in concentrated form in this area of arts and entertainment, and because one cannot answer the questions posed without first having found a road to a genuinely Christian lifestyle, I shall have to deal with some rather general matters in this book. Perhaps the absence of a tradition in the reflection on art and entertainment will make it easier to trace a new path here.

However, because I cannot follow a tradition or a shared opinion, my views must by necessity also be strictly personal. That is why I have not entitled this book something like 'The Christian and art' or 'Biblical norms for our approach to art and entertainment', while adopting or opposing some established method. A fuller title might appropriately have been 'A Christian's approach to art and entertainment', but our times demand brevity. The questions concerning our dealings with art and entertainment may justifiably be called urgent, because it is precisely in this area that we make very direct and essential contact with the contemporary world.

A special reason for writing about art (the connection with entertainment will follow gradually and quite naturally) is that the struggle of the spirits is concentrated in this area. The field of politics has been amply outlined in keeping with familiar codes and has become a matter of agreed techniques; there is only a faint suggestion of this battle of the spirits there. It undoubtedly takes place in economics and the natural sciences, but there too the battle lines are often not so clear and no decisive ground is gained one way or the other. Where philosophy is concerned, the struggle of the spirits is studied by a small group and the battle waged by an even smaller one, except in connection with art. So, to mention just one example, the philosopher Sartre wrote many stories and plays in order to elucidate his philosophical ideas.

Precisely because art is still in many respects free – a field as it were in which virtually anything is possible, where little account has to be taken of mass opinion, statistics, regulations and traditions – it is in and through art that the struggle of the spirits is the most conspicuous and the most bitter. Less than a hundred years ago a discussion of art provided a pleasant and erudite way of passing the time because art was something separated from ordinary life, as pleasure was separated from the serious matters of the day. Nowadays a discussion of art quickly becomes a heated debate that touches upon the deepest questions of life. Art seems to have taken over the place of revelation and religion. Art expresses one or another life or world view and evokes strong assertions about these by those who hold them. Thus art can no longer be discussed without serious commitment.

Crisis in contemporary culture

It must be asked whether the crisis in orthodox Christian circles concerning a Christian way of life is connected with the much vaunted crisis in Western civilization. Have we ended up in crisis because the world in which we live has been seeking new approaches and putting its old values at risk for the sake of new principles, which are often irrationalistic and relativistic? The world view of our culture is often ours as well. We are not isolated from the times in which we live. We live 'in the world', but in what degree are we also 'of the world', 'of' this great Western world that is in such confusion today, whose children no longer know how to judge and have no answers for so many questions?

We should realize clearly that it ought to be easier for Christians to distinguish themselves as being different, strangers and sojourners, during times when the culture of the world around them is in spiritual crisis and prone to unwholesome expressions than during times when they do not have to be disturbed by the ruling culture of the time as it crosses their path. And we should always remember that unbelievers are often equally disturbed by developments. Yet believers have a firm foundation in knowing themselves to be children of the living God – why then should they not act creatively and prophetically to help? Or have we become too closely identified with the humanistic Western culture in which we live?

In order to arrive at answers to such questions we shall have to provide a much more incisive account of what the crisis in Western culture really means. I want to begin by examining a modern work of art with you, a woodcut by Escher.

In 1947 M.C. Escher made his *Other world*. With this and other works he experienced great success, and rightly so considering his brilliant, well-considered and elaborate compositions. Later his fame was overshadowed by the new art of the 1950s, the international style which is probably best typified by the term 'Abstract Expressionism'.

What is it, then, that Escher expresses? Why did his work speak so directly to people shortly after the War? If we look at the print we see a kind of portal that offers a view of a landscape, somewhat like a moonscape, cold and uninviting. Beyond it we see infinite space stretching away. In the arch of the portal sits a bird-like creature with a human-like head. Upon looking more closely we notice that precisely the same scene appears twice more, once viewed from above and once from below.

What motifs does the artist employ here? The first is that of the landscape or vista we just described. It is a motif we encountered already, albeit less tellingly, in such Romantic painters as Caspar David Friedrich (c.1800). Such a theme is relevant and meaningful for both the artist and the modern viewer because it expresses what one experiences in the world, the reality one knows: it is alien and un-heim-isch, a world in which the modern person does not feel at home. The unending space above the vast plain contributes to this suggestion for, far from affording them the experience of freedom, such emptiness seems instead to oppress modern viewers, since they know themselves to be lost in it.

Next we notice the strange, bird-like creature with human characteristics. It is remarkable that we often come across birds in modern art. If one might venture to say that nineteenth-century Holland could be typified by Henriëtte Ronner's 'sweet' cats, then twentieth-century life could be said to be best expressed by bird-like creatures. After all, the bird is an animal with which little or no human contact seems possible, inasmuch as it almost always reacts in an entirely unpredictable way: aggressively when we approach it in a friendly manner, and amicably just when we expect it to attack us. The rooster is therefore a particularly apt symbol for our times. Escher's print here features a bird which, oddly enough, reminds us of a man while at the same time it suggests qualities of a metallic instrument. Is human being so strange, so mechanical, one is compelled to ask.

Yet the most important aspect is Escher's playfulness expressed in the perspective, which he applies with an absolute purity that permits him, at the same time, to set it up as relative. The portals form transitions that create spatially 'impossible' situations, such as the not falling of the top bird-man, at least as long as one views the work as a whole, which in view of the repetition cannot be the intention . . . and so on. In short, there is a toying here with the old rules of perspective, the human mathematical control of space as we have known it since the Renaissance. Escher questions that. Is it correct to say there can be only one vantage point, of which the starting point is always man, looking out and observing the world from where he stands? Is this old view of the world inherited from the Renaissance still valid today?

It is this inherited view of the world that is called into question here. In a lithograph Escher once drew a very clear and naturalistically precise picture of a hand. But the rendered hand is busy drawing another hand on the same piece of paper. Again the trusted old way of representing objects, by means of which people believed they could grasp reality and thereby apprehend it intellectually, is presented as being conditional, turned into a game and thereby robbed of its claims to absolute validity.

In the first place the crisis of the twentieth century is this: a large and sometimes threatening question mark looming behind the picture of the world inherited from earlier times. Both people – humanity – and their view of reality are relativized, and values that previously seemed self-evident lose their validity.

One must not imagine that anyone in the seventeenth century could have engaged in such trifling. Not that playfulness was alien to people then, but *this* would have been impossible. It would have violated a trusted understanding of the world which they had no reason whatsoever to call into question. Not until the nineteenth century would there be a few precursors of this art, people like Granville, but they did not go as far as Escher and we will not consider them here.

Now it is certainly not wrong to subject one's own views to critical scrutiny. But in all that we have discussed here so far there have been only question marks raised and no new content added. This is consistent with the experience of twentieth-century persons who more often than not live in a world that they experience as something from the past, one which they cannot do without but in which they at the same time no longer believe. They regard it as arbitrary.

One can also set out to destroy the accepted world picture and, in the absence of a new conception and direction in life, endeavour through experimentation to design new images in which inherently a new world understanding is depicted That is the path of the Experimentalists, of Abstract Expressionism.

Those who seek a deeper insight into this approach can benefit significantly from a particularly astute little book by Platschek. In it he writes of Wols, one of the most important predecessors of the latest art:

> [Wols works in] a nadir whereby not only painting but also the characteristics of reality are rendered superfluous. To Wols this is the very centre of his existence, and the art of painting is the embodiment of doubt ... This view not only put the art of painting at stake, but more than that: the symbols of reality and the elements of one's own existence. That these paintings nevertheless came into existence was in any case an act of self-preservation. Only by virtue of the fact that Wols committed the outlines of objects to the canvas could he liberate these objects from their given forms of appearance and subject them to his own view.[4]

No wonder that it had to be said that Wols 'painted . . . without joy'! A few pages later Platschek continues:

> Here one can speak of destruction. The possibilities of meaning of the symbolic signs, as one may call the accents that give the painting its physiognomy, are destroyed, although the painting does in fact actually contain the remnants of these possibilities of meaning. Here the only question that remains is that of what must still be portrayed and what destroyed. The answer would be about as follows: if there are forms in the painting that remain legible (such as the circle as moon in Paul Klee), then this legibility becomes problematical when the form is destroyed, but the possibilities of identification are thereby rendered moveable and exchangeable, they now indicate and 'name' conditions.

He also writes: 'Painting and figure are stripped of formula and protocol in this way, while the possibility nevertheless remains, while standing in front of the painting, to find formulations, which each person does at his or her own cost and risk.'[5]

As we can see, the new reality is utterly irrational; one can call it whatever one likes and arbitrarily read into it any meaning. Yet no given meaning becomes 'truth' for anything can be truth at any moment. Such painting proceeds from the destroyed image of the world – all old values have vanished, the world has become values-less and hence valueless – which has been exchanged for full-blown relativism, the arbitrary giving of meaning to the meaningless. Meaningless, for if nothing is sure, if no truth is really true, then every intention and every effort to discover meaning is meaningless. And it abolishes itself – what is the use, after all, of seeing meaning in something if there is ultimately no meaning at all?

René Huyge once wrote that the modern in art can be characterized by the words: 'We feel ourselves floating in empty space.'[6] That was in 1947. A few years ago [in the late 1950s] we had the première of a play in which people looked out of a spaceship at the earth and watched it explode as the spaceship continued on its way. This portrayed how modern persons experience the meaning of their own life. It is no accident that the piece was accompanied by modern jazz.

We feel as if we float in empty space, that is how the world is pictured by the person who says with Heidegger that he or she is 'thrown': we have arrived here, in time and space and in this form, by accident. The accident destroys all meaning – which is contrary to what the Scriptures say about people, namely that they have been placed in this world, called to a meaningful existence.

Surrealism surrendered the traditional picture of the world to irrationalism by taking ostensibly real shapes, which were intentionally rendered in the familiar way, and connecting and grouping them in a bizarre, coincidental and unreal manner. Thus a mirror is held before us with the suggestion: You may think this is crazy, but is it any more crazy than your 'ordinary' image of the world? And why, after all, should this not be considered the normal one? Nowadays one proceeds from the irrationalistic starting point, mentioned above, and destroys through the act of painting every 'ordinary' view, evoking as if by happenstance images that could serve as symbols, if they themselves were not at the same time destroyed again. And this is intrinsically consistent, for no meaning is deemed present, nor possible.

The following citation is a poetic statement that accompanies a drawing by Karel Appel:

> In connection with certain paroxysmic effects of modern painting some have employed the notion of the 'aesthetics of the scream'. In a painter like Karel Appel, who has turned colour into a virtual apocalypse, this cry is a scream of embitterment. The reds and the blues of the furious animals he has made knock us squarely in the face, the tortured colour unleashes a grimacing horde of monstrous creatures poised to trample and devour whatever crosses their path. Maelstroms of ink flood the landscape and consign even the human face to the fury of the elements: the limits of expressionism are pushed back into the infinite by this rage to destroy.[7]

Apocalypse

'Apocalypse' is a biblical word. It is aptly used in the citation above, for it expresses something of the anguished cry of modern people: mountains fall on us (Revelation 6:16). We see here what the Bible calls the 'man of lawlessness . . . [who] will oppose and will exalt himself over everything that is called God or is worshipped' (2 Thessalonians 2:3-4). It is clear that this new irrational picture of the world arises from a nihilism that imagines it has settled accounts with God. Thus it is no wonder that everything is considered meaningless – without values and without value.

Sometimes the effort is made to construct a new kind of myth. But Christianity through its preaching has already unmasked all such efforts far too thoroughly, denounced them too severely (as in Isaiah 44 [see v. 16, where from the sacrificial remains 'he also fashions a god']). 'Sacrificial remains', one modern sculptor entitles one of his pieces (*Tajiri*); it remains an empty piece, a myth that is no myth, concomitantly unmasked until nothing is left of it but a form, an all too human product, a scream.

Who can find words to express how much angst, how much flight, how much hate has been laid into many of these so-called non-figurative works (that is, works that portray nothing in any way of the reality around us)? This is painting as a form of profanity, of cursing! In a gnostic manner God is reproached for having made a rotten world . . . or no, even that is impossible, for God is no longer there. It is paradoxical that in that case we must believe in that other myth of the present age, and one that is claimed to be scientific, namely evolution, in which everything proceeds from lower to higher. And 'high' turns out to be meaningless, essentially nothing but angst and pain and hate and emptiness.

Modern painting is form alone, so it is said, just colour and composition, a free human creation. But is the person who has to avoid every appearance of naturalness indeed natural and free? How much of a desperate clinging on is there, of hypocrisy as well, all for the sake of being accepted. This art is apparently easy because its techniques are easily imitated. Then coquettish spots of colour appear, and. . . with that we find ourselves merely in a present-day Salon,[8] amidst today's commercial art, of equally little value as the despised naturalistic art of the nineteenth century with its *lupanar obligatoire* or compulsory whorehouse mentality, as Gauguin once bitterly and keenly observed. This art is perhaps equally dirty, though in an entirely different way.

But we must not stare ourselves blind at the sick peripheral phenomena that accompany modernism. It is indeed telling that the irrational, flight and angst could become fashionable. Behind all this, however, are the formative, hidden spirits of our age which we have allowed to have their say. To disparage them and simply dismiss them as charlatans is to abandon the spiritual struggle – after all, one does not wrestle seriously, body and soul, with frauds. At the same time, that gives them free rein to infect our world and environment. In this way we have thrown away the key that enables us to understand our own times. For all these things are happening not only in what is called the 'avant-garde' milieu of the artists; they are also manifest in the spirit that is tarnishing almost all cultural work today. Culture is not a party game for a handful of so-called intellectuals. It is the mould into which life is unremittingly cast.

How then are we casting? Are we at work finding a meaningful form in and for today's world? Or are we leaving it to others whom we quickly dismiss in a denigrating manner as charlatans?

The Bible today

Well then, we must put on the armour of belief and take the helmet of salvation and the sword of the Spirit, which is the word of God (Ephesians 6:10–20). But what does that mean concretely? Does the Bible tell us how we are to fight or, practically, what we must do? Does it indicate a direction in these matters, even *the* direction? These are the questions that surface again and again.

Often it is as if we no longer can read the Bible. The short answer is then simply: Learn to read the Bible and, in order to do so, wipe the theological and legalistic mist off your glasses! Stop looking for 'principles from the Bible' by which to live and act in a Christian way. In the long run no one can live on a set of theoretical inferences; they are stones for bread![9]

It is certainly so that whenever we separate the Scriptures (that is, to read only extracts from them) from the One who is the bread of life, from Christ, then the Bible becomes a pile of dead letters – and that is not without danger but, as Paul observes, can kill.[10] It was a part of his life's work to deeply and powerfully oppose such a separation between life, the 'walk' of Christians, and Christ. That is the substance of his polemics against the Judaists, who expected to receive everything through the fulfilment of the Law. And what do our own theologisms and principles achieve but to drive us to do works of the Law in this sense, if indeed we separate them from the living God and from his truly risen Son?

The Scriptures give us laws so that we may find life, and the Holy Spirit bears witness to this in his self-witness in the Scriptures.[11] The moment we begin to think that God's word does not provide sufficient guidance and wisdom for our everyday lives, we have already begun to scorn his laws which leads to the chilling of love (Matthew 24:12), starting with our love for God. And is that not the result of a lack of trust in the One who promises that he will keep his word to us?[12] Do we not in that case proceed as if we are consigned to ourselves, to our own interpretations and achievements, and as if he (considering the results) simply allows us to muddle on? And with respect to these results, are they maybe none other than the fulfilment of the words 'You do not have, because you do not ask God. When you ask, you do not receive, because you ask with wrong motives' (James 4:2–3)?

And if it should prove possible to abstract faultlessly from the Scriptures the principles and norms for every sphere of life – suppose one could do that – then with that we would have lost the freedom we acquired in Jesus Christ. We would no longer live through him, no longer work in God's strength, made perfect in our weakness,[13] but in our own strength and wisdom. We would put on again the heavy yoke from which he had so recently freed us (Matthew 11:28).[14]

We must try to grasp these things before we can go on to discuss what it means concretely to be children of the living God. This is not to sermonize but to indicate the firm foundation for our work, that we may not face the spirit of the age unarmed. I may have appeared to speak sharply and to generalize when I used the term 'legalistic' – but let us at least take a good look to see if we are not infected by legalism as members of the Reformed tradition. It would indicate a lack of strength and explain the failure, already evident, of many of our works to bear fruit. For legalism binds us to the laws of the fathers, traditionalistically understood, with which we endeavour to pave the way ourselves (cf. Colossians 2:22–23[15]). Legalism is one of our greatest enemies, a traitor in the community. Only a real love for the Lord, Christ of the Scriptures, can save us from it and lead us into true freedom. Only by starting there can we find the way in our day and age.

As I explained above, the Bible gives us laws so that we may find life. God provides us with wise counsel to follow the way and puts up warning signs where we might deviate from the right path and commit ourselves to things that do not belong to life as he intended it. Consider the Ten Commandments (or better, the Ten Words). Each one of them contains wise advice, not prescriptions to be legalistically fulfilled but the sort that will keep our lives healthy, spiritually and physically, and bring us to full maturity if indeed we listen to them and obey them.

Such advice includes the commandment to rest on the Lord's day. It belongs to the richness of God's guidelines for our lives that the how and the what are not constantly prescribed. He did not tell us precisely what is involved in resting on Sunday, for two reasons that I can think of: first, because it is impossible in our ever-changing circumstances (of time, situation and personal status) to frame laws that would apply to all cases (the Bible would have become an inextricable tangle of little laws and commandments); and second, because he has so created us that we are able to find the way in these matters ourselves. We know very well what it means: rest, do not work.

I would like to clarify that with an example. Johnnie's father has forbidden him to go to a certain street. Naturally, Johnnie's father has good reasons for this. But the little boy also knows very well that if his mother should ask him to run an errand and, in order to do it, he has to be in that street, in such a case he is allowed to be there. Or should he suddenly need to fetch the doctor from that street, then too he need not ask permission to enter it. The boy is not restricted in his freedom by the commandment of his father.

Such restriction would exist if there were no bond of love between the father and the child, or if this were broken. Then little Johnnie would reason as follows: I know that father is strict and that he will punish me if I enter that street, and that is why I will not do it. In that case he can never enter the street, not for an errand and not in an emergency. He has lost his freedom. As a result he will say to his father that, of course, he will never enter that street, but that it would be good if his father could identify more precisely where the street begins, at this house or at that stone . . .

In the same way, when love for the heavenly Father no longer exists, casuistic questions become important, whether we may do this but perhaps not that.

The commandments that God gives us are very concrete – but they can only be grasped and followed in the freedom of love, with the engagement of our whole being, our whole heart, our whole soul, our whole understanding. That is what it means to do his will in true freedom.

Only in this light does it make sense now to go further and inquire into the nature and meaning of entertainment. In this pursuit we shall not engage in casuistry, we shall not aim to frame principles and construct theories by which to live.

2
The Meaning of Art and Entertainment in Human Life

Entertainment

Entertainment is joy, the relaxing joy that follows our work. Entertainment includes parties, going out together, listening to Bach, Beethoven, Louis Armstrong, an organ concert or a popular song; it includes reading a detective story, an informative article, a textbook about America, the works of Dostoyevsky or Shakespeare; it includes watching television, a street parade, a flower pageant or immersing ourselves in modern paintings or the etchings of Rembrandt or the engravings of Dürer. I leave aside here active relaxation such as pottering around doing a hobby or making music, although much that follows will apply to that too.

We must be careful here not to create a false tension between our work and our entertainment, as if between seriousness and fun, burdensome duty and the pleasant life, between what must and what may, concentrated thinking and absent-minded jollity, financial necessity and unencumbered possibility, and so forth. If this is the case, our lives become a caricature of socialistic-humanistic ideals which find their meaning in the exercise of free time and vacations.

No, entertainment too can be serious and difficult, and our work too can give us joy. Our work belongs to the mandate given to the first man on earth, it belongs to life in the covenant. There is a judgment on our work, to be sure – we work in the sweat of our brow [Genesis 3:19] – but entertainment is not without problems either. There are difficulties in our entertainment as well as in our work if we take both seriously, seriously, for example when we immerse ourselves in a composition by Bach in order to understand how the piece is put together. Such difficulties are inherent in our creatureliness; they will not interfere with our joy but instead may deepen it. The problems we experience as a result of sin and its effects are of a different order: here joy is spoilt when an undertaking is not successful, and there is sorrow when we can no longer untangle the knots.

For all that, entertainment is the serious diversion needed to follow our more ordinary daily exertions, both mentally and physically. The (same) bow long bent at last waxes weak.

Entertainment is essential to human life. Hence the Lord provided for it. Did he not at Sinai prescribe feasts for Israel, regular times of rest and relaxation – the Sabbath, the Passover, the Feast of Tabernacles?

(Deuteronomy 16, Leviticus 23, Exodus 23: 'Then you shall rest from your labour and rejoice before the face of the Lord!') Moreover, he gave his people special feasts, for instance after the passage through the Red Sea. How tense the days must have been through which they had lived: first the flight from the army of the Egyptians, then the passage through the sea with the waters threatening from both sides, the Egyptians again close-by, and then the safe arrival on the far bank. These people were no 'heroes of the faith' for whom all of this was just a matter of course; the events would have taken their toll on nerves and bodies. Thus relaxation was needed, including dances and a new song: 'And Miriam . . . took a tambourine in her hand; and all the women went out with her with tambourines and with dancing' (Exodus 15:20). That was entertainment, joy, even if the new song was not so easy to learn and the party brought a tiredness of its own.

Joy belongs to being a 'child of the Lord'. 'Rejoice . . . always,' proclaims the New Testament (1 Thessalonians 5:16), but as a fruit of faith and not as a determined effort to conjure up happiness for ourselves. For today still it is true: 'For to the one who pleases him God gives wisdom and knowledge and joy' (Ecclesiastes 2:26). And again in this same book which so beautifully deals with human life in its concrete form, 'it is God's gift that all should eat and drink and take pleasure in their toil' (Ecclesiastes 3:13; cf. 9:7–10).

No, depth in human life does not come from melancholy, problems, tragedy, sadness, heaviness. Romanticism has tried to convince us that it is so, but that is not true. The authentic Negro spirituals are happy songs but not therefore superficial or unchristian; far from it. The music of Bach or Schütz is happy, sometimes almost airy, but permeated with a biblical depth, especially when it is joyful. The psalms too, that were sung in the sixteenth century and contributed so much to the spread of Calvinism, were happy songs. Queen Elizabeth I even mockingly called them 'Geneva jigs', dances from Geneva. The deepest quality in the life of the Christian is joy, even though there will be times when those who are happy may sigh. (Isaiah 24:8: 'The gaiety of the tambourines is stilled, the noise of the revellers has stopped, the joyful harp is silent.') There are low points in life, but they are not for that reason the deepest moments of life.

The question we must now consider is what we should or may enjoy, or what the content is of that which the Lord gives to us for our enjoyment. Nowadays we are offered a tremendous amount of entertainment, and it is self-evident that problems will arise when especially this aspect of human living is largely in the hands of those who have strayed furthest from the Lord. These difficulties result from sin and its effects, and we cannot expect that it will ever be possible to give a 'solution' to the 'problem' of entertainment. Sin is a destructive power, so how can it ever be solved as a 'problem'?

We must also remember that we are strangers on this earth, living between the time of the Fall and the New Day. Later I shall have more to say about this. First I want to try to provide an initial answer to the question of whether there are norms for art and entertainment.

Norms in the choice of our entertainment

The first question concerns what entertainment is appropriate in given circumstances, according to the function, purpose and task of the occasion.

With respect to music we can distinguish, for example, between the serene music of a string ensemble that can create a festive air in a restaurant – as long as it is not too intrusive and their choice of music not too complex or demanding for listeners – and marching music – can you imagine national celebrations without brass bands? – 'music while you work', and concert music. Light music, as in the popular Dutch broadcast 'Vitamins while you work', is not always bad or wrong. It would not be appropriate to bombard housekeepers doing their morning chores with Beethoven's *Missa Solemnis*. That does not fit with dusting and being interrupted by the doorbell. And if a public parade should suddenly be accompanied by the sounds of Bach's sixth *Brandenburg Concerto*, even though this music is upbeat, it would be out of place. For there are norms for the choice of entertainment, for the sort of music to be played. Someone enjoying a cosy evening at home will leave Mahler's Kindertotenlieder or Schütz's *Symphoniae Sacrae* on the shelf and play something light instead. Records of the latter sort should certainly not be played when one is having a musical evening – different music fits such an occasion.

The same is true of books: a detective story cannot be compared with a work by Dickens, Mauriac or Hella Haasse. But anyone who considers Wodehouse less worthy and thinks one should never read anything but Marlowe, Goethe or Vestdijk lacks discrimination; the distinction between good books and bad ones is not a distinction between the weightier, more serious ones and the lighter ones but a distinction that cuts through all genres . . . there are good and bad serious books, and there are also good and bad books devoted to the lighter muse!

The same principle applies to images as well. A joke that is drawn – a 'cartoon' as we see them in newspapers and magazines – can be something very special indeed, a delight that one can savour slowly and repeatedly. Here the requirements differ from the requirements for a light-hearted illustration or wall decoration. But anyone who would place a cartoon, even the best cartoon in the world, in a golden frame and hang it in a museum would be playing a truly dadaistic game, calling into question the value of all the other works on display. A masterpiece is never a joke, no matter how funny a piece it may be. The material medium of which it is made is also of importance. Albrecht Dürer knew that unfailingly: for the erudite circles he wished to reach, he created prints from copper engravings, while he chose a woodcutting technique, usually simpler in structure and less complicated in content, for the more general public. This is not to say that the latter would be of a lesser artistic quality; they just represented less value in terms of money.

Genre and function are thus closely connected and require a regard for sharp boundaries. These boundaries would become blurred and it would lead to the devaluation or inflation of individual values if we were to place a cartoon at the same level as a Rembrandt, even if we were to assert while doing so that the Rembrandt is the greater masterpiece. In the visual arts too the dividing line between good and bad art runs through all genres.

A cartoon would not necessarily have less 'content'. Certainly in this genre there is a great deal of genuine humour – the importance of which for human life we should not underestimate – but all too often the way in which something is portrayed, with biting scorn, denigrates humanity and violates human dignity. In cartoons we often come across a manipulation of 'ordinary' images, as in the work of Escher; yet a myriad times more often we are confronted with those images that go much further and spoil the meaning of what they have pictured by giving it an irrationalistic twist. One of best cartoonists and one of the most famous in this field must be the very influential American caricaturist Saul Steinberg: in an almost frighteningly intelligent way he is able to play scornfully with human values, sometimes just by the way he draws things. I am thinking here of his 'strange' (from the point of perspective) stations. A grim nihilistic game is also going on in his 'old documents', pieces which he writes illegibly with lots of flourishes and thereafter furnishes with pompous and equally illegible signatures. Are not many historic agreements, written with just as much swank and signed by bands of fancy gentlemen, just as worthless, just as empty as Steinberg's designs, these cartoons seem to ask. Once one has seen them, it is difficult to muster much respect for all the memorials of treaties, drawn up with great effort, the results of 'higher' political action.

In the same vein we can also understand the meaning of another cartoon I have in mind. By the way in which the artist there draws an old interior or museum, its meaning is leveled. The approach is crude but awesome in achieving its goal. Precisely because Steinberg had no shortage of skill but knew exactly what he was doing, these little works took on a meaning of their own. They testify to a grim Dada-humour which finds its continuation in the work of the Dada movement, which by around 1918 had levelled all cultural values and all symbols of authority and equalized all that was worthy of respect, proclaiming it to be nothing. This was a work of demolition, effected through black humour that undermined all symbols of prestige, of every highly esteemed thing. Who is not reminded of 2 Peter 2:10 [' . . . those who follow the corrupt desire of the sinful nature and despise authority'].

We chose an example like this one in order to show that humour too, even when apparently no more than a joke, can be laden with meaning, with ideological insights. Jokes, as in Steinberg's work and, in another way, in the work of Chas Addams, destroy every belief in the established values by their irrationalistic emphasis on the absurd, the compulsively neurotic, the demonic, and by placing these phenomena on the same level as higher cultural values. The *demasqué*, the unmasking of values that began in the nineteenth century, appears here as a macabre game of destruction, trampling underfoot all that is held to be authoritative or valuable, in essentially the same way as postwar painting did and continues to do.

But let us not on account of these powers of the large-scale and thorough revolution of life and lawlessness forget what is truly valuable: happily there is still a great deal of that left, even if the undermining effect of what we have described above is not insignificant. We must certainly be fully alert to guard our minds against it. To submit would bring us only loss. But by the same token we should also not in blind fear shy away from every contemporary thing, lest that which is valuable escape us.

In all the genres mentioned above, literary works or popular romantic novels, artistic masterpieces or cartoons, there are standards to be distinguished. I do not mean this so much in a qualitative sense as with respect to the nature of each genre. The standard can be higher or may have to be lower, with a view to the public, considering the degree of difficulty. In music, for example, it is clear that programmes for youth concerts and popular concerts have to be planned quite differently from those for music lovers. For a youth concert an overture by [Carl Maria] von Weber would probably be a good choice, but do not serve up something like that to experts. It is too light for them, they know the piece through and through; it has little more to offer them. But by the same token the most recent work by the most modern composer or that recently rediscovered piece by Monteverdi does not belong in the programme for the youth concert: not only are such pieces far too difficult but it is also impossible for the audience to have any notion at all of the true value of what they are being offered.

Thus the purpose and the circumstances for which the work of art is used, and the standards or level of development of those who are going to be confronted with it must be important factors in our choosing. Anyone presenting a Greek drama at a wedding would have to be very ignorant, but a wedding reception might be planned to include a fragment of Shakespeare's *Twelfth Night*, for example, if it were fitted in appropriately.

What does our own level depend on?

If the choice of entertainment depends on the function or purpose for which it is chosen and on the level of the 'users', whether others or ourselves, then it is important to know what factors determine that level. I believe that in this regard we must take into account the horizons both of our experience and of our knowledge, together with our understanding of the nature of what is offered.

That the horizon of our knowledge plays a role both in our choice and in our enjoyment of entertainment is virtually self-evident. I have a gramophone record with a song by Orlando di Lasso called *Todesca* (pronounced 'todeska' and meaning 'German'). To appreciate the subtle humour of this little work, and its value, requires quite some background. The more at home one is in the things I shall proceed to mention, the more filled with nuance one's pleasure in the piece will be. The more complete one's understanding of the work, the better one is attuned to savour it. By the way, this is in refutation of the notion that one can 'simply' enjoy art, and music in particular, without having fulfilled any conditions beforehand except that of opening up one's sentiments to it. There is a very great deal more involved in music than feeling alone. (I selected a song here for a particular reason, namely, that I might otherwise have had to illustrate my words with musical notation and in so doing have transgressed against the very norm we are discussing here!).

Orlando di Lasso's *Todesca* was written at a time when there were many German troops in Italy acting as a kind of occupation force. Naturally these soldiers flirted with the sweet maidens, so the composer has such a man sing a serenade to a signorina. He commences his song however with the words 'Matona mia cara', thereby addressing the girl as if she were a matron, a somewhat sturdy lady of the house. Subtle and spirited is the strophe:

> Si mi non saper dire tante belle razon,
> Petrarcha mi non saper, ne fonte d'Helicon.

Here we must know of course who Petrarch was, and why he is mentioned here, and what kind of a mountain Helicon is. The more at home we are in the cultural history and the better we know Italian, the more we will enjoy the song.

The same is true for literature. Who can hope to grasp Multatuli's *Max Havelaar* without a modicum of knowledge of the circumstances under which the book was written? Likewise, with respect to paintings, even an ostensibly simple landscape can be enjoyed according to its worth only if one knows at least what a landscape is.

I write all this not in order to discourage anyone but to show that enjoyment in the field of entertainment and art cannot be taken for granted and that it requires some effort of us. Yet those who start out by thinking there is no way they can understand it and that they therefore must remain at the lowest level impoverish themselves even more. They allow this life to shrivel into uniform emptiness, the fruit of which may be intellectual or spiritual impoverishment. By the same token those who regularly read the Bible seriously gain so much to think about that, because of this alone, they can never fall to a desperate level. A proof of this we can find in the Christian songs of the poor and simple black country people of the American South (listen, for example, to Blind Willie Johnson).

Everyone can garner spiritual riches by studying the Holy Scriptures and by becoming acquainted with sensibly selected art and entertainment. If people who call themselves Christians have no spiritual wealth at all, then they have left their Bibles closed (Sunday preaching alone offers something, but the very least of the minimum) and have not truly lived in this world, but disdained the good that God has given them.

The horizon of our experience is the second thing I wanted to mention. If a work of art tells about situations we have never experienced, things about which we know nothing at all, a world in which we have never lived, we will be able to judge it or assess its worth only with difficulty. (It may still be worthwhile for us to consider it, but more about that later.)

How can I grasp a poem written from the viewpoint of a deep-sea diver, or at least be somewhat in a position to test the depth of the observation and the accuracy of the situation presented? The reader of a book has it a bit easier, since the writer can surreptitiously introduce the uninitiated to all kinds of detail that will enable them to experience some empathy. But how will anyone be able to understand a character sketch of a 'hero of the faith' or be able to assess the truth of what is presented if he or she has no personal experience of real faith?

It remains to be added that it is not really necessary to have experienced everything in order to be able to judge it fully. Every work of art tells of human vicissitudes and realities, and as a minimum we all have our humanity. This can be the entrance to an understanding of what has been written or painted. Proceeding from our own human experience we can sense and empathize with and feel and reflect upon and think about what appears in any given work of art, even if we have never witnessed it ourselves. Is there anyone who, though he or she has never participated in a war, would not be able to comprehend much of the struggle and moods of a soldier at the frontline? Yet someone who did experience war would be able to judge more deeply and incisively.

The final factor I want to mention that determines our own level in the matter of entertainment and art is our knowledge of the structural laws that are proper to it or of the nature of what is offered. Anyone who really wants to enjoy art must know something about its nature, about its structural laws. Someone going to an organ concert does well to know something about the construction of an organ: one who does not know what registers are and what they are used for, misses a lot. Someone going to a flower pageant will enjoy the procession much more if they are knowledgeable about flowers: a grower is able to construct a float using certain blossoms or others, and by overcoming certain identifiable difficulties he or she can amaze those who are able to observe this, in contrast to those who just look at the pretty flowers.

Indeed, the more we know, the broader and thereby the deeper the satisfaction and the greater the joy derived. Here too I would hasten to add that these things are not written to discourage readers. For it is always the case that one who is truly open and willing to listen or observe will gain much more from an experience than those who, though ever so knowledgeable, let things wash over them, muttering, 'I already know that, so why don't they come up with something new?' Such people are the poorer, in spite of all their so-called riches, because they are not using their talents in the right way.

Thus we need not know everything and have extensive familiarity with the techniques before we can enjoy things. There must be a minimum, of course, but those who row with the oars in hand will attain a certain fullness of understanding, as long as they do not stop after looking or listening once, but work instead to move persistently ahead. We must also avoid turning our looking or listening into some kind of analytical game, an extreme danger that we do well to warn one another against. Analysis, immersion in the given structures, should always be in the service of understanding the art on its own terms. Analysis serves to enable us to arrive at true entertainment and must never be an end in itself. Yet effort devoted to it always repays itself many times over.

Entertainment?

As you may have noticed, I make no essential distinction between art and entertainment, since to my mind distinction can only be made as to function and genre. Nowadays the term 'entertainment' is often used in a denigrating way that leads us to think of kitsch, of empty hollow sounds, or of the frivolous diversions of the tabloid press. Entertainment in this sense requires little knowledge, for it is based on everyday experience and is usually so simple in its composition and structure that it takes no effort at all to see through it. Everything here is minimal: no effort, no imagination is asked of the reader or listener and no problems are posed.

The reason for the rise of this novum in cultural history is in fact not so easy to uncover. To look into it would also carry us far afield. Perhaps it is simplest to see it as the flip side of the coin that is modern art. For modern art has often become such an esoteric religion, presumes so much cultural development, is so full of allusions to earlier art and requires so much knowledge and critical sense to understand it that the average person today no longer can or wishes to make the effort. Modern art is also often anything but a joy to behold. Authentic folk art no longer exists in Western culture, and what we have is a surrogate that has replaced it.

We observe the flip side of the modern coin in another sense too. Those who opt not to peer into the abyss of the modern feeling about life, those who seek joy but who cannot find it in themselves because there is nowhere in their life and in their view of life an identifiable basis for it, those who experience the meaninglessness of all humanity in the manner of the existentialists but who have no desire to leap into the abyss of suicide or adopt the nihilistic myth, will choose instead a variety of problem-free art or entertainment. In that case entertainment becomes a flight into the emptiness of raw sexuality or pure rhythm, and we end up with rock-and-roll and the beatniks.

Present-day entertainment in its function of bringing conviviality has all too often become art in the service of Mammon. Such amusement is hollow because it has been commercialized. In America we have Tin Pan Alley where, with great knowledge of psychology and publicity, the latest hits are concocted. Art is not the goal there, and beauty less so, and truth least of all. All that counts is the almighty dollar. In that case entertainment is made to fit the greatest common denominator of the souls of the greatest mass, because such entertainment makes money. Those who produce such 'art' have sold their own souls to the devil of money and therefore turn out, in the most refined way, something that is really nothing. This is a curse of our times.

Yet the public they sell it to wants it that way, some say. Why? Again, because in our time there is little else on offer.

The age is long past when great art was at the same time popular art, as in the seventeenth century. Rubens' art is art for connoisseurs, for devotees and experts, but whoever wants to look at it without all these specialist talents can also enjoy it. It is not without reason that this art was meant to bring the masses back to the mother church. As art of the Counter-Reformation it is in perfect harmony with its goal. And the art of the Reformation? Our own Dutch seventeenth-century art, Vermeer for example, offers a great deal to digest to the most brilliant professor, but his art is also a source of joy to the simplest farmer or artisan who passes through the Rijksmuseum. In the period when they were new, such paintings did not adorn the homes of the culturally educated alone. Those who could not afford to own such works had prints in their homes instead, copies of the great works or original engravings, which continue to this day to astonish modern art historians and experts for their great depth and beauty and meaningful content.

The loss of all this reveals a great deal about the deep break that nineteenth-century Romanticism brought about in Western culture. It shows something of the emptiness prevalent in people's hearts today. But let us not direct our reproaches exclusively to one side. The spiritual breakdown is also a result of the decline of faith inside the churches, of believers being swept along by the spirit of the age, of great neglect amongst Christians of social and cultural problems. Much prayer, much love, much faithful action is needed, looking to see if, instead of eliminating us, God may be gracious to us. 'Us', that is, the spiritually impoverished West. Ortega y Gasset has portrayed something of that in his *Revolt of the Masses*, but he believed that he was above the masses himself. Do we really realize how much 'mass' mentality has affected each of us? No, haughtiness and condescension to the lack of taste of the masses can not help us or our Western culture, only real belief and loving prayer to God can do that. Or did some suppose that by our labours alone we would be able to solve the problems of the crisis of the twentieth century?

Our wisdom in the discussion with and about art

Entertainment and art must always be chosen in such a way that what is offered should satisfy the goal, fulfil its function. At a wedding, as I said, we do not stage a Greek drama but we might, for a cultivated company, adapt a fragment from a Shakespearean comedy. On a relaxed evening we may play pleasant records or listen to nothing at all, but no *Missa Solemnis*. If it is our intention to listen to music together, then we leave the popular tunes in the drawer and take out something like the *Brandenburg Concertos* or Heinrich Schütz's *Auferstehungshistorie* or another work we can appreciate together that will also enrich our minds.

It all depends on our own level, as we have said in an earlier section. Because we are now approaching the heart of the issue, I must go into it more deeply. The trio of elements that I have identified as our knowledge horizon, our life experience and our understanding of matters I shall now gather together under the term 'wisdom'.

A group of people can know themselves to be united by a common life and world view. Among Christians, God establishes this unity through the fellowship of the Holy Spirit. Christians express this by speaking of the 'communion of the saints'. Yet in unity and in communion there are still great differences in wisdom. For wisdom is the individual (I do not say 'individualistic') forming or shaping of that common life and world view. Depending on our character, our social 'background', our education and our experience, depending also on our knowledge and on the breadth and depth to which we pursue knowledge, our individual wisdoms will differ. Wisdom is the individually concretized and sharpened life and world view. Important components of it for Christians are their experience of the fact that God exists, that he answers prayer, and that all he created is good but that sin ruins much.

When we have put matters in these terms, then we recognize that wisdom is also to be found in the makers of works of art. The content and nature of their work is coloured by it. We must not take an all too individualistic approach to an artist, because he or she too is borne by a cultural group and is the bearer of a tradition and a member of a cultural community.

Hence when we look at a work of art or are confronted with a perspective in a novel or find ourselves trying to understand the distinctive character of a piece of music, a dialogue can arise, as it were, between the author or composer and us. Given our wisdom we engage emotionally and intellectually, aesthetically and religiously, socially and culturally with the artist who in his or her wisdom conceived and realized the work.

That dialogue is often far from simple. Therefore we cannot carry on the discussion alone. Who said that art is a strictly individual affair? One cannot argue about taste, so it is said. But that holds only for similar cases that are comparable in level and nature. Surely that saying does not mean that at a given moment one might prefer a cup of tea to an etching by Rembrandt?

We cannot carry on the discussion alone. We experience entertainment together, in company. That holds not only for a party but also for a concert. Why do we like to go to such events in the company of others? Surely not just because we prefer not to be out alone in the dark but also because we enjoy discussing what we have heard and exchanging thoughts with someone about it during the intermission and afterwards? That is just as true of a book. Once we have finished it we are not yet done. We talk with someone else about it, discuss it. That is important, because in that way we digest it, and we digest it together.

The importance of art for life

Processing a new experience together is of great value. Every work, whatever it may be, penetrates our humanity, our knowledge, our wisdom. Often a work of art will help us to know and understand a world which was previously unknown to us, for instance when reading a book about Eskimos, the Inuit, for the first time. The content enriches our lives as we learn how different people act under different circumstances. Or how someone with a certain viewpoint, the writer in this case, regards a certain problem or state of affairs. In short, by virtue of the subject it presents, the work of art broadens the horizons of our knowledge and experience.

The misconception could arise here that I value a work of art only for its didactic aspect, for its being useful and instructive. But that is by no means the case. The example I chose of a book about the Eskimos could have that element, even if that were not in the least the intention of the writer. Moreover, there are many works of art having almost no such element at all which nevertheless can be of great value. For art may not only teach us little things and bring us into contact with worlds otherwise unknown to us; art may also, if it is good, open our eyes to much that is beautiful and much that is worthwhile in everyday life. One of the most important social functions of art is precisely this renewing of our emotional experience of familiar things and situations, this opening or reopening of our eyes to certain beauties, this integrating of new elements into our life and experience, by making us notice them in their emotional meaningfulness and connectedness. I use the term 'emotional' here to indicate a full experience of reality in which the intellectual has its place but is not all-dominating. Perhaps one of the causes of the crisis of the twentieth century is that art fulfills this function far too little nowadays. Because the artists neglect to work with the realities around us and because for this reason art has become something remote and arcane for most people, it can no longer perform the function in question. And to avoid another possible misconception, this task of integrating the experience of reality, or of being an 'eye-opener' to put it in less academic terms, will be best fulfilled by art precisely when artists think least deliberately about it, but instead just allow themselves to be inspired by the things around them that they find gripping.

Statistics and surveys cannot help us here, precisely because art works so quietly in this respect. Something in particular may assume a large place in our life, a poem (or just a few lines from one), a melody, a novel featuring a hero fulfilling the role we imagine to be our own calling in life, or a painting that shows us certain visually observable beauties.

It has been said that the inhabitants of the Southern States of America in the early nineteenth century shaped their lifestyle to the Romantic ideals as they appeared in the novels of Walter Scott; their heroic approach to fighting during the Civil War in the 1860s would also have been inspired by these ideals. And surveys have shown – yes, even surveys can serve at times to make things clear – that movies influence older schoolchildren in their lives and in their ideas of love. 'We would not be so passionate if films did not show us passion,' these teenagers have been reported to claim. The societal ideals of Ruskin and William Morris, utopian idealists, would not have found their form if they had not been so fascinated by the beauties of Gothic architecture and art. Ruskin even made it a part of his political programme and distributed a fragment of his *Stones of Venice*, entitled 'The Nature of Gothic', as a pamphlet amongst the workers.

No, art is no luxury, no marginal phenomenon of life. Art is at the centre. Naturally, one can make do without it. We can also make do without forks and glassware, and without chairs and tables, without umbrellas and bicycles, without books or Sunday-go-to-meeting clothes, but that is not to say that all such things are without value. On the contrary, together they shape our lives as cultural beings. Beauty and joy and forms and sounds and ideas and images all belong to our lives. They are also inseparably interconnected.

> Diaphenia like the daffodowndilly,
> White as the sun, fair as the lily,
> Heigh ho, how I do love thee!
> I do love thee as my lambs
> Are beloved by their dams;
> How blest were I if thou would'st prove me.

This is a stanza from a little poem by Henry Constable dating from the beginning of the seventeenth century. And not much wisdom is to be gained from it either, we might think at first glance. It is just a play on words by a man in love, or one pretending to be so, for perhaps Diaphenia never existed, and if she did she certainly would not have had such a name, and yet . . . Here we do not learn to be in love, although a young man might run such lines as these through his head for days, but the little poem does show us something of an open and cheerful, playful manner of looking at things. It has the effect of a refreshing bath, because our spirit is washed by it, as it were, and things seem again as if new. But the theme need not always be one of love. Let us read:

> It's pleasant in Holy Mary
> By San Marie lagoon,
> The bells they chime and jingle
> From dawn to afternoon.
> They rime and chime and mingle,
> They pulse and boom and beat,
> And the laughing bells are gentle
> And the mournful bells are sweet.

This stanza, the first of three from a poem by John Masefield, opens our ears to the charming and distinctive sound of tolling bells, again something perfectly superfluous and yet at the same time indispensable. It is as if we were somewhere in southern France. For a moment it is as if we were on vacation. Conversely, it could perhaps come about that while actually on vacation our ears would pick up something like that and that we would recognize its beauty precisely because we knew that little poem (and so not say, 'Ugh, I can't even hear my transistor radio above that stupid noise!').

Where my own personal experience is concerned, I suspect that I love the English countryside, Dutchman though I am, because I have read so many English poems and novels. I say this in order to justify partly or at least explain my selection of these particular stanzas.

Because art plays a significant role in our lives, more important even than we sometimes imagine, it is necessary not only that we choose our art well but also that we examine its contents (together), looking more closely at it and so assimilating it into our experience. That does not mean that we have to become members of the esoteric art clan of our day: there is truly a lot to talk about in the presence of a Jan van Goyen, a Jan Steen, a Weissenbruch, or a poem by Geerten Gossaert. In the end a debate about a painting by Picasso will probably give us much less; we may learn from it to understand something of the spirit of our age, and that is important enough, but our own experience of life and our view of the world will probably be little enriched by it.

You will perhaps have noticed that in all I have said so far the facts as such have not been the focus of our attention. The fact that bells toll in southern France may be of interest for a geography lesson, but we do not need all these lines by John Masefield to tell us so. Happily, indeed, life is richer than so-called brute facts and figures, and art can remind us of that.

Therefore we will now proceed to analyse the structure of a work of art in order to see how such a work is connected with reality. We shall see that the actual content includes not only objectively portrayed facts, which may be described in a few words, but also its artistic treatment, its form and composition. These elements contribute to the significance of the work as it impacts us and possibly anchors itself deeply in our lives.

Works of art in relation to reality

This section presents a theoretical discussion of these matters. Anyone finding it too technical may move on directly to the concrete examples that begin with Jan van Goyen's landscape.

Here we choose painting as our point of departure. Most other art forms have equivalent elements. Occasionally we shall also refer to those.

The art of painting is rooted in three basic facts of human life, three aspects of the creation ordinances given us, namely the aesthetic, the iconic, and the visual experience. There is something to be said for beginning with the last of these since painting is based on what we can see, observe and understand through our eyes. The matter of order is not so important.

By the 'aesthetic' element we refer to the fact that humans are endowed with a sense of form, an ability to discriminate between good

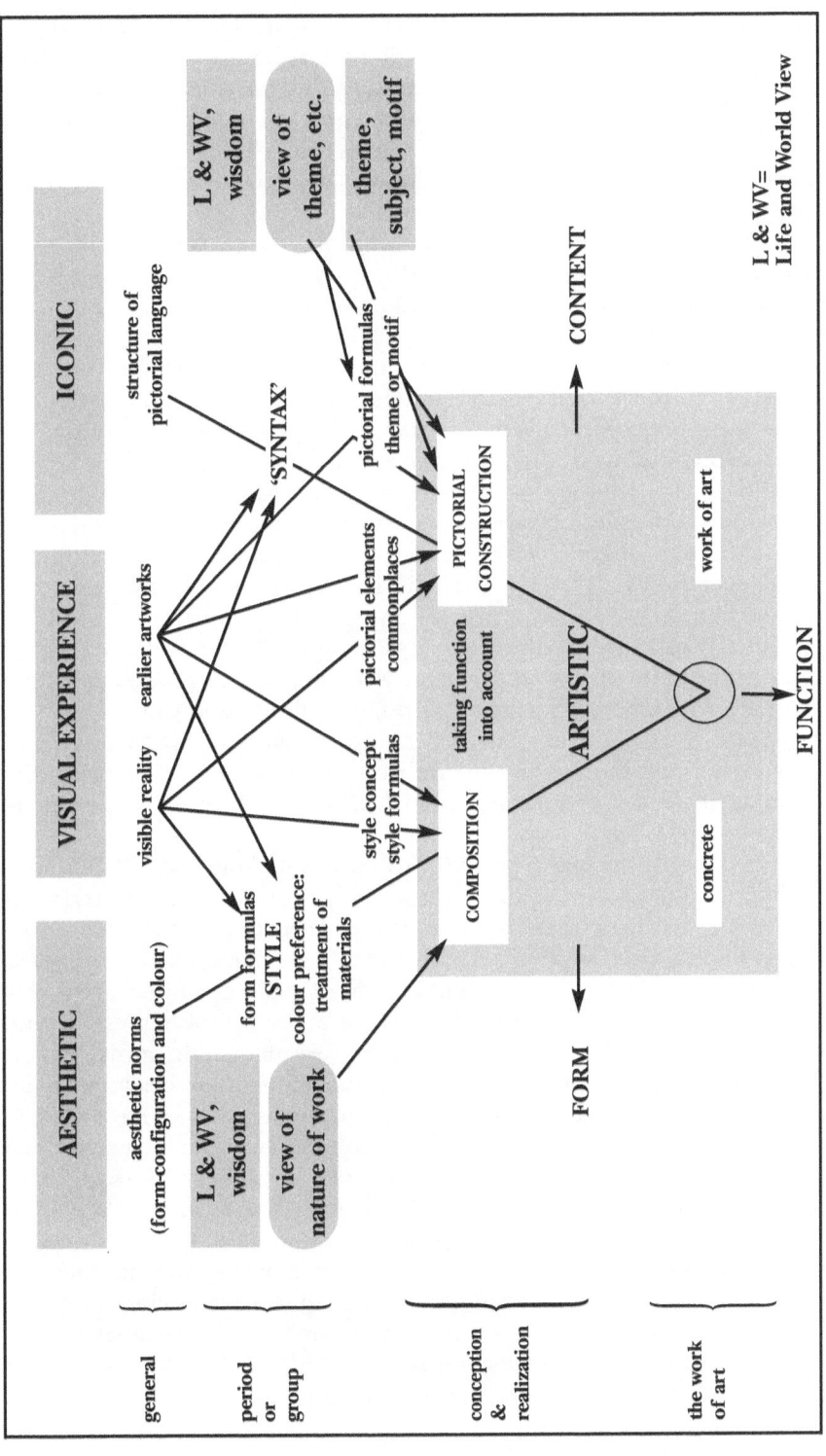

and bad colour combinations and a sense of proportion. The way in which a line is drawn, with a bit of colour to it here or there, whereby a certain coherency of forms is manifest, can fill us with joy. That we can speak of colours which go well together, and in contrast of colours that clash, indicates that there are norms here, rules of combination given in the creation order which an artist may violate, to be sure, but at the peril of producing something ugly.

This aesthetic element is something that we encounter daily even outside art and aside from the splendours of nature. Beautiful handwriting, a lovely colour, a well-formed vase, a nicely laid-out page are not the sorts of things we would call 'painting' or 'drawing' or 'sculpture'. Yet they have aesthetic meaning. The aesthetic element exists in its own right in ornaments, in decorative arabesques, in attractive typography. This is important, but it does not yet mean that we are dealing with art in the proper sense of the word.

The norms in question, the ones which are valid for all times and known to all peoples because they have been given with our human life, take a different shape in different periods; every period (or sometimes a particular people group only) has its own taste, its own sense of proportion and its own sense of using colour, aspects of what we commonly call style. A distinctive style is also reflected in the choice of materials, in the way by which paint is applied to the canvas, with bold or fine strokes, yielding a rough or polished finish, and so forth.

We can naturally achieve something stylistically only by using our eyes, observing the colours in the world around us and studying the mutual interconnectedness of forms. Without visual experience, nothing is possible.

The iconic element pertains to pictorial language. This too is something we encounter times without number, every day, outside the world of art in either the stricter or broader sense. All visual communication presupposes that it is possible to communicate by means of lines and/or colours or a combination of the two. Letters are a very simple example, as are traffic signs. There are scores of matters that we can communicate more clearly with a picture than with words. That is why teachers like to use chalk boards in education. A good example of an image that imparts data about reality is a map – but then we must *read* the map. Then, by its use of more or less traditional pictorial language (blue for water, brown for mountains, green for forest, red for roads) that describes or represents countryside, cities and villages, one can 'see' their respective locations, surroundings and importance.

As in the case of style, a more varied forming of this pictorial language is possible. The example of the map makes this clear. Not only older maps look different; current maps are not all of the same sort either. Anyone who has examined a maritime chart knows that it presents data in an entirely different way from our familiar atlas.

As in speech we may distinguish different languages, so too in the 'language' of cartography. In language and cartography there is a similar relation between reality and its representation. Words differ from language to language: what in Dutch is a *bos* is in English a 'wood' or 'forest', and in German a *Wald* and in French a *bois*. Likewise one can indicate a forest on a map by means of little trees or just by the colour green or brown – or in a painting in some entirely different manner. We will not elaborate further upon the many different ways in which forests have been depicted iconically through the ages.

Sometimes there is a certain direct relation between the image and what it represents. Thus when the grass in a painting is green, that does not surprise us. There are however also paintings in which another colour is used without causing confusion: consider grisaille paintings that are done entirely in brown or grey. Nor does anyone ask why in a black-and-white painting a roof is not red but grey or why white is used on a blackboard against the black background.

It is therefore incorrect to describe the iconic in terms of a visual relationship. Someone who makes a figure of a man by drawing just like little Johnny has to put the arms, the legs and the head in the right place, but that is not a question so much of copying or plagiarizing the visual data as it is one of making clear the structure of a human being. In the iconic, one depicts the make-up of structures. Language can only accomplish this with many, many words, whereby an appeal must still be made to the listener's visual imagination. Just try to explain to someone who has never seen an anchor what it looks like without drawing a picture of one or evoking a virtual mental image of one by suggesting comparisons! On the other hand, through language one can explain many things which could not be explained through images, for example the gospel.

The various iconic elements must be fitted together in a particular way, just as words are in language. The word that we shall use here to indicate that fitting together is 'syntax' (grammar). As it turns out, syntax varies from one period to another. Since the Renaissance the various components of the visual 'story' have been spatially connected with each other using perspective as the means to suggest relative space. The fact that depth was pictured iconically in so many different ways through the centuries already indicates that perspective itself is a syntactic device. Thus Japanese prints are difficult for Westerners to 'read' spatially, since they do not employ perspective in the Western sense (and also portray no shadows).

As we delve further into the history of visual communication (e.g. in paintings) we will see ever more clearly that the relation between what is expressed iconically and the reality it represents is not so simple that a term like 'visual relationship' can explain it. Just consider how light is used in art. In Romanesque or Gothic pictures one sees that light (daylight, lamplight) plays no role at all. Even at the beginning of the fifteenth century an artist telling of the birth of Jesus could still show that it was night by putting a candle in Joseph's hand while leaving all else as bright as day. Rembrandt accents the most important group or person by flooding them with light, as it were, against a dark background. But Carel Fabritius and Johannes Vermeer, in practically the same period, often let the most important figure stand out darkly against a lighter background, thus just the reverse. Different examples of still other syntactical elements could be given. But one can study these matters for oneself by asking, for example, how an advertisement communicates its message to us.

When artists set out to make a painting, they must tell their story clearly, relating what they want us to see and at the same time constructing a composition that is aesthetically responsible, that is beautiful – otherwise the result will not be a painting but just another picture. Every element in a painting implicitly works in a twofold way: it is at the same time both an iconic element of image and an aesthetic element of composition. The red in a little hat is at the same time the hat and a spot of red colour occupying a more or less important place in the whole composition (just as in a poem every word has an objective meaning but, at the same time, is an element in the construction of the poem as to rhythm, assonance, consonance, etc.).

In every good painting this duality will be such that the two elements form a perfect whole: the main figure will look like the main figure because of the place it occupies in the composition and, according to the rules of syntax, it will also have to be important in the story. Where this twofold character is absent I may still be able to infer from the story alone that the figure is important, but in that case the artist has not succeeded in confirming it to me. In the structure of the painting the artist must combine the elements in such a way that his or her 'story' is clear. The story, or theme, is what has to be incorporated in the painting. As such it has no artistic significance and will only acquire that when it has been incorporated into the work of art.

Sometimes the way in which something is represented is entirely prescribed by tradition, by a fixed pictorial formula. Precisely because of the stability of such a formula one can recognize it directly, in medieval art, for example, even if one has only been engaged with it for a short while – the Crucifixion, the Entry into Jerusalem, the Last Judgment, the Birth of Christ, the Baptism in the Jordan, and many more. The pictorial elements in these cases all have a fixed place which one cannot change without altering or impairing the meaning of the given facts. One can compare this with the Apostle's Creed, for example, which is even less open to change without violence being done in some way to the truth contained in its confession. Yet just as one can utter this creed in various languages (Dutch, French, Latin, etc.) so a medieval artist could develop an own style and to a certain extent also a distinctive way of using the pictorial language in his own times.

The pictorial formula itself is no more art than the pictorial language as such is art – and an aesthetic figuration as such equally is no visual art, however pretty it may seem as ornamentation or surface decoration. (We will return to abstract art later.) Only through its artistic assimilation, whereby the aesthetic and iconic elements are unbreakably united with each other, does it become a work of art, which as such may be a success or a failure, beautiful or ugly. Thus the artistic, which distinguishes visual art, is brought forth only in a close interweaving of the aesthetic and iconic factors.

The remarkable thing about all this is that the aesthetic-iconic way in which the theme is treated implies a view of that theme. This manifests itself even in the choice of colours and the composition. If Bruegel paints the story of Christ bearing the cross and then places a great host of people on the canvas in such a way that the entire scene with Christ is engulfed and becomes lost in it, as it were, then he may very well have fulfilled the requirements of the standard pictorial formula – he had to do that or else he would have failed to make clear to us what he was portraying – but he is showing us that to his mind this event means little in the course of history. He makes this even clearer by placing a windmill on the top of a mountain, which suggests a familiar saying, that the windmill's vanes keep whirling, that life goes on in the same old way. It is worth noticing that in this short discussion I really have been unable to keep the aesthetic and the iconic factors separated. In this painting the composition and pictorial construction do indeed work perfectly together to produce the desired effect.

In what follows now I shall not go into any more detail than is absolutely necessary. Above we have endeavoured simply to show how a viewpoint can be expressed in a work of art, or what the relation is between a work of art and reality. The traditional concepts of form and content are approached in a different way here and referred to in their coherence, in their quality of being naturally and logically interconnected – see figure 1 – and it may also be clear that from the moment the artist began to think about a work, he or she would have considered the function it was meant to fulfil. We also might have adopted a position right next to the artist, there where the word 'ARTISTIC' appears on the chart: he or she chooses a form in order to make a particular content clear, with a certain function in mind; or she or he seeks a certain theme in order to express a certain content; or it is even possible that one should proceed from the configuration of a certain form and then seek a content or a theme in which to realize it.

The sense of reality in a work of art, the view of reality expressed in the work, and its clarification of a certain interconnectedness are brought to life by the artistic realization of the theme. We will now look briefly at two more examples in order to illustrate this.

A landscape by Jan van Goyen

Jan van Goyen is one of the most brilliant landscape painters of all time. He was productive between 1620 and 1656, the year of his death. His art improved in a direct line, and the works he made after 1640 are virtually all masterpieces. We shall discuss one of his paintings from 1646, *Approaching storm* [see Plate 1].

Jan van Goyen is almost unrivalled as a master of representing space. He was in complete command of the devices that had been developed for this since the beginning of the modern period, and he applied them brilliantly. In the first place there is his perspective – figures appear smaller the further away they are from us – but possibly even more important is his atmospheric perspective – the tone and colour of an object that is further from us is lighter and softer than that of a similar object viewed at closer range (compare the sails of the boats in this painting). He also uses *repoussoir* – setting a lighter object against a dark background or a darker object against a light background so that it thereby appears to be located to the fore while the background is pushed back (*repousser*). And, finally, he uses lighter and darker strokes in the water so that a clear spatial arrangement is achieved and things are put in their right place, as it were. In this painting we see the repoussoir in the sails as they stand out against the sky but also in the dark boat set against the lighter strip of water, which is thereby clearly pushed back. Through that repoussoir the artist can make things clear and define them distinctly in their interconnectedness. Jan van Goyen knows how to use this device in such a way that we hardly notice it, it seems so natural. Only upon looking more closely do we discover the mastery and realize that it is not a simple matter of course.

It is remarkable how the painter is able to use the darkly clouded sky to draw our eye towards the back, where the lightest part of the painting is at the most distant horizon. In the clouds too one can point out repoussoir (one against the other). Yet it is still more remarkable when we come to realize just what van Goyen accomplishes with the clouds, how he divides them as dark tones across the flat surface to thereby reinforce the entire construction of his composition.

With that we have arrived at the real problem, which led us to select this painting for discussion which at first glance may appear to be just another representation of a scene one could have witnessed any time, and possibly still can, somewhere in the Netherlands along one of the great rivers or the former Zuiderzee or Haarlemmermeer. For Jan van Goyen knew, perhaps better than anyone else, that a painting is in the first place a flat surface on which we work with our painting materials to call up our picture. In spite of the fact that he knew infallibly how to use the depth-depicting devices we have described, the syntax of his times, one can never accuse him, as some modern artists have reproached the old masters for doing, of tricking us by suggesting a 'hole in the wall', namely a real depth. On the contrary, Jan van Goyen knew not only how to maintain the surface but also how to use it in a wonderful way to serve his purposes.

Van Goyen's compositions are very tightly constructed and guided by an almost symphonic feel for form. Left . . . yes, one 'reads' a painting from left to right. This probably is because of the direction in which we write (and it would therefore be the reverse for, e.g. Chinese people). Naturally we can look at a painting from right to left or in any other way, but only after we have read it in the right direction first. In a similar way we have to read a sonnet first from top to bottom, and only after we have done that can we go back and re-read one line or another, and figure out how the way the sonnet ends is prepared and called up in earlier lines. The correct order of reading is presupposed in the creative process. But to return to our earlier discussion: at the left of the landscape we see the 'introduction' by means of a little boat, which draws us into the space and positions us on the water, as it were. Then we come to the first theme, which we could call 'distance with storm cloud'. Next we have the transitional theme in the pair of slightly larger sailboats, precisely in the middle of the canvas. Following that we come to the second main theme: ships tied up at a mooring, at a harbour, suggested by a few houses entirely to the right, which at the same time form the light coda. The main element in the second theme is the ship with the large dark sail, which finds its direct 'response' in the somewhat smaller and lighter sail just behind it. That second theme is more loaded, busier and manifests more movement, and it fixes our eye on a less remote distance parallel to the surface of the painting.

And now, if we look at the clouds again, we see that, like a kind of countermelody, a bass line, they follow the themes, and so also the main organizing principle of the painting. Thus the 'reading direction' from left to right is anything but arbitrary. We cannot turn this painting around – just try holding the page up to the light on which it is reproduced here and look at it from the back. It immediately becomes difficult to see the two themes. It is still possible to do so in this case, but much more difficult in many others. That it is still possible here, at least to a degree, is due to the serenity; it is not possible where ships are in motion, with their sails fixing the direction of observation.

Typically, the second theme has much more complex, and plural, constructive elements. Moving from left to right, one discovers that matters also often become more complex in a painting. It can be compared in this respect with a novel that begins with a single character but in which gradually an ever larger number of people come to play a part.

In this painting we therefore do not have some kind of copy of reality, not a photograph of what we would have seen had we been there. Rather, we enter another world, the world of the painting. And Jan van

Goyen has clearly set the world of painting off from our own world with a 'threshold', the dark strip in the foreground.

Thus this world does not offer us exactly what we would have seen in reality with our own eyes, had we been there. Rather, what we have here is Jan van Goyen's view of what was there, his own poetic view of a slice of reality, his own 'song' about the beauty at the calm mouth of a river. The things he notices and shows us are not necessarily self-evident, we must learn to observe them. And if Dutch people today cherish such beauties – and often, happily, they do – then they have to thank for that the lessons in observation that they learned from this artist (and those who followed after him), even if they are not conscious of it and, yes, may indeed never have been personally involved with such art. Once eyes have been opened to something so real and pure, so true, in which there is so much humanity and in which justice is done to all the elements, it is not easily forgotten. Fathers pass it on to their sons.

It is remarkable that this unifying effect, the distinctive quality of this 'symphonic poem in paint', arises in the composition. It would carry us too far afield to introduce a great deal of comparative material here. But it is precisely the use of two themes and the other elements we discussed that call forth this effect. By simply drawing a certain view of a wide river we cannot achieve such artistic content and such a suggestive result. It is therefore no surprise, as becomes evident when we examine Jan van Goyen's works carefully, that the artist seldom stuck closely to a precisely identifiable phenomenon. His art is not topographical, it does not portray exact locations, although he occasionally incorporates a 'citation' or visual reference to an existing tower, for example the one in Dordt. What he shows us, rather, is the structure of the landscape, in this case of a river-mouth or a lake, where the beauty forms an integrating part of the whole.

Could this view of reality not have had something to do with the Reformation? Could it be a fruit of our having opened ourselves up once again to reality as we learn to know it in the Bible? The Reformation liberated art from the chains of the domination of church and devotion, and it did so without secularization, without seeing the world as something detached from God. Such a hymn to the unity of creation, in its beauty, in its multiformity, in its richness and intimate connection with humanity – without idealistic exaltation, without making the world a sort of humanistic paradise where one is always on vacation with no difficulty or care – is something we can look at with jealousy today. No, this is no vacation paradise, no world of labourless rest and 'ideal beauty'; it is much more sober. It is as sober as the music of Heinrich Schütz can be, without frills, direct, and always with complete unity between means and ends.

In a painting like the one we have been discussing there is a complete unity between the iconic elements and the aesthetic structure, such that the content of the work cannot be considered apart from the manner of artistic realization: the theme is not an excuse to paint something, and the composition is not just coincidental, an embellishment of something that could have been said just as well in a few words.

We said that we might be looking here at one of the fruits of the Reformation. The painting reflects the spiritual climate in Holland during the first half of the seventeenth century. And it does so despite the fact that van Goyen was a Roman Catholic. His view is conditioned by the world in which he lived, and the word 'Counter-Reformation' has no meaning in connection with this river scene. Nor has it any meaning in connection with the work of van Goyen's son-in-law Jan Steen. Compare Steen's art with the art of Rubens and the difference will be even more clear.

Jan Steen's St Nicholas morning

As a second example we will discuss here briefly and not at all exhaustively this famous painting from the Rijksmuseum in Amsterdam [see Plate 2]. Unmistakably, Steen conveys us into the home of a Catholic family: the little girl has been given a doll of a saint!

What is the problem or difficulty for the painter? That he should depict so much movement and confused activity in his painting. We must recognize that he wants to tell us, 'Yes, that is what it is like.' Yet at the same time everything must be neatly laid out and clear, for with a disorderly painting one does not achieve this effect. Nor may anything appear to have been posed. The painter cannot arrange all his figures in a row, for example. Neither is the painter interested in creating a snapshot. So much would never actually be happening at the same moment. His work of art must present a comprehensive picture of this typically Dutch event.

How did he achieve all this? Partly by constructing his composition along fixed lines. The centre-point at the bottom is indicated by the little shoe. From there two slanted lines run: one runs towards the upper right and is shown by the little stick that the pointing boy has in his hand and comes out where the corner of the mantelpiece intersects with the upper edge of the painting; the other one runs toward the upper left and is shown by the handle of the bucket and comes out where the middle window jamb intersects with the upper edge of the painting.

Now, if we take the lower left-hand corner as our point of departure, we can see a clear line that runs past something orange in the bucket, past the mother's head, and along the arm of the boy who is showing his brother that Black Peter had come through the chimney. A second line runs from the lower left-hand corner past the head of the girl, the grandfather and the grandmother, toward the point already mentioned where the corner of the mantelpiece intersects with the upper edge.

From that point there is a clear vertical that comes out at the leg of the chair below. The intersection at the lower edge of the painting is indicated by the underside of the huge ginger biscuit in the right lower corner of the painting. From there another line runs past the head of the girl and the boy, who received the rod.

The many repeated V-forms give this painting its tremendous liveliness. Next we would still want to analyse how the artist created depth in the painting and assigned every figure its place in such a way that everything is unambiguous and clear.

In this way we discover that Jan Steen was able to tell his story precisely through his tight composition. With great psychological insight he has been able to portray the grandfather for us as he follows events with satisfaction, but also with a certain detachment, and the grandmother, who still has something hidden away in the box bed for the boy who got the rod and who is now being teased by his brother and sister, and the trio by the chimney who are singing 'Thank you, Saint Nicholas.'

A final observation: notice how here too an introduction is provided by the beautiful still life at the bottom left, and how the left half of the painting is simpler and has fewer figures in it than the right side, which is almost too small to fit everything in. The chair with the ginger cookie functions as the conclusion.

3
Art and our Life and World View

Let us return, then, to our subject of the association between human being and art and entertainment. I have tried to show in the first place how our understanding of art and entertainment is connected with our wisdom, and how in our viewing of and listening to both art and entertainment a dialogue of sorts arises between the maker of the work and ourselves, in which both the artist's wisdom and ours are at stake. I asserted that for this reason we need to confront art and entertainment together [as a Reformed and evangelical Christian community] inasmuch as we cannot carry on that dialogue alone. And then we became involved in a discussion of the nature of art, especially in order to counter the misunderstanding that in art, and the ensuing dialogue, only the subject of a work should be an issue.

No, art does not depict reality, it speaks instead in its own way *about* reality, says something about the subject, explains the motif. As examples we chose two paintings which seemed at first glance to be perhaps as faithful to reality as one could possibly come. Yes, and they are so, but not in the sense that they confront us with direct depictions of the visual data. Rather, we are engaged by a view or outlook or perspective, and no less so than in a Picasso, a Michelangelo or a Surrealist work. Yet here the view is so pure, so truthful, here justice is done so fully to the reality that we seem to be viewing that reality itself. That is why everyone can understand this art, even without knowing anything about the analysis I presented above. The works themselves are clear enough. That is the greatness of the art of our golden age, of seventeenth-century Dutch art, a ripe fruit of the renewal of life brought by the Reformation.

Yet for the very reason that the dialogue in question has so much to do with our wisdom, it is sometimes difficult for us to 'work together' in this field with those of a 'different mind' – more difficult, in fact, than in many other so-called serious matters. Because so much of our own wisdom and that of others is formed by a highly individually concretized life and world view, and because that is the crux of the matter, I will next examine the significance of life and world view for art.

As the term indicates, it concerns our view of human being, the world and life. It concerns our search for insight and understanding in and through the world around us, from a desire to establish our proper place and meaning, and the significance of what we see. It is clear that to this end people need to observe and immerse themselves in reality itself. Understand me well, this is not a matter of science and theory but of practical, pre-theoretical perception and experience, albeit that science may have a word and sometimes an all too obtrusive word to add, such that in our culture one must sometimes speak of an overly theoretical or 'theoreticized' approach to life, of life conditioned and dominated by theory. However that may be, the focus is on reality and life itself. It is a view in its own right, that outlook on reality, concretized anew in every age, which rules all forming, undergirds all culture and cultural activity and is determined as such by human subjectivity. Determined, that is to say, by the deepest human impulses, by the direction of a person's life, by a person's response to the primary questions of life, whether clearly formulated or merely sensed. Determined, in short, by a person's religious outlook on life, a person's acceptance or rejection of God as mentioned in Romans 1, a personal recognition or negation of certain powers or forces or gods that give meaning or determine life. One's life and world view depends on what one believes and on where one seeks anchorage, even on the denial that there is any anchor to be found anywhere at all.

This may all sound somewhat theoretical, and in its formulation perhaps that is so, but what I am talking about is a concrete outlook that determines how people react moment by moment to what comes at them from the outside, that governs their actions again and again in the acceptance or rejection of everyday things.

This outlook on life, the life and world view of which we are speaking, is first and foremost an insight into reality itself, or at least an effort to form such an insight. However, to be sure, not everything is logically reasoned out. Religion and belief do not necessarily determine a person's outlook in a logical manner from beginning to end. People's outlook is co-determined by the way in which things were presented to them in the past and by their own surroundings. In the outlook of a modern person, even of one who desires to live consistently by existentialism (the experience of the meaninglessness of everything), there is a great deal that is the fruit of Christianity. If we claim that our civilization is built on the Reformation – let us not forget that the Counter-Reformation too was a consequence and in part a fruit of the Reformation – then this means that even though many in our civilization may no longer draw directly on the foundational principles of the Reformation in their living and thinking, what it brought us in form and insight and outlook has not vanished and continues to influence us concretely in ever so many ways in our actual lives and vital insight. However, where the foundations of this civilization have long been repudiated, demolition has been slowly under way. Perhaps this is one of the most important facets of the crisis of the twentieth century: to live in a world that can be called post-Reformational and postchristian. And even if there are happily still some Christian influences at work, perhaps many more than we suppose, we must add at the same time that much of what today is called Protestantism has likewise departed from a basis in biblical Christianity and repudiated the Reformation.

Now, few have sunk so low that they would consciously and deliberately avoid the truth and follow the lie. Most people desire in subjective honesty to attain a correct and true insight into reality. They will seek the truth even while going astray and disregarding the Truth. Therefore there is much also in the insight of non-Christians that is realistic and does justice at least to a part of reality. If this were not so, non-Christians would not be able to find their way in this world in which they have been placed. Their insight will be expressed primarily in human wisdom, for in their experience of life they will endeavour to correct their life and world view at various points where it falls short and fails to fit the true state of affairs. Reality itself will teach them insight.

In everyone's view of reality there will thus be a great deal of truth, even where the foundation, according to Romans 1, is to deny the living God, a view that is accompanied by much darkening of the understanding. People's view of reality will also be manifest in their art, which expresses their wisdom of life. Therefore it is impossible to draw sharp dividing lines and not so easy to speak of 'Christian' art. It is better to speak of art that does justice to reality and then to distinguish gradations in this regard, the more so since the wisdom of Christians is also not always perfect, not even of those who keep their Bible open as a given of God and an infallible commentary on reality. For Christians too sin has obscured much. Inasmuch as the surroundings of Christians offer them broken fragments of insight or no insight at all, and inasmuch as they will never be more than partially able to correct or fathom the situation, they too will fail in many respects. In this regard Christians too are fully children of their time.

The point of this discourse was to show that in people's understanding of reality, reality itself, as it is and as it was disclosed by an earlier (Christian) generation, plays an important role. We must not become victims of (historicistic) subjectivism by maintaining that our subjective attitude can fully determine our world. However much people might resist the fact, their subjective attitude can at most have no more than a superficial influence, even though they may want to claim a one-sided disclosure and neglect certain given phenomena. Reality itself will compel people to capitulate, time and again, because reality is God's creation, the world in which he has placed humankind. Our subjective insight can never alter that essential fact.

Finally, we must keep in mind that the life and world view that holds sway in a particular period or over a large group of people may justifiably be called 'the spirit of the age'. In that respect it may sometimes be very enlightening to be mindful of the 'spiritual forces of wickedness' of which Paul speaks in his epistle to the Ephesians (6:12). It helps us to understand that ideas that fall short of doing justice to reality and truth can grip people for a long time. Moreover it shows that the notion of our wrestling 'not against flesh and blood, but against principalities, and powers, against the rulers of the darkness of this world' is no theory, and that Christians are well advised to take this seriously into account – these spirits can be dangerous!

Thus human insight into reality has its limitations: places, facets, fields, points where no justice or less than full justice is done to reality. It goes without saying that this will be reflected in art, not only in the choice of theme but also and especially in the way in which a subject is handled artistically.

Humanism, for example, holds that humanity is essentially good. That is the belief of humanism and its confession of faith. There is thus a shortfall of insight into human corruption, into sin and its power. This we find depicted in many ways in art. From the period between 1500 and 1800, for example, to pick some round figures, we find hundreds of paintings of an ideal world, the world of which humanists dream. Such art reaches out for paradise and shows what humankind is, in essence or by nature, according to that view, or at least what humankind ought to be. These paintings are idealizations, a fact that keeps alive, of course, an awareness that this world is not so beautiful after all and that people fail to live up to the wonderful dream. Moreover, sin as a reality is relegated to somewhere outside the world view or otherwise people could not have painted this way. Instead, they would have realized that what was presented was a lie, a distortion of reality. A lovely, ideal world, a sunny vacation resort, where naked or scarcely-clad people with beautiful bodies perform heroic and noble deeds or simply enjoy their existence, is held up as that which is really meaningful. In allegorical or heroic form it pictures the ideal for our lives.

This world, which is not to be encountered in everyday reality and which cannot be realized, is found in the myths and stories of antiquity, which the painters draw upon as a resource. I think particularly of the story of Arcadia, a poetic creation of Virgil, who was the first to depict this distant land of shepherds and shepherdesses and unspoilt noble simplicity, an ideal world, a 'humane' daydream as a remote and lost ideal. Unrequited love and death do exist in this world – no humanist is so estranged from reality as to ignore this entirely – but they are firmly consigned to the past or relegated to the future.

The Renaissance rediscovered Arcadia. And in the eighteenth century we find Marie Antoinette setting out to 'play' this world, turning it playfully into reality – a reality in the beautiful park at the Petit Trianon at Versailles – an alternative to real reality. Guercino, an Italian painter who worked in the first half of the seventeenth century, a typical artist of the Counter-Reformation, gives us impassioned paintings of the ideal of saints in their contacts with a higher world. Sometimes in themes borrowed from Greek mythology he shows us something of that ideal of superhuman life. Around 1625 he made a painting of Arcadia, in connection with which he was the first to use the phrase 'Et in Arcadia ego.' In this painting we see Arcadian shepherds walking through their lovely world and then suddenly, to their consternation, coming upon a skull. 'I too am in Arcadia' is in this work a seventeenth-century rendering of a medieval idea, of the memento mori (remember that you must die). Poussin, the great French painter who worked in Italy, classicist and humanist par excellence, gave this subject an entirely new interpretation about fifteen years later in a renowned piece that may now be viewed in the Louvre. In it a number of shepherds and shepherdesses, lovely forms without anything boorish or rough, are engaged in examining an inscription on a tomb. We sense in the painting something of the soft evening mood that belonged to Virgil's Arcadia, the hushed mood of an elegy. They read the inscription 'Et in Arcadia ego.' Through the construction of the work, through the motifs employed and the composition – we see here once again how the content of a work of art does not depend on the theme alone, but especially on the way in which it is treated artistically – the motto has acquired an entirely different meaning than it had in Guercino. In contravention, to be sure, of the rules of Latin grammar, people quickly began to read this saying in a different way from Guercino's rendition. Here it became instead: 'I too was in Arcadia' (that is, said by the one in the tomb). Death is present here too, yet dying is not a threat for the person living now in the present age; it is something of the past and far away. Poussin's painting speaks of the greatness and glory of being human, even if tempered by the thought that death is not entirely absent. Yet it is not a memento mori. To the contrary. The tomb embodies a beautiful dream that speaks of the great classical past. In the eighteenth century, under the influence of this painting, people could erect classical tombs with this same inscription in parks, which in that age were designed to evoke various moods and daydreams but certainly not to remind people that they would soon die.[16]

Existentialists, however, the people of our time, we may characterize as disappointed humanists. They have lost their faith in humanity. Humankind aspire to absolute freedom but collide with reality, which limits them in their movements and possibilities. Existentialists can no longer perceive the glory of such a reality. Not only is everything meaningless but also everywhere and at all times the same. We can perhaps comprehend existentialism when we think of the tantrum that a child may have when he or she has been exposed to too many impressions and is exhausted. Then that child can no longer pay serious attention to anything, but scoffs and jeers at all values. At a higher level and in a deeper way this is the 'nausea' that Sartre talks about.

And then there is the idea, often unexpressed but also sometimes stated in so many words, that 'we live in a rotten world.' This world is bad in itself, an enemy of humankind, a threat to their essence, a violation of their dignity, a thief that steals the meaning of their existence. Humankind are thrown into this chaotic situation, where death and suffering and difficulty and aggravation reign, imprisoned as in a hell, and the highest they can freely achieve is to resignedly take their existence upon themselves and strive to become gods while knowing themselves doomed to failure. To strive to become a god is, as the Zen poet put it, 'to have the sun and moon in your pocket, and the universe in your hand'.

A 'rotten world' is the world as the gnostics already saw it. A world miscreated, in which evil like a curse forms one of the essential characteristics of existence. Some Christians think that what we have here is an understanding of the curse in Genesis 2, and that these existentialists understand better than the old humanists the truth about being human. That remains to be seen. For although it may embarrass Christians to find the word 'cursed' and the idea of hell revived by these people, it is equally true that in their thinking neither notion bears any connection with the biblical preaching on the subject. This world is not rotten, and there is not only a vast impoverishment but also a lie in the words of the Japanese Zen master who expresses his view of reality poetically in the words:

> Mount Loe in mist and rain, the river Ge at high tide,
> Only by being there can I still the pain of longing.
> I went there and came back again.
> It was nothing special
> Just Mount Loe in mist and rain, and the river Ge at high tide.

How brilliantly in this poem is an entire situation depicted in just a few statements, and how frighteningly in this short space is the full dignity of humankind dismissed. Zen Buddhism has become a fashionable current today, which is entirely comprehensible when we realize that it is a sect with a close affinity to existentialism. I cite from this world of thought because things have seldom been said in a shorter and more artistic way. Zen has a tradition that is centuries old, something European existentialism still lacks.

Christians who assert that truth is nonetheless spoken here do not fully understand that God made this world *good*. Therefore it is no more true or correct to speak constantly about the death, curse, anxiety and negativity in the world than to pass over sin as some kind of *quantité négligeable* or unfortunate accidental circumstance, as the earlier humanists preferred to do.

The Scriptures say that Christians are strangers in this world. But that does not mean in this creation! On the contrary, in this creation Christians are at home, because God created the earth for humans and we fit here. It is neither improper nor unessential to enjoy the beauty of the clouds, of a rolling countryside, of the surf, as if in doing so we would be superficially ignoring what is the more proper understanding, namely that at the same moment, somewhere, a death's cry might be heard. In the Psalms, in the book of Job, in the words of the Lord Jesus when he talks about the beauty of the lilies, so that 'even Solomon was not arrayed like one of these,' the beauty and the grandeur of creation are celebrated again and again. The human children of God are at home in creation.

Alas, sin not only obscures much of the good, so that 'the whole creation has been groaning . . . right up to the present time' (Romans 8:22), but many have also turned their backs on the Creator, who is revealed in his works (Romans 1), many who will not accept him as King and Lord of creation. In the midst of such a generation the believer is a stranger, and it is in this sense the Bible speaks of believers as strangers in the world. Later, in the Day of the Lord, the glorious liberty of the children of God will be revealed (Romans 8:21). Then those who hate God will perish.

No, existentialism may be a deepening in unbelief, in realizing oneself to be accursed, knowing oneself to be not at home in this world as God's creation, but that does not make it a correct insight into reality. We must neither detract from the glory of creation, nor misjudge the destructive power of sin and the sway death holds. Yet sin and death are not the essence of reality but alien elements in it, toxic, a sickness, an evil from which we can be saved, thanks be to God, through Jesus Christ. We will see the rich fruit of this salvation in its fullness after the Day of the Lord, when the original situation has been restored and death as the last enemy has been swallowed up in victory (1 Corinthians 15:54).

But let us pick up again the thread of our argument. We have shown how an unbiblical point of departure may interfere with a healthy view of reality, so that the correct and true elements are damaged which people can know simply by looking and observing. That can go so far that art is deprived of its general human character. Truth is always general to humanity, while lies are always just subjective opinions, even if sincerely believed (a matter we will discuss more extensively in chapter 4). Nowadays modern art has convinced many of the view that the world is rotten, but just how relative that notion is will eventually become clear to everyone. And not only eventually! Even now there are many, also outside Christian circles, who do not agree with the message of contemporary art. Why else would there be so many people who seem to find it impossible to connect with the art produced by their own culture?

But that lack of a general human element is usually not recognized by a movement's contemporaries, and certainly not by those in it who are driven by the same spirit. Only later on does it usually become clear. More and more people, for example, begin to perceive the relativity of Romantic art, of nineteenth-century music with its heroic struggle of mere mortals against the overwhelming powers of nature and society. This heroism, this struggle, this passion was real and alive but people have begun to be aware, increasingly, of their limitations, of the fact that these sentiments had a characteristic connection with a particular period. People come to understand that Romantic music is not universal to all ages on the basis of its general human truth, but that it expresses instead a particular attitude towards life.

We have tried to show how a particular life and world view brings with it limitations in the perception of reality, and how that is naturally directly reflected in the content of the works of art produced by those who bear that life view. Yet sometimes we can no longer speak in all honesty of a life view but must just say, instead, that sin is served by the maker of a work, that he or she went looking for sin in order to let it reign. The work may be wrapped in idealism and it may seem to be justifiable culturally especially when it claims to unmask hollow notions, but that does not really make a difference. I have in my possession a gramophone record with a prayer to the dollar, a blasphemous piece of unadulterated mockery of all religion. Here we can no longer speak of ideals, and I believe the maker had no deeper intention than to scoff to his heart's content. It reminds one of Romans 1:32 ['who knowing the judgment of God, that they which commit such things are worthy of death, not only do the same, but have pleasure in them that do them']. In the same way we occasionally come across a book that is thoroughly pederastic and that praises homosexuality as the most natural and wholesome thing in the world. Somewhere in North Italy there is a villa with a room in it decorated with frescos depicting a pederastic 'ideal world'. We may at times object to the content of a humanistic painting that conveys us into a sort of ideal world with naked gods and goddesses, but that is quite a different matter. The representations on these frescos are only lies and sin, and there will be very few people indeed who feel themselves at home there.

A different judgment is called for in the case of a book that depicts the lives of these unhappy people and deals with the problems brought about by their sexual inclination.

In this section we discussed the matter of a life and world view as it is expressed in a work of art. If our formulation has perhaps been somewhat abstract, that was necessary in order to arrive at a more general insight. For the wisdom we mentioned earlier is so individual and so conditioned by various circumstances that one can hardly discuss it in more general terms. In studying a particular work by a particular artist, one can better speak about his or her wisdom than about his or her life and world view. Not that the latter would not exist very concretely as a motivating spirit – the life and world view as such is not theoretical – but it belongs more to larger groups, to streams or movements.

In a certain sense a similar distinction also applies to what follows. Based on their life and world view and in response to the situation, people will adopt a certain attitude to life. That is, they will have a certain sense of calling and responsibility, a certain insight into what is meaningful and worthwhile to do or not to do. Here too one will see a clear pattern arise within a group or movement, but at the same time every individual within such a group will have her or his own mentality. In the following section we shall try to determine what attitude to life has been of importance in more recent art.

This attitude to life, the concrete effect in people's lives of their life and world view, will manifest itself more fully in their lifestyle. Where do they seek their friends, their pleasures, their fulfilment in life? How do they stand in everyday reality? Are they commonplace, respectable and bourgeois? Are they snobbish, looking down on the bourgeois, and do they aspire to greatness or are they happiest when living in a solitary, cloistered existence?

Finally, and so directly related to their life and world view that it may be called a facet of it, is their sense of reality: how do people perceive reality. Do they feel at home in it or do they feel themselves strangers in it, and if so, in what sense?

In the following sections we will devote some attention to these facets of life and world view; in the process, various problems relating to art will engage us.

Art, the spirit of the times and the artist's attitude to life

Art has not always been simple handicraft, and artists have not always seen their task as completing commissions to the best of their ability, which is to say making beautiful works and works fulfilling the requirements of a (societal) function. Thus in the nineteenth century artists often assumed an attitude of prophets, as if they were presenting a revelation of the deepest truths in the cosmos. Or we might better say that various philosophers and art critics assigned art a lofty place and that this view gradually worked its way into practice. Idealistic philosophy, the theoretical thought belonging to Romanticism which one might even call the theology of Romanticism, moved in this direction. Schiller, Goethe, Wackenroder, the Schlegels, and also such professional philosophers as Fichte and Schelling have virtually declared art to be a revelation, the highest religion, the cosmic principle whereby the deep contradictions, the rift between nature and freedom, between determinism and rational morality, are resolved in a higher certainty. Through the work of Schopenhauer [1788–1860] and of Carlyle [1795–1881] this Romantic intellectual heritage was extended so as to make art aware once again, at the end of the [nineteenth] century, of its high calling. The art of the Symbolists about which even Kuyper lectured in 1898 aspired to be a revelation of deep reality; in the symbol people hoped to be able to lay hold of the meaning of reality. This revelatory art-religion became the secularized religion of people who no longer knew the God of the Scriptures.[17]

Remarkably enough, this art is strictly individualistic and subjectivistic and demands of artists that they lay bare the deepest stirrings of their soul. Only in this way would the artist, as someone who by virtue of his or her genius and artistic sensitivity can sense reality more competently than ordinary mortals, be able to reveal the deepest truths.

It is impossible to say how much damage this idea of the artist has inflicted on artists themselves, and how much of its proper function art has lost as a result of such inordinate elevation. It is one of the causes of the abnormal position of modern art, of the chasm that exists between art, borne as it is by an esoteric clan, and the lives of 'ordinary' people.

Artists are compelled to present an often shameless analysis of what lives within them. In the forum of the art world they fight to work out their personal problems, until the most extreme consequences are reached. Meanwhile the art critics often assume that it is their task to analyse the drift and meaning of an artist's struggle. This is even more true for literature than for the art of painting, where this attitude expresses itself in a slightly different way, more as a search for extreme originality, for being at all times perfectly oneself. The feverish quest for originality is frequently mentioned in studies of modern art, and it has done considerable damage to less gifted artists capable of winning a position only in a forced manner. In the name of honesty – above all else to be yourself – much dishonest art has been produced.

Given this desire to express as directly as possible one's own personality and psyche, we cannot help but think of a verse in Proverbs: 'Fools find no pleasure in understanding but delight in airing their own opinions' (18:2). This saying is sharply critical, to be sure, but its scriptural wisdom will often help us fathom the meaning of some modern artistic statements.

There is another remarkable consequence of the doctrine that artists are meant to reveal the spirit of their times and express its most essential values. If that is indeed true, then there is only one art that is truly modern. Everything that does not seem to measure up to it is to be discarded, decried as out of date, a mistake, worthless. It has brought about a kind of 'dictatorship of the latest trend', which again only serves to tempt many who are less talented to howl with the wolves.

I want to present two objections to this sense of dictatorship. In the first place, our times are by no means unified in a spiritual or intellectual sense, although that does not mean we have to go so far as to say our times are chaotic in contrast to earlier periods. In most epochs various and even countless tendencies have existed side by side, some more important, some borne perhaps by only a small group. When we look at the past from a distance there sometimes appears to be an amazing unity, but what we then see is only the overall effect, the smallest common denominator of the many things that were quarrelled about in that period and were pursued as ideals. Culturally this unity is also the smallest common denominator of all the work that was done and of the enduring results that were created. In short, just as little as in the past there was ever anything approaching perfect unity, except in marginal, disclosed societies and cultures, but rather, always, upon closer inspection, a conflict between tendencies or a struggle for contradictory ideals, so also in our own times there is no unity. And therefore it is impossible that everyone today should regard the same things as beautiful or be expected to support the same things and find them worthwhile. That can only produce snobs and dishonest people while at the same time dooming as fruitless, useless or culturally ineffective the work of many who, for whatever reason, do not belong to the stream that has been pronounced 'the' contemporary tendency. It is hardly conceivable that under such circumstances there should be a fair chance for everyone with talent. (Happily the politics of the matter are felt almost exclusively in the field of art; in many other fields the situation is still rather more open, and more possibilities exist.)

A second and weightier objection is that it is impossible to discern who or what tendency represents the spirit of the times best, what has laid bare this virtually apotheosized spirit most tellingly. Would it be the most revolutionary figures? Is it the art that is most dissimilar to anything produced in the past? Is it found where the most radical break has been made with the past, since that represents the most 'original'? Are the most appropriate questions not rather: What is the best? What is borne by the most positive values? What content is the purest and most precious? To be sure, answers will differ, but given such questions the spiritual struggle will unfold in the fairest way. The question of truth, the question of meaning, the question of the content and significance of things must be posed again and again, and our answers, whoever we are, must be the main issue in our cultural labour for each of us in the place assigned to us and with the talents given to us. In this way only can we all, each in our own way, in honesty, openness and freedom, shoulder our responsibility.

The idea that the artist is a prophet, a sort of antenna that can pick up the slightest movements of the spirit of the times well ahead of others, to present us with a new outlook on reality, is a lie, to put it bluntly. An artist is an ordinary person, just like anybody else, who can go astray despite personal insights and ideals. All that artists can do, as individuals amongst others, is to give form to their own view, their sense and understanding of reality, to express their grasp of things in an artistic way. In this way an artist can sometimes help us as viewers to see things more sharply, can make clear to us what a particular outlook entails, can tell us how a certain group or movement thinks about and reacts to the encompassing reality. That is already a great deal. Yet the question of truth must always be posed. For there is no guarantee that an artist has not been gripped by some misleading philosopher or doctrine. An artist can help open our eyes to values or their absence, yet in all of this she or he remains, as I have said, a person but not in the least a prophet, and at most a preacher. The question concerning the content of the preaching remains, and for that the artist's work must always be evaluated.

It is possible that we have said too much here. Or rather, that the bar has been set too high. Would it not be much more worthwhile if the artist simply set out to sing, as it were, in his or her own way, of the beauties of creation and the richness of life under the sun? Then, unobtrusively and dependent on the wisdom of the artist, something of a view would appear. That would not be so bad, but we may not find in art any longer to such a marked degree that which is popular, stressed, in many ways foreign to art itself. No, assigning art too high a function, proclaiming art a religion, has not been profitable for it. A possible objection to the above notion – we have quietly slipped back to the question of a choice of position in the present, but how could it be otherwise if we are people alive in our times – would be that precisely in our times people can appreciate everything, can enjoy and value everything. That is undeniably true. Just walk into a good gramophone shop and see what is for sale there, or see what your friend who collects gramophone records has on his or her shelf. Standing next to one another you may well find the music of Bach, Beethoven, Debussy, Honegger and Bartok, music from India, from Africa, and from Amazon Indian territory, music that originated in the Middle Ages, the Renaissance and the great seventeenth century. And even if a true music lover may not have all of this in her or his cabinet – unable to afford it or restricted to a specialist field in order to be able to listen to all of that – then he or she still listens to all sorts on the radio and to everything played at a concert. Surely present-day means of communication have made all this diversity possible, and who would venture to challenge its value?

It is no different with the calendar of exhibitions. Anyone who is a little active can view within a short period of time the art of the Aztecs, of Rembrandt, of Frans Hals, of the Venetians, of Africans, of primitive tribes from Indonesia, yes, and ever so much more. We can appreciate all these things and have an understanding of them all.

Does it make us rich, we may ask. And how did this 'omnivorism' arise in the field of art? Certainly historicism, a facet of existentialism, has had something to do with that. After all, historicism claims that there are no fixed norms, that every age and every group creates its own norms and hence must be measured according to its own values. Everything is valuable if only it reveals signs of truly creative activity, reveals how humankind have been able to create their own world for themselves and construct their own world picture. In short, those who know how to constitute themselves, who know how to be the bearers and developers of their own values, are held in esteem. Believing is permitted but is considered to be a purely human invention. One's beliefs may be expressed in one's art and some may even say that this is necessary and good.

Thus this omnivorous, all-is-equally-valued habit does not occur without a presupposition: the preconception of the historicized norm.

Yet something else also had to happen in order to make this attitude possible. It was namely necessary to place the full emphasis in all art on its aesthetic quality, on the artistic creative activity, and to regard content as of merely subsidiary importance. In order to place an equal value on Bach's *Mass in B minor* and the last part of Beethoven's *Ninth Symphony* one should not go into the content of the words or ask how the words are served by the music, the composition and musical treatment. For then it becomes virtually impossible to find the work of the believing Protestant and of the idealistic humanist equally good or beautiful without distinction. Both are creations of genius. But is there not an issue of what people do with their genius, of what they have to say, and of what fundamental values they serve with their work? If that is not an issue, then one may go so far as to regard the aria 'In diesem heiligen Hallen' from Mozart's *Zauberflöte* as a humanistic confession of faith par excellence, or as neutral, or even as Christian, or to deny that it is unchristian.

When people pay no attention to the way the text is presented, to the content of the art, yes, then a mass by Mozart and Bach's *Mass in B minor* can be placed on the same level, since both are beautiful renditions of the same text. But those who ask which of the composers has really done justice to the content of the text are compelled to take a position. They can go so far as to say that Mozart's music is certainly very beautiful, particularly if one does not pay too much attention to the words; but that would imply that they might prefer an aria (preferably not the one mentioned above) from one of Mozart's operas, for example from *The Marriage of Figaro*, precisely because the content is less important there.

In other words, in art it is not the aesthetic quality alone that is important. Art is not a purely aesthetic affair; its every fibre is tied to the fullness of human life. Art is connected in many ways with the life of the person who made it, and with the group or function for which it was intended; and sometimes, in the lives of those who know and love it, it plays an important, many-facetted and much more encompassing role than its aesthetic aspect alone could warrant, although that is no excuse to underestimate it. Yet art that is only beautiful, only aesthetic, as some abstract modern art aspires or pretends to be, is impoverished and is in fact no more than an ornament, an element of beauty. As art it falls short. Certainly there is a difference between a lovely vase and a painting that we call a masterpiece. Try to look at Rembrandt's *Jewish bride* without taking into account the human content of the painting, the lovers in their mutual relationship. I am persuaded that the old masters started with their theme or content, whatever it might have been, and then cast about for adequate artistic means to present what they had to say.

It goes virtually without saying that the choice of theme as such is not arbitrary. Artists will choose their subject in such a way that in its artistic treatment they will be able to express their view the most clearly. They will choose it in such a way that it contributes to expressing what moves them most deeply, what is relevant to their view of life and reality. That really goes without saying. No one will devote their powers to telling about something that leaves them cold. Thus, as we saw in the examples presented above, the themes are often loaded with meaning as a result of their being connected directly with the life and world view of the artist – or of a group of which he or she is a part, for we may never consider artists too individualistically as if they were solitary figures, choosing or inventing things in a strictly personal way.[18] Yet only through the artistic treatment does it become clear what in the chosen theme was relevant, connected spiritually to the deepest motives of life.

And this does not apply to the old masters only. How honest and real it sounds when Mahalia Jackson, the renowned singer of Negro spirituals and gospel songs, explains why she does not sing the blues: 'Anybody that sings the blues is in a deep pit yelling for help, and I am simply not in that kind of position.' How much more correct is this insight than that of Christian people here in Europe, who become angry when you say that the blues have nothing to do with Christianity and that in that worldly song of the African-American an entirely different spirit speaks than in the spirituals. It does not detract from the fact that the real blues can have superb qualities, but that only becomes clear to us when we take a good look at the songs. We will not do that here.

Art can be purely aesthetic only if content is unimportant, if every theme is really no more than a pretext to paint, since a work makes an aesthetic statement only and says nothing in fact about what is represented. In that case art is also terribly impoverished.

Lifestyle and art

In order to be clear, I have chosen examples that are in shrill contrast to each other and examples full of content. It would not have achieved the same effect had we compared purely instrumental pieces by Bach and

Beethoven, for example a work for the harpsichord and a piano sonata, although in such works too something of the composer's outlook on life is expressed. Such works too are meaningful in content and have a significance that contributes to our loving them or being indifferent to them or even being negative about them. I mean by this that it is a matter not just of the text or the theme but of the spirit expressed in the work.

A landscape by Rubens looks very different from a landscape by Paulus Potter, and the viewer is aware of a difference of nuance in the content as well, without necessarily being compelled to take a stance for or against it. This example could be multiplied many, many times. For instance, line up beside each other portraits by Jan van Eyck, Raphael, Titian, Frans Hals and Quentin Latour, and as many worlds are represented. Yet it is not necessary to choose between them, although we may prefer one or another, depending on too many factors, too many nuances within ourselves, than we could analyse right on the spot.

These differences depend on the lifestyle of the artist and on the milieu in which he or she moves. Especially in this respect we react sensitively to slight differences. Who people are appears from the way they dress, the way they spend their leisure time, the places they frequent, and the world in which they feel comfortable. These will also be reflected in their art. A landscape by Rubens introduces us to the painter as grand seigneur, a man of the world, a man of passion and heroism, a man full of life's grandeur with a broad outlook; Potter's landscape, by contrast, is a typical product of our middle-class seventeenth-century society, of a modest lifestyle, standing amongst and not above people and things. Rubens shows us his tenants, Potter, his friends; Rubens shows us his possessions, Potter, the charming open countryside of the polders where he wanders, enjoying the light, the sight of the cows, the panoramic view and not least of all the rural serenity.

When we read a book in which the main figure is given little to do besides seducing girls and going to bed with them and in which he is surrounded only by others who do the same, then that indicates something at least of the lifestyle of the writer, and at the same time of his or her outlook on life. Are there really no other ideals, is that the point of life? It may make us feel like strangers. Perhaps while reading such a volume we become acquainted with a different world, perhaps it is a terrific book, perhaps it is even entirely true and the circumstances the writer describes are exactly as he or she typifies them. Yet we may still put the book aside after a while in a state of mild irritation. Perhaps we prefer the romantic heroes and lovely maidens of Walter Scott, even though that world is far less true to life.

We also see in all this something of the great richness, the many-sided nature of human life. Not all people are alike, not all settings are the same, not all people emphasize the same priorities and uphold the same set of values. In order to be able to enjoy all this and judge things for what they are worth we need not be neutralistic and, in the modern spirit, overlook all differences as if there were no norms. A book about guerilla fighters takes us into a different world from the one we normally inhabit, and had we found ourselves in such a world we might well have chosen the 'other' side; yet we can understand that in that world certain values are esteemed and certain habits rule which are not ours, even though we 'accept' the whole situation. Yet we do not have to look that far. Those who have travelled and have kept their eyes open know about such differences from personal experience and therefore know too that often we cannot say that one thing is better or worse but only that it is different.

Sense of reality and art

Finally, a person's life and world view expresses itself very concretely in his or her sense of reality: what does it feel like, how does he or she relate to things, to people and, more importantly, to trials and tribulations, to setbacks and problems? Does a person know how to take his or her burdens to Christ, to bear a cross patiently, to live with his or her own deficiencies and illnesses, shortcomings and limitations? Or is one constantly in revolt, feeling shortchanged, wanting to change things right now, in a revolutionary manner, to satisfy one's own ideals?

The old ideal that we encounter already in Genesis 3 with the Fall, the desire to be God, to have our destiny in our own hands, to have all our wishes fulfilled immediately just as we want them, is still alive and kicking. Carlyle, the nineteenth-century philosopher, put it beautifully, wittily and aptly when he said that even the shoeblack needs basically for enduring satisfaction and fulfilment in life simply this: God's infinite universe entirely and exclusively to himself, in order to entertain himself in it without end and satisfy every wish as fast as it arises.[19] Modern people seek freedom and in doing so encounter reality, which they call 'nature' but which should properly be called 'creation'.

I believe it was Sjestow who once said he did not want it to be so that $2 \times 2 = 4$. And that is understandable, for in accepting it we have to bow before what is given, before that which limits our freedom – that is, our humanistic freedom, freedom in the sense of being equal to God. There is something heroic in the struggle for a new world and culture, solely determined by humankind, as one forerunner expressed it, a struggle intent on 'destroying this unworthy world in order to re-create it'. In what is perhaps one of the finest definitions of much modern cultural work, someone described John Davidson as follows: 'the honesty and courage of a spirit that courageously dashes itself to pieces against the closed, barred door of an unknown and perhaps nonexistent reality'.[20]

Modern people, who are in essence no different from people throughout the ages, have come into an intense conflict with reality itself. To be convinced of this we certainly do not have to listen just to the philosophers. Around 1900 it was the artist Gauguin who said pithily:

> I know, just like everyone, and just like everyone will always know, that two plus two equals four. But it is a long way from the convention, from knowing, to understanding: I resign myself, and just like everyone else I too say: two plus two equals four ... but that lies heavily upon me and robs me of much of my judgment.[21]

It is from this attitude towards reality – an attitude of not accepting what God has created, simply because he created it and people in their freedom did not – that the modern artistic way of working has arisen, the main lines of which were likewise already formulated by Gauguin in his last years, around 1900. And seldom has a spiritual will been so faithfully executed to the letter as in this:

> And as to the work, a method of contradiction, if you like, venturing into the strongest abstractions, doing all that was forbidden, and reconstructing more or less happily, without any fear of exaggeration, even with exaggeration. Learning anew, and then, once having learnt, learn again. Conquer any timidity however much ridicule it may occasion. In front of his easel the painter is no slave, either of the past or of the present, either of nature or of his neighbour. He is himself, again himself, always himself alone.[22]

Again and again one finds the same thing in commentaries on modern painters, and then not by opponents or by those who do not accept modern art but especially by those who stand fully behind them. It is the best refutation of the often heard thesis that art is ultimately nothing more than a purely aesthetic matter of beautiful versus not beautiful, about tasteful proportions in line, colour and surface. Thus we read in a book about the Dutch painter Corneille the following: 'We see that the matter is one of a conscientious choice, an existential choice of position. Altogether refusing to copy reality, which means trying to present a never previously offered solution to what people call the conflict between man and nature'.[23]

The art of painting during the years following the Second World War is certainly more than a mere playing with paint. Sandberg, the well-known director of Amsterdam's Stedelijk Museum of Modern Art makes that clear: 'The period of suppression and falsification in which we live does not solicit our response but screams out for protest – that protest, shrill and piercing in music, gripping and often murky in book and play, breaks out cursing and seething in the art of painting and in sculpture shows ruination alongside new, burgeoning life.'[24]

Consider finally what Paul Tillich, the American theologian and philosopher, has to say. He wrote the introduction to a book that seeks to clarify the contemporary view of human being through modern artworks:

Where are the organic forms of the human body, the human character of his face, the strictly personal in his individuality? And finally, when in abstract or non-figurative art the form disappears entirely, one is tempted to ask what has become of man. Humanity is not something that man simply has. He must fight for it with every new generation, and he can lose the fight. There have been few periods in history when a catastrophic defeat was more threatening than in our own ... There are demonic forces in every person that endeavor to take him in thrall, and the new view of man shows faces in which the condition of possession is disturbingly clear. In others the anxious fear of such possession or anxiety at the thought of being alive is all-determining, and in yet others there are feelings of emptiness, meaninglessness and despair. But there is also courage, desire and hope, a reaching out into the unknown.[25]

Notice the closing words, 'a reaching out into the unknown', the search for a new insight into life that ignores the familiar, namely the traditional and certainly also the biblical, revelation. Yet it is certain – and the seekers know this too! – that humankind will never be successful in recovering their own humanity if they mean to do it in their own strength. Only through the work of the Holy Spirit and in redemption through Jesus Christ is there salvation and true, liberating freedom, and true and genuine humanity.

What does the development in art since the seventeenth century teach us?

We will now try to examine more extensively the course of events that led to the modern crisis situation and to see, in particular, what art can teach us about it.

To begin with we must understand well what the old paintings pictured in reality. What, for example, is it really all about when in fifteenth- and early sixteenth-century art countless stories are depicted from the Bible, and of saints dressed in the clothing of the painter's own period? Is the painter so naïve as to think that people once, long ago, really looked like this? I will try to be brief. Never for a moment did these painters intend a kind of reporting of facts, to show us what we would have seen had we been there. This is true for a Nativity scene, a Crucifixion, an Entombment and for a depiction of Christ in the storm at sea. What the painter does offer us is best compared with a sermon on the subject. Without desiring to tamper with the historicity of the subject, for example the Crucifixion, it will still not be presented as just any event from very long ago, as we might speak about events associated with the battle at Issus or Anthony's visit to Cleopatra. No, the crucifixion is not purely something that happened in the remote past; it is something that happened which continues to have everything to do with now, today. The story of the Lord Jesus with his disciples in a small boat on the sea of Tiberius during a storm tells us more than the fact that some 2,000 years ago a kind of miracle-worker did this or that on one occasion or another. This story teaches us something that is still true today, something that can comfort us. When Negro spirituals sing of Joshua at Jericho or Daniel in the lions' den, then that does not signify that black Americans are avid historians who want to show that they know what happened a long time ago in Canaan or in Babylon. In short, and that is why I used the word 'sermon', these stories have something more to tell us than historical content alone – more than reporting what a person was likely to have seen had he or she been there then. The historical element is very important, to be sure, and woe to us if we forget that and turn these biblical stories into myths, interesting truths dressed up in stories, more or less historically true, for in that case what is important for us in them would vanish at the same time.

While discussing Soviet attitudes towards history, Gollwitzer once said that the moment one starts to regard Plato, for example, as an interesting piece of history, entirely outdated now however, and certainly without importance for today's world, then every reading of his work becomes a waste of time. The person who reads Plato carries on a dialogue with him about the deepest values pertaining to humanity and the world system in which we have been placed. One can therefore disagree heartily [with Plato], for that does not detract from a one-to-one dialogue, communicating across the ages.

That is true even for non-biblical history. But it does confront the painter with a problem. How must he or she depict these biblical historical events in such a way that they express, beyond just the historical element, also that which is so directly important for me? Before the end of the eighteenth century people had resolved the question by depicting events in a fully concrete way – no vague visions, no sketchy ideas – that stressed the palpable and the visible, the it-happened-here-on-earth quality of events without attempting any reconstruction of the past. They took no trouble to show with the help of the clothing, setting, landscape or buildings how things actually were at the time. They only showed that what happened was authentic and true, very real, and that it is of direct importance for us, with an importance that transcends the purely historical element. When in a woodcut Dürer depicts Christ crowned with thorns, then that is no portrait, no record of history, but rather a testimony, a sermon if you will, a view of Christ in his importance for us. In viewing seventeenth-century paintings, for example, we must also be ever mindful that the painter paints more than what is directly visible and uniquely accurate. Jan van Goyen seldom if ever paints a riverscape that one could actually see from a particular location, but he shows us the structure and associates it with something more general than a particular instance. Moreover, as we want to show in the continuation, when Rembrandt paints Bathsheba, he is concerned not just with events surrounding this woman a long time ago, but he paints something about the glory of womanhood [see Plate 6]. He uses his brush to tell us about it. Even a simple still life is not just made up of a number of objects, but through the objects something of general human interest is communicated – for example, a Vanity painting speaks of the futility and transience of material things, while a so-called breakfast or still life with fruit tells us about the the richness and glory of life.

We can best understand this if we imagine the picture of the world of a seventeenth-century person. Perhaps a very great deal of the Platonist intellectual heritage was still incorporated in it, perhaps it was more clearly biblical and Christian, expressing the idea that all things are constructed, with norms, by God; however it may be, there was a concept of what constituted general truth: the ideas, general principles, general human realities that were not engineered by people but created and given by God. Individual things and events were understood to be the concrete expression here below of the individualization, the deposit of these ideas and principles. Schematically it would look as follows:

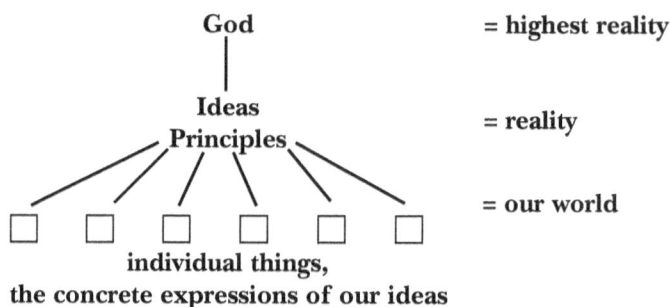

When in Rome in the seventeenth century a reporter observed that the presentation of an address by the pope in a particular chamber had been a manifold revelation of wisdom – referring to the piece that the pope spoke about from the (apocryphal) book of Wisdom in his persona as the embodiment of the highest Wisdom, Christ, here on earth and to the paintings depicting wisdom on the ceiling – then that is a purely Platonic account. From such an account we also learn that the allegories people painted at that time involved a great deal more than a pretext to do some decorating.

More directly biblical statements were made in the works by Jan van Goyen and the Dutch still life painters, as well as in the way Bible stories were painted during that period – I think especially of the art of Rembrandt. In all these cases truth is expressed that still holds for us today, a meaningfulness that is important for every person, a general rather than strictly individual idea that did not originate in one person's mind but was simply given to humankind.

In the seventeenth century, however, humanism, reflecting on its own foundations, banished God from the scheme of things. God was still named, but then as a sort of basis or cosmic principle, perhaps still as Creator and Sustainer, but then more as an inventor who constructs and maintains a machine. God as a Father, a personal God with whom we can and must stand in direct contact, no longer exists for the seventeenth-century humanist. Such was the world picture of Leibniz and Descartes.

In the eighteenth century the Encyclopedists thought things through further in this direction and drew more consequences. The age of Enlightenment settled accounts with the old world picture and precisely on that account believed itself to be 'enlightened'. God as an actual reality was set aside entirely and even some general principles had to yield, reduced to human inventions, to principles inferred from the observation of individual, materially given things. Schematically it now looked as follows:

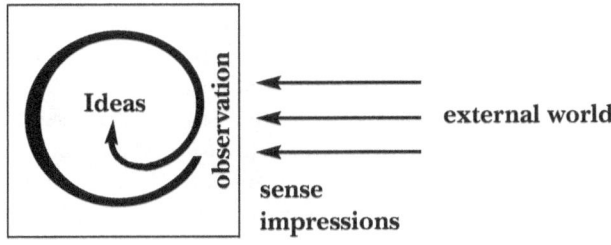

Thus ideas arise within people, also . . . God. This is approximately how it is with Hume, and that line of thought is carried through ever more consistently. In the old, albeit somewhat Platonically conditioned, world picture God was first, then Creation, including both matter and general principles, and only thereafter the realization of the structural principles or ideas in matter, the substance of reality in which we live. Also concrete humanity was placed there. But now all that changed, and God and these ideas became the subjective inventions of people. In the new scheme of things humanity is first, and God and all the rest are secondary, figments of human thought. So people reverted to the old sin of regarding their own idols as gods, their own ideas as generally valid principles.

This is not a history of philosophy but a view of reality that intruded deeply into the human world picture, first of the elite and then gradually into the minds and especially the hearts of people in general. It involved a revolution of values, a revolution that is still far from finished. It is most extreme with the so-called 'avant-garde', much more so than with the general public. Perhaps their direct contact with reality interrupts this degradation. Where the Bible is read and believed there is naturally a powerful brake against this development.

These changes are clearly mirrored in art, a proof that something more than an academic matter is at stake here, something that affects more than just a handful of thinkers. We notice it already in the eighteenth century, when the genre pieces are invested with a different nuance than in the preceding period, a difference that is difficult to describe but that is certainly connected with this altered outlook. We notice this change most clearly in French art – then already avant-garde in this sense. The genre pieces no longer present a perspective on values and realities of importance for human life, more or less moralizing, disapproving or laudatory, but instead we are given little glimpses of situations that are often amorous in nature. What saves this kind of painting and makes it fascinating is the fact that this amorousness, this sensuality is turned into a refined game: were not the words 'galant' and *esprit* coined in this time and environment? This art conveys us into a world in which the ladies are amiable and charming and the gentlemen gallant and spirited. Yet Venus is no longer the goddess of beauty and love, but a sweet, disrobed amourette, presented in the way in which the gallant gentleman on the prowl, ready to pay her a full-spirited compliment, liked to see her in her boudoir.

Against this lifestyle and this art – Diderot already complained that you see far too many nipples and thighs! – opposition arose towards the end of the century. Masculine strength, loyalty and patriotism, those were the values that deserved to be depicted. No longer the frivolity of the Rococo, but instead the discipline and noble simplicity of classicism. When David spreads this ancient world with its republican ideals out before our eyes – and keep in mind that the bearers of these ideals were the men of the Encyclopedia, those who, whether conscious of it or not, were preparing the Revolution[26] – he wants to grant us a look into that ancient past in such a way that if an ancient Roman were to see it he would recognize it, David explicitly said, as his own. In this way painting now becomes a reconstruction of the past. And in that ideal, or rather idealized past, idealized people walk about, often naked. Winckelmann and the other builders of classicism sung the praise of the Greeks, who still possessed a beautiful naturalness that we, sadly, lack. But, different from earlier centuries when nudity was a heroic vestment, a reflection of the meaning of life, of the ideals implicit in images meant to be understood allegorically, it now became an indication of concrete historical reality. These heroic scenes from the past thereby acquire an entirely different accent from those, for example, of Poussin in the seventeenth century. Now it is more as if we had been transported to a nudist colony. In David's painting of the Sabines struggling with the Romans the naked warriors have a somewhat less than credible, unreal quality because they are, more than undressed, naked. It indicates that this art is essentially illustrative only, naturalistic, and as such no longer a rendering of ideas.

The shift is especially clear in religious art. The eighteenth-century Nativity scenes, the most beautiful of which were made in Naples, show through a great many figures a picture of the world in which the artist lived, of the hustle and bustle in a real market of the day. But in about 1800 that changed and instead we are shown reconstructions of the past, with men dressed in burnous, Arabs in white garments, as people were then thought to have dressed when they went about their business in the time of the Lord Jesus.

Understandably, it is no longer the divine persons, no longer the importance of what happened in the past, no longer the meaning for us of the deeds and figures appearing before our eyes that receive emphasis; rather, all attention is directed to human beings, and the religious quality depends, as it were, on them. I am thinking of Tassaert's painting *The unhappy family*. We see a mother and her daughter sitting mournfully together. The mother fixes her gaze and heart on Mary, beseeching her for help – that is the meaning in this painting of her looking up at a little print of the Madonna on the wall. We have to understand what this painting actually offers us. If we were to look for parallels from the past, we would find virtually nothing. And that is entirely comprehensible since the direct parallel of this work insofar as content is concerned is every Madonna painted before 1800. In those Madonna paintings, Mary, as the one who brings comfort, was presented to the eyes of the believers in an image that represented this holy woman. Now, however, she has become a mere print on the wall; all attention is focused instead on the believing person. It is not the content of faith that is painted here but the believing person, no longer the supra-temporal reality as this is believed, but belief itself, the subjective human quality in its relation to whatever it is that people adopt as object of their belief.

Again and again it is as if divine persons or holy events and things are placed outside the frame of the painting. I would like to characterize that by using a term borrowed from mathematics: extrapolation. The proper subject, according to the earlier art and biblical message, is nowhere to be seen but has to be imagined. A quite extreme example is provided by the English painter Holman Hunt, who does not show the grace of God, his disposition to forgive, in a Crucifixion or some other scene from the Passion intended for our edification but, instead, shows us the scapegoat in the wilderness in a minutely detailed painting of a goat painted at the shore of the Dead Sea. And he was astonished when people did not understand the message in his work! Another extreme example that borders on blasphemy is Tissot's peculiar painting of the Crucifixion. It shows us what Christ saw from the cross, and thus it was possible for the painter to render a Crucifixion in which the heart of the matter, that around which everything turns, does not appear in the painting but lies outside of it and has to be imagined by the viewer.

The religious art of the nineteenth century constantly gives us reconstructions of the biblical past. 'That is the way it was, then and there,' just as in literature writers like Renan and Hall Caine perpetrated reconstructions of the life of Jesus precisely as they supposed it would have been historically. Now the remarkable thing is that the biblical reality is not thereby made more concrete and real for the beholder, but instead becomes more distant: it is just history, after all, something that happened a long time ago. Its connection with us in our time has vanished from it. The believing person is now at the centre, for that alone is concrete and true in the present age. Therefore we see the believer again and again in scores of paintings, praying, sitting in the church, even dying as a hero for his faith. Yet in every instance it is the person and never what he or she believes, the believing and never the content of belief that we see.

The naturalism of the nineteenth century, which in art aspired to present visible reality or a reconstruction of the past as it would have been visible at the time, thereby gradually lost its human value. The only truth it still preached was that of the purely visible and purely natural. The dearth of content became increasingly conspicuous. What a pity that the Protestant Christian world connected with precisely this nadir in religious art for its Bible pictures and illustrations! It is no easy task to say what was lost to our spiritual lives as a result of this development, or how it carried over into the souls of all those people who filled their imagination and their knowledge of the biblical past with such images.

Undoubtedly there are difficulties here, and it is moreover often not possible to connect in a positive sense with modern art. That many have sought refuge in the etchings of Rembrandt is accordingly understandable and above reproach. Yet this situation remains a testimony to our own poverty and powerlessness to produce acceptable and meaningful art again for ourselves, in the sense discussed, at whatever level. Happily the numbers are increasing of those looking for solutions to these problems. Let us support their efforts. We thereby serve not only art but also, most importantly, the faith of many who through thorough-going historicization have lost contact with biblical reality.

For nineteenth-century people, in the period during which belief was so subjectivized and the contents of faith removed so far from human consciousness that they could scarcely be experienced as reality, reality often lay elsewhere. By way of an aside, have you noticed how the term 'reality' has changed in meaning through the course of time? For Plato and those living in the Christian Middle Ages, God, ideas and general structural principles, in short, the supernatural was reality, and earthly reality was just the reflection of that. The Reformation, to the extent that it broke with scholasticism, understood that God put us in this reality as a reality in its own right, while the supernatural reality of God the Father and Creator and the general structural principles continued to be considered as reality as well. With the coming of the apostasy of the eighteenth century and the influence of humanistic principles, first in philosophy and then also in the general life and world view, however, that supernatural element which in the biblical world picture was always upheld as the highest reality was rationalized, and finally declared dead – consider Nietzsche. As a result, reality is now just what is still materially and visibly here, and only that may justifiably be called reality. Realism in Greek philosophy thus turns out to be something entirely different from realism in the nineteenth-century sense. For the latter I prefer to use the term 'naturalism'.

Nineteenth-century reality lay in the purely individual, in the subjective and human; at bottom reality was to be found only in nature. It is therefore no wonder that nineteenth-century art is strongest when it paints nature, since it is only in nature that it truly believes. That is why the art of landscape painting blossomed; and it is especially striking in this regard that people showed great interest in the changing aspects of nature . . . observing how a particular tract of land looked in different kinds of weather, summer and winter, rain and sunshine, or even how it changed at the end of the day – things that an earlier art, more concerned with the structure of the landscape, had never depicted. A typical example is Turner's *Rain, storm and speed*, which shows us a train crossing a bridge during a heavy rainstorm, while the train itself is hardly visible.

In this connection it is also instructive to compare the series of etchings made by Callot about the horrors of war in about 1630 with the series Goya made on the same theme shortly after 1800. For Callot, righteousness and justice are anchored firmly in God himself. We see plunderers, and also how they meet their end through the death penalty. We see that in spite of all the horrors, including the fact that as a result of the circumstances wicked human passions are let loose in war, reality itself ultimately never changes and that norms and values retain their significance. With Goya that is all entirely different. For him there are no fixed norms to be detected in war, but only blind passion, merciless in its murderousness, crime, cruelty, all without any deeper meaning and without any higher perspective.

On the second page of this series *Disasters of war* we see two poorly armed men fighting against well-equipped French soldiers. The caption reads, *conrazón o sin ella* – 'with or without reason', or 'rational or irrational'. There is no way of telling whether what is happening is meaningful or not. Remarkably, this etching is strongly affinitive in its composition to the renowned painting *The execution of Spaniards by the French, May 3, 1808*, so that the content of that work likewise becomes clearer for us if indeed it was not already obvious: it is not about serving justice or upholding a just order, and even less about martyrs, people who have risen against tyranny and then died in the fight for a good cause. No, what we see is only a murderous firing squad, anonymous and without emotion, and a group of desperate people being butchered, nothing more and nothing less.

So too the companion piece that deals with events at Madrid a day earlier, the struggle with the Mamalukes, Napoleon's elite troops, near the Puerta del Sol at a great square in the city [see Plate 7]. Lafuente Ferrari writes correctly that this masterpiece is entirely different from all earlier historical paintings, not only because Goya draws his inspiration from an event in his own time and place, something he could even have experienced himself, but also because he presents a historical piece without any hero and without any underlying idea, *una deshumanizada crítica anti-contenutista*, a dehumanizing vision from which all human normative content has been removed.[27] Goya achieved that through the construction of his composition, which is entirely different from the earlier humanistic portrayals of history: here we are forced to see, as it were, a detail from the conflict, a murderous slaughter in which it is virtually impossible to distinguish the parties. It is precisely the absence of a fixed structure emphasizing certain parts in this painting that evokes this image of undirected and therefore senseless slaughter, without motivating ideals, loveless on the one hand, but then on the other hand also without hatred. Precisely because of this new vision, Goya's art was something unprecedented, and for this reason too many have justifiably come to regard him as the first modern painter.

In official circles of nineteenth-century French painting people still endeavoured to keep up the appearances of the humanism of the classical tradition, acting in a reasoned academicism as if they still wanted to achieve the same as before, as in Poussin's day. Yet they did not get much further, as we have seen, than the making of idealized or sometimes purely naturalistic reconstructions of the past. The destruction of Babel, the decadence of the Romans, and many death scenes, as of the death of Queen Elizabeth, were favourite subjects. Yet because of the pretence, and because the theme was often not much more than an excuse to paint sultry women, it was inevitable that such classicism would one day be thoroughly pilloried and a mockery made of its ridiculous unreality. Daumier was the man who carried out this sentence: in a series of lithographs he shows us the classics 'as they really are' – an idealization in reverse – a swaggering Alexander, an exhausted Apollo, a bruiser of an Oedipus with a most unpleasant virago named Sphinx, an anorexic, nearly dead Narcissus, a pining Penelope, all figures excelling in ugliness, wispiness and the contradiction of all that is heroic. This was the death of classicism, but more than that, of the art of painting as it had been understood earlier, in the seventeenth century. From now on no self-respecting painter would dare to depict a

Hector or an Achilles as the great heroes of a better age, and it was even less possible to use such figures to give form to general ideas or ideals.

Thus when in the last quarter of the nineteenth century the effort was made to overcome naturalism and to let the art of painting be the art of painting once again, people felt compelled to hold on to realism, the representation of ordinary reality. The work of Seurat, Cézanne, and Gauguin means the conquest of new possibilities for art, it means regaining the insight that painting is a language, and understanding once again of what I earlier called the iconic element. But while art thus becomes art again, the view of reality as such does not change essentially. These painters tried to depict the ordinary everyday reality in which only the subjective human element and nature are truly real using new, non-naturalistic means, and no longer to imitate it. Nevertheless, a world persisted without God and without deeper values. The supernatural was and remained dead.

Art was now a purely aesthetic activity in which people indulged their creativity and freedom to the hilt. Early in the sixteenth century Giorgione painted a Venus, and she was a true Venus, not just a naked sun-bathing woman. In the eighteenth century she became a coquette who used her nakedness to parade and seduce; in the nineteenth century, with Ingres, she became an odalisque, the favourite concubine of a sultan. It was still far away and outside our world, but it was a reality and not in the least an ideality or the image of a deeper human value or truth; the *Olympia* of Manet from around the 1860s was unabashedly a prostitute, staring at us somewhat insolently. But even this reality was soon taken away. She came to be called simply Nude and the reality that this represented became ultimately a purely aesthetic one, a play of lines and forms devoid of further significance. That is how we may understand the work of Matisse called *Still life with nude*.

L'art pour l'art had meant in the nineteenth century that art was detached from higher values, that artists were free to paint reality as they saw it, raw, direct and including everything bad or immoral. This was a fully secularized art in which only the artistic quality was still upheld as a norm.

The consequences of this tendency may be observed in so-called abstract art, art that is no more than line and form and in which no image is presented of any visible reality. The question is, however, and we must be mindful of it, honestly and without mincing words, whether this art is so purely artistic after all, or whether in and with this art something is still stated about reality. I believe something is said after all, and in the first place it is a negative statement, that reality is not worth the effort to inspire or fascinate us.

Yet there is more. One of the most important builders of non-figurative, non-representational art, Kandinsky, wrote in 1912: 'Clash of tones, lost balance, falling principles, unexpected drumbeats, great questions, apparently purposeless striving, passion and desire apparently ripped to pieces, smashed chains and bonds that make a unity of diversity, contradictions and rebuttals – that is our harmony.'[28] As this makes clear, the interplay of line, form and colour is not at all internally harmonious but is full of tensions, full of conflict, full of loss. Abstract art is more than the purely aesthetic alone. It is first of all a negation, a negation of the value of the reality around us. Next, it is an effort by human beings to create something in full freedom, to build something detached from reality. Finally, people still have something to say about that project, namely that they know no inner rest, no balance, no peace, least of all with reality.

Upon taking a better look at modern art, one is struck by how closely abstraction and Surrealism or Dadaism are connected. Historically, in the first place as to the leading figures who shaped these developments, figures who were in good contact with one another, and secondly as to the pictorial language and the sentiments that inspired them, and also as to what they express in their work. Of the two, Surrealism is easier to explain and understand since it endeavours to say precisely how it interprets reality, while the abstractionists seem to shut their eyes to reality – not only because they have no interest in being inspired by it but also because they do not wish to participate in it. With some abstractionists this is only pretence. Anyone who has noted the prophetic tone of the articles in *De Stijl*, the magazine of Mondrian and his circle in the 1920s, knows very well that behind all their so-called quest for pure beauty a revolutionary spirit was enthroned, together with a hatred for reality, especially for nature, and for the established order of society – an attitude that would be inconceivable if one were not, for all that, continually participating in it oneself.

In 1947 René Huyghe, the renowned French art historian, wrote an article about modern art, and in particular about Dadaism and Surrealism.[29] It is interesting to quote several citations from it, especially in order to make clear that the ideas expressed above are not uniquely my own contribution but that they have been expressed much more widely. In this article Huyghe advances his own view of the development, a view that corresponds in many ways with my argument, by typifying modern people in their relation to reality as follows: 'In this universe, of which we imagined ourselves the future masters, which appeared to be at least a familiar habitat, the illusion is shattered: everything remains closed against our intimacy and resists our efforts to attain to an understanding of it.' And so it comes about that we 'feel ourselves drifting in empty space.' 'Contemporary man has given up attempting to attain to any thing besides images of terror, . . . and "anxiety", "despair" and "absurd" have become the words whereby he struggles to disclose the mystery (of reality).' Huyghe goes on to quote from Sartre and Camus in order to arrive at the conclusion: 'So human life is sterile, thus absurd, and it knows that it is absurd. The greatness of man consists in despair at the fact, that the capacity for clarity that he accepts is overcome by that capacity itself.'

And finally Huyghe writes a passage in this important article that I recommend to all for consideration, especially those who are here called 'good souls':

> There are good souls who are continually outraged by the expressions of 'modernism' and who see in it fraud, yes even financial combinations. However, people are never more easily misled than by their own mistrust, and nothing leads better to gullibility than one's own skepticism. No, good souls, people are not trying to make fools of you! This art, this literature is no more frightening than present-day science, which you esteem because you only see its results; they obey the same unavoidable fatality. They are also undergoing the crisis of the irrational; they too experience or proclaim the bankruptcy of our ever so trusted Reason, they too contribute to its meltdown, the results of which are as yet unforeseeable. They obey the ineluctable law of the present age, namely, that of the absurd.

Before we go any further I want to make two observations. First, I do not believe that the law of the present age is ineluctable. And the proof is easily given. It lies first in the fact that many people today (still) refuse to see reality as the modernists see it, judging from their art. If absurdity really were the law of the present age that would have been impossible. But not only do these 'good souls' still see an 'ordinary' reality, even Picasso still does so – and shows it time and again alongside his better known, more typical work. He too obviously still knows ordinary reality, although in his other work he usually says terrible things about it. And we would do well to understand that as soon as the view that Picasso paints in his 'crazy' works is accepted as normal and ordinary by everyone, his crazy paintings must lose their meaning. For their meaning resides precisely in their protest, in the besmirching, in the destroying of the image of reality given people in their everyday experience. The moment Picasso can no longer refer to such ordinary experience, he can no longer continue with the way of working he has adopted until now. The message in his work would be silenced.

That it is not ineluctable to see as modern science, philosophy and art do, with a nihilistic gaze and no regard for God, who is kept at a safe distance, is also apparent from many present-day works of art which are not modernistic but which for all that are still of this age and not a parroting of the past. We will return to this later.

Second, I want to observe that in this discussion and also with reference to the words of René Huyghe the matter is not one of our developing interesting ideas about art, or of carrying on philosophical or literary discussions concerning things that people should know but cannot see, 'see' in the most literal sense. No, all these things may be seen in the art itself. Just browse through some illustrated works on modern art. Better yet, pay a visit (not too short a visit) to a museum of modern art. Better than all the words printed here can describe, you will be able to see and experience in such a place what 'modern' means.

Now, we still want to ask ourselves how it is possible for us to see all this in modern art. Recall that we discussed nineteenth-century art from which all content had been drained away, that Venus could no longer be an allegory or goddess but had become a real, undressed woman, that the painter had to create a slave market or some such situation in order to justify painting such figures. We also discussed how in connection with so-called religious art the proper content was often extrapolated from a painting so that only the believing people were portrayed. In short, we discussed how all belief in higher values external to human being, in the reality of God and angels and so on, was gone, and how the painter was thus forced to fall back on reality itself, though disfigured. Only in that which was given in immediate experience, in people's direct contact with the things they can see, weigh, measure and feel was there truth and reality, all the rest was at best a human figment, a human invention, and as such exposable as nothing more than a concoction meant to satisfy 'natural' principles and desires.

But when reality is robbed in this way of its value and bereft of its meaning, then it unavoidably becomes meaningless to paint what one can see. Hence naturalism was quickly doomed; in fact it was already doomed at the moment it was born. For what could possibly be the significance of slavishly painting visible things that anyone can see just by looking at them? What is the sense of painting things that have no deeper meaning than their visibility itself?

The twentieth century simply goes on to draw the consequences. Not the theme, the subject, but the manner in which a work is presented, the style in which it is painted, is now most important. What is given in reality has become no more than a pretext for the work of art, for in the things as such one now finds little that is valuable or meaningful. Therefore art can become abstract, the female figure an arabesque, a landscape a few daubs of colour.

The twentieth century draws the consequences by painting pure subjectivity and by demanding the direct expression of individual experience, since that at least still shows that people possess subjectivity and can experience freedom. This freedom, freedom in the humanistic sense, is the essence of modern art. And in the name of this freedom there is a great deal that must be destroyed. Picasso occupied himself in this way for several decades with a series of works in which he paraphrased old masterpieces by Velasquez, Courbet and Cranach, conjuring them into a play of forms in which all content, all beauty, all reflection of reality is smashed, besmeared, trampled underfoot. In this way he shows what every past view means to him, so little in fact that in a sort of nihilist iconoclasm its every value may be destroyed. Where every belief in the meaning of things has gone, it cannot be otherwise than that the modern person who wants to express in art what he or she regards as valuable will want to clear out of the way every bequeathed depiction of reality!

A revolutionary feeling is expressed in all this, a feeling of an uprising against God himself that vents itself in hatred for what is given, for the reality that blocks the path of human beings in their passion for freedom and their will to self-determination. This makes Picasso's nude *Portrait of a lady* comprehensible. In this piece not only the time-honoured form is destroyed, the image of woman given in art at least since the Renaissance twisted and profaned, but more: this work says no to the creation. A painting such as this is a curse! It is an expression of hatred. Of Picasso it certainly cannot be said that he is meek or humble, or poor in spirit, someone who in awareness of his own weakness and dependence comes to God for salvation, someone who can be called a peacemaker because he thirsts after the righteousness of which the Bible speaks.[30] This work is an outburst of hatred levelled against all beauty, against all human warmth, against every value held in high esteem for all ages, while one searches in vain for traces of respect or prudence.

On the occasion of a recent exhibition, one reviewer wrote about this and similar pieces: 'Grim, mostly drab paintings they were, which sometimes gave us the impression of a scarcely veiled, furious assault on a part of our society (especially *Portrait of a lady* aroused this impression), a critique of our own planet.'[31]

Now, it is worth noting that this work by Picasso is not beautiful, that it is a piece of revolutionary sentiment, hatred, declension, and destruction of all that is lovely, but therefore certainly art – which is to say a work by a man whose talents are above all doubt and who knows how to realize or present his view comprehensively. It is not beautiful, and therefore it is entirely unnecessary to do as so many do, who stand in confusion in a museum of modern art and ask themselves: Am I supposed to think this is beautiful? Am I so dumb that I do not understand my own time and cannot see the beauty in it? No, you saw right: art is no secret doctrine, no abracadabra that people can approach with a modicum of understanding only after years of practice. It is indeed ugly, it is a curse, it is a tearing down of all values, but it is also art, an honest expression by a person of our times. You do not have to agree with him, but you can engage with him in an open discussion, in and through his work, in order thereby to come to understand something of the spirit of our age. In order to learn as well, better than ever, to tremble before this spirit from the abyss, this spiritual malevolence, this rebellion . . . against the Creator, which is manifest precisely in the refusal to accept the most primary and self-evident human values.

In this way we are made mindful of something we probably never saw so clearly before, namely that human values even such as the acknowledgment of woman's beauty and the importance of love are not in the least self-evident in themselves but are originally the fruits of Christianity. For it was Christianity that first restored woman in her honour and assured her of a proper, fully worthy place in life.[32] One learns to understand the grace that leads to a renewal of life if one can call oneself meek and an anti-revolutionary in the whole of one's life perspective and struggle. However, there is no reason whatsoever for Christians to consider themselves above these moderns, whose revolutionary breakthrough was certainly a consequence in part of the negligence of Reformational Christians to become engaged, openly and with a warm heart, in the areas of art and culture and to be of service to their neighbours in these areas as well.[33]

4
Norms for Art and Entertainment

The Scriptures do not say much about art and entertainment. We are told how two men made the tabernacle and all its furnishings and that their work was good. We hear of David who knew how to play the harp and write poetic psalms. We hear about blowing on pipes and trumpets of ram's horn and similar instruments at ceremonies in the temple. There is talk of beautiful cities and rich palaces, of the beauty of the Temple, of the 'sea of brass' and of the capitals of the pillars. All this is told in a matter of fact way as if everyone simply knows what is good and beautiful in this area.

And I believe that is exactly how we have to put it. To have knowledge of certain norms and laws and to know how various things ought to be is simply part of our being human. We may be reminded here of Romans 1 and also of Jude 10 which speak of things we know naturally. The Scriptures give us wise advice and show us the way in our lives, but they do not tell us (literally) how to walk, how to make a plough, how to hitch a draft animal to a cart. All of that is unnecessary. We can know it, and if we do not, we can learn it from someone else or discover it by experimenting. In the Bible it is assumed we are people who can invent things ourselves, people who know how things must be done. It is accordingly not necessary to give us manuals for building houses, for example, although we are advised to take safety into consideration, as in fitting railings to houses with flat roofs.

Implicit in the paucity of prescriptions is a condition of human freedom. To this freedom we are called and the Lord has left us free to discover things we need for life: construction methods, techniques, and much more. This is a freedom whereby we must always make use of the possibilities given in creation and respect natural laws in order to achieve a result.

Now, this holds not only for the things we would gather together under the term 'technology' but also for the norms of society. We must do justice and we must therefore punish a thief, says the Lord, but a juridical definition of theft is not given. If one is needed, we can make it ourselves – that is, we can give form to the norm that is established in creation and that we all know simply because we are human. Therefore it is not necessary here to get into all kinds of epistemological and theoretical questions. As human beings we know not only the natural world that is visible around us but also the norms that apply to our lives as we associate with other people. Be humble, says the Lord, and friendly and meek; comfort and encourage one another and say a good word where one is needed (see Ephesians 4:29, for example). It is assumed that we know naturally what that means and how to do it. We are offered no lessons in tact, psychology or character analysis, let alone in elocution or mime.

We need to consider all of this carefully, for then we will be able to understand why the Scriptures also do not give us norms in the narrower sense when it comes to art. It is not denied, to be sure, that such norms exist, but by experimenting in freedom we may discover these for ourselves. As human beings we are equipped to do that. We can even give these norms a special form of their own. There is no law that we have to use oil paint on canvas, and a painter who decides to try chalk on sandpaper, for example, or earth on wet cement is breaking no law. One can discover for oneself whether a method is useful or not. Even less are we told that if we want to emphasize a particular figure we should place it in the middle of our composition. If one can achieve the desired emphasis by putting the main figure to the side or even at the edge, then that is smart and perhaps even outstanding in a particular situation. The same is true of colours. There are beautiful and ugly colours, colours that match and colours that clash – colours that curse at each other, as a Dutch saying would have it. But that is also something we can discover for ourselves. In this area we are free to act as we please.

So those who look through the Scriptures to find formulas for judging art, those who ask for laws governing composition and other artistic devices, will be disappointed. Happily so! Happily, for the Lord speaks to us as mature people who can and may go about our work in the arts in freedom.

Yet there are people, so the Bible says, who find their ruin in what they know naturally (Jude 10), who as rational beings use the possibilities they have been given and the freedom they possess to deal with things not for good but for evil. They misuse the possibilities that exist in creation to achieve sinful goals. To mention an example: a person may be able to use an axe skilfully to fell a tree with a minimum of effort, but it is also possible for that person to use the same axe efficiently to murder someone. In our field good use of the artistic possibilities is demanded of every artist. The issue then is one of how artists use the possibilities and of what they do with them. It is a matter furthermore of what they have to say with their art, of what they express with it and of whether they edify their fellow human beings or poison their spirit. Here too people know very well what the norm is, but there is also much, as in all human knowing, that has been obscured, much of beauty and nobility that has been destroyed by sin. To do evil in any field, art not excluded, always means violating norms that people as human beings know by nature; yes, it is often a conscious violation of the norm, an act that finds its meaning and purpose in the violation. See Romans 1:32 ['Who knowing the judgment of God, that they who commit such things are worthy of death, not only do the same but have pleasure in those who do them'].

God fundamentally shows us the way by giving us wise counsel and by placing warning signs along our path: thou shalt not, thou shalt not . . . He teaches us as people to be truly human. The basic norms and commandments, the good counsel and demands are not outlandish and incomprehensible assignments that we have to carry out unthinkingly, even though their meaning and significance may sometimes elude us. On the contrary, walking in God's paths is the most natural and ordinary and, of course, also the most human thing to do. His commandments are not heavy, his burden is light and his yoke is easy. One who keeps these commandments shall live, says the Lord, and one can discover and experience how much humanity and freedom and naturalness and openness one gains by keeping them. The Devil sometimes fools people to think that the ordinary and natural is boring and dull, but that is a lie. For the commandments do not chain us, do not kill initiative; on the contrary, they give people enlarged possibilities and infinite freedom to act. Violating them, in contrast, always restricts us and robs us of our freedom. Thus it is much more difficult, for example, to make a drawing that suggests nothing than a drawing that represents something: in the first instance one has to watch anxiously lest there be a possibility that someone could read something into it. To be open to reality is easier than to try, with a blindfold on, to call up beautiful proportions from within oneself.

But enough! Our question was whether we could find commandments and norms in Scripture for the development and method of art. It will by now have become clear that one should not look for them there. Thank God that he gave people complete freedom in matters of technique, artistic laws and questions of artistic means and methods. Yet Scripture does guide people in all their activities, showing them the good way. This is essentially no different for art than for other areas of life. Art is communication, the announcement of observed beauties, the calling of attention to human values, the bestowing upon one's fellow human beings of beauty, singing and testifying, rejoicing and praising, opening eyes and building an outlook truly worthy of human being. And therefore the same thing is true for art as for every other area where human relations are manifest – and what area of life would be excluded!

In the following Scripture text we find formulated what to my mind is the shortest and clearest norm for art, and therefore of course for entertainment too. (And it surely does not just apply to these areas alone.) I am thinking of Philippians 4:8: 'Finally . . . whatever is true, whatever is noble, whatever is right, whatever is pure, whatever is lovely, whatever is admirable – if anything is excellent or praiseworthy – think about such things.' In the sections that follow we will endeavour to discuss in connection with art and entertainment each of these norms, each of these pieces of advice for artists active in the arts and entertainment and for those of us who as viewers desire to assess a work.

Whatever is true . . .

Is it possible to speak of truth in connection with art? One would like to answer this question with another question: Why should it not be possible to do so? Art is a human activity, after all, and one that is bound up directly with the human spiritual condition. Only one who believes that it is never possible to speak of truth or lies in connection with human working and striving will be able to deny the existence of these categories in art.

Yet it is no wonder that people sometimes take that position, especially in our day, now that people no longer regard the subject as important and consider only the artistic treatment as worthy of critical assessment. With respect to the aesthetic element, of course, one would not be able to speak of truth! Anyone saying that, however, has narrowed truth to an ethical category or to one that can only obtain in science or theology. Yet truth is not a matter that can be limited to particular areas of human life. Truth (and its negative opposite, the lie) confronts us in and through everything that is human, thus including art.

One can therefore certainly speak of truth in connection with the purely aesthetic or artistic element. Critics often call it 'honesty', but that is nothing other than a more subjectivistic name for it.

In a work of art the form must serve the content, and for each of these aspects no greater pretension and no deeper value must be suggested than is really present. This norm is violated when the work is not made with honesty, when the artist acts as if gripped by a particular form or idea, as if having something to say while in fact making something only in the hope that it will bring some sort of success and support.

Honesty is therefore required in the use of the materials, which must be used adequately. There must also be honesty in the choice of theme, of style, of suggested content. Many nineteenth-century works that people currently call 'salon art', because it could be viewed at the official exhibitions in Paris called 'Salons', fall short here. They put up an appearance of wanting to uphold the old values, but the makers did not believe in those values themselves. Because viewers quickly see through this surface semblance they have the feeling they are being deceived. The work is not honest; the norm of serving the truth, even in art, has not been satisfied. If one claims to be painting a Venus but can present nothing more than a scantily clad lady, a painting with a rather shallow, boorish content, then the maker lies. Then the painting lies!

We again chose an example that could give the impression that satisfying the truth is mainly a question of theme. Indeed we do believe that the theme is central in art – not so much on account of the thought as it can be described in words, the iconographic element, the theme or the subject, but always because of the theme as it is presented. In our example the work indicated was a lie because it made a pretense of representing Venus, while in fact the artist was saying something entirely different with the – please note – paint-written forms on canvas.

Still, even where there is no theme at all one can speak of lies. We see this already in ornaments. What is a kitsch brooch or vase except an artistic lie? Kitsch presents itself as art, suggesting content and values, but it is empty and commercial. This comes about because the goal it serves is not beauty but Mammon. The problems that arise here are essentially the same ones we have already sketched in our discussions of modern entertainment.

Another example of theme-less art is found in the work of Mondrian. There the content serves the form absolutely. In it the artist devoted all his great talent to the service of realizing a certain aesthetic harmony. Therefore every square centimetre is well thought-out. Only live viewing and, for example, comparison with the work of imitators and forgers can teach us the truth about a Mondrian, namely, that his harmony is real and not the trick of a charlatan, that every line and every colour says exactly what it claims and that it is always in its proper place, never just cranked out, but always deliberate and deeply felt.

The reason why this is so deeply felt is undoubtedly because as the source of his inspiration Mondrian drew upon a truly profound outlook on life and upon philosophical principles. Yet one cannot actually see these here. One can call his art impoverished in this respect and believe that he allows vast expanses of reality to lie fallow and that he was too rigorous in restricting himself, yet the fact remains that his works as they appear before us are absolutely honest, that they are what they pretend to be. The values contained in them are very particularly those of pure harmony, and those are fully realized. One can acknowledge this without subscribing to Mondrian's philosophy of life and also without concealing the fact that his art seems to fall short with respect to warm humanity.

Mondrian is a borderline case. Because all he set out to do was to express harmony, his art has beauty, although the underlying world of ideas does not have an opportunity to shine through.

How then should one judge a work in which human values are trodden underfoot, a work that simply lies, such as Picasso's nude, in which falsehoods are proclaimed about humanity and the Creator? Here we can speak of honesty, but not of truth. And we hasten to add that honesty is to be highly esteemed and that the artist deserves our respect. If an artist is bold enough to say precisely what he or she thinks or feels about things, then we must at least acknowledge the subjective truth, the honesty. We can hardly expect of a nihilist that he will hold high values and truths in which he does not believe! We must not ask someone to be a hypocrite. How frustrating it is to engage in a probing discussion, while someone else conceals their real thoughts behind a veneer, mincing words and ideas.

Thus one can speak of an artistic truth, a truth that lies in what an artist expresses about his subject. A Baptism in the Jordan is not a true painting simply because Jesus was actually baptized in that river. For a painting presents in its artistic treatment, in its structure and composition, an exegesis of the theme. The question of truth is thus not one of applying theological or ethical standards. We are not going to judge the work separately according to those standards after the questions of artistic honesty, beauty in colour and line, and adequate use of iconic means have already been answered. No, the question of artistic truth has been answered when full justice has been done to the artistic qualities.

Now I do not deny that this raises a new problem; yet it will turn out to be essentially irresolvable. For we live in the midst of a broken reality where sin has laid waste a great deal so that we now live, as it were, amongst the ruins. And it is possible that a composition will prove entirely adequate as to its content, artistically upright and true, while the question of the truth of the content remains unresolved.

To elucidate this problem we will turn our attention to the statue of Saint Theresa by Bernini in the Church of St Maria della Vittoria in Rome. It shows us the holy woman in ecstasy, about to receive the divine love from a cupid-like angel with an arrow in hand, ready to pierce her through the heart with it. The language of the form is that of the Baroque with its humanistic (in the sense of derived from Renaissance culture) conceptual language and sense of form. Yet seldom has what someone has reported about their experiences (of a mystical vision), including the erotic symbolism and the exaltation above the material and terrestrial, been so purely translated into artistic form. Artistically the image is absolutely true. Nevertheless, questions arise for anyone who does not accept this Roman Catholic mysticism. These do not concern the artistic image, but the message. We cannot deny, however, that this woman who was proclaimed a Saint had visionary experiences, even though we will be inclined to stress their purely subjective character. Still, we have to come to the acknowledgment that Bernini has done justice to the story of Theresa.

The moment the artistic element falls short in the portrayal of such an event, however – in this case one of the most difficult assignments ever confronted by an artist – then it raises a question mark or even, if we are confronted with a breathless, swooning woman and a somewhat too sensual angel, an outright lie. This sculpture of Bernini's however is a work of art both because he was a brilliant artist and because he truly believed in what he had made; had he doubted for a moment, he could not have been honest and in this case would have short-changed the truth.

More can be clarified by considering paintings of the Madonna. Wonderful paintings have been made on this theme, and the museums and churches in Italy are filled with them. Sometimes they are deeply moving in their beauty and true because the artists had the capacity to realize in a telling way the position and function of the Mother of God in Roman Catholic religion. Yet those who see too many of them will make the remarkable discovery that they sometimes acknowledge the truth of the paintings not because the artist has succeeded in painting a real Madonna but rather because the artist has 'only' made a truly charming image of a mother and child. Meanwhile, they will gradually get enough of all this candied beauty and these stereotyped 'icons'. In the end truth will not be found in these paintings. For artistic truth cannot maintain itself in endless repetitions of the same theme when people set out again and again to express something that does not exist in reality.

Naturally a visiting Calvinist will undergo this experience sooner than a Roman Catholic. Yet it is striking that many present-day Roman Catholic artists have a great deal of difficulty creating images of Saints and Madonna figures. The reason is that the truth of what they want to make – granted that they are believers and do not doubt the dogma as such – seems problematical to them. Their dilemma appears to be virtually insoluble: either make a sweet Our-Loving-Lady picture or statue (think of the image from Lourdes) that the artists in question experience as pure kitsch and that appears immune to 'improvement', or else make a genuinely felt true image that does justice to the facts and that is therefore artistically responsible. These people have been worn out by a surfeit of artistic lies, repeated for centuries. Probably the most beautiful images in this area were made in times when people did not in fact do full justice to their theme but dared rather to reproduce genuine womanly beauty in the earthly sense. The content has thus evidently not been able to acquire an adequate form, except in a few exceptional cases such as Raphael's Sistine *Madonna*.

Piero della Francesca's *Baptism in the Jordan* may serve as a vehicle for further elucidation [see Plate 4]. It is noteworthy that this painting is of supreme quality and makes an immediate and convincing impression on us, so that it takes some time before we become conscious of its idiosyncrasies. The work is executed namely with the help of two scales of proportionate sizes: Jesus, John and the angels have been done in one set of proportions and the surrounding landscape in another. This is clear at the spot where the feet of the baptized figure stand in the Jordan. There it looks as if the artist painted a ditch instead of a river. If we imagine the scene without the figures we see that the landscape as such is well proportioned and that the river is indeed a river.

In applying this method Piero built on a long tradition. It was employed to say that sacred events are of a different dimension from natural ones. Yet questions arise here. If the events were supernatural – in the sense of good Roman Catholic scholastic insight – would the figures, yes, including the angels in the upper left-hand corner, have had such a natural appearance? Or did the Renaissance ideal trick this fifteenth-century painter into making these figures too earthly and material? Christ is almost, though not quite, a hero of antiquity, although the proportions have been influenced by the renewed study of the ancient world. Perhaps the persuasive power of the painted artistic truth of which we spoke has its origin, paradoxically, in the fact that the painter falls short, namely that he did not succeed in realizing the view of this event in a form that depicts the supernatural as entirely supernatural – yet he did succeed in making the message acceptable! Perhaps that should not surprise us, since the human nature of Christ occupies the foreground in this gospel story.

Is the use of two formats, of two sets of scaling then not a violation of the truth? We think not, because in that way iconic means are used to make clear that what we have here is not just any arbitrary baptism, not just any person being baptized by any preacher. To those who are at home in the world of the medieval formulas that I mentioned earlier, this is more than clear: Piero made a typical Renaissance painting without abandoning the old formulas. He did not proceed as did many of his contemporaries from Florence, in whose works the genuinely biblical or ecclesiastical content went lost in a purely earthly view or, more accurately, through the use of the old formulas in the service of a purely this-worldly focus and concern.

So, what exactly is truth, or what does it mean to say that a person, a painter, *does* the truth? We say that not only to do the Scriptures justice[34] but also in order to make clear that truth is not just a matter of intellectual correctness. Truth is much more than that. Only an outlook, an act that does justice to the given structures, to values and norms, can be called true. Truth signifies being in agreement with reality, including spiritual values and realities. Moreover, truth means being truthfully situated in reality: a work of art is not true just because it represents the structures correctly (about which we will say more below), it must also fulfil its function correctly. Presenting a genre painting as an altarpiece would be a lie, however lovely and true a work it might be in itself.

Truth means thus that in a work of art justice is done to reality. But we must not deceive ourselves here. That does not mean that a painting must be a copy of reality, that it must reproduce the visual details with finely spun precision. It already became clear in the previous chapter in our discussion of naturalism that this approach often short-changes the fullness of reality and thus also of the truth. This is also apparent in the work of Piero della Francesca. How far removed a work may be from what is given visually before we say that it has distorted reality, and hence short-changed it, may appear from the following example, which at the same time provides a comparison with the *Baptism in the Jordan* discussed above. It is a miniature that depicts the same subject [see Plate 3]. How did this artist from around AD 1100 tell the story? In the centre stands Christ, to the left (as we look at it) there is John the Baptist and to the right, an angel or a prophet. We see that Christ does not stand in the water – that is, the painter did not paint him like that – but that the water gathers itself around him in the shape of a mandorla, the form in which Christ was so often portrayed during that period in the tympana of the great churches, in the so-called Maiestas Domini presentations of 'Christ in glory!' The artist is offering a commentary, as it were, on the baptism: he is saying that the Lord showed himself there in his divine majesty. The water flows from two pitchers held by naked figures: these are the old river gods, used here as personifications, as symbols. (In the lower area of this composition we see the wedding at Cana, but we will not discuss that now.)

We see little in this miniature that is 'natural' in the sense of something we might have observed in reality with our own eyes. Yet justice is done to the given structures of the human body, the water, and so forth, and a view is given of the event that is certainly not incorrect. To the contrary. The natural aspect did not interest this painter in the way it interested Piero; he certainly wanted to represent the supernatural only, as in some kind of formulation of dogma. Yet here too the persuasive power is great, both through the adequate artistic realization and through the comprehensibility and assayability, yes, the correctness of the artist's view (even if we do not fully share it). In the long run, as a result of endless repetition during the course of the years, such works could not escape ending up as apparently schematic products created according to a formula, partly through too great detachment from the sacred, detachment from the reality in which the Bible story happened. But for that artist in that period that view was still absolutely vivid, and the supernatural had not yet been relegated to some faraway space approachable only in a more or less philosophical or visionary way. For the artist this was reality itself, and the ordinary earthly element hardly counted.

When we look at these two examples again, we can discover even more about the meaning of the idea of artistic truth. For it is clear that at many points in these works of art not all the data have conformed precisely to historical reality. In Piero's *Baptism in the Jordan* we see the baptism, to be sure, but the landscape behind it looks very much like that of the artist's native country in its structure and composition, and probably very little indeed like that of the real Jordan area, which the artist did not know. The more we study such works, the clearer it becomes that the artists had no interest at all in that aspect. When

Rembrandt etches Abraham and Isaac on their way to the top of Moriah, we can be certain that he does not render that mountain precisely. He could not have done so, even if he had ever been to Palestine. After all, Jerusalem was built there later and no one can say what it looked like in the time of Abraham. But Rembrandt does more 'strange' things. Thus he has dressed Isaac up in a kind of Persian carpet. Whether such things already existed in ancient times we do not know, but if they did, would Isaac have put one on? And Abraham is wearing a turban. Rembrandt wanted to make it clear that the story took place in the East, and we should not read more into it than that. Truly he did not set out to reconstruct what one would have seen had one been there a long time ago, like some kind of delayed news report. We already called attention earlier to the fact that in this the artist faced and faces a special problem.

Yet one ventures to speak of truth in connection with such works not because the artists are engaged in some kind of biblical archaeology but because they have set out to make clear to us what the Bible story has to tell. Rembrandt's etching contains an interpretation, an exegesis of the biblical history, but it does not present a reconstruction of what we might have photographed had we been there. The photograph is also true, but then that is more a truth of a natural scientific nature. Rembrandt and the early artists presented a view in the human sense. And so that is what needs to be discussed.

It is peculiar that the nineteenth-century ideal of presenting a kind of reconstruction of the past, a sort of photographic report similar to those given by Renan and Hall Caine in literature, should have worked its way through so strongly as an ideal that people still use it today as a basis for evaluating older works of art (which appears from the fact that these are all too often dismissed as naïve or primitive in outlook). It is difficult to free oneself completely from this ideal. Yet from our earlier discussion of these matters it will be clear that we may have lost more than we have gained.

In the cases mentioned thus far it has still been fairly easy to form a judgment. How does the question of truth appear when we have to deal with works that have sprung entirely from the imagination? I have in mind, for example, Dante's *Inferno*, or a fairy tale in which things happen that are not possible, or a piece of fiction in which characters appear that have never really existed.

In all these cases I want to reply that one does no justice to these stories by testing them against historical or natural scientific standards of correctness and exactness. Whether Dante's *Inferno* is true does not depend on truth in the historical sense of the story and perhaps not even on whether we should think of hell in that way; it depends on the answer to the question of what view of life and death is given in this work and of whether in that respect justice is done to the full reality in which we live.

Thus a fairy tale can be singularly true if it describes human passions and ideals correctly, in short, if it does justice to human motives and ways of acting and reacting. Therefore I want to emphasize here that it is artistic truth that is the issue, and that it has a different meaning from the truth demanded by the historical and natural sciences.

Therefore we need have no objection, on the whole, to measuring with two different standards, one for the figures and another for the landscape, as in the work of Piero della Francesco discussed above. And we need not find it odd that in the French miniature Christ is not standing in the water although he is surrounded by it. We need not ask ourselves whether in Rembrandt's works depicting nature light could have fallen or shadows have been as dark as his paintings indicate. For he did such things deliberately in order to present his view, his interpretation, his pictorial representation of the theme.35 We must take into account subjective truth, the subjective insight of artists: they can express their view with much force and do so uprightly and in perfect honesty and still violate the truth as such. In that case tension will appear in the dialogue that arises between the work of art and us, in the first place because there is a discrepancy between the view it expresses and our own view. If we hold a similar view to the artist it becomes much more difficult to recognize the subjective side, or even the failure of its truth. But where there is a discrepancy it is possible – and here we have a consequence of the fact that we live in a broken reality – for us to say in a particular instance: 'How beautifully the artist has realized his view, but I have to say I do not agree with him in the least.'

Getting along with works of art is just like getting along with people: there are subtle humanists, faithful and honest Roman Catholics, keenly observant pagans, and all the joys but also all the difficulties we experience in getting along with those of other persuasions turn up also in a similar way in our contact with works of art.

Furthermore, I want to say emphatically here again that naturalism and realism are decidedly not the standards against which we are required to evaluate the 'truth' of a work of art. It does not mean that what a work of art expresses may be permitted to ride roughshod over truths from other areas of life – it was not my intention to imply that. I believe that when it is well done there would be no real contradiction. Every truth that is functionally determined, whether scientific or theological or artistic, refers beyond itself to the fullness of Truth in which the meaning and structure of reality are anchored. In all these areas people will endeavour to serve truth, in accordance with the nature of that area. It will always be truth as it is humanly understood, and when healthy it will be in direct relation – even though that may not be easy to verify – to the truth of the reality of God and the meaningfulness of creation.

Now we must not inadvertently revert to subjectivism. All people, no matter who they are and what they believe, live in the same world and are creatures of the same God. Romans 1 tells us more about that, but we shall not go into it here. Yet if we all live in the same world, then realistically speaking we should all see and experience the same world, even though our view may not be clear and, for whatever reason (be it consciously or unconsciously as a result of sin), may not do full justice to reality.

This explains why in the work of all artists we may occasionally see, alongside subjective and false opinions artistically expressed, also surprisingly sharp and accurate details. Thus during a large part of his career Picasso continued to make, besides the work we might call 'typically Picasso', also other 'normal' work, including portraits and figurative pieces. These refute the notion that all Picasso did was to employ another way of representing reality, one to which we could get accustomed and which we could come to accept as commonplace. I do believe that Picasso developed a new pictorial language, but I also believe that the essential thing is what he said with it. And I believe that we will never be able to grow accustomed to it unless we overlook the cursing and revolutionary Picasso and thus lose sight of the essence of his art. Yet his other work demonstrates that ultimately he also knew and lived in the reality in which we all live. Happily so.

We can make the same observation about the art of the past. A sixteenth-century Mannerist whose art proclaims that his times are in crisis and that he has a negative sense of reality will suddenly surprise us by painting, right in the middle of his distorted and strained depiction of reality, a keenly observed Florentine street girl – I have in mind a figure from Pontormo's *Joseph in Egypt* in the National Gallery in London.

In general we can say that people, artists, will endeavour to realize their vision in their art through images that are relevant to them, and that they will choose their motifs and themes in such a way that these will express clearly what they have to say and what strikes them as being true. Yet it will often happen that in works which are not so laboured with intentional meaning, for example in sketches, artists will show that they have been struck by something in the reality that surrounds them. Then this less important piece may turn out to feature a penetrating truth that the artists' other works possibly lack because of their subjective starting point. Such pieces, which are likely less important to the artists, may then have a general import that is absent from the artists' 'greater' works. They came about only because the artists succumbed to the sheer joy of creative activity. Or because they were inspired by a genuine love for the motif or subject. Love often breaks through the boundaries that people set for themselves in their subjective thinking. Someone should one day investigate the portraits that artists have painted of their loved ones and spouses; such a study may well discover that in these portraits the artists have expressed wonderful things about reality that will not be found, or will be found only partially, in the rest of their oeuvre, which represents the themes and contents they considered to be important.

Thus it does not seem strange that in our day and age the best and most enjoyable works are often discovered amongst so-called minor pieces or in advertising or even in purely decorative items such as the designs of printed textiles. There the artist is constrained by his or her assignment, which requires being considerate to and mindful of others, fellow human beings, through which the work rather gains in meaning and importance, in truth and beauty.

We need to keep this observation firmly in mind when discussing contemporary art. We may not say dogmatically that everything made by an existentialist always does violence to the truth. There is more than enough to enjoy, to admire, and to support within the world of modern art: it may be wonderful colours; it may be a marvellous, fantastical shape; perhaps an aptly and tellingly rendered detail; maybe a surprisingly beautiful creation; or something given in reality that we had overlooked ourselves but to which the artist has opened our eyes; or something purely poetic that touches us in a way that is impossible to translate into words.

Whatever is noble ...

This requirement is not about being affectedly distinguished, smooth, expressing an exclusive cultural position, being respectable. Sin can and must be mentioned in a work of art – otherwise it would lose truthfulness by skirting the facts of reality – but it must be done in a reserved and pure manner, and without too much preaching. Sin must be presented in such a way that it is not encouraged by being aroused.

Whatever is noble, or honourable, means taking into account the function a work of art is meant to fulfil. Those who make the paintings for a church must be mindful of what they are doing, so that people cannot criticize them later for having made things that are inappropriate for the surroundings.

This brings us to the question of what we are to think of so-called religious songs, such as those presented by people like Piet Sybrandi. A song like 'Silver threads among the gold', a sentimental song that celebrates a beloved person in their ageing, can touch a chord with even the most hard-headed lover of classical music if it is good in its genre and tastefully rendered. Why not? But it is quite something else when somewhat sentimental 'Christian' texts are sung in this manner. The style in which these songs are presented is adopted without change from a genre of entertainment that in itself is not without its problems; but what may still work in the entertainment genre cannot work as a Christian song without demeaning the latter's religious character.

It is sad to have to observe that what in America is offered honestly and uprightly as entertainment in the field of spirituals and hymns (a genre that is equally open to criticism but that at least is honest about its intentions) is often presented here in Holland at a different level and in all seriousness. The songs of a Johnny Desmond, who presents himself honestly as an 'entertainer' and who alongside top hits also from time to time sings a hymn in a sentimental way, are not burdened by any serious, deeply religious pretension. However, when the same sort of songs are sung in the Netherlands and given pious sounding titles, wires are crossed that short-change the dignity of belief and the majesty of the Lord who is addressed in such songs. Our judgment can be quite different when hymns are sung freshly and directly, without embellishment and without sentimentality. Then we do not need to apply the highest aesthetic norms, for that would be inappropriate. We must always be mindful, as we said earlier, of the function and nature of what is offered.

Perhaps it is good to say a bit more about these matters. Why is it that these new religious songs are so popular amongst the youth? In my opinion, what we have here is a fierce and rather undirected reaction to the fact that church people's (singing) mouths have been muzzled in the Netherlands. In every age believers have celebrated in their songs the deeds of the Lord which they witnessed and recognized. They were creatively engaged in doing so. Such creativity is typically human. Gollwitzer said somewhere that if one deprives a person of his or her creativity, of the possibility to be creatively engaged, then one short-changes and impairs that person in his or her humanity. Thus Miriam sang and made a new song; thus David and an entire school of poets and composers sang about the works of the Lord in their time; and thus Christians have done throughout the ages. Consider, insofar as Holland is concerned, the rich treasury of songs from Valerius' *Gedenkklank* memorializing the mighty acts of God in delivering his people during the Eighty Years War against Spain (at least one of which has been adapted as an American Thanksgiving Day hymn).

How it has come about therefore that in many circles everything bearing the name 'hymn' is suspect I do not know. [In the Netherlands, Reformed churches traditionally sing the Psalms only, in order to avoid worldliness and subjectivity in worship.] Whether what we have here in this resistance to 'hymns' is a sort of perfectionism, or a sort of false shame at expressing oneself, or a misunderstanding of the nature of such songs, which people want to measure by the norm of biblical purity to such a high degree that no one can approach it, or anxiety at the notion of singing something subjective and personal and even mistaken, or ordinary fear of free creativity and cultural work, including elements of an Anabaptist-like aversion to such work, is unclear. Possibly the answer lies in a combination of several of the factors suggested. In many orthodox Protestant circles people hold the Psalms in high regard and forget that these songs, in the translation in which they are sung, sometimes fall far short of the norm of purity – or people do not forget it but, remarkably, put up with it – and that the melodies used are old and sometimes outdated. It is magnificent sixteenth-century music, yet not always suited as the vehicle of living song for today's believers. Opinions may vary in these matters but not, I believe, in this: that people have forgotten that belief needs its own voice in song or it will weaken and wither. Might not the fact that the Dutch people as a whole sing so little and so poorly and have almost no repertoire of any scope and significance have something to do with this state of affairs? What young people (and old) can contribute in this regard on appropriate occasions is distressingly little. The English and especially also the American people with their rich treasury of folk music and hymns prove that it can be otherwise, even in our day and age.

Thus the crisis of belief that we discussed at the beginning of this book has given birth to this new kind of church song, and more so because no tradition existed for this new kind of song to build upon, or only a tradition that had become so outdated that it had lost its appeal. Also, in searching for present-day forms people have been unable to call upon anyone for support. They have not been able to call upon the contemporary composer, who from the remote heights of the esoteric art clan does not deign to be concerned with this sort of folksy music; nor upon good writers of poetic texts (would anyone today want to write suitable texts in such a way that these would be useful and comprehensible?), perhaps because they fear they might touch real depths and stir up problems no one knows how to deal with any more as a result of the crisis. In short, this situation exists because poverty reigns in this field of endeavour. Thus it was almost inevitable that people would seek the desired renewal in something far below par.

In text and melody and especially in style of delivery people know no better today than to present a sort of Christianized version of the music of present-day entertainment. That too could hardly be otherwise: for where apart from this genre can one find a living folk music, a genuine art that is popularly and generally understood? Perhaps people do not dare to be creative themselves, to seek ways of their own that are different from the current fashion, which is either the music of modern art, which is virtually unusable, or the music of entertainment. Or do people not dare because they no longer understand what it is to make things themselves?

We must not judge too harshly. Even if we sometimes cringe at the results, one thing is encouraging: namely, that a search is under way again, that something is being done. Perhaps in this way a living song can arise that is truly Christian and truly good in style. Those who have some talent, composers and poets, should therefore not stand aside but should roll up their sleeves and work to produce something good that can be popular at the same time, in the good sense of the term, which is to say comprehensible and singable for ordinary people today. Something of the sort can already be seen to be happening here and there. Let us take note of it then, not as critics but with an open ear and an open heart.36

Above all let us pray, in the awareness that in this field we too are poor of spirit and unable to accomplish the task by our own strength. Pray that the Lord in his grace will deepen belief into a veritable reformation and not withhold his Holy Spirit in the work.

What is of no avail here are indifference, of the kind that says 'just see how empty and hollow the spirit is in those circles'; lack of interest, as of a spectator looking on from a distance; fear of making mistakes and of making or saying something which will not stand the test of time; and resistance to anything and everything that is undertaken creatively and enthusiastically. Rather, what is needed here is a genuine love for one's neighbours, so that one approaches them in openness with a will to listen. And where there are talents, these must not be hidden away. Only then, and by waiting upon the Lord (and that may decidedly not be just a hollow, traditionally pious expression) in constant prayer and by reading and listening to his word in the confidence that he is not only the God of David but also our living God, may we expect any good thing here. But in this way this part of our lives too – art in the most direct sense of the word, connected with the life of faith and the life of the church – can contribute to the awakening, the reformation we all desire. Not only must we hope for it but, once again, we must pray for it. For only in this way can the crisis in our own circles be overcome.

Yet we do not have to depend exclusively on the dubious genre of the new religious song, albeit negatively considered, in order to understand something of the norm of honourableness. If we take notice of what is accepted today in Reformed circles as visual art in the decoration of calendars, the illustration of gospel tracts, the prints we give our children, the posters we hang on the walls of our meeting rooms, then we see that we have landed in an environment that is essentially no different from that of the song we assessed above. The causes will not differ much from what I enumerated there. The connection is sought with what has proved to be a nadir in art, namely, with the naturalism that was in vogue less than a century ago in a more or less fashionable milieu (I mean the 'official' art of the time). Do we realize that this style is also a feature of the most artistically dubious posters that we see all around us nowadays – promoting some brand of stimulating, refreshing drink, for example, that we are being cajoled into buying by a very attractive young lady and a gentleman with nothing better to do than quench their thirst; do we realize that all manner of highly questionable papers and magazines, for sale at the news-stand, are illustrated in a similar way? Are we blind to this popular style, which is just as little honourable and fitting as the music of Sybrandi? And do we want to do nothing about it? Are we not stuck here in the same sort of dead end? It is no simple matter to offer a solution either. A solution can be found here too only in the knowledge that, poor in spirit as we are, we must prayerfully expect the will and the means and the result from the Lord our God alone.

Let us furthermore not fail to cultivate some good taste ourselves by improving, for example, the typography used in our church papers. Or do we talk about such matters in the same way one sometimes hears people speak of songs in the church, namely, what does it matter as long as it comes forth from a believing heart? But that is the view of mysticism and shows a disdain for the wise counsels of the Lord as given in the Bible text we are discussing. Persistence in this attitude can only lead to further attenuation of our religious life and a worsening of the crisis in which our church life finds itself. Or do we find it impossible to imagine that young people (and older people too) never get around to reading the church magazine because it is such a measly, miserable rag? If that were the case because of hard times, of persecution or poverty for the sake of the faith – as with our brothers and sisters in Spain, Columbia and China, who perforce cannot address these matters – then that would not be so bad. But we consider ourselves to be well off, to possess so much . . .

Anyone who thinks that in the ecclesiastical sphere and in matters of our religious life we can afford to be cheap skates who make do with bargains and with shallow, graceless songs and with an equally tasteless way of decorating and preparing our publications and visuals and of constructing our churches and all the rest forgets that we cannot do that without paying the price, because in doing that we are neglecting a part of our lives that we received from the Lord. Bargains are not noble, not honourable and not appropriate in matters of faith, which are cheapened by inferior 'packaging'.

Whatever is right . . .

Whatever is right, in the sense of whatever is just, does not mean that in a novel things must always work out well for honest Johnny and badly for the scoundrels. That would not agree with the truth. It would also be superficial. The Scriptures speak more soberly and more deeply, very much more deeply, and more urgently. We must do justice to things. Anyone who presents Christ as a 'sweet' Jesus in word or picture undervalues the dignity and worthiness of Christ to receive that which belongs to him.

As we write or poetize we must proceed soberly from reality itself and then do justice to people, things and situations. That means we must not call sin good. We can make it clear by the way we speak about something whether it is straight or crooked. Only by letting the norm speak and by portraying evil for what it is can justice be done to its reality.

Whatever is pure . . .

It is clear that the issue here is that of purity and decency in relations between the sexes, of avoiding what is unnecessarily arousing, what is likely to provoke others to sin. These are the matters that are dealt with in the Heidelberg Catechism, Sunday 41.

Now, there are questions in this area. That is especially so in our time, now that so many changes have taken place. Just compare the images of bathing in the sea today with those from half a century ago. What was considered indecent then will seldom be judged so today, in the 1960s. And that may be a good thing. In other respects, however, there have been many losses.

The Seventh Commandment, also in the extensive form of the catechism answer, certainly does not mean that the sexual and erotic may have no place in human life. The Bible itself makes clear that they belong to the healthy relationship in marriage between a man and a woman. In Proverbs the man is counselled to be satisfied by the breasts of the wife of his youth: 'May her breasts satisfy you always; may you ever be captivated by her love' (5:19). No, the Scriptures do not teach us that purity means being silent or secretive about this important part of human life. On the contrary, the Scriptures speak openly and forthrightly about it again and again. For in our Bible we also have the hymn to sensual love called 'The song of Solomon'. And when upon their entry into the promised land the Law was presented to the people of Israel (Joshua 8:30–35; Leviticus 18), sexuality was discussed in very direct and unguarded terms.

Purity or its opposite is expressed whenever the subject matter is concerned particularly with the relationship between the sexes. It is impure to defile this tender relationship by robbing it of its dignity, by lowering it directly or through innuendo to pure pleasure. Professor Schippers has shown very clearly in his book about Calvinistic morals and manners[37] just how much is at stake when we fail to assert our humanity in this respect and to do justice to the wealth of facets in the play of love. When one person sees in another nothing more than an object of desire or means of satisfying his or her lust, then the other is dehumanized and something lovely is turned into something low and vulgar. In that case purity too suffers shipwreck and everything that is part of the relation between the sexes is turned into lasciviousness.

For art, all arts and certainly also the visual arts, many questions crop up here. Let us begin with the assertion that custom plays a great role. What is permissible in one time and place is not permissible at other times in other places. In fact, impurity is often indecency, which is to say it transgresses the norms and boundaries that have been formed and concretely fomulated in a particular time and for a particular environment.

We must constantly keep these factors in mind when we read literature and view art, alert to the fact that customs everywhere are comparable in content but do not always have the same concrete elaboration. To Balinese sensibilities our girls and women walk about shamelessly since they do not cover their legs, while in their own culture women who go about their business with their upper bodies bare are really not behaving indecently. Naturally, it is possible that the custom itself is not in agreement with the norms that obtain for all ages and peoples universally. Yet one should not rush into judgment. To be able to judge, one should be well informed about the meaning and significance of diverse customs and practices. Whatever one's final judgment may be, customs will be found at least to form a brake against people's lawlessness, of which in this context the worst imaginable outcome is immorality.

In our own world these matters are immensely refined and differentiated, given the advanced level of cultural opening or disclosure. In our society a girl can walk on the beach in a skimpy pants and top, together called a bathing suit, and – depending on the character of the pieces and the manner of her wearing them – be well dressed. In other circumstances the same dress would be considered brazen, and it would be so! These boundaries are known to all of us because they belong to our being members of Western culture. Those who violate these norms also know them, for it is precisely in their violation that the sensation and daring lie that they consciously seek.

We want to go on now to ask what is meant by 'shame', since that word is at the core of all the questions about purity. For an answer we are directed more often than not to Genesis 3 and the aftermath of the Fall into sin. Adam and Eve saw that they were naked and were ashamed. It is difficult to tell exactly what that meant, difficult especially because for centuries people were influenced by spiritualistic Greek philosophical doctrines that regarded what is bodily and sexual as base and sinful. What would this account mean? Could it not be so that it was not so much their nakedness in the sense of not being dressed that they saw, but rather their frailty, their defencelessness in contrast to the animals, which have fur and natural protection, but also more deeply, their nakedness, their lack of protection, their being on their own before the face of the Lord? They were aware of their weakness, their dependency. They were ashamed, an expression that can be used in two senses today.

Then God clothed them. Being dressed gives people a sense of self-confidence, and clothing is a part of our personality so that we can hardly imagine people without thinking about clothes. The extent to which that is so is clearly illustrated in a humorous manner by Carlye in his *Sartor Resartus*, in which he explored what it would mean indeed if parliament had to convene naked tomorrow. Where then would the dignity of the gentlemen [and ladies] be? An absence of clothing reminds us of our frailty and our weakness. To be naked and at the same time proud and purposeful seems almost a contradiction. Yet this shame certainly also bears some connection to the sexual. Personally I suppose God ordained matters in this way in order to protect people against themselves: is shame not a protection for a girl in our times, and is manly reticence not its counterpart?

Nakedness and shame certainly have something to do with each other. Yet the concrete manner in which they are connected depends on the place and the time, depends on how people have given form to the commandment, the norm. It would be difficult to formulate a generally valid definition of precisely what nakedness is. In our day and age in Western Europe bare breasts are naked, something that arouses shame and modesty; at other times other people, however, have not experienced matters this way. In some circumstances people do not connect nakedness and shame at all. There are nations where people bathe together naked without any implication of immorality – and that does not mean they have no sense of shame.

Nakedness that engenders shame virtually always involves the kind of uncovering that puts the erotic relation between the sexes at stake. Where bathing is concerned, being naked can be natural and acceptable according to traditional usage while, among the same people, there may be great prudery in language and practice where companionship between the sexes is concerned. Shame and modesty arise where something is 'discovered' (literally and figuratively; cf. also Leviticus 18), and this puts a brake, as it were, on erotic 'curiosity'.

Our conclusion can be that shame is always connected with what is primary in sexuality. By all peoples and in all ages shame is in the most direct sense associated with the pudenda, the things we are ashamed of, that is, the sex organs and the sexual act. At the same time, we must always keep in mind that shame has something to do with our frailty, with our unprotected state both in the everyday and the religious sense.

Purity does not mean that what is erotic and sexual may not be discussed. Purity lies in avoiding all shamelessness. An absence of a certain reserve will virtually always mean that our sexuality is degraded and reduced to the level of pure (but essentially impure) lust. The issue is about our conduct in entering upon and dealing with this important area of human life and about the question whether the boundaries set by custom are respected.

In our time there is a great deal of literature in which these boundaries are needlessly tested and violated; naturalism or realism, with its notion that a writer is free to describe every situation, has sought to cover a great deal of lawlessness and shamelessness under the mantle of love. By the same token this revolution in morals has thrown overboard much false shame and unhealthy prudery (as revolutions often tidy up matters that have outlived their usefulness). Nevertheless, the motive behind this revolution is often the idea that it is essentially the sexual aspect that determines and gives meaning to everything else. The danger in this view is that what has been gained may be lost again if the erotic is robbed of its human quality, i.e. that which identifies it as being more than direct and absolute lust.

It is now time to concern ourselves with the question of the value and meaning of the nude in visual art. We came to the conclusion above that shame is connected with the sexual, and often very directly with the sex organs themselves, or with those parts of the body that people in company do not 'dis-cover' because of the erotic implications. When we consider sculpture and painting from this vantage point, we can observe several things. In the first place, people in virtually all ages have complied with the moral code. Nude female images either have a small covering over the primary sexual organs or simply do not feature them at all. That applies to both the Greek images and to those made since the Renaissance. And things continue in that vein until the nineteenth century when, with the rise of naturalism, we witness an abrupt change. Then the rendering becomes more natural, so that pubic hair and so on are depicted. Along with that the meaning of these images also undergoes a change. No longer are they general personifications or poetic portrayals of an idea but instead they become direct representations of observed reality. As a result a certain vulgarity seems often no longer avoidable, and the question arises why a painter has made a particular work if not for a purely erotic reason. Often these works evoke shame and we may feel that boundaries have been violated. Shameless, for example, are certain of Hodler's female nudes, but not the *Venus* of Praxiteles. With respect to the male nude we can say the same thing. Naturally there is always a suggestion of the private parts, yet always very modest and without emphasis.

In short, one encounters violations of the norm of shame and modesty from time to time, especially following the heyday of naturalism in the nineteenth century, which recognized no limits. Such images inevitably make a crass and unpleasant impression. The phallus is very seldom depicted, nearly only in cases where one might speak of pornography, or else in situations portraying a kind of religious veneration of the sexual aspect as in ancient times with the satyrs and fauns. Yet even then people were often quite reserved. On the other hand, there is no call to idealize Graeco-Roman antiquity: the *Barberini faun* is perhaps the strongest example of an image in which all the boundaries in question are disregarded.

In principle we can distinguish two kinds of nude in the visual arts. The nude can be used to express frailty, nakedness in the metaphorical sense. That was the case in the Middle Ages. Perhaps it is in keeping with this that in some medieval images and paintings the pudenda are indicated, the women have pubic hair, and so forth. Here the image portrays precisely the shame and nakedness, albeit metaphorically.

In contrast there is also an entirely different form of nude, the heroic or glorified nude. We find this in the art of the Greeks and, in imitation of the Greeks, in European art since the Renaissance.

A most remarkable concatenation of these two conceptions – the one generated essentially by an attitude that focused entirely on humankind and their glorification, and the other by Christianity with its perception, based on Genesis 3, of human being as frail and impoverished in spirit – appears in seventeenth-century Baroque art. The Baroque as the art of the Counter-Reformation aimed to harness the culture of the Renaissance to the service of the supernatural and the proclamation of the sacred. In this period people often painted Mary Magdalene doing penance. According to legend she would have done her penance in the wilderness and have taken off her clothes for ascetic reasons. There she was, naked and frail in the Christian sense. And all she wanted to do in this disrobing was to express without any erotic allusion her relinquishment of the things of this earth. (I leave aside here any discussion of the question of the truth of the legend or of whether this form of asceticism is biblical.) Yet in these paintings we see in fact a naked woman whose body is beautiful. There is a remarkable ambiguity in these pieces, but by far the greater number of them violate the norm. This concatenation cannot be realized without tarnishing the honour of Mary Magdalene; the saint cannot be glorified in this way.

Somewhat greater success is achieved in the depiction of such saints as Sebastian or of Christ himself. Use is made of the heroic and glorious nude in order to honour the Lord and to present him through the medium of painting as great, powerful and mighty. One is reminded here of the work of Rubens: his Christ on the cross is less frail than fifteenth-century artists depicted, yet we can follow Rubens to a certain extent in his honest intentions.

Decisive for all these cases is what the nude expresses or what it is meant to say. That will also determine where the boundaries of purity are located. These Magdalenes are almost always unchaste, even when the nakedness is largely covered or disguised. The simple uncovering of just a small part of a breast creates a titillating and erotic effect. In contrast, in *Abduction of the daughters of Leucippus* Rubens composes a hymn to femininity without doing the least violence to purity [see Plate 5].

To be sure, we need to understand what Rubens is showing in that painting. He was certainly not particularly interested in the story as such of the mythical Leucippus and his daughters who were seized by the Dioscures, even though in his day such stories probably had much more emotional impact than they do today. He chose this story because through its theme he could raise a 'hymn in paint' celebrating the significance of the feminine in life. The men with their fiery steeds form a kind of wreath of honour, a grandiose *epitheton ornans* around the female figure at the centre of the painting. The lower female figure, pictured from the back, forms both an introduction to and a spectacular underscoring of the central figure. Everyone can understand, from the way the material is composed to form a whole within the boundaries of the work and from the improbability of the situation and the tone of the piece, that Rubens had not set out to report what some shepherd boy saw while peeping through the bushes one day. Such an idea is too vulgar and totally inappropriate to the grandiose rhetoric of this work. In it Rubens extols womanhood and tells how man passionately pursues and seizes woman and what a tremendous place she occupies in life. Yet he does not tell this in a way that would imply that everything 'revolves around sex', as if the sexual act were the only thing that drives people. Even a Freudian commentary about sublimation of the sexual in this warmly human confession about woman's great importance in life, erotic in the broadest possible sense, demeans Rubens. He shows us an idea, sings his song of praise, and that is not the same as painting a pipe dream. It is not a dream that Rubens shows but a reality, an idea that can materialize more or less well in our reality. Nevertheless, there is something about that painting with its glorification of the flesh that makes us as Netherlanders, with our Calvinistic past, rather uncomfortable to say the least. The reason is that in one way or another the human aspect is too highly rated.

In that case we can better take our recourse to Rembrandt as he paints his *Bathsheba* [see Plate 6]. He joins the same Renaissance tradition, although we should think then of the artists of Venice more than of the artists of Bologna and Michelangelo, who were decisive influences on Rubens. But however that may be, how different is his nude! How much more sober and realistic is Rembrandt's view of women. He does not paint an ideal floating high above human reality of which our experience can only be a faint shadow; yet with his figure he too personifies a general human reality. Rembrandt's Bathsheba is more than the portrait of a disrobed woman. We must certainly conclude that with his painting he wanted to proclaim something of the same sort as Rubens did, namely, something of the important position and significance of woman in life and of the great values that are given in the relation between man and woman. Yet Rembrandt has not adopted this theme by accident. On the one hand he joined a tradition here that was already more than a century old, in which this story was often the pretext for painting a female nude – in its own way the sixteenth century was as preoccupied with the erotic as our own. On the other hand there is something else here: it deals with the great importance of love and the erotic, but with the knowledge that also great dangers threaten of sin and seduction. Already with respect to this facet Rembrandt is more sober and faithful to reality than Rubens is. Rembrandt proves to have a better insight than Rubens does (who within his Roman Catholic view thinks ever so much like a humanist) into what human life knows of toil and trouble alongside wealth and joy.

Rembrandt's *Bathsheba* is a hymn to the woman in the man-woman relation, and although the painting speaks of warmth and humanity, the woman is not idealized – to the contrary. And the artist's picture of reality with respect to the erotic is thereby also not idealized. Therefore Rembrandt is deeper and more true, more true to life and more sober, and also more beautiful, albeit less grandiose. Rembrandt rendered similar content on more than one occasion – one is reminded of his *Danaë*, which is warmer and more real and yet, precisely in all its erotic openness, perhaps more chaste and pure than Giorgione's *Venus*.

Chaste and pure are indeed the appropriate terms. Here I want to say, by way of an aside, something that may be of importance for our subject. I have spoken many times with Reformed Christians about these matters, examining reproductions of these works and discussing their beauties and defects. Remarkably, no one has ever raised an objection. Remarkably, I say, because people still often believe that these things should be excluded from our circles as titillating. It is as if everyone is always concerned about others, while regarding oneself as mature enough to discuss the material openly and uprightly. I believe that this attitude is entirely uncalled for. Paintings like the two Rembrandts and yes, even the Rubens, teach us to understand important aspects of human life better. They open our eyes figuratively and literally to values and beauties. They do not sully, because they express nothing vulgar, because they satisfy the norm of purity.

That is otherwise when we look at the art of the eighteenth century. Anyone who has been engaged intensely for a long time with the French art of this period – art about which we already had occasion to make several observations in the previous section – risks no longer being able to look at a woman openly and honestly. This art leads us to violate the commandment against adultery in the sense in which the Lord Jesus speaks of it – 'anyone who looks at a woman lustfully' (Matthew 5:28). Rubens addressed the erotic in general and Rembrandt the healthy and honest man-woman relation including its dangers; eighteenth-century artists, to put it bluntly, practically elevated the gallantly adulterous to the norm.

During the nineteenth century, with its pulling down of all these general principles of life, a great deal was lost as to this aspect as well. Ingres, the most classical of all the nineteenth-century painters, is virtually unable to paint a Venus any more. He calls his nudes *Odalisque* – the name of the sultan's favourite concubine in his harem. In that way this sensuality, or should we say this voluptuousness, has become the content of his Venus figure. Love and the erotic are thereby degraded, for the woman has become no more than an object of lust, albeit also an admired and respected one. In essence she is a slave, no longer on the high plane to which Rubens had lifted her and even less fully human as in the biblically Christian position that Rembrandt gave her.

We will not go into detail. By the end of the century we are even further removed from the rich fullness that once existed in these matters. Woman has become purely an object of desire without any remnant of ideality. We see this in a painting by Corinth in which he presents a paraphrase of the Rubens piece.[38] Here one actually sees two rather strangely dressed randy soldiers on an old nag invading a nudist camp to carry off a girl whose own intentions are decidedly less than honourable. For why else would this woman have been walking around naked? The naturalism in the style lends the content something base and coarse. Here we could practically speak of pornography, for this work certainly slings mud at sexuality. Such paintings are not pure. They defile our minds because they tear down things that are lovely and clean and declare them to be nothing but salacious passions.

It is no wonder that by the time there was nothing more left to discover in woman and the erotic than what Corinth depicted around 1900 a following generation had no desire to prolong such coarseness in their paintings. People went on to deal with such things in a different way. Now the nude became a direct inducement to the kind of playful painting we see in Matisse. And we end up with Picasso who paints his hatred of this debased hollowness, debunking all the ideality behind the lust and chastising the hypocrisy of all who want to see more behind it, in short, who paints his nudes while cursing a no-longer-lovable reality.

A modern painter once observed that people today really object only to the manner in which artists express themselves and much less, if at all, to what they have to say. And there is a great deal of truth in that. We can understand that, for while in essence the content of Corinth's and Picasso's work is not so very different, many viewers still prefer the former. I personally would prefer to look at the Picasso, if only because he has moved so much further away from reality and thereby confronts us less directly with this devaluation of values. Yet here too we must not generalize about the art of our times. There is also much else, and much that is different, to be discovered. Consider, for example, the work of the young etcher Veldhoen, who in his nudes, couples and even births tells us so much that is beautiful about human sexuality, all the while plucking in a most positive way the fruits of the openness that has become possible in that area in our times.

With respect to the nude we should not take offence so directly at the aspect of being undressed, for it is not there that the impurity as such is to be found. We must instead always ask ourselves what a work is saying about people and the erotic aspect of their lives. Then we must say that the brothel is impure and degrading, short-changing the truth, defying the full human truth of the man-woman relationship, while the Rubens and the Rembrandt can be called pure.

If we object to the nude in ancient times and since the Renaissance, then our quarrel is more with the glorification of humanity than it is with the nude as such. Thus we may assert, perhaps rather crudely, that Michelangelo's great *David* in Florence (1504) is a shameless statue. That is not because the figure is entirely naked – there is hardly an erotic implication in the work – but shameless because this person no longer knows anything of his frailty. Central here is the greatness of man, whereby a sort of humanistic confession of faith arises from the Renaissance idea, here considered in its deepest sense as the emancipation of humankind from God.

Why do we always think of shamelessness and impurity as naked and disrobed? The sex bombs used as eye-catchers on the covers of our magazines are usually adequately dressed, but in their blatant sexual prickling and intent to titillate they seem to be personified violations of the commandment to be pure. Here shamelessness is evident in the detachment of sensuality from humanity in its fullness, in subjection to norms and in the acknowledgment of values.

Whatever is lovely . . .

It may seem remarkable in view of the context that this is also to be found in Philippians 4:8. For this passage does not deal with art in the first place, although that facet of life is not excluded. If we want to understand this, we must be mindful that beauty and loveliness are not just properties of works of art, not aesthetic qualities per se. Nowadays people often talk as if only beauty can be found in art, while setting aside and dismissing as irrelevant the rich variety of concrete values and meanings in works of art. What is retained is only some kind of abstraction, and this abstract beauty – which is also sought in some kinds of abstract, non-figurative art – is seen as real beauty.

I believe we may say that this view impoverishes us, and that we would do well to listen once again to the old philosophers, such as Plotinus, who were able to tell us a great deal more about beauty than beautiful relationships between planes and colours on a surface or, as in the case of sculpture, masses and volumes can do. The old philosophers are so taken with beauty and have so much to say about it that they hardly get to what we would call aesthetics, to theoretical reflections on art and beauty.

Calvin too joins this older tradition, and it may be instructive to take on board the significance of Wencelius' summary of Calvin's view (presented in the chapter of his book about Calvin's 'aesthetics' that deals with beauty and sanctification) as follows: 'The work of art that is our holy life is beautiful as a result of the harmony that exists between the parts that compose our personality.' The passage continues with a discussion of how we come to a holy life, through trials and cares, and by taking up our cross in following Christ. We can speak of beauty in being human itself (I leave aside any discussion of whether Wencelius interpreted Calvin correctly).

This human beauty, which with the ancients I could call the beauty of the soul if there were no need to fear calling forth a legion of misunderstandings with such a term – this subjective human beauty is very closely connected with love. Therefore we speak of a beautiful act, of wonderful cooperation, of a lovely evening, for example if we have discussed a passage of Scripture together and everything has transpired in harmony and mutual love and unity, in such a way that God's truth has become clear to all of us in an abundant way – and so on.

That is all beautiful. Then there is the loveliness that the Bible speaks about, for the inner beauty, that loveliness in subjective human behaviour, will surface and be expressed. It is true, to be sure, that a beautiful act can consist of writing a little letter on ugly paper – but it is unthinkable that anyone wanting to help someone else would purposely send a soiled paper. It is absurd to want to show someone our love and friendship and then knowingly send them an ugly piece of rubbish.

Love and beauty go together. To speak of a beautiful act is thus to my mind not a metaphorical use of terms. Because the act was in obedience to the Second great Commandment, to love our neighbour as ourselves, it could also be beautiful, in the sphere that for want of a better word we refer to as the aesthetic.

Loveliness is something we should seek, says the Lord. That speaks for itself: it is inappropriate for believers who desire to love their neighbours and to be salting salt to go through life snarling and growling! A person who is truly mild-tempered will exhibit that quality, perhaps without even being aware of it – or no, almost certainly without thinking about it – in a friendly voice (what else could this expression mean), in a calm and controlled way of commanding, quite the opposite of swearing up and down at someone.

It is not only in books and radio plays that scoundrels have unpleasant voices, an ugly way of moving, a leering stare, etc. Although in reality matters are sometimes uncannily tangled up in a hopeless knot of sin and wretchedness and goodness and beauty, it is remarkable to see how love can ennoble someone's face, so that someone who is not very attractive by nature can still be regarded as very beautiful, as having a kind of beauty that is not based directly on the harmonious proportion of shapes but that is all the same striking. On the other hand we can sometimes see very beautiful women whose beauty is hard and pitiless, cruel in sensuality – think of many photos of film stars or of women in advertisements. One is confronted often enough with this sort of 'ugly beauty' (I do not mean to generalize or say this is always the case).

Thus we come to the remarkable problem of whether sin and beauty exclude each other mutually. Can a tyrant build a beautiful city? And our answer must be yes, and no.

First the yes. It is certain that beauty can exist in the world even where sin holds sway. Sometimes it will even be feverishly sought there. Every sovereign likes to appear in beauty, in an entourage that suggests more than wealth and power, that in its harmony aspires to justice and humanity. Babylon and the other great cities of the ancient world were beautiful cities. The Bible also describes them as such [Isaiah 13:19]. We can also say without objection that the Greeks built beautiful temples for their gods, and we must observe that of course people never honour their gods with ugly buildings!

In general we can say that only seldom do artists not seek beauty. If they want to succeed and to gain status, they simply must try to make the most beautiful work that they are capable of making. So they must defer in this area to the norms that are given in creation. Yet there is a flip side to this. The pompous architecture generated during Hitler's Third Reich does not appear in books about the history of architecture. After all, nothing truly beautiful could be found in it. The desire to make something striking and impressive and perhaps also a fear of falling out of grace with the Party (if their work was labelled as 'corrupt art') constrained the artists to such an extent that their work seems bogus, dishonest and ostentatious.

Beauty in the service of the tyrant, beauty that thereby becomes creepy and not inspiring confidence, is often found in fairy tales and 'science fiction', everywhere in fact where human fantasy sets out to describe how rulers with unlimited means at their disposal furnish their surroundings. Aesthetically they may be magnificent, but they have a cold, cruel beauty that stands in sharp contrast to the true beauty of the good sovereign and, in the fairy tale, of the even more beautiful daughter.

In fantasy literature the image of the idol is always something hideous and gruesome. And that is in keeping with the truth. The images of the demonic gods of the Hittites and of many other pagan cultures are totally repulsive. The good god may be beautiful but the real powers are usually destructive and cruel, like Shiva in contrast to Vishnu. In this way what is ugly in a moral and religious sense, the demonic, the deification of the negative in the cosmic order, leads not to beauty but to the creation of a sort of fantasized deliberate ugliness. What do you suppose the god Moloch looked like (Leviticus 20:2–5; Acts 7:43)?

Historically it has seldom reached the point that artists have been free to use ugliness to create their own picture of reality. Yet our century has managed to accomplish that (see Picasso's nude to which I have alluded several times before). Here we discover direct connections between hate and anxiety and 'nausea', in short, all manner of negative feelings, and the ugly and disharmonious. Our times provide a rich treasure of examples in this regard. Just look at Grosz's album from the twenties in which he draws, heckles, loathes, accuses and spews his bile against postwar Germany, and the connection between ugliness and a lack of love will become clear. I take this example because Grosz is an artist still only relatively modern in the language of his forms.

That example leads us to offer a little word of caution: do not think that Picasso and those around him make ugly art because they do not work according to naturalistic or time-honoured principles. The twentieth century has its own pictorial language, its own iconic syntax, which we encounter in advertising, illustrations, etc. without there being any possible objection to it. To the contrary. Yet the issue is not the dialect one speaks but what one has to say.

We could also point to Daumier, an artist who in the middle of the nineteenth century is hardly out of tune when considered from a purely stylistic vantage point – he did stand head and shoulders above most others – but his view of all manner of authority figures and people whom he strongly disliked, bluestockings for example, was so unmerciful that people are hard put to find his work beautiful. Yet Daumier's work is so impressive that our picture of the French politics of his day, of people like Louis-Philippe and Guizot, is strongly coloured by his view, which was distinctly revolutionary and socialistic (in the language of our own times it is perhaps more apt to call it 'communist').

In this way someone can create things that are at the same time both ugly and artistically great, for these artists know how to present their view so convincingly, so penetratingly clearly, that one is compelled to recognize their greatness. We accordingly also honour Picasso, and Wols, and Appel.

In the injunction to seek whatever is lovely we find a direct connection with the Second great Commandment, which contains all the Commandments within it, namely, that we must love our neighbour. We can ask ourselves whether it is not from this Commandment that the greatest and most fundamental objection arises to various kinds of modern literature such as Kafka's *The Trial* or to some kinds of modern music such as atonal *musique concrète*, which makes us sit on the edge of our seat and makes our flesh creep as we listen to unresolved dissonants and so on, and thus testifies to a less than loving attitude toward the listener or reader. If such music is an expression of anxiety, powerlessness, frustration, melancholy and dissatisfaction, then it can be totally honest, then the artist can perhaps make his or her view powerfully clear, but the question remains: Does one have the right to draw one's neighbour into the pit into which one has landed oneself? Here to my mind lie the deepest questions concerning modern art, once we concentrate on its message and allow its content to affect us. May one transmit one's hatred to another or impart one's own angst to one's contemporaries? Is that not unloving? Culturally and humanly speaking, the moderns make no bones about it, like Dubuffet who wrote: 'This art that mocks the creature has just as little respect for the Creation.' This is clearly the opposite of being salting salt.

Before going further I want to make a final observation in this regard. Do not draw the conclusion from what I have said thus far that I suggest only cheerful and pleasant pieces should be written or performed. Practice already refutes such an unjustifiable demand, for it often happens that a tragedy produces joy and a comedy sorrow. It all depends on the truth the work serves. I once saw a comedy in which everything was stood on its head: the so-called virtuous character was a caricature of horror, and the bad character was virtuous – truly a piece to make one weep. And many a tragedy, by Shakespeare for example, evokes joy because in its own way it does justice to reality.

If there is any virtue and if there is anything praiseworthy . . .

The above will by now have made clear what this is all about. We must think virtuous, excellent thoughts. It is remarkable that in our day such an idea can sound suspicious. Virtue is dismissed as bourgeois and held in discredit. Yet it is good to proceed from it if we want to contribute something to our culture. Perhaps we should understand 'if there is any virtue' (NKJV) to mean that in general it is best to abide by existing good manners and customs. For virtue is that which is consistent with good manners. An expression like 'if there is any virtue' opposes revolutionary destruction. Let us support and build what is good and only fight against sin, for that is the task of human beings. Then there is no danger of stagnation since manners and customs will certainly change over time and with circumstances. When we seek what is good and avoid evil or endeavour to block its course we are culturally engaged. Who can tell what the fruits will be? Let us not be concerned about the outcome. This world is about deeper ideals than originality and renewal. Nowadays there is a considerable overestimation of culturally formative work, as if not the work of the person who makes something good were more important but that of the person who makes something new, albeit that the meaning is questionable.

Anything praiseworthy – naturally this refers to everything that serves one's neighbour, in which things are built up and not torn down. In general we may say that this means we must honour those who endeavour to give the best they have, who serve their fellow human beings, who desire to make something lovely and good. And we do not always have to be severe. Criticism is sometimes so unmerciful! Why can we not be gentle instead? Why can we not honour effort, even where it does not succeed, and offer criticism only where appropriate, where there was a lack of honesty and love. And then only if our criticism too is given in love. There is no place for murder by criticism.

5
Norms in our Association with Art

In the previous chapter I endeavoured to develop some insight into the norms for art, and from that angle it was indeed possible to take a close look at several issues. We must keep in mind, however, that all that still says very little about the norms for our association with art, although this is in fact even more important, for it concerns our practical everyday lives. As far as I am concerned, the heart of what I want to say lies in what follows here. No one needs to share my views on the works of art and schools of thought discussed above. These can, may and even must be discussed, for that is the only way to move ahead and help one another, on the basis of our own experiences and insights.

As I argued earlier, discussion is important for us as we seek to absorb what we have seen and heard. It is important precisely because art occupies such a significant place in human life, even if people are not always conscious of it. The discussion must always be conducted honestly and openly and with an awareness of the impermanence of one's own point of view, which can become outdated or prove to be incorrect and therefore limited. To be sure, that last observation does not mean it is meaningless to talk about these things simply because no one can ever discover the full certainty and truth about them. Such absolutism would put an end to all human work. In the Bible the book of Ecclesiastes teaches us otherwise. With an awareness of our limitedness and of the vanity of our labour we can still maintain that it nonetheless can be meaningful. That is, if we take as guideline for our work and for our discussions Philippians 4:8, in other words, if we seek the Lord's will in our work and do not inhibit the work of the Holy Spirit through unbelief and sinful self-interest.

What I discuss here in this final section seems to me the most compelling. This is not just an opinion that is offered, a view, open to discussion. For the issue here is that of our walking in the ways of the Lord according to the Scriptures and of listening to what he requires of us in these matters. In this we may not approve anything short of the truth, as unveiled by the word of the Lord.

How shall we judge concretely?

In judging a work we must in the first place never hack about wildly, as it were, with a machete. We must look and listen with an open eye and ear to what the other person has to say, with a view to recognizing and honouring the qualities that are present and to doing justice to the work in question. What is beautiful and true deserves respect, and even what fails to satisfy in this regard must not simply be cast aside without further ado; rather, we must ask ourselves if there are not still other values implicit in the work that did not fully ripen or that were not entirely realized. Nothing is more merciless and pernicious than snobbism in the contemplation of art. Remember that a second-rate work may still be of importance, if only because it gives us joy. We must try to recognize the spirit that speaks in the work and give free rein to the dialogue with the art and about it that we alluded to earlier. Only in this way can it enrich us.

Let us be aware, furthermore, that a work of art is a piece of reality, that it forms a part of the entire pattern of our times and culture, and that it may have either more or less importance. Every work attests to a reality, to a spiritual reality – the spirit that compelled a person and was sacred to her or him.

Finally, works of art may tell of realities, realms, beauties and horrors, loves and hates, circumstances and touch on areas in which we may not feel at home at all. Let us therefore in all circumstances judge modestly, acknowledging where appropriate that we are hardly in a position to judge because we do not know the world of which the work speaks, cannot understand the spirit that inspires the work, and can scarcely imagine the importance the work might have for someone else.

In short, here it is certainly demanded of us that we judge in mercy and in love, meekly, hungering after righteousness, after that which is right in the eyes of the Lord. Never may we haughtily cut a work to pieces, never peremptorily dismiss the work of another who may have poured his or her soul and years of life into it, simply because we do not recognize it for ourselves, because it does not fit our chosen areas of indulgence. We have the Holy Scriptures as a light unto our feet, to be sure, but they were not given us as a club for beating others over the head. Those who desire to engage in dialogue must begin by loving their neighbour and by realizing that they encounter that person not as a judge but as a fellow human being.

I believe that the last point is very important. It strikes me as a good rule never to attempt to judge, let alone condemn, the artists, the makers, who are responsible for the work. Let us remain sober and focus rather on what we can see standing or hanging in front of us. How can we know what possessed its maker? How can we penetrate to the depths of the artist's soul, which he of she may have concealed more than revealed in the work of art? How can we know if the other, misled or insufficiently capable, aimed at something quite different from what we can detect or surmise in the work? Let us keep in mind that God has reserved judgment to himself: 'God will judge those outside' (I Corinthians 5:13).

It is a difficult matter that we introduce here. We have grown accustomed in our subjectivistic times to focus on the person, the maker.

Literary critiques in particular are sometimes virtually psychological analyses; and artists sometimes wrestle with their personal problems before the forum of an erudite and cultivated public. Let us restrict ourselves to the given work and just attempt to assess that. That will engage us in the struggle, the spiritual struggle, against all manner of spiritual malignancies in today's world. Artists are of course present in their work and they wage their struggle too – even if we may not be able to follow their banner – but it is the work as such that in the first place exercises its influence, it is the artists' weapon or at least the first fruits of their effort.

Perhaps it is better not always to think in terms of struggle. Let us simply open up and judge fairly and uprightly the things that are put before us. Then it will be obvious if at some point we are called upon to fight for truth and beauty, for righteousness and love. What should be key is a love for creation, for our neighbour, for essential values, for our Father in heaven and, most of all, his Son.

Above all we must allow a work to speak for itself. We must be mindful as we proceed that a work of art always depicts precisely what it represents and that the content of a work of art is fully expressed in its own idiom; in the field of art there is far too much reading of one's own ideas into another's work. In the case of art from an artistic source or movement that we still barely know, it can sometimes be necessary to immerse oneself in the backgrounds in order to study its peculiar language. Art history and art criticism can be of assistance to us here, helping us to avoid misunderstandings and unfair judgments; but there is no need to look to psychology. Certainly, a psychology of artistry is interesting, and it can be illuminating to know what was going on in the other person's mind as he or she created the work of art. Yet that will teach us precious little about the work of art as such, or about its impact. A third-rate artist can be more interesting psychologically than a great master, and the spiritual depth of a more modest talent greater than that of a virtuoso. To this we must add, however, that genuine masters will always be intelligent and deep figures whose work will have depth and be richly faceted. However that may be, to round off this subject, our concern must be first with the work and not with the person.

No prescriptions are given

In the preceding chapter I endeavoured to find guidelines for judging art. I tried to formulate norms that obtain for art. I did so not in order to dictate to anyone but in order to initiate a dialogue.

We must not read any prescriptions into this, for even if I were entirely correct, then still . . . I did not present any formulas that could be applied to a work of art in order to arrive at a judgment. To judge art, or rather to look at a work of art in order to see if we can have any pleasure in it, or if we will love it or want to have it around us, is an extremely personal and subtle affair. That process can never be captured in a formula.

Here I want to interject two observations. The first is that the process may very well require some effort; it may demand practising our taste and deepening our insight. This does not happen by itself. We must cultivate our judgment and develop ourselves in this respect.

We may very well make mistakes. That is not nearly as bad as snobbishly parroting someone else's opinions or deciding that something is nice just because it is of our own times or just because our forefathers thought it to be so. It may very well be that for a while we admire the content and qualities of a particular work and that precisely for this reason we are eventually able to move ahead and discover that the values it represents are limited after all and that another work that we did not understand at first is deeper and more beautiful. We may perhaps be able to understand the second work only because we have worked our way through the first.

The second observation I want to make is that debates about taste are certainly in order, although not where matters of similar quality are involved. Nobody needs to justify why they prefer Bach's *B minor Mass* to his *St John Passion*; one may certainly do so. Another person may like the cantatas better and someone else may prefer other works by this master. Someone who prefers the *St Matthew Passion* of Schütz to that of Bach, as I do, can hardly argue the case. Those are questions of taste in which our character, our personality, our development and a great deal more play a role.

There is, however, most certainly something to argue about where differences of level are concerned. Anyone who ranks Aubert above Beethoven or who considers Léhar a greater musician than Debussy, anyone who places Ferdinand Bol above Rembrandt is simply ignorant. We need not judge anyone harshly here. Inexperience may play a role. Yet to take an absurd example, anyone who stands in front of Zadkine's great statue in Rotterdam and professes to see only a chunk of bronze is not normal. Qualities are real values, and even though our judgment will always be subjective, it is certainly subject to argument.

If in the fullness of human experience it were not possible to appeal to norms, then any discussion of art would be meaningless and anyone who might still want to mention it would be a monomaniac. What would be the point of talking about Bach or Rembrandt if all that could be expressed were utterly individual feelings, and if nothing about truth and correctness in one's judgment and understanding could be discussed?

In that case we could close the museums, for we would not be able to see in them anything but works of art that someone once considered important. But the museum, the artistic expertise, and every critique and history of art invoke and attest to the existence of norms. We can sometimes get it wrong, but that only means we have wrongly applied the existing norms and short-changed the truth.

Let us return to our subject. We cannot provide prescriptions because we may not bind anyone to any law apart from the Scriptures. This is the realm of Christian freedom. We are free in our salvation through Jesus Christ, and we may never deprive another person of that freedom, not under any circumstances, and certainly not for the sake of idealistic pretexts.

The first and foremost norm for our association with art is that we may not bind one another to someone else's judgment, no matter whose. If we do so, we are thinking hierarchically and reintroducing the distinction between the priest and the laity and taking away our fellow human being's dignity to have a say. We are taking away something he or she received from the Lord.

'Is this not dangerous?' I am often asked concerning my offering no prescriptions. Undoubtedly it is very dangerous indeed. Mortally dangerous, in fact, in the deepest sense of the term. Anyone who does not live close to the Scriptures and who does not truly love the Lord, who in these matters cannot show any fruits of faith for the simple reason that she or he has no faith, acquires in this way a freedom that may be fatal to her or him.

Must we really be concerned about someone, who does not genuinely love the Lord, going astray from the godly path, and must we therefore be willing to bind not only him or her but our entire Christian community by our petty laws? Surely it is not our task to protect, maintain and keep the church? That is something our Lord reserved for himself! Let us therefore simply trust him in these matters.

'Fear of man will prove to be a snare, but whoever trusts in the LORD is kept safe,' says Proverbs 29:25. Therefore let us have confidence that everyone who is a child of the Lord has been given the Holy Spirit (Romans 5:5–6). We do not walk as orphans; the Lord is very near us by his Holy Spirit! We may also be certain that the Lord will not allow our prayer to go unheard. Those who doubt and do not know whether they may enjoy something, whether they may go into a certain field or avail themselves of a certain work of art or entertainment and devote their time to it, may confer with their friends and fellow believers; but they must, before all else, in prayer ask God for wisdom and the guidance of the Spirit. They must pray that they may know God's will. They must ask to know what is good for them in their circumstances. In their circumstances, for not everything is generally valid: personality and individuality count. God did not save us in order to make us all alike but precisely in order to make each one of us fully human with a character of our own. Therefore it is mortally dangerous to say that no prescriptions can be given. It is mortally dangerous for those who are lost. Yet it is even more dangerous to trivialize the work of the Holy Spirit and to underestimate the importance of believing prayer. How are we to bind where the Lord says that that may not be done?

Consider that this freedom, this Christian freedom, is different from humanistic freedom. One is reminded of that telling citation from Carlyle to which we alluded earlier.[39]

Humanistic freedom is at base the old sin of Genesis 3, of human desire to be like God, to be able to do everything one wants, to be tied to nothing. Whenever people set out to realize such freedom they inevitably run into reality, God's creation itself, which permits them human freedom but no divine characteristics. Reality then becomes a sort of prison, an alien and disagreeable power that curtails people in their possibilities – it reminds us of Gauguin becoming angry at having to accept that 2 x 2 = 4. As the expression of a form of humanism that has arrived at the deepest introspection and rejected God entirely, modern art also bears witness to this. People have sought frantically for an absolute art form, namely an art no longer bound to anything 'natural' as given in reality. Non-figurative art appeared to give the artist this kind of freedom. Yet persons who desire to make something valuable must take aesthetic laws into account. And they must at the same time always guard against their work becoming 'bound' again to the reality of creation in identifiable things or beings. Read again what I have said earlier about Wols, who in his art always seeks to destroy the image of reality.[40]

Goya was quite right to inscribe one of his etchings with, 'El Sueño de la razon produce monstruos' – 'the daydreams of reason bring forth monsters'. Where the mind has lost contact with reality and freed itself from creation in order to try its own wings, that which is ugly and monstrous will appear. I already alluded to that in speaking of sin and ugliness. People can also take their recourse to pure abstraction, to empty super-ornamentation. In that case they may very well be free of nature, but they will be able to do no more than reveal their own poverty, that there is nothing more to say. And if there is then still beauty to be found in this sort of art, as in Mondrian's work, it will lack humanity and will owe the beauty it has to respect for the norms given in creation. Or else the abstraction bears witness itself to a loss of balance, an inner chaos, or rather, the experience that the essence of reality is chaos, as in the work of Kandinsky, of whom I also spoke earlier.[41]

In short, modern art teaches us that the humanistic kind of freedom cannot be realized. Such freedom delivers people into anxiety and desolation and a sense of not being free, as Sartre's work so penetratingly demonstrates; it reduces people to the slavery of the so-called 'absolute' and turns reality into chaos.

Christian freedom is entirely different: it is the essential freedom of human beings to develop themselves as human creatures. In Christian freedom people are saved from the original sin of desiring to be like God. Let us re-read the gospel on this point.

The lesson of Colossians 2

In seeking to understand the foundations of Christian freedom a closer study of Colossians 2 is most instructive. There Paul first presents in a very concentrated form the main points of the gospel.

He begins, in verses 11 and 12, by talking about the importance of Christ's work for us: we have received in him immeasurably much; with him we have died and been buried and have risen again – a very abridged version of what Paul discussed more extensively in Romans 6. In this being-one-with-Christ's-work our sins are forgiven (v.14), certainly, but in this passage Paul emphasizes that our being in him means much more. And that is something that is often neglected in the proclamation of the gospel: that we have undergone, as it is expressed here, a spiritual circumcision 'in the putting off of the sinful nature', which died with Christ on the cross. Thus we have risen with him to new life (cf. Romans 6:6) and have been freed from the power of sin.

Herein lies the foundation of all sanctification and hallowing of life. Thank God, we do not have to mope around hopelessly accepting the fact that we have a body that is dead, a humanity that in and of itself is dead through transgression and uncircumcision, but we are saved from all that to a new life through Jesus Christ (v.13, cf. Romans 7:24–25). The gospel is indeed 'good news'. It saves us from ourselves, from our own 'carnality', so that the way is opened to a new life according to the Spirit (cf. Romans 8:1–17), if only we remain in Christ (Romans 8:9). Here we are reminded directly of Jesus' words in John 15:1–8, that we must abide in him, as branches in the true vine. When we live through him and bear fruit through him we are useful and good members of his body, salt that salts.

Horatius Bonar formulated that in an unsurpassable way in his classic book, *God's Way of Holiness* when he said:

> Most hateful also must that old life of ours be to Him, when in order to abolish it, He delivers up his Son; and most dear must we be in His sight when in order to rescue us from the old life, and make us partakers of the new, He brings forth all the divine resources of love and power and wisdom, to meet the exigencies of a case which would otherwise have been wholly desperate.[42]

Now what does this mean in practice? It means we must not try in our own strength to set up some kind of works-based holiness. It means we must not try to do good apart from Christ and his work in us. According to the gospel our sins are forgiven when we bring them to the Lord. Yet if we fail to see that the gospel means more than that, namely that we have acquired a new life in order to walk by the Spirit, then we narrow Christ's work. Living from the salvation that is in Christ we must at the same time attain to holiness of life, the fruit of Christ's work and not of our own toilsome striving.

Thus we must not only take our past sins to the Lord in order to receive forgiveness but we must also pray that he will enable us, who are in him and who with him have risen from the dead, to be the fruit of his work: that we may walk in the light (I John 1:7). Those who endeavour in their own strength to lead a life devoted to God will discover that they do not succeed. But those who seek refuge in Christ and live from his redemption discover that the fruits come as of themselves.

That is all the more so since Christ has triumphed over the devil and spoiled the spiritual 'principalities and powers' that constantly seek to draw people away from the Lord and from the good that he requires of us.[43] Therefore, if we are 'zealous for God' but with a zeal that is 'not based on knowledge' as Paul puts it so sharply in Romans 10:2–3, then despite our own best efforts we will not taste Christian freedom and happiness, imprisoned as we are. Instead we will remain sorrowful at the discovery of our persistent failure.

We must live close to him. For if indeed we are not in Christ, if we are not a branch that bears fruit through being grafted into the vine, if the Spirit of Christ does not dwell within us and we do not walk in the light, then we can better no longer call ourselves Christians and no longer claim to know the gospel at all. If we are not truly children of God we should not expect the fruits of the Spirit.[44] To the contrary, then we have to fear . . .

The confession that we live close to Christ, from his strength, may not be permitted to fade away into just so many words, pious rhetoric without content. Then we make God a liar (1 John 1:6). That confession must mean that we live in prayer and fasting (Matthew 17:21): in prayer not only for forgiveness of our sins but also in concrete matters for the guidance of the Holy Spirit and the strength to do what God asks of us as his children. Then we walk in the light. We must surrender our entire life to him and be prepared to renounce everything that is not in keeping with his will or that obstructs our fulfilling our task as believers.

Only then can we take up our cross and follow him, our difficulties, our sins, which he has left with us as reminders that we can only live in reliance on him (cf. Hebrews 12:5–7), and only then will we discover that his yoke is easy and his burden light (Matthew 11:30). We will see then that it is no idle slogan to 'rejoice always' (1 Thessalonians 5:16). We will find that the freedom of which the Scriptures speak does exist in our world.

The preceding short Bible study was intended to confront us clearly with the meaning of the gospel. We need to get away from superficial talk, as if it only meant that God always forgives everyone all their sins if they but confess. That is true too, but it does not mean he forgives when we ask light-heartedly without turning to him in conversion and without truly loving him. The gospel means so much more: it is a power for the sanctification of life as the fruit of the completed work of Jesus Christ. Prayer and a readiness to make sacrifices are an indispensable part of it, and opening ourselves to the guidance of the Holy Spirit.

After Paul has brought all this to life again for the reader with a few words in Colossians 2, he goes on to say, 'Do not let anyone judge you by what you eat or drink, or with regard to a religious festival' – which I would paraphrase as 'in respect of art and entertainment' – 'the reality is found in Jesus Christ' (v. 16–17). And a little further: 'Since you died with Christ to the basic principles of this world' – that is, the spirit of sanctification by works – 'why, as though you still belonged to it, do you submit to its rules: "Do not handle! Do not taste! Do not touch!"? These are all destined to perish with use, because they are based on human commands and teachings' (2:20–22). This is the foundation on which I dared to assert in the preceding section that no prescriptions may be given and that Christian freedom is an unassailable good.

'Since you died with Christ' . . . that is how this text began. Without that it is meaningless to speak of biblical norms in our association with art. Yet if we are indeed in Christ, then it is as if we are still walking in conformity with the world to ask for commandments, for human doctrines or rules. We must think very seriously about the statement: 'why, as though you still belonged to it, do you submit to its rules.' Paul goes even further and adds the warning: If you must have prescriptions after all, then know that they make a show of wisdom but serve only to satisfy the flesh! (2:23).

Let no one say that this freedom will only produce lawlessness. Certainly, this freedom belongs only to the believing children of God. In the next chapter of the letter to the Colossians Paul discusses what the new life means (as a fruit of faith, in the full freedom of the children of God) but we will not go into that here.

There is no other possibility to speak about our association with art than within the framework of this freedom. However, we must also mention the necessity of belief and conversion at the heart of the matter. Apart from a life in the Holy Spirit there is no Christian freedom and no possibility of speaking meaningfully about Christian conduct.

At the beginning of this book I referred to the crisis within our orthodox Christian world, exactly with respect to the practice of the Christian life. Does this provide and answer for the collapse of faith? It appears that neither better methods, nor better prescriptions applied to the situation, nor a deeper thinking through of the norms for art and entertainment, nor an appeal to the traditions of our fathers, nor anything in such a spirit can be of any help. For what we need is not better prescriptions and doctrines, which are always the work of people, but life in Christ, freedom, not in our own strength but in dependence upon him, poor in spirit as we are, deploring our own brokenness but glorying in the work of our Saviour and in the power of the Holy Spirit

– not better doctrines but true faith, and conversion where that is necessary. Without such belief we should not expect anything. Our commandments and prescriptions . . . do they not prove that we are living as if we are of the world, attempting in our own strength to erect a defence against all unrighteousness and ungodliness?

Those who wish to think and speak in a Christian way in this area can therefore do no better than call for renewed faith, for reformation, for conversion, for the renewal or regeneration of life. Yet whoever neglects to speak of the saving work of our Lord forgets to speak of the very foundations. Is not a great deal of our speaking saltless because we assume to be addressing Christians, while in reality many hearts are thirsty because people have lost their way and really no longer know what God's beautiful gifts mean concretely? Our crisis is perhaps above all else from a lack of understanding on our part of the work that the Lord has done for us. For years people have discussed many matters but kept silent about this foundation, which they considered to be self-evident. The result has been that the connection between concrete everyday life (also with respect to art and entertainment) and belief is no longer perceived or understood. And for many it has come to appear that matters of belief are good only for preaching and meditation and clergy's chitchat, with no reference to reality!

Thank God we have a living God. He is not an apotheosized fate or an unfeeling Ruler; he is our Father in heaven, to whom we therefore do not pray in vain (cf. Matthew 7:11).

Our life in freedom

This heading is not an otherworldly slogan but must become sober, everyday reality if we hope ever to escape from the impasse in which the Christian life has landed in so many respects. I now want to explore what this could mean for us in connection with art and entertainment. If a work of art suits us in its nature and level, if we understand the content of the work and can support that, it is not only easy to arrive at a positive judgment but we can also enjoy that work to the full, without any ifs or buts. Without difficulty we can then proceed to pore over and lose ourselves in artistic qualities we know and appreciate. That is wonderful! Then we feel at home with the work.

I did not say it was necessary that the work be related to our own life and world view, nor did I demand that it be the product of an environment like our own. Such circumstances could be beneficial to a positive contact with the work, to be sure, but they are not a condition!

Is it not striking, for example, that in viewing and discussing seventeenth-century Dutch works we are seldom led to account for their religious or philosophical backgrounds, for the artists' outlook on life? Could this be because the artists had such an open attitude towards reality, such a positive disposition, that through it reality itself is shown to full advantage? Because they speak of a world we also know, of human experiences we all have in common, no further explanation of the how and why are needed here.

That holds for all art that acts in truth, that comes to us openly and honestly from a loving human understanding of things. Earlier I already mentioned that we can also find that quality in the work of artists who for the rest give evidence of living in conflict with reality. Really, it is not necessary to drive them back to their own consequences again and again, to ask incessantly about the how and why. Let us just take things as they are offered to us. We need not make it difficult. I am thinking of a little portrait etched by Picasso, something we may all just look at quietly and find beautiful, and we may enjoy it. We may enjoy it without any further ado. Even the questions about the period in which it was made and about the circumstances of its creation we may leave blissfully aside. Seldom do the stories surrounding a work of art assist us in fathoming its value. More often such considerations simply distract us.

It is when a work deviates from fully human normality, no matter what its style, that questions arise. That is the case, for example, with the questions raised in connection with modern art, even of works which their makers say present nothing but pure aesthetic forms, pure abstraction without content. People seem to not want to believe them. The debate is heated. Questions are also raised about all kinds of contrived art from the past, about the Mannerists, about the classicists with their exceptionally well developed coolness and self-imposed restrictions based on obedience to academic rules. These questions make it interesting to engage with such art, but sometimes they also take away our pure pleasure in it. The moment one starts to ask, while listening to a piece of modern jazz, why the rhythm is so frenetic, why it has such a remarkable though almost indefinable quality, why there are so many unresolved dissonances and why the melodies are so erratic and whimsical, the moment one does that, pure pleasure in the music vanishes and listening can become a difficult cultural activity. That can arise from ignorance: any Westerners who for the first time make the acquaintance of gospel songs as they are rendered by the Spirit of Memphis Quartet or by Mahalia Jackson may ask themselves what these really contain, or what the meaning is of the unfathomable and sometimes seemingly unaesthetic ferocity in their manner of expression. Those who consider the matter more closely will learn, however, that there are no strange tensions here, that there is an open and emotional, direct expression of faith that does full justice to the reality of faith, that we here encounter a living Christian musical culture in the environment of the African-Americans.

In short, I want to break a lance for listening, looking and reading with eyes and hearts that are open. Tasting, and enjoying where possible.

We must not let ourselves be deprived of the possibility of enjoying a work that we find beautiful by theoretical cultural considerations, by cultural history or our own knowledge or expertise. This would be another way in which to lose our freedom.

If the work with which we are engaged does not connect with us, or if it contains elements we find dubious, then the dialogue can arise to which we referred in an earlier chapter. Engaged in that dialogue we need not fear landing up outside the limits of the rules that our neighbour, who may be called a critic or theologian or ethicist, may seek to impose on us. Let us speak openly and honestly, investing the whole of our personality, our humanity with all its wisdom and shortcomings. Here too we must be on guard against losing our freedom.

This means that we have the freedom to say no, to turn the radio or the gramophone off, to walk past a painting in a museum, to slam a book shut. We need not surrender our freedom in order to act like snobs!

For the freedom we discussed in the preceding section does not mean lawlessness or an absence of norms. This freedom means that we will continue to listen as children of God and continue to carry on the 'dialogue' in that capacity – not as if compelled and not anxiously, but openly and honestly. And then it may turn out that we break off the dialogue because the 'other', in this case the work of art in question, curses, or because it treats sins casually, as if it is the most commonplace thing in the world.

We have the freedom to lay a book aside if it leads us into sin. It may very well be that that is a personal matter. If a book presents a character that re-awakens feelings of hatred or revulsion that I experienced in my youth or that activates my erotic fantasy in an unwholesome way, then I am free to close the book, even if that has nothing at all to do with its writer. Our reactions to what is offered to us are a highly personal matter, and for that reason alone it is impossible to articulate generally valid rules. Art criticism, even the best Christian criticism, can be no more than an effort to express a general judgment. To give marks, as in some Roman Catholic criticism, seems to me to ignore the reality of individual personalities, which may react to various things quite differently from what a critic suggests. In short, we must develop the necessary self-discipline. What one person can cope with may be beyond another's capacity, and what is good for one may have the opposite effect on another. I am formulating the contradictions in broad terms, but in human reality matters are infinitely varied. Individuals have to fight their own fight and keep themselves untainted by the world and by sin.

A consequence of all this may be that at times we have to abstain from something. We may have to ask the Lord to give us the strength to restrain ourselves, so that we use our freedom in such a way that we do not stray from him. It is sometimes said that we ought to act as the Lord Jesus would have done in the same situation. That seems to me to be a strange demand. How can we know what he would have done? For we must also keep in mind that he had a calling and task of his own, so very different from ours. No, it seems to me clearer or purer to say that we should always act in such a way that we would be able to account for our behaviour should he suddenly drop in for a visit. That reflects the real situation, for the Lord is always with us and knows what is going on inside us, where we are and what we are doing. We cannot hide ourselves from him, not even for one moment.

Now, what does this mean in practice? Imagine a street in which believing people live. At a given moment they are all tuned in to the radio play on their radios. It is a strange tale, an existentialist story in which situations are described and views are presented that are far from ideal. What will happen? Number One turns the piece off after a short while, saying 'Bah! What nauseating stuff!' Number Two listens to the piece with great interest, asking himself all the time what solution would be given, from that particular view of life, to the problem raised . . . the more so since he has a friend who is wrestling with just such a problem and whom he may perhaps be able to help as a result of gaining a better insight into the situation through this piece. Number Three turns the piece off immediately, unprepared to think through the difficult problems of others since she already has enough problems of her own. Number Four listens to the piece with great pleasure till the end. He is hardly aware of what it is about, though he found it rather heavy going, but then one must not always be satisfied with light material. Number Five listens with fascination, since in her studies she is currently dealing with similar questions, yet turns it off anyway after a short while because at this moment she cannot cope with a work in this spirit. Number Six also turns the piece off at a given moment, because something appears in it that reminds him of something that happened not so very long ago that he no longer wants to think about. Number Seven turns the knob off just before the end. There is something in the piece that sets her fantasy to work in an unhealthy way, and she wanted to begin her daily Bible reading shortly with an open heart. And so one might continue.

The one turned off the radio and that was good; another left it on and that was also good; and in between there were many possible options. Now, we can think through our example still further by having all these people meet up the next day and letting them discuss what they heard. Then we will discover that there are nuances in the assessment of what they heard but definitely a certain concurrence as well. For the different reactions did not arise from a difference in understanding of the piece or in a great discrepancy between views of the obtaining norms; the different reactions resulted from the different situations and circumstances in which these people found themselves. Through this example I have wanted to show that chaos does not have to result if we are obedient to the Lord in the defence of Christian freedom.

I would like to give another example, this time a true story. At Easter

1956 an opera singer was converted to the Lord. One of her first questions to the counsellor who had led her to the Lord was whether she could continue to sing. What would you have answered? We must be mindful that the issue here was not the resolution of an abstract problem about whether opera and Christianity could go together, but a much more concrete one about possibly breaking off one's career. Her counsellor gave her the only possible answer: he said he did not know. The Bible does not talk about it. But he did discuss with her the portions of Scripture that deal with the Christian walk, with keeping oneself untainted by the world (James 1:27), with being a letter of Christ to be read by others. He also spoke about prayer and about the leading of the Holy Spirit. Perhaps the Lord would call her to bear witness to him there in that environment by her walk and her conversation, perhaps he wanted to use her to bring people from the world of the opera to the gospel. But perhaps that would turn out to be impossible for one reason or another, or at least not the will of the One who was now also her Lord.

For a while she simply continued to sing. Later she began to concentrate on works like Handel's *Messiah*. After a while she returned to opera and it became increasingly clear to her that she could not go on down that path, not because the surroundings were unchristian or because she could not live as a Christian there, but rather because she discovered that it is extremely difficult to sing the role of Isolde in a Wagnerian opera (her specialty), since the part features a paean in praise of adultery. It was not her surroundings but the content of what she had to sing that finally made her work impossible.

She proceeded to act as subtly as a serpent. 'If I just stop,' she thought, 'people will say that I am seeking refuge in belief because my career is not going well.' Therefore she sang on until in Naples she played her role brilliantly before several thousand people. Naples is the entrance to the La Scala in Milan and therefore represents something near the pinnacle of any opera career. Only after that success did she announce that this would be the last time she would appear. In England and America this made large headlines in the newspapers and she gained the opportunity to tell many why she was doing this and to bear witness to her Saviour.

So she ended her career in 1959 because her Lord asked it of her. Since that time she has worked as an evangelist and led Bible study groups. She is able to do so because during the first years following her conversion she did not stand idly by but studied hard and read a great deal in the Bible, in Christian books, in commentaries and much more. Now her life, her works, and also her spiritual insight radiate a testimony that the gospel truly means a renewal of life.

Her name is Jane Stuart Smith.

Her life is to walk in the freedom that is in Christ. She did not leave opera because anyone told her to do so but because the Holy Sprit himself convinced her of the truth and of the will of God in this matter.

Thus we are free. If our conscience condemns us, then we know we are doing something that is not right (cf. I John 3:18–24); and when to our mind something is wrong, we should not do it even if a brother is convinced, rightly or wrongly, that it is permissible. In such matters the rule of life in Romans 14:22–23 is a good guideline. If only we do not give things up for the show of it, in order to be seen (cf. Matthew 6:16).

There is much to enjoy

Sometimes I object to using the word 'enjoy' when we are talking about art or entertainment. It makes it seem as if someone who has chosen his or her profession in this direction, be it as an artist, an art historian or an art critic, is some kind of a hedonist, someone who pursues pleasure as the goal of life. Anyone who knows anything about how artists live, whatever their arts genre, knows better. It is hard work and hard study, not only to earn a living but also to produce something worthwhile. And it is not pleasure but idealism that drives those who are professionally engaged with art. No, someone who wants to enjoy life should not choose his or her profession in this direction.

Yet we also need not object to the term 'enjoy', for art and entertainment are given by God to people for their enrichment and to beautify their lives. Beauty and joy belong to the Christian life. It would be ungrateful to our God to claim otherwise.

It is true that in this area there are snares and traps, but for anyone who is willing to expend a little effort there is a great deal of beauty to enjoy. Enjoy it freely and 'undogmatically'. We do not need to question first, Does it have a Christian origin? Was it made with good intentions? Is it in keeping with God's will from beginning to end? If you like the colours in a painting by Karel Appel, then do so, and do not let anyone else throw you off stride. Perhaps they are beautiful colours, even if in general the content of his art is less so. It may be less pronounced in some of his works than in others, or even absent. Or it may be there and elude you. You are allowed to enjoy what you are able to enjoy.

There is a great deal of beautiful and very positive old art. There is also old art that is less easy to accept. The old is not good simply because it is old and has stood the test of the ages! There is also contemporary art that fully deserves our attention.

At an exhibition we may find ourselves confronted with a little work such as a watercolour by van Goethem. It is an example of how a younger generation of painters is exploring the possibility of bringing something of reality into a work while retaining the techniques and directness that were developed in the experimental art of the postwar years. Notice how elegantly this picture was made, as if with a single stroke. Perhaps the little farm is a weak point in the whole, too deliberate and less direct in origin than the rest. That is something we could quietly discuss.

We can also refer to the beautiful work of the young etcher A.J. Veldhoen, an artist who says reality is too dear to him to pursue abstraction or Expressionism. Yet he produces entirely original work and does not simply repeat what has been said for centuries. It is remarkable how he can render nudes, couples, and even childbirth without being coarse or unclean. A breath of purity wafts through this work, which thereby helps us to grasp something more of the greatness and beauty of the life God has given us. Whether he would claim this himself in such terms is a question we need not ask. What he does say we may cite from letters written at a time when he was doing his work in operating rooms, letters in which he tells how beautiful and fascinating a physical organism is, how beautiful a heart that beats. We can see that enthusiasm in his etchings. [Plate 8] shows an etching that he made a number of years ago at an airfield. He was gripped by the theme of the fighter pilot, almost overpowered by his outfit and panoply of equipment, yet still a real human being. Why should a fighter aircraft not be fascinating, including the remarkable jet opening at the tail end? That does not have to become a surrealistic vision of anxiety. It can be looked at openly and warmly.

We must restrict ourselves however and not write an entire chapter about Veldhoen's work, his cactuses etched in Ibiza, his view of Lelystad, and much more, every work created afresh, original and new, without deformation, without violence to the truth. Here is work that we can support virtually without reservation, not only because of its content but also because of its high artistic quality.

We can perhaps also do ourselves a favour by turning to art with which we feel less at home. Sometimes there are considerable benefits to be gained from that, not just from an artistic vantage point but also in terms of content. I will give you an example from my own experience. I visited an exhibition of the works of one of the greatest sculptors of our time, Marino Marini. I walked about amongst the pieces for a long time. They were strong in statement and construction, truly not in the least superficial or empty. It was fascinating work, yet it repelled me. I asked myself what this man really had to say with all these remarkable figures. What drove him and what was at the heart of his art? Finally I came to the conclusion that here we had to do with a kind of strained nihilism. Whether I was right or not is not what matters. I am still not sure about that myself. A few days later, however, when I overheard a few characters in black leather jackets talking, I understood that in his work something is typified that belongs quite decidedly to our reality. In particular his riders, as I now saw clearly, express the spirit of the modern person, of the motorcycle maniac, of the beatnik biker on his roaring machine, of the empty joy of thundering along, fast and making a senseless racket.

Because I had experienced Marini's work, I could understand their world better than before. Now, it is not easy to say just what this work embraces; Marini said it in a purely sculptural idiom and words must therefore fall short.

Thus art can bring us into contact with entire worlds. Often we are relieved not to have to steep ourselves in them. Sometimes it is good that a particular piece is located in a museum where we can enjoy it freely, since it would be difficult or impossible for us to view it in its original place, where it fulfilled the function for which it was intended. I have in mind the statue of an idol. Seeing it as such, we are horrified – imagine, for example, people bowing and praying to the *Venus* of *Milo!* – yet one can freely enjoy that statue as a work of art, independent of all that, and discover in it an enriching human beauty and truth. But someone who is unmoved by the work does not have to pretend otherwise . . . that would be snobbery.

Perhaps I am already talking too much again about great art. We can expand the field still further. Think of a beautiful vase with a beautiful glaze and lovely form. What joy it can give! It does not need to be an expensive museum piece. Outside the scope of the visual arts in the narrower sense there is a great deal of beauty to discover and enjoy as well. Those who enjoy browsing through antique shops can sometimes pick up things that cost little and are nice and fascinating, beautiful and interesting.

That also applies to entertainment, to art with a small a, to light literature, popular music and the like. Anyone who makes the effort to look for something good and attractive will surely be rewarded. Someone who just takes what is offered, who is lazy in this area, will have to be satisfied with less. And that is a great pity.

We must not imagine that all this beauty can only be discovered and enjoyed by highly educated people or by those who have a special talent for it. Moreover, association with beauty is not at all a privilege reserved for people with well-filled wallets. Nothing could be less true! To be sure, cows do not catch hares, which is to say that anyone who wants to discover beauty will have to keep an eye open for it. Otherwise one can walk right past even the finest things and never see them. Just look at the crowds of people in the museums, at the tourists who feel obliged to stroll past every painting in sight. Happily there are some who really enjoy what they see and who benefit from it; but many go away with little more than the possibility of saying they visited the Rijksmuseum. A lost opportunity! If they had taken the opportunity to look a little longer at just one work that attracted them instead of walking past countless more, they would have enjoyed their visit far better.

Thus we do not need to be afraid of involving ourselves with art and entertainment, not even if what is offered us is questionable for one reason or another. I believe the scriptural word applies here too: 'It is not what goes into a man that defiles him but what comes out' (Matthew 15:16–20). It is not what we read, hear or see that makes us impure but what lives in our hearts, what proceeds from us in thoughts, words or deeds. For those, we are responsible. Manifest in them will be the use we make of the freedom that has been given us. The things that proceed from us should reveal our new lives. I am not responsible for what the writer of a book that I read had in mind or what he meant to achieve. I am certainly responsible for my own thoughts that I have acquired through my reading. I repeat, I may lay the book aside because it stimulates my fantasy in an unwholesome way, while that is not the writer's fault at all and was never her or his intention.

Why we must involve ourselves with art and entertainment

No one is obliged to find Bach's music beautiful, to study Picasso's work, to read Steinbeck or to enjoy the experimental poets. Who would dare lay any such yoke upon us? Yet I believe we may not remain simply oblivious to everything that is offered us, even if such unmindfulness were possible.

Then we would be poorly prepared to fulfil our task, our task of living as human beings and Christians in these times. We need to understand our own world, to know what is going on in people's hearts and minds. If we do not know that, how can we help or offer an answer to the issues of life that are hurled at us, give answers to the problems posed in our world, work together to find solutions to the difficulties with which the world confronts people today? Without knowledge we cannot love our neighbours, cannot help them, without that it is even difficult for us to proclaim the gospel. For in doing so we must be a Greek to the Greeks and know what is going on in the inner world of our contemporaries. In our speaking about the works of God we must be able to connect with the common experiences of good and beautiful things. Otherwise we miss our common basis, as expressed in Romans 1, of what we can see and experience of God's works, while a critical observation about a work of art that does violence to the truth can often break the ice or open another person's eyes.

We also desperately need the association with art and entertainment to know the spirit of the age for our own sakes. Through that association we not only may learn what concerns others; we also may be made attentive to sins that live in us. By reading about people who have devoted their lives to the acquisition of an impressive title and career we may perhaps discover something about ourselves. If we recognize ourselves in an existentialist novel, then we learn that even we cannot remain free of this spirit. If we ask what in the world has happened to people in their current travel habits – so many thousands of kilometres per vacation – then we will probably learn that we too have been affected to some extent by this spirit: we do not want to really cherish something, to tie ourselves down; we want to escape boredom and not really immerse ourselves in anything. Truly, we must not walk through this world with our eyes closed, for then the spirit of the age will overcome us before we know it. And we can get to know this spirit best and most directly through that expression of life called 'art'.

Finally, we must consider the following. May it not be the case that modern art, particularly visual art, so clearly and emphatically expresses a totally secularized attitude towards life because we Reformed and evangelical Christians have held ourselves completely aloof from this area of life? If modern art is indeed unchristian, then does the blame not lie with us rather than with the world that gives birth to and sustains it? Simply by our showing some interest, by our participating in the viewing and discussing, we might have had the effect of salt that salts and served as a brake on the influence of the spirit that is not of Christ. If we really want to mean something for our world, then as Christians living by faith we must empathize, take an interest, and learn to discuss what is at stake with an understanding of the issues and insight into the nature of things. Keeping off to the side and offering bitter, possibly even irrelevant, criticism from a distance is no help at all.

The same is true for the field of entertainment in the broader sense, an area that is daily becoming more and more important for our culture as a whole now that we have ever more leisure time, more ready money and improved, generally available means of communication.

Sojourners

By engaging our times we discover more and more what it means to be a stranger and a sojourner.[45] It is not just that we abstain from some things the world does and do a few other things the world leaves undone. It goes much deeper.

If being a Christian means nothing more than abiding by a few rules – do not touch, do not taste – and for the rest distinguishes itself only by going to church once a week, then it is poor. Perhaps in that case we are no less worldly than the child of the world. The neighbour who lives across the road, a thoroughbred humanist, also never goes to the movies, has no television and leads a pure life. Where then is the difference between us?

Our sojournership goes deeper. It means, negatively expressed, that we cannot bow before the spirit of the age, and positively that we have a God in whom we trust, in whose ways we want to walk, close to him and living in the redemption that is through his Son. It is precisely in this last matter, in the renewal of life that is not of our own strength, that the uniqueness of the believer lies and this is what distinguishes believers from unbelievers.

We are at home in this world, the creation, the Creator of which we honour as our Father who is in heaven. And the very fact that unbelievers are sometimes so negatively disposed towards reality – 'we live in such a rotten world' – causes us pain, since we feel that this is offensive to him. We are at home in this world, which is now cursed to be sure, bringing forth thorns and thistles, but which is still good as God's creation. We all look forward to the full revelation of the richness of his work. Consider Romans 8:21–23.

Perhaps art can serve to make us mindful of these things. Anyone who walked around the exhibition of ancient Mexican art that was held a few years ago could see what an abyss and darkness appeared in that heathen world, such cruelty, such terror. It will have led many to praise God that he delivered us from such devilish bondage to fear and an idolatrous theology. There will be few who thought we could have been better people if left to our own devices.

Our freedom and our effort

We should now be able to pose again the question that has engaged us throughout this book. Where do we stand with respect to art and entertainment in our world today? For it is undeniable that particularly in these areas, more than others, unbelief and apostasy have the upper hand. Where does one find genuinely Christian entertainment? Where does one find wholesome and good relaxation? Something is offered us in that direction in Bible illustrations, literature and song, but most of what people dare to put before us is far below standard. Truly, any effort to make, discover, support and build up something better and more meaningful and more wholesome would be worthwhile. I said it before: let us not constantly regard with scepticism everything that is undertaken in this direction, but let us instead offer positive criticism and be constructive and helpful!

For the time being, however, we shall have to make do with what we can find in the world today, even though there is precious little out there that is Christian. Nevertheless, there is a great deal to be discovered that is positive, if only we will look for it with open eyes and hearts.

Also, we do better to begin with ourselves and to ask ourselves how we will stand. And that gives reason enough to be saddened, which is better in any case than sniping at the sometimes really honest work of people who no longer know God; and let us add directly that sometimes that is our fault.

The Holy Scriptures say positively who we ourselves are meant to be and negatively how we are meant to stand in a world of sin and unbelief, a world that we cannot and should not leave. Positively the Scriptures teach that those who believe in the Lord, who find their only comfort in knowing themselves to belong to Christ, are 'free from the law of sin and death' (Romans 6:6 and 8:2). Through Christ we were 'bought with a price' (1 Corinthians 6:20). We are not slaves of the spirit of the age, not of prejudices, not of slogans, not of public opinion or the judgment of others, not of gravity or of superficiality, not of our work but also not of our pleasure, no, we are no longer slaves but free. Free to listen to God's word and to act according to it, which is not a new slavery but a truly human freedom, because then we can be what we were meant to be and may do what we were created to do and what we were given the gifts to do. Though we may be free of the law of sin and walking in the light, we cannot say we have not sinned without making God a liar (1 John 1:10). That is our difficulty. It is for this reason that no 'solution' can be given for our pleasure, for our association with art and entertainment. Warfare between the new and the old person (see Romans 7) will always persist, and things will remain that way until we are entirely renewed on the Day of the Lord.

From this warfare, this division whereby we are renewed in part but are not yet entirely delivered from our sinfulness and our old nature – the meaning of which we find explained in Hebrews 12:7 – from this situation that finds us on an earth that is cursed, with sin in us by nature, living between the Fall into sin and the new Day, the twofold message of Scripture is comprehensible. Be not of the world (John 17:14–16); but neither should you go out of the world (1 Corinthians 5:10). Test all things (1 Thessalonians 5:21); but avoid bad company (1 Corinthians 5). All things are lawful unto me; but not all things are expedient or edifying (1 Corinthians 6:12 and 10:23). Rejoice with those who rejoice; but there will be times when all the merry-hearted will sigh (Isaiah 24:7). Be a Greek to the Greeks (I Corinthians 9:20 and 10:32); but avoid splitting hairs, getting into foolish questions and contentious debates (Titus 3:9). Let every person be fully persuaded in her or his own mind (Romans 14:5); but let not your good be spoken evil of (Romans 14:16). Rejoice, O young person, in your youth but remember that judgment is coming (Ecclesiastes 11:9).

All things are lawful; but not all things are expedient or edifying (1 Corinthians 6:12 and 10:23). The situation in our world is always extremely complicated, a tangled reality of sin and sorrow and of good and beautiful. Art and entertainment too are more than something purely aesthetic; they are directly connected to a fully human situation. This situation cannot be regarded exclusively from an individualistic vantage point, for it is one in which our behaviour has a direct effect on the behaviour of others. We do not stand alone; remember again the passage of Scripture: 'Do not allow what you consider good [thus also your freedom] to be spoken of as evil. For the kingdom of God is not a matter of eating and drinking [however good these may be in themselves] but [there are greater things at stake] of righteousness, peace and joy in the Holy Spirit' (Romans 14:16–17).

Righteousness (that is, doing good and helping the weak and not bringing them into temptation),[46] peace and joy, therein lies the kingdom of God. That kingdom can be present only through the Holy Spirit and through prayer.[47] If indeed it is there, then the trademark of Christians, of believers, will make itself known, namely in unity and love.[48] The wonder of it is that this unity and this love do not destroy our Christian freedom; on the contrary, this freedom is indispensable in the mutual bond of the fellowship of the saints.

Unity, love and freedom, these characterize living together in a Christian way. It means that our association with art and entertainment cannot be individualistic, as if we could maintain our lofty position, as if we could look down our noses at the masses who know nothing of the Law of the kingdom of God.

Unity, love and freedom, that means that we may have confidence in one another, for the Holy Spirit also guides the other. Let us not find fault with one another; let us not deprive others of their freedom because we believe we can see things so much more clearly. Perhaps at a given moment we will be the one who is weak and the other the one who is strong (Romans 14). We must not 'judge another man's servant', someone with an insight different from our own.

Often Romans 14 is interpreted to mean that those who at any given moment think differently from what is the prevalent custom in an environment should conform without further ado. That is one-sided argumentation with a vengeance! For it is not at all Paul's intention to put freedom in a straitjacket again, as if the weak should be the dictators in the community of the saints. No, unity means that we must trust others, approach them in love, be prepared to listen to them and not judge them too hastily when we do not immediately understand what they are saying. Others, however, will try not to give offence, will take their brothers and sisters into account, and will discuss quietly with them all the things that are needed or expedient. Without unity and love, for the sake of which we must sometimes wait for one another and pray for one another and occasionally admonish one another, no Christian fellowship is possible; without that there is also no freedom. We can also turn this proposition around: if freedom is curtailed and a new legalistic slavery is built up, then the unity and love have already gone. Then we no longer work alongside one another as the members of a body do, perhaps with quite different tasks (cf. 1 Corinthians 12:12–31), but some want to dominate others and consider themselves superior.

Legalism is our greatest enemy here. It is right of us to act or refrain from acting because we can do nothing else, because our whole human frame desires nothing else. We also pray for this and implore the Holy Spirit to guide us. This is better than to commit or omit deeds because we know the Law and force ourselves with difficulty to behave in conformity with it. That will sometimes be necessary in our struggle against the sin that lives in us (Romans 7:20). Yet in that case too it must not be the commandments of men but the will of God that rules.

Every legalism is our greatest enemy. If I should do or refrain from doing something, also in the area discussed in this book, merely out of obedience to Reformed customs, to our own Calvinist commandments, but I lack love and do not seek unity and do not know freedom, then all my deeds are nothing, like the tinkling of a cymbal; they are self-righteousness. By contrast, those who act or refrain from acting for the sake of love and unity, even without seeing the need to do so, are free and are making good use of their freedom. That builds strength and brings blessing. Those who refrain from doing something, even though others do it, because they believe it is not good for them are also doing the right thing. Yet others who believe they can listen or read or observe are equally free and do not need to be disturbed because their brothers or sisters judge differently.

Unity, love, freedom: that bond is part of belonging to the body of Christ, of being a branch abiding in the vine. Unity, for we have one Saviour and one Holy Spirit that dwells in us; love, for we love one another as fellow creatures and as fellow believers; freedom, for we do not want to deprive one another again of the freedom that our Lord gained for us.

Let us therefore guard against depriving one another of our freedom through legalistic preaching, asking one another to live according to the law, not of the Spirit but of the letter, a law moreover that is mainly made by people: this law of the letter kills, actively kills!

Then we may speak of the fellowship of the saints, of the community of the children of God, sanctified in Christ. But if we may not proceed from there, then what sense is there in talking about norms in our association with art and entertainment? If we talk about the Christian life and walk, about the fruits of faith and that faith is not there . . .

Indeed, if that faith is not there then we really should be making little rules and regulations in order to stem the tide of lawlessness. Or better still, let us endeavour to win our neighbour back to Christ through our actions and walk and, above all, through our prayers for them. The following is a fact of experience, although it is self-evident: if someone is not committed to a Christian way of life, then we should not attempt to convince him or her of the appropriateness of all our little laws, of the customs prevalent in our circle, however good these possibly may be (it is not a foregone conclusion that they should be so), but we should instead talk to him or her about our Saviour. Often we will then discover that something is amiss in the relationship with the Lord. Frequently we will encounter real spiritual need. 'Falling behind in grace' our fathers called it, or 'backsliding' if you will. Misconceptions perhaps, as in the story of the Reformed girl who went off the rails for a period of time and lived a totally worldly life, more worldly than the world in some respects, until a deep discussion made clear what the root of the problem had been: she had tried very hard to live a holy life but discovered that she could not. And since she believed that if she did not lead a holy life she could not belong to the Lord, she had given up the struggle and done the only thing that made sense in that case: to eat, drink and be merry, for tomorrow we die. A clear proclamation of the gospel and an opening of the Scriptures (e.g. John 3) opened her eyes. Since then she has taken up her cross and followed her Lord. Moral sermonizing and exhortations against this or that were entirely unnecessary after that.

Conclusion

> A man can do nothing better than eat and drink and find satisfaction in his work. This too, I see, is from the hand of God, for without him, who can eat or find enjoyment? To the man that pleases him, God gives wisdom, knowledge and happiness, but to the sinner he gives the task of gathering and storing up wealth to hand it over to the one who pleases God (Ecclesiastes 2:24–26).

This text summarizes everything I have wanted to say. There are no satisfactions, no joys apart from the Lord. He gives them all to us. And we must thank him for them all.

Noteworthy is the last sentence of this text. Remember it when you are in a museum looking at the ceramics of heathen or unbelieving peoples: astonishingly beautiful is a celadon dish made hundreds of years ago in China! Fascinating and sometimes almost thrilling are the polyrhythms from Africa: the sounds may very well have been created for the exorcism of evil spirits, but we may enjoy them freely. As long as there is no open and blatant cursing in art and entertainment, as long as people endeavoured to make something good, we can enjoy it freely, thanking God.

Yet we shall have to learn to do this as believers. It is certainly not a superfluous luxury to move forward in the matter of a Christian lifestyle or to surmount the crisis discussed in our first chapter. For we live in the last days, an era that is not easy. If we do not stand firm, we will be swept along by the world.

We must face the situation. A general liberal religion is growing. Liberal Roman Catholics, liberal Muslims, liberal Hindus, liberal Zen

Buddhists, liberal Protestants and liberal humanists will find each other – in a liberal religiosity.

Religion is something people need, that is a fundamental tenet of this liberal doctrine. According to this doctrine people are natural beings who originated through evolution. The world develops and moves according to natural laws. The most important is the psychological structure of human beings. There are moreover no fixed norms, for in every age people will again give new form to their life's potentialities, and thus historicism remains true. Forms of government, technology and culture are expressions of being human on the one hand, and they give a pragmatic form to human necessities on the other. Human beings evidently possess – in spite of the fact that science teaches that there are no miracles and that everything is built upon natural laws – a religious function. Without religion people are apparently incomplete and not happy. In their myths humankind have humanized their instincts at a higher plane. Thus it makes no sense to speak of eternal truth: people can boast only of truths-for-us, of useful, operative insights.

Through all the ages people have fulfilled their religious needs in their own way, according to this doctrine. Thus the religions arose, although they are essentially all the same, shaped by one and the same psychic need for belief, for certainty in the religious sense. In this functionality lies the meaning of religion. Whether Jesus ever walked the earth or whether he ever truly, historically rose from the dead are therefore not meaningful questions. Perhaps it was actually so and historical science may one day give us an answer, but it is only important religiously speaking that he was once on earth. That strengthens believers, and it is good to believe it. Yet it is a myth, which is to say a profound truth, namely, one attuned to people's needs; for indeed they invented it themselves.

Thus according to this doctrine all religions are essentially one and the same. They complement what the sciences, which will discover actual truth, leave aside, namely people's religious needs. Indian religions, which have long proclaimed such notions, connected with Western science form a remarkable syncretism on a psychological basis – proceeding from humanity and denying the real and concrete existence of a God who cares about people, although some speak of the Numinous or even of God in order to build a better world based on human rights, with recognition that religion is indispensable to human happiness – such is this liberal religiosity.

In the United Nations building in New York there is an empty room for meditation or prayer, for people of all religious persuasions. Naturally it is empty, for it serves the smallest common denominator, as it were, of all religions, and that is not much, hardly more than religiosity and a feeling of dependence. Feelings and myths play their role in life. Let us, so the liberals say, therefore not argue about theological problems, about doctrines or confessions of faith, for it is meaningless to speak about things that are purely subjective. Let us rather discern and recognize the great treasures of wisdom that have been bequeathed to us by the various religions and ecclesiastical denominations, for each of them has grasped only a small facet of the real, in essence mythical, truth.

Such is the new world religion that is now taking shape. Jung is its prophet, Eastern teachings point the way, Asians are often the preachers (Yogi Yogananda, for example) and to the extent that Christianity is involved, we must look to the liberals – who genuflect to the venerable old traditions but are by no means prepared to go to the stake for them (the age of religious wars is long past, a sort of barbarism that has now been superseded) – and to those who claim that the most important doctrines, about creation and redemption, belong to the *Urgeschichte*, the 'primal history', which means a sort of supra-temporal reality that only in a religious sense has anything to do with the world in its physical and temporal existence.

This religious humanism, warm and humane, respectful of science and taking a psychological view of human being and a subjective view of truth, is growing and spreading its wings everywhere.

This new religion will be the enemy of all who do not subscribe to its quest for unity, of all dogmatists and of all who think they know better, of all who affirm in opposition to science and subjectivism that Christ truly rose again – that is certainly a deep thought, some say, but not really an event that one could have witnessed at a particular moment in history, true in a historical and physical sense.

Let us therefore hold fast to what the Lord has taught us and not be carried along the road of such Bible criticism in this science-worshipping liberal direction. Let us pray to God that he will give us the insight to 'test the spirits, whether they be of God'.

Only a firm faith will enable us to stand against this rising world religion. Only a truly established Christian lifestyle, the fruit of faith, will enable us to counter the poisononous effects of the preaching of this human wisdom. For art and entertainment are the revelation and the catechization of this religion: we are bombarded, practically every hour of the day, by all modern means of communication – usually called cultural forming, it is in fact often nothing more than very effective brainwashing.

But enough of that! There is every reason to be on our guard, that is what I wanted to say. There is also every reason to pray that the Lord may give us the wisdom, the strength and the faith to overcome the crisis in our own Christian world.

In the meantime, I cannot give you a solution for our difficulties because there is no solution for the opposition between evil and good, between death and life. The opposition is not just a problem, it is a concrete reality.

Happily, we know the living God, the Saviour seated at his right hand, and the Holy Spirit who never leaves us. Believe in the Lord! And then you have the promise of the return of the Son. Well then, may an awareness of our situation as the poor of spirit lead us to pray even more urgently:

Come, Lord Jesus, yes come quickly!

Part II

THE CREATIVE GIFT

Introduction to the First Edition: The Centre of History[49]

We live in a wonderful world – a world that discloses itself to us through our senses, but is at the same time far more than what our senses alone can reveal. We see something moving, we recognize certain shapes and we know that a human being is standing before us. Yet the merest glance tells us far more. By his or her clothing, actions or expression we can tell what sort of person this is. So when we talk about 'seeing', we mean much more than visual perception. We can 'see' love or hatred, the beauty of a landscape or the nobility of a sacrificial act. We can know someone has great faith, even though we cannot perceive it with our eyes. Although these things do not, scientifically speaking, belong to the senses, they are part of our daily experience; reality comprises much more than our senses alone can apprehend.

Even if we use all our human faculties, and add to the senses our experience and our knowledge, these can show us only a small part of the things that exist, for reality goes deeper than our familiar world. Many things in the world we see point to this other world. As the psalmist said when speaking of the forces of nature: 'There is no speech or language where their voice is not heard. Their voice goes out into all the earth, their words to the ends of the world' (Psalm 19:3, 4). Within this world is evidence of the other side (Romans 1:20), including the realms of heaven where God dwells and his angels and a whole order of reality. Yet God is not confined to the other side, for he is also the Creator and Lawgiver of the world as we know it, including everything we call secular and even our own selves.

This same God has revealed himself to us, telling us who he is and what he expects of us. Through the men who wrote the Bible God has given us a glimpse of what is behind our empirical reality. He has provided us with insight into our world, its principles and structures. Because of this revelation, we have knowledge beyond the mere reach of our human faculties, but also more than we should have had even if humankind had never fallen into sin. We know, for example, that the world is not a closed system but open; that it does not exist on its own; and that its centre is not on the humanly visible side of reality.

God gave such a glimpse as part of his revelation to St John. Revelation 4 is John's account of what he saw, difficult as it must have been to express in the language of this world and in relation to limited human experience. It is a vision of God, the Almighty One, sitting on his throne and surrounded by his heavenly servants. The vision ends with a song of praise to God, who created all things out of his own will.

Here, and nowhere else, is the real key to understanding our world, the heart of the matter, the crux of the good news told to all people: there is meaning because God exists, and he created all things.

Just as the book of Revelation provides us with insight into the heart of all creation, it also gives us a key to understanding the flow of human history. History is not just events, mere historical cause and effect. It is not a long list of dates in a textbook. Ultimately, history is the work of Christ, the Lord of history, and it unfolds itself because he acts within and into it.

A reading of Revelation 5 discloses this. We see Christ and the power of the Holy Spirit. Christ, the promised Messiah, is the Lamb 'looking as if it had been slain'. He is the Lord who died on the cross and rose from the grave. He is with God and receives the scroll, the book of Life. He takes the book and opens it, removing the seals one by one, and gradually unveils human history.

All this is described in language that is difficult for people of the twentieth century to understand. John's language is symbolic, images taken from natural reality in order to describe a level of reality beyond the reach of human sight or understanding. What John writes about is not just thoughts or fantasies.

Revelation seems indeed an obscure book, but it is less so for those who know the prophetic books of the Old Testament and are familiar with Jesus' prophecies of events to come. In this sense Revelation is not a new book, for it adds nothing to the Bible that has not been mentioned elsewhere. Rather, it is a reminder that many of the things described by the prophets are still to happen, even though many prophecies have been fulfilled in the life, death and resurrection of Christ. Revelation can be seen as a great collection of Old Testament quotations, using the same language and images. It shows everything in its proper perspective: history unfolding itself from the day Christ rose from the dead to later ascend into heaven, on to the present, and then on again to the Last Judgment.

History is not a 'nice story'. Jesus himself spoke of wars, famines and earthquakes to come. In Revelation we are told that he is to come in the midst of all these things, events that even in the heavenly realms are described as 'woes' (Revelation 8:13). Christ is purifying the world, preparing it for the day when all things, even death, will be subjected to God's dominion (1 Corinthians 15:24 ff.) and the new earth will come into being.

We stand in awe as we realize that all these great things – including the death and resurrection of God the Son – will have been necessary in order to bring about final victory over darkness and evil and the complete restoration of justice.

As awesome as this all sounds, it does not take place without the involvement of people and their actions, whether great or small. The unseen world is inextricably intertwined with the natural world, and each has a significant effect on the other. Often we brush aside as unimportant the little sorrows and pains of life, as well as its good and positive moments. But the Bible assures us that they all have meaning.

Introduction to the First Edition: The Centre of History

In this book we shall consider our actions, our history, our culture, our creativity – the little deeds of little men and women, all incomplete and imperfect (Romans 8:20). Yet they are crucial and have their place in God's great scheme. We can sit down and think about our work, our calling, and know that it is real and full of significance. Our actions have far wider results than we could ever have imagined. We are called upon to play a role in an immense drama, in the great tribulations of our era as well as in the little adventures and battles, whether spiritual or material. This is no game, but reality itself.

Part One:

Being a Christian in a Broken World

1
Our Calling in God's Creation

God's hand in history

There is indeed more to history than meets the eye. While it may be easy to go along with this proposition, it is frequently difficult to discern the 'more'. Pious believers often devaluate history by regarding it simply as the story of how God saves sinful men and women; others view history as a random sequence of events – human greed leading to violence and warfare. But the final truth about history goes deeper.

The Bible – especially the book of Revelation – offers a perspective on the whole of history. It shows God at work in creation and then in judgment, the warfare against him waged by the powers of evil under their prince, God's work of redemption and deliverance, and the assurance of a final victory in which his children will share.

Although there is this meaning to be discerned behind events, there is in the biblical view no ultimate duality, nothing Hegelian. History is one; within the 'little' things that happen God's great purposes are being fulfilled until finally his Kingdom will appear, unchallenged, untarnished. (1 Corinthians 15:24–28 briefly tells the story.)

Within the theatre of history, people are neither puppets nor passive spectators. Even if both the decisive victory and the final triumph must be acts of God, since weakness and sin disqualify human beings from such an achievement, nevertheless God, after his work of deliverance in the coming, death and resurrection of his Son, calls people to action. God invites them to help prepare a new world in which all things will be unified in Christ (Ephesians 1:10).

Few people today take seriously an event at the beginning of history which has affected everything since – the Fall. Human beings, tempted to be like God, to be their own master, broke God's one basic commandment and set in motion a series of momentous events. Death came into the world. The creation, now cursed by God, became subject to futility (Romans 8:20). How little Christians have studied the implications of this curse.

Although we quite rightly study the meaning of God's grace, we often fail to deal with issues like Ecclesiastes' description of the vanity of human activity. Yet despite all frustration, futility and suffering, our daily life still has meaning and is waiting to be set free from the bondage of decay (Romans 8:21).

Adam and Eve must have had an extremely limited understanding of the great things God prophesied in that ominous moment just after the Fall. Even today sin and death distort our understanding of reality; as

Paul says, we now see things in a 'poor reflection' (1 Corinthians 13:12). Nevertheless, our hope is that one day we will come to full understanding.

All humankind await salvation from the curse, from the power of evil, from the futility of human work; we look forward to the fulfilment of the promise that all creation will one day be cleansed and liberated. Meanwhile people are called to work. God's world is still there, and it is still our responsibility to till and keep it (Genesis 2:15). We are also to create, within the framework of our humanity.[50] It is for human beings to activate and realize, to discover and give form to the world's inherent potential.

This is all possible because, in spite of the curse, God also gave hope. The 'seed of the woman' was to conquer the serpent, Satan. As history progressed, God made it clear both through his prophets and the work and teaching of Jesus that it was Christ who was to be this 'seed'; and although the serpent was to bruise his heel, the woman's seed would attain the victory.

Ever since God said that liberation would come through the seed of the woman, humankind have been looking to their offspring, the next generation, to overcome the results of the curse. Eve looked at Cain in this way: would he be the redeemer? Cain proved instead to be a murderer. Yet even Cain was not simply put aside, nor were his offspring deprived of their humanity. The cultural mandate, that all humankind were to develop and utilize this world, remained in force. God cancelled neither his plans, nor his creation; he continues his great work of restoration. And although this must now be achieved the hard way, through suffering, pain and death, there is also the resurrection of Christ, making possible the resurrection of all who in him have become new men and women (Romans 6:8–11).

Thus the cultural task of humankind remains, but in history there have always been two ways of fulfilling this task, represented on the one hand by the line of Cain and Lamech, and on the other by the line of Seth and Enoch.

Human work in history

Cain and Lamech – self-sufficient human being

Cain and Lamech are the forebears of all those throughout history who do things their own way, without reverence for the God who made them. We read of them in Genesis 4:17 ff. In the activities of these men and their descendants we soon find a development: people discover possibilities and give them a specific form. This opening up of culture is the making of history. We read of the invention of shelter against sun and rain, of the beginning of animal husbandry, the beginning of music and the use of tools. People start to make themselves comfortable.

Lamech immediately begins to misuse these tools. He brags about his weapons. God had given Cain protection; but Lamech boasts that he can do even better and uses his strength to take more than one woman. Already at the beginning of history we have sex and violence, in the line of Cain and Lamech, just as we find them today, described in the newspapers with their stories of crime and prostitution, or in books, theatre, movies and art – except that our 'enlightened' age does these things even more powerfully than Lamech.

'Man himself; man through himself!' sings Lamech. His power and cunning will win. And because in his day sex also meant children, man would become strong and powerful through his children. Deliverance and freedom would come through man's seed. Such freedom, however, is the freedom of the strong and means the enslavement of the weak – the weaker sex, those weaker in battle or the economically and socially weak. Humankind thus begin to look for freedom, dreaming of a new world and a salvation made by themselves, to be achieved by the strong.

People even begin to long for the unity of all humankind. After the Fall this unity had immediately been broken; there was the family of Adam and the family of Cain. Later the breach between people became even greater with the episode of the Tower of Babel which was, ironically, a desperate bid for unity. Thereafter unity could be achieved only through power. The great empires of Babylon, Persia and Rome do indeed show a certain unity – a unity often brought about through the suppression and enslavement of many surrounding peoples. But these empires never achieve a true unity, for humankind are shattered. In spite of attractive principles and theories, unity rarely means more than that connections and relations can be established, however temporary or insubstantial.

Faith in progress. As people strive for a better world, they choose their own gods. These gods are meant to make them great. A glance at any history book will show that one of the great driving forces behind human behaviour is faith in the god of progress. People believe that through their offspring progress will be achieved. They try to change others, either through ideas or through force, hoping for the emergence of a better world. They try to change human systems, only to find that this also is not the solution. Still, in desperation, they go on. Wars and revolutions, violence and suppression are the fruits of the human faith in progress. All too frequently sincere idealists are superseded by power seekers who misuse even the best things to reach their own goals.

Meanwhile, in their quest for progress, people develop techniques and crafts, create cities and works of art, think deeply about life, write books, sing songs and organize their world into all kinds of systems. More and more they have learned to utilize the wealth of materials and the potential present in nature.

In themselves these things are not to be despised. The Bible never belittles beauty or refinement. It praises the beauty of the cities that are destroyed: Babylon, Nineveh, Tyre and Sidon. Listen to the description in Ezekiel 27 and 28 of the wealth, the skill, the abundant goods of Tyre. We are certainly not encouraged to look upon these achievements with contempt. In fact, we are told to lament because they are gone, destroyed. Their wisdom was even greater than Daniel's (28:3). They were destroyed because Tyre was 'filled with violence, and . . . sinned . . . [its] heart became proud on account of [its] beauty . . . [it] corrupted [its] wisdom because of [its] splendour. By [its] many sins and dishonest trade [it] desecrated [its] sanctuaries' (28:16–18). Also, Tyre had said, 'I am a god' (28:2).

Human achievements. Who has not seen the treasures of those days and admired the skill of their artisans, the ability of their engineers, their development of trades and the work of their sculptors and painters! The great bulls with human heads which act as watchmen at the palace gates of ancient Mesopotamia are more awe-inspiring than reassuring (imagine what it was like to go through the gates of a tyrant's palace!) but they do testify to a great culture. They achieved something worthy of respect. But precisely because such beautiful things were used to support tyranny and the lust for power, they seem the more horrible.

Throughout history many discoveries and techniques – the 'opened potentiality' – are handed down from one generation to the next. We still employ many of them today. It is sin which turns these good things into a curse, when they are used to serve the Moloch of progress.

We need not discuss our own era, with its great achievements in micro and macro physics, its superior technological developments – and yet inner decay, a growing number of dictators, endless abuse of power, perhaps even less by states than by vast international companies, which are demonic in their anonymous greed, their uncontrollable activities for which no one seems to be responsible. But the understanding that both the gods and humanity are dead is something new, and a sign that history is hastening to its end.

Our era is characterized by a spiritual wasteland, such confusion as has possibly never before existed in history. Christianity has been cast aside. Secularization is the keyword of our age, in spite of the many who are searching for another religion or myth to live by. Society itself is held to be neutral. We talk about a 'pluralistic society' in which everyone holds private views which have no further meaning or impact on public life. At least, that is what some would lead us to think.

Revolution. Never before in history has there been such a widespread belief that revolution is positive, that by violent change a new world can be brought in. Already during the French Revolution – the first in a long line – the revolutionaries felt this and introduced a new time scheme beginning with year 1 of the Revolution. The fact that this scheme was so short-lived proves that the Revolution in the end did not achieve its goals. Yet people return again and again to this false hope. Young people today are caught up more than ever in these expectations; this is their ideology. They want to change humankind by changing the structures of society – mainly the economic and social structures. For them being human is defined not in relation to the gods or to God himself but by their place within an economic and social order.

Revolutionaries cannot wait for changes to come gradually. They want immediate results, trying to achieve equality by eliminating those who stand in their way. Certainly we would agree with them that all people are equal, but we mean equality before God and before the law. Truth and beauty are also the same for everybody. Revolutionaries, however, extend these truths into a demand that power should be given to the lower classes in order to achieve equal power and wealth – equality in everything! To achieve their ideal they are even prepared to sacrifice individual freedom. Too often in reality this has meant that everyone was equally suppressed by a tyrant or dictator.

Revolutions are unhappy periods, times of uncertainty and lawlessness in which more is destroyed than built up. In a way, they are a sickness of humanity. Sometimes they are caused by the wrongdoings of the ruling classes, by an unacceptable gap between the wealthy and the poor and the suppression of those who are economically and socially weaker. During revolutionary periods, everyone looks forward to the time when all will be settled and life will return to 'normal'. Sometimes – even often perhaps – something is achieved in a revolution. We must not think, however, as the present generation does, that this is the direct fruit of revolution; at best, the revolution paved the way so that these new gains could be realized. A certain development had come so far, until greed or conservatism or lack of concern blocked the way. Then revolution gave it a chance.

If a person is sick, he or she may have a crisis, followed by a gradual restoration to health. The healing is not the result of the crisis itself, but of the body's driving out the poisons that have been afflicting it. After the French Revolution, for example, more power went to the middle classes, and in general freedom was increased and oppression reduced. No one would deny that these things were positive. But because the Revolution was also a time of terror, and later of dictatorship, these beneficial changes were almost halted. Such things happen because revolutionary people have no patience to bear burdens or to wait for God to act. They want immediate results.

Besides the crises of revolution, there are also what I would call the fevers of growth. While they may include some marks of revolution, they are essentially times of heightened creativity. One example is the birth of the Dutch nation, which freed Protestantism and liberated the nation from the very conservative force of Spain. Or consider the birth of the United States of America: growth and development had come to the point that the American colonies were now to be accepted as equal to the motherland, not colonies anymore. But the Old World did not understand, and the result was the War of Independence.

Seth and Enoch – salt in a decaying world

Growth. In the line of Seth and Enoch, as in that of Cain and Lamech, we also find development and change. But here is no dream of bringing about a new world through revolution or human endeavour. The children of God are called, along with the rest of humanity, to work towards the unfolding and realization of this world's potential. But they are given the added understanding that in the time between the Fall and the return of Christ, nothing good can be achieved without at the same time taking into account sin and its results. We can accomplish nothing without a continual battle against evil. Christians are called to be the salt of the earth, to preserve and add flavour to what is good, and to bring a measure of healing where people are sick and broken.

Alas, the church has too often ignored the suffering and oppression of the poor, and neglected its calling to help the needy and sick. We are to work concretely for peace and freedom. The message of the prophets has always been: Repent! Turn back to the Lord, and show that you love him. Do not just offer sacrifice and praise, but *do* the truth (John 3:21). What does the Lord require of us but to 'act justly and to love mercy and to walk humbly with [our] God' (Micah 6:8).

Here one finds a basis for unity – the communion of saints. Here the redemption of the world begins. Although even here sin abounds and no Christian can say that Christianity as such will bring in the new world, still, much good has been achieved. Many of the world's wounds have been healed through the sacrificial lives of thousands of saints – saints in the sense used by Paul and others, saints because their sins were forgiven by the Lord and because they achieved something through the renewing power of Christ's work.

In the line of Seth and Enoch the Lord has sent great men to show the way: Moses, Elijah, David, Daniel, the apostles, Augustine, Luther, Calvin, and many more. There have also been great scientists and artists. And although even the best works of all these men are tinged with sin, our Western culture owes them a great debt – the West which is presently in a state of decay because people have fallen away from God, but where we still find laws requiring monogamy, and laws which presuppose charity and trustworthiness.

Science too was a fruit of Christianity, which saw nature as separate from the God who had created it and therefore open to exploration. And in the seventeenth century, when there was a Christian consensus, art in northern Europe reached a peak that has never been surpassed.

The art of that century has a richness and technical brilliance yet to be fully investigated, even though our museums are full of 'old masters' and many books have already been devoted to them. People may be critical of all these achievements, but they usually use as their measuring rod Christian ethics and Christian standards, thus paradoxically demonstrating the depth of Christian influence.

As we have seen, the line of Seth and Enoch does look for development and renewal; but unlike the other line of humanity, it realizes that these things must come through a gradual *growth*.

Although the line of Cain and the line of Seth work so differently, both are working within the same framework of God's creation, towards the goal of realizing its potential and thus making it a good home for humankind, ultimately overcoming evil and the curse. Both lines form part of the same humanity with the same basic calling.

Renewal. Ultimately, complete redemption from evil will come with the judgment of God, when the seals of the book of Life are opened, letting loose all the woes described in Revelation. Meanwhile, the work of developing and maintaining the world is often done mainly by the people of the line of Cain and Lamech. That does not mean that the line of Seth and Enoch is to withdraw from participation in the world, as will be clear further on. But the special task of the line of Seth and Enoch is to be 'salting salt' (Matthew 5:13, my rendering). Salt is used to preserve, or at least to postpone decay and corruption. Christians are called to show by their words and their lives that God exists and that Christ is his Son. Saltless Christianity will be thrown aside. Judgment begins with the church (1 Peter 4:17), and anyone who becomes a Christian just to have a kind of supreme insurance policy is badly mistaken! Not those who say 'Lord, Lord' will inherit the kingdom of heaven, but those who actively love God and their neighbours (Matthew 25:31 ff.).

Christ did not die simply to make people Christians. That is not enough; his work is too great. He died so that we might be human, living and acting in a human way, as God originally made us to live, in love and freedom. Christ is not just the Redeemer of the Christians, nor the guru for those who follow his cult, nor the Lord of 'our faith' – we should not have faith in faith – but he came to redeem and restore the whole creation, and to be its supreme Judge.

The decay we see around us can be halted only when with God's help and a life of prayer we appropriate the power of Christ's resurrection to live as renewed human beings (Romans 6). God's call to 'seek righteousness, seek humility' (Zephaniah 2:3) is certainly not a matter of conquering the world for God but rather of beginning, ourselves, to walk in obedience.

Real fruit in the Christian's life can only be achieved as we are sanctified through Christ's work. Redemption does not merely mean a 'spiritual' blessing, something which happens to our soul so that we feel the Lord close to us. Of course, the Lord *can* be near his people, answering their prayers, and can be present with them in a special way when they are persecuted (Luke 21:12 ff.). He forgives their sins and leads them in his way by the Holy Spirit. But these graces are not to be an end in themselves. They encourage those who are working in his kingdom, helping them to go on doing the things he told them to do in this world. Freedom in the midst of this world's troubles, and miracles of God's intervention can have meaning only within the context of sacrificial obedience to him, doing as well as hearing the word (James 1:22).

Humility is the keyword. Power, riches, greatness are not ends in the Christian's life, nor even means. Christ is our example: born in a manger, surrounded by lowly people and growing up in a place remote from the cultural centres of his time. His life and work were of the same quality, sacrifice and service – washing others' feet! His end was death on the cross. What appeared to be weakness was his triumph! We must never confuse humility with softness and passivity, for no weakling could have denounced the Pharisees or opposed hypocrisy, corruption and dishonesty as Jesus did.

Christ's death was not a theological proposition or a statement of creed. It was and is reality, the centre of history, for in Christ God redeemed the world, conquering sin and death. Christ's death is the fulfilment of all history, and the realization of all potential, all promises.

Our common humanity

Looking back over so many thousands of years, we must acknowledge that something has been achieved. Hygiene, comfort, freedom, wealth and justice have been attained by people, although these things are so precarious and even scarce that they have to be continuously defended.

Human accomplishments are important, even if they are not absolute, and they certainly form part of God's plan for a great future. The task to subdue the earth and have dominion over all creatures (Genesis 1:28; 9:1, 2) has been carried out, if only partially, and in spite of sin, pain, sorrow and tears.

The question, however, is often asked: how is it possible for an unbeliever, a non-Christian, to do works that are both good in themselves (even though done by a sinful person) and at the same time acceptable to a Christian, who is a child of God? An answer is often given in terms of 'common grace', suggesting that God gives a special kind of grace, grace in a general sense, so good things are possible. This common grace is sharply distinguished from particular grace, through which the Christian gains salvation, the forgiveness of sin and the power to do good.

I feel that this is a wrong question, leading to a wrong answer. Non-believers are not devils, devoid of the possibility of doing any good, even if they are sinful people. They are above all human beings who may or may not see that they need salvation. They certainly wish for a good and fine world, even though they may have only a distorted idea of what that means.

Since non-believers do not accept God as their Saviour, and since they want to make a better world in their own strength and wisdom, they may cling to strange beliefs or an unfounded optimism. But they are not master of God's creation. Their insights do not constitute reality, although they colour their achievements and their attempts to make a better world. Reality remains as it is. If people want to achieve something lasting they must capitulate to reality and its God-given structures, and this may cause them either pain or joy. We cannot call it grace, unless we call it grace that God has not yet removed every unbeliever from this world as not belonging here. This will happen only at the end of history, when the rebels will experience a second death and be denied a place in the new earth.

Non-Christians are still human, in the full sense of the word. Even if sinful, they can work in this world and create things of value and intrinsic quality. (And, just as with Christians, sin will mar all they do.) If they are philosophers and want people to hear them they must say something sensible since no one cares to listen to nonsense (this is part of the capitulation to reality). If they are artists their art must be beautiful or they will run into problems and their art will become a strange phenomenon remote from reality – something almost unknown in history apart from modern art. Politicians too must at least try to deal with actual problems and work for a just economic situation, otherwise they will be tyrants who constantly live in fear of revolt. Likewise, traders must carry on their business with some honesty and some positive rules or they soon will have lost all their customers!

There is a deep difference between Christians and non-Christians, but we must not look for it in the wrong place. The difference lies ultimately in a person's basic attitude, hope and understanding of his or her task. But when it comes to any specific activity, the Christian may be foolish and sinful and the unbeliever wise and right. Essentially, the Christian and the non-Christian are travelling down totally different roads, but as human beings living in the same created world and in the same history, their differences may be less black-and-white. That means we can truly communicate with each other.

Summary – no shortcuts
The road to complete fulfilment of the goals of creation is a long one. God chose the road of growth and progress – giving people creativity and the freedom to be his co-workers. Having made people in his own image he has called them to participate in a process which leads them to eternal life. It is a way of obedience, marked by love, freedom, truth, justice and beauty.

The Devil has always preferred shortcuts: you can have it now; be like God; just eat the fruit. We all know what happened. The Devil presented Christ with the same temptation in the desert (Luke 4): bow down before me and you will be Lord over this earth. But Jesus knew that God's way to Lordship led through suffering – a longer but more certain road.

When man and woman ate from the tree of Knowledge they did get to know good and evil. God did not change his plans because of this, but now the road has become cursed, a way of suffering, pain and death (Genesis 3:15,23). There is also now the enmity between the seed of the woman and the seed of the serpent, the clash between good and evil. History has become a long story of violence and war, injustice and revolutions, but also of idealism and good deeds. Inseparably entangled in a complex knot, the seed of the woman and the seed of the serpent together make history. Those who, with Cain's offspring, try to take the shortcut of revolution, to have it all now, inflict deep wounds which make the world ugly and end in new sorrows. People cannot be their own redeemer, and if they reject God's reign they may find themselves bowed under a rod of iron. God will bring the redemption that people themselves can never achieve. Meanwhile, we are to go on with our human task, accepting suffering and the less-than-perfect. In this way, although we may not understand it, we will be working towards the fulfilment of God's purposes.

Freedom and authority

Unless people are prepared to accept chaos they must achieve some agreement about objectives, a certain unity. We call this a consensus: moral aims and laws to strive for which constitute a social and political basis for society. The weaker these become, as we see happening today, the less freedom there is and the greater the threat of chaos. Witness, for example, the rising crime rate in our big cities, and the resulting need for caution which hinders our freedom to go where we like.

Because it is a dream to think all people are good and working towards identical objectives, God in his wisdom has given us the state to punish the criminal, to preserve public security and to uphold justice in relationships between people. The world needs some power that possesses authority, as Paul makes clear (Romans 13:1 ff.).

Authority re-evaluated: the position of women
Immediately after the Fall, God instituted authority. He placed the man over the woman and told her that she was to look to him as the master. The man was to protect the woman and work to provide for her. The man became ruler over the woman, over his offspring, over nature. The woman was to help the man and be the mother of his children. The Fall

thus necessitated some loss of freedom, just as it brought suffering into the world.

These words in Genesis, however, were not a command or a law; they merely stated a fact that was henceforth to colour the reality of man and woman. The Christian should try to soften this reality and make the burden lighter; no man has the right to be a hard taskmaster, and women were not intended to be a kind of cattle. Men, however, being the more powerful, often behaved as the Marquis de Sade was later to preach, using their superior physical strength to gratify all their personal whims.

The biblical position is very different. In its history of the position of women, we have an excellent example of the meaning of growth, as opposed to revolution. As early as the laws of Moses we find many rules governing the position of women, laws in which there is no revolution, no immediate break with the past or present practices of society. But inherent in all these God-given laws is a growing tendency towards monogamous marriage and a better position for women.

These things cannot, however, be enforced in a day, with one stroke. Real change takes time, for it involves not only outward obedience to a law, but a change of mentality and attitude. Without an altered mentality, sinful people will only find ways to circumvent the laws and make the situation even worse.

After the law of Moses, the New Testament brought more changes along the road to more freedom for women. Today in the Western world monogamy is the law. In many Muslim countries and elsewhere, where people follow the ways of the West, women have been gaining more freedom, even if the end has not yet been reached.

However, when women try to force the pace of emancipation in a revolutionary manner, it often makes things worse. The women's liberation movement has turned the gains of the past, in which women were gradually gaining more equality, into a battle of the sexes. Instead of the closeness and unity between men and women, involving a recognition of the wonderful diversity each has received by creation, we have hatred. Women begin to act in an ugly way and are no longer themselves because of imitating men.

Today, as Christianity is slowly pushed aside, we see a gradual loss of those values which began to be realized in the laws of Moses. The position of women is threatened; free love and permissiveness abound, and easier divorce laws are leading to greater breakdown of marriages. It is women who will suffer most from all this.

I am not of course suggesting a return to the laws of Moses; that would be retreating to a bygone position. We must see those laws as pointers, to prevent an even further retreat! Ours is the long way, the way of patience and perhaps of suffering, as we defend what has been realized. But this gradual process has had great results. Even today, despite all attempts to undo the process, we find that these ideas and principles are deeply engrained in people's minds and deteriorate only very slowly. Monogamy is still the rule. Women are still safeguarded from the evil of men.

Authority's rightful place

As we have seen in the position of women, when the Bible teaches us to accept authority it never means that the bearers of it can do as they like. Their authority is always related to God's commands. A person in authority must not say, 'Do what I say,' but rather, 'This is the norm or rule, and I am bound to it as well.'

The world still needs authority and protection. Injustice and chaos can result from too much equality. The family, for instance, is important and so is the rule of obedience to parents! That the new psychologically-oriented teaching methods say otherwise is one reason why we currently have a crisis of authority in the world. On the other hand, we must be very careful that our view of authority does not degenerate to the relationship between a ruler and his slaves.

We live, then, in a revolutionary era. There is socialist egalitarianism which would turn people's rightful equality before God and the law into a demand for equality in all respects – even going so far as to bypass the great differences between men and women. There is women's lib. There is the call for a new democracy, which is often anarchy, recognizing no authority whatsoever. And there is also Marxism with its utopian idea of making a better world through revolution, but it has brought tyranny, glossed over with the promise of a better world later, 'for your children'!

The easy-chair mentality

During the Enlightenment a new quest, a new mentality, started to become part of human thinking. We may call it the 'easy-chair mentality'. I hit upon this expression when I noticed that before the eighteenth century, easy-chairs were never made, not even for the very rich. The easy-chair is not a feat of modern technology; people could have made it in the distant past, but nobody did. The easy-chair is the result of a new mentality that demands all ease, all comfort now. Maybe in the past people accepted discomfort too easily. Perhaps in an almost fatalistic way they did not try to overcome the cold, the lack of water, the poor accommodation and the slow means of travel. We certainly cannot object to the quest for more comfort, running hot and cold water, a good heating system, and improved roads and transport; we surely would not put up with the services offered in the ages before the Enlightenment. As human beings we are participants in the development of these new conveniences, and as Christians we have no reason to say no to them.

But we should say no to the *mentality* that is involved; it sometimes drives people on too far, into absurdity. The developments themselves may be legitimate, but sometimes they cost too much. We must establish priorities; to insist on the good things here and now, while others suffer poverty and live far below our level of comfort, makes us unjust, overdemanding, and even cruel.

This is the mentality which says everything that can be done *should* be done. If we can build planes that go slightly faster (even if they cause more pollution and more noise), then we ought to have them – even if no one really needs them! We say, 'It's absolutely essential,' which often means, 'We want to have it, and we won't wait, even if social evils are the result.' Or we insist that we must remain competitive in the world market. But may not competition itself sometimes be evil?

As long ago as 1831, Carlyle accurately described this mentality in *Sartor Resartus*:

> Man's Unhappiness as I construe, comes of his Greatness; it is because there is an Infinite in him, which with all his cunning he cannot quite bury under the Finite. Will the whole Finance Ministers and Upholsterers and Confectioners of modern Europe undertake, in joint-stock company, to make one Shoeblack happy? They cannot accomplish it, above an hour or two; for the Shoeblack also has a Soul quite other than his Stomach, and would require, if you consider it, for his permanent satisfaction and saturation, simply this allotment, no more, and no less: *God's Infinite Universe altogether to himself*, therein to enjoy infinitely, and fill every wish as fast as it rose.[51]

I think Carlyle is right. But that means that the shoeblack is doing the same foolish thing as people did at the Fall, wanting to be like God, wanting in fact to be a god themselves – in order to get their wishes fulfilled.

Ours is the age of the instantaneous. The advertisements cry, 'Take this pill for instant relief!' The generation of the sixties was sometimes called the 'now generation'. When they bumped up against a wall of reality which did not obey their whims they fell back into apathy, despairing because their desires could not be met immediately. They had no patience, certainly not the patience of waiting for the Lord.

Christians too have been infected with this mentality. We have all the comforts, life is easy, and every wish can be fulfilled – if we belong to the happy rich. Our economy has done so much to make everyone wealthy, more wealthy even than the kings of old, whose palaces could not compete with our bungalows in comfort. We have all this. But not everything is in our hands. Some things are beyond our control: good health, a happy marriage, and a sense of achievement. So we call on the Lord and ask him to provide them for us, as if he were a magician on a string – our string! How often people have asked me what is meant by 'answer to prayer'. In probing the questioners, I have found that they are often looking for the immediate fulfilment of wishes beyond their power. I have also often been asked what the 'fear of the LORD' means. There may indeed be a lack of clarity in communication here, as the word 'fear' in this sense has become obsolete. But the question also shows that people today have lost the understanding of a great God Almighty who commands our awe and wonder. We find it difficult to bow deeply before the Supreme God and say, 'Thy will be done.' Too often we have made Christianity into a happiness system, guaranteeing success the easy way, with God there in his power to fill in the gaps.

Science

Modern science also has been affected by this mentality. In its early phase, science developed because people wanted to understand the world in which they lived, and to use this knowledge for practical purposes. In the words of Susanne K. Langer: 'Practical gain, dominion over nature, were [Science's] early motives; its motives were intellectual, they lay in the restless desire of an ever imaginative mind to exploit the possibilities of the factual world as a field for constructive thought.'

This attitude changed with the new secularized mentality of the eighteenth century. Now science became two things. First, it was a way of knowing things, or rather the *only* way of knowing things, whether natural or human. Second, science began to try to take control of all things for the benefit of humanity. Says Langer: 'We know that knowledge is power, that it is something more than mental satisfaction, that it enables us to use the facts of life and the secrets of nature for human benefit. Knowledge makes us able to do things, and so add to the sum of human wellbeing.'

Nowadays we enter our home, turn on a switch, and billions of electrons move at the fastest possible speed to give us light. This can be the result of a legitimate desire to know facts in order to put them to use, possible only if we ourselves submit to nature and its laws. But we can go too far, and want too much, in the process becoming natural facts ourselves, caught in the laws of nature and the laws controlling society and economy.

Political-economic systems

Like science, Marxism has also fallen into the easy-chair mentality. It too looks for a way to force nature to serve humanity. And people themselves are forced to exist in subjection to a social-economic order that completely rules their behaviour and even their thinking. People want to rule nature but they have lost their status as a steward, as described in Genesis 1:28 ff. and Genesis 2:15. As a result, nature is against them, to be subdued almost as an enemy.

Socialism, the offspring of Marxism, has been much more fruitful because it accepts that this world has to change slowly if it is to change at all. It has done much good in its concern for the economically weaker. Socialism tends, however, to overstress the economic, and assumes too readily that happiness can be achieved through centralized plans, which leave too little freedom to the individual. It is too egalitarian, seeking to make all people the same, at least in the economic sense.

Even if the Marxists or socialists think that Christianity has been too slow and has accepted pain and inconvenience too easily, they must recognize that many of their ideas and ideals have their roots in Christianity. In a way, these are Christian heresies, claiming that the benefits they seek can be achieved by human endeavour, without God. Often they are anti-God, and certainly antichristian.

In the Western world capitalism also continues to be very strong. With its *laissez-faire, laissez-aller* principles, its belief in free enterprise and the positive aspects of competition, it too assigns too great a priority to the economic side of life. In fact, it has called into being the bourgeois way of life. Capitalism in itself is certainly not Christian and has caused many of the injustices we see today. It too has been coloured by the easy-chair mentality.

Our Western pluralistic society assumes religion to be irrelevant to our public life, to political, social and economic reality. While this view of religion as a field in which the individual must decide for him or herself offers Christians valuable freedom, we must not fall into the trap of leaving this world to be run by the principles of Cain, while we carry on our private lives as the line of Seth. Not only does such behaviour imply a restricted view of God; it will not work. We cannot continue to enjoy the fruits of a long process in which Christianity has played a decisive role if the foundation of our world order, including morality, becomes divorced from obedience to God. We simply cannot live our daily lives in a closed world order, totally naturalistic and without God, and then on Sunday proclaim that the world is open and that God and his kingdom are true realities; such a position is schizophrenic. We are one, and the world is one.

The Christian's task

Preservation of the world

Christians must accept the good things that have been done by the line of Cain and Lamech. Humanity has been given a great responsibility, in the interests of a great future. We must beware of taking judgment on these matters into our own hands (Romans 12:19; 1 Corinthians 5:13). The Christian's task is not to change the world – wonderful as this would be if it led to better morals, better justice, better management of the world's resources – but primarily to keep the world from decay and corruption, evil and suppression.

Christians live in tension. On the one hand, knowing that people are sinful, they do not expect a utopia. They accept the world as it is after the Fall, knowing that it is unnatural, subject to pain and death and crying out for removal of the curse. They know that only Christ can bring renewal. On the other hand, Christians can never merely accept this malfunctioning, this pain and suffering. They may never abandon their duty, but are called to follow Christ's example, to relieve or fight the effects of evil. In this sense Christians are protesters, but theirs is a protest in love. It takes wisdom and love to know when to accept the less than perfect and when to press on for something better.

Christians cannot be revolutionaries. The Bible teaches us to be patient and not to take up the sword. While there may be some exceptions, they must be very strong in order to justify violence.[52] Christians are not even to assassinate tyrants; think of David, who in spite of a unique opportunity, refused to kill Saul (1 Samuel 24). Both the Bible and experience teach that violence only breeds more violence. Christians should be peacemakers, though never of a 'peace at all costs', which leads to evil and oppression.

If Christians want to draw others to accept Christ, they must demonstrate what it means to be a child of God. A child of God is not someone who is always happy and content and without psychological problems, someone who refrains from looking at bad things and lets the world go its own way because it appears to be rotten anyway, someone who defends the establishment as such, just for the sake of peace (Jeremiah 6:13–15).

Far from retreating into a kind of Christian subculture, leaving the world to its evil, Christians not only can but *must* take part in the world's activity. This could even be called pre-evangelism; it is indeed the only way that evangelism itself can ever be really fruitful. It means doing our work with honesty and care, excelling where possible, never cheating, never letting the ends justify the means, being always responsible and reliable.

Above all, our involvement in the world means perseverance. If we want to work towards a change in the right direction we must realize that it cannot be done by one person, nor in a few years. It is an endless task for all Christians in all ages. Only in this way can God use us. Our work will not be in vain, even when we have no hope of seeing results in the near future and must wait to see fulfilment later, perhaps only on the new earth.

Christians should be better than other men and women, not to call attention to themselves but because they have such a great God. Their sanctification must be evident in the fruits of the Spirit. Not that Christian men and women are to work for success and prestige, the world's criteria of greatness. Often they will be second-rate in the eyes of the world, just because being 'salting salt' takes so much energy!

2
Our Calling in Culture

Christianity and culture – a false dichotomy

There is no shortage of books on Christianity and culture. Unfortunately, reading them often tends to leave one with a sense of dissatisfaction, as if the most important aspect of the subject had not even been touched upon. In spite of every effort to show their interrelatedness, Christianity and culture have remained alien to each other. Is it perhaps the very plan of most of these books, articles or lectures that is to blame? First comes a beautiful, clear definition of Christianity, then a definition of culture. Finally there is an attempt to confront the two, to unify them or set them over against each other. The titles of the books highlight the problem, taking as they do the form, 'Christianity and . . . (be it Science, Economics or . . . Art)'.

Have we been making a mistake? Can an abstraction like 'Christianity' really have any meaning? Might it not be better just to consider Christians, weak and strong, profound and superficial, who are thinking and working? Culture also can be understood in these terms, rather than by means of an abstract definition. Our attempts to relate Christianity and culture sometimes fail precisely because we have mistakenly thought of them as separated from the beginning.

The problem of Christianity and culture has also often been approached historically, in an attempt to show how people acted in different ways at different times. This approach is useful and helps us to see what a living faith meant in the struggles of a particular period. But sometimes we become too critical when we do this, and in pointing out a period's shortcomings, as for example the asceticism of the Middle Ages, we fail to do justice to the good that was also present. This happens because standing, as we do, at a distance, we see very easily how 'they' were children of their times; yet, unaware of the difficulties they faced, we become overly conscious of their failures and of what we – from our viewpoint – see as shortcomings. On the other hand, in studying a period when God gave his blessing there is the danger that we may misapply its attainments to reinforce or defend our own personal views. There is thus the very real danger of ending up with self-imposed problems or hasty conclusions unrelated to past or present reality.

Defining 'culture'

The Christian's environment

There are two ways of discussing Christianity and culture. First we may consider the attitude that the individual Christian and the Christian community should adopt towards the surrounding non-Christian culture. This problem is met where Christians live in a world guided by consciously non- or antichristian principles, as in Russia; or one that is not consciously antichristian – such as the pagan world – where nevertheless the norms and ethics of life are different from those of Scripture. An issue that arose in such a situation was dealt with by Paul when he discussed the problem of eating meat that had been offered to pagan gods.

Wherever the gospel has been preached and taken root, it has necessarily involved the demythologizing of the pagan gods, exposing them to be no gods at all, or perhaps only impersonal forces like those of nature. Instances of such demythologizing in the Bible include the story of the god of the Philistines that fell to the ground when the ark was brought into its temple, or the words of Isaiah declaring the folly of people bowing before something which they themselves have made (Isaiah 40:19 ff.; 44:9 ff.). Christianity has liberated the world by demonstrating that all things – even the highest and strongest – are the creation of God. In this sense Genesis 1 is the greatest liberating force in all history.

However, in any culture where Christianity has been preached, exposing the old gods as false, we must expect to find a subsequent decline of faith accompanied by secularization. This is the special problem of the Christian living in a world where Christianity is the nominally accepted standard but people no longer live accordingly. God's world, his creation, remains, but people simply pass him by and ignore his life-giving words. The position of Christians in such an environment is difficult. What can they accept? Where should they draw the line? Clearly they must not take part in the sins of the culture that surrounds them. But what is the difference between those who simply live an autonomous life and those who commit outright sin, deliberately disobeying one of God's clear commands? The Christian can share neither of these lifestyles. We must realize that although Christianity has an ethic it is not in the first place an ethic. The rightness or wrongness of our way of life is to be measured against this principle: love God, and accept his Son as the Saviour.

The Christian's activities

The second way to consider the relationship between Christianity and culture is to examine what Christianity itself produces. Has a specifically Christian culture been produced? Is this something Christians should attempt?

At this point we should try to formulate a definition of the term 'culture'. Over the last few centuries a restricted use of the word has been adopted, restricting it to the arts and the world of scholarship. This narrow application grows out of the inherent dualism of our culture. On the one hand are the strong forces of science and technology, which people today do not think of as culture but simply as life and reality. On the other hand are scholarship and the *fine* arts: music, poetry, painting – interesting perhaps, but of little real consequence. (Maybe even religion belongs here.) Culture then becomes only an embellishment of life – an ornament, possibly even an enrichment, but never a necessity.

How far Christianity since the eighteenth century has reinforced this idea would be difficult to say. All too often it has looked on what is now called culture as something superfluous or even dangerous. At the same time, it has accepted modern science and technology with great naiveté as 'neutral ground'. Christians have too easily left the field of scholarship and the fine arts when they found that here the forces of unbelief were very active, forgetting that it is precisely at the front line that one has to engage the enemy. Consequently in some of these fields Christianity has relinquished almost all influence – for example, in the visual arts – and non-Christian ideas have found an almost undisputed freedom of expression. This has happened not only in the fine arts, literature and philosophy but also in 'entertainment' – films and television and the mass media in general. Thus the non-Christian mentality, world view and lifestyle have had such a powerful influence that people speak today of living in a 'post-Christian era'. Certainly the influence of Christianity has waned.

The term 'culture', however, should not be restricted to intellectual and aesthetic pursuits. Such a dualism underlies the disharmony of our modern civilization. Life should be one, and culture is simply the creation of life's forms, customs, and institutions, as well as our utilization of nature and its resources. When farmers cultivate, their methods and tools are all part of culture. When composers write songs, that is also culture. They choose sounds and express ideas, creating a form whereby people can express themselves. As the popular song of the thirties said, 'Without a song, there ain't no love at all.' Human beings are creatures who have their own place within God's creation. There are innumerable areas in which they may be occupied: language and music, but also law, liturgy and economic systems. Involvement in these is inescapable, for people are cultural beings. If they have instincts at all, those are only very weak; their life is far from being predetermined like that of the animals. People must build themselves homes, grow their own food and develop ways of cooking. Also, they need to find patterns for social intercourse. Whether they express their love for one another, demonstrate politeness or friendship or assume roles in a hierarchical order, they do all these things within the special forms and customs which are part of culture.

Adam and Eve already set the pattern long ago. Adam gave everything a name and soon after the Fall both he and Eve were making clothes. Later on, script was developed in order to write things, including our Bible.

The Christian's participation in culture

Involvement unavoidable

Christians should not disdain participation in culture. It may sound pious to say that the way we sing is not important, but to me it is almost the same as despising God. If one loves him, should one not try to sing good songs with good tunes? Moreover, to sing badly, for whatever reason, is also culture, even if only poor culture. For Christians to make a duality in their life between on the one hand their spirituality and faith and on the other the 'neutral', more or less a-Christian activity of their daily experience, is to impoverish their existence. It denies God sovereignty over a large part of one's life and creates a dichotomy that is dangerous to our spirituality.

Asceticism, which entails becoming a hermit and escaping from the 'world' and 'culture' into a cave in the desert, should itself be recognized as a pattern of culture. In the early Christian era this attitude led to the rise of the monasteries. In trying to save itself from 'the world', the church avoided all cultural activity. This may explain why it was so long before the masses of 'lay-people' became properly educated and the rough world of the Dark Ages was replaced by something more refined and beautiful. Perhaps it was precisely because of this dualism in the mentality of the Christians that the new non-ecclesiastical culture – the Renaissance – which emerged at the end of the Middle Ages was so secularized. I say perhaps, because this is a complex matter about which I hesitate to make sweeping statements. But we can never totally avoid being cultured and creative beings; it is inherent to our humanity.

Christianity, or at any rate the Christian community, when it is small or its principles greatly at variance with those of the surrounding culture, is bound to develop a kind of subculture. I do not think we should be afraid of this; it is almost unavoidable. Yet we should also not see it as an ideal, and be content just to cultivate our own little garden. The Christian community should never behave as a 'we-group' or an 'in-group'. It should not be proud of its lifestyle, its forms of worship, its ways of speaking or singing, for non-Christians may see it as odd, old-fashioned, and maybe even incomprehensible. Instead, Christians should always be open towards the world around them and maintain contact with their contemporaries. The church should never be a closed community, removed from the world; after all, the mark of the world will always be within it and may even manifest itself in the sin of pride!

New creatures in Babel

Many of the problems which arise when we discuss the relationship between Christianity and culture come from treating them as separate entities; others result from confusing two different questions. The question of the place of a Christian in a non-Christian world is a very different one from the question of the attitude of the Christian towards living creatively. In the second case, the only legitimate question is *how* can it be done? How can we creatively express our faith, our hopes and principles, our perspective on life? How does the Lord want us to work, think, create, and live?

Even in the early church there was already confusion about the two approaches to the relationship between Christianity and culture. The great question then was whether or not Christians should affirm solidarity with the surrounding culture. The Christians of those days, and particularly the more refined members of the upper classes, were raised and educated in the thought patterns of Graeco-Roman civilization. For them the question was how to regard this great culture, and particularly the philosophy which expressed its basic principles.

Two answers were formulated, in the words of Popma: '(1) a more synthetic one, which acknowledges elements of truth in Greek philosophy and wants to make use of them, and (2) an antithetic attitude which condemns philosophy and the whole of pagan culture, and which considers a training in Greek philosophy to be useless, and even dangerous for a Christian.'[53]

Those who accepted the first position found that, in one way or another, their understanding of the Bible became coloured by the philosophical insights of Plato and others. They laid themselves open to the criticism that their thoughts at some points were more like a pagan's than obedience to Scripture should allow. According to Popma, both for our understanding of Philo's theology and for our understanding of Clement's and Origen's estimation of culture, it is of the greatest importance to recognize that the syntheses of the latter, which favour cultural solidarity, are based on a purely pagan religious basic idea.

However, if we look at those who opposed this solidarity and who rejected classical culture, we see that they, perhaps even more than the others, made a synthesis with classical culture and were thus working from non-Christian principles. To quote Popma again:

> Tatian has been struck by the Word-revelation, he has come to believe in Christ ... For him, that involves an evaluation of culture characterized by extreme opposition to cultural solidarity. He must have failed to realize altogether that in this way he was actually engaged in bringing about a synthesis. As is evident from his preserved writings, Tatian remained faithful to the subtleties of rhetorical training, and, in addition, his estimation of culture clearly betrays the Cynic marks of contempt for the world.[54]

(The Cynics were a Greek philosophical school, of which Diogenes of Sinope has become the most famous figure, who held all culture, laws, customs, etc. in utter contempt.) As the attitude of these early Christian church leaders has strongly influenced Christian thought through the ages, it is not surprising to see these ascetic and anticultural tendencies persisting throughout the history of the church. They are still not dead. We must realize that this anticultural attitude is not biblical. It comes from classical pagan philosophy.

Our attitude to culture as such must not be confused by our attitude to a non- or antichristian culture. Christians must acknowledge their task as 'salting salt' (Matthew 5:13), not to shun culture, but to try to purify it or at least preserve it from decay. That is, if we can and if we are allowed to do so by God and by the world around us.

We are children of our age. Whatever culture or age we live in, we are influenced by its ways of thinking, its language, manners and patterns of life. Therefore, we have no excuse for feeling superior to the early Christians. We should remember the words of Scripture: 'Do not be overrighteous, neither be overwise – why destroy yourself? Do not be overwicked, and do not be a fool – why die before your time?' (Ecclesiastes 7:16, 17). We can never analyse everything conclusively – how well Ecclesiastes reminds us of this! – but we should also remember that we ourselves are sinful beings.

Yet we cannot just live as those who surround us. Certainly, so far as we achieve insight into the thoughts and ways of our times, we must beware of accepting them where they are incompatible with Scripture. Failure here prevents Christians from fulfilling their role as a people hungering and thirsting for righteousness, prophets recalling their fellows from the path of disobedience which leads to death – in short, from being salt. Sin manifests itself as greed, lust for power, corruption, misuse of people, racism – and as simple lack of concern. We have to fight these sins in ourselves, but also in the world around us. To be a child of God certainly implies that we can scarcely ever be at ease with the world around us. We may call this attitude the 'prophetic pessimism' of the Christian; but it does not entail either accepting things as they are or being perpetually despondent. There is always the hope that sin and its results can be checked or at least mitigated, just as pain can be alleviated even when death is ultimately inevitable.

The Bible contains no criticism of culture as such. Solomon hired people from the pagan world to help build the Temple. Perhaps that could be done in those days. But God's people are always reminded not to follow the pagan gods or fall into pagan religious practices. A culture becomes unchristian when the wrong gods are revered and served. Today the gods are pleasure, sex, power, and money: this is the Moloch which Allen Ginsberg denounced with power and accuracy in his poem 'Howl'. These gods blind us to the true power of sin. The results are becoming plainer every day, as a non-Christian culture reaches maturity and works out the full consequences of its principles: 'The earth is defiled by its people; they have disobeyed the laws, violated the statutes and broken the everlasting covenant. Therefore a curse consumes the earth' (Isaiah 24:5, 6; see also Hosea 4). In Ginsberg's own words:

> They broke their back lifting Moloch to heaven!
> Pavements, trees, radios, tons, lifting the
> city to heaven which exists and
> is everywhere about us![55]

Indeed the last thought here makes clear the difference between the human-made city with its idolatry and the kingdom of God.

The biblical symbol of such an evil culture is Babel, where sin and idolatry have come to fruition, although happily never completely so. It is a place of tyrants and impending chaos, a world where the worship of power goes hand in hand with anarchy, where people do what seems good in their own eyes and where everybody wants complete fulfilment in this life regardless of what happens to others. The Bible is full of such examples, among others Psalm 73; Isaiah 32:6; 1 Peter 4:1 ff.; 2 Peter 2:19. Wealth is Babel's coveted status symbol, bringing power, pleasure, and immediate satisfaction. We also read of Babel's riches and luxuries in Revelation 17 and 18. Again, it is not the wealth in itself that is sinful but the impure passions, the spiritual fornication, the purposes for which the wealth is used – and the dealing in human souls.

So the Bible warns: 'Come out of her, my people, so that you will not share in her sins, so that you will not receive any of her plagues' (Revelation 18:4). The catchword is, 'Beware! Don't take chances, like Lot whom God had to lead out of the evil city of Sodom. Take no part in her activities, do not bow down before the beast, do not imitate her sinful ways.' Here is the real antithesis: not between culture and Christianity, but between the sinful idolatry of this world and loving obedience to God's laws.

'Come out' cannot mean that we should withdraw from this world, letting it go its own way. The Bible calls God's people to care, to help, to be concerned; we are reminded of this in the story of the good Samaritan. Our friendliness must be known to everyone (Philippians 4:5).

Peter's letters teach very clearly how Christians should live in a non-Christian world. 'Mere common sense,' we may say, and we would be right, but it is biblical common sense! How effectively Peter shows that love is not something simple, and certainly not being soft, sweet, and unprincipled. In 2 Peter 1:5 ff. we are told to build knowledge upon virtue. Knowledge here does not mean rationalistic knowledge, but rather wisdom and insight into who we are, and what is right or wrong. Upon knowledge is built self-control, and on that perseverance. Then we come to godliness, leading to mutual affection, and finally on to love –

love for everyone (the kind of love described by Paul in the famous passage, 1 Corinthians 13). Although many things have changed since Peter wrote, the wisdom of these words of God is never outdated and can still show us how to live in this world.

The prayer of Jesus for his followers was also quite clear in its intentions: 'My prayer is not that you take them out of the world but that you protect them from the evil one' (John 17:15). Later he refers again to their way of life and asks, 'May they be brought to complete unity to let the world know that you sent me and have loved them even as you have loved me' (verse 23). To live as Christ prayed should be our most forceful and convincing testimony.

Understanding that the Lord made the world good and that it therefore belongs to him, we should work toward a realization of its concrete potential in the customs we follow, our thought-forms, the lifestyle we adopt, our use of natural resources, our discovery and treatment of beauty. This entails taking action against sin, destruction, corruption and the lust for power and self-satisfaction. We must forsake Babel, not in order to gloat over her lostness, nor to withdraw our concern for those who still belong to her, but in order to help. We must avoid the pollution of this world not in order to feed our own pride and self-esteem (that would itself be gross pollution, the sin of the pharisees of all times) but to be better able to help, as the salt of the earth.

It is vital that we understand the gospel here. God's gift to us is a Saviour who is able to cleanse hearts and forgive sins. Repeatedly in the Bible God urges us to turn back to him and be redeemed from the sins that separate us from him; he wants our relationship with him to be restored and open. Ezekiel 36:25 promises, 'I will sprinkle clean water on you, and you will be clean; I will cleanse you from all your impurities and from all your idols.' But the text does not stop there, for God says, 'I will give you a new heart and put a new spirit in you; I will remove from you your heart of stone and give you a heart of flesh.'

We find the same gospel summarized in Colossians 2:11 ff. We read again of renewal of the heart, this time in the metaphor of inward circumcision (also found in Jeremiah 4:4). Man becomes a new creature (Romans 6). We read again of forgiveness of sins, and then of the Devil's forfeiture of his power. Here then is the gospel: that the power of sin and evil is broken, through the Cross.

The importance of this good news goes beyond its offer of salvation for the individual, and even beyond the promise of a new heaven and a new earth. It has immediate relevance for us, because here and now we as a community can be a healing force. Life begins *now* for anyone who has accepted Christ (cf. John 5:24) and for whom death has lost its power; Christ's renewal allows people to live. Though perhaps they may face the danger or even reality of persecution and will certainly not find ease and total acceptance, the Christian community as a whole has been called to demonstrate that Christ is truly the Saviour and Renewer. It is only on this basis that we can begin to solve the problem which some call 'Christianity and culture', but which we could better describe as 'Christianity's place within God's creation'.

Even the word 'problem' sounds too academic, too intellectual. This is a real-life issue, not a problem to be solved in theory at the writing desk. It is the tension in the life of Christians between on the one hand their love for the beauty of God's creation, their fellow creatures and their Lord, and on the other hand their battle against sin and death – a tension further complicated by the knowledge that sin is not only 'out there' but also 'in here', within themselves.

We must recognize that sin goes much deeper than moral failure. As we have already seen, the Bible points out that following false gods is the real source of the trouble. We read, 'The Israelites did evil in the eyes of the LORD; they forgot the Lord their God and served the Baals and the Asherahs' (Judges 3:7). Again and again in Deuteronomy Moses warns the Israelites not to be faithless to the Lord. They were promised cities, vineyards, all the good things of life – we would say 'cultural benefits' – but they could enjoy these things rightly only if they did not pollute the land with idols (Deuteronomy 6:10 ff.).

This problem of culture can be solved only in Jesus Christ. Not in a rejection of the world – that is more a Greek than a Christian solution. Nor in a following of the cultures around us, with a dash of 'Christian religion' thrown in – a God for Sunday and 'quiet times'. It is a matter of getting our priorities right. Our surrender to God must be without ifs and buts, without restrictions. The other things will follow. God gives his commandments in order that we may live; he is the Creator of life. Jesus said, 'If you remain in me and my words remain in you, ask whatever you wish, and it will be given you' (John 15:7).

A colleague of mine once gave a very important lecture, discussing at length the sources and meaning of asceticism. His study, 'Culture and Salvation', deals, although in a more specific context, with the issues we have been considering. Here is his conclusion:

> Shall we say that both are right? Shall we say to the ascetic: the cultural mandate has been given to us, and when we act upon it we are always safe? Yet the ascetic will – quite correctly – counter with the objection: you misjudge what culture has come to mean since the Fall. What is to be the solution? God tells us in the creation story and Christ explains to us in his sermon on 'taking no thought': cultural mandate, acceptance of culture, well and good, but first remember that I am the meaning of all culture and that accordingly you can accept culture only when you desire my kingdom and love me more than yourself. See Matt. 6:33, 'But seek ye first the kingdom of God ... and all these things shall be added unto you'; see also especially Mark 10:28–31, where Jesus elaborates, as it were, upon the words just cited: 'Then Peter began to say unto him, Lo, we have left all, and have followed thee.

> And Jesus answered and said, Verily I say unto you, There is no man that hath left house, or brethren, or sisters, or father, or mother, or wife, or children, or lands, for my sake, and the gospel's, but he shall receive an hundredfold now in this time, houses, and brethren, and sisters, and mothers, and children, and lands, with persecutions; and in the world to come eternal life. But many that are first shall be last; and the last first.'
>
> Here Jesus explains concretely that even in this life, houses, lands, etc., will, for his sake, fall to the lot of those who believe in him, provided they first give up everything for Christ. The tragedy of the ascetic was that he neglected to read the words 'in this life', or exegeted them away, because he failed to understand that Jesus restores the things of this world to us if we have but once given them up for his sake.[56]

Indeed, provided we have no false gods and are clear about our priorities, we can creatively engage in cultural activity. But in the same text in Mark we also find a warning that there may be persecutions, and that we may have to lose everything, including our lives, just *because* we have set our priorities right. Nevertheless, the promise holds for a great and real future.

As Matthew 7:13,14 reminds us, there are two ways. One goes through the narrow gate that leads to life, and the other has an open and easy entrance but leads to destruction. The narrowness of the gate does not mean that the gospel is not open to everybody. The gate is narrow in that when we go through it we must leave behind our pride, our self-reliance, our autonomy. (Many people would prefer to be asked to make difficult sacrifices or be given special assignments because that would make them special people, part of a respected in-group with grounds for pride.) The broad way seems to be open and easy, for it coincides with our deepest longings and strivings; it promises to fulfil our wishes and free us to do as we please. The breadth of this road is deceptive, for it soon takes away our freedom and leads to destruction and death.

A person's choice at the crossroads is not just a religious one, set apart from the rest of life in a kind of supernatural 'spiritual' realm. It has concrete consequences, a harvest, the 'fruits' mentioned in Matthew 7:17, 18, 20. What are these fruits, if not what we in our time call culture: the way we live our lives – our style, our influence, our insights, our convictions and, flowing from these, our actions?

Finally, it is not our work but God's to judge the world, as is clear in the Old Testament, in Revelation and in the last addresses of our Lord (Matthew 24). Our calling is simply to help our fellow beings, to love them with deeds rather than with words. Ours is not the dilemma posed by Camus in his book *The Plague* – that if human ills were sent as a judgment by God, then doctors go against God's will when they relieve human suffering. Camus was right when he showed that the plague had something – a great deal, in fact – to do with God's actions. The priest was right in calling the people to repentance. But the doctor was also right when he tried to alleviate their plight. The Bible tells us that God is acting in history, and that suffering is part of the curse. But judgment is not our work. We are merely to help, and to explain the truth in a prophetic way.

Today the Christian community has a special place in the midst of hardships, when the Four Riders of Revelation 6 are passing over the earth bringing famine, war, and death. We need not fear, for like the Israelites whose houses were sealed with blood on the eve of their departure from Egypt, we too are sealed (Revelation 7). The Lord knows who are his. In the beautiful story in Jeremiah 45, Baruch, the secretary of the prophet, looks with dread into the future; but the Lord has a special message for him: although judgment is coming, God will protect Baruch.

Meanwhile, we are to 'Seek righteousness, seek humility' (Zephaniah 2:3), acting with integrity, obeying God's commands, and not compromising with the ways of the world. There is no room for the pretension that we can change history or even save ourselves; our involvement in culture must not be with the idea that God needs the assistance of our great accomplishments. Humility implies looking to him for shelter in the day of adversity, as Zephaniah suggests. His words are nearly the same as those of Christ: to seek God's kingdom first, and the rest will follow.

Part Two:

Freedom within a Framework

3
Creativity in Love and Freedom

As we saw in the last chapter, culture is concerned with economics, social conditions and everyday life. Yet it is far too often considered something special, rather odd and impractical – all very well for an elite that has the time and brains for it. In our own time a noticeable split has occurred in which certain activities, including art, have come to stand apart from and outside of economic and social life.

When culture is seen in this way as something special, then creativity becomes something special too. It becomes a hobby for those who are looking for recreation. Here we can sense the influence of Romanticism, which regarded art as a kind of religion – deep, yet remote from reality – and the artist as a high and sublime creative being, a high priest of culture.

We have seen that it is important to think directly from a biblical world and life view about our work, our creative powers, and our lives as human beings, beginning by acknowledging our need of God. We shall now specifically consider creativity, how with our own personalities and God-given freedom we can help to shape reality, and how this leads to culture.

In doing this, Christians are not doing something special or peculiar. Non-Christians also feel free to talk about their work as human beings living within a cultural framework – or perhaps moving towards a new framework. They do this from their own world view. Why should a Christian not do the same? We need not feel apologetic in the face of approaches that call themselves scientific or scholarly, for our starting point is the full reality of the world, made by a Creator who has revealed himself in human language, in Scripture.

Christ the Creator – made in his image

John 1 and Hebrews 1 affirm that the world was created through the Word, meaning Christ, and that nothing can exist without him, for he is the foundation of all that is. As the Creator, in whose image all people are made, Christ is therefore also the source of all human creative powers.

Furthermore, Christ's Lordship over creation is also the model for our human relationship to it – a relationship of love and freedom. Humankind were created unique, the crown of God's creation, with all created things at their disposal. The uniqueness of their relationship to both God and the world is at once apparent in the name-giving with which man started his activities (Genesis 2), for giving a name is more than just labelling things in an arbitrary way. It means ordering, finding relationships and perceiving individual qualities. It means discovering, not inventing (for people do not really invent anything), what the created world in its inexhaustible multiformity and variety has to offer.

God's framework for human creativity

One cannot, however, make such discoveries without respecting the given realities of the world. No human activity can take place outside the appropriate structural laws, whose presence in creation provides people with a norm for all their undertakings. Language and expression, thinking, administering justice, acquiring knowledge, making or recognizing something beautiful – all are possible only within structural laws. We cannot live and work outside them. They give meaning to all our activities, whether we are simply feeding animals or boiling water. Even someone who wants to commit suicide has to take these laws into account, otherwise his or her attempt will fail.

We should not see these laws as a deterministic system that compels us to do certain things. That is why I prefer the term 'norm' to describe them. Because they are founded in Christ and determine the reality in which we live, we as creatures can work well only if we act according to them. Nevertheless, our relation to them is not one of compulsion but one rather of love and freedom.

Freedom and love are inherent in being human, part of our essential nature. They are at one and the same time a gift and a guideline to enable us to live effectively. God 'commands' us to love and to be free (Galatians 5:1); and although the word 'command' for many connotes restriction, God's words are not meant to be a prison but the exact opposite. People were not created for the Law, but the Law for people (see Christ's words on the law of the Sabbath in Mark 2:27).

The command to love provides the true basis for freedom. To love our neighbours involves allowing them their rightful freedom as human beings and, at the same time, using our freedom in ways that are good for them. To love creation includes thankful use of its potential, ruling over it as lords rather than as tyrants.

The structural laws which constitute the world in which we live cannot be dissociated from our relationship to God. God gave human beings everything, including life with all its potential, and said 'It is good' (Genesis 1). Because the whole structure of reality is based on Christ (cf. Colossians 1:15–19; Ephesians 2:20–22), people cannot live outside of Christ without ruining life and bringing about destruction.

The Fall: God's framework distorted

The Fall meant, essentially, that people wanted to be like God, to determine their own course of action. Ceasing to love God, people also refused to accept all they have as his gift. Instead of lords of creation, humanity became tyrants over reality – creation reduced to mere 'reality', a terrible impoverishment. Their view of things thus reduced, people tried to manipulate them, violating their very nature. And as we see very soon after the Fall, their failure to force animals and human beings to do what went against their nature drove them to cruelty, slavery and even murder. The man or woman who wants to rule in tyranny finds that reality itself resists and frustrates his or her activities. Then not only is love dead, but freedom is lost as well.

Fallen humanity refuse to see that reality is founded in Christ. Isolated from their true Source, things and actions become merely accidental, part of an attractive and entertaining game but without any positive end or purpose. Instead of a wonderful totality, displaying unity in diversity, reality loses touch with truth and becomes a mass of unrelated facts. Perceiving phenomena as things in themselves, totally unrelated to Christ, human beings futilely try to distinguish order and meaning. They may even conclude that whatever order they discern is of their own making, a result of their attempt to escape chaos. 'What is the meaning of meaning?' asks modern philosophy, paradoxically forced to think about meaning upon realizing its absence.

People, however, cannot live with the full consequences of this situation. Though they may claim that nothing is worth fighting or dying for, if someone they love is hurt, their emotions are inconsistent with their philosophy and they react with indignation or sorrow. People who refuse to recognize God nevertheless continue to seek a foundation and meaning for things, even if their starting point provides them with no basis for doing so. This tension causes the lives of thousands to remain empty, superficial and unpredictable; what they accept one day, they reject the next. Without a foundation even acts of goodness have something accidental and arbitrary about them.

When people abandon the root or core of reality, not only theoretically but in their understanding and experience of life, then they lose their connections, their relation to things. The result, spoken of in modern philosophy, expressed so strongly in modern art, is alienation: life in an absurd world, surreal, among strangers. Even the reality of other people's existence may become oppressive, for they limit me. The world is a strange prison with no exit, no way of escape, as described in Jean Paul Sartre's famous play. Reality is bizarre, irrational, incomprehensible.

Once things exist independently like this, alien both to us and to each other, they are accompanied by death. Paul asserts in 2 Corinthians 3:6 that 'the letter [of the law] kills'; apart from God and his love, the Law (including the structural laws mentioned above) only shows our weakness, our shortcomings, our helplessness. It shows that we are lost.

Separated from the lawgiver, law becomes a deadly tyrant. The norm, the Law intended to lead to life can, when given a concrete form, become a harsh demand whereby a person in the end is dehumanized into a thing 'under the law'. People become slaves of the very systems they have constructed (often with the best intentions) to make everything go smoothly and be of maximum usefulness to them. We see this concretely in our own culture since the Enlightenment, when people have been reduced to 'cogs in the machine'; we also see it in current dictatorial political systems which devalue people to instruments of the state.

Apart from Christ, the norm becomes a source of frustration, a hindrance. This happens when the relationship with a personal God has been replaced by idolatry; a person who does not recognize a transcendent Creator has to choose in God's place something immanent, something belonging to the created order. Everything then becomes related to this god and, since people cannot change the real structure of the creation, everything is distorted. This god may be nature or some other natural force (naturalism), reason (rationalism), morals (moralism), fertility (either the old worship of Venus or Astarte or the modern worship of sexuality), and so on. Finding themselves caught in a demanding ideal of their own making, people again try to break away to recover their humanity and their freedom by dissociating themselves from the norm, the structure which they formulated for themselves. The inevitable result is lawlessness. The composer John Cage 'wrote' a piece of music, 'Four Minutes Thirteen Seconds', that consists of total silence for that duration of time – 'silence which may then be filled up by the sounds of the world itself'. Yves Klein made paintings which are just uniformly blue, leaving the beholder completely free to give them their own meaning. Certainly freedom is won in this way, but it is a meaningless and essentially inhuman freedom since there is no possibility of communication. As such it means death and absolute alienation; it is a possibility only if we say with John Cage, 'Here we are. Let us say yes to our presence together in Chaos.'[57]

Christ the Redeemer – his restored purpose

From this state of misery, described in the Bible and observable in human experience, Christ can redeem humanity. He can liberate them from death and alienation and sin. Being redeemed in Christ is not just a subjective experience, a 'leap in the dark'. It is described in some profound words from the Old Testament, quoted by Paul in the Epistle to the Romans: 'The just shall live by faith.' These words have a concrete relevance to our lives. Being 'just' means (among other things) being in a right relationship to the structural laws of our reality. 'Faith' means being founded in Christ and directed towards God. 'Live' means standing in freedom, openness and love, responding to the norm with understanding rather than being bent under the law in an enforced obedience.

Life

All people are concerned with life; and God himself wants to be known as the 'God of the living'. Life, however, is something much greater than the biological phenomenon studied by the scientists, although of course life includes this. Life is more than the heartbeat, more than being able to move about and observe things. Conversely, we can understand something of what life means when we think of the expression, 'to lead a dog's life'. A person may be biologically alive but his or her existence totally joyless. Never was this better expressed than when a young hippy asked, 'Is there a life before death?' This is typical of the conflict facing modern people: they want to live, but they have rejected the foundation of Life. They long for life and try to reach out for it in adventure, in sex (called 'free love'), in lawlessness, but all they find is death. This is the tragedy of our times. One would have expected that autonomous humankind would extol their life without God as something beautiful and good. Sometimes they do try to find something positive and optimistic, but reality forces them to admit their misery and alienation. Martin Esslin says at the end of his book *The Theatre of the Absurd*: 'The dignity of man lies in his ability to face reality in all its senselessness.'[58]

Life before death can begin only with the new birth in Christ. Only he can restore people to a meaningful relationship with reality. He gives them the power and the desire to do what is right, to act in love and freedom.

Love

Love stands alongside those other basic realities which are the essence of human existence – life, truth, righteousness, freedom and beauty. The one is not possible without the other. To define love is difficult if not impossible, for it affects us too closely to be summed up in a few words or sentences. Nevertheless, as human beings we do recognize, experience and in a measure understand, love.

Usually we notice love only in very intensive forms, like the growth of passion between a man and a woman, a response of delight to something beautiful in the world, or the wonder of new converts when they discover what God has done for them. We often fail to realize love's full significance until we are without it and life has become cold and ugly.

Paul has given us some penetrating observations on the absence of love in 1 Corinthians 13: if there is no love, then all wisdom, righteousness, purity, truth amount to nothing. They become noise, idle sound, devoid of meaning. Paul wrote these words as a warning to Christians who would give the impression that as long as doctrine is sound, everything is all right. Here is where so many church people fail; they seem to fear love as a mark of weakness.

When this happens it shows how little they have understood the nature of love. For if their love has not expressed itself in the form of gentleness, patience, regard for others, meekness, and perseverance (the marks of Christian love according to 1 Corinthians 13:4–6, Galatians 5:22, and 2 Peter 1:5–7), then all their righteousness is empty, their exertion for the church fruitless, and their purity of doctrine useless. The kingdom of God can never be built in this way.

The four freedoms

Freedom without love would be licentiousness, but love without freedom is not really love. Together they determine what it is to be human. Again and again in his epistles Paul explains the basis of real freedom. In Colossians 2:11–15 Paul shows first that human life is renewed in Christ; he refers to Jeremiah 4:4, which speaks of circumcision of the heart. Then he declares that people's sins are forgiven (v. 13). Finally he mentions the defeat of the Devil (v. 15).

Paul continues with a magnificent passage on Christian freedom. Christians who make rules for other Christians to obey, or who accept such rules, show how little they understand the renewed life offered in Christ. They are worldly, says Paul (Colossians 2:20). One might even say they are secularizing the Christian life. As the apostle says elsewhere: 'You did not receive a spirit that makes you a slave again to fear, but you received the Spirit of sonship. And by him we cry, "Abba, Father"' (Romans 8:15).

Freedom is a fruit of the Spirit. It means that we are *free before God*. Like Jesus, we may call him 'Father'. John speaks of our 'confidence before God', which means an open and straightforward relationship, without fear (1 John 3:21). Although our freedom must not be confused with forwardness and impudence, we may stand in love and confidence before a personal God. For no matter how some Christians have unfortunately regarded him, God is not Fate, a bogy, or a sadistic spectator eagerly waiting to punish our every failure. The Bible would have us see him as a beloved Father whom we regard with reverence and awe, and try not to grieve.

If we have founded our lives in Christ and are free before God, we are also *free towards ourselves*. We need not be afraid to be ourselves, for Christ has accepted us as we are, with our own personalities. We are free to develop our own individuality. Frustration and self-mortification do not belong to the gospel, as Paul points out in Colossians 2:16–23. Yet self-realization is also not the aim of those made new in Christ; for them life is both a gift and a task addressed to each one individually.

Freedom towards the world is another privilege of the Christian. Christians may suffer in the world, because the world also made Christ suffer (1 Peter 4:12–16); but Jesus said we should not be afraid of the world, which may kill the body but cannot kill the soul (Matthew 10:28). We need never seek an undesirable compromise; we have true freedom because we are in God's hands. He has counted the hairs on our heads and knows our needs (Matthew 6:25–34). As his servants we can perform our duty, but we need not worry as if the fate of the world depended on our actions. This trust in God liberates us from the need to calculate and determine everything ourselves.

Because God wants to work through our weaknesses (see 1 Corinthians 2:1–5, and the verses preceding) and has pledged himself to answer our prayers liberally, we as his children are free to work without pressure, without fear, without superiority or inferiority complexes. We are not alone, and we do not depend on our good works to gain us a place in heaven.

The Heidelberg Catechism makes the same point in regard to the church. 'From . . . beginning to End . . . the Son of God gathers, protects and preserves' the church.[59] It is not our responsibility. Responsibility for the church would be too heavy a burden for its leaders, who would feel a need for rules, ecclesiastical policing and spiritual tyranny.

Only God can give people the freedom we are describing, and enable his children to live together in this freedom. He maintains and protects them – and even adds to their number. Christians may preach the gospel, but it is God who calls people to himself. God's children may admonish and support each other, but it is God who maintains his church. It is disastrous when those who think they know better try to maintain the church themselves, like the minister who wrote to his friend, 'Things are going well here; the church is getting purer, even though fewer and fewer people come to the services.' One remembers the figure of the Grand Inquisitor in Dostoyevsky's *The Brothers Karamazov*: the church leaders had corrected the mistakes of Christ, who was too idealistic! In all ages this way of thinking has perverted the church – Roman Catholic, Eastern Orthodox and Protestant churches alike.

How much religious strife would have been avoided if Christians had understood that it is their task to be kind, patient, gentle, humble, regarding others better than themselves. Although church people may have their responsibilities, all final judgment is reserved for God (Romans 12:19).

Finally, freedom in Christ gives people *openness towards nature*. God's creation lies open before us; and because he is Lord we need not fear it as a malevolent force. It is also not a system that runs by itself, explainable in terms of a mechanical law of cause and effect. Such laws may describe how the world functions, but they stop short of touching its deepest reality: the world is open, and God is active in it (cf. Deuteronomy 27–30). That is why it has meaning to pray for blessings, to give thanks before eating and to have a national Thanksgiving Day.

By contrast, the mechanistic universe of modern science is indeed something to be feared, for it functions as an entity completely unrelated to human actions or will. Admittedly we do not understand everything in nature and cannot provide a theological rationale for every plentiful harvest or natural disaster. But that does not mean that everything happens by chance, by natural laws unrelated to the human situation. Because the world is open we must take into account the curse and God's judgment.

But even if we here arrive at the limits of our human understanding, if with Job (Job 40:6 ff.) we stand awe-stricken at God's wisdom in nature, we need not see nature as a prison that frustrates our plans and activities; this occurs only when we make demands upon it that go against its created order, those structural norms we have already mentioned.

So we can be free towards nature, since as God's creation it is the environment he gave us to inhabit. We are at home here. Alienation is unnecessary. Contact with reality at a deep level is part of the Christian life. Christians enter into reality rather than escaping from it. The flight from reality is a mark of Eastern and classical mysticism, not of Christianity.

Of course, our freedom is limited by the curse (Romans 8:18 ff.) and also by sin. Because of the Fall nature is not fully as God intended, and we must put restraints upon it. Nature's occasional hostility and recalcitrance show that the curse is real. But the curse does not have the last word, for in Christ there is the promise of ultimate renewal, and even now our relationship with nature can be marked by renewal and restoration.

This may all sound rather obvious. Yet anyone who has understood even a little of what is involved in the pursuit of autonomous freedom – with its alienation, frustration and sense of imprisonment in one's own existence – will understand that such freedom and openness are anything but a matter of course. (See chapter 5 below, on Buñuel.) Nor are such freedom and openness cheap; Christ had to die to give them to us. Outside of him, the love and freedom of ordinary humanity are lost.

The Christian's battleground

Christ's coming into the world has brought back the possibility of life, love and freedom, but these are not to be had without a struggle. The Christian must wage war on two important fronts, the first of which is within him or herself. Sin is in our bones; it tries to drive us back to self-determination, self-protection, self-reliance. It tries to draw us away from God and tempts us not to use his gifts, nor to believe the promise that he will answer our prayers.

But sin is also outside us, in the world, where the effects of the Fall are still a hard reality. Christians therefore must fight against the misery and imperfection around them – injustice, falsehood, corruption – things that take away human freedom and put people in a cage of fear, frustration and guilt.

True humanness in Christ

The new life in Christ is all-inclusive. It means living creatively with God's help, through prayer. In Christ, God gives us the opportunity of living; it remains for us to build on this possibility, this foundation, with the talents we have been given – to sing, to paint, to build or to manage a home. But in order to erect a building that is more than hay or stubble we must let Christ produce the fruit of the Spirit in our lives. That is what it means to be truly human.

Creativity in everyday life

Creativity, then, is what we make of our own lives. Each life is an individual possession, but each life also touches the lives of others, in community. Christians speak here of the 'communion of saints'. At every point we are involved with others, working in and for the world to renew and maintain it, to set things right, to restore peace. We are to do this not primarily on a large scale, but in a small way among the people around us, which is the most difficult thing of all!

This is what it is to serve the truth, in love. Truth is not a concept to be formulated and defended; it is something to be *done* (John 3:21). Doctrine that is sound must express itself in godlike behaviour, for God considers mere lip-service abominable (Isaiah 29:13). He wants to involve us in restoring relationships and situations. We will have to work and think, seizing the opportunity to benefit other people within the realm of everyday experience.

Often this sort of work is anonymous; the people connected with it may know of the effort involved, and one may perhaps receive some public honour, but even then the work (making laws or roads, building houses or organizations, even producing works of art) is ultimately unacknowledged and meant for the benefit of others. Whether our work will last or will continue to be honoured is unimportant. At this point, the wisdom of Ecclesiastes runs directly counter to all human striving to make an eternal reputation.

Such work will always be in conflict with evil and the Evil one. By fighting against the incompleteness of the world, by renewing and improving it, we are taking part in the very real struggle against evil and destructive spiritual powers.

Creativity in the narrow sense

Besides the more general matters mentioned above, there is a more limited kind of creativity that leads to a particular creation like an invention or a work of art. Between the kind of creativity discussed above and the latter, for which the term is usually reserved, there is no material difference.

Looking in the Bible for an example of the narrower kind of creativity, we find Bezalel and Oholiab who are mentioned in Exodus 31.

Bezalel is described as being 'filled with the Spirit of God, with skill, ability and knowledge in all kinds of crafts' (verse 3). Oholiab has the skill to carry out the designs of Bezalel. Since Bezalel makes designs, he is a shaper of culture *par excellence*. He is a man who discovers new possibilities; he opens up creation and cultivates it, and he does so with wisdom and understanding. Wisdom is the capacity to see relationships, understand what is and is not possible or meaningful, what contributes to humanity, dignity, righteousness, purity, harmony – in short, everything which serves life in a positive way (Philippians 4:8).

Inspiration. Creativity in any specific sense does not come of itself. Inspiration is necessary. Nowadays, the old conception of inspiration as a spiritual influence from outside a person has completely vanished. Even if the word is occasionally used, its real sense is denied. It tends to be employed to indicate a certain physical condition during the act of creation, when everything goes well for instance, and the artist is able to concentrate. But the idea that there might be any influence on a person from outside is not considered at all.

Without inspiration, creativity becomes a continual search to find something new, without any concern to make a real contribution to humanity and the conditions of life in this world. In their creativity people may be inspired by the Holy Spirit as in the case of Bezalel; indeed, God's Spirit is needed to produce what is truly beautiful or positive. Yet God can also give the Spirit to non-believers, to inspire them in their creativity. This gift never comes automatically, although to the non-believer it comes unsought. It comes because God thinks a certain thing necessary for his creation, for the benefit of men, women, children, and animals (see Jonah 4:11). The latter may not belong to his people in the more limited sense, but they do belong to his creation.

When speaking about creativity we need not think only of the work of the artist. We can also include the work of inventors. Surprisingly often such people describe how a long-sought solution has flashed upon them from outside, through inspiration, in a sudden moment of clarity. There is evidence of remarkable guidance in their research. R.E.D. Clark gives some striking examples in *Christian Belief and Science*. He quotes men like Helmholz, Faraday and Gauss, the latter asserting that although it was he himself who achieved certain results, he cannot explain how.[60]

Much creativity also occurs without the guidance of the Spirit, especially in this day when people prefer to be emancipated from God. They want to do things themselves and regard the consideration of forces and powers outside human subjectivity as antiquated superstition. But without God, without Christ, without the Spirit, our work lacks purpose. It becomes neutral and cold. This can be seen in Darwin's autobiography, wherein he describes how as a young man he used to love poetry and music, but that he can bear them no longer. Even the appreciation of natural beauty is almost entirely lost for him. 'My mind seems to have become a kind of machine for grinding general laws out of large collections of fact.'[61] He notes that the loss of his taste for art has affected his happiness and certainly weakened his emotional life.

Without the influence of God's Spirit, people have to rely on their own subjectivity to provide the creative force. Often they try to achieve this by transgressing all intellectual and moral boundaries, giving free rein to their passions, perhaps using drink or drugs to stimulate their subjectivity. This results in creations which would not otherwise have come into being. It cannot be proved that a clear mind and judgment would have led to something more profound and lasting, but such a conclusion seems obvious. We can also trace the preference for improvisation and spontaneity, for all that is unstudied and unreasoned, to this modern predilection.

Lastly, we may mention the possibility of inspiration by diabolical forces. There are truly devilish crimes, which are sometimes even committed out of a kind of delight in the perverse. Literature gives us examples, like the character of des Esseintes from Huysman's *A Rebours*, written in 1884, and the strange inspiration which led de Sade to conceive and write *Justine* (1791). The character of Faust may be similarly understood.

In real life such phenomena occur more frequently than is often realized. One must be prepared to recognize that the 'spiritual forces of evil in the heavenly realms' (Ephesians 6:12) do indeed exert an influence on the lives of human beings. (The more one considers these matters, the more one realizes how much even Bible-believing Christians have been brainwashed by contemporary patterns of thought which deny the existence of objective spiritual forces. How great is the consequent impoverishment of their understanding.)

In view of all this we can see the importance of praying, 'Deliver us from evil.' The fact that our Western world is still relatively free from evil forces like black magic and occult occurrences may be the result of this prayer. If people today think this unimportant, the reason may be that people in previous ages did pray this prayer with understanding. For the Germanic tribes who became Christians between AD 500 and 1000, this deliverance from the devil and from evil forces, often equated with the old gods, was the centre of Christ's work. This can be seen when one carefully studies early Romanesque art.

Artistic freedom. Even granted the presence of inspiration, there is no creativity without freedom. If people always have to ask, 'What will people think?' or 'Have I taken this or that into account?' they will achieve nothing, for they will be relying on laws and rules made by others rather than those belonging intrinsically to the thing they are creating, the content already present in God's creation. The person who would be creative must be free from legalistic thinking; how, for example, could anyone compose songs in a milieu where all but sacred hymns were considered evil?

Whoever would create must be free from the tyranny of past, the present and the future. Such a person cannot do things just for the sake of tradition, although he or she may work within traditions and even uphold them. One need also not be a slave of current fashion, although one may appreciate its contributions. Nor should one be concerned only with the future significance of one's work, stifled in creativity by a vain search for glory.

Although a work of art comes into existence in a contemporary situation, and is perhaps made for a certain purpose, it must not be forced into an imposed framework. Artists must be free to realize the commission in their own way, their own style. A person who gives a commission may ask for a piece of music of a certain length, for a book on a certain subject or for a wall decoration of a certain size. These are requirements belonging strictly to the commission and they may challenge the artist to find the right solutions. They do not as such take away the artists' freedom, but rather give them a chance to do something meaningful, something with a function. However, artists must never be asked to comply with norms which they find altogether alien and which are outside the scope of a given commission, as for example, 'A Christian novel must always have a happy ending' or 'A Christian should write only sacred poetry.' If the group to which an artist or any creative person belongs is censorious, either his or her talent will be stifled or else such an artist will be forced to leave his or her own native milieu.

There must also be freedom in a person's use of materials necessary to accomplish the creation. Within the limits of the task assigned, a free use of materials may lead to development of new materials and new methods.

Basically, one should be free to do what is right. Christian freedom is not freedom *from* something, but freedom *to do* something. It means openness, freedom of movement, exploration and mental adventure.

Responsibility. The freedom we have been describing can never exist apart from love. We never create in a merely individualistic way, in a vacuum. Love means that we have a responsibility, as God's servants, to direct our creativity for the benefit of others. If we ourselves fail to remember our obligation of love, other people may have to curtail our freedom by appealing to our sense of responsibility. This is certainly much more than a mere theoretical possibility within the (orthodox) Christian world. Freedom never means sinful licentiousness or a stubborn individualism that makes us indifferent to the effects we have on others.

Creativity is nothing special

As we have already pointed out earlier in this chapter, when we speak about creativity we do not mean art only. Creativity is part of everyone's work, wherever the best solution to a task is sought in love and freedom. This applies both to our contribution to social relationships and to our specific work in engineering, in science, in theology – wherever things have to be made or problems solved.

What do we mean when we talk about Western civilization? Is it not what we, Western people, have created? Creativity means growing bulbs, designing a new car, building a computer, discovering certain relationships within molecules or writing a sermon; all these activities and a thousand more, like town planning, architecture, road construction, but also office work and cooking.

All of these can be done in a creative way. Of course, we must understand that all these activities have their economic and social aspects, and each of them has its place, function, and significance within a larger context. Once the component parts of each aspect are harmoniously related to one other, providing also that the relations between the various aspects themselves are harmonious, then everything is in its proper place. But if, as happens in twentieth-century culture, strong contrasts have developed between on the one hand 'culture' in the narrow sense of the word and on the other hand science and technology, then the result is a disharmony which afflicts us all and which constitutes the crisis of our civilization.

There should be no dichotomy between anonymous works and the creations of individuals, between 'industrial design' and what has become autonomous art. This dichotomy stems from the disharmony just mentioned, and is in many ways the consequence of a strongly humanistic view of life.

Christians, having been renewed in Christ, can help to restore the unity of our civilization. They are called to be creative – in their daily lives, in Christian organizations, in their jobs and the fulfilment of their calling. Although some of their activities may look insignificant in the eyes of the world, the historian or the snob, they may prove very important for human society as a whole and even for the kingdom of God.

Christian culture is not something special or sacred with a kind of halo around it. On the contrary, it means nothing more, and nothing less, than the building of a civilization within the structures, laws and norms given by God. In the end it is all very commonplace and ordinary – what could be more ordinary than the healthy and the good? But as history and experience tell us, these are precisely the most difficult things to achieve in a cursed world populated by a sinful people.

The way is so simple and yet so difficult – so difficult that Christ had to die so that some of it could be achieved now. When as Christians we bring forth the fruits of the Spirit in our lives, we can begin to influence the spirit of human social institutions. Our work may help to form customs and traditions in a positive way, and renewal instead of legalism may help to heal relationships.

These things will come about only if the Lord blesses our efforts and gives us a place of influence (Deuteronomy 28:13). This is not a mechanical process; we could better describe it in organic terms, as the Bible does. A rich general culture, alive and many-faceted, can result as a fruit of the fruit of the Spirit (Isaiah 32:15 ff.) – a secondary fruit if you like, but nevertheless an important sign of the vitality of Christ's finished work.

4
Authority and Permissiveness

What has happened to authority?

In the last chapter we talked of the freedom of the Christian to live and create. But, as we shall see, this freedom is very different from what most of our contemporaries mean by freedom.

The world we live in is rapidly changing. The structures of society have been radically criticized, and many things rejected. The demand is for a new society, characterized by permissiveness, which is what most people mean by the word 'freedom' today.

The relative speed of all these changes has left many people perplexed; they want to know where the sudden landslide of collapsing values has come from. And what does it mean?

The old world view

Directly linked to this change in modern life – in fact, the very key to it – is an altered world view, a new attitude to life. During the past three centuries, since the Age of Reason, human understanding of the world and life has changed out of all recognition. If we go back to a time before this world view began to change, let us say to the seventeenth century, we find that the people of those days looked at the world as follows:

>   GOD
>   The Cosmos
>   Angels   People
>   Devils   Animals
>   Plants
>   Things

This is also the basic view of the world which we find in the Bible.

Even more important for an understanding of our topic is the fact that this world view included *norms*, laws which were universally valid. There was a difference between good and evil. There was *order*, there were structures, there were absolute values. And because these structures existed there was also authority, an authority that was universally accepted. This authority was based on a norm that was just as applicable to the person in authority as it was to the person subject to it. This meant that the one in authority did not get his or her power as a result of personal qualities; every ruler, whether liking it or not, exercised rule by the grace of God. The whole of society was based on what Paul said in Romans 13 about obedience to the government, for 'there is no authority except that which God has established.'

People at that time also recognized the existence of sin. They knew that they could not reach perfection in this life, and because of this – and because of their Christian duty to love their neighbours – they had a certain forbearance towards those in authority, recognizing that leaders too could make mistakes.

However, a new attitude began to appear in various humanistic circles, an attitude that became more noticeable as the seventeenth century progressed. In the next century this new philosophy materialized as the Enlightenment.

The Enlightenment – a new world view

With the Enlightenment the old world view disappeared. The God who had been recognized at the summit of all things disappeared. Whether he – whose name had been totally emptied of meaning by the deists – really existed or not was of no importance. There was no longer any need for him. God was removed from the world, and with him went the angels and the devils as well. With him also vanished the norms which he had established, and which had potency and validity only because of his existence. Finally, along with the norms, the absolute distinction between good and evil faded away, for one could no longer be certain that such a distinction existed.

Thus we have arrived at the world view which our modern age also accepts as the true one. The whole supernatural portion, the 'unseen world' of the old framework, has been removed. All that is left is humankind and the nature which surrounds them.

A new view of human being

People since the Enlightenment have become autonomous. No one has authority over them; they are free. But there is more to be said. They are free at a price. The fixed norms have gone. Where are they to find certainties and security? Only the subjective is left. How can they know when something is true? What, if any, is the standard? Humankind, lonely and isolated, must try in their own strength to solve the problems of existence, to find meaning in a life where things have lost their structure.

In the old encyclopedias all information used to be classified, arranged under 'animal kingdom', 'plant kingdom', etc. But now that God has disappeared from our world view, nothing has its fixed place any more. In the famous *Encyclopedia* of the Enlightenment, edited by Diderot, we find everything for the first time arranged in alphabetical order. The connecting link has gone. Is a human being more than an animal? That is difficult to say; a human being has more understanding, but does that make him or her more significant?

A process of atomization has taken place whereby things now exist independently of each other. The hierarchy of people and animals, things and ideas has been lost forever.

This change has also had repercussions in art. When the Spanish artist Goya depicts the rebellion of his countrymen against the French regime in 1808, the theme is no longer the struggle for freedom, freedom fighters on one side and oppressors on the other. No, men are killing men – that is all that can be said [see Plate 7].

Who solves the problems in a normless society?

When all norms break down, one of the first effects is in the administration of justice – how can it still be done? Above all, how can one exercise authority? From whom does one really derive one's power?

The first philosopher to take on this problem was the Englishman Hobbes, who lived in the seventeenth century. In his book *Leviathan*, published in 1665, he describes the state as a monster. A still more influential figure was Jean Jacques Rousseau who wrote about a century later but who, unlike Hobbes, was optimistic about the possibilities for humanity without God in their lives.

The 'social contract'

Rousseau declared that humanity are autonomous, completely free. But because a society made up of strictly autonomous people would rapidly lead to chaos, this new society also needs norms. What can be the base for these norms? Rousseau's answer was the 'social contract'. According to him, sovereign humanity in early times handed over their rights to authority to the government. This means that all governments are republican in origin. Having first drawn up the laws, the people willingly subjected themselves to these same laws. The authority of the state is thus derived from the authority of each individual. The next step is for the interests of the state to become the norm. This means that, following in the footsteps of Rousseau, we repeatedly come up against an unsolvable dilemma: issuing from the autonomous freedom of humanity is either chaos – in which case freedom loses its meaning – or dictatorship – whereby people essentially lose their freedom, no matter how they may disguise that in beautiful words.

We see that there simply is no real norm. A norm can be a norm only if its authority is greater than that of individual people. A true norm must be one that exists outside of, and issues from something greater than, humanity themselves. All agreements on the basis of what is rational (i.e. what can be understood by reason and accepted as being just) are by necessity relative. Our opinions change, our agreements vary, and the structure of society changes as well.

If there are no norms left, then one can obviously no longer use words like 'sin'. The social sciences have reduced evil and sin to environmental or social structures. Evil surely cannot be metaphysical, can it? The structures will have to be changed. But who is to do this? That is obviously the duty of the state. The state has to come up with the answers. The state must attend to economics and general prosperity. It must encourage and promote the wellbeing of the citizens.

A world without fathers

The state is still with us. But where is authority? *There Are No Fathers in the World* is the name of a book by Hans Müllerschäfe, in which he discusses how the world has lost a legitimate hierarchy of authorities. Family ties are broken, people are cut off from one another, everyone works as an individual. Life is atomized. The family no longer has a real father, there are hardly any true teachers and educators left, and last of all there are no true statesmen anymore. We have plenty of experts in the social-economic field – we have experts in this and experts in that – there is no shortage of technicians. But there are no more great leaders.

Our society today no longer has any concept of *office*. An office is directly related to the fact that we are made in the image of God – prophets, priests and kings; officeholders are something more in their official function than they are as individuals. They have authority not because they do something particularly well themselves, nor because they are infallible. No, they are in a position of authority because they have been placed there. The norms which they apply, and which also apply to themselves, are not meant to give the impression that they themselves hold all the laws, but that these originate from an authority higher than the officeholders themselves. And the justice that they dispense derives its validity ultimately from the judgment of God which is to come.

Without such an 'office', people in authority must justify their own position. Their authority can never be rationally proved. Who gives them the right to occupy a particular position of control? Are they competent? Is authority only a matter of the personal prestige of the people in authority, or is it decided by factors other than individual ability? If personal qualities are the only criteria for leadership, then leaders have no real right to prohibit anything, for that would make them guilty of pure paternalism.

Love grown cold

Our life, then, has become atomized. This also explains the growing crime rate, the violence and murder which are a direct consequence of a waning respect for the law. The boundaries between society and the underworld have become blurred, a process that has been accelerated by the presence of the 'Underground',[62] the subject of so much modern literature. Loss of norms also leads to an increasing hardness of life.

Officials today are not allowed to make mistakes; if they do, they are lashed by a storm of criticism or a hate campaign.

Through the mass media we are increasingly confronted with evil. And kindness has gone. Where is the love that overcomes evil? Matthew 24:12 says, 'Because of the increase of wickedness, the love of most will grow cold.' This is the order in which it is written, and this is the order in which we see it happening in our society.

The age of permissiveness

The idea of permissiveness consists in the freedom of each person to lead his or her own life. Where that may and does lead is summed up in a book by Roscam Abbing, *Real Challenges to Christendom*. After he has described practices in our society which are on the increase, while not so long ago they were not even discussed, let alone carried out, he says, 'Irrational and emotional objections will carry less and less weight. Many will rapidly become accustomed to these practices.'

To many people, protests against modern practices indeed seem 'irrational'. If we look at these things 'rationally', what after all is wrong with prostitution, homosexuality, pornography or drugs? Human reason is the final authority, and reason has no standard by which to judge anything and eventually reject it.

No involvement

Much of what we see happening before our eyes at the moment, the whole drift towards a society where everyone has 'come of age' and is able to decide for him or herself what to do or not to do, we can also find discussed in 2 Timothy 3 and 2 Thessalonians 1. There we find that sexual matters are discussed very emphatically, sometimes much too emphatically, in our opinion. But if we find the first verses of 2 Timothy 3 overdone, we must ask whether we ourselves have not been infected by this spirit of permissiveness. We must not forget that the letters of the New Testament were also directed to people who had 'come of age'. Time and again it is pointed out that because Christians are free they are not bound to all kinds of rules and regulations. Mature Christians are led by the law of love, by a feeling of responsibility for their neighbours.

The refusal to bear responsibility for one's neighbour is also evident in the current businesslike approach to sex. One can make sure that intercourse has no biological consequences, and there need also be no emotional consequences because people are not involved with their full humanness. Some years ago in California so-called 'sex weekends' were organized. During these weekends in the country everything was allowed – with one condition: there was to be no talk about one's private life. At all costs the participants had to prevent a real meeting in which they would actually become emotionally involved with the other person.

The writer Wayland Young shows how there is a very close link between sexual customs and religion. He divides societies into two categories: orgiastic and non-orgiastic. In the latter, of which our Christian civilization is (or was) an example, where monogamy is the custom, we find that human personality is strengthened by the love one bears for one's partner. We see a parallel to this in that a personal relationship can also exist with God, a situation in which one can love and be loved.

Essential to an orgiastic society, however, is the orgy which takes place several times a year, orgies in which people give themselves to a total stranger in a completely impersonal way. Alongside this goes an impersonal religion – everything becomes diffused.

Lost identity

In the orgy people lose their identity. It does not matter with whom one has sexual intercourse, for who is one oneself anyway? Loss of personality by means of the orgy is also the aim for which many drug users strive, an aim that has apparently been aroused by the greater influence of Eastern mysticism in the Western world. These phenomena are evidence that there exists in our present culture a drift towards an orgiastic society.

Many customs and habits have become emptied of their meaning and force. You can read about this everywhere; there are many examples of 'modern living'. The restraints which in former times may have made a person refrain from free sexual intercourse today hardly play a role. People have lost sight of God's judgment. Pregnancy can be prevented with a pill; warnings from the home – 'You'll be put out of the house if anything happens' – mean very little today. In many cases the family structure itself has broken down.

Changing taboos

Some time ago *Newsweek* featured an article, 'The Permissive Society', in which it stated: 'There is a shattering of taboos in language, fashion, and manners. It is part of the larger disintegration of the moral consensus in America.' As a result, the citizens of a state distrust their government, and Roman Catholics no longer feel bound to what the pope and the curia lay down about birth control, etc. Meanwhile, the family, formerly the place where children were taught certain values, increasingly fails to fulfil its function. It has become instead an arena for the conflict between the generations.

As stated in *Newsweek*, many taboos based on language have also disappeared during recent years. Pornography has ceased to be chiefly bad language, or to be sold only under the counter. Anything can now be bought which would have been forbidden a few years ago. But the function of profane language has also changed. Even the better writers have turned to the use of obscenities, because they need the most powerful language to express the chaos of modern life. Norman Mailer writes about conditions in the United States: 'I have indeed used many obscenities in my books. And I must, although I hate it. But such language is the only metaphor that can express the situation which has brought about Vietnam.'

The word 'pornography' has come to have a broader application than it used to. One finds books with titles like *The Pornography of Evil* and *The Pornography of Power*. Power has become something dirty, and it makes those who wield it dirty.

Of course, there is another side to permissiveness. New taboos have arisen to replace the old – for instance, the taboo about death. (Death must not be discussed; that would not be good manners in our modern society.) Moreover, there are many who precisely because of too much freedom get into difficulties – those who get a neurosis from modern life, or are shipwrecked in some other way.

Realization of this fact has produced, in a kind of vicious circle, a reaction of idealism and utopianism. Again the structures get the blame for all the misery, so the structures must go; long live freedom! But often the philosophy behind this is anarchy, the theory based on the doctrine of autonomous human being. As we saw in the case of Rousseau, however, because the problem for the anarchist is that of how to renew the structures, how to allow people their freedom but still ensure that society functions, one finds in all this striving the seeds of a new dictatorship. We find repeatedly a tension between freedom and chaos on the one hand, and order and dictatorship on the other. And no one knows the real answer.

The bourgeoisie

A question that is often asked is why all this is happening just now? Why, so long after the Enlightenment, is the 'cultural revolution' under way just at the present? The answer to this question also must be looked for in the past. The revolution which we now see is really a reaction against the bourgeoisie. The bourgeoisie, which arose just after the Enlightenment, for a large part were convinced by the philosophers that we could do without God in our world view. Most people after Darwin were also convinced that humanity had an evolutionary past, and that human reproduction took place in the same way as it did with animals. The bourgeoisie, however, were not prepared to alter their lifestyle to bring it into agreement with this new vision. They wanted to go on living as if nothing had happened. Instead of an honest treatment of sex, consistent with their evolutionary view of human being, came the Victorian morality with its refusal to discuss sexuality. Morals turned into moralism; people had to be respectable.

Much of what we now see is a reaction to all of this. People want to live in accordance with the life view that they have. They refuse to put up with dishonesty any longer.

And why does this have to happen just now? For years philosophers have laid the groundwork. Throughout the twentieth century artists and writers have preached first anarchy and later the absurd. Particularly after the Second World War a very realistic style in art (and 'naturalism' in literature) began to predominate. The theatre, films, and other media have also helped to pave the way. Television has brought relativism into our homes; news reporters present the news without any moral commentary: this is life as it is, these things are going on at the moment. And nothing more. All together, these influences – along with the crises of our century – have brought us to where we are now.

One can also no longer turn to the state to solve the problems of society, for the state has also lost its face, its image. It is involved in the same crisis. How can the state bring any order into society without possessing authority?

The Christian minority

If we deeply feel the extent and the scale of the problems with which our modern society is faced, one question remains: Do we have an answer?

Yes, we do have an answer; we must have an answer where the world does not. Our answer has two aspects, two levels: the personal and the governmental. On the personal level we must understand that as Christians we are a small minority in this world and can no longer – as previously – decisively influence the rulings of the state. We shall have to accept our pluralistic society as it is. The Apostle Peter tells us how to live as a small minority in a non-Christian, scarcely Christian or antichristian world. In 1 Peter 3:13 ff. he clarifies our position in regard to authority, including non-Christian authority. And he says clearly that Christians may have to suffer for righteousness' sake.

On the organizational level, where each of us has our own proper place, we must simply do what we can: be salting salt. What we are not called upon to do is defend the establishment as such; in fact, many aspects of it could be attacked, and rightly so. Often there is much humanism in the forms of society which some Christians so earnestly defend.

What we are also not called to do is to cling to all kinds of rules and regulations as ends in themselves. Legalism is not a Christian virtue. Christianity is not a morality; it is not something static, but something vital and dynamic. It means life with Christ, new life, new humanity. As Christians, we must have the mentality of the Beatitudes. We must hunger and thirst for righteousness, and never compromise. Where possible we must try to exert positive influence in our pluralistic society. *And we must never ask for the fruits of faith where there is no faith.*

It takes wisdom for a Christian to be involved in society in a fruitful way. It will mean doing all we can to resist the reduction of people to numbers. It will mean defending everyone's freedom, for the Christian too may sometimes require the freedom to oppose issues which the majority favours. It will mean joining forces with those concerned about ecology, the energy crisis or social injustice. It will mean fighting for healed relationships and a responsible use of creation for the benefit of humankind, who – whether they know it or not – are made in the image of God.

5
Art and Freedom – Buñuel and the Bible

A message of absurdity

The horror of Buñuel's vision

In this chapter, we shall consider a film by Luis Buñuel, an example of how belief in unlimited human freedom can lead to a vision of life as meaningless, absurd. The value of considering such a film is that it confronts us with questions so deep that all cheap answers become impossible. Also, it helps us to discover what the gospel really means when it tells us that we are free in Christ. It gives us so much more reason to thank God for this freedom and to be on our guard that it not be taken away from us and our fellow Christians by anyone, not even by leading churchmen.

Interest in the absurd is not confined to modern philosophers, nor to poets and writers. Visual artists were first in the field, and even before 1914 there were examples of absurd art. By the late 1950s and early 1960s the theatre of the absurd had become almost a rage, with plays by Pinter and Albee being performed everywhere. In view of all the propaganda involved and the tone of the artistic discussion, it was almost a new religion, modern, non-Christian, sometimes even decidedly antichristian. Yet the theatre of the absurd has existed for a long time: Alfred Jarry's *Ubu Roi,* one of the first absurd pieces, was written as early as 1896; it has clearly anarchistic tendencies. And in 1928 Luis Buñuel, later to become very famous, made his debut with a short film, considered since to be of major importance, *Un Chien Andaloux* ('The Dog from Andalusia').

Men like Sartre and Camus have long contended that this world is absurd. It is, they argue, so full of contradictions that it cannot fulfil the demands which modern people would like to impose upon it. Although human beings know they are human, they cannot account for the fact; it must be true, yet it can't be true. Sartre is certainly right when he says that rejecting God renders the world meaningless. He is also right to recognize that this world, God's creation, will not (fortunately!) allow people to organize it according to their own ideas. Remarkably, Sartre's language is very beautiful and grammatical French. Despite his message, the form of his thinking and writing is not absurd.

In the theatre, however, the impact of the absurd is not experienced in words alone; both the acting and the production reveal the writer's thoughts. Actors can give direct expression to the absurdity of our world: its contradictions, futility and self-deception. Again, in a way, they are telling the truth. The remarkable thing is that they truly communicate;

the spectator may not understand what they see or hear, but they are nevertheless overwhelmed by the message.

This 'message' is central for Buñuel. He was disturbed by the critics who had discussed *Un Chien Andaloux* exclusively from the viewpoint of artistic form. They had called it 'interesting' and 'fascinating', a kind of supreme play which they could talk about quite calmly without having their hearts touched. Or rather, they would not admit that they had been touched for fear that they might not be thought 'in'. Buñuel denounced these snobbish connoisseurs as 'that crowd which has tried to call "beautiful" and "poetic" something which is basically nothing but a desperate cry for murder.' The film shows a frustrated love which does not really go much deeper than sexual passion. It shows sadism and murder, viewed by spectators who are indifferent or only curious without really being moved. It shows a world full of death, rottenness, fear and pain; lacking not only joy but also any solace or hope of a solution; a world which is evil to the very depths of its being. A more detailed description of the film is not possible, for it is a series of apparently disjointed scenes, strange and nightmarish. According to Buñuel there is no judgment to set right what is wrong.

Citizens of a welfare state, sitting in our comfortable chairs, only too well cared for, we tend to see Buñuel as abnormal – sadistic or possessed. All too easily we suppress our deep anxiety about the possibility of war, of economic crisis, of personal death. Buñuel is in fact possessed, not in the medical sense, but by a faith, an idea, a conviction which in this film is expressed with a crude and dogmatic Surrealism. In his more 'normal' later films he says it again: the order of this world is rotten through and through; and unless church and state, laws and norms pass away, a better world can never appear and people will never be free to do any good. Buñuel is a real anarchist, who believes in terror and revolution and who preaches lawlessness. Yet as a human being he is extremely gentle and in no way eccentric or mentally unbalanced.

This makes it all the more clear that he confronts us with very deep questions. How does God answer these in Scripture? Here, too, we find misery and suppression, covetousness and hypocrisy, sensuality, sickness and war, and not just in a simplified scheme whereby only the wicked fare badly. The psalmist, for example, speaks of the prosperity of the godless (Psalm 73) and the misery of those – including believers – beset by injustice and imminent death.

The wrath of God

The Bible is realistic, perhaps more realistic even than Buñuel and his companions, when it describes the misery of humankind. I do not mean this in a merely theological sense. The Bible puts it this way: 'The earth is defiled by its people; they have disobeyed the laws, violated the statutes, and broken the everlasting covenant. Therefore a curse consumes the earth; its people must bear their guilt' (Isaiah 24:5, 6). Sin always and immediately brings suffering and injustice, heartlessness and mercilessness (Romans 1:28–32). That is why 'the grave opens its mouth without limit' and 'both low and high [are] humbled, and the eyes of the arrogant brought low' (Isaiah 5:14, 15). Although there are mockers who dare God to hasten his judgment so that they can see it (Malachi 2:17; 2 Peter 3:3, 4), when the anger of the Lord is kindled against all this immorality, the mountains will tremble and the dead bodies will lie in the streets like dung and refuse (Isaiah 5:25). But when God hides himself and lets peoples for the time being pursue their own course, that is even worse. The God who hides himself is an angry God (Psalm 89:46; Isaiah 57:17). In that situation sin is momentarily allowed to go unpunished, but divine blessing is withheld.

God, the Lord of lords of the Old and New Testaments, displays his wrath against evil because it should not be there. Evil prevents human beings from living a full life in God's creation, and God's love for humankind makes him hate the sight of evil.

There is a solution, but not in a revolution, which although it might bring a better social or economic order would still leave people corrupt and inclined to evil. The Bible speaks not of revolution but of redemption. People are called to repentance. 'Repent, repent before the judgment is upon us,' is the cry of the prophets. Above all, do not try to cover things up, saying, 'Let us eat and drink, for tomorrow we die' (Isaiah 22:13). This is cheap, and no solution.

The Bible apparently agrees with Buñuel about the condition of the world, but would reject his solution. The psalmist might address him with the words, 'The fool says in his heart, There is no God. They are corrupt, their deeds are vile; there is no one who does good' (Psalm 14:1). So biblically speaking Buñuel is a fool. How does a man arrive at this point of foolishness? The book of Ecclesiastes appears initially to agree with Buñuel: 'This is the evil in everything that happens under the sun: the same destiny overtakes all. The hearts of men, moreover, are full of evil and there is madness in their hearts while they live' (9:3). Nor can we dismiss this as only a matter of appearances. If our experience is not sufficient, then Psalm 44 says it clearly enough. We have no excuse for fighting Buñuel in a cheap way by declaring him a sadist or accusing him of inhumanity.

The Lord himself burned with anger against death at the grave of Lazarus; his anger flared again, against dishonesty and greed, when he drove the money-changers out of the Temple. Jesus warns us that we will face struggles and dangers, and nowhere does he promise a sentimental peace. He is moved with compassion for the multitude – needy, doomed, ignorant. Buñuel also hungers and thirsts for righteousness. But for him there can never be any righteousness in the world; that is the horror of it.

Buñuel does not know about full-grown love, beauty, or real compassion. Perhaps he believes, contrary to his better knowledge and judgment, in the possibility of a new anarchistic order that would bring freedom and righteousness. Or are we still trying to see Buñuel too much as a dogmatic Marxist? He may be in favour of the Communist Revolution, but he nowhere depicts the realization of such a society.

More than once Buñuel blasphemes in his films. Perhaps we should remember that he is a Spaniard who spent much of his life in Mexico in voluntary exile, so that his blasphemy may be more anti-clericalism than anything else. His priests seem to become human only when adversity forces them to stop preaching cheap grace and pointing futilely to heaven. Here too the Lord Jesus would be on Buñuel's side, for Jesus denounced the Pharisees and accused them of unrighteousness, hypocrisy and even of despising the Law.

Anyone who knows the story of the Grand Inquisitor from Dostoyevsky's *The Brothers Karamazov*[63] will understand why Buñuel protests against that sort of Christianity; it only confirms what he says. This particular point is not where our difference with Buñuel lies. Surely it is part of a Christian understanding of life that evil and suffering are realities; Paul uses the present tense when describing how the entire creation is in travail and pain (Romans 8:18, 22).

A song in the night

Despite this, the Bible does not in general appear dark and pessimistic, full of black humour, misery and despair. Nor does it merge sexual desire and the death wish, and still less does it present terror and revolution as positive social action. The Bible never tells us that we are caught in a world where love cannot exist and where nature in all its aspects is hostile to human being.

The person who believes the Bible is appalled by pronouncements like that of de Sade, that for him the greatest torture was his inability to offend or hurt nature. Buñuel, who is spiritually related to de Sade, sees reality as black, awful, rotten, without comfort or escape. The hell in which Buñuel immerses us, where people behave like deadly scorpions, is far from the world that the Bible describes.

We cannot sidestep the discussion between the Bible and Buñuel. In talking about art, we cannot stop at form. And the form, however clever and controlled, is fairly straightforward in Buñuel's work. He himself forbids us to flee into pure abstract contemplation of autonomous art forms; his art is loaded with meaning. How, then, does the Bible contradict him?

We need look no further than Genesis 1, where God himself says that the world is good. Nature itself declares God's glory and proclaims his handiwork (Psalm 19). It does this so clearly that Paul in Romans 1 is able to conclude that people have no excuse if they refuse to recognize God. Even the writer of Ecclesiastes can say that we should be thankful to God for the joys of this life and go on doing our work, 'because nothing is better for a man under the sun' (Ecclesiastes 8:15). The kingdom of God, as preached by the Scriptures and the whole of nature, is righteousness, peace and joy (Romans 14:17).

Although evil, sin and judgment are realities, there is room for love and beauty. Although it may seem that the wicked flourish, we should consider their end (Psalm 73:17–20). And if God does send judgment, it is so that people will repent and understand his will (Ezekiel 6:10; Revelation 9:20, 21).

Our task is to love our neighbour as ourselves; not to repay evil for evil, but to think of what is honest, proper and noble in everyone's sight; and to pursue peace (Romans 12:17, 18). We must leave the path open for God's wrath, not taking it into our own hands (Romans 12:19).

Possibly the deepest error and sin of Buñuel and the other anarchists is that they themselves want to eliminate evil, to terrorize it away. They hate their fellow human beings, instead of loving them in their weaknesses and helping them towards what is good. To hunger and thirst for righteousness means to promote goodness and justice, not to trample upon our neighbour in hate.

Happiness, beauty and love belong to people, who are created for them and can enjoy them, even today, in the midst of God's curse pronounced upon sin. This is the testimony of countless believers down through the centuries. That is how Rinkart, a minister who had seen and lived through all kinds of misery during the Thirty Years' War and had buried thousands of dead, could create the song which is so well-loved in the German- and English-speaking worlds: 'Nun danket alle Gott' ('Now thank we all our God'). That is how Schütz in the midst of that same misery could write such beautiful praises to God, using either the words of the Psalms or texts written for his own time. He refers directly to this most horrible war when in 1641 he composes 'Aufer Immensum, Deus Iram' ('God, let Thy terrible wrath pass away from us'). Nor should we forget that the golden age of Dutch art coincided with a long war. And who could forget the message of the Negro spirituals, a testimony that is especially miraculous because they were sung by slaves or by those who, although perhaps emancipated, were still suppressed and miserable? Cannot everything we have said be summarized in a sentence from one of those 'gospel songs': 'I have lost all I lived for; God bless all I live for'?

Although the Christian knows about the good, the true and the beautiful, the humanist also speaks about these as ideals. People of all ages have known joy in great and little things. I have already quoted elsewhere the line from a well-known musical in the thirties: 'Without a song, there ain't no love at all.'

That sound has not been silenced today; its testimony is still there, in songs, in comedies, in cartoons, even in advertisements which go against the fashion of celebrating the blackness of misery and death – a fashion which recognizes Buñuel as one of its exponents. In spite of existentialism, anarchy and dread of reality, people in our age have made much that is positive, beautiful and good.

Many beautiful things have also been created in painting, music and film, either serious or as 'mere entertainment'. The evidence against Buñuel and his kindred spirits – the creators of 'modern art' in its more narrow definition – is enormous. The testimony of the Bible, of believers and many unbelievers, of humanists past and present, is that the whole of creation and all humanity were intended to be beautiful, good and joyous.

In a paradoxical way Buñuel himself also testifies to this. Although his whole work stems from the belief that misery is indeed inescapable, and that this world is irredeemably bad, he does not want to resign himself to the world and senses the horror of what he has said. He is in rebellion against this world precisely because he cannot accept it as he sees it. Nor can he find a way out of its misery. The strange thing is that one can talk of misery, injustice or deceit only on the basis of a known and accepted norm which reveals these things for what they are! Buñuel is not a devil who loves evil, but a person who with his whole being rises in protest against what Christians would call sin. In church-historical terminology, he is a gnostic, a person who believes that life on this earth as such is contemptible. But he no longer knows how to be redeemed because he has cast God aside; there is no exit and no freedom. Buñuel claims that it was Surrealism that taught him to see that people are not free.

So we have arrived at our subject: freedom and art. We have tried to confront Buñuel's vision with the biblical outlook, for the depth of his questions demands no lesser answer than that of God's revelation.

Freedom and art

Modern art: people in a cage

The reader, who may have concluded that this chapter is about freedom or the lack of freedom and not about art, should be reminded that in modern art we meet these ideas in many forms. Buñuel is not alone. He is closely allied to the Surrealist movement, and thereby to such prominent artists as Picasso, Miro, Ernst, Dali, Breton, and Joyce. But even those who may not have chosen exactly this style express similar ideas. Sartre does it in *Huis Clos*: 'Hell is other people;'[64] Henry Miller in *Tropic of Cancer*: 'If I am inhuman, it is because my world has slopped over its human bounds, because to be human seems like a poor, sorry, miserable affair, limited by the senses, restricted by moralities and codes, defined by platitudes and isms.'[65] And he makes it clear that such a vision has everything to do with art: 'Anything that falls short of this frightening spectacle, anything less shuddering, less terrifying, less mad, less intoxicated, less contaminating, is not art. The rest is counterfeit.

The rest is human. The rest belongs to life and lifelessness.'[66] Do we realize what Miller is saying? What he presents us with is art, no matter how horrible; anything else would be human, would mean life. But it would then be a lie, a fake, a false reality.

To show that we meet this idea not only in modern authors but also in the visual arts, I would prefer to lead you through the rooms of the art galleries and confront you with Raysse, Rauschenberg, Paolozzi, Couzijn, Guston, Wols, Baj, Saura, Tapies, Dubuffet, Richier, Matta, Lam . . . we could extend this list without any trouble. Perhaps a quotation will clarify what I mean. Hans Platschek, an intelligent German artist and admirer of Wols, wrote about the latter: 'With Wols the proper theme is . . . the possibility of catching images even when not only the protocol of art, but also the protocol of reality is denied by it.' That is why 'to him the art of painting is the embodiment of doubt.' Wols, who committed suicide in 1951, is known now as a herald of the informal abstract painting of the 1950s.

Consider also some words of E. Rosenthal, author of a small collection of essays about modern art. Rosenthal sees new freedoms and great possibilities as a result of modern psychology, beginning with Freud. But within this very framework he also deals extensively with human being and the insecurity characteristic of modern art, for example that of Paul Klee. 'Fear is something we find everywhere in modern art, and it is directly related to hellish feelings which have their origin in the unconscious,' wrote E. Rosenthal. Maybe the best definition of the work of these artists is found in Holbrook Jackson's description of the work of a predecessor, the English poet Davidson: 'The strife of the artist for a new expression, a new poetical value, is too evident . . . the courage and the honesty of a mind valiantly beating itself to destruction against the locked and barred door of an unknown and perhaps nonexistent reality.'

Never has freedom been discussed so frequently as in our times; in itself perhaps the best indication that freedom itself has been lost. Buñuel knows this. Others, to their despair, know it too. Does not Sartre speak of humanity being sentenced to freedom, when he asks whether the freedom which people have to take upon themselves is not a curse, and itself the greatest lack of freedom? Over and over again, implicitly or explicitly, freedom and the lack of freedom are the issues confronting us when we focus our attention on modern art. Have not fear and despair, the realization of being caught in a world which in essence is bad and rotten, everything to do with the loss of human freedom? Are they not the very signs of its loss?

We must return here to Genesis 1: God created a world which was good. Then came the Fall, and with it both judgment and redemption. Sin, the fruit of desire, came under judgment and led to death. Salvation from this misery came from God himself, first in the promise, and then later in its fulfilment in Christ. But no matter how deeply sin has penetrated the world and defiled it, people have remained human beings and God's world the creation, and the norm retains its value. Because of our shared humanness we can understand something of what moves people in our times to promise themselves and others freedom, while in reality they are slaves of corruption – not just in a theological sense or according to a Christian interpretation but according to their own experience and words (2 Peter 2:19).

In the first chapter of this book I have talked in much greater detail about the two lines in history: the line of Cain and Lamech, and the line of Seth and Enoch. These two lines are responsible for two types of culture.

All culture is the fruit of human activity. People are driven by motives deep down in their heart to shape life on the basis of the way they understand it. In the line of Cain culture will be the fruit of unbelief; in the line of Seth it will be the fruit of belief. Unbelief produces all the horrors – sin, hatred and death – which we find summarized in Romans 1 (see also Isaiah 5:15, 16). Yet, because people remain human beings they can never go to the utmost limit. Neither Sartre nor Buñuel can lead the life they preach about. Buñuel himself cannot even bear to kill an animal. What is it then that keeps him from breaking through his godless ideas and accepting reality? The answer is simple: he is caught in sin. We must realize that the words of Paul which say that in Christ one can be freed from the law of sin and death (Romans 8:2) are true not only in the pulpit but in the totality of life, and thus for cultural matters as well. Artistic leaders need Christ's liberation just as much as anyone else.

The decline of Western culture

The truth is the same for everyone. The church has often forgotten this. In the words of G.J. Dippel:

> Why is the church the way she is? Because in the church the same pseudo-myths of cultural and social behaviour are honoured as they are in the world ... The same ideas seem to manifest themselves, the same unacknowledged presuppositions.
>
> No matter how much the church twists itself in innumerable coils of Christendom, she misses her basic assignment when she refuses to call culture, politics, and public opinion to repent ... This is the only meaningful form of revolution open to man. This is the revolution which calls for ... the giving up of those false securities which have led to death. Western humanity is threatened by the products of her own hand, based on wrong securities and customs.

The revolution which Dippel describes means abandoning faith in the things we call obvious, which on weekdays fill us with more confidence than the certainties we profess on Sunday. Are freedom from or slavery to the law of sin and death indeed matters that affect 'normal' reality?

Let us look first at our Western world, the world we have to live in, and consider the fruit of the Reformation in our Western culture. As one fruit we must certainly mention the Counter-Reformation – the renewal and purification of the Roman Catholic Church. A second fruit would be the stimulus to humanism, which although it claimed its roots in classical antiquity was essentially something different. A third fruit was renewal in the moral and social spheres after the restrictions of the Middle Ages. A fourth fruit was the artistic freedom which came when art became unshackled from the church, and artists were freed to discover new frontiers in their work.

It was during this period that our Western culture as we know it was built, a culture which although far from perfect was also a fruit of faith. Of course, people were sinful in those days, but at least there was a consensus, a general agreement about norms and morality and an understanding of reality such as has rarely been demonstrated in history. There was richness, openness and freedom, grounded in the reality given by God at the creation, and therefore neither sectarian nor private. Tragically, all too soon the world of the Counter-Reformation was marred by absolutism and the dreaded Inquisition, and freedom was destroyed.

Meanwhile humanism was attempting to deepen its foundations and supported its attempts to reform the world on theories such as the ones of Descartes. In the eighteenth century the humanistic and cultural thrust of the Enlightenment found little resistance from Christendom, weakened as it was by mysticism and traditionalism, as well as by the corrupt absolutism with which the Roman Catholic Church tried to maintain its position alongside the secular power of the monarchies.

The cultural influence of the Enlightenment stemmed from the declaration of humanistic people that they no longer needed God. Only very gradually were the consequences of this new mentality realized. First the whole structural consensus of Western culture as it had been developed during the preceding centuries had to be broken down, a process which has happened so slowly that it is not complete even today. But we can see now more and more clearly, particularly in art and philosophy, the fruits of this new tendency based on the conviction that God is dead and that people are free to build in their own strength.

We have chosen Buñuel's film as a twentieth-century example of this process. To grasp the nature of this new culture we may simply consider the issue of freedom, which is, after all, a broad concept. First, driven on by a positivistic approach to reality, people studied their own life and actions to find the basic laws of their being; is a human being *really* any different from animals and nature? The result was that people found themselves inescapably caught in a determinism growing out of their own positivistic world view, and thus trapped in the technocracy about which so many books have been written!

Still, human beings remained human. They tried to retain their freedom and fought desperately against this mechanistic philosophy. Modern art is one of the most eloquent testimonies to this fight, as is existentialism, which has submitted the human predicament to an exhaustive analysis.

Human freedom, assert the existentialists, exists outside of, beyond, alongside technology. Perhaps people are no more than atoms, but they know about their existence, their 'being'. They know that they 'exist unto death' *(Sein zum Tode)*, and in this knowledge lies their opportunity to transcend their 'thrown-ness' *(Geworfen-sein)*. 'Thrownness' is a term invented by Heidegger to describe the situation of humankind as 'thrown' into a world which they cannot comprehend and which they had no share in making. People achieved a kind of freedom in this way; they had desperately looked for it and passionately affirmed it. But it was only fragmentary freedom, gained mainly by declaring the greater part of reality to be senseless. The consequent dialectic between nature and freedom is inhuman and unpalatable. So modern people try once more to escape and grasp again their true, full humanity.

This situation, complex but concrete, affects not only philosophers but also many young people. Awareness of it helps us to understand some of the things that are happening in our world, the tensions and stresses in the field of culture and science, and even the conflicts in the personal and family life of thousands. We can understand the rebellion of Buñuel and his sympathizers; they cannot accept the situation, but they know of no way out. In their desperate search for freedom, modern writers and artists have tried to break through all the norms and structures of life. But the end result has been a still greater lack of freedom, so that many find themselves asking whether even art itself has not been lost.

More than once I have been asked – and not only by 'bourgeois' Christians – whether all mainstream modern art is not in essence like Hans Christian Andersen's story of 'The Emperor's New Clothes'. One is tempted to sympathize with this question, but to answer yes is to pose another problem: how do people get into a situation so devoid of freedom that they think they see clothes where none exist? How else can we describe the horrors of modern drama, and films like *Un Chien Andaloux?* How else does the work of a Raysse get into a museum? Almost inescapably, these modern works present themselves as fruits of the modern attitude toward life.

Our basis for art

Art can flourish only in and from freedom. And it can gain warmth and joy only from love, not hate. Our task as Christians should be to work on the basis of the freedom which we have gained in Christ's redemption. We must ourselves be creatively involved. Far too often we are content to watch the activity of the world – admiring, amazed or irritated! We must look for positive ways to express a true vision of reality, and in searching for new forms we can breathe life into them so that they bring joy to our needy contemporary world.

Yet first of all we cannot do this in our own strength. Any Christian work which is begun without looking to the living God for help, strength and insight is doomed to powerlessness. We must never forget Jesus' words that apart from him we can do nothing good or meaningful (John 15:5, 6).

Secondly, when we ask for Christian activity in the arts, we are *not* calling for a sectarian style, the art of a subculture. We ask for art that is fully art, which springs from the fullness of what we are, and which takes into account the whole reality in which we live, a reality immeasurably greater than simply the total of nature plus human being. Such art will express joy and beauty, it will give honour and praise – but it will never close its eyes to sin and misery. It will be, in short, an art born of the freedom given to human beings by God. Art should be a form of play, rejoicing before the face of God (Proverbs 8:30).

Thirdly, nobody could imagine that the road we have just described will be easy and smooth. People do in fact long for freedom; but because they prefer darkness to light (John 3:19), enmity – or at least resistance – will be in store for us. We could go into this in more detail, but a reference to 1 Peter 3 must here suffice.

Fourthly, artistic freedom is a human freedom, that of a creature, and therefore not absolute: since the Fall people have longed to be equal with God, yet our freedom exists within the human limitations laid down by God. Without a norm for life there would be no point in talking about art or beauty; they would mean nothing without some regulating structure.[67] Paul in Galatians 5:23 mentions the fruit of the Spirit; 'against such things there is no law.' This certainly holds for artistic norms. It is only when we try to break the norms that we lose our freedom. The advice in Philippians 4:8, 9 to think about those things which are 'true . . . honest . . . just' (KJV) in no way hinders our work. On the contrary, it opens the whole world before us.

Some dangers to freedom[68]

When we talk about freedom, we usually mean freedom *from* something. One freedom we still have in the West is the freedom to produce art independently of political or other coercive social influences. This is the legacy of seventeenth-century civilization. Everyone knows how this freedom has been threatened in the twentieth century. We should not think here only of Nazi Germany or Soviet Russia but also recognize the dangers of a politics of subsidies, however well intended. We must really defend artistic freedom, demanding it even for works which we may not approve of.

Again and again, fearing that freedom might be misused, the church has tried to tie Christians to new laws. Christians have recoiled from Paul's passionate appeal to live out of the freedom in Christ, arguing, 'We never know where things may end up.' This legalism is the weakest point in modern Christianity, a striking proof that God's laws are wiser than human ones. And it is exactly here that the world, including Buñuel, most violently attacks the church. Christian freedom is not lawlessness but it is openness, the right to realize all the potentiality of our talent. Paul spent his life defending this freedom – he felt it basic to the Christianity he preached – and this in itself proves that even in those days people found it difficult to live by faith in the finished work of Christ and by trust in God. People always want to play it safe, and Christian leaders with the best intentions repeatedly tend to replace freedom with legalism. There are pharisees in every age.

Freedom should mean liberty to experiment, to walk in new paths and even to make something which goes against the ideas of a former generation. It also means the latitude to make works of art that are not perfect. Some critics may be long-suffering, but the rigid ones and especially the moralists should understand that perfection cannot be demanded – not immediately, at least! Such a demand cripples spontaneity; perhaps this explains the remarkable dearth of artistic activity within the church. To grasp freedom is to take a risk. God himself took a tremendous risk when he placed man in creation *with* his freedom. And in spite of its misuse since the Fall, God still preaches freedom, through the mouths of the prophets and apostles, and through Christ himself (John 8:32). Are we not trying to make ourselves wiser than our God if we refuse to take the risks implied in the freedom he has given us?

Freedom also liberates us from every historically conditioned cultural ideal. It is ridiculous to maintain that at any given time a person may work only in such and such a way if what he or she does is to be meaningful and to the point. We are never completely bound within a particular situation, although of course we cannot live totally outside it. We need never be dominated at a given period by one style or manner; there are always other possibilities and other answers. Historicism, which says that people are caught within the norm of their own time, kills every kind of free creativity. I think we see this in our time, when so many feel obliged to follow the latest fashion and the most way-out art. This is mere snobbery and shows a lack of courage to accept the responsibility of freedom.

We are free to choose whatever subject matter, style or technique we find useful; free to be traditional; free to try something entirely new; free to illustrate biblical stories or noble ideals, and free to focus on the smallest flower. The art historian of the future may perhaps be able to trace where the tradition came from, what was the source of the new art;

he or she may even find that something truly new has emerged. But the artist should not be worried by fear of future art critics. The artist should be driven by what seems appropriate and sensible at a particular time.

The artist also needs the freedom to create art which is connected to life. One of the strongest disagreements we have with modern art is its belief that the artist is a prophet, and art a kind of revelation. This kind of thinking has been responsible for many modern works which are not so much works of art as arguments in a kind of theological debate, often of a nihilistic or anarchistic character. Little inspiration seems to come from the reality in which the artist lives. As in the case of Buñuel, whose surroundings seem a long way from the setting he depicts in his films.

Modern art is supposed to be autonomous, but there is an impoverishment, a loss of freedom, when we cut art loose from its ties with life and place it in a vacuum, a kind of scientific laboratory. The full reality of human life is infinitely removed from the 'reality' of modern gnosticism. There is no need, every time an artist makes something beautiful, to rap him over the knuckles saying, 'Don't you know about the atom bomb, about Vietnam, about the injustices of our society, about our country's heartless bureaucracy?' We are not saying that artists should never portray evil and depict the unreal and the sentimental. But a nihilistic theology offering a counterfeit reality cannot be forced on us for no better reason than that it is the style of our time. We can achieve a much deeper and better understanding of reality than those who speak of *échec* and *nausée*.

What a gulf there is separating *Un Chien Andaloux* from, for example, the blues of the African-Americans, those 'songs of sorrow and frustration'. When the black people sing 'The sun rises in the east and goes down in the west, you never know what is best,' they are using poetry to express a troubling situation; but they evoke a compassion seldom achieved by Buñuel.

Christian artists must not be misled by the spirit of the age with its anarchistic lack of freedom. They should investigate everything while retaining the good (1 Thessalonians 5:21). This will lead them, perhaps unwittingly, to function as salt, inspiring others to work out the full meaning of their true humanity, unrestricted by a narrow philosophy or theory. It has always been the task of Christians to unmask pseudo-gods or false ideals and to reopen a vista towards the fullness of reality.

This is not an invitation to look nostalgically back to some golden age of the past. Instead we should have our eyes focused on the future in the hope of a fresh, new vision. We must beware of traditionalism, and instead accept our responsibility towards the future on the basis of a living faith.

We started our discussion of Buñuel by asking whether what he showed was, in fact, reality. We conclude by saying that if the Bible is true, then Buñuel is wrong. The strength of Christianity lies precisely in the fact that it offers joy in the midst of suffering because of its certainty that justice will finally come. It knows that evil has *already* lost the battle and will eventually be totally defeated – not by people who may have good intentions but by the living God through the work of Christ Jesus (see Romans 8:18 ff.; 1 Corinthians 15:20 ff.). We must therefore take hold of the freedom that Buñuel has lost. It is the freedom to love our neighbour, to perceive creation as beautiful and fascinating, and to reckon life worth living.

6
Does Art Need Justification?

A new secular religion?

Somewhere between the Middle Ages and our times, art became Art. The visual arts had always been understood as a craft, even if a very special craft. In the fifteenth century, however, and specifically since Giotto, the position of art began to change. Artists began to aspire towards more recognition, hoping to see painting take its place with poetry, scholarship and letters and even be introduced into the circle of the seven liberal arts. Some great artists like Raphael, Leonardo, Michelangelo and Dürer nearly achieved this status, but for lesser artists it was out of the question.

In the eighteenth century, however, art finally took its place as a form of 'high culture'. To be an artist could mean to be a genius, one of the great leaders of humanity, a seer, a prophet, a high priest of culture. Art with a capital A even came to challenge the place of religion itself, becoming a new religion in a secularized world. Also, the term 'culture' took on a new meaning, separate from the natural sciences, economics and technology. (Someone who is favourably inclined might say that culture involves high human pursuits, removed from the practical things of daily life. Someone less sympathetic might call culture a pastime for the rich, or the *nouveau riche* middle class. Expressed negatively, culture has no real meaning at all and is the hobby of a snobbish coterie.)

For the few really great artists, this change was no obstacle. They came to be revered as superior people; their works were sold and discussed in the learned and cultured circles. For the vast majority of artists, however, the change was almost disastrous. Although their profession was regarded as high and important, and surrounded with the aura of Art, often their works could not live up to such a high standard. Certainly a less prominent artist could not survive on the income from work regarded by most people as inessential. Art was something to look at or, in the case of the musician, to listen to or, in the case of literature, to read. Visual art especially was certainly not something to spend much money on. As a result, many artists were very poor, and even important works could not be produced without high subsidy. Now art, or Art, has become elevated and refined but must be kept alive in a highly artificial way. (Note the implications of the very term 'artificial'.)

Another result of the present situation is that along with Art, a new kind of artistic category has emerged, a type of work which is confined to the realm of the crafts but which is often not recognized as valid primarily because most artists of quality tend to despise it. We refer here to popular art, which is often called 'commercial' or 'entertainment' art. To entertain seems to be one of the great sins in art. Yet if we hold such a position we are challenged by the quality of a waltz by Johann Strauss or the jazz of Duke Ellington; and in commercial art there are such outstanding figures as Toulouse-Lautrec and Cassandre.

Not only the artists but art itself has suffered from this shift. Placed too high in the total culture, art has lost its ties with reality and therefore its meaning. Abstract art is one result of this change. Also, because art has taken on religious significance, it has given birth to some very strange offspring. As a result art has for most people become an esoteric activity, extremely intellectualistic on the one hand, and fostering irrationality on the other. It has become confined to the museum.

A museum is a place where one usually finds objects which have lost their function in contemporary life. The modern art museum, however, has almost become the nihilistic temple for an anti-religion. In a way, this is also true of the museums of the older arts, like the Metropolitan Museum in New York or the National Gallery in Washington. 'Cultured' people know the famous works of art in order to refer to them just like Christians quote Bible texts.

As a result people have come to examine the true meaning and function of art. What is art, really? What is its importance? Why bother with it at all? Certainly in teaching, one must deal with these pertinent – or should we say impertinent – questions. And many answers have been formulated. Art teaches us deep things. But, say some, art should not be didactic; it is meant to enrich life. Is art, then, only for the rich or for snobs? For those who have the time, the money and that peculiar gift called artistic sensibility? Can art never be for the toiling, hard-working men and women, or for those who live far from all cultural centres? Oh yes, most people do have paintings on their walls, but that is only decoration; one could certainly not call it Art. Art is too high and special. Indeed, art has become something lofty and removed, and even the interpretation of art has become a strange and difficult pursuit, since one must read into the works meaning that is certainly not evident to the 'unenlightened' masses.

The elevation of art to its current position is in itself a sign of the crisis that exists. High Art has become strange and esoteric; popular art, with which most people are surrounded, is often very low in quality, revealing and even promoting the spiritual poverty of our age.

This crisis makes life very difficult for many artists and art students. For many, art has become a gratuitous activity. Nevertheless they continue, often searching for their own identity in their work, like the philosopher depicted by Max Klinger: a man looking in a mirror at his own image.[69] Art is said to be an expression of a person's innermost being.

But what if there is nothing inside? The artist is supposed to be a genius, and geniuses cannot be taught. Young artists are frequently left to themselves, to find themselves and their own forms of expression. They often reach a point of despair; but when they cry for help they are thrown back upon themselves and many crumble under the load. Unless they are really strong and endowed with great talents, or filled with a powerful ego-drive and able to carry off a profitable programme of self-promotion, success in the art world will elude them.

A hedonistic pastime?

Art is in crisis. This is no less true in the Christian world, where perhaps the crisis is even doubled. On the one hand Christians are children of their own times; on the other hand they tend to regard the arts as the very epitome of the non-Christian spirit of our age. Two different responses then follow: either one abstains from the arts altogether, and leaves them to the 'worldly pagans'; or one enters the art world, hesitantly and with many questions and doubts. Each of these positions requires some justification.

The justification of the first attitude may be that after all, a person's real calling in life is to be a witness for Christ and to live the 'spiritual' life. And since art does not enter this realm, it can be ignored. The interesting thing is, however, that having taken this attitude, one cannot really avoid art. For having discarded art, one still uses a stained-glass window in the chapel and one illustrates an evangelistic pamphlet or church paper, using either 'old' art (like a copy of a Holman Hunt painting) or popular art. That the pamphlet therefore looks cheap does not seem to bother anyone. After all, the message is the only thing that counts!

The second attitude, that of the Christian who does enter the art field, is often difficult to defend in the face of the first. 'Isn't it sinful to devote a life to the arts, which are worldly anyway, only for giving pleasure?' Many a Christian who is active in the arts is made to feel like a kind of hedonist, someone who never works (art is not work!) and who is in constant danger of falling into the evil snares of this world. Usually he or she is seen as a person of strange or impractical ideas. After all, what has art to do with the realities of daily life, especially 'Christian' daily life?

Many fine Christians who have a talent or an interest in the arts are forced to defend their involvement by saying that art is an excellent means of evangelism. When art is used as a tool for evangelism it is often insincere and second-rate, devalued to the level of propaganda. I would call this a form of prostitution, a misuse of one's talent.

A gift of God?

Art is not a religion, nor an activity relegated to a chosen few, nor a mere worldly, superfluous affair. None of these views of art does justice to the creativity with which God has endowed people. It is the ability to make something beautiful (as well as useful), just as God made the world beautiful and said, 'It is good.' Art as such needs no justification; rather, it demands a response, like that of the twenty-four elders in Revelation who worship God for the very act of creation itself:

> You are worthy, our Lord and God,
> to receive glory and honour and power,
> for you created all things,
> and by your will they were created and have their being.[70]

The supreme justification for all creation is that God has willed it to be. And so there is no need to justify, let us say, a tree. A tree is there and is meaningful because God made it. Of course a tree has many functions: birds sit on its branches, cattle rest in its shadow, and people use its wood for building houses or making fires. What would the world be without trees? Yet even if the tree is indispensable to many ecological cycles and useful to humankind, none of these functions alone, nor even their sum total, can provide the justification for and the meaning of the tree. The tree has meaning simply because God made it; that meaning surpasses all its functions. If we do not see this we are not far from accepting naturalist evolutionary theories, which are all based on functionalist assumptions.

God's creatures require no justification. God has given them their value by including them in the totality of his creation. In the same way, our personal human qualities and activities need no justification. To love is indeed a command of God, but a justification for it is not given. To marry, to praise the Lord, to till the ground, to prepare meals, to talk, to feel, to think – all need no apology within the context of 'Hallowed be thy name, thy will be done.'

In the same way, art needs no justification. It is meaningful in itself, not only as an evangelistic tool or to serve a practical purpose or to be didactic. Art must be free: free from politics (including church politics); free from traditions of the past, free from fashions of the present, free from the judgment of the future; and free from our economic and social needs. Art cannot be turned into a mere function of any of these without losing its indispensable place in human life. After all, Christ died for us in order to restore our humanity, and to give meaning back to God's creation. Not only is evangelism Christian, but all of life is Christian, unless we would make Christ very small.

But if art needs no justification it also does not follow that art is to be art for art's sake. Just as a tree, being more than the totality of its functions, nevertheless *has* functions, so art is not just there to be art, but is bound by a thousand ties to reality. Nothing is simply autonomous. A tree, a human being, a work of art – all are part of that wonderful fabric which we call reality; no thread can be missing without impoverishing the whole.

So even if art has meaning in itself, it can never be on its own. It would wither and die. It is tied in two ways to reality. On the one hand, art deals *with* reality; it is *about* fear, hope, joy, love, our surroundings, the things we love or hate. On the other hand, art is used *in* reality. Music, rhetoric, poetry make up a large part of our social functions and religious activities; and architecture, furniture and textile design, interior decoration, painting and illustration provide the setting for our movements and actions.

No matter whether art receives a prominent place or serves in the background, the fascinating truth is that the more it becomes engaged in reality, and the more concrete its manifold ties with our daily life, the more we will recognize that it needs no justification.

Appendix : Letter to a Christian Artist

Diemen, The Netherlands
August 23, 1966

Your letter reached me yesterday after its trans-Atlantic voyage, and I propose to answer you directly. Your request touches on a problem I have been thinking about for a long time. Maybe what follows can be of help to you. I'd like to approach the matter in a schematic way, pointing out some principles.

Your questions concern your wish to paint – that is, to work as an artist – as a Christian. It really is remarkable that you decided to do this when you were just converted. Many times new Christians just drop their artistic careers because they think painting and art today are incompatible with being a real Christian. I'm glad you made this decision and hope to help you by suggesting the following principles for Christian artists:

1. If God has given us *talents* we may use them creatively – or rather, we *must* use them creatively. A Christian artist is not different from, say, a Christian teacher, minister, scholar, merchant, housewife or anybody else who has been called by the Lord to specific work in line with his or her talents. There are no specific rules for artists, nor do they have specific exemptions to the norms of good conduct God laid down for people. An artist is simply a person whose God-given talents ask him or her to follow the specific vocation of art. There may be circumstances when love towards God would forbid certain artistic activities or make them impossible, but the present moment in history does not ask for such a sacrifice. Quite the contrary. We – the Christian world and the world at large – desperately need artists.

2. To be God's child means to be offered *freedom* – the Christian freedom Christ himself and Paul in his letters say much about. This freedom is most important for anybody who wants to do artistic work. Without freedom there is no creativity, without freedom no originality, without freedom no art, without freedom even no Christianity. This freedom can exist only if it is based on love towards God and our neighbours, and if we become new people through the finished work of Christ, and the Holy Spirit is given to us. Without this base, freedom may easily mean being free from God and consequently free to indulge all the cravings of the sinful heart of an unredeemed

person. (For more on this matter of freedom, see Paul's letter to the Galatians.)

Christian freedom is different from humanistic freedom, the freedom people give themselves to build a world after their own devising (as was tried by the Enlightenment and the humanist development after that time in the Western world). Humanistic freedom leads to all kinds of problems, as our Western world is now learning from experience. Freedom in the biblical sense is in no way negative – shun this, don't do that, you must leave that alone, keep away from this. Christian freedom has nothing to do with a set of rules by which you must bind yourself; indeed, such rules may easily be pseudo-Christian. Freedom is the necessary basis for creativity, for creativity is impossible when there is timidity, when you allow yourself to be bound by narrow rules. Do not think the modern art world is free – but we will turn to that later.

Freedom is positive. It means being free from tradition, from the feeling that everything you do has to be original, from certain fixed rules said to be necessary in art – but also from the thought that to be creative you must break all kinds of rules and standards.

Freedom means also that there are no prescriptions for subject matter. There is no need for a Christian to illustrate biblical stories or biblical truth, though he or she may of course choose to do that. Artists have the right to choose a subject that they think worthwhile. But non-representational art provides no more freedom than the most involved allegorical or storytelling art.

Freedom includes the right to choose your own style, to be free from tradition but also from modernity, from fashion, from today and tomorrow as well as from yesterday. Yet there is no need to slap the contemporary in the face, as some streams of art nowadays deem necessary. Christian freedom also is freedom from the sinful lust for money, from seeking human praise, from the search for celebrity. It is the freedom to help a neighbour out and give him or her something to delight in.

3. There are *norms for art* that are a part of God's creation. Without them art would be an empty word without sense. To say a person has been given a feeling for art and beauty (everybody has, to a certain extent), that he or she has been granted a strong subjective sense of artistic rightness, is but another way to say that he or she has been given an understanding of certain norms God laid down in his creation, the world in which we live. We call this taste, a feeling for design and colour, the ability to

grasp the inner harmony of a complex of forms and colours, the understanding of the inner relationship among elements of the subject matter, the ability to recognize the indefinable dividing lines between poor and good art, between worn-out symbols and fresh ways of saying things that are important to people.

These norms do not stand in the way when we want to live in Christian freedom; they are a part of our world and our nature. Only when people revolt and do not want to be creatures, when they want to be God and not human, do they feel constricted by these norms. For those who love the Lord and rejoice in his good and beautiful creation, these norms provide the opportunity to live in freedom and to create. As one cannot act and live free as a woman if one is not a woman and has not the nature of a woman, so the norms for beauty and art are at the same time the opportunities to see beauty and create art.

4. When God created – and in that way made the perception of beauty and the human creation of art possible – he gave art (or any artistic endeavour) a place in this world in which we live; and that world he called good. (I added artistic endeavour because we have to think not only of the rarefied museum type of art called Art with a capital A today, but also of all other types, including ceramics, dance music, pictures used in Sunday schools, and so on. We shall come back to this.) Art is here because God meant it to be here.

So art has its own task and meaning. There is no need to try to justify one's artistic activity by making works with a moralistic message, even if one is free to emphasize moral values. Nor is there any need to think one has to serve as a critic of culture, or always provide eye-openers to the non-artists, or teach, or evangelize, or do whatever other lofty things one can think of. Art has done its task when it provides the neighbour with things of beauty, a joy forever. Art has direct ties with life, living, joy, the depth of our being human, just by being art, and therefore it needs no external justification. That is so because God, who created the possibility of art and who laid beauty in his creation, is the God of the living and wants people to live. God is the God of life, the Life-giver. The Bible is full of this.

Art is not autonomous. 'Art for art's sake' was an invention of the last century to loosen the ties between art and morality; that is, to give art the freedom to depict all kinds of sins as if they were not sinful, but simply human. The human understanding of depravity, of morality, of good and bad was thereby undermined or erased. The results we are seeing today, in our century. The meaning of art is its being art; but it is not autonomous, and it has thousands of ties with human life and thought. When artists cease to consider the world in its manifold forms outside the artistic domain, their art withers into nothingness because it no longer has anything to say.

Much abstract art today is art, yes; but it has little meaning because it is *only* art. All its ties with reality have been cut. This applies as much to a ceramic product as to a painting. Art has its own meaning and needs no excuse. But it loses its meaning if it does not want to be anything but art and therefore cuts its ties with life and reality, just as scholarly work loses its importance and interest if learning is sought for its own sake. Art and science become aestheticism and scholasticism if made autonomous. They become meaningless idols.

The artist's work can have meaning for the society in which God put him or her if the artist does not withdraw into an ivory tower or try to play the prophet or priest, or – turning in the other direction – in false modesty consider him or herself to be merely an artisan. The artist has to make art while thinking of his or her neighbours in love, helping them and using his or her talents on their behalf.

5. Most art today expresses a spirit, *the spirit of our age*, which is not Christian. In some ways it is postchristian, in others antichristian, in still others humanistic. Here and there are Christian artists who try to do their work in a godly spirit. But often their brothers and sisters leave them alone, distrusting their creativeness or doubting that they are Christians. False art theories that have pervaded the Christian world – the artist as an a-social being, a nonconformist in the wrong sense, a dangerous prophet, an abnormal being who lives in an alien world – are often responsible for this attitude. But some Christian artists themselves hold these false views and look down with contempt on their fellow Christians. Anyway, there is a lot of confusion.

That the art of the world at large is also in a deep crisis does not make things easier. We live in a society where there is a break manifest between the mass of common people and the elite, and another break between the natural sciences and technical realities on one side and religion (most of the time rather mystical) of a completely subjectivistic and irrationalistic type on the other. We who live in this world cannot act as if these deep problems did not exist.

There is *no real Christian tradition* in the arts today to turn to. If an artist wants to work as a Christian and do something that he or she can stand for and bear responsibility for, such an artist has to start with the freedom based in a true faith in the living God of Scripture. Such an artist has to make art that is relevant to our day. Therefore, he or she has to understand our day. And, in order to gain from all that is good and fine today and yet avoid being caught by the spirit of our age and its false art principles, he or she must study modern art in all its different aspects deeply and widely, trying to analyse the language modern artists use, their syntax and grammar, in order to be able to hear correctly the message they profess to speak. To analyse, understand, and criticize lovingly, loving people but hating sin, in order to avoid their mistakes but gain from their achievements – that is the Christian artist's task. A new Christian tradition, as a fruit of faith, can grow only if artists who understand their work and task, their world and its problems, really set to work.

6. But what has the Christian artist to offer the world? The artist has *a freedom to do something*, not just the freedom for freedom's sake. What should such an artist aim at? Let's be careful not to lay down new rules. There are no biblical laws that art must be realistic or symbolic or sentimental, or must seek only idealized beauty.

The artist as a Christian is free, but not with a purposeless freedom. The artist as a Christian is free in order to praise God and love his or her neighbours.

These are basic laws. What do they mean in practice? May I refer, this time without comment, to Philippians 4:8 – 'Finally, brethren, whatsoever things are true, whatsoever things are honest, whatsoever things are just, whatsoever things are pure, whatsoever things are lovely, whatsoever things are of good report; if there be any virtue, and if there be any praise, think on these things' [KJV]. Here we read what a Christian standing in freedom as a new person, in God's strength and with the help of the Holy Spirit, must search for. This also applies to the Christian as an artist. It is up to him or her to work, to pray and to study, in order to realize as much as he or she possibly can of these truly human and life-promoting principles.

In the Lord,
H.R. Rookmaaker

Part Three

Creative Sharing of the Gospel

7
Communicating the Gospel to Modern People

Over the years, in L'Abri Fellowship and elsewhere, I have talked to many young people coming from a wide variety of backgrounds. Often they have asked me what I thought about evangelism, whether there were principles to go by or methods to follow. In this chapter I should like to consider some questions that are often asked and to suggest some principles for communicating the gospel to others.

Our point of contact

A Christian is human
Being a Christian is not a matter of wearing blue earmuffs with polka dots. It does not mean wearing red socks, or putting on a false nose. How often the world thinks, 'There go those Christians! He is a decent fellow, and she is friendly. They may go to church on Sunday and pray before meals; but thank goodness, they're pretty normal otherwise.'

If this is all it means to be a Christian, then we are indeed only ordinary people with an extra something added. Just a little strange, a bit odd in some ways. If this is the way we want to witness then there is no point in even beginning. What should make Christians different from other people is that they are more fully human, more what God intended people to be when he created them. Not people with odd rules that only isolate them from their neighbours or beliefs that have nothing to do with daily life but seem appropriate only for the soul, the future, or for the crises in life.

The gospel is more than a mere opinion, a personal discovery or something our fathers or forefathers dreamed up. It is the *truth*. Only then is it worth talking about.

Furthermore, the Bible which contains the gospel is very definitely not a religious book or a collection of devotional texts. The Bible is about reality and has something to tell us about life and relationships today. As such it is our standard, the basis of our practical and intellectual decisions. It is crucial that we remain willing to submit our words and actions to its correction.

Know the other's world
In telling others about Christ, we must keep in mind whom we are speaking to and be familiar with their world. Paul said we must be a Jew

to the Jews and a Greek to the Greeks. Many misunderstand these words to imply a compromise, as if we should think and act just as the others do and then hope they will be prepared to listen to the little extra we have! But Paul is talking about something completely different. He spoke to Jews very differently from the way he addressed the heathen on the Areopagus at Athens. Because of their different backgrounds and occupations, their knowledge and the framework of their thinking, they had different interests which had to be taken into account.

Therefore, just as missionaries have to learn the language (which involves some knowledge of background and mentality) of the country they are sent to, we too must learn to speak the language of the other people. Like the 'Jews' or 'Greeks', our neighbours have their own language – even though we may both speak English. When we say, 'God says this' or 'God says that', what do our listeners understand by the word 'God'? The Supreme Being? Nature?

There are many gods in this world, but they are utterly different from the God of Abraham, Isaac and Jacob, the Father of Jesus Christ. We must make clear who God is. Otherwise, when we speak of him our neighbours may have a totally different idea of God in mind. We must be sure that all our terms are understandable to the other people; this involves a genuine sensitivity to the framework of their thoughts and feelings.

For example, a person who has been brought up as a Christian may find it quite obvious that people are sinful. But if a Christian uses the word 'sin' he or she cannot be sure what others associate with the word. Even if they see it as something very terrible, it may still not be what the Christian meant. Nor does it really help to use a statement from the Creed or the Authorized Version of the Bible. These may have a certain connotation for churchgoers, but the language is likely to be incomprehensible to our neighbours, seeming to come straight out of the Middle Ages!

We should, moreover, never begin evangelism by discussing matters that are secondary to the gospel itself, like church attendance, the Christian way of life or the ecumenical movement. It is of no use to talk of these things to someone who does not yet know God. Witnessing is not advertising; our goal is not to get members for our church, our community, our cause. Our message is not for the benefit of institutions we hold sacred, but for people.

A different world view. Modern people have a radically different world view from that of the Christian. People's understanding of the world and of themselves has profoundly changed, particularly since the eighteenth century. I am not talking here about theories or intellectual ideas far removed from life. The world view of modern persons is the result of many generations of teaching during which certain assumptions and principles have come to form the foundation of their outlook on almost everything. Although they may not know the names of the great philosophers, past and present, their starting point when thinking about human being is humanism, and their presuppositions about nature are derived from the natural sciences. Even the present crisis in humanism itself and the failure of science to provide adequate answers to life do not drive them back to God but make them turn (sceptically perhaps) to the most recent modern movements in the scant hope that they may offer a way out of their dilemma.

In their lifestyle and goals modern people are very different from us as well. This does not necessarily make them wrong; on some points they could well be right. (Sad to say, it has often not been Christians but unbelievers who have taken the lead in issues like ecology and the energy crisis.) We must get to the very basis of modern people's thinking and see what can hold before God within the reality he has created.

It is no use closing our eyes to the world view of the unbeliever. We have to be open. We must be willing to put our insights and knowledge to work, and to study. Contemporary Christians who know nothing, for example, of Marxism are neglecting a vital area of the battle. If they fail to understand the Marxist position, they will never be able to enter into discussions with Marxists nor answer the problems they pose.

Modern people are aware of the world's many injustices and hypocrisies. They see oppression, abuse of power and the economic dictatorship of big business. If they blame Christianity for these things, we must not defend the present order by pretending that it is Christian. We must stand alongside modern people against the decay and downfall of our Western world. But we can also show them what has gone wrong, and that true deliverance can be found only in Christ, who died to make a better world possible.

Indeed, a great strength of the biblical message is that it is directed not only towards the individual but also towards the community and the nation. The gospel is for every nation, tribe, people and tongue (Revelation 7:9). Some Christians have forgotten this.

Christianity is not a mystical consolation to help the individual escape daily reality. Instead, it urges us to go even deeper into reality, which has been created by our Father. This is why I stress that we must be so careful with our use of certain words. We preach a real Christ who felt real anger at injustice, greed, and hypocrisy, and who died on a real cross.

It is difficult to communicate with the truly modern person, who is often to be found among the working classes and the intellectuals. As a result many Christians have given up trying to reach either of these groups. We have been reaching only the middle classes, those who still have some knowledge of Christianity and are willing to sit in a stadium with thousands of others and listen to a comforting old message. But in spite of difficulties in communication, modern people will have to stand before God one day to be judged and see the results of their sin. If we have not warned them, God will require their blood at our hands (Ezekiel 33:8; 1 Corinthians 10:11).

The 'silent majority'. Many of our contemporaries are not really 'modern people', but what we could call bourgeois; they are part of the 'silent majority'. These are the people who want to avoid the gloomy conclusion that unless something drastic happens, our society will soon be finished. They believe in humanity and want to live a 'normal' human life. Optimistically they insist that even if the present is not very rosy, humankind will still be able to build a great future. After all, have not new times of prosperity always emerged after periods of crisis? Bourgeois people want to be happy, and their gods – small but powerful – are money, sex and comfort. But bourgeois people have no real basis for their optimism and they pay a high price for their comfort – namely real life, real humanity.

What are their standards? Maybe they stand for law and order – after all, there are so many crooks who may try to rob them of their security and their ease! Even if their basic philosophy is not so different from that of modern people they try to avoid seeing the consequences, the death and the dirt. They close their ears to the groans of the poor and the oppressed – though they may occasionally give money to charity to ease their conscience.

The bourgeois has no consistent standards. What stops Mr Smith from committing adultery? The danger of being found out. (What would happen to his career? What would the neighbours think?) He tells his son to dress neatly. Why? Because of what the neighbours might say. But if neighbours represent the only norm for life, then the son is likely to say at a certain point, 'I will do as I please; I will dress as I choose and go to bed with the neighbour's daughter.' This is his protest against the pragmatism, the utilitarianism of his father who has only practical reasons for not committing adultery. There are many such sons – and daughters – today.

Bourgeois people lead a very normal life. They have a few children. They go on vacation. They receive a gold watch after twenty-five years on the job, and a pension when they reach sixty-five. After that, there are a few years in an old people's home, and finally the grave. We must admit that Christians are often like this. That is why the protest of modern people has often been aimed at Christians – not only because of their bourgeois ways but because they have failed to provide any alternatives.

An old Beatles' song describes Eleanor Rigby, whose task it is to darn the minister's socks. Finally one day she dies. The minister buries her and washes his hands. 'All the lonely people, where do they all come from?' Why do Christians keep their mouth shut? Have we nothing to say? We should be concerned for these lonely people, and also for the bourgeois who have lost the way of life.

I speak of them as bourgeois rather than as middle class, because in this sense of the word many intellectuals and working-class people are also bourgeois. Bourgeois people are even harder to reach than modern people. Modern people know about the lostness of this world, but the bourgeois try to deny it. All the songs of the protesters cannot shake them out of their comfort. They even manage to harvest some fruits from the protest culture, making money from pop music and posters.

We must certainly not preach the bourgeois an 'easy gospel' that satisfies their spiritual cravings, fills their emptiness and even offers them security in the next life! A mystical type of Christianity, stressing that all worldly things will pass only gives them false security. They feel confident that they can live what they call a 'normal' human life – they even have a foundation for it. But the gospel is truth, not a psychological tranquilizer! Becoming a bourgeois to the bourgeois means telling them that their dreams are legitimate, but that ultimate peace and happiness cannot be found by closing one's eyes and ears to the evil in the world.

Modern artists and thinkers have also tried to wake up the bourgeois and make them see the world as it really is. Martin Esslin, writing about the modern theatre of the absurd, says:

> There are enormous pressures in our world that seek to induce mankind to bear the loss of faith and moral certainties by being drugged into oblivion – by mass entertainment, shallow material satisfactions, pseudo-explanations of reality, and cheap ideologies ... today ... the need to confront man with the reality of his situation is greater than ever. For the dignity of man lies in his ability to face reality in all its senselessness; to accept it freely, without fear, without illusions – and to laugh at it.[71]

The Christian would agree about the bourgeois, but never tell them to laugh at their lostness; that would be cruel. Better then to let them sleep.

We must make the bourgeois see that this world is in turmoil because of what humankind has done. We are not just discussing 'secular' matters, but events that can be understood only if we see in them the active working of God. Isaiah 9:18 describes the situation: 'Wickedness burns like a fire.' Yes, what people do is destructive, but God adds to this (verse 19): 'By the wrath of the LORD Almighty the land will be scorched.' As Revelation teaches us, when Christ opens the seals and the trumpets sound, judgment will come over a world which has turned from God. Nevertheless, there is hope. It is possible to return to the Lord in repentance, with a genuine hunger to see justice done. This goes far beyond merely seeking to save one's own soul and is the heart of our message to the bourgeois.

Lost people are still human

Everyone is searching for humanity and truth. And everyone lives in the same world as the Christian, bearing God's image. This is the point of contact between the Christian and the people of today. We must never forget that the other people are also human. Perhaps sometimes they want to forget that themselves; they try to say that humanity means nothing and that love is only sexual attraction. But in their heart they know this is not true.

At this point I would like to tell a true story that took place in the 1950s. A boy and girl, students of Jean-Paul Sartre, were sitting on the left bank of the Seine, weeping. Why? Because they loved each other and wanted to express their love. But they had come to believe that the words 'I love you' meant only 'I have a sexual urge.' False reductionist theories had told them that love was no more than a bourgeois façade meant to give respectability to the animal instincts of procreation. And so they wept, because they were denying what their experience told them was true – that love does indeed exist.

This couple, like many other people in our modern world, could not abandon their humanity, and their tears were a protest as well as a sign of despair. Though truly persons, they were unable to live as such. People long for humanity because they are human. They cannot explain sin but know that it is there and sense that it brings death. Truly modern people have begun to realize that they cannot create a better world with their knowledge. They perceive that in spite of their great knowledge they have destroyed everything. As Peter Gay has said:

> Eighteenth-century thought had liberated man from his filial dependence on God and made him part of nature, but the philosophical anthropology of the philosophes (like Diderot), which promoted man from servitude, ironically enough demoted him at the same time – from his position little lower than the angels to a position among the intelligent animals. While man seemed on the point of conquering the worldly domain through his critical intelligence, he was faced with a second expulsion from his terrestrial paradise, and this time the avenging angel was man himself.[72]

Yet leftist theorists and activists continue to long for a better world. They point out injustices like the heartless use of money and power, the manipulation of desperate people by propaganda and other destructive practices in our society.

Indeed, modern people acknowledge many injustices. But they no longer understand that sin originates with disobedience to God and a lack of love towards one's neighbour. That the abuse of money and power, corruption and crime are not recognized as sin may even be the basic mistake, a sin in itself, whereby people continue to talk 'objectively' about the structural ills of society. I do not mean to say that such structural faults do not exist, but more is wrong with the world than just organizational or sociological weaknesses. Sin goes deep and defies analysis. And unless sin is 'cured' at a very deep level (which is what Christ came to do), all human endeavour to better society is in vain.

People long for an ideal world, and to realize such a world they are willing to sacrifice both freedom and human lives. But in their hearts there is despair. Knowing that humanity is not won this way, they still try, even against all odds. They keep hoping that human being itself can be changed if the order of the world is altered.

We must admit that there is validity in their longings, and we may even admire their persistence. If God did not exist and Christ had not come as the supreme Protester – One who would not accept this world full of sin and death, but was and is able to do something definitive about it – then we too would feel compelled at least to try to make a better world ourselves, even if deep inside we knew the effort was hopeless.

Our contemporaries' craving for justice proves their humanity, and we may add that it is Christianity which has made people aware of the injustices. Without the preaching of the gospel, the leftist ideology – which is in effect a secularization of the gospel – would not have existed.

Why then are so many modern activists antichristian? Because Christianity has often forsaken its calling, and followed the ruling powers. Because Christians have accepted existing injustices. But also, let us add, because some Christians who have done more than most people realize may not call attention to their own good works. And finally, because history taught and studied for two centuries from a humanistic, secularized, so-called neutral point of view has made us forget what the Lord has done and what fruits faith has brought forth. We overlook the spiritual force that motivated the Reformers, and we have learned to explain their works in terms of social and economic forces and natural circumstances.

The fact remains, however, that most leftists are not optimists, but are basically existentialist in their outlook on human being. They – at least the deeper thinkers – know that a Saviour is needed. They know what is good and true because all reality testifies to it, including their own humanity. But the terrible truth is that, knowing what they know, they still are not converted (Revelation 9:20, 21). They know they are forfeiting their humanity; yet rejecting God's solution, they still seek answers in places where they cannot be found and continue on the road to final lostness. Paul describes this in the first chapter of Romans (verses 18 and 19), where he speaks of men who by their wickedness suppress the truth. Like all sin, this is incomprehensible. For sin takes away freedom; it destroys; it relegates people to an unnatural and broken world that lacks the very things they yearn for.

The situation in which we speak the gospel to our fellow human beings is critical. But in the midst of almost insurmountable difficulties we also find the point of hope that, because the other person is searching for humanity, we have something in common, a basis for communication. We can talk about good and evil, life and death. He or she will certainly know what we are talking about. And we can tell him or her what God has meant humanity to be, and what it still can be if we live as God's creatures in the open world which he has given us.

These things are not mere theories. Modern films and modern books (even pornographic ones) show that sin – the human quest to be free to indulge in lust and to search for happiness – is inevitably linked with disillusionment and death. Through it all echoes a scream of anguish. People are caught. They can find no adequate answer unless the vicious circle is broken by true redemption as they bow before the Creator and Saviour whose words give significance to life.

Summary

Today people are indeed caught in a vicious circle. We have already referred to the dilemma of the bourgeois. Their mentality, often marked by a Victorian morality, leads to the anti-bourgeois protest, 'Don't you see you are no more than a cog in the machine, a number in the computer? This is true reality. Your morals have no foundation – science has long ago disproved them. How can you go on living as you do?'

But even the protesters themselves gradually realize they cannot accept human being as nothing but an object of nature. They cry out for freedom, identity, humanity. But by then they can no longer discover what is true, for truth consists only in what science can prove.

Rebelling against this, modern people try to find their humanity by leaping into the area of existential freedom; they want to jump out of the box of technology in which they are caught, whereupon they find that even this little bit of freedom is an illusion. Some, like Timothy Leary and Allen Ginsberg, have extolled LSD as the open door to the mystical experience of freedom. Ironically, however, this 'freedom' is dependent on a technological product, a pill. But even Leary and Ginsberg were saying nothing new. In the 1920s Aldous Huxley wrote *Brave New World*, which describes a beautiful new world – beautiful, but unliveable; drugs were needed to make it bearable.

The use of drugs is further evidence that reality and humanity without a reference point are too much for modern people. They are willing to sever their contact with reality, to reduce their own consciousness of it, in the hope that it will become less of a burden. This, however, is an escape, not a solution.

Why do people go on in this way? Because they are human, and cannot stand still; they strive for real humanity. Our message to them must be that true humanity can be found only in the gospel.

Sometimes people finally do get to this point, only to discover all too often that Christians, individually and in the church, have reduced humanity again to something bourgeois. They are disappointed when they come up against a bourgeois Christian, for it means that Christianity has lost its flavour, its saltiness. Bourgeois Christians say they believe but live as if faith were nothing but religion, valuable only for the future life.

Our task, our calling, is to be human. Life has meaning, and love for our neighbour is possible. Our certainty lies neither in ourselves nor in nature; it lies in God, with whom life is an adventure.

We must let others see the consequences of their own point of view. We must show them how they have thrown away their humanity. We must tell them that God has a real answer to these questions, and that he, too, has no use for a lukewarm church (Revelation 3:16).

Some basic questions

There are some specific questions that non-Christians often ask, good questions which we cannot with honesty avoid. The present form of these questions may be different from that of the past, for modern people are influenced by modern thought forms. But the questions as such are not new; they come back in every age and are the very questions which the Bible answers.

I once had a Bible study with some thoughtful non-Christian students. They were existentialists. As I started with Romans 1:18, they began to ask questions. The amazing thing was that these were exactly the questions which Paul answered in the process of his own discourse. Sometimes the students even used almost the same words! As we continued, not only did they 'reconstruct' the whole letter up to chapter 8, but they also began to see that Paul was dealing not only with his contemporaries but with questions for all time, concerned as they are with the nature of human being and the world.

Here are some of the more recurrent questions, together with the main thrust of the biblical answer. It is most important to be clear about the nature of evangelism. Evangelism is not telling someone what a wonderful experience of Christ I have had, nor even what Christ has done for me. It does not mean saying, 'Look at me; am I not wonderful!' and thus hoping indirectly to show something of the Lord. No, it is instead standing alongside the non-Christian as a fellow sinful human being, also needing a Saviour. Then one can share the good news that the Saviour has come. Our Christian life is, at best, a means to show that what we preach is a reality.

Can we be sure that God exists?

In one way, the answer to this question must be no. Even if all his creation points to him, God is not part of it, nor of the things that people can see, understand or experience.

People often ask this question because they want the kind of proof which modern science would give. However, the approach to reality which accepts only those things we can weigh, measure or perceive with our senses will never lead to a proof of the existence of God. Indeed, the entire modern system of rationalistic thought was constructed to exclude God from this world, or at least from those things which scientists considered worth thinking about. There is no way to discover God by means of a system which deliberately denies him! God does not exist in the same way as the world exists; he is the Creator of that world, of all that exists, the Maker of existence itself.

It is preposterous for people to try to prove God. Rather, it is human being itself that has to be 'proved' before God. Today people try to prove theories in order to put their knowledge to use in practical ways; science and technology are closely related. One could conclude in this context that if we were able to prove God, we would then be able to manipulate him! This would perhaps be possible if God were lower than humanity, if he were impersonal – a kind of immense power-house. But we know that God the Creator is a personal God, a God who lives. In biblical terminology he is also a jealous God who is not going to share his place with any other god, and certainly not become the servant of a new god called 'human'.

We should never try to answer people when they ask whether God's existence can be proved. God is the Father, and his Son is the way, the truth and the life. They cannot be put on a level with anything on earth that people try to prove, whether a biological hypothesis, a sociological theory, or a philosophical speculation.

A quite different question is whether we can see God's work, his actions. Here the answer is yes. Just open your eyes, if they are not too dimmed by sin, prejudices and the excuses people use to escape considering whom he is (Zephaniah 1:12). Human doubts of God's existence are almost absurd for he has given a full and overflowing revelation in the Scriptures, where we find not only his words recorded but also his actions in history. He reminds Israel again and again: 'I am the LORD your God who brought you out of Egypt.' And there is so much more. The Scriptures are full of the objections of God, that he has sent his servants, his prophets, in vain and that people have refused to listen to him and tried to live as if he did not exist (Hosea 11:1–4). People will never receive a fuller answer about God than that given to Job: 'Where were you when I made this world?' People want a sign, but Christ said that the only one they would get would be his resurrection. The sign, in our midst for centuries, has been evaded ever since (Matthew 28:11–15).

If people can no longer see God, it may be because he is indeed hiding himself; but if so, then this is itself a judgment (see Isaiah 57:17 and Micah 3:5 ff.).

If God is a God of love, why did he make this world full of sorrow and suffering?

God's original creation was not a world full of pain and death; it was good. But the Evil one tries with human help to turn it into a horrible chaos. Nevertheless – and this is most important – God cannot accept the sufferings of men, women and children. When people talk about the evils of the world, they almost always mean the big things: war, famine or pestilence. Often they forget the sufferings of everyday life: unkind words, lack of love or freedom to communicate, lack of hope – all the many thousands of so-called 'minor injustices'.

God does not forget them. And he is angry. Christ, the supreme Protester, was incensed when he saw all these things (see, for example, Matthew 23). When a person protests, his or her words are feeble because a person cannot really alter things; his or her attempts often make the situation worse. Christ, however, was not only angry; he was able to do something.

This is the very heart of Christianity. Christ came to change things. He came, he died, he rose again from the dead, and his great work has continuing effects, described both in 1 Corinthians 15:20 ff. and in Revelation. If our protest is right and honest because our hearts are filled with sorrow, then we share the mind of Christ, whose protest was motivated not by defiance but by love.

The recent activities of extreme leftists, like the protest movement of the 1960s, have shocked many people, who cannot understand why others have rejected the beautiful world they are trying to build. But Christians can be shocked only if they have failed to hear the cry of the oppressed, the weak and the poor – the wretched of the world. Non-Christian protesters are much closer to where humanity should be than are bourgeois optimists who keep hoping that everything will turn out all right in the end.

If God is good, how can he accept the world as it is? Why does he not put an end to evil?

This question is closely related to the last, and has already been touched upon. Certainly we must empathize with its urgency, for the Bible itself is full of the cry, 'Awake, O Lord! Why do you sleep? . . . Rise up and help us; redeem us because of your unfailing love' (Psalm 44:23–26). The same cry is heard in the New Testament, as in Revelation 6:10, where the martyrs cry to God to avenge them and restore justice.

The Bible assures us that our cry is not in vain and that God indeed acts in the world. First Corinthians 10:1–4 is one of many biblical passages that remind us of this. However, it often seems to us to take very long before some things are corrected. That is because God in his patience wants to give humankind the opportunity to change. We must wait expectantly for the day when justice will finally prevail (Psalm 73:17 ff.). God hears the cry of the martyrs' blood and the groans of those who suffer unjustly, and will come in his glory to set everything right.

The thought of the Last Judgment fills many people with fear, but we should remember that it will be a great day, a day when order will be re-established, and no act of cruelty will pass unnoticed; the balance will finally be restored. We are told to look forward to that day, and to pray that it may come soon. God is waiting for many to be added to the number of those who have been forgiven in Christ and will stand in glory on the new earth (Revelation 7:9–17).

How can a loving God bring judgment over people?

Interestingly, this objection is the exact opposite of the last one. It is precisely because God loves that judgment must be. Love is not something soft and sweet. If God had said he was sorry that people had fallen, but then went no further, it would mean that he cared neither for humanity nor for his creation. There would have been no gospel, for the heart of the gospel is that God made the world and is still interested in it. Therefore God must come with judgment, for he is the only one who can put a stop to evil.

Judgment is not an arbitrary act, unrelated to the things people do. Judgment is a way of cleansing and preserving this world. Moreover, when God sent death as a part of the curse he put a check, a limit, on sin and evil. As a result, humanity can never become totally degenerate; they know how vulnerable they are, especially to death. The other side of the coin is that evil itself is never allowed to grow to complete fruition (Romans 8:19 ff.); humankind and creation have been spared its full consequences.

If one loves something, one cannot bear to see it destroyed. God loved his creation, but he also loved humankind and wanted them to be what they were originally created to be. He could not settle for a lower standard. If there were no judgment, we should have to accept humanity as being less than they really are. If we love people, we cannot do this.

We should turn the argument around and see that we human beings often underrate sin and evil; we just do not see their seriousness. While we talk flippantly because we are indifferent, God's imminent judgment shows that to him at least the world is of much more than casual importance. Reality is more than we realize; every human thought and action are significant. This should fill us with awe.

If the claims about God's omnipotence are true, how can people be responsible? Can a person have real freedom?

Indeed, this is beyond human understanding. We cannot understand how God is three and yet one; how Christ can be fully God as well as man; and how there was nothing, and God spoke, and there was. Yet these things are not irrational or absurd. It is true that although we may grasp the meaning of these words, we will never be able to explain them fully. How could anyone explain how God created and maintains the world? How is he able to set the times and the seasons while simultaneously allowing so much freedom everywhere that people are even able to turn against their Creator? We cannot explain these things, but how could they be otherwise? Our knowledge and experience testify that God really is the great God he claims to be, and yet we are free. We can do what we like, including evil, within the framework of human limitations and options.

The trouble is that we compare God to ourselves. We can create things, but they are always determined, bound by our designs, our programmes. Think, for example, of the computer. God, however, is the great God he is precisely because he was able to create a universe in which all things move in freedom, and yet without chaos!

This particular question is really the age-old one which all philosophers have tried to answer: the problem of freedom and determinism. All recognize that both exist, but no one can explain how. Even the Bible does not try. It is just beyond human understanding. We should have to be on an equal level with God and comprehend his depths if we were to know the answer.

We also face this question in our own human experience. The Bible refers to it, without trying to account for everything in an all-embracing theory. I am thinking here of the wonderful words of Paul, which are so true to the believer's experience, and yet so inexplicable: 'Work out your salvation with fear and trembling, for it is God who works in you to will and to act according to his good purpose' (Philippians 2:12, 13).

Because people are finite and restricted, human achievements are less than perfect. Is this imperfection sin?

We humans are restricted. In spite of our freedom to choose, we have certain limitations because of the kind of creatures we are: we cannot swim like a whale or fly like a hawk. We are also limited by time and space: we cannot be in two different places at the same time. There is nothing wrong with these limitations, for they were also part of human being before the Fall. Only God is infinite and unrestricted in his power.

However, this question could indicate that we are still bound to the sinful wish that led to humanity's fall: the wish to be like God. People want to do those things which God said were wrong, and which go against their own nature. Ever since the Fall people have constantly done things that oppose their own freedom, their own understanding and love (Romans 1:18, 19; 7:21). Our creaturely limitations, given when God made us, are not wrong or sinful. We do wrong when we refuse to be what he has made us.

But happily this is not the end of the story, for our deliverance in Christ means not only that he has forgiven our sins, but that he has conquered the evil in us and set us free to become what he originally intended. The gospel has restored our true humanity (Colossians 2:9–15).

Principles of personal evangelism

We ourselves cannot convert anyone; only the Holy Spirit can change hearts

It is our responsibility to give honest answers to honest questions. We cannot expect others to believe us just because we have strong convictions, nor ask them to take a leap in the dark. The responsibility of sharing our faith is overwhelming. We cannot convince anyone; who are *we*? That is why we must accompany every discussion with the silent prayer that God will convince the other person; perhaps the Spirit will lift the veil of the unbeliever's sinful wish to suppress the truth, and allow him or her for just one moment to look reality – even his or her own reality – right in the face.

Jesus, speaking of his disciples' difficult confrontation with possessed people, said, 'This kind can come out only by prayer and fasting.' Fasting means being willing to sacrifice something, to set some things aside for the sake of one's petition. In his words in the upper room, described in John's Gospel, Jesus says more about prayer: 'Soon I will go away, but understand that I do these things because there is a three-way bond between the Father, myself, and you. I do these things because I love you, and I love God. This is all done in order that your prayers may be heard' (John 14:13 ff., my paraphrase). John's Gospel repeats this five or six times. Jesus died not only to forgive our sins but also to make us new people. He died so that our prayers might be heard, including our prayers for our neighbours.

Imagine that your boss, a humanist, is coming to visit you one evening. Before she comes, you might pray, 'Lord, guide our conversation so that we may have a chance to talk about you. Let her see that the Bible is not out of date, and that the gospel is concerned with the ordinary events of life.' Once you look behind another person's mask, you may discover many difficulties. It may be possible for you to talk about one of these problems, and to give an answer. God can use such a visit to build his kingdom, but not without prayer. When Christians realize their dependence on God in these matters, great things can happen.

The Lord does not, however, answer all our prayers immediately. Sometimes we may have to wait, perhaps because we ourselves need to learn something, or because the other person must learn to trust us as real human beings. Whatever the reason, we must not give up too easily.

Our faith is not in the Bible itself, but in the Lord who reveals himself through it

Christians should not put all their trust in the Bible; it cannot be their god. Our faith is not in words, nor in commands or parables, but in the living God. The reality of God, who rules this whole universe and a great unseen world of which we know next to nothing, is too immense to be contained even within the Bible.

Christianity is certainly a 'religion' with a book, but that book is not simply the story of a cult, nor a collection of devotional poetry. God has used the Bible to tell people about himself. The Bible speaks primarily of the reality of this world, of the God who lives, of a Saviour who really exists and who accomplished something on a real cross, not just for the souls and feelings of people but for the world in all its fullness. Because Christianity deals with reality it is not only for Christians that these things are true.

To accept the biblical message is not to deny one's intellect

Bultmann and other theologians have said that to accept an unaltered biblical message in our day would be a sacrifice of the intellect. It is indeed true that we have many things today that did not exist in biblical times: television, cars, aeroplanes. But these things do not undo the truth of the Bible, nor make it obsolete. It is true that our modern thought-forms are often not in line with those of the Bible, but perhaps it is modern people themselves who have sacrificed their intellect and lost the way to understand the world. We have limited our horizon to what we can understand and know with the help of our human brains and senses.

The Bible, though far from supporting rationalism, is not contrary to reason. It does not ask us to believe strange things far removed from all human experience. Can a woman bear a child without contact with a man? No, says the Bible, this never happens – only in one case, and this is therefore a once and for all exception. Can a man return from the grave? No, says the Bible. Only Christ was able to overcome death, because he was also God; his resurrection was an exceptional event.

Can miracles happen? The greatest miracle is the wonder of God's creation. But can a man walk on the water, or heal the sick? Can fire come down from heaven as happened during Elijah's sacrifice on Mount Carmel? Why should a man not be able to walk on water if that man is the Son of God? If God, the Lord of creation, wants to show that he is Lord by sending fire from heaven, why should that be strange? Such a happening would be strange if he did *not* exist; but since he does, would it not be peculiar if he were unable to do these things? The Bible is not unreasonable here. There may be some things in the Scriptures we cannot explain, but they are never against reason when we first acknowledge the great God who has revealed himself. Part of believing in God is recognizing that he has the power to do what we in our own strength are unable to do.

The Bible does not ask for a sacrifice of the intellect. It begins to be inexplicable only when I insist on denying all the things which I cannot actually see in the world around me. Even in biblical times these miraculous things were not common. Just count the number of people who ever saw an angel (and their amazement when they did!). If God did not come to Abraham, how was it possible that so many years before Christ he believed those great promises for the future of his folk – believed because God had told him so? If the things the Bible relates did not occur, how did the Bible itself come into existence? The very unity of its message and the events it describes are surely comprehensible – even if the message could never have been conceived by a person (Isaiah 55:8, 9). By accepting the word of God we begin to see and understand, for the fear of the Lord is the beginning of wisdom.

Again, how can the Bible be false when on so many pages it asks us to inquire, to look, to investigate for ourselves whether the events it describes are true, or coming true according to prophecy? (See, for example, Matthew 24; Luke 1:1–4; John 2:22; 20:27–31; Acts 1:3; 4:20.) If the Bible is not true, then Jesus was an impostor, a liar, or at best a fool misleading himself by making such great claims. How can people say that Jesus was a great man and at the same time deny his claims to be the God-sent Messiah? If the Bible is not true, then according to its own standards we had better call it a strange and impossible deceit. Can we really imagine the apostles sitting down to make up the story that Jesus rose from the dead, or constructing legends to create propaganda for a dead idealist? What would they have to gain? Most of them lost their lives for what they said. And certainly the period that elapsed between the things that happened in Jesus' time and the first gospels and epistles is too short to allow such a legend to gain credence. Also, the idea that the Old Testament is full of 'prophecies' written after the events occurred creates more problems than it solves; the Bible's plain message is easier to accept. Psychologically, historically, we run into great problems as soon as we try to deny the veracity of the biblical witnesses.

To accept God is much more than merely to believe that he exists or that the Bible is true

The question that modern people so often ask about the existence of God is closely tied up with epistemology, for it asks the question in the terms in which it was formulated during the Age of Reason. As such it is a wrong question. It is also unanswerable; God cannot be put on an equal level with the realities of his creation. God's existence is so abundantly clear from all creation – even apart from the Scriptures – that it is hard to deny his being. Of course, without Scripture it would be difficult to say anything positive and precise about him; that is why we need revelation.

A positive answer to the question of whether God exists is only a small step toward truly following him. One does not become a Christian by believing that God exists – the devils know that, too (James 2:19). To be a Christian means that we love him and want to follow him even if it proves costly and difficult.

We should accept the Bible as God's revelation if we want to be his followers. But saying that the Bible is true also does not make us Christians. We are not only to accept the word as truth, but to *do* the truth (John 3:21). It is not enough just to say yes to a system.

Love is the only legitimate motivation for evangelism

Our calling is not to tell about the church, nor about ourselves or our experiences. It is important to emphasize this because of the many misunderstandings which exist. The only reason I talk about Jesus is because I love my neighbour. My neighbour is not just a modern person in general but much more specifically, John, with whom I work, Mrs Smith next door or the man sitting opposite me in the train. Am I going to condemn them to be lost because I am too wretched to speak? Because I love my neighbour, I want to help him or her and pass on freely what I have received from God.

The following story sounds almost like a caricature, but it really happened. One day a young man offered to help an elderly woman cross the street. As he accompanied her home they got into a conversation and she told him how she had once belonged to a church, but because of her husband she had given up attending. Now that she was old, she had begun to think of these things again. All the young man could say was, 'Isn't it a bit late to ask for the address of the true church?' A response like this is totally without love. Nothing can happen if we lack love.

Some Christians evangelize in a legalistic way, only to fulfil their duty, their witnessing all too often sounding like a phonograph record – grinding out the same lines, and slogans without any real interest in the person before them. They pay no attention to his or her questions, problems, personal situation. It is a sin to do missionary or evangelistic work legalistically. As Paul says in Galatians 2:15 ff., we are no longer subject to the law. This is not just a theological statement but a truth we can accept with great joy.

The only reason for telling other men and women about Christ is that we know it will be good news – an answer to their personal needs. Christians should love their fellow human beings, whose need of God is just as great whether they are criminals or immoral or just people of another type or class than themselves. Christians are sometimes very harsh on people whose lifestyle they find low or degraded. It is as if they have not read what the Lord said about the harlots, the wicked and the poor who needed him and should therefore not be sent away, but helped. The same is true of unbelieving family members. Our guide should not be what others think but what the Lord says, and he told us to care for the lost.

Whenever we see a person destroying her or his life through sinful foolishness, we should weep. At the same time we must understand that such a person can really change only through the work of the Holy Spirit. Only after Christ himself has become a person's Lord and Saviour can we try, carefully and tactfully, to lead her or him in a more godly way of life. A new Christian will often need our help to show him or her gently what the Lord asks of his followers – not a whole string of dos and don'ts but true fruits of the Spirit.

Evangelism cannot be limited to one method or approach

Because people are different, and their backgrounds and experience vary so enormously, no one method can reach everyone. We can never communicate if we do not reach people where they are. What is right and appropriate in one situation can be totally inept in another. This makes life fascinating, but it is also why methods can be so deadly. If, however, we are driven by love, the Holy Spirit can show us how to act.

This does not, however, mean that study is unimportant. On the contrary, we must have knowledge of the other people's world if we are ever to make meaningful contact with them. And of course we need to study the Bible in order to know what we are talking about. Although we shall never have complete knowledge and know all the answers, we have no excuse for being lazy. Without such study it is dishonest to ask the Holy Spirit to lead us, for God is too great to be used as a kind of servant to carry out the things we have failed to do.

In our own lives, meanwhile, must be evidence of the fruits of the Spirit. Otherwise, we cannot honestly claim that Christ has overcome evil. The Bible says that anyone who claims to be God's child but goes on sinning is walking in darkness (1 John 1). This does not mean that we must be perfect; we shall all continue to need forgiveness. But some change in our lives must be apparent.

Not everyone is called to be an evangelist

In many Christian circles, evangelism is seen as the first and probably most important task of the Christian. I do not agree. The Bible does make clear that whenever we are asked about our faith we must give an answer and not deny the Lord by acting as if we do not know him. There can also be no argument as to whether the church, the body of Christ, is called to proclaim God's message. A Christian community that is not interested in the furtherance of the gospel is in need of careful self-examination.

This does not mean, however, that every Christian is called to be an evangelist, or that there can be no Christian life without direct acts of witness and testimony. Some people are called by God for this special work, and in answer to prayer he gives them particular talents and opportunities. But not everyone is called to be an evangelist. Many Christians are deeply frustrated because they have been told that the first law of the Christian life is to evangelize, and yet they do not know how to go about it. They feel inadequate and the Lord never seems to give them opportunities. Their frustration is the painful result of a hard legalism, and it is unnecessary.

Like the Old Testament prophets, some people in the New Testament – like the first apostles and Paul – are specifically called to preach the gospel. But we never hear of a general command to all of Christ's followers. Paul exhorts his congregations to live a good Christian life; but as sharp as he could be in pointing out their shortcomings, he never rebukes them for not evangelizing. He also does not command them to do so, but explicitly states that God has called him and other specially appointed people to do that demanding job.

A Christian can bear fruit for the kingdom of God in many ways. There are rich variations in our callings. One may be a scholar or technician, a housewife or teacher, a musician or painter, a bookseller or a farmer. Those who are not evangelists or preachers, theologians or missionaries are no less Christian than those who are. Nor is their work unrelated to the gospel. In this day, marked more and more by the absence of a Christian lifestyle, we find that honesty, truthfulness, reliability, wisdom, and insight into the basic truths about human life are becoming ever rarer. We have the opportunity to show clearly that what we do is different, and that our goals are not conformed to those of the world around us.

Everyone is called by the Lord to 'full-time Christian service'. We are God's children twenty-four hours a day, or we are not Christian. But full-time service can be in the kitchen, at the helm of a boat, doing accounts, helping sick people or looking after the plumbing system.

We can also say this in another way. Paul speaks about the Christian community as a body, made up of various members (1 Corinthians 12). If we compare the evangelist with the mouth, it becomes obvious that more is needed to make a whole body. Perhaps your calling is to be a foot, an ear, an eye or even some less conspicuous member. We cannot all be evangelists, as there must be a body behind the evangelist – helping him or her with money, with prayers, but also with insight and knowledge, maybe by analysing the spirit of the modern age, or by making the building or decorating the interior of the room he or she speaks in. Also, if the evangelist is to speak of new life in Christ, he or she must be able to point the listeners to a living church made up of real people. There ought to be cooks, teachers for the children, musicians, caretakers – a wide variety of people, each of whom helps to complete the body of Christ. How can we do without them? Let us not build a surrealistic and absurd church, made up of mouths only.

We can sum up all we have been saying in one sentence: Christ did not die merely to make us Christians. He died that we might be human – men and women in the fullest sense of the word.

The danger of Christian utilitarianism

Having understood these things, we must beware of the danger of Christian utilitarianism. This is a most appalling trap, into which one can easily fall. If we believe evangelism to be the ultimate and only real Christian work in the world, this means that any other work must be second-rate, and at best only an aid to evangelism. Art – fine, but what can it do for evangelism? Business – nothing wrong with it, provided it can be utilized for evangelism. Why do we live? – in order to evangelize. We smile, not because we are happy, but because we want to be regarded as happy Christians. And so on. This means that all these things, which are gifts of God, lose their intrinsic beauty and are prostituted for evangelism.

If the supreme purpose of art is no longer to sing the praise of the Lord and be a joy to our fellow human beings, but to provide a tool for evangelism, we soon do not ask whether art is good and beautiful but only whether it can be used to convert people. We are then not far from trying to manipulate the people we want to reach. Another trap is to give the people merely what they want; art is not seen as important in itself, but only as a means of carrying a message, and the artist is asked to do things that fail to meet the best standards. Music, graphic art, other forms of communication are dragged down to a level of mere usefulness for evangelism, but fail the test of honesty, beauty, and integrity.

Art has its own value. The music of Bach, for example, is certainly Christian, but it was not composed to attract a large crowd to be preached at, nor to stir up emotions so that people would more easily accept the message. The music of Bach, and the art of Rembrandt, are in themselves a witness because they show what it means to adopt Christian standards, to use one's talents in order to make the very best work one is capable of; this in itself honours God. Call it pre-evangelism, if you like.

Here is a challenge for us, the challenge to show that the end never justifies the means. We must not sacrifice our honesty, failing to make quality work because we fear it may not appeal to popular taste. In the very act of denying our own standards we also insult the human beings we want to reach, as if they cannot see through our cunning little devices. I have spoken to many people who have been hurt, and estranged from Christianity, in this way. I have also seen Christians distressed because they wanted to find a place where the Bible was really taught, but heard only evangelistic talk in the churches they went to, talk which led people no further than conversion.

What is an evangelist?

After all we have said, we must not forget that the Bible does assign a particular role to the evangelist. What does it mean to be an evangelist?

How does his or her work differ from that, for example, of a missionary?

The missionary is a man or woman sent to a country, a people, a nation that does not know the gospel. He or she must bring the good news into a society and culture completely moulded by a non-Christian religion and mentality. Yet the missionary must be careful, while preaching God's message, not simultaneously to be introducing Western culture, an especially important consideration at a time when Western culture itself is in a state of crisis and has drifted from its former Christian foundations. He or she cannot be a proponent of Western supremacy, for anything that indicates a colonialist or racist mentality will be detrimental to the work and will contradict God's message that all are in need of salvation, regardless of racial or social position.

The evangelist has a quite different task. He or she addresses a Western world that has heard the gospel, a culture that once was Christian but is now falling into apostasy. (Hosea 4:1–3 describes the situation perfectly, even including pollution.) Everywhere people are ignorant of the word of God; they think they have 'come of age' and do not need it. The position of the modern evangelist differs only superficially from that of the Old Testament prophets. The prophets were speaking to the Jewish people, who had received a specific call from God but were often far from God-fearing. In the midst of their heathen practices they dared to believe in continuing peace and success. The prophets called them back to God, quoting passages from the Law to warn them that if they did not put an end to their greed and idolatry God would come with judgment, concrete and inescapable. However, the prophets also preached that God is a God of mercy; there is a chance for individuals to return, though they must be prepared to face social pressures and perhaps even persecution. In such circumstances, God has a special message for them (see Jeremiah 45 and Zephaniah 2:3). The prophets also spoke of a way of return for whole nations, a way which could lead to blessings instead of the threatened afflictions.

The same warnings and promises apply in our age. Today's evangelist is the prophet of our time, speaking to people who have forsaken God, the Giver of so many blessings. The twentieth-century prophet needs to study the prophets of the Old Testament, and echo their call to repent: Repent and accept the true God; give up your wrong philosophies and false religions. Stop suppressing the poor and the socially weak. Stop putting financial security and personal happiness before the glory of God. Reject dishonesty as a part of politics. In short, turn from the modern mentality in all its ungodliness. The words of Micah to his generation could not be more timely:

> With what shall I come before the LORD
>   and bow down before the exalted God?
> Shall I come before him with burnt offerings,
>   with calves a year old?

Will the Lord be pleased with thousands of rams,
> with ten thousand rivers of oil?
Shall I offer my firstborn for my transgression,
> the fruit of my body for the sin of my soul?
He has showed you, O man, what is good.
> And what does the Lord require of you?
To act justly and to love mercy
> and to walk humbly with your God.[73]

8
Dürer's Apocalypse: An Artist's Message to his Contemporaries

The time just before and after the year 1500 was marked in Europe by decisive developments and an extreme richness of achievement in art. Following the preparatory endeavours of the fifteenth century, the grand tradition which was to last until the end of the eighteenth century took on its final form. In this period, known as the High Renaissance, lived a number of the greatest artists in world history: Leonardo da Vinci, Raphael, Michelangelo. To that company also belonged Albrecht Dürer.

Leonardo da Vinci, a typical Renaissance thinker who placed human being in the centre of the universe, created a new art as an attempt to solve some of the problems inherent in a humanistic world view. He also made use of the new possibilities in the naturalistic portrayal of reality, making exact drawings of anatomical details and technical tools for scientific purposes. Raphael was a typical High Churchman, whose altarpieces and work for the Vatican Palace set the standard for Roman Catholic art for more than three centuries. Michelangelo, who grew from a humanism with Neoplatonic philosophical implications to a more Christian position in the course of his long life, made during the early years of the sixteenth century his famous *David*. This sculpture was perhaps the greatest monument to the Renaissance person, facing the future without fear.

Dürer's accomplishments included some magnificent paintings, portraits and altarpieces. But his greatest achievement lay in his graphic work, his woodcuts, his engravings and even some etchings, and in a large number of brilliant drawings. In addition, he wrote some of the earliest works in the German language dealing with human proportions and perspective, with the intention of providing a sound foundation for art.

In his own day, Dürer was a man of great fame. The Emperor Maximilian employed him in large projects. Raphael sent him a bundle of drawings as a legacy, and he even had to travel to Venice once in order to guarantee the copyright of his graphic work, which already during his lifetime was being forged extensively. For the centuries to come his fame seldom waned; his graphic work was collected, many of his figures imitated, and his books used as textbooks. He became famous almost overnight when he published his *Apocalypse* in 1498.

Dürer's breadth and depth of subject matter are truly unique. He depicts biblical stories, the lives of saints, historical events, fashion, elements of social life, classical mythology or allegory, animals, plants, heraldry, as well as making portraits, landscapes, fantastic ornamental borders, and even depictions of dreams. No other artist ever treated such a wide variety of subjects while at the same time introducing many innovations. All this richness comes together as if condensed in his lofty and fantastic portrayal of John's book of Revelation.

As mentioned before, the early fifteenth century had seen the introduction of naturalism, an attempt to respect reality as it was seen, including even its depth and space. In Italy we call this the Renaissance. In the north its centre was Flanders, the home of great Flemish artists like van Eyck and van der Weyden and other Flemish masters wrongly called 'primitives'. Dürer knew both streams, felt their influence and in many ways even furthered their achievements.

A problem inherent in naturalism is that just because it starts from the rendering of the visually given, it is a difficult medium for depicting the supernatural, things that are never seen and beyond human visual experience. The struggle to depict biblical, devotional or dogmatic subjects makes up much of the history of fifteenth-century art and also, in a way, of Baroque art. Fifteenth-century book illustrations, devotional prints, etc. often kept to the 'iconic' mode of representation, a more 'flat' symbolic way of representation than was common in medieval art. This means that lines, colours etc. are not a *copy* of what the eye receives, but a *symbol* representing it. Letters are also symbols, and we see that often in this period letters and renderings of symbols like the cross or the chalice were used together in engraving.

In his *Apocalypse*, Dürer was able to achieve a unique fusion of the naturalistic and the iconic systems, depicting his fantastic subject matter with an extreme precision of naturally rendered details. Not only did Dürer's work surpass the older portrayals of the Apocalypse in blockbooks or early book illustrations, but he introduced a completely new approach to the art of the woodcut. Paradoxically, the more naturalistically precise his figures, the more visionary and fantastic they became. Thus, he was able to depict almost unimaginable visions in a natural and convincing way.

Dürer's work is also unique in that it has never been repeated, except for some more or less free copies. The naturalistic mode of art made these scenes almost impossible to render. If it was tried, as by Cornelius in the nineteenth century, it became too realistic – even when he based his work on Dürer's example – or it resulted in fantastic visions resembling hallucinations, totally subjective. Dürer, however, managed to achieve complete objectivity; he let the visions remain something which a man, St John, had seen outside himself, and not only in his mind.

The fifteenth century was, for Germany, a particularly difficult time. Social injustice, the result of suppression and taxation of the people by wealthy bishops, was universal. The church itself was secularized and decaying. The beginning of a reformation by John Huss was suppressed, and Huss himself martyred. To make it worse, there were plagues, famines and other natural disasters. Also there were wars, and the imminent threat of the Turkish Muslims who stood at the borders of the German Empire.

Christians in those days read the Bible, and particularly the Revelation of St John, as a book of consolation and of hope. Dürer must have come out of such circles, where there was much prayer for a renewal of the church, for renewed understanding of Scripture and dogma, and for a new and better world to come. In this pre-Reformation age, pregnant with expectation, Dürer's work was loaded with meaning. His *Apocalypse* is not a work of art which shows primarily how he was challenged by the difficulty or beauty of the subject matter. He made it because of his conviction that the message of Revelation was so appropriate to his time; he wanted to warn and console his contemporaries.

Dürer chose the technique of the woodcut because it was a medium both popular and cheap. He hoped to reach many people. Maybe just because these fifteen plates were made not for their own sake, but loaded with a meaning not only important to Dürer himself but, as he saw it, necessary for his time, this work has become one of the world's most beautiful works of art. (Personally, I find it the most beautiful work of art there is.)

Dürer published his *Apocalypse* in 1498. It was a book, actually the text of John's Revelation in German, intended to appeal to a large audience. The book was illustrated with fifteen large plates (39.2x28.2 cm). The technical quality of the plates is unsurpassed. In 1511 a second edition followed, this time with a Latin text, making it a more international edition. It is impossible here to deal with the book in all its details, but a few remarks are necessary. It is important to realize that the original plates appeared with the appropriate Bible texts beside them. If one takes one's Bible, reads the text, and compares it with the plates, one finds oneself reading the text just as carefully as Dürer himself did.

1. *The Martyrdom of St John*

This is the only plate that is not based on the Bible but on legend. According to the legend, St John was brought before the emperor, who condemned him to be boiled in oil. Miraculously, the torture did not work, and St John survived. The emperor then banished him to the Isle of Patmos. Note that the emperor has a turban on his head. He is equated with the monarch of the Turkish Muslim Empire which was threatening Europe, and therefore Christianity. The whole scene thus becomes the confrontation of the pagan world and Christianity, in which the former tries to undo the latter. Humanity is looking on; we see representatives of all types of people, including a converted man from the East.

2. *Revelation 1*

Read the description in the Bible. This is one of the last plates in the series made by Dürer. It is much more accomplished, and has a grandeur lacking in the following plate, which is one of the earliest conceived. The later plate looks simple, as if made with great ease. This testifies to its quality, for the greatest art always looks simple and, as it were, obvious. Note the treatment of space here, with the well-designed candlesticks (Dürer's grandfather was a goldsmith) one behind the other, while at the same time the whole lofty scene is kept on the surface, reminding us of pre-Renaissance imagery. Even though this scene is depicted naturalistically, it is not realistic. It keeps its iconic quality. In this way a clash between the naturalism in style and the non-realism of the subject (as naturalism would define realism) is avoided. Note also how beautifully the darker and lighter passages are distributed over the surface. Dürer uses clouds just as the High Renaissance does: as a symbol of the supernatural realm. St John kneels amidst the candlesticks, before Christ.

3. *Revelation 4*

Here we find a division of the supernatural and the natural – nature and grace – which is not present in Dürer's later work. The doors of heaven are opened. St John kneels for instruction by one of the crowned elders. Chapter 5 is included here as well, for we see the Lamb of God near the Father, being given the book with the seven seals. The heads in the clouds represent the winds. Also notice the rich and beautiful landscape.

4. *Revelation 6: the Four Horsemen of the Apocalypse*

This is one of the most famous of the series, and rightly so. Note the speed of these riders, and how this effect has been achieved. Here is a supreme example of how Dürer, while very precise and natural, is at the same time able to preserve the visionary elements. Notice how the horses seem to have no tail ends but are fused with the clouds and with the mantle of Death, sitting on the very lean horse. Also note how the whole of humankind is represented by no more than six people. A bishop is being swallowed up in the mouth of hell.

5. *Revelation 6 (second half)*

Here we see the souls of the martyrs under the altar, and then a faithful rendering of verses 12 and following, in which humankind tries to hide in the caves in the mountains. The many details become clear when we read the Bible text in conjunction with the plate.

6. *Revelation 7*

This plate depicts the four angels at the four corners of the earth, and the sealing of the 144,000. The faces in the clouds again represent the winds.

7. *Revelation 8 and 9:1–6*
Here we see the four trumpets, and then the fifth. If one reads the chapters for oneself, one notes the inclusion of every detail.

8. *Revelation 9:7–21*
In the sky one can see the four horses, and on the ground the four angels.

9. *Revelation 10*
Again, careful reading of the chapter reveals how precisely Dürer has followed the text. His portrayal of the eating of the book is magnificent. The angel in the sky is the 'voice from heaven'.

10. *Revelation 12*
Here appear the woman and the dragon; the latter is equated with the beast of Revelation 13. In the Middle Ages, and later in the Counter-Reformation, the woman here is equated with the Virgin Mary. Dürer follows the treatment of her that was traditional in his day, adding wings. From the plate it is difficult to tell whether or not Dürer believed the woman to be Mary.

11. *Revelation 12*
This plate portrays the battle of Michael against the dragon and its followers.

12. *Revelation 13*
Humankind adores the dragon.

13. *Revelation 14*
The Lamb appears with the 144,000.

14. *Revelation 17 and 18*
Here appear humankind and the whore of Babylon, sitting on the dragon. The woman is dressed in the Venetian style. This was not a random choice, for Venice in those days well fitted the description of Babylon in these chapters. Venice wanted to become the centre of the world and attempted to get the pope to live there.

15. *Revelation 20 and 21*
Here are illustrated the binding of Satan, and the new Jerusalem.

After making his *Apocalypse*, Dürer made many other important works which we cannot discuss here. However, I cannot conclude without quoting the text of his moving prayer, written in 1521. Dürer had had a yearly pension from the Emperor Maximilian. After the latter's death, Dürer hoped to get the same from his successor, Charles the Fifth, who was to be crowned in 1521 in Achen. For that reason he travelled to Antwerp in 1520. In Belgium he was received with great honour by fellow artists, visited several highly-placed people, saw an exhibition of

American treasures in Brussels, and had a very fruitful time. He kept a diary, invaluable in spite of its dullness of style, telling what he spent, how much he got for a portrait, whom he met, which engravings were sold to whom, etc.

In 1521, however, Dürer heard rumours that Luther had been taken captive (rumours later found to be erroneous – he was taken by his friends in order to keep him safe from his enemies). Dürer, having begun his diary entry in the usual way, could not refrain from letting his thoughts go. His entry becomes a prayer. This piece is very difficult to translate, as thoughts tumble one over the other in Dürer's mind. It was, of course, never written to be published. It gives us a clear insight into the mind of a man who was a true child of the Reformation. His *Apocalypse*, made long before the dates which textbooks give us for the Reformation, already testified to a reformational spirit – his deep interest in and obedient submission to the Bible text, his being moved and consoled by its message and wanting to share it with others.

The entry from his diary which follows here testifies to the same spirit, and shows how closely he followed Luther from the moment he arose to lead the Reformation:

> On the Friday before Whitsuntide, 1521 [May 17], news reached me at Antwerp that Martin Luther had been treacherously taken prisoner. For, being accompanied by the herald of Emperor Charles, he had trusted the Imperial safe conduct. But when the herald had taken him to the vicinity of Eisenach, an unfriendly place, he said that he would no longer be needed, and rode away. Soon appeared ten knights who carried [Luther] away treacherously, a betrayed man, pious and enlightened by the Holy Ghost, a successor of Christ, and a follower of the true Christian faith. Whether he is still alive or whether they have put him to death, I know not. He has suffered for the sake of Christian truth and for having condemned the un-Christlike papacy, which obstructs the redemption of Christ with its oppressive man-made laws. Also because we are deprived and stripped of the fruit of our sweat and blood that is consumed so shamefully by an idle and blasphemous clique, while the needy and sick die of starvation.
>
> It is especially depressing to me to imagine that God should want us to continue listening to the false and blind teachings written and invented by men called 'fathers', who in many instances have misinterpreted the Word of God or else neglected it. O God of Heaven, have pity on us. O Lord Jesus, Rex Christe, pray for your people. Deliver us in time and sustain our true and proper Christian faith. Gather your widely scattered flock by your voice, the divine Word of the Scriptures. Help us know your voice, so as not to follow the piper's call of human error, so as not, O Lord Jesus Christ, to go astray. Call together the sheep of your pasture, those still in the fold of the Roman Church, and also the Indians, the Moscovites, the Russians, the Greeks who were cut off by the oppression and the avarice of the popes and the false aura

of holiness. O God, redeem your poor people who are forced by heavy ban and edict to do what they dislike, as it would violate their conscience to disobey. O God, you have never so greatly burdened a people with laws made by humans, as us poor ones under the [rule of the] Roman See, who should be redeemed each day by your blood and be free Christians. O highest Father in heaven, through your Son, Jesus Christ, pour into our hearts the light that will permit us to know which rules we are to obey and which, in good conscience, we may lay aside because they are a burden, in order to serve you, eternal God and Heavenly Father, with a free and joyful heart.

And if we should lose this man who has written more clearly than anyone in 140 years [since John Wyclif], and to whom you have lent such evangelic spirit, we beg you, O Heavenly Father, once more to give your Divine Spirit to another who will then unite your Holy Christian Church everywhere, so that we may again live in Christian unity. And that by our good deeds all nonbelievers, Turks, heathens, Calcuttans will want to join us voluntarily and embrace the Christian faith. But Lord, you willed before you judged, as your Son, Jesus Christ, died by the hands of the priests and then rose from the dead to ascend into heaven, that in like manner your follower, Martin Luther, would be slain in perfidy by the Pope and his money, and that you would resurrect him. And as you, my Lord, then ordained that Jerusalem be destroyed, you will, likewise, destroy the self-assumed authority of the Roman See. O Lord, give us thereafter the new beatified Jerusalem which will descend from heaven as told in the Apocalypse; the divinely pure gospel, untarnished by human doctrine.

Whoever reads Doctor Martin Luther's books must needs observe the clarity and lucidity of his discourse on the Holy Gospels. Wherefore his writings are to be held in great honour and should not be burnt [as had occurred at Cologne and Louvain after the publication of the Papal Ban], unless his opponents, who fight against truth, are also cast into the fire with all their *opiniones*. For they would make gods out of men, even as new Lutheran books are again printed. O God, if Luther is dead, who will henceforth expound the Holy Gospel so clearly? Ah God, what might he have written in the next ten or twenty years?

O all you pious Christians, help me to lament this divinely inspired man and pray that another enlightened one be sent us. O Erasmus of Rotterdam, where will you stand? Do you not see the result of the unjust tyranny of worldly power and of the forces of darkness? Hear, you knight of Christ, ride on beside our Lord Jesus, guard the truth and win the martyr's crown! Else you will be just a dear old man. But I heard that you have given yourself two more years of activity. Use these well for the benefit of the Gospels and the true Christian faith. Make yourself heard, and the gates of hell, the Roman See, as Christ says, will be powerless against you. If then, like your master

Christ, you suffer shame at the hands of the liars and therefore die a little sooner, you shall that much sooner arise from death to a life glorified by Christ. If then you drink out of the cup from which He drank, you will reign and judge with justice those who failed to act wisely.

O Erasmus, act so that God may speak of you with pride, as it is written of David: For if you are capable of acting, indeed you shall be capable of overthrowing Goliath. For God stands by the Holy Christian Church, even as he supports the Roman [Church] according to his Divine Will. He will help us attain everlasting happiness; God the Father, the Son, and the Holy Ghost; one God, Amen.

O you Christians, pray to God for help, for his judgment draws near and his justice will become evident. Then we shall see those whose innocent blood was shed and who were judged and damned by the Pope, the priests, and the monks. Apocalypse! They are the ones who were slain and now lie beneath the altar of God, crying for vengeance. The voice of God then answers: Await the full number of those slain innocently, then shall I judge.[74]

Part III

ARTICLES ON HISTORY, FAITH AND CULTURE, LIFESTYLE AND SCHOLARSHIP, AND THE WESTMINSTER DISCUSSIONS

The Constituent Factors of a Historical Deed[75]

'Monsieur V.! It's time to wake up!' V. had been waiting for Ursula's voice even while he slept. 'I was awake, Mademoiselle Ursula', he called back. 'No, you weren't,' the girl laughed, 'but you are now.' He heard her go down the stairs and into the kitchen. V. put his hands under him, gave a shove, and sprang out of bed. His shoulders and his chest were massive, his arms thick and powerful. He slipped into his clothes, poured some water out of the ewer, and stropped his razor.

We may ask ourselves whether we have in this quotation a description of a historical deed. Does it make any difference who the V. in this fragment is, whether he is one of the many nameless ones in history or whether he is a very important figure, without whom we would not be able to understand the development of art history? Does the fact that the main character in this little piece of history was Vincent van Gogh make the event described a historical event?[76] We do not think so. And yet, it cannot be denied that there is a historical facet to this event. Apart from the fact that the language spoken was used in a certain country in a certain period of time, both the manner of waking someone as well as the fact that V. shaves himself in this or that manner are historically determined and dateable. But what does not happen here – and that is crucial for our discussion – is an action that is of any importance for the development of civilization. Yet we cannot deny that van Gogh had to sleep, get up and shave, in short, that he had to live and work in his contemporary world in order to be able to create those works of art which have been so highly formative and have left their mark on events in such a way that their artistic style strongly determined the development of art during the following decades. We may say that a historical deed is a deed that has a formative impact on the course of events.

Before we continue it is desirable that we first determine more precisely the difference between two concepts of history. History in the diachronic sense comprises all that has happened in the past, from the most momentous to the most trivial events. Van Gogh's getting out of bed really happened and therefore it belongs to diachronic history. The truly historical, however, although it undoubtedly is a facet of all that has happened in the past, refers to the formation by responsible people of that which does not develop 'of its own accord', or 'naturally'. It is the formation of certain possibilities, by which a certain shape is given to what is as yet unformed, to what has not yet been put into concrete form. For that reason we can also call the truly historical, formative. It refers to that aspect of reality that is qualified by controlled formation. From this it follows that not every deed is truly historical. Dr H. Faber describes history as 'a complete set of changes of or within a certain entity'.

Relating this to a person or a people, he continues:

> The circumstances, which he did not choose himself, but which befall him, and also his deeds, or, in Heidegger's words, the possibilities that he chooses; behind those lie the motives that guide him to his deeds, and the inner emotions in which deeds are born; connected to those are the standards for his actions, which he accepts and tries to accept; and finally his faith, in which these standards are anchored.[77]

In my opinion precisely that which makes something truly historical is not grasped in these definitions. This is because history is without doubt a large collection of deeds, from the very trivial and repetitive to the extremely unique and radical. Undoubtedly all the elements Faber mentions play a part, but that does not mean that he has put his finger on what is typically and truly historical.

The question is always whether it was those deeds that effected the changes – because even without historical development changes take place, for sure: people grow old and die, young people take their place, all kinds of natural events change the face of the earth. Deeds done in the past are not necessarily historical deeds as such. We would characterize historical deeds as follows: human formative action in a responsible, controlled activity, whereby latent possibilities are opened up, disclosed, and where shape is given to the latent resources available.[78] Accordingly, when we wish to determine those features that constitute such a historical deed specifically, then we are not concerned with just every action in the past but only with those actions that intervene in a controlled manner to effect a formative change in the status quo.

In other words, we are interested in those deeds which consciously effect changes in culture and which, therefore, together with the unsurveyable system of historical forces constitute the development of civilization. We would like to emphasize that a historical deed is a deed that was once done, in a specific situation. It is not the historian who gives meaning to what happened in the past by scientifically studying it and placing it in its context.[79] No, a historical deed is true and real. It does not coincide with what can be perceived physically or psychically, which are only aspects of the historical deed. It encompasses the whole event in its full structure, of which also the historical, the lingual, as well as the economic, and the ethical are aspects. On the other hand, it is not the task of historical science to investigate the event in all its aspects, since only the historical aspect constitutes its specific area of research.[80] When analysing and investigating a historical deed, we do it according to the element that makes a deed historical, namely the formative, whereby the remaining modalities as such are not investigated.

If, for example, a lecture is of far-reaching meaning in a historic course of events, then the historian does not investigate how the speaker's tongue formed the words – this is something that the biologist or the linguist may be interested in. Nor does the historian investigate the economic aspect as such – the costs of the radio broadcast, or how much the bookseller earned with the sale of the printed lecture. Such factors are taken into consideration only insofar as they had an impact on the course of events within the formative, and therefore functioned in one way or another within the historical modality. Thus the deed is not investigated in its total reality structure but only according to one of the modal aspects abstracted from that totality. The deed that we would define as historical is precisely so because of the meaning that attaches to it in the formative aspect. Its relative importance and historical significance can only be ascertained with reference to a historical norm and never by consideration of its psychical or economic aspects. That is not to say that the latter facets would be irrelevant for the deed as it occurred according to its full, concrete structure. When we assess historical research we need to ascertain whether the events under consideration, as they are set out according to their historical aspect, really did happen in the way discussed, and whether their formative character was truly seen and elucidated. The science of history when true to its calling thus undoubtedly abstracts one aspect out of the concrete actions and events of the past, but it invents nothing, it does not assign meaning, and thus elucidates truthfully one aspect of the concrete events as they once occurred.[81]

All sorts of circumstances can determine the course of an event. It can happen that seemingly trivial deeds suddenly have a decisive effect, or that objective historical events such as natural disasters, disease or death make their influence felt or turn the scales in cultural or political power struggles.[82] The latter – natural disasters, etc. – are not part of our subject and requires no further justification, for they are not conscious and controlled events that presuppose human activity. Yet the first category too of seemingly trivial deeds falls outside our investigation.

For example, if a soldier on watch played with his rifle out of boredom and accidentally discharged a fatal shot that precipitated events which affected everybody, that soldier was not consciously committing a historical deed. He merely created, unintentionally, a situation in which the responsible leaders were forced to choose a position. In this case, they were the ones who committed the actual historical deeds. We do not want to underestimate the significance of such actions that are in and of themselves insignificant and only become important because of their consequences. Nor do we want to underestimate objective historical events in the course of history. But in this study we want to limit ourselves to the historical deed as we understand it in this article, namely one in which people have a certain goal in mind and act deliberately to achieve it.

A historical deed we now want to define as a deed whereby formative action is undertaken by a responsible history maker in a given historical situation. The deed involves giving a positive shape to norms, or the disclosing of as yet latent possibilities – whereby in either case the aim is to solve present problems or difficulties. The actual reality structure of the historical deed will be constituted, or determined, by the situation in which it occurs and to which it reacts, and also by the abilities and characteristics (i.e. the personality) of the history maker and by his or her world view. By further analysis of the elements summarized above we hope to gain insight into the factors that determine a historical deed according to its character and shape. When studying a chapter of history and investigating a historical deed we will also have to take into account the role of sin and its effects if we wish to obtain a correct insight. We should not consider this a new element in addition to what has been mentioned before but, on the contrary, we should view sin as a cancer that touches and damages everything and reveals its destructive effects in all human activity. We need to understand, for example, that history makers do not properly take into consideration the situation in which they commit their deeds.[83] By the very nature of sin it is understandable that a world view, driven by an apostate religious motive, often misses the point, both in misunderstanding the situation as well as in its posited ideals. The order of reality, however, i.e. God's creation order, does not allow itself to be distorted into any scheme of human contrivance and will assert itself. That is why a historical deed can only seldom be understood simply from the world view of the history maker. Many of the inconsistencies of a given deed, measured by that world view, will be the result of the fact that human beings have to capitulate to reality itself.

The formative aspect of the historical deed

The goal of the historical deed is formation. Struggling will be necessary to this end, using 'spiritual' means or [physical] weapons, using means such as organization, strategy, tactics, writings and arguments. Formation is aimed at affirming a certain status quo against attacks from the outside or bringing about a new situation. We now want to direct our attention to the historical deed in its formative aspect, either as disclosure or positivization, for formative action consists of and is directed to these two aspects.

a) Disclosure. With disclosure, possibilities contained in the creation order are opened up and realized. In the first place we think of disclosure of the natural aspects of reality, whereby nature is made serviceable to humanity through technical formation and adaptation, as in discoveries and inventions which can sometimes cut deeply into the historical state of affairs. These seem to be fully determined by circumstances and possibilities, and a person's world view seems to play no or only a very subordinate role. Yet this is only partly so. For inasmuch as world view determines a person's attitude to life and directs cultural activity, the selection of particular possibilities is certainly not dependent on 'natural' factors only without regard to the subjective attitude of the person. For example, it is not by chance that the machines capable of increasing production which initiated the Industrial Revolution were invented in eighteenth-century England.[84]

It is very seldom that we meet with 'coincidences' in the events of history. For the attention of the inventor or discoverer has to be directed to finding a solution to a certain problem or providing an instrument in order to fill a certain need. The anecdotes woven around the most important inventions clearly illustrate this. For example, Archimedes in his bath was not the first to discover the law named after him, noticing that a body in water undergoes an upward pressure. This phenomenon had already been used for centuries in shipping. But as Archimedes' attention was focused on the discovery of natural laws he suddenly realized which law of nature constituted the basis of this phenomenon. Similarly with the story of the invention of the printing press, when Koster or Gutenberg dropped a letter on the sand and suddenly discovered that an impression was created. For similar observations had doubtlessly been made many times before, even apart from the fact that the use of wooden blocks for printing on fabrics had been known for a long time. Though still a very important invention, the significance of their observation is in fact limited to the realization that they could make use of this for the printing of books. As a discovery it should be explained in terms of the demands and questions of their time and not just as an 'accidental moment of insight'. The role of inventors in the historical developments in which they consciously obtain a position is thereby further emphasized.

Disclosure is not limited to the realization of possibilities that are contained in nature. Possibilities that are latent in the normative aspects of reality can also be disclosed.[85] A connection with world view is here often much clearer and more direct. In the greater majority of cases, having a world view implies that certain facets of reality very emphatically receive full attention. Coupled with this is a neglect of other areas of reality, although we won't go into that now. For example, it is undeniable that the importance ascribed during the last hundred years to economic and social concerns, partly through the activities of the socialists and communists, has brought these aspects under closer attention and has led to further disclosure and development. The economic and social sciences can be the obvious proof of this, among many others. The history of the art of portraiture is also enlightening in this respect. We tend to see a development in portraiture whenever personality as such plays a large role and receives popular attention. Even though the people of the thirteenth century were technically capable of solving this problem – the series of pictures in the cathedral in Naumburg can prove it – it was only in the course of the next century that portraiture as such was 'discovered' and further disclosed as a possibility. So we see in such cases a strong connection between disclosure and the cultural ideal, and indirectly the world view of the leading groups in a certain period.[86]

b) Positivization. We should now direct our attention to what we call positivization.[87] In the first place we want to discuss positivization, the giving of a concrete, positive content to the leading principles and ideals in the various modalities, because when that happens the historical formative act is of the greatest and most comprehensive significance. It is undoubtedly the case that the cultural ideal itself also needs positivization, but we wanted to delay treatment of this in order to look at it in the context of world view. In the event of the cultural ideal having been given form in conformity with the world view of the groups which possess historical formative power, those groups will also strive to actualize this ideal in the remaining, historically-based facets of reality.[88] A man like Forster, who was not a leading or significant figure but in taste and insight completely held to the prevailing opinions, clearly exhibited such a connection between world view, culture and artistic ideal in his *Die Kunst und das Zeitalter* of 1790 in which he gives a summary of the classicistic artistic ideal as follows: 'The moral characteristics of the Schiller-Humboldt humanity: worth, nobility, purity, and moderation demand the corresponding aesthetic characteristics of the Winckelman–Lessing artistic ideals: limitation, strict form, dignified unity, noble purity, elegant proportions, clarity, the masterly and exemplary with the rejection of the uncontrolled, the unbalanced, turmoil, rank growth and wilfulness.'[89]

We shall leave it at this one example in order to point out that the culture makers have certainly not completed their task by posing such ideals, even though they have formulated the decisive principles. For, the ideals also have to be realized in continued cultural activity. The unruly reality, the indecent material, must be reshaped in such a way that it conforms to the demands contained in the posed ideal. In the struggle with tradition – the struggle by which continuity is effected[90] – and in continual cooperation with or opposition to the situation and the reality as given at any moment, a positive form is given to the norms, which are valid for each one of the relevant modalities. Sometimes, as is clear for example in the area of jurisprudence, such an activity is aimed directly at the positivization of the norm, as in the case of legislation. Very often, however, matters stand quite differently. With respect to the aesthetic, for example, it will only rarely happen that the norms as such are positivized directly, that is to say, apart from concrete works of art. It is rather the case that the great, leading artists, in their striving to create works of art that meet the posited ideals, call into being a certain style. Their style becomes normative. The development of style – and style is nothing but the positive realization of aesthetic norms – occurs in specific works of art. Such creations are epoch-making: the creation of the specific work of art is a historical deed in this case.[91] The situation can be even more complicated in other areas. Consider, for example, the formation of language and the struggle involved in gaining acceptance for the introduction of new spellings. These are matters that involve much more than a simple agreement about how certain words will be written from now on. The supra-arbitrary norms that are to be positivized can never be given a shape that would go against their meaning. A positive norm cannot itself be anti-normative! For example, a cultural ideal carried by an apostate attitude to life can never become a binding positive norm for all cultural endeavour. An apostate cultural ideal remains but a subjective opinion, precisely in as far as it is apostate, no matter how great its influence on those who give it cultural expression.

Intention and responsibility

A historical deed by definition has an effect on historical events, and so influences the course of affairs and has consequences. Prior to the event, one can at most suspect, but never fully anticipate, what the results will be, which consequences the disclosure of certain possibilities or the positivization of norms will have for development, which will next become the norm and determine the character and quality of human actions over a longer or shorter period of time. It is true that people can posit their ideals and shape things in a certain way, because they desire to be active in a truly edifying manner, since then all possibilities would be optimally exploited and all demands would be met. But it remains to be seen whether the things mentioned would really unfold and be realized according to expectations. A historical deed is like the opening of a door, of which we can only suspect what lies beyond. Perhaps we expected to enjoy a beautiful sunset on a peaceful terrace, but then we were attacked by a pack of hungry wolves or the panorama was overtaken by the approach of a most dangerous tornado.

Putting aside these metaphors, we would like to point out that a historical deed can create a whole new situation, perhaps deviating completely from the original intentions, which in itself can give rise to something totally new or different. For example, in the nineteenth century, in close connection with the positivistic views of history and culture,[92] ethnology as a science underwent a strong development whereby many materials were gathered together. As a result whole series of primitive works of art could be seen in various museums. But in the study and exposition of these works the aesthetic aspect constituted only an incidental factor. At the beginning of the twentieth century, however, these works were 'discovered', almost simultaneously in France and Germany, precisely as masterpieces of art. Since then the specimens of primitive art, gathered previously by museums, have been able to exert a great influence on Western art without such an intention ever having arisen in the minds of the original collectors. In the same way one could point to the profound influence Japanese woodcarvings had on late nineteenth-century French art, which itself put its stamp on all of Western European art. When America in 1852 broke violently through the Japanese isolation it was certainly not with the intention to give new impulses to Western art in this way. Such an outcome was not at all contemplated.

From all of this it is obvious what a great responsibility it is to act historically. The results can always be foreseen only very imperfectly. That is why people have to be accountable before the deed, so that their actions are not a leap in the dark. Of great significance here are insight and knowledge of the norms that are valid for human actions. Finally, it remains the case that the laws which the Creator has placed in his world order for our actions must be obeyed while truth may not be held down in unrighteousness.

Judging historical deeds

When judging a historical deed we should not have the intention of the history maker as our starting point. In the first place, this intention is not decisive for the historical deed as such. For the aim of the history maker does not need to be directly connected with the cultural-historical meaning and context of his or her deed. The deed itself must be tested by the relevant norms. In the second place, such a starting point for our assessment would entangle us in all sorts of difficult problems which, even if we could solve them, are totally unnecessary and would not make us any wiser with respect to the historical deed itself. For we would immediately have to ask whether the intention of a murderer such as Balthasar Gerards (who killed William the Silent), who is subjectively convinced of the correctness of his deed, should be called 'good'. The subjective starting point of posing the problem in this way would lead us into a maze of nearly insolvable questions.

The assessment of historical deeds, however, is not in the first place a matter of ethics, as is often claimed. Undoubtedly these human actions function in all aspects of reality, and therefore also in the ethical. For this reason it may well be possible to judge every deed ethically, but that will not ultimately teach us much about its historical significance. A judgment about a deed, particularly as historical deed, ought to direct itself to a testing by the norms that are valid for cultural formation without neglecting the other aspects in which it functions. It also bears consideration that it may well be possible in our broken reality for a deed to be historically[93] anti-normative, while ethically speaking there is nothing wrong with it in the first instance. I said 'in the first instance' since, considering the inter-modal coherence and dependence, it is not very well conceivable that a formatively unjust action should not, on closer inspection, be called ethically reprehensible as well.

However, and this is the flip side of what we have said so far, it is of course the case that people can only be responsible for what was implied in their own endeavours or was indissolubly connected with them. For example, we cannot make Walter Pater alone responsible for what a group of young people have read into the postscript of his *Renaissance*, namely a programme with which they could cover their own deeds.[94] This ideal of life and art was, in the first place, those young people's own responsibility. The question of whether Pater was co-responsible can only be answered once we have determined whether the ideals that the young people read into it were really contained there, independent of the fact that Pater himself refused to accept the consequences. From this example it is also clear that the judging of deeds and the posing of the question of responsibility in practice, both in daily life as well as in the discipline of history, is sometimes far from simple. We emphasize this so as not to give the impression that we think these questions always have an obvious answer.

The historical deed is not determined

A historical deed as such is never predictable. There is no historical law or pattern that could force its arrival. Circumstances can order us to pose deeds – since otherwise things would go awry – but they do not force them in the real sense of the word. There is such a thing as historical causality, but this cannot be established without applying historical cultural norms and therefore is not the consequence of a natural law. We surely should not think in terms of inevitability here: the deed is, according to its actual reality structure, not completely dependent on the circumstances that causally called it into being. But this is not where we want to direct our attention: the question that concerns us now is whether there exists any 'rationality', or law, by which a particular person inevitably acquires a certain place. For example, could anyone in 1918 have predicted that Hitler would become the 'big man' in Germany? Or further, because of the limitations of our calculations, was in that respect any 'cosmic' inevitability involved? We think not. People can never claim that by arguing from the situation. For there is no historical norm or law that determines that a particular person has to act in a specific manner. Neither could one say that there had to come a person who would act according to one or another intention or ideal: a Vincent van Gogh, a Michelangelo, a Charlemagne, a Francis of Assisi did not appear on the scene as the result of a regulation similar to a law of nature.

The history maker is a person with an above-average desire to shape. We may even say, with a compulsion to shape which may sometimes become an obsession, as in the case of Vincent van Gogh. This compulsion, this awareness of calling, although it concerns the formative aspect, is directly founded in the psychical. However, similar to the formatively responsible desire for power, the desire of the history maker is not determined by psychical impulses of the emotions. This desire for power ought to be tested by the norms valid for cultural development and will always be interpreted from the point of view of the historical deed and its consequences. The will of the history maker cannot be explained causally from the historical situation alone, precisely because it acts formatively in the latter.[95]

Who can posit a historical deed?

It would be possible to initiate an extensive and also important investigation into who posits a historical deed, a person or a group, and if the latter, which conditions would have to be met. However, as we do not want to analyse the historical deed as such we will not go into that. It should simply be noted that groups can indeed posit a deed, although it will be a requisite that such a group has to form a connection that is able to act as a unity. Unrelated individuals cannot posit a historical deed together; they would first have to connect with one another in some way. It can happen, as can be seen repeatedly in history, that in different places a similar deed is posited simultaneously. This can happen if all, or at least a great number of the factors that constitute a historical deed are equal or closely related.[96] Differences in the actual 'how' can then be explained with reference to differences in one or more of those factors.

Significance and influence of the historical deed

It is possible to ask which elements are determinative for the significance and influence of the posited historical deed. This too is a question that we cannot deal with extensively, otherwise we would stray too far outside our brief. Summarized briefly, we could say that the influence depends on the degree to which the deed solves an actual problem, although very many questions will remain unanswered in saying so little.[97]

Implicit in what has been written so far is the fact that historical deeds can vary in size and significance. This can only be discovered by testing, using intrinsically historical norms. Testing by non-historical norms will not be helpful here. For example, in the history of art the question about aesthetic quality will never decide the art-historical meaning of a particular work of art. It could be that the work in question, though ever so beautiful, has not played any role in the events of art history. For example, it might have been concealed for a long time. Or it might have been merely an especially successful example of a movement in art that already fully possessed the historical power and dominated the times without showing any new stylistic characteristics.

On the other hand it is true that in general a work of art will not gain any art-historical significance if it is not also of aesthetic importance. If that is not the case, then the historian has a new problem, namely how a work of such a low standard could have come to exercise so great an influence.[98] Here again we encounter the inter-modal coherence of the aspects of a historical deed.

We now want to move to an investigation of the constituent factors of a historical deed: world order, the situation, the personality of the history maker, and world view, to investigate their significance for the historical deed.

I World order

In our day the paintings of the Surrealists and others show that modern people are sometimes nauseated by the existing state of affairs. It bores them. It is meaningless in their eyes. They feel restricted, imprisoned as it were in a reality that does not offer them the opportunity to behave as freely as they would really want to. Nor does it offer them any opportunity to flee from the threatening difficulties – except in their dreams. Which is often the chosen escape but always very disappointing in the end. For every dream ends with an awakening and the dream is simply not reality. Moreover, the awakening cannot be delayed forever. The world situation in which we are placed simply forces us into a confrontation with harsh reality. People feel thrown into a world of which they understand neither its meaning nor character. They feel alienated and only reluctantly commit themselves to it. In that way the simple act of accepting their existence has become a problem for them, even a problem of guilt.[99]

But precisely this situation in the world today cannot fail to revive the awareness that we, as people, are bound to a certain world order, which we cannot change by our own free will, according to our own insights. Our situation is fixed, but not by ourselves: we can only accept it or withdraw from it by committing suicide. Even this last possibility is one which in its anti-normative character is prescribed by the existing order and which cannot be created apart from that order.

The natural aspects

Although it might seem to go without saying, we may just as well point out that a historical deed is in part determined by all kinds of natural laws. These natural laws may be used by people to realize their own goals but they can never transcend their limitations. We think, for example, of such evident facts as that a person has only one body and can be only in one place on earth at any given time. Moreover, a person is limited in the speed by which she or he can travel from one place to another, and can do only so much work because of the need to consider the biotic necessities of eating and sleeping.

Less obvious is the fact that the speed of cultural development is similarly limited. Nowadays people are of the general opinion that the speed at which history changes has increased in our times. There is no doubt that the 'events of the day' do to a certain extent take place faster. Announcements and suchlike can be spread around the globe much faster than ever before, so that reactions can and must come with greater promptitude. However, people still have to digest the massive volume of information now available. Even if we accept that modern people have more intellectual knowledge and a greater capacity to adapt than medieval people, for example, it still remains the case that the volume of information that they need to digest has become so great that they can hardly keep up.

The question remains, however, whether historical development, the actual cultural formation, has really increased in speed. When we think, for example, of the influence of America on Europe, it makes little difference whether a book or a film is transferred in a few days or a few months. Finally, the influences have to be assimilated by people who have a certain capacity for assimilation and who need a certain amount of time to do it. These factors may have changed a little on account of the qualities of modern people mentioned, but there are biotic limits that cannot be exceeded.

Indeed, we do believe that in one period growth and changes may occur faster than in another. For that reason, in order to come to a considered judgment about the speed of cultural development, we should compare our time with another, when things were also in fermentation and commotion. We think that a study of the sixteenth century from this point of view could clarify a lot. In general, development will take place most intensively and quickly where new ideals are in competition with one another to conquer the cultural power, and where old forms are finished and done with and are being replaced by new ones.

When we look at the field of art and see, for example, how quickly Gothic art developed and spread over Europe, and we compare this with the speed of the formation, change and spread of Baroque art, classicism, Impressionism or modern architecture, then we do not believe that we can perceive a great difference in speed. And when we compare the artistic revolution of the years 1890 to 1915, which led to modern art, with the revolution that took place at the beginning of the fifteenth century, which in turn gave rise to Italian Renaissance art and the art of the so-called Flemish Primitives, then the difference in speed is not so striking. What is perhaps more remarkable is that the intensity of cultural influence now is hardly greater than then. Even in our time there are areas which, despite all means of communication, remain behind, provincial and hardly touched by the developments in the large metropolitan centres. Only a larger spread *is* noticeable: Gothic art spread over all of Europe; modern art or derivatives of it can be found virtually over the whole world, although even now there are areas, and we don't have to think of the jungles of Africa, where the influence of the development of modern art is small or negligible.

With respect to art, therefore, we do not believe that the process of positivization has accelerated noticeably. The question is, of course, to what degree this applies to other areas of cultural activity. We are of the firm opinion, however, that with respect to the work of positivization, the question of the speed of development should not be answered too hastily and without proof in the sense of a truly measurable acceleration. But it can be argued with much greater certainty with respect to disclosure, especially disclosure of the natural aspects in technology and the natural sciences. Here we see the radical effects of more intensive and faster communication in the development of civilization. However, we should not overlook as a factor of great significance the intensive, and often rather exclusive, interest of modern society in these areas.

Capitulation to the order of nature

No matter how we answer the question above, the historical deed is co-determined by place, time and biotic-psychical laws. The limitations put on the speed of action by these could be modified to some extent by further disclosure of nature, but they will always pose boundaries. People simply have to take account of these boundaries if anything at all is to be done. People have to submit to this world order which, as we believe, is a creation order, created by the Lord our God, who also provides for it and maintains its structure.

Normative aspects

The preconditions for life as prescribed by the laws of nature – although they are inevitably closely connected with the normative order founded in the natural aspects – can never be negated by people without bringing their existence into immediate danger. It is even possible to make use of this fact in order to act decisively in a historical event: think of hunger strikes and suicides, etc. It is different in those modalities of reality where a norm is valid instead of a law of nature. A norm as such can be transgressed. And yet, even here human freedom is not at all absolute. It is possible to act anti-normatively, but in doing so we remain bound to the structure of reality: political acts remain political acts, irrespective of whether they were good or bad and whether the one who acted wanted to regard them as such or not. If someone is active in a truly historically formative way, then he or she cannot do anything other than disclose the possibilities that have been put into the creation order or positivize the norms that are suited for such formative activity. Justice or injustice, faith or unbelief, speaking or silence, being sociable or unsociable, all these can exist only because of the fact that there are modalities or functionalities in a normative order, norms to which every subject is and remains subjected. Absolute irrationality is as impossible here as in the natural aspects. And whether they want to or not, people have to submit to the reality in which they have been placed, to the order of creation where they have been included as creatures.[100]

Normativity in the historical aspect

The historical deed as such can exist only because of the fact that a historical modality has been placed in the world order. This implies that historical deeds can and ought not only to be tested by a historical norm but, moreover, that even the ascertaining and understanding of such a deed is only possible by seeing it in relation to the norm-complex of the historical modality.[101]

Historical phenomena such as tradition, progress, reaction, revolution etc., can only be understood in relation to the norms contained in the historical modality. What, for example, would be the difference in historical significance between the French Revolution and some or other South American revolution if we should take note only of the physical-psychical, i.e. the visible, aspects and should leave out of consideration the norms for all human action that are just as much a part of the world order? Nor will we be able to find such a difference by paying attention only to the subjective ideas of the history makers. Would the fact that they thought they were acting historically correctly and sought to improve the world really achieve this outcome? A man like Manet did not really intend to bring something new into art; the thought of revolutionary deeds was foreign to his mind.[102] But did he not make works that were extremely radical in art history when he created his *Déjeuner sur l'herbe* and *Olympia*? On the other hand, would a subject really achieve great things by thinking he or she was doing them?

In history we find an intertwining of the human desire to form and the supra-arbitrary normative principles that need to be positivized. A peculiar complication of the foregoing results from the fact that apostate people do not wish to subject themselves to the norm or that, in absolutizing one aspect of temporal reality by choosing other gods for themselves, they have come to a 'twisted', distorted attitude towards this law. For a historical deed can generally exert a great influence only if it tallies with the world view of the leading groups. In such a deed, reality will be brought into closer conformity with their ideals. If, however, the leading groups are apostate, unbelieving, then this law will change into a law of sin. For this deed will not remain without consequences. If an attempt were made to elevate the anti-normative into a norm it would precipitate unforeseeable and, perhaps, as the act of elevating the anti-normative into a norm, sinful results, for a great tension would come about between the supposed positive order and the normative principles that are in the creation order.[103] If, for the time being, such results were not forthcoming – for example, because of the position of great power of those apostate leading groups – then this would be taken as an excuse for continuing in the direction of realizing ideals that were actually foreign to reality. Only a radical conversion would be able to halt this process of continuing sinfulness – until a reaction sets in, in fierceness, depending on how far they have moved along this sinful road, that will make them opt for new gods again.

As the normative structure of reality is maintained, it makes it impossible for humanity to fully express their sinfulness. It ensures that in any case only the demise of a culture itself would be brought about. That is why people have to submit to the creation order, which allows itself to be only very partly forced into the wayward schemes of humanity. It means that every historical deed is a knot that can hardly be disentangled, consisting of sinful and good threads (which we cannot do without), of sin and – enforced – obedience.

Understanding historical events always implies relating them to the norms that are valid for what is formative, since otherwise we would lose their historical meaning and significance. In this connection we always have to pay attention to what extent form was given to the supra-arbitrary norms of creation, how the apostate attitude to life, in tendency and partiality, asserted itself, and to what degree people continued to realize a culture that was marked by sin.

The work of positivization also has norms

We now want to ask ourselves whether, in connection with the positivization of norms in a post-historical aspect, we may talk about historically correct or incorrect, responsible or irresponsible, or whether we are allowed to test this form-giving activity only by the norms that are valid for that specific aspect. For example, can the formation of law be tested juridically only, or does a historical norm also come into consideration here?[104] Is a new direction in art subject to aesthetic standards only or also to historical cultural norms?

We will attempt to find an answer by directing our attention towards the controversy that is taking place in modern art. It is striking that only a small part of the argumentation, especially of those who have declared themselves opponents, relates to actual aesthetic factors; the new movement is being tested not only on the purely artistic value of the works of art but also on whether or not people are departing from the correct way, whether or not the aesthetic formation is being guided into the wrong cultural path, and whether the results might not be disastrous for art and culture. With respect to Expressionism one author, who has few appreciative words to say about modern art but who, nevertheless, is sober and knowledgeable enough not to lump them all together, writes:

> Again we have the 'purity of the direct sensation', the direct transfer of sensation to canvas without the intervention of the mind: the happy notion that 'true feeling makes true art' – the Expressionist war cry which has

become the painter's panacea and his silencing answer to the layman. This notion lends authority to that brand of self-satisfaction posing as genius; allows for every imaginable kind of stupidity and lack of knowledge, and raises children, freaks and incompetents into the ranks of the masters.[105]

This kind of reasoning, which we encounter in a variety of ways, shows that people condemn such a movement precisely as a movement, an attempt to give form to or positivize norms. As proof they often point to the low quality of works created by the disciples of the principal exponents – it is always their bad influence that is pointed out. To continue the quotation: 'One of the most mischievous influences in this direction is . . .'

What happens in such a formation of style, from the point of view of its formative aspect? Earlier we claimed that, if a movement has given shape to a certain cultural ideal in a – modally understood – historical power struggle, then its real task is only just starting. For the complete positivization of the functions or modalities that are founded in the historical modality, in accordance with this new ideal, still has to be completely settled. In artistic life also, i.e. the unorganized cooperation between artists, critics, art dealers and art lovers, the way will lie open for the bearers of this newly positivized cultural ideal. Not that it would all happen without a struggle; on the contrary, the 'power of tradition' will often present them with considerable resistance.[106] But the possibility for historical deeds in this area has been gained and can be realized by competent style-makers. In the area of art, those who speak authoritatively demonstrate their competence by their talent and insights.

The activity of style formation that will take place, then, has many aspects. For us, however, the formative and aesthetic aspects, which at the same time are the qualifying aspects, are especially important in their mutual coherence. We discovered that in the struggle for modern art, the purely cultural (historical) element was brought to the forefront repeatedly, more so than the aesthetic element. And understandably so, for the work of positivization is and remains normative, to be directed at the realization of the normative principles that are inherent in the creation. Every attempt to destroy artistic values or to leave the way open for what is ugly, immature or uncontrolled is incompatible with the norm that is valid for the deed of style formation, precisely according to its formative aspect. A negative judgment about a movement can sometimes go together with an appreciation for the works of the style-making personalities. They are condemned as history makers, while being honoured as artists. That is how Craven (quoted earlier) writes about Manet, whose talent is beyond doubt in his opinion: 'Manet was a painter of surfaces; his art was ready material for shallow imitations. And by the close of the century he had begotten a school of flashy painting machines who needed for their mechanical transcriptions neither mind nor imagination.'[107] Hence Manet's position in the development of culture is criticized rather than affirmed. Whether you agree with the writer or not is of no importance. What matters here is to show that indeed the formation of style, perhaps even in the first place, ought to be tested by a purely historical norm. Indeed, we can only judge whether truly artistic demands have been met in the actual historical deed if we pay attention to this aspect of reality as well. We are dealing here with an intimate coherence or interrelation of the various modalities in the created world order.

We have undoubtedly found a striking example of what we wished to demonstrate in the controversy concerning modern art. One of the reasons for this is that modern art at the time it originated – approximately between 1900 and 1920 – formed the vanguard of a new movement. The controversy about modern art was an initial and therefore intense, controversy about the cultural ideal, the historically formative power. It is a controversy that is not yet finished, although the main front has now moved to the area of philosophy and literature with its vanguard in existentialism. But we cannot here elaborate on this.[108]

The forced submission to the norms that are valid for the formative – also by those who preach lawlessness

We have drawn attention to the character of the historical deed as being subject to norms, especially in its formative aspect. Norms are rules for how things ought to be done and they can therefore be transgressed. Norms command; they do not force. But, to express it paradoxically, they do give a compelling directive. If history makers would indeed try to trample all historical norms underfoot their deed would be doomed to unfruitfulness already from the start. If they wish their deed to have a good result, they will to some extent have to submit to those norms. A true 'lawlessness' would place itself outside the world order, which makes it impossible. Even prophets of lawlessness, the philosophers who are in favour of being 'loose from all norms and laws', will still have to keep the relevant norms if they wish their opinions to gain acceptance. For example, anarchists will have to strive for the formation of a group. They will have to carry on a power struggle with the ruling cultural powers. They will have to subject themselves to the norm of historical continuity and to numerous other valid norms if they do not want to render their struggle fruitless from the start. If they should gain political power, which is requisite for them to bring their ideas into practice, then they will find themselves as historical persons in power, placed in the institutional position of authority. This position will force precisely those normative structural principles on them which they had denied or combated in theory.

In this way Lenin and his followers, who had theoretically propagated a stateless and classless society, were forced, after their successful October Revolution, to build up a Bolshevist state organization on the historical basis of monopoly by the power of the sword. Their anarchistic theory was changed into an eschatological ideal, while any appeal to this theory was temporarily suppressed by the power of the sword. The communist theories regarding marriage and property were apparently forced to adapt to the normative structural principles of a differentiated society. The principles of a bourgeois rule of law turned out to be stronger than the anti-bourgeois Marxist doctrine. The revolutionary history maker came up against the norm of historical continuity at every turn.[109]

In this connection we could also point to the attempt by the Experimental artists to positivize new attitudes relating to art. Things like beauty are considered obsolete concepts. Art should be the most direct and spontaneous human expression. What people achieve, in reality, is often not art in the strict sense of the word. They often make what could be called 'psychograms', in which they indulge their desire to draw without any reflection, like a child does or we ourselves do when doodling on a piece of paper during a telephone conversation. These scribblings are then elevated to an actual creative deed. As 'psychograms' they are perhaps very direct expressions of the personality and as such of interest to psychologists and psychiatrists. That is not to say that these 'creations' would not also have an aesthetic aspect to them and therefore would not also be subject to the norms of beauty. In spite of the anarchistic theories the norms remain applicable to such expressions of art. This movement may claim to want to put an end to artistry and to make creative activity universal, but they already give in to the relevant order in that even the Experimentals exhibit their works in museums and exhibitions and introduce themselves as representatives of a new artistic direction. They try to gain a position in the world of art and are rightly judged by art critics on their merits.[110]

Historicism and the normed character of the formative aspect

We saw that the historical deed is subject to norms, principles of normativity which, although they are intended to be positivized by humans, are not arbitrary because they are founded in the divine world order. Even historicism, which we cannot discuss extensively here,[111] cannot break through this order and can only partly ignore it. The historicist cannot be consistent here, at least if she or he wishes to remain a historian. Because how else would any historical study be possible? How would we be able to understand the past? And how could there be any sense in speaking about such things as family, state, art in past periods of time? Or are we, in fact, only reading our contemporary ideas into the past? Can we, in general, have any valid insight in the real course of events in the past or do we read only our own cultural insights into the past? Indeed, it is impossible for historicism to avoid these epistemological questions. For historicism claims that everything, including every norm as such, is historically conditioned. It can answer these questions only by means of a radical scepticism. If you want to be a truly consistent historicist you cannot recognize any criterion of truth that claims to be elevated above the subjective opinions of a certain period. Oswald Spengler was someone who openly accepted this nihilistic consequence.

On this view every historical study has lost its meaning. And cultural philosophy would never be able to progress further than what Troeltsch called the 'current cultural synthesis' (*gegenwärtige Kultursynthese*).[112] As long as people have a subjectivistic starting point and look for law in the subject, which in this case creates the norms in historical formation itself, they will never solve the problem first formulated so clearly by Dilthey, namely how the historicity of values can be harmonized with the demand for a universal truth and lasting values. In the meantime it seems that historians never want to accept the results of historicism in their professional work. They will maintain the correctness of their findings until these have been refuted by additional evidence or alternative explanations that do greater justice to the existing evidence. What historians really take into account is not fundamental relativity but rather relativity that results from the limitations of every historian himself (or herself) whose work, after all, can never be perfect or completely irrefutable.[113]

World history. When discussing world order the question arises whether there really is or can be one world history,[114] in other words, whether there is only one development of civilization in history or whether various developments take place alongside each other. The question of whether or not it is possible for events that are decisive for the future to be played out intensively in a limited area, outside of a direct connection with cultural developments elsewhere, is beyond the scope of this discussion, although undoubtedly connected to it. The answer to the first question, we believe, is that world history is a potentiality, a possibility that may be realized. There have been times when there was little or no significant contact between the various large culture zones, either because the means of communication were so limited or simply because people were ignorant of one another's existence, or because people from either or both sides avoided and resisted any closer contact. Even now there are indigenous tribes in the Brazilian interior who stand completely outside of world history because they reject all outside contact.

The issue of cultural contact between East Asia and Europe before the modern age is a complex one. These were fairly closed cultural areas with boundaries between the two, each with its own development of civilization. Not that there were no influences active between them, whether directly or via an intermediary, but interchange happened extremely slowly, so that even technical discoveries made in China became known in Europe only after centuries. Think of the manufacturing of paper which we have already mentioned as an example. The procedure was discovered in China in the fourth century and passed from one country to the next until it finally became known in Western Europe around a thousand years later. It would have been possible to have had closer contact – the potential just needed to be disclosed. That this did not happen owed less to geographic and transport obstacles than to the fact that China and Japan resisted any intensive cultural contact and influence until late into the nineteenth century. The few contacts that could be mentioned from earlier times in the areas of art and science are incidental and of little significance. The influence of political deeds in the one area on the other were fortuitous and not intended. We think, for example, of the course of events during the great migrations of the Eurasian peoples which received their impetus when the Chinese chased the Huns from their borders, or of the history of incursions by the Golden Horde or the Turks.

The intended potential possibility for a unitary world history is based on the fact that people, wherever they live and work, are bound to one and the same world order, the creation order established for humankind. Disclosure and positivization can therefore differ greatly and be guided by totally different principles, so that mutual understanding can be extremely difficult. But the influences in the areas of art and politics between East and West show that these areas cannot be regarded as so independent of each other that there is no possibility of a genuine world history.[115] The contacts and influences that can be documented also show that the chasm between East and West was not based on a fundamental difference in the structural ordering of reality, which set the norms for the behaviour of people both here and there according to its character. Recent history shows this convincingly, now that the possibilities of contact have been realized to a certain degree.

Does the course of world history run lawfully?

The question arises whether we can discover a determinant law in the development of world history. Much has been thought and written concerning this question.[116] Troeltsch also thinks it is a very important problem. He deals with it in both his *Historismus und seine Probleme* ('Historicism and its Problems') and his *Historismus und seine Ueberwindung* ('Historicism and its Victory'), formulating it as follows: 'How do we get from the empirical use of a specifically historical concept of development that can be logically sound, to a universal world thought, in which our own creative direction is simultaneously normed and objectively founded?'[117] Such a search, in which people try, from the facts, to find laws that determine the course of all world events, seems to us not only unfruitful but also likely to be dangerous. Winckelmann, for example, saw a parallel between the development of art in antiquity and in modern times. In his vision of the art history of antiquity, and the presupposed parallel between this development and the development of the West, he was as it were forced to depreciate all art after Raphael, whereby every unprejudiced judgment was nipped in the bud. As a result the art of Carracci, in particular, was completely misunderstood and undervalued.[118] An almost forced distortion of the facts was the result of this a-priori-ism.

We think that the search for such determinant laws in the course of world history is actually nothing but a search for the law in the subject, in humanity itself. For the course of history as it unrolled itself by the formative activity of one generation after another is being elevated in some way to the status of a law. In the subjective course of history there is no law to be discovered. There is only a norm – or rather, a complex of norms in a specific structural coherence. This structural coherence is valid for all people and all times, whereby each successive generation gives it a new positive shape. It can be observed that in the course of the centuries, by the continuing formative activity of people as they continue to build on what the previous generation had achieved, a continuing disclosure of both the natural as well as the normative aspects of reality takes place. But that does not provide us with a law for the course of development in the sense of evolution to a better future, or something like that, nor can a three-stage law as in Comte be distilled from it. This is already clear from the fact that loss mutations can occur, whereby some achievements in the past are lost or purposely destroyed. We notice a tendency to the latter direction in the modern art movements that are focused on revolution, such as Futurism.[119]

Even less than we can discover such laws in the disclosure can we discover them in the continuing work of positivization. New world views and new cultural ideals appear and attempt to reform reality to their way. No law or prescribed pattern can be found in either the succession of world views or in reality-changing activity. For, alongside the new dominant streams the older ones often continue to exist – just consider the problem of the discontinuities between generations.

There is only this 'determinant law', that the world order – and with it also human nature – does not change, that people are at all times and in all countries bound to the same basic modal norms and structural law, which carry an imperative character in the natural aspects and force people to submit again and again to the normative aspects if they do not want to go under or, with all their striving and labouring, to 'strike a blow in the air'. On the one hand you can leave a challenge unanswered[120] – but you will pay for that negligence, at best with a loss of influence, at worst with the loss of viability. On the other hand it is impossible and senseless to break through the structure of our cosmos and try to put oneself outside of this order.

Thus we discover a continuing condition of being bound to an order in the course of history that was not created by humanity. It is not possible a priori to construct progress according to a determined course of events. At most we can notice an increasing disclosure, combined with an enlargement of the terrain of which people have knowledge, and an ever increasing complexity of problems, both practical and theoretical.

Order and coherence in world history

And yet it is not the case that the course of history, though not running according to natural law, is a meaningless succession of generations, each with their own opinions and views.[121] God has a plan and guides history according to his ordinance. Some of it is revealed to us in the Holy Scriptures. But this is no law to which humanity just happens to be bound; we are not being taught determinism here – it is prophetic revelation of history in advance.

Also revealed to us are some directives of God's character and behaviour, for example in Deuteronomy 28. But even here we find neither laws to which God would be subject in his actions nor a discernible law in the subjective events. These directives are most closely connected with the revealed will of God, the norms he has given for all human activities. In Deuteronomy 28 it is said, for example, that if people disobey, the Lord will come with his judgments in many ways, in his time – for he can in mercy delay judgment – unless the people repent. Yes, the aim of all judgment always remains conversion.[122] So God intervenes in events according to directives that he chose to reveal to us,[123] but we should never see a determined law or fate in this. Not because the Lord's actions are irrational, but because they are not subject to the law at all. We must never elevate the unfolding of God's decree into a norm. We have to take note of the facts, and then bow before his sovereign will.[124] It should be enough for us to know that he has given us norms for our behaviour that we should obey.

We cannot discover general laws by which world events take place. In the course of history we are concerned with a complicated interaction of historical deeds, which in historical causality have influenced the course of events. Each of those deeds was individually dependent on all kinds of factors. The deeds might have been good or bad, submitting to the norm or anti-normative. Each deed contained a certain element of inexplicability. All these historical events certainly do not take place without coherence and connection. The fact that people have to adapt constantly to historical norms, whereby it is not possible for them to overlook continuing power relationships or to ignore tradition or not to act in historical causality in response to the actions of allies or adversaries – for all these reasons there is a coherence to all human history from the beginning to the present. It is this coherence which ensures that the development of civilization does not proceed without a certain order.[125]

The subject-side of reality

The subjection to one and the same complex of natural laws and norms in its various modalities constitutes an order and coherence in the course of world history that is in itself neither bound by laws nor determined. In the preceding treatment of the law-side of our cosmos we also had to bring the subject-side into the discussion. We now turn to specifically consider the subject-side of our topic. According to the subject-side people do not live independently from each other. On the contrary, we are all related and our lives and work take place on one and the same earth and within the same era.

All of human history takes place on planet earth, which has a certain geological composition and a certain distribution of flora and fauna which people may utilize in their cultural work of disclosure, which demands a great deal of work. We may never forget that we are dealing with a cursed earth that brings forth thorns and thistles, and that man shall make a living by the sweat of his brow, according to the divine word.[126]

Although born of one father and mother and therefore according to the flesh of one race, humanity has been divided spiritually by the Fall. The struggle of the antithesis between the seed of the serpent and the seed of the woman as proclaimed immediately after the Fall takes effect in two ways! In the first place there is the struggle between the 'old man' and the 'new man' in the heart of every believer. In the second place there is in world history in principle a twofold cultural unfolding. Both the race of Seth and the race of Cain are working at the cultural mandate, which remained in force after the Fall. A very special place has been given in history to the race of Seth, God's people, later the people of the covenant: to be 'a salting salt'. By keeping the revealed word of God and by obeying his commandments, walking in his ways, it will have a preserving, decay-resistant function in the development of civilization.[127]

Cain's race, i.e. the 'world', is working at the cultural mandate in their own fashion, yes they have often considered precisely this (the cultural mandate) as the meaning and purpose of all their striving and work. In doing cultural work people try to build their own paradise, to gain mastery over nature, to be king. However, the aim of all work is then no longer to reveal the glory of God or do his will, but the human achievement itself. In a continuing realization of their aims, constantly driven on the paths of disobedience by the prince of this world, becoming more and more conscious of their own strivings and starting point but also subject again and again to the world order as maintained by God – sometimes assisted by an apostate race of covenant children[128] – this race is building their own culture by directing disclosure and positivization at human being as such, at people's happiness, comfort, freedom and desire.

The history of this one human race, the whole of humanity, in which the struggle of the antithesis comes to expression sometimes fiercely and sometimes barely or not at all, runs its course between the Fall and the Last Day. This means that sin will always remain a real factor. It will be impossible to create a paradise on earth. The struggle of the antithesis will not end until the last day and the Last Judgment make an end to history in this present age.[129]

With respect to the struggle of the antithesis – which, as we said, is not always fought equally fiercely – we should keep in mind what we may call the world-historical periodization, which does not always have to be the same everywhere. It makes a difference whether we are looking at a nation that lived before or after Christ, and if the latter, whether or not they had already come into contact with Christianity. In the first case, the struggle of the antithesis plays a role, in the latter it has not yet come to actual manifestation.

In his divisions of the history of European philosophy, Professor Vollenhoven takes account of this periodization to arrive at: a time before the spread of Christianity (pagan philosophy); a time when antichristian streams occurred side by side with ones in which people tried to take account of the Scriptures (the time of the Church Fathers); the time of synthetic philosophy in which a dominant Christianity adopts pagan elements (the Middle Ages); and finally, the modern times, in which he distinguishes, besides the Reformational and synthetic directions also new antichristian streams.[130] However, these 'periodizations' will work out differently when we speak about America from the way they do when we speak about primitive peoples. For example, before Columbus America still lived in a pagan period. Finally, at the Last Judgment all people from all races and times will be at the same point.

Every historical deed is done by a member of the human race, under the norms of the world order created by God. If we attempt to analyse the constituting factors of such a deed, it becomes clear that the actual situation in which it takes place will exercise an influence. We wish to devote our attention to this in a separate section.

2 The situation

Every historical deed is limited according to its character by the norms and laws present in the world order and occurs at a time and place set by world history. In its actual, subjective reality structure it will be an answer to the actual historical complex of circumstances arising at that moment in history. Every deed of formative significance stands in a relation of historical causality with previous deeds and can never be separated from the total situation of the time in which it takes place.

When we speak about the situation, we direct our attention to all those factors which the person doing the deed has not called into being him or herself. It is the 'facts' of the actual circumstance that compel. People can never, except to their own disadvantage, avoid or ignore them. We may never close our eyes to the factual circumstances at the base of every historical deed, even if we should do so from a seemingly lofty idealism.

Fact and world order

'What is a fact?' we may ask. What one person calls fact, another calls interpretation. The question arises whether there is such a thing as a fact, independent of a subjective judgment. It seems one can talk without objections about the so-called facts of nature, while one usually distinguishes between facts and subjective judgments when discussing the normative aspects of human life. We now wish to look at some of these things more closely.

It is indeed true that the laws of nature are laws that maintain their validity, even if we were to try and escape from them. People have to accept them whether they want to or not. This becomes especially clear when we meet thinkers or artists for whom this state of affairs has become an ongoing problem because they experience this order of the laws of nature as a restriction on life, a prison, an irrational fate. We have in mind here the irrationalists amongst modern thinkers. But this 'negative concept of reality' occurs more often than we might suspect among artists, especially the Romantics, mystics and the moderns.[131] To give an example, think of Mallarmé, whose *Un coup des dés* is very instructive in this respect. The work is very dark, since he attempted to express the unreal in it.

At the same time it is often impossible to speak meaningfully about facts, even those relating to natural events, without a subjective judgment. If we read in a report on a flood in which many lives were lost that it was a disaster, then there is more than the simple fact of a numerable number of dead and a loss of cultural goods that can be expressed in figures. It is possible that someone could say: 'Ah well, what is a handful of people – a disaster?' That is why it is only partly true to say that facts compel. A person is, after all, more than a pure 'natural being' and that is why in her or his actions all kinds of other factors, besides survival instinct, fear of death and hunger play a role. The question is always how a person will react to the actual circumstances of nature. She or he will have to accept them as facts, but the subjective human judgment makes them meaningful only as a starting point for human action. In the case of a natural disaster many different reactions are possible, e.g. attempts to control the circumstances to such a degree that as much as possible may still be saved, or to let everything take its course and escape. Only rarely can one talk about a genuinely instinctive action. That happens only when nature overwhelms a person in such a way that he or she has to react immediately and no time is left for any subjective insight. This may happen if a tidal wave were to fall on the house. The more sudden and direct the natural event, the more complete the subjection to the natural order and the more 'instinctively' people will react, in other words, without subjective consideration or judgment, just following their survival instincts.

This is a case where nature acts as a historical object, to which people, as historical subjects, have to react. That becomes especially clear where a natural disaster has a much larger effect than could be explained by the factual circumstances. That the earthquake of 1755 destroyed most of Lisbon (Portugal) lies in its factual structure. However, that these events would deeply affect and occupy the minds of Europe when people were debating the question of theodicy and natural religion can only be understood from the cultural circumstances, not from the fact of nature itself.[132]

Therefore, we see that with respect to a natural event according to its objective-historical aspect, it is hardly possible to speak of indisputable facts. How much more problematic will it be to speak about subjective factualities in the normative aspect. And yet, there too, people usually distinguish between facts and judgments. We will now investigate whether such a distinction is meaningful, and which criteria need to be applied.

Imagine someone saying: 'It is a fact that so and so at that time acted wrongly.' It is possible that someone else may reply: 'You judge him in this way, but I think he did the right thing.' The question then becomes whether the first speaker spoke correctly of a fact. Or again, someone may say: 'However you may judge the content of the report, it is a fact that he spoke Dutch badly.' To which someone else may reply that it was not at all noticeable or that it was not true. However that may be, you can see that many facts are being stated on the basis of judgmental norms.

This will always be the case with the normative aspects and hence we may pose the thesis: no knowledge of the facts without insight into the valid norm. People like to exacerbate this particular problem into a dilemma of 'norm or fact'. Therefore we wish to draw special attention to the connection between knowledge of the facts and knowledge of the norms.

If you state as fact that a murder has been committed, this is meaningful only if a norm has been made valid that one person may not kill another without legal cause. If this were not so, we could get no further than to establish that one person injured another, whereby the other lost his life. Nevertheless, not every act of killing is murder, even when it happens intentionally. Think of self-defence, death by misadventure, the execution of a death sentence, war etc. There are no facts standing apart from values and judgments.

Historicism

The issue discussed here does indeed form the central question of historicism. Since historiography is dependent on knowledge of the facts, and those in turn cannot be separated from insight into the relevant norms, history writing itself has become problematic for every viewpoint that denies the existence of enduring norms. Troeltsch gives as a first solution to that problem that the history writer has to test deeds by the norms that were in force at that time.[133] But even this leads us into difficulties. For in this way we could understand why a person like Raphael became so great but it remains a deep mystery why another painter from that time, whose work was carried out by the same approach, was appreciated much less and exercised a much smaller influence. In order to understand this we have to make a qualitative judgment ourselves, and we can do that only by making comparative judgments.

But it becomes even more difficult if we wanted to test and understand, in this way, new formations that depart from the positive standards that had been valid until that time. In historical scholarship it often happens that people judge events differently from how the contemporary person judged. Think here of the art-historical judgment about the significance of van Gogh. If tested by the norms that were in force at the time, then words like 'tragedy', 'under-estimation', 'unjust snubbing' would become meaningless terms. If we measure van Gogh's art by the standard for art that was valid in his time, then the contemporary rejection of him is more than understandable. The fact that van Gogh positivized the norm and would become one of the guiding spirits in Expressionism at the start of the new century remains completely unintelligible in that case. It is also difficult to ascribe the later appreciation for van Gogh to the positive norm that was valid in the decisive years 1900 to 1910, since van Gogh's art itself fell short of this by a long way. Besides, even if one wanted to persevere, there are still other difficulties. For, what was the positive aesthetic norm in those years? The opinion of this or that group or of the general public or only of an elite group? Or will it suffice to take account of the opinion of a numerically very small group of 'avant-gardists'? It is clear that in this way we get only further entangled in the difficulties. Van Gogh's own place, his significance and influence, are understandable only if we judge his art on its artistic merits and thus measure it by universally valid aesthetic norms. The change in positive standards detracts nothing from the fact that the aesthetic character of the various criteria maintained itself. Therefore, there must be constant modal principles of beautiful harmony, which during the course of time make differing actual realizations possible.

How is agreement possible when stating the facts?

If we can accept the thesis that a knowledge of the norms is necessary before the establishment of facts (in the normative aspects) or, formulated more broadly, that a knowledge of the facts is dependent on insight into the world order, then the difficulty has moved to another area. For then the question becomes one of depth and kind of insight. If there is agreement over the validity of certain norms people will be able to state in principle the same facts or accept them as such. If no agreement exists about the recognition of norms the factual statement will be experienced as a subjective judgment, a subjective value judgment, which cannot claim universal validity.

As we hope to explain, insight into the world order and hence also a principled view of law and norm are dependent on world view. Nevertheless, it is possible in various respects to obtain agreement between bearers of different world views with regard to the facts. Consensus is possible insofar as there is agreement about the positive validity of natural laws and norms. Beyond that people will have to speak of judgments. For example, an orthodox (believing) Christian and a humanist will have little difference of opinion regarding all sorts of factual data relating to the area of the state, justice, rules for social behaviour and the like. But the fact that the Lord Jesus Christ is now sitting at the right hand of God and reigning as King over this earth will be no more than a myth for the humanist. On the other hand, the believer will view as a deceptive illusion the humanist statement that humanity is the final arbitrator of good and evil in their autonomous reason.

The boundary placed in social relationships between 'universally valid fact' and 'subjective judgment' cannot simply be found in the subjective event, but only in the presence or absence of a consensus of opinions. How can this develop between the bearers of different world views? In the first place, by submission to the world order. Why submission? The answer is, because reality cannot be ignored for ever, nor can the truth in every respect be suppressed in unrighteousness, since then one would not only fundamentally but also obviously be at variance with reality itself. The consensus of opinions thus reached is of great importance for the whole of society, since without communal acceptance of inviolable truths and the recognition of universally valid norms for behaviour there would be no possibility of human society, *koinonia*.[134]

This consensus of opinions also comes about because in any particular cultural area there is always a historical coherence that ensures agreement on a number of matters, at least in social relationships. In Western European society it is true that Christians and humanists live side by side, but the latter are not imaginable without the profound influence of the former. Whatever that coherence may be, it is undeniable that through this there is agreement with respect to a series of norms and principles that control the basic traits of our modern Western European society. For it is in this historical coherence that the positivization of norms took place, undoubtedly not without conflict. Thus the positivized norm is valid for all. Earlier we gave the example of speaking Dutch badly, a fact that can only be tested by positive norms of language. In other words, through our communal endeavour we all have the same language, irrespective of our world view, just as we all have to respond to the same norms for social behaviour and for morality etc. within the area of general social relationships.

The situation is itself not normative

We may conclude from the foregoing that at every moment there is always a real, actual state of affairs, irrespective of our vision of what it may be. But people see it, and see through it, more or less correctly depending on their insight into the structure of the world order as it really is. With respect to the latter it is possible, in any particular cultural area, to achieve a certain degree of common agreement as people test occurrences by the norms in their positive shape. Is it then possible to call the thus viewed situation normative in the sense that it follows from the situation of the moment itself that a certain decision ought to be taken? No, the question is put incorrectly, in principle, because the subjective situation as such can never be the norm. But we are able to say that the situation ought to be judged in a certain way, and that we then ought to do deeds that are meaningful and just in this situation, i.e. in accordance with the norm. Say one power attacks another – as for example Germany did when they invaded the Netherlands in 1940. The correct judgment of the situation is that an act of aggression took place. The norm is valid that says that the territory of one's native land ought to be defended with the power of the sword against an unjust act of aggression. The authorities, soldiers, population, each in their place, have to act rightly, i.e. in this case, to cooperate as much as possible in defence. In general, we may conclude, norms are always valid in respect of a factual situation. They are not general existences or substances or ideas apart from reality, nor does their validity have actual meaning everywhere and always. If a man is single, he may marry a wife. But it would be bigamy if he entered into a second marriage. Norms and laws are meaningful only in connection with the subject-side of reality and receive their actual significance only in a certain actual situation.

Troeltsch again, and the testing of historical facts by the norm that was valid at the time

In connection with the foregoing argument we can point out here that the methodical postulate of Troeltsch, i.e. to measure the events of the past by the norm that was in force at that time, is also meaningful. For when we read that a French monarch ate with his fingers, we may not conclude that he was a barbarian – if we are reading about one who lived in the Middle Ages, when our present table manners were unknown. And we do not need to argue the fact that we should not test the administration of justice in the seventeenth century by our contemporary laws. But, and this is where our difference of opinion with Troeltsch surfaces, whatever positive law looked like in the seventeenth century, injustice can never be justice. Therefore, there must be constant legal principles that do not change with time. The norm principles in the creation should always be kept in view, even though contemporary people (correctly) measure by the norms in their positive shape as they are in force in their time. Besides, since in the positivization of norms shape has been given to enduring principles of norms, there will be no opposition between them. Adultery can never be called good, whatever the opinions of the time may be, even though the order of marriage in a polygamous society will have a different shape from that in a monogamous society.[135] And a truly beautiful work of art will always remain beautiful, however much the artistic opinions may change.

However much we should keep hold of the latter, if we are not to get lost in a directionless historicism and also, as we argued, if history itself is not to become unintelligible, we have to admit there is one more element of truth in what Troeltsch has said. We should indeed take account of the contemporary opinions when we are studying a certain period of time. If in a certain period of time people refuse to see sin (i.e. what exists in conflict with the norm put in the creation order) in a certain context, or even not only tolerate but laud this sin, then deeds done in this sense will not provide any direct occasion for historical reactions. In such cases one always reacts to the actual situation, and if that is seen as normal or just, then one will not easily take action. In the late Middle Ages, when prostitution was very common, one will not expect to find people starting an association to fight the trade in white female slaves.[136]

Summary

We began with the thesis that insight into world order determines insight into a situation. However much we are convinced that this insight is dependent on world view, we pointed to the relative character of it in the sense that, again and again, there will be a submission to the world order whereby only rarely a fundamentally unjust insight will be carried out in a consistent manner in all areas and in all depth and breadth. A certain communal opinion arises about valid laws and norms, partly through living within the same cultural community with its own historical tradition. This makes the establishing of facts communally possible. The situation is maintained as it is true according to the world order, irrespective of human insight. That is why people will continually have to submit to the world order if they do not simply want to 'live past the facts' and make their own work meaningless or ineffectual. This is why the actual situation is of such great influence and significance for the historical action.

The situation in a specific period of history

Our thesis was that a historical deed would be constituted partly by the situation. It is clear, however, that a deed will only seldom be done consciously with an eye to world history. More often an action will take place within the cultural sphere of the narrowly bound terrain in which a person moves and feels at home. Before we go into this more deeply, however, we must look at a tangential problem, i.e. whether it is correct to speak of a uniform cultural development even within a closed cultural area. Will there always be cultural unity?

We think that this will only rarely be the case. Such a situation could arise only if one of the historical powers had gained such an ascendancy that all the others had to take their cue from it. But even then, as for example in the time of the medieval ecclesiastical mono-culture, one comes across subsidiary movements when making a more detailed study. If we look at the nineteenth century we see a number of cultural movements alongside each other which had developed to a certain degree independently of one another. These cultural entities standing alongside each other are of two kinds. In the first place variously qualified cultural powers will move independently of each other, without any noticeable mutual influences. We think for example of art and the church, which had little or no cultural connection in the nineteenth century. In the second place we see movements develop next to each other which are guided by completely different goals, often accompanied by a profound difference in world view. That is how in the nineteenth century in the Netherlands both socialism and the Reformed political movement developed alongside each other, both perhaps in opposition to the same ruling party but not defined by that in their aim. The first-mentioned difference arises out of the different work terrains – whereby within each of the terrains various groups will fight over the formative power – the second cuts right across that and comes about as a result of fundamental differences in cultural ideals.

Yet it cannot be denied that on the other hand the above-mentioned movements, which were differentiated by world view only, moved only very partly independently from each other. For not only was their position of being in conflict, by which they found themselves positioned over against each other, an important form of cultural-historical contact from which they all derived important influence but they also had a communal cultural heritage. What they had in common was the degree of disclosure of the natural aspects, for it is almost unthinkable that one group would monopolize certain technical possibilities, although that can happen.[137] On the other side also, at least to an important degree, people would have been subject to the same positivized norms. Here we think of language, behavioural norms, law etc. I said: 'to an important degree'. For even here individual differences remain. As to language, we may think of a jargon that is exclusive to a group. And the formation of a group will involve its own internal law-formation. But in any case, there is to a certain degree a communal culture, also as a result of a commonly experienced national and international history.

Next we must deal with what is not held in common. It goes without saying that faith differences can be big, but divergence is not limited to matters of faith. The 'worlds' in which people move are very different. Think of the journals you read or for which you write, the leading figures that you esteem and follow, the occasions such as congresses you attend, etc. People make their own history within their own group, and also have their own history. For the Reformed part of the Dutch population, for example, the *Afscheiding* ('Separation') of 1834 and the *Doleantie* ('Lament' or 'Protest') of 1886 still have enormous significance, while for others they are mere facts from the past that are hardly known, since they seem to be of no interest to them. And, to give an example illustrating the other distinction, for everyone who is concerned with art, the work of Gauguin, regardless of how that person thinks about it, is of great importance because he was one of the pillars on which modern art was built, while there are many scholars and politicians, from whatever movements, for whom Gauguin is at best a known name. Thus we have a particular history alongside a communal history which is connected with the limited cultural horizon of human beings, who can only consciously live, strive and work in a limited area.

All this is fundamentally important for our insight into the character of the historical deed. History makers too will take their starting point in a particular situation and will develop their activity precisely in that limited area where they feel at home. Physicists, for example, will build on what has been discovered in physics and will make their discoveries there in cooperation or in competition with their professional colleagues. They will make their discoveries known and within the group of colleagues and initiates they will be honoured for them and will make a name for themselves. This is just as valid if the discovery were of world-historical importance: the outsider will hear about it though he or she can usually not judge the relative greatness of the discovery as a personal achievement and often does not even know the name of the physicist.

As an example in another area, consider that in the fifteenth century a lot of diligent study and hard work was being done in several studios, especially that of Verrocchio, with the aim of achieving and perfecting a certain artistic goal. That goal was to represent reality as accurately and as objectively as possible. The new possibilities disclosed by them had a significance that went far beyond the limited area of the art of painting.

Also Leonardo da Vinci received his training there. Later, and as a direct result of this, he was the first to put this possibility in the service of science, in such a way that since that time science can hardly function without the use of exact drawings and has continued using it, even though the art of painting itself developed in very different directions. In this way an artistic activity, which in the life of art had an undoubted but nevertheless limited significance, became a deed that bore fruit we still enjoy daily – which thus acquired world-historical perspective.

Historiography and the current situation

All of this has significance for the task and place of historiography. A historical deed presupposes two things. In the first place a linking up with the past – it is neither possible nor permissible to ignore the past and everyone has to build on what has been attained. In the second place a historical deed arises out of the current situation. A knowledge of history is necessary for both. In order to know and understand one's own situation, to distinguish different movements and directions, to perceive the sometimes delicate nuances in the terminology used, behind which sometimes very profound differences of opinions are hidden, and to become aware of what the different parties desire – for all of this a knowledge of history is essential. For that reason, apart from general history, it is a particular history that will have our full attention. For example, the history of the origins and growth of modern art will be of fundamental importance to people who have anything to do with modern art and who therefore need to determine their attitude towards it, especially art critics and artists. This is so because it is impossible to gain an overview or make a judgment of the situation today without this background. And, drawing the circle even closer, it will be especially important for them to pay attention to what has already been said or done by kindred spirits.

For this reason historians from various groups or directions will make a subject choice. They will struggle with their own set of problems connected to the questions of the day in the context of the particular situation in which they find themselves. In order to reflect on the character and meaning of the current questions of the day, and to investigate possible ways of solving these questions, people will have to direct their attention to similar problems in the past. Those who take a new direction will search for analogous cases in the past in order to reflect on the complications and difficulties this could incur. Especially the particular history will be an obvious field of investigation. When you read through a history of historiography such as the one by Fueter, it is remarkable how closely the subject and its related range of problems cohere with the current, particular situation. We think of Lecky, who concerned himself with the history of rationalism, and of the Bollandists, who were especially concerned with hagiography in order to assert the truth against imputations of error.

It is not at all a limited or narrow view that in this way motivates the historian in his or her work. Very often, writings borne out of the needs of one's own time and place become the best and most influential. We think here of the work by the Bollandists, as mentioned already, Groen van Prinsterer's *Unbelief and Revolution*, Voltaire's *Louis XIV* and others. It is true that such works are sometimes rather one-sided, since the study was undertaken with a certain goal in view, but on the other hand there is much understanding for the problems of the past since they are understood to be also the problems of the day. Moreover, historical studies that are motivated by an inner conviction and necessity are often more profound and inspired than those with nothing more than the detachment that characterizes a purely formal, scholarly interest.

Troeltsch's cultural synthesis ('Kultursynthese')

Troeltsch's thinking about the 'contemporary cultural synthesis' (*gegenwärtige Kultursynthese*) can be meaningful here. The study of one's own past, together with the struggle that sometimes takes place in order to gain a correct insight into certain events, brings clarity to one's own endeavours and objectives and provides a definite criterion for recognizing errors and irrelevant lines of investigation. Historical research can and must, in a serving way, but sometimes decisively, make its contribution to the solution of the problems of one's own group. This not in the way Troeltsch suggests,[138] namely that the historical investigation will yield norms for today, but in that it can make its own contribution both to insight into the situation as well as to the norm.

In the light of this we can understand the more or less fierce debate that has been carried on around the figure of Groen van Prinsterer. The conflict was not just about Groen himself and his contemporary history – in the particular history of Reformed people there are many others who could draw our attention – but the concentration of attention on Groen can be explained especially from the fact that he laid the foundation on which the Anti-Revolutionary Party [political party] built all its activities. Consequently, valid insights into aims and opinions of this party and its people cannot be obtained without studying his work. Therefore the struggle for Groen is not in the first place a scholarly debate of historians but also a struggle for today regarding the direction to be taken and the correctness of various principles. It is the situation today that demands reflection and a choice of position.

In general, this is why the historical investigation into a certain piece of history will often be connected with current points of conflict – whereby the study of history as a whole will benefit, since in this way areas of study that were hitherto little known may be brought to the attention.

Internal and external causes of the historical deed. Having shown that the historical deed stands in a very direct relationship to the situation of the group or movement to which the history maker belongs, we should now consider which elements constitute the situation in such a way that a deed will be done. We may distinguish between internal and external causes.

In the case of an internal cause a development takes place within a given group that calls for a decisive response. For example, if one tried to push or force art into a certain direction by holding on too tightly to certain principles, by being too one-sided and passing by other equally worthwhile elements, then a reaction is bound to come from others who will try to set their own course. Their deeds will be the result of the situation in the specific area of the arts. Think of the continual conflict, especially in France, which was carried on last century by leading artists against the academy system, and the politics connected to it of judging pieces submitted for the annual big expositions, the Salons. We will return to this later, but here too there will exist a connection with the overall cultural situation. The acting persons are not independent of this and they will take their place in the power struggle that is carried on for the cultural ideals. Both the occasion and the shape in which the deed takes place, however, are primarily guided by the situation that exists within artistic life.

However, it will happen more than once that the deed is not guided in the first place by circumstances within the group but by external influences. For no single group, no matter how private or distinctive their development may be, is independent of other culturally significant entities. There will always be close intertwinings. Circumstances that are in no way artistically determined can force the artist to look for new ways to solve new tasks, to find the correct answer to problem situations which have come about by external circumstances. A political power that suddenly acts in a totalitarian way may give us the most telling example – think of the development of art in Germany after 1933. But it can also be that social circumstances cause adaptations in, say, architectural style which present the artists with new tasks – e.g. making monumental wall paintings. Such tasks may be quite foreign to the art of painting at that time and something which its internal development did not necessarily demand. To give another example, consider the art in the second half of the sixteenth and in the seventeenth century in Italy which would undoubtedly have developed differently if there had not been an ecclesiastical Counter-Reformation. The latter provided the artist with new tasks as well as restrictions.

The power relationships that determine the situation. It will not be necessary to subject the various factors that determine the situation as such to analysis. We do want to consider more carefully the power relationships that determine the situation in the context of our subject. It goes without saying that foreign politics especially is dependent on this; in the first place we do not wish to pay attention to this. During our discussion we have already came across a remarkable development. There are two completely differently constituted power types involved in the struggle in the area of culture. In the first place there are the groups whose activity is qualified by different aspects of reality which come to actual and diverse expression by way of cultural formative endeavour. Alongside these we encounter mutually antagonistic directions which differ in their cultural ideals, which are usually intimately connected with differences in world view.

The last-mentioned groups will fight each other for historical formative power in order to realize their cultural ideals, a power struggle which repeatedly dominates all of cultural life. The debate, or other attempts to gain influence, will take place both in general as well as in specific areas of life. Occasionally the struggle will wane and every movement will try to gain positive results within its own circle. The divergent developmental tendencies may then become all the more sharply delineated. The only instance when this will not occur is when the work of positivization embraces every person without exception, as in the work of legislation by the authorities and, perhaps to a lesser degree, in economic activity. The coexistence of different movements also shows that history does not move along one line of development but rather coheres in a complex of lines, which at any given time together determine the situation.

It is no less important, however, that the various differentiated typical cultural circles form power centres that function alongside each other. Each of these will more or less direct the formative cultural activity, dependent on the power that they possess at any given point. At the time of the Italian Renaissance art enjoyed a dominant position of power.[139] At other times it played a subordinate role in cultural life. Today economic relationships are very important, whereas they were less significant in earlier periods such as the High Middle Ages. In our time the practical influence of the church in the struggle for cultural ideals has greatly diminished. By contrast, in the Middle Ages the church provided leadership and unity of direction to all of cultural life. The role played by science as a cultural power in the various periods also differs greatly. In modern times, cultural life has been bound more and more intensively to the powerful development of science. For us the significance of science is incalculably greater than it was in ancient Rome. It would be possible to multiply such examples to support the thesis that the unfolding of power of a specific cultural circle exercises a historically variable influence on the whole of cultural life. If you keep an eye open for this you will notice, when studying art history, that now these, then those external factors will have a decisive influence on the course of events.

Once again, the situation as occasion

We have repeatedly noted that the situation is the occasion for the historical deed. We now wish to look at this subject from another angle. In general we could state that a historical deed will be pre-eminently a reaction to an actual situation. There are either new possibilities that bring forward new developments, or an existing state of affairs comes to be experienced as unjust. Shortcomings become evident and people think they are on the wrong track. It can also happen that the historical development has led to a situation that produces new problems which cannot be solved, or that makes demands that cannot be met by existing practices. We have already dealt with some of these, so we do not have to elaborate on this now.

Only the second possibility in the relationship between historical deed and situation requires further explanation. The necessity of an act of intervention in the historical event will be very strongly felt if there is, indeed, a yawning chasm between the actual positivization of the norm and the cultural ideal that people profess. Those 'people', a certain group, carried along by a certain world view, will, if there is a possibility of gaining cultural power, undoubtedly try to capture it with the aim of adjusting the positivization to their own idea, and to change the existing system drastically. The shortcomings will usually be felt particularly in a certain sphere, e.g. in the political or ecclesiastical sphere, or in science or art, and it is in that particular area that the initial skirmishes will take place. If these are fought successfully, awareness will slowly deepen that also in other areas of cultural life renewing action is needed. At the time of the Reformation in the sixteenth century there was initially a concern only for the situation in the church. Only after the success of the initial struggle were people free to realize the same ideal in other cultural areas and could they pay attention to this. That is how it came about that a movement that was at the beginning, and by design, an ecclesiastical movement had such a deep influence on almost the whole positive structure of human life in all its facets.

From this it is also understandable that leading personalities, striving for renewal with all their power in their own sphere, can act and think conservatively or even in a reactionary manner in other spheres. Just think of Luther's attitude towards social and economic questions.

Prophecy

Such a discrepancy between the demands set by one's own world view and the current situation will, in the first place, give rise to prophecy. In prophecy, failures and abuses are laid bare and ways of renewal are declared. Such renewal can only be possible if it is carried by a living faith. Prophecy will involve the evaluation of a situation, whereby it is tested on the basis of one's knowledge of, and insight into the operative norms. We are using the term 'prophecy' in a general sense here, although a distinction will have to be made between true and false prophecy. Moreover, prophecy will also point to the history that made the current state of affairs what it is. The true prophet will not be content merely to depict the improvement and renewal, which will result when the preached insight into the norm and world order is accepted. No, he or she will try to show how the present-day depressed circumstances are the result of following unjust ways, determined by a false cultural ideal that is connected to a world view that is rejected as untrue. There is no genuine prophecy without delineation of the history that has led to the present situation.

Prophecy is not just an explanation or propagation of principles to be followed. On the contrary, justice and truth have to be defended (whatever one considers these to be). Prophecy shows how justice and truth have been violated in the present time by striving for false or wrongly posited ideals. One prophesies about injustice and lies and prepares oneself to serve justice and truth – and in the actual striving it will become clear what the motivating principle is. Prophecy will always speak about actual situations and failures. In doing so, it will put forward very clear-cut and defined ideals and demands. The principles that prophecy expresses and the cultural ideal upon which it is based will be exhibited in and through both what it rejects and what it requires.

Such prophecy always precedes every spiritual revolution. If the words are heard and accepted, then through the resulting activity a situation will arise which was indeed prophesied, in the more narrow sense of prediction. For justice and truth will indeed be restored or, in case of a false prophet, injustice and untruth will prevail.

Gauguin was such a prophet. The quotation that follows can hardly be called a description of what came to expression in his own art, as he knew very well, but it was rather the formulation of the way that he thought art could and should be renewed. He wrote in 1902:

> While taking into account the efforts and the investigations, even those of science, it was necessary to think of a complete liberation, to break the windowpanes at the risk of cutting one's finger, to leave it to the next generation, henceforth independent, free from any shackles, to solve the problem completely ... For this purpose it was necessary to risk body and soul in the struggle, a struggle against all the schools, all of them without any distinction ... And as to the work, a method of contradiction, if you like, venturing into the strongest abstractions, doing all that was forbidden, and reconstructing more or less happily, without any fear of exaggeration, even with exaggeration. Learning anew, and then, once having learnt, learning again. Conquer any timidity however much ridicule it may occasion. In front of his easel the painter is no slave, either of the past or of the present, either of nature or of his neighbour. He is himself, again himself, always himself ... I flatter myself to imagine Delacroix having come to earth thirty years later and undertaking the struggle that I have dared to undertake with his fortune and above all his genius. What a renaissance would take place today![140]

Here the prophet takes up his position in the midst of the contemporary situation. He notices failures and shortcomings by testing these against the ideals. He places himself over against them and wants to point the way to a better future. He believes this will come if people will follow him in his insight, which he has proclaimed with such conviction. He does his best to obtain an art that is, in his opinion, purer and better, and in this his starting point comes implicitly to expression, though for the philosophically learned reader it is very clear. The situation, measured according to his insight into the norm, is the starting point for his historical deed, whereby he urges others to act in a similar spirit. The direction that is being indicated, carried by his conviction, however, does not belong to the situation anymore – for it puts itself against that and wants to change it drastically – but is totally dependent on the world view of the prophet. For this reason we will not follow this subject further here, but will return to it in the section on 'World view' below.

3 The personality

'There is no history writing without a cult of heroes.'[141] This saying summarizes what we wish to discuss in this section. However, the saying itself is a strong overstatement, for it is not at all necessary to glorify the formers of history in order to gain an insight into history. On the contrary, such an overstatement of the significance of the leading persons can only falsify the historical perspective. We may easily lose sight of the fact that they were dependent on the situation in which they were placed, and that their most profound convictions, for which they fought, were not their personal possession. The fact that they gained followers and adherents proves this; it would never have been possible without agreement on this point of conviction. The glorification of leaders can make us forget, and probably completely overlook, how they failed, what faults they had and where they took a wrong turn. There is no doubt that such leaders must have possessed great gifts, talents and possibilities to do their work. The question, however, is always what they did with those talents. Leaders are bound by the same norms as anyone else – they have to subject themselves to the norms, even more so when they have gained a leading position, for their responsibility will be very great indeed. For many years they may, by their enormous influence, move many people in a certain direction, perhaps even for centuries. The genius ought to take heed that his or her influence is a good one.

'A cult of heroes', while subjectivistic, all too easily blinds us to a correct perspective concerning their actions and the actual content of their achievements. Besides, in the historical struggle into which the great figures have thrown themselves, creating their works or positing their deeds, they were not in the first place concerned with their strictly personal character. They were even less concerned to impose upon the world their good or bad characteristics or to make their talents normative, but they were concerned with justice, correctness and truth, no matter how deficient their insight may have been. Just look again at the passage by Gauguin cited above.

The national character

In the introduction we posed the question about who posits a historical deed, a community or an individual? Whatever the answer, it is always the case that both a group as well as a person form part of a larger entity, a people with their own history. Here we can think of groups of people who have their own world view – e.g. the Reformed people, or the socialists and such – as well as the people integrated into a group on the basis of national unity – e.g. the Dutch, the English, and so on. The history maker comes from such a national and a population group, and should keep this in mind. Thus insight into national character has meaning for our understanding of a historical deed; it will not be without influence on the form, and even the style, in which it is delivered. Whether the history maker speaks with big words or expresses him or herself in a modest and businesslike manner, aspires to profundity or to effect, delivers affectations or seeks to be inconspicuous, such characteristics are not of minor importance or without significance.

The national character is not a 'mythical' given, there once and for all, unchanged throughout the centuries. It has also been shaped by the influence of a number of natural and cultural factors and can change under pressure of incisive historical events. Any apparent constancy arises from the fact that it shapes or adapts itself under the influence of truly profound happenings only or through long-standing influences in a certain direction. Therefore we can say that national character possesses a relative constancy. Transitory influences of less important events will mean very little in this context. This constancy of national character also constitutes the continuity and, in a certain way, the homogeneity of cultural expressions within a certain cultural area. It enables our national past to be a truly national past. Our forefathers were not only our forefathers by blood but they also had qualities similar to their descendents. That is how they can be understood. The vestiges of our national past have a familiar quality to us, resembling what we see around us.

But if revolutions of a profoundly spiritual kind can substantially influence national character, then the result will be that the time before such events will have less to say to the later generations. Forefathers who lived in those earlier times will be strangers in some way, that is to say, almost as foreign as a person from a different nation. Therefore it should not amaze us that a Dutch person today in general can hardly appreciate the history before the sixteenth century, which was marked by such decisive changes as the Reformation and the Eighty Years War (1568–1648), as national history. In the Reformation our nation received a spiritual background very different from the previous one. It was only after the Eighty Years War that our national unity arose. It is true that we may speak of a medieval Dutch culture, which started with the formation of a Dutch linguistic area, but the Dutch nation with its particular national character has grown through their conflict with the Spanish tyrant, whereby the Reformation played a very decisive role in the formation of a national character, distinct from the other nations of the medieval Dutch tribe. Just compare the Dutch with the Flemish!

In some Roman Catholic countries, by contrast, such as Italy and Spain, the medieval past does have a real meaning as a living factor in the national tradition. In England we see an intermediate case, where the Reformation was established very gradually and less consistently, without a strong break in historical continuity. Especially in England, therefore, people feel the meaning that the past can have for the present. It is experienced as a living tradition, binding the English together and moderating any revolutionary passion for renewal. But here too, people should abstain from every myth. This past is and remains alive only if it is being continually made known to successive generations, and if they consciously accept the national 'heritage'. Here also lies a task for historical scholarship.

What influences determine national character? We cannot go into this in detail but shortly would like to formulate our answer as follows: national character is determined by religious conviction, natural conditions, and by a politico-historical sense of unity. The positivistic school (Taine) has especially emphasized natural conditions, but, although theses factors may certainly not be ignored, their influence is often difficult to determine with any precision.

We wish to elaborate a little on the influence of religion, with reference to a study by Hoffet,[142] in which he analyses the influence of faith on the formation of the national character, especially with an eye to the differences between Protestants and Roman Catholics. He points to significant differences in outlook between Protestant and Catholic persons, also when they are only nominally so. He demonstrates a large difference in attitude towards the law, the loose opinions of the Roman Catholic over against the much more severe and stricter ones of Protestants. He also draws attention to the difference between *le vice protestante et le vice catholique*. He points to the differences between Protestant and Catholic countries with respect to the division of poverty and riches, hygiene, literacy, etc. He shows how the Protestants have a democratic disposition, whereas in the Catholic nations democracies are much more like 'dictatorships in eclipse'. Finally, he points out that even now these differences determine the relationships between European nations: 'Not that they still play an important role in their conscious form, where beliefs and practices are concerned. But in their unconscious form of moral types, of psychological structures, of families of sensitivities, they trace more important boundaries than our political maps.'[143]

We have to look for an explanation for this fact in different positivizations of the norm and disclosure guided by faith commitment. Catholicism and Protestantism each entail a totally different cultural ideal. Even if faith or the church itself would no longer have any significant historical power, the power of tradition, the connection with the national past, which they influenced in a formative way, would still mean a great deal. Think of how leaders in the various areas, also the ones who consciously abandoned the faith, in their opinions on a number of matters – most strongly perhaps relating to those areas of life where they do not specifically move around – are nevertheless shaped by the milieu from which they come. And very often that was, and still is, a Christian milieu. Here we mention a succession of German historians, such as Herder, Hegel, Ranke, Burckhardt, Justi, of whom one even was a preacher and two others enjoyed a theological education. Besides, more generally manifest is the great influence of pietism on the German Enlightenment. To close our series of examples we point to Comte – Troeltsch among others pointed to the typically Catholic characteristics in various of Comte's theses.[144] It has already been said often that modern humanism is a secularized Christianity.[145] This implies that Christianity, i.e. that which has been secularized, in many respects continues to play a decisive role in humanism.

When we look at the influence of religion on national character we should not lose sight of the fact that it is very well possible that more than one religion had worked in shaping the national character. Often a more or less clear line of demarcation can be drawn between one part of the population, influenced by one religion, and another part, influenced by the other. In the Netherlands, for example, we speak of the Protestant North and the Roman Catholic South. In the latter case it is clear that the historico-political connection, provided that it is really rooted in the national conviction, integrates such profound religious differences into a national unity. The history maker cannot be understood apart from the spiritual background against which her or his work ought to be placed. In attitude to life and opinions about a thousand-and-one matters, even where it is almost impossible to point out how they were shaped under the influence of certain religious convictions, which in the perception of her or his contemporaries hardly have any relation to these convictions (because they have become common property of the whole population, irrespective of individual confessions), this history maker cannot be imagined apart from the nation from which she or he arose. Thus, the national character is one of the factors in the forming of the personality of the history maker, and this will also influence the character of her or his historical deeds. Besides, even if free, by reason of character or milieu, of the bad habits and positive characteristics of the people among whom she or he lives and works, these will still have to be taken into consideration in order for her or him to gain acceptance.

The significance of the personality. We have quietly assumed that character is not just something unformed and strictly individual. We will not investigate the question of hereditary traits here. But we think it is safe to say that the character and disposition with which an individual is born undergo immediate formation through upbringing and education. Apart from national character many other influences come into play here. They include milieu, economic circumstances, school, physical health. The character formed in this way will, in the immediate context of disposition, position and milieu, co-determine the lifestyle of the person concerned. This will be a factor, sometimes even a decisive one, in respect of the feeling of responsibility, the awareness of having a task with respect to a certain group or with respect to certain problems. All this will put a stamp on the activity developed by the former of history. There is a remarkable illustration of this state of affairs in the person of Anton Rafaël Mengs, the painter who already at his baptism was dedicated by his father to the task of reviving the art of Antonio Correggio and Raphael. His whole upbringing was directed to this purpose, and indeed, Mengs seemed to possess sufficient talent, up to a point, to satisfy his calling. It was how he saw himself and how others estimated him.

Notwithstanding what we have already said, it cannot be denied that the strictly individual disposition and the typically unique features of someone's character – short-tempered or peaceful, sanguine or melancholic etc. – are of significance for the manner and form in which the deed is done.

On the other hand, the exact characteristics of a person, yes, even down to the looks and the voice, co-determine their influence as history maker, and therefore the significance of the deed performed. This applies especially when personally known during his or her lifetime. With time and greater distance these factors will play less of a role in his or her continuing influence and the work will increasingly speak for itself. Think of the influence Plato and Aristotle exert even today, persons whose personal character and appearance are now hardly known.

We see a remarkable case of influence that was especially linked with the personality of the leading figure in Gauguin, especially during his early career. The following quotation from Maurice Denis testifies to this: 'Gauguin . . . was the uncontested master, the one whose works people were collecting, of whom people were peddling paradoxes, whose talents they admired, his loquaciousness, his gesture, his physical strength, his nastiness, his inexhaustible imagination, his capacity to imbibe alcohol, and the romanticism of his disposition.'[146]

Finally, talent plays a big role. Similar deeds will have a greater or lesser significance depending on the quality of what has been delivered. An aesthetically more important work will have greater influence than a less important work. In subjection to the world order, high aesthetic achievement – being in greater conformity with the aesthetic norm – will be recognized as such, provided that the power of sin has not become so great that even in this the truth is suppressed in unrighteousness. The talent, the gift, entails that people, in subjection to the law, can attain the highest level of achievement. The question is always how these talents are used. Talents may be used to further progress in the direction of sin or they may be used to result in a positive cultural formation, either obediently and willingly or in forced capitulation to the reality of the world order.

Sin

A final motive, which people are often inclined to overlook but which in many cases is of decisive significance, is sin in the heart of the history maker. Lust for power, ambition, vainglory, love of money, a tendency to constant contrariness, cruelty, a tendency to fulfil dissolute sexual desires, and so many other human tendencies not only colour the deed in a certain way but may be its deepest source of inspiration. The question could be asked whether Gauguin would have gone to Tahiti if he had not been led by his ambitions, especially his desire to live out his sexual passions freely. How would the lives of Napoleon and Hitler have run their course if they had not experienced a desire for power?[147]

Two more remarks need to be made here. In the first place it is true that sin colours the deed and, perhaps, may have motivated it, but it is the situation which particularly explains the 'object' of desire. Today there are few people who, no matter how ambitious for power they may be, dream of being a monarch. In the twentieth century one would rather be a financial magnate or a political leader. Gauguin would have expressed his passions quite differently if he had been brought up in another milieu, and if he had not possessed that exceptional artistic talent. He probably would have become a philosopher like Nietzsche. Some passages in his letters lead one to suspect he had great inclinations in this direction. In the second place it should be pointed out that sinful desires only seldom fully determine the deed of the history maker. In this present age, sin cannot be fully realized. There will always be an element of subjection to the world order. Every deed done by a human being is a sometimes indissoluble compound of sin and misery on the one hand, and well-intended endeavours and tendencies on the other.

All this must be taken into account in the investigation of a historical deed. It can save us from hero worship. If we remain free from that we will be better able to judge the deed itself. The tendency to go into rapture, and to judge as good any action by the revered person, simply because she or he did it is then cut down at the root. Finally, what makes a deed good is not the subjective good intentions but the obedience, intentional or unintentional, to the norms put into the creation. Besides, where does the boundary lie between the well-intentioned deed and sin, if the good intention as such is in conflict with the norm? Perhaps it lies in the intention? It is true that people often know how to sublimate their own propensities, or to reason in such a way that their own evil will become a lofty and good ambition, at least in their own eyes. It cannot be denied that the subject in his or her particular character puts a personal stamp on the actual shape of the historical deed. Nevertheless, every situation in which the history maker him or herself is envisaged as not being subject to the norm ought to be rejected. Otherwise the way is open to preach complete normlessness and, with it, the meaninglessness of all events.

The strictly personal sinful tendency or desire often drives someone to action. Culturally speaking, however, the question of strictly personal motives is less important than whether the formative intervention into events was according to the norm or anti-normative. However, the one cannot be separated from the other. History makers, working alongside each other and following one another, being inclined to all evil, will in their formative work strive to satisfy their deepest desires or to allow them full play. They are, however, not independent individuals, but – also in Cain's line, to which we restrict ourselves here – each one of them is a member of the human race who has fallen into sin and thus, animated by one spirit, prompted by the prince of this world, attempts to put the stamp of their own insights, wishes and desires on culture. People seek to build a world in which they have as much freedom as possible to satisfy the passions of their sinful hearts, passions to which they seek to give continual expression. However, sin will never be able to fully reveal itself in this creation. Again and again people have to be subject to God's world order. Moreover, the decay-resisting effect of the race of Seth, who have kept and carried out God's word, can make its rich blessings felt. This may only happen for as long as this race has not become 'saltless' by being conformed to the world and neglecting their task. The formative activity of Gauguin, orientated towards initiating an art in which artists can express themselves freely, not bound by any norm, is much more important than Gauguin's personal passions, even though these cannot be completely separated from it, even as he built on the work of his predecessors and was stimulated by his contemporaries, and he himself through the influence of his thoughts and works motivated young people along in the direction he had adopted.

With this we have touched on problems, however, that reach further than the subject of this section and that we will now consider more closely.

4 World view

'All world views regularly contain the same structure. This structure is in every case a coherence, in which, on the basis of an outlook on the world, the question about the meaning and significance of the world is decided, and from which the ideal, the greatest good, the highest principles for the conduct of life are derived,' wrote Dilthey, a thinker who has been profoundly occupied with the questions we now wish to consider.[148] Two points are especially emphasized by him: first, the subjective attitude of people with respect to the world that surrounds them and, second, a factor which is often not seen in its significance, that 'every world view has a development, and the latter constitutes the explanation of its contents.'[149]

A person is not a totality or coherence of functions. No, a person is one, a unity, an 'I' with certain functions in a certain structural coherence. By this structural coherence people express themselves and find their way in this world, the place where they have been put. The Philosophy of the Cosmonomic Idea has introduced the scriptural term 'heart' for the concentration point of the human personality, the 'I-ness' that a person does not have but is in him or herself.[150]

People are now placed, with their whole physical and mental structure, in this world with its order and its more momentary situations, determined by time and place. People need to determine their attitude towards laws and norms and, intricately connected with this, towards other creatures. A person's world view is her or his attitude towards life. People have to specifically determine their standpoint towards, or in, the given world order. We intentionally avoid the word 'opinion', for that would give too much of an impression that a world and life view is a question of reflection, of philosophical reflection. It is much more than that. We could even say that the reflection itself is guided and directed by a person's attitude to life. On the other hand, we would affirm that the world and life view[151] does not bypass conscious reflection on the deepest questions of life.

Precisely because a world view is not a philosophy and not a systematically thought-out system, but involves the direct relationship between people and the world that surrounds them, it is so difficult, or rather impossible, to define. A person's world view only becomes manifest in his or her attitude to the full reality of the context in which he or she thinks, works, acts, loves, believes, and so forth. It reveals itself in the direct and actual expressions of life. It is like an old-fashioned typewriter. We cannot say with certainty what the typeface will look like unless we depress the keys and find out. Only then can we see clearly the actual result of a letter printed on the paper. However, when we do this we straightaway have an indication of what the remaining letters will look like. Likewise, only in reaction to events, and in the answers given to questions, and in the responses to given problems and difficulties, be they scientific or more practical, can we receive an insight into the structure and actual character of the world view in question.

We said it was people who determine their attitude in this world. That means that people orientate themselves in the positive world order and situation from within themselves, their heart, with the help of their body and spirit. Hence there are two factors determining the world view according to its character: the heart and the reality outside of them.

The religious power manifest in the world view

People make their religious choice in the heart: there, in the fullness of their life, they determine their attitude to their Creator, their God. They love him with all their heart – that is why they are sorrowful when they act according to the 'old man' – or turn away from him to serve other gods, i.e. to look elsewhere for the foundation of the cosmos and human life. It is this firm structure embedded in the creation that has made them into religious beings. Hence they can never avoid the question deep in their heart, i.e. whether they are for God or not for God, even when subjectively they deny its reality and existential meaning.

Humanists who do not want to know about the Lord their God are in the deepest sense always seeking themselves. Two ways are open for them. They either surrender themselves totally to reality as it presents itself to them, become totally absorbed in it and allow themselves to be guided by it[152] – this is the way of least resistance. By following their nature they hope to do as they please and to satisfy their sinful desires without conflicts. Or they attempt to determine their attitude in complete freedom, they become their own lawgiver, not bound by anything or anybody – free human self-determination then becomes the deepest motive for their actions.[153] Neither of these standpoints can be carried out without loss. In the first case they lose themselves, their being human with an own place in the world. In the latter case they can no longer live nor carry out any meaningful work. That is why, as they capitulate to the structure of reality that is neither determined nor determinable by humanity themselves, they again and again lapse from the one standpoint into the other, whereby an inner religious dialectic comes to expression, caused by religious starting points which are polar opposites and which consistently seek to exclude each other.

In the successive world views the deepest motives of human action will manifest themselves with increasing consequence in the course of history. As humanity attain an ever-increasing self-awareness in these successive world views the religious dialectic comes to expression in new forms, each time, in an unstable balance. In humanism we see, in principle, two world views next to each other.[154] These are ultimately founded in the internally divided starting point of people who seek themselves. The first world view is the scientific ideal, where the dialectic itself, by ruling over the nature motive, comes to expression in the ideal to dominate nature with the help of science, and thus to proclaim human kingship over it. The second world view is the personality ideal, where the freedom motive dominates. It wants to use reality as material in order to manifest itself. In both cases there is an inner tension that produces a continual instability as the dialectically connected, but exclusive, poles repel each other. The unstable balance is constantly lost and – in subjection to reality, which does not allow either pole to be consistent in its effect – a new balance is sought. Usually the emphasis will then shift to the counter-pole.

World view and world order

A world view is not an abstract entity that floats outside of reality. No, it is the actual attitude to life of people as they orientate themselves in the world that surrounds them. Therefore it will be closely focused on this reality. We will first look at how a person focuses on the world order, in which are contained the constant norms to which everyone is subject, no matter who they be. Then we will see how this world order is positivized in a certain way through human formative activity, by disclosure and positivization, and how this activity influences world views in connection with the subjective historical state of affairs. Therefore, the time and place in which a person is placed plays a large role.

If people do not know or recognize the revelation of the Word and reject it, and therefore do not understand that the whole order which they perceive around them is created, and not 'self-contained' but pointing to the Creator and Lawgiver of all things, then it is inevitable that in their attempt to understand something of this ordered creation they will do violence to the truth – which they suppresses in unrighteousness (see Romans 1 and 2).

This apostate humanity, driven by their heart, will choose for themselves gods in a pistical fantasy. These could be real gods (idols) – such as the heathen have, and the old civilizations had. Alternatively, in more disclosed civilizations, where through discursive thinking more insight has been gained into the structure of reality often one or more modalities or complexes of modalities will be considered as the founding principles of the whole cosmos. This pistical fantasy will exercise a great influence on the whole vision of reality as it is contained in the world view. One could say, for example, that the normlessness present in the lives of very many modern people is in many cases undoubtedly connected to a certain historic insight.[155] When one aspect of reality is wrestled from its place in order to exalt it as something that gives or determines meaning above all else, while denying the meaning character of all of creation, then it cannot but exercise an influence as far as the innermost texture of the world view is concerned. Consequently this influence extends its insight into laws and norms, and to events in this world and our task and place in it.

World view and situation

We shall now draw our attention to the relation between world view and the actual historical state of affairs, the situation in which people are placed. For that is where they will first of all choose their attitude. Of course, people do not stand alone or as the first in this world order. The life experiences[156] of very many generations before them have a formative effect on the way they shape their insight and attitude. And yet, the ever-changing circumstances ensure that world view is not something static. It is not an entity that remains constant – not even when the religious starting point and the scientific insight into the world order remain in principle the same. Along with further disclosures and positivizations, as well as changes in the actual historical situation, there will also be modifications in the world view. These will usually be slow and, as long as the basic attitude of the human heart does not change, in an ongoing process of adaptation or reaction to changes in the situation. For example, industrialization and the rise of modern technology in the nineteenth century, the rise of the body culture in the twentieth century, the First World War, each of them have had a great influence on world view, which has therefore undergone change, but not in a radical way. The latter only happens when there is a fundamental change in religious starting point.

Undoubtedly, insight into situations is also co-determined by world view, since the judgment of the situation is dependent on our knowledge of norm and law. And yet, this subjective attitude can only partly assert itself and 'capitulation' to real states of affairs will repeatedly take place, as was explained earlier. It is true that in the world view in its actual form there is a lot of 'capitulation'. There is much that does not arise consistently from the basic attitude or in agreement with it but is guided by other factors.

Thus world views are shaped on the one hand by circumstances, but on the other hand they also shape circumstances, as we will shortly explore in more depth. This has the result that situation and world view often cohere to such an extent that the question of what was determinative for a historical deed may have the appearance of a 'What comes first, the chicken or the egg?' kind of question. Their view of life and outlook on the world sometimes prompt people towards deeds of new disclosure, which in turn, because they affect world view, call for further modifications of their view of life, which again lead to new deeds. For this reason the world and life view character of a deed, also for the person who is doing the deed, will not be conspicuous. People only become strongly conscious of this when a world view is in strong contradiction to the actual situation which, for example, may have arisen as a result of cultural endeavour produced under the impulse of another world view.

The connection between religion, world view and reality

In the course of the historical process of formation, reality, the positive order – in its disclosure and positivized norm – will more and more exhibit the stamp of the world view of the group that has the formative power, both in its character and shape. It is not merely that a situation, which has been changed by formation, disclosure or positivization, will result in a modification of the world view by way of adjustment. Rather, also reality itself will be distorted a little in line with this world view. The driving power at the heart of a world view is, after all, the religious position of choice, in the heart itself. This compels people to continue in a certain direction in an increasingly consistent and conscious way. As people continue to 'impose their will on the world', they become increasingly conscious of their deepest motivations: thus they will attempt to annihilate the element of 'capitulation' to the order itself. They do this in two ways. On the one hand, by trying to put a distinct world view stamp on reality through disclosure and positivization, whereby in a certain sense capitulation becomes less and less necessary. On the other hand, by attempting to liberate more consistently the world view itself from this element.

The religious motive in their ever more conscious, subjective experience of their own world view urges people to shape reality more and more in conformity to that world view. This shaping takes place primarily in the formation of ideals for every area of life, which then have to be actualized in reality. The next question is to what extent the latter, the actualization of ideals in reality, is possible. This will after all depend on the greater or lesser degree of agreement and adjustment of the ideals to the real structure of the world order in both the normative side as well as the subject-side. If an ideal is foolish or impractical because it is in conflict with the order itself it will not be realizable. With sadness, people will have to admit their inability, and nothing will be left for them but to capitulate. This is because the reality structure maintains itself and cannot be changed by the subjective attitude, wishes or will of a person. We see such a delineation of ideals in the utopias we meet with from time to time. When it comes to carrying these ideals into practice, people are forced to 'adjust to reality' in a significant way, and all the more to the extent that the desired utopia was unrealistic, more in conflict with the actual structure of the created order. If such an adjustment does not take place, and people persist in a certain direction guided by their religious starting point, a conflict will arise. This conflict will be between subjective endeavours and an 'unruly' reality, as we find it expressed in the characterization of the work of the modern poet-philosopher Davidson as 'the courage and honesty of a mind valiantly beating itself into destruction against the locked and barred door of an unknown and perhaps non-existent reality'.[157]

Such a conflict has become especially acute in our own time, now that humanists have become extremely aware of their own deepest motives through the cultural work being done in a certain direction, which has been going on for centuries. Reality, as ordered and disclosed in the spirit of the scientific ideal, is an oppressive restraint, especially for those who claim absolute freedom for humanity. Modern works of art exist as confessions of faith in people's own freedom, which they want to hold on to at all cost. These works proclaim human sovereignty over reality and absolute freedom in the creative process. But reality keeps on fighting against them, and hence there is this conflict that expresses itself in existential angst, a feeling of meaninglessness and absurdity in all events which simply do not want to conform to the subjective insight of modern people. At the very moment when people have become most conscious of their own motive and have seemed as if they could shape their world view completely autonomously, without any capitulation, in complete self-determination, a completely opposite situation has arisen. For this perception of life, with its angst, and this picture of the world, with its feelings of absurdity and meaninglessness, is fully due to and dependent on the world order – to which people refuse to adjust – and the actual situation.[158]

The people who adjusted themselves religiously and completely to reality, which they endeavoured to organize and disclose radically for the wellbeing of humanity,[159] in order to control it and to make it serviceable for their own convenience, have also ended up in a crisis, though possibly in a less acute one. This reality, into which they, in many respects, had a false insight because they ignored the revelation of God, now begins to rule over them and curtail their freedom to such an extent that through the course of events all joy and happiness, so passionately sought, threaten to escape them. In some cases even their existence itself is brought into danger.

The attempt to gain more and more knowledge of nature and to explain everything scientifically, human being included, has also led to a state where in a continual process of self-confrontation[160] people have discovered their own deeper nature. They have become acquainted with the deep abyss in their own being, an abyss full of horror. In this way being human itself has become restrictive and there arises an inclination to the 'superhuman', which in truth often means the 'subhuman'.[161] In this way humanism tends towards its own abolition. Some of the leading artists, those predecessors and champions of a new world view, have said things like, 'Very early in life already I found man ugly,' and (another), 'Man is an unsuccessful experiment of nature,' or (a third one), 'Man is an animal.' They even speak of the 'ugliness of nature, its impurity'.[162]

These inner tensions become only more complex and painful through the fact that both tendencies, each of which threaten to overturn its opposite, do not stand next to each other but dialectically opposite each other in the heart of one and the same person, sometimes emphasizing one tendency and at other times the other. In a freedom that has led to ruin, and in the discovery that people cannot control reality to make a genuine improvement, to build a paradise, humanism has annulled itself. This has become very obvious with the 'avant-garde'.

The spirit of the times

More than once the remark is made that such or such an act was due to the 'spirit of the times'. The question arises, also in connection with what we have just discussed, of what should be understood by this 'spirit of the times'. There are two possible answers. First it could be said that the spirit of the times is the greatest common denominator of the world views of the leading groups. About it a profound and all-embracing agreement will exist. Deeds driven by it, or in agreement with it, will be able to count on general acceptance and, if one of these is a truly historical deed, can exert a deep influence. This is because there will be no resistance to overcome at world view level, since the people will be able to concur with its direction and content. However, it should be noted that outside the leading groups there will always be those whose world view diverges from the spirit of the times. In such cases, they will not accept such a deed but will attempt to resist and fight it and its consequences. Yet it might make sense to talk about the spirit of the times as including these groups. Thus we arrive at the second answer to our question, whereby we have to fall back on something even more general and commonplace. Indeed, in this case the greatest common denominator will not be able to go any deeper than an agreement with the positivized norm. Here we think especially of the anticipating moments in the various modalities, the ideas and ideals that give direction to the activity. We could think about the cultural ideal, the artistic ideal, the moral ideal, etc. If something is carried by the spirit of the times conceived of in this sense it can become truly popular. Examples include certain posters and products, songs that become a hit and bestselling books. This spirit of the times also manifests itself in all kinds of habits and customs. For example, in our time, it will be manifest in the way we spend our holidays, the sports we enjoy, the style of interior decoration, etc. It will often be difficult to distinguish between simply following the spirit of the times and acting according to the positivized ideals and norms, on the one hand, and the world view, on the other.

It is very understandable that a deed, which in its character coheres with the spirit of the times, is usually not seen as being determined by the world view, neither by the person doing the deed nor by the community. In later times the historian will be struck in his or her research by how much the deed was motivated by the world view. The deed can then be used as a symbol for that period in history. For example we may think of the origin of the torso in sculpture, or the rise in importance in the nineteenth century of caricature as a separate art form. The fact that world view played a large role in these developments is clearly noticeable to us, but for the contemporary people it was not at all evident. And yet, a person like Sedlmayr can adduce these phenomena precisely from this point of view.[163]

Wisdom

A world view is the insight and attitude to life of a group or movement. It is not the possession of an individual but a characteristic of a collective group. Wisdom, by contrast, is possessed by a person individually. Wisdom may be defined as a world view deepened by life experience and reflection. The person who possesses wisdom has a deep insight into humanity in all their expressions, endeavours and works, in the coherences, dependencies and conditions, in all kinds of contexts of life. It includes a knowledge of human nature and a profound understanding of what is happening in the world. One could say that wisdom is a world view refined by experience. If this world view were to contain an incorrect insight into the real structure of the world order, then there would be a deeply felt element of capitulation in this wisdom, probably expressed in an awareness of the relativity of one's own vision, the impracticability of one's own ideas, and the dependence on factors that are not controlled by humans.

In wisdom we find a very tight intertwining of world view and personality: wisdom is a person's most personal possession, but at the same time it is a vision of life and the world that may never be considered individualistically and subjectively as an outcome of character. Apart from the situation in which it is posed, the character and direction of a historical deed are thus constituted by the wisdom of the history maker.

In the writing of history the quality of a work will, in the first place, depend on the wisdom of the historian. His or her wisdom contains a depth and breadth of vision and a greater or lesser insight into historical events. Hence, the value of the historian's work will not just depend on the world view of the writer nor just on the writer's talent but, rather, on how well-considered his or her judgment is, on his or her spiritual maturity, feeling for restraint, contact with the particular situation in the world of the day, in which and for which the history is written. This applies also to work done in other areas.

Is world view something that is subject to the norms?

Since we reject all relativism, we cannot consider all world views of equal value. That would be pure subjectivism. We said that world view is determined by the positive order as well as by the religious starting point. The positive order can never just be seen as a norm for the world view, precisely because the world view itself has had so much influence on it: positivization and disclosure could have taken place in a manner that was too fragmented or too one-sided. World view should therefore always be seen in relation to the whole created, normative order that is designed for positivization. As we said, world view is the result of people's attempt to orientate themselves in this order. The more or less correct their insight into the world order is, the greater or lesser will be the correctness of their world view. It is normative for a world view to have a correct insight into the world order, if the place and task of humanity, as well as the meaning of events and existence, is to be understood correctly. Since in this latter the religious starting point is already taken into account, we need not explicitly state that world view should also be tested by the revelation of God.

Prophecy

As we already noted, world view also gets shaped. We should now pay some attention to this. It is especially the role of the prophet in the historical event, as we emphasized in the previous section, that we should investigate more closely here. Prophets form and, insofar as this is ever possible, formulate the world view. They do this as spiritual leaders who evaluate their own time and milieu, testing these by their insight into the world order and, from their own situation, point the way to a better ordering of that situation. Or, in order to come to a better insight into the meaning, purpose and state of affairs in living and working, leaders pre-eminently provide a sharpened insight into humanity and their situation in the world order. They do this in accordance with the motivating centre of life, the religion in their heart. They motivate people, at least, those who listen to them, in the direction of a closer realization of the ideals in reality so that they might be better adjusted to the world view, which itself will become a more and more clear and consistent expression of the religious standpoint. To summarize, the prophet points the way and motivates people in the direction of a continuing activity with the purpose of making what is positive reality, with the world view and religious attitude in unity without contradictions or disharmonies, and the prophet calls for repentance when people have departed, in her or his opinion, from the true religion.

Although determined by context and choice of religious standpoint, this shaping and delineating of the world view does not function so rigorously as to make it impossible to speak of a free human activity. That is why differences in its shape are possible and that explains how, from within the same religious starting point, various groups can arise and coexist, each holding somewhat divergent insights into humanity's task and place in the world order. These groups are separated from each other by differences in world view, which once was shaped by a prophet or leader. The world view of each of these groups – which will know its own prophets and leaders – will in the course of time, as the particular history continues to develop, be more sharply delineated. Alternatively, it can also happen that these groups will come closer to the outlook of another group. The latter will depend on various influences, which we do not need to investigate here. The possibilities are endless and richly varied, as actual history exhibits in a superabundant diversity. For it is also possible that a movement, whose origin and past were determined by a small number of leaders and circumstances, will split during the course of its further development under the influence of a highly complex process involving the interaction of internal and external factors. In the long run it may result in different, even opposing, groups. We think here of the origin and development of communism and socialism. There would be very little purpose in elaborating the problems extensively here and illustrating them with examples. That would also lead us too far from our subject.

The prophet does not, in the first place, disclose and positivize.[164] The prophet calls on his or her followers to do that. It is likely that prophets will themselves be active in some area as philosophers, statesmen, theologians or artists but, although this will certainly play a role in the influence that they will exercise, their significance do not lie primarily there. Marx and Engels acted prophetically when they published their *Communist Manifesto*. Their scientific insights may have been refuted and have lost their actual significance, even amongst their followers, but as spiritual pioneers who pointed to a direction and task they still remain of great significance. They did not just formulate insights into the state and society, even though this is what they paid most attention to, they formed a world view that has directed the life and work of history makers in all sorts of areas.

Even though prophets may not often have acted in the process of positivization themselves they can certainly have an enormous significance in the course of history, depending on the degree of influence of their words. Whether it will be an influence for good or for ill will depend to a large extent on their wisdom and insight, and the agreement and harmony of their message with the relevant norms.

The cultural ideal[165]

If a prophet makes a positivizing intervention – and therefore acts as a history maker in the stricter sense of the word – then this is usually as a shaper of a cultural ideal in which the course of action for all formative activity is already contained. Yes, perhaps we may even modify the thesis above to say that prophets, in many cases though not all, owe their great significance especially to this. The positivization of the cultural ideal is of tremendous significance, as we have already stated several times in anticipation of our present discussion.

We called Marx and Engels prophets because 'the *Communist Manifesto* opens perspectives for a whole new way of looking at the world . . . It is a revolutionary doctrine, a break with all idealistic world views.'[166] Therein lay, and still lies, the fundamental power of this publication, even now when various of the theories contained in it have been refuted and a large number of the primary demands have been fulfilled.[167] There is no doubt that a totally new cultural ideal is proposed in the *Manifesto* in which the revolutionary view of life comes to expression. The writer of the introduction was able to state: 'In all countries it is now the communists who are the bearers of progress and a new civilization.'[168] This involves considerably more than just political and social ordering. Indeed, communism is much more than that. It is a cultural ideal, as already contained in the *Manifesto*, something the authors themselves recognized when they wrote: 'The communist revolution is the most radical break with the traditional relationships of property, no wonder that in its course of development it makes the most radical break with traditional ideas.'[169]

The historical power struggle between various groups will initially be fought in order to obtain the power to give the particular shape to the cultural ideal that is considered best in a given situation. This will be the ideal of a positive direction of disclosure and positivization that will lead to a positive ordering in accordance with a person's own world view. Once this power struggle has been won, and the positivization of the ideal has truly been settled,[170] cultural activity is far from finished. The task of actualizing these ideals in reality is only just starting. Positivization and disclosure have to be brought into harmony with the ideal; ideals must be realized or, after a time, they will become empty and vacuous words.

Reality is so complex that it is beyond our full scrutiny. For this reason it is hardly conceivable that someone will positivize the cultural ideal with an eye to the whole world order. That is why history makers will usually shape ideals within their 'own terrain', that area of reality that they oversee and where they are most acquainted with the shortcomings and needs. In other words, the cultural ideal will in very many cases come about within a particular history. Here we are not so much thinking of the particular history of a group distinguished by a world view, for that will almost always be the case. Rather, we are especially looking at the particular history of a group whose activity has been qualified by a certain aspect of reality. Very often, such a group – or, depending on the kind and manner of association, such an organization, movement or trend – will be active in the political arena, since that is where the positivizations are the most binding and inescapable – especially here then any deviations from the personal ideals are most strongly and painfully felt. We may consider in this respect the preaching of a new political order in the eighteenth century, or of Marxism, as we just mentioned. In general it is the case that people form ideals according to which they will direct the activities within their own terrain, in order to be forced, as it were, because of the coherence between the various modalities, to revise the cultural ideal in agreement with it.

Although a new cultural ideal may arise repeatedly within political movements this does not necessarily have to happen. During the Renaissance the new cultural ideal was hardly noticeable in the political arena, at least initially, but it cut very deeply into the scholarly and artistic terrains. That is where it first received its shape and where it was first actualized. And the re-shaping process of the cultural ideal by the

Reformation, which had an even more profound effect, did not start with politics but with the church. With respect to Romanticism, we see the new ideals first come to expression in the areas of art and philosophy, which were accorded a leading place within the culture that people wished to shape.

Art also played an important role in the formation of the modern cultural ideal, first of all by being a consistent revelation of what was seen as a deficit of Western culture, by which at the same time the real crisis of this civilization was demonstrated. People tested the status quo by their own world view and prophesied the failure of the cultural ideal that glorified science in a humanistic way. They did all this with purely artistic means, staying completely within their own terrain. People soon saw that this was not enough. They pointed to the necessity for an all-encompassing revolution – whereby a cultural ideal was advanced that could lay the foundations of the artistic ideal. Such was the vision of Redeker, who expresses himself as follows:

> What art made visible and what it inexorably unmasked was the malady, the deficiency of the West itself ... Art evoked in western man: the experience of conflict between his own reality and his own possibilities, inner resistance and inner unbearableness. Art made man understand what had become of him, as a precondition for finding out what he really should become, sought in the image of what 'man really is'.[171]

He continued,

> The crisis of art as artistic despair comes to symbolize a total and fundamental crisis of the West and its 'tradition'. The impossibility of a purely 'artistic reply' confirms the view that only a resolution of this crisis in western life, and a healing of its brokenness, can rectify a situation in which modern art has become ensnared. The crisis in art is more than an artistic crisis only: this is the greatness and the fate of the current artistic situation. Seen against the horizon of the life to which it belongs, art is the radical experience of the western deficiency to its uttermost consequences. In a fundamental manner, art first forces this deficiency on our consciousness and into crisis, to which at the same time it already is an 'answer'.[172]

'Modern art owed its blossoming of the "isms" to its "function" as symbol of the rebellion against the western tradition and reality . . . Thus it became the zone where this rebellion was experienced in a fundamental way, and carried this rebellion along in the innermost part of her being.'[173] However, art itself was incapable of carrying out this revolution. It hit on boundaries which it revealed but could not break through. It called for a revolution, which is 'a radical and fundamental turning over, which, seizing the deficiency of what came before by the root, can understand itself as a radical consequence of what has gone before, and which touches and puts in doubt all the elements of the "old" – concepts, institutions, values, norms and authorities'.[174] We intentionally quoted rather extensively in order to do justice to this complicated state of affairs as Redeker set it out. It was our intention to show, at least to make it plausible, that art has played an important role in formulating the new cultural ideal, more than in any preceding period, while remaining art and not going beyond the truly artistic.[175]

Continuing disclosure of the cultural ideal itself

In the positivization of the cultural ideal, the meaning of the historical development is deepened and brought into an ever closer relationship with the world view. In the progress of historical development, disclosures take place that become more and more consistent and heartfelt. Accordingly, the tie between the latter and the religious starting point will become ever tighter. In the old cultures the tie was not yet so tight. It is even possible to question whether the ancient Babylonian culture knew a cultural ideal in the sense of our discussions here. There was indeed a culture. Who would deny that? And the disclosure of latent given possibilities was sometimes directed according to the demands posed by religion or statesmanship – think of the development of astronomy in the service of astrology or of the art of soldiery. But an actual shaping of the whole social system was hardly constituted by one deeper lying principle or ideal. The power struggle was mostly of a purely political kind, almost exclusively determined by the desire for kingly power and hardly ever by a clash of ideals.

In the course of history, purposeful power struggles increasingly exhibit the character of contests determined by more profound motivations that have their basis in world views. These become more than just political struggles. Already during the Crusades the armed struggle had connotations different from a pure concern for the expansion of power. These wars of religion in the early modern era were probably the first where the struggle was about principles. The wars fought during the French Revolution were also motivated by an idea, namely to make 'liberty, equality and fraternity' a common European property. If that were not so, then the acts of those who welcomed the French as liberators into the Netherlands (and they did not think this was an act of betrayal) would be completely unintelligible. But we do not have to restrict ourselves to wars as a means in the struggle for power. Politics in the modern age are more and more founded on principles. Much earlier, principles did play their role, e.g. in the politics of the German emperors in the Middle Ages. But there is a lot of truth in the assertion that it is only since the American Revolution that 'governments, statesmen and politicians [are] . . . expected, and even required, to justify their existence and their policies by principles, reasons, prophecies, and performances.'[176]

We were able to choose our example from politics because there is always a direct connection between the formation of ideas in the various areas of life and the formation of the cultural ideal on which this is based. We could just as easily, however, have chosen our example from the area of art. There too we are able to perceive that from antiquity to our times there has been an increase in the actual, conscious formation of ideas in direct relationship to the world view. It is true that in the Middle Ages art also stood in direct relationship with the then dominant world view. However, only in more recent times, roughly since classicism found its formulation, has it been true that various artistic movements have allowed themselves to be consciously guided by certain ideals, which brought art into a direct relationship with world views, of which art was presumed to be an expression. Only in this way can we understand the many manifests in the more recent history of art.

Summary and perspective
The cultural ideal comes ever more consciously and consistently into a direct connection with the world view, revealing ever more clearly the mark of the religious power that motivates people in their cultural endeavours. People strive to realize a harmony between religion, world view and reality. Where the religion is apostate, this law fully functions as a law unto sin. The 'demonic harmony' that would arise in this way, however, is never realized in the present age, since humanity have to subject themselves to the world order, which does not allow itself to be re-shaped according to human schemes that distort reality – that would result in hell becoming a reality here and now. If it were not the case that sin is found in the heart of every person, such a harmony would likely be actualized in a religious attitude to life that was directed to the God of the Scriptures. However, the 'old man', still active in every believer, ensures that a paradise on earth is not possible in this present age. Since in reality both basic positions, the apostate one and the one directed to the Lord through the work of Christ, occur alongside each other there will be a continuing struggle, the struggle of the antithesis, that will also, or rather especially, be fought in the cultural arena.

Epilogue

Historiography
The evaluation of the relative significance of the factors constituting a historical deed will differ according to the starting point of the historian. A historian who is strongly influenced by scientific thinking, such as the positivist, the naturalist and, in a certain way, also the Marxist will especially emphasize the element of the situation. For the Marxist the world view itself will to a great extent be determined by this. The pure subjectivist in the individualistic sense, however, will emphasize the element of the personality. She or he will attempt to explain world view in terms of the character and personality of the history maker. Finally, the historicist, in the spirit of Dilthey, will consider especially the life and

world view element, the subjective judgments and the values on which they are based, to be of decisive significance for the historical deed. I consider that we ought to do justice to all the factors mentioned here, since their coherence is determined by the structure of the world order itself. We will have to recognize that sometimes one and at other times another facet will be of decisive significance, depending on the deed that was actually done.

If the writing of a historical study itself is to be considered as a historical deed, then the same factors analysed above would qualify its character and quality. At the same time it will become clear why a historical period will have to be described again and again. The reasons for this may be summarized as follows: a) the limitations of each person and hence also the history writer; b) the progress of scholarship, whereby new elements and sources are discovered and new problems emerge; c) new problems will arise, apart from the internal development of scholarship, through shifts within the world view and through changes in the situation. If it is the case that historians write history in order to understand their own situation and time – as we suggested when we discussed the 'Situation' – then the emergence of new movements and questions in general and particular history will also involve new tasks for the discipline of history. This is how, for example, the origin and development of modern art has stimulated research into certain phenomena in late eighteenth-century art that were previously considered to be of secondary importance.[177] d) Even if no changes in outlook had occurred and no new facts were found relative to a particular field of research, the historian would still have to reflect on certain problems and developments. This is an important point. Suppose the impossible became a reality and a completely conclusive book was written on a certain subject, even then research on such a subject should not cease. For the life of scholarship itself is at stake here. The moment we think we have described everything and consider our scholarly task completed, at that moment scholarship will be dead. For scholarship has a task within life and it can only be fulfilled if the scholars are actively addressing the problems, and thus are able to bring forth the 'treasury of achievements' and make it serviceable for today.

Relativism

No single theory will be able to reason away the fact that among the historians we meet, different world views exist. Each of these will involve a difference in insight and knowledge of the norms, which in themselves will result in greater and smaller differences in the judgment of facts and events. Different visions of the past are not just possible; they really exist. That is an undeniable fact.

However, this does not mean that we have to go along with relativism and accept its consequences. They are unavoidable as long as people accept subjectivism and refuse to recognize any norm outside the subject. But as long as we maintain the normed character of all human activity and therefore continue to recognize that for every judgment and world view the content of their truth must in principle be tested, a principular relativism can never gain status.

However, once again, differences in insight depending on differences in world view are unavoidable. Every attempt to find a solution that involves denying the fact that there are different world views, or to invalidate its results in order to arrive at a presuppositionless, objective historiography, is herewith declared unfruitful, since these differences themselves, when it comes down to it, are based on the divergence of religious choice. That the latter is a fact cannot be reasoned away or invalidated by scholarly research. It is the result of our living within the span of world history. We are living in the time between the Fall and the Last Day![178]

Besides, and this is the other side of the picture, it is not as bad as it seems. If people really were to think through the historical-relativistic attitude in a consistent way it would be impossible to understand the work of others, to say nothing of expressions by people from the past, whose witness we need at every step of the way.[179] In reality, we see here a continuing 'capitulation to the world order', whereby even the most convinced relativist will be able to discover truths and events from the past for him or herself, and will also be able to hand over to others materials in an understandable, verifiable, and as far as materials of fact are concerned, (i.e. matters about which our insight agrees) in a completely useable way.

It will never be possible to attain to a real neutrality of science, since every study is determined, not just in broad outline but also in detail, by the world view (or rather, the wisdom) of the researcher. Neutrality as a demand for being scientific is only meaningful insofar as we understand it to mean that researchers will try, as far as possible, to eliminate their personal preferences or disapprobations. Whether they consider a person likeable or not will perhaps play a role in their final judgment, but they ought to strive to do as much justice as possible to all people and elements and hence to do no violence to the known truth, no matter what the considerations. The facts – all the known facts that are considered significant for the course of history – should be allowed to speak. Historians should not in any way be consciously tendentious in order to allow their own prejudices to rule over and above reality and truth, even though this reality may show their own sympathies in a worse light or refute their own hobbyhorses.

Historians must stand in service of the truth. They must stay conscious of the fact that there is truth, independent of their opinions about it. They should know that their own world views, just like their own subjective attitudes to life, should be tested for their correctness. All work and actions remain subject to a norm that we ourselves have not devised. It could be the case that at a given time, after having gone back to the deepest, the religious starting point, still the scholarly debate may not be able to advance beyond the simple acknowledgment that an unbridgeable gap exists. Only on the Last Day the final judgment will be pronounced on the innermost stirrings of every human heart.

This writer is fully aware that his work is thoroughly guided by his world view, apart from the particular situation in which he is placed and his own personality. It is founded on his recognition of the Lord, Creator of heaven and earth, as his Lord and God. Religion cannot be reasoned away, neither in his case nor in any other. Therefore he considers that the revealed truth in God's word may not be neglected in his work, least of all in such a scientific work that carries so much responsibility. For it would be the greatest audacity to ignore, in an opinionated and wilful way, the insights into the world order and the norm contained therein as provided by the Holy Scriptures. It would be wrong to hide the light received under a bushel. We would be doing an injustice to honesty and sincerity, emphasized here as normative for all our work and, moreover, a prerequisite for all scholarly work. It would also transgress the norm that God put in his creation and revealed to us against our better judgment. Even without such transgression my own work would already be relative, fragmentary and open to disputation.[180]

• Summary: The Constituent Factors of a Historical Deed[181]

In a survey of the past it is necessary to distinguish the totality of the successive events of bygone times from the cultural development of history. The latter is the formative process observable in the development of human society.

The past, as such, comprises all that ever happened, no matter whether it was a simple daily activity or an important action. Such an action may or may not have been deliberate. But the present inquiry is concerned with the determining factors of a truly historical deed, i.e. with the actions of a responsible former of history, deliberately interfering with the course of events.

This interference bears a formative character and lays bare latent possibilities in what is merely potential in the historical datum.

In connection with the immeasurable complex of historical powers and forces such actions constitute the cultural development. The relative importance and meaning of an action do not depend on its ethical sense or its economic value or on its physico-psychically perceptible aspect. This importance can only be understood when evaluated according to norms of formative activity.

The opening process discloses and realizes possibilities inherent in the divine order of creation. In this order the norms to be positivized are only given in principle. If a particular movement seizes the historical formative power, it will try to realize its cultural ideals. Its leading principles and ideals will be given positive concrete content in the different modalities. Then the attempt will be made to concretize these ideas in continued cultural activity. The actual situation may further or check historical development, and tradition – though making for historical continuity – gives rise to a struggle for power with the new tendencies. Eventually the result is that new norms are found whose positive content holds in each of the relevant modalities.

A historical deed must be judged according to the norms valid for all formative activity. Such activity will have to obey God's laws and commandments, and to disclose and positivize the possibilities of created reality in accordance with its meaning. This positivization must not be directed by an ideal that is alien to reality, nor by an idolatrous motive.

A historical deed is not the result of some natural law. Circumstances may necessitate an action, but they do not force a person to a certain action. There is something like historical causality. However, this causality can only be discovered with the aid of cultural norms because it possesses a cultural meaning and is not qualified by a natural-scientific aspect.

The factors constituting a historical deed that will be considered in the sequel are the following: the divine world order, the actual historical situation, the personality of the former of history and his or her view of life and the world.

I The divine world order

We live in a world order to which all our actions are bound. We cannot change this order at will according to our subjective insight. This state of affairs is also decisive for a historical deed. Thus the fact that a person has only one body and can only be in one place at a time and do a definite and limited amount of work is one of the factors determining the tempo of historical development. A former of history will have to reckon with influences, to assimilate the data at his or her disposal, etc. Cultural formation requires time.

The question may crop up as to whether the historical tempo has been accelerated or not. It is possible that the power of assimilation has increased in comparison with former times, but we must not draw hasty conclusions. The inference of an accelerated tempo will have to be based on a comparison of our times with another period in which everything was in a similar state of fermentation, and when there was also such a fierce struggle for cultural power in progress.

The old forms have been worn out and must be replaced by new ones, just as in the sixteenth century. However this may be, we do not believe that in the field of art there has been any change of tempo. If we compare the tempo of the rise, development and spread of Gothic art, Baroque, Impressionism or modern architecture we find little difference. Even the intensity in the spread of these styles shows little change; its extent has increased on account of the closer contact between the various geographical units.

As to the normative aspects, human formative scope is likewise restricted within comparatively narrow limits. People can only disclose and positivize possibilities and they cannot ignore or infringe the norms with impunity. In the normative spheres people have to capitulate to the divine order of creation.

In history people's formative will and the super-arbitrary normative principles to be positivized are closely interwoven. A formative action has influence only if it is compatible with the life and world view of the leading circles of society. Then the positive form-giving activity will be increasingly in consonance with their ideals. When, however, this view of life and the world is apostate this law will turn into a law of sin. For if the action is an attempt to elevate the anti-normative element to the position of a norm, the consequences are as unpredictable as they are sinful. The result is a great tension between the intended positive order and the super-arbitrary principles inherent in the divine world order.

People will continually have to capitulate to this order of creation into which their arbitrary scheme can be realized only very partially and imperfectly. Every historical deed is therefore an all but inextricable tangle of sinful and indispensable law-conformable actions, a mixture of sin and forced obedience.

We may ask whether the work of positivization is to be judged by formative standards or exclusively according to the norms of the particular aspect to which this activity was directed.

The answer is that formative standards also should be applied. The struggle that is in progress in the field of art is a case in point. Here it is very clear that the formation of a style is usually not judged by merely aesthetic standards but that the formative activity of the leading artists is also involved. Historicism looks upon every norm as exclusively the product of human formation and becomes entangled in 'the antinomy between the claim of every view of life and the world to universal validity and the historical conscience' (Dilthey).

At this point we are confronted with the problem as to whether there is only one line of development or whether there are more. Is there only one history of the world? In any case world history is a potentiality based on the fact that people are bound to one and the same world order wherever they may live and work. No attempt should be made to find some law-like regularity in the course of the history of the world. For then we should always be trying to find the law in what is subjective, namely in the course of history up to and including the present moment. This is not saying that history is a meaningless succession of generations, each with its own opinions and insights. On the other hand, history is not a phenomenon wholly determined by the laws of nature.

God guides and directs the course of history in accordance with his divine plan. Holy Scripture reveals something of this plan, but it does not disclose a law to which people are inexorably bound. The Scriptures do not teach us any determinism. Yet some leading ideas of the character and the manner of God's guidance of history have been revealed, e.g. in Deuteronomy 28. But they are not to be considered as laws to which God himself is subjected. And they do not represent any law-like regularity in subjective events. God controls every event, but this fact is by no means to be interpreted as a kind of fate or as some deterministic regularity.

The course of history comprises a very intricate interplay of historical deeds that are connected in a meaningful coherence. Because people always have to comply with historical norms it is impossible for them to ignore existing relations between the historical powers. They have to react to objective historical events and to actions on the part of their supporters and their opponents. All these circumstances give rise to some kind of coherence between the various events from the earliest times to our own day.

As a result there is order in the course of cultural history. In accordance with the subject-object relation in history people are not independent of one another. On the contrary, humankind have been made of one blood (Acts 17:26) and its members live and work on the cursed earth in the same space of time between Paradise and Doomsday. Since the fall into sin the conflict has continued between the *civitas Dei* and the *civitas terrena*, especially in countries where the gospel has been made known.

2 The situation

A historical deed is occasioned by a concrete historical constellation or it is an answer to the 'challenge of the moment'. Facts are inescapable and urge people to action. The question is whether there are any facts independent of our subjective judgment. Even an objective historical event cannot be considered apart from human judgment. In the case of events determined by normative aspects there will always be subjective appreciation which must be regulated by norms. A knowledge of facts will always depend on the knowledge of and the insight into the norm. The agreement upon a particular norm will enable us to establish and verify the same facts. If such agreement is absent every individual appreciation will be considered as a subjective evaluation lacking 'universal validity'. The presence or absence of a consensus opinion is the line of demarcation between a 'universally valid fact' and 'a subjective judgment'. It does not denote the structure of the judgment or the matter to be judged. There is often a consensus opinion, not infrequently among those who have a different insight in law and norm, or a different view of life and the world. This consensus is the effect of the historical coherence in which the general principle of human beings having to capitulate to the divine world order plays an important part.

Historical development is not a *einheitliches* process (i.e. a uniform and unified process). Various historical powers exist side by side, just as there are various contemporary movements originating from different views of life and the world. The state of affairs within each of the separate cultural spheres is called the 'particular situation'. It will generally give the impulse to historical action. This is not saying that the importance of such action is restricted to its original limited field.

A historical deed may be a reaction to a concrete situation, in which new possibilities must be actualized and elaborated; new problems are raised and new demands are made; maybe it is suggested that there are shortcomings and that civilization is on the wrong track. There may be a decided break between the actual postivization of the norm and the prevailing cultural ideal, especially when the view of life and the world has undergone a fundamental change. In the case of such discrepancy the demands made by the personal outlook and the actual situation will first of all occasion the proclamation of a new prophetic message. The faults and abuses of the times are laid bare – of course as they are seen in the light of a personal insight in the norms. The cause of the trouble is sought in the now rejected outlook. New methods are proposed, but at the same time the necessity of a living faith is set in the light. A spiritual revolution is generally preceded by such a prophetic message. Gauguin's writings are an illustration of such an epoch-making message. They were a prophecy of what was realized in modern art later on.

3 Personality

The personality of a former of history is determined by his or her individual qualities and peculiar talents and influenced by the national character. The latter is relatively constant, i.e. it is only affected by very fundamental changes in the circumstances of the national outlook. The influence of this outlook is discussed in F. Hoffet, *L'imperialisme protestant: Considérations sur le destin inégal des peuples protestants et catholiques dans le monde actuel* (Paris, 1948).

The formers of history in the successive generations working simultaneously or in succession will try to satisfy and give free scope to their deepest desires. They are sinful human beings, inclined to all manner of evil, also in their formative work. Those who follow in the footsteps of Cain are animated by one spirit and urged on by the prince of Darkness, and will try to develop a culture giving them free scope to indulge the passions of their depraved hearts. But they will always have to capitulate to the divine order of the creation.

On the other hand, the true believers of the word of God will be the salt of the earth by their faith and obedience.

4 The view of life and the world

A life and world view is the result of people's effort to orientate themselves in the reality of their surroundings. This view is manifest in and through their behaviour and their utterances. Their personal outlook is determined by their religious commitment and by the actual positive order in which they find themselves. People who do not believe in the God of the Scriptures are always at bottom seekers of themselves. They try to satisfy their own desires by surrendering to 'nature' or they seek the absolute freedom of self-determination. Thus a religious dialectic is started which is concretized in the successive life and world views that try to maintain an uncertain equilibrium between the two poles of this dialectic. A shift in the religious dialectic as well as changes in the positive order will entail a change in the view of life. Often such changes in the positivization or in the opening process will be correlated with the impulse of the religious outlook. The attempt will be made to mould reality in accordance with the new views of life and the world, and to purge existing conditions of the element of capitulation to the divine world order. At the back of this tendency is the urge in people to establish harmony between the religious starting point, the personal outlook and the reality of the positive order (cf. part 1 of this essay).

Ultimately this tendency in apostate people will never be fully realized. The impact of reality leads to conflicts; hence they have to capitulate to the world order. In modern people – so very conscious of themselves in a religious respect – a serious crisis arose, formulated by existentialism with its nuclear concept of 'dread, meaninglessness, death'.

The spirit of the times is the smallest common factor of the life and world views entertained by the leading circles in a particular period of history. Or, to put it in a more general way, the spirit of the times is the generally accepted positive cultural ideal in a certain period. Wisdom, on the other hand, is a strictly personal acquisition, a life and world view purified by experience and, of course, one of the determining factors of the historical action of a former of history. A life and world view is formed especially by prophets who point the way to realize the religious principle in the actual situation (cf. the last part of section 2). Often a prophet will give a more exact and concrete form to some cultural ideal. Marx and Engels' *Communist Manifesto* is a case in point. In the course of time such a cultural ideal will be more and more intensively integrated into the faith and the religion of a particular cultural sphere.

Epilogue

The significance of the above-mentioned factors for the insight into a historical deed is considered in greater detail, especially with an eye to historiography. Any kind of relativism is rejected, just as any attempt to reason away the differences in the various life and world views are rejected, as well as any attempt to put these differences out of court in a scientific discussion. All such attempts are found to be futile.

Faith and Culture

• On being salt that salts[182]

Our task in this world is given in the words of our Lord Jesus Christ: 'You are the salt of the earth.' That is not something that we must become, in one way or another, but something we already are, if indeed we are numbered among his faithful followers, his people. To be the salt of the earth means to be a preservative, to prevent decay, to make food palatable. That is not an extra task or some difficult assignment that is laid upon us, but this: that you let your light so shine before men, that they may see your good works. To be salt that salts does not mean to solve, with our Calvinistic wisdom, the difficult problems of the world, to know the right answer for every difficult problem, to look down on the world and think that we can always help them out of their difficulties because we have a lease on wisdom and possess, after all, the right rudiments and principles. That is not the way it is, for very often the problems that confront the world are a tangle not only of sin and its effects and wretchedness but also of good endeavours and things that are indispensable. These problems are not susceptible to a simple resolution, because they arise from an often incomprehensible combination of forces and powers, they exist because we live on an earth that has been cursed, where sin and judgment pull things out of whack.

Let us not be pretentious in this regard. That is not necessary, for we are already salt that salts if only we are faithful and keep his commandments. Thus 1 Peter 2:13 states: 'Submit yourselves for the Lord's sake to every authority instituted among men . . . For it is God's will that by doing good you should silence the ignorant talk of foolish men.' And Paul states in Colossians 4:5–6: 'Be wise in the way you act towards outsiders; make the most of every opportunity. Let your conversation be always full of grace, seasoned with salt, so that you may know how to answer everyone.' Salt that salts is what we are if we seek his kingdom, as we wrote on an earlier occasion. It is being prepared at all times to give an account of the hope that is in us, to live a holy life and to walk in his way. It is to be worthy, as a worker, of one's wages, even if we labour in the employment of a person of this world. It is to pay the full wages of the worker we may have hired. It is to call immorality immorality and not, as the world does, an 'affair'. It is to be honest and upright and to call injustice injustice and therefore also to stand up for the rights of the oppressed. It is to be steadfast and immovable, always abounding in the work of the Lord, doers of the law, for we know that our labour is not in vain in the Lord (1 Corinthians 15:58).

This may all seem self-evident, and it is when we live close to the Scriptures. Yet it is precisely in these things that we may see clearly how far we have wandered from his paths over the years. How many do not find great political activities in this world more important than simple work in his church, to strive for righteousness and justice there? How many do not regard the science of the Christian so highly that a scientific argument possesses more power to convince than a simple word spoken according to the Scriptures and our confession? Science, politics, and the like, are often held in higher esteem than obedience to the 'everyday', 'ordinary' commandments given in the Scriptures. Do we not often occupy ourselves with all kinds of remote problems while neglecting to unmask vain philosophies, so that the Lord's people may thereby be protected from false doctrine? Are we not often so preoccupied with all kinds of work that the Lord has not assigned us that we neglect to prophesy, which is to speak in such a way that we edify, warn and encourage people?

To be salt that salts does not mean to pursue grand schemes and unleash tremendous events; it is nothing other than to fulfil the task God has given us, namely, that we keep his commandments, that we be legible epistles of Christ and that we do our work within the community of the saints. Our task in the last matter is to instruct one another, admonish and teach one another from the Scriptures . . . and to forbear one another in all longsuffering and meekness. Christ himself taught us in the washing of his disciples' feet that we are to serve one another, and we do that by strengthening one another in the faith, by calling attention to dangers, by admonishing when necessary, by providing support in times of difficulty, by building together towards a reformation!

Reformation

'Reformation' is a grand word with an appealing sound to our ears as children of the great Reformation. A grand word, yes, but let us keep in mind what the word means. It does not mean developing ambitious activities in all the various spheres of life, although it may be compatible with that; it means nothing more and nothing less than conversion, returning to the Lord and once again placing our trust in him. It means putting aside everything that cannot stand in his presence; it means breaking with sin.

Reformation means listening to the call of the Lord when he says: 'Repent! Turn away from all your offences; then sin will not be your downfall. Rid yourselves of all the offences you have committed, and get a new heart and a new spirit. . . . Repent and live!' (Ezekiel 18:30). Thus Reformation can only occur when we know that we have sinned, that we have wandered astray from the paths of the Lord. For if we believe we do walk in God' s ways, from what then are we to be converted, and how can there be a return to the Lord? Therefore we must always listen, again and again, to what our Father says to us in his word and assess our works; therefore we must listen when he sends prophets and teachers to us in his churches to show his people the way (Isaiah 30). Therefore too we must pay heed when the Lord chastens us, his people, confronting us with his judgments and destroying the work of our hands, so that we may confess that he is the Lord our God. Then we can sing with Psalm 119: 'It is good for me to be afflicted so that I might learn your decrees,' for woe betide us if we should fail to heed and take it to heart, so that the Lord would have to speak of us as in Isaiah 42:25.

How grateful we should be that we do not have to rely upon ourselves, but that we can trust in our God because he has promised to protect and maintain his church. We must be ever mindful that it is the Lord who gives strength and that it is not by our own might and the strength of our own hands that we achieve what is good (Deuteronomy 8:17–18). Reformations are therefore not something we have to bring about ourselves. God will give them to us. 'The LORD your God will circumcise your hearts and the hearts of you descendants, so that you may love him with all your heart . . . You will again obey the LORD . . . Then the LORD your God will make you most prosperous in all the work of your hands.' These words revealed to us what reformation is according to Deuteronomy 30, where it is also written that he will have compassion on us and overturn our captivity, and gather us from all the nations where we have been scattered . . . promises which we ourselves have seen fulfilled in the history of our churches in the recent past.

Reformation, conversion, returning to the Lord, that means trusting in him again and not in our own strength and wisdom (Isaiah 30:15–16), it means learning again that he is our Father in the covenant, the Lord of lords, who will honour those who honour him, but who will send judgment upon unfaithful covenant children and an unfaithful people (Deuteronomy 28). It is putting into practice what we so often confess with our mouths but so often neglect to really believe, that is, to find our starting point in the Scriptures and to test everything by the Scriptures. For reformation is turning from our sins and following God's commandments.

We and God's word

How often have we in fact not scorned the simple reading and acceptance of God's word! And have we not thought that science and theology would show us the way and disclose and make clear the norm? Having read the Scriptures in order to find principles we then left the Bible closed, for, we thought, by then we had the good principles – principles which were indeed sometimes good, but apart from the Scriptures are broken vessels incapable of holding the living water. Returning to the Scriptures – how often have we not understood that to mean using more and more commentaries and thick books while reading the Bible, so that we might become even more scholarly . . . but perhaps absolutely none the wiser when measured against the wisdom that one can boast of because one knows God.

How often have we not lived according to so-called scriptural ideas: we have had our notions of the kingdom of God, of walking in the ways of the Lord, conceptions of our task in the world, and ever so much more. We lived according to an idea of the covenant expressed more or less as follows: 'we are all sinners, and Christ forgives our sins if only we believe in him,' such that we read past the Scriptures when they clearly and directly admonished and indicted us. And therefore we were also not converted from our sins. And because of this we also read past the wonderful comforting passages that God gave in his word to us who live in very difficult times ... 'for we are all sinners, are we not, and the Lord Jesus shed his blood and forgives us all our sins.' That is true, yes, but he also guides and rules our lives, is ever near us, is angry when we deviate to the left or the right of his way, watches over us, keeps us from all evil and turns it to our good. We so often forgot, because we lived by an idea of the covenant instead of in the covenant, that God rules and guides the world even in ordinary and concrete events, even in times of war and insurgencies of Colorado beetles and pestilence in the chicken coop and the Liberation of our churches[183] or whatever.

We often constructed our own lines of reasoning according to our own, sometimes no more than putatively scriptural, theories and then attempted to solve the problems these produced by going to the Scriptures. We put our questions to the Scriptures instead of letting the Scriptures interrogate us. Sometimes we posed dilemmas unknown to the Scriptures and therefore forgot to examine the dilemmas the Scriptures do know. Our attitude towards life was often so theoretical that we turned the most ordinary everyday difficulties and questions into theoretical scientific problems. We did that, for example, with the so-called problem of the movies. We wanted to solve the difficult problem of the relation between the Christian world view and the newly disclosed possibility of moving pictures, so we hauled out theories of culture, world views and much more and, in a word, framed the matter as a scientific, theoretical and general problem, forgetting all the while to answer the question concerning the position a simple urban church member should take toward the cinema around the corner. Yes, we often did not know the answer to that question ourselves, because we wanted to see the question solved at a general level first and then, from the scriptural theory, to infer the scriptural answer.

Let us then in practice and in truth return to the simple word of God, that word of which it must be said, and then not only in our theological proceedings, that it is perspicuous, efficacious and sufficient (which is to say clear, powerful in convincing us and refuting error, and revelatory of all that we need to know). We must really have confidence, even in our common daily reading of the Bible, that the Scriptures are transparent and clear and sufficient and that their meaning is accessible to everyone who reads them believingly, even without theological, scientific preparation.

And if in this way we begin to read the Scriptures again as the simple, clear word of God, if we begin to live close to the Scriptures, not just saying so, but actually seeing the world and the churches and the times and ourselves through the open Bible in our hand, if we judge the questions to see if they are scriptural, and count our own problems and ideas as dung and loss, simply trusting and believing what is in the Scriptures and obeying God's commandments without raising objections . . . then, then unprecedented perspectives will open.

Problems will melt away like snow in the sun, we will be freed from all manner of overly burdensome tasks that we have set for ourselves and one another under the influence of certain concepts of the kingdom of God, which in turn entailed a certain notion of obedience. Questions we did not know how to cope with will resolve themselves. We will learn to see who our Lord is, how he rules the world, how he reigns over the world in his judgments and how he protects and keeps his people . . . If we begin to live close to the Scriptures this way and to seek his kingdom, and to be salt that salts, then we will again know our place and our task and learn again to be forbearing and meek and modest and also steadfast, not tossed to and fro and carried about with every wind of doctrine. Then we will also be thoroughly equipped for every good work (2 Timothy 3:17).

Scriptural discernment

Then, when there is truly a reformation and a listening to the word of the Lord, God has promised us in Malachi 3:18 that we will once again be able to discern between those who serve him and those who do not serve him. In this way we will learn to judge better and more in keeping with the Scriptures: our judgment will be much milder on the one hand and much sharper on the other. We will take a milder view of those who serve God in a manner not precisely our own, who are perhaps even caught up in various misconceptions and unscriptural ideas, for we know that we too were attached to many opinions, and we know that the Saviour also forgave us a very great deal indeed. Then we will also no longer look down upon the 'multitude' who do not know the law, as a Pharisee condescends to a publican, but on the other hand we will discern more keenly where the Christian or his science is set upon too high a pedestal, where people are promoting concocted ideas about the kingdom of God and all the rest while not really trusting the Lord, and thinking they have to erect barriers to 'contain' communism and all the rest themselves, or where people exhibit a genuine lack of scriptural humility.

We will free ourselves of the idea that reformation begins with and consists of studying harder, addressing more difficult questions, and being more principled and theologically purer. We will see that reformation is not founded upon science or even theology, but rather the reverse, a true reformation of scientific thought will be the result of real reformation, of conversion. We will learn to value science and theology correctly within the community of the saints and to assign them their proper, rather modest place.

Once we have returned to the Lord in this way, God our Father will watch over us again, to our blessing and salvation. And once we have heeded again in this way the commandments of the Lord, it may be that he will make us the head and not the tail (Deuteronomy 28:13). He will honour those who honour him and pour out showers of blessing on the work of our hands. And we? We will fulfil our task, with his help, in all simplicity, as faithful servants . . . and so lay up treasures for ourselves in heaven.

• **Faith and culture**[184]

a) Obedience, not religiosity

God, an exalted and great power, a mighty being, with whom we must endeavour to live in harmony. God, an exalted being we cannot avoid, whom especially after death we shall encounter, which is why we must see to it that we are in such a state that we can appear before him. Therefore, let us be devout and be careful to give him what is his due. This is the way people often, we might even say usually, talk about the Lord of lords.

And then the question of course immediately arises: what does this God want, what does he ask of us, and how and in what respect can we get on the right side of him? Naturally, so people reasoned, he is so exalted, so far removed from our petty human affairs, from all earthly and ordinary doings, that he does not want to have anything to do with 'lower' things, with matter, with the 'ordinary', with our everyday lives. He has nothing to do with all that; he stands apart from that. Rather, he regards us in the higher, the deepest and innermost, part of who we are, in the core of our being – that is where we must focus on him, see to it that we are pleasing to him: therefore let us be devout, and religious. Yes, religiosity, wherewith we please him, let that be the area in which we give him everything he wants. For no, God does not concern himself with ordinary everyday affairs but with our religious lives.

This is the way many generations have reasoned. And after having followed the inspiration of their own hearts in that way and after first having relegated God to a place outside daily life – on the pretext that he stands above it – these apostate generations attempted to make themselves acceptable to him through their religiosity. And that religiosity belonged to a sphere apart, to something extending outside and above daily life: that is how it came about that people set out to find ways themselves to please him religiously, by sacrificing much to him, by giving up everything that was dear to them. Wilfully and waywardly people decided for themselves how they would come before God – without regard for what he so often said through the mouths of his prophets: 'Not burnt offerings and sacrifices, but obedience I require, not religiosity, child sacrifice, hard penance and abstinence from the so-called lower sphere of life, but, where sin reigned, a broken spirit and a contrite heart, and further, a walking in my ways.' This is the way too in which we must understand the verse: 'Religion that God our Father accepts as pure and faultless is this: to look after orphans and widows in their distress and to keep oneself from being polluted by the world' (James 1:27). The world, that is of course the lower and the lesser aspect of life, that which is not noble, so many generations of people have reasoned, but James puts it differently. He talks about the way we speak, the backbiting and adultery, about sin as it reigns in the world of the unbelievers.

How have the thoughts which we have attempted to report here, the contrivances of the apostate heart that we have attempted to sketch here, slain their thousands! We have in mind here not the heathen but the children of the covenant, the people of God: Israel, people who wanted to have a sacred high place in every locality, who multiplied the prohibitions and religious rules, against God's explicit command; we have in mind the Pharisees, who regarded themselves so highly elevated above 'ordinary' people, since they knew the Law, after all, and lived so religiously – something the common people had no time for, bound as they were to struggling for their daily bread and doing their daily things, including, for example, baking the bread for the Pharisees' own meals.

St Anthony. No, then hermits like Anthony were more consistent. They left everything and radically shut themselves away from the 'world'. Into the desert, in caves, they fled from the world, put aside all pleasures and wanted no thought about their bodily needs to reach them. They fled the world and wanted to live only in the religious realm, fighting to make themselves acceptable in God's eyes. Yet while they did indeed cut themselves off from the world, they forgot that their sinful heart went with them and they forgot that as they obstinately pursued purification for themselves without holding Christ's great sacrifice to be sufficient, the devil would claim them for himself. For who can stand before God? And it is there that the devil will begin his assault (for he also torments his own), it is there that the wicked heart will manifest its perverse tendencies, where God's commandments are violated the most. That is where there is contempt for the creation, for the 'lower' facets of life, as if they could be impure in themselves. And therefore it is hardly astonishing that hallucinations and visions tormented St Anthony, the first among hermits. Every tendency to yield to the natural desires and needs of the body, the so despised lower sphere of life, seemed to him after all to be a temptation, and so it was precisely those never to be satisfied needs of his body – thus that which simply never can be 'religious' – that made him sick and brought forth the most perverse daydreams. And the vexations of the devil which continually prodded him to seek himself, to persevere, to reason on consistently, and for all that to regard his own religiosity as something of the lower aspect of life, as something of this world, made life an agony, a strange nightmare, a horrible fight against himself for himself.

'The temptation of St Anthony' is a theme that later would be picked up again and again by those who recognized in it their own fight and their own self-will. Perhaps this is to be found at its most brilliant in Flaubert's book of 1874. Flaubert depicts for us in a breathtaking way Anthony's hallucinations and anxious dreams, his striving to attain sanctification on his own and his fight against nature, against what is natural. I want to share a fragment with you. At the end of the book we see Anthony standing between two women. The one is voluptuous and beautiful and says, as she bares herself before his eyes: 'Come, go with me, for what does all this matter, let us eat and drink and follow the lusts of the flesh, for life is short and the end unavoidable.' Here we have a perverse dream, an unbearable strain for shattered nerves. The other woman is old. She shows him an empty pit and tries to persuade him to commit suicide, saying: 'Think about it: he created you, and now you are going to destroy his work, you, with your courage, in complete freedom. Your joy will be full, and moreover your body has opposed you enough that it is time at last you took revenge on it. You will not suffer. It will be over quickly. What are you afraid of? A big black hole? Perhaps it will prove to be emptiness!' In this passage we see how Flaubert, a Roman Catholic writer, has plumbed very sharply the depths of self-willed religion and seen even how in the end this man was seeking himself and rebelling against his Creator and therefore also eventually doubting everything, including even the salvation that he fought for so bitterly.

This Anthony lived in about AD 300 and the Roman Church numbers him amongst its saints. Naturally, they could not tolerate this individualistic mysticism, this self-seeking piety; yet they also did not struggle radically against it. They tried instead to regulate it. And so the first monasteries arose.

b) The monasteries

In order to be able to understand something of the monasteries, we make a leap to the heyday of the Middle Ages, when in the thirteenth century the church and scholastic theology were at their apogee and everything was being systematized. Philosophically speaking, realism held sway, built on the notion that everything in this world is subject to a universal, all-embracing world order. This notion was borrowed from heathen Greek philosophy, and this world order is accordingly not the same as the law order that God has revealed in his word – quite disrespectfully, according to this scholasticism, even God is subject to this order and cannot do otherwise than create according to its laws! In the system that people now designed we encounter again the division between a pious realm, that of religion, and another realm, which stands loose from God and his word, the realm of nature. One can perhaps grasp this best by thinking of the regulations and the theoretical justification of a Sunday-go-to-meeting type of Christianity. The spheres of grace and nature are separated, and life is divided into the areas of piety and of nature, where human reason rules. It is in that respect a purely Roman Catholic notion that is expressed in Amsterdam in the Kalverstraat where a sign in front of a church says: 'Every day 20 minutes for God!' The rest of the time, presumably, people may live according to the laws of nature.

The church, the institute of grace, is naturally the higher that encircles and governs all the lower. For the lower, nature, is seen as a preliminary stage of grace, where everything must be directed towards the highest good, towards salvation. Everything in this life, state and society and marriage and family are in the service of that realm of grace and ought to be directed towards the highest goal, the church, and therein towards eternal salvation, and is thus subject to it, no matter the extent to which it is also a sphere having its own laws and belonging to the lower, to nature. The church distributes the means of grace, the sacraments, and only obedience to the church can bring salvation. That also applies to the monastic communities, which at the same time, however, through their devout works and prayers accumulate a treasure of grace, which the church can then in due course distribute in the form of indulgences, for example for the benefit of those who because of the fact that they are lay people, thus people who commit themselves to the lower sphere of life, do not have the time to devote themselves entirely to the pious life with its devout meditations, constant prayers and doing of penance. For here too grace must be earned by pious works, it is our religiosity that must make us acceptable before God, and the lower sphere of life is an indispensable aid, to be sure, but has no value in itself.

However, it was inevitable, in spite of the Inquisition that was set up to see to it that everything was indeed, and would remain, obedient to the church in the framework of the system, that a tendency quickly arose, first of course within the monastic communities, to earn salvation oneself, outside the church's means of grace. Did these not also belong to the lower sphere, the secular, and was not all that mattered after all the piety and useful religious works that one performed oneself? The old principles, already taught and ardently lived out by Anthony, could not be disowned. Thus it soon came about, in the fourteenth century, that individualism started to run rampant: an individualistic mysticism arose that wanted by no means to undermine the church – the church was good, after all, for the lower folk, for those who still lived in the world – but that actually did so in spite of itself by disesteeming the church's importance.

Especially in the monasteries along the Rhine this sort of mysticism blossomed, the basic characteristic of which is always that people seek God in their own way and by means of their own religiosity, outside his word – that word belongs to the lower sphere as well, so people thought, as it is merely a 'dead letter'. Because God's word is scorned and one's own (so-called pious) heart is the point around which everything revolves, it can come as no surprise that in this environment all manner of heresies soon began to flourish. Led by the pious fabrication that the Holy Spirit enlightens the elect – directly, naturally not by means of the word of God which was consigned to the lower sphere – the most extreme individualistic doctrines were eventually cherished here: humanity themselves were apotheosized and proclaimed the centre of all endeavour and work. In this way both life and theory were secularized, often under the guise of piety: humanity's subjectivity, their centre, the highest in them, was free, free not only from the external world but also from God, whom people would now endeavour to serve in their own way.

The Modern Devotion. In the fifteenth century a centre was established here in the Netherlands where such an attitude held sway. We refer to the well-known so-called 'Modern Devotion'. Given what has already been said, the following citation requires no further explanation:

> The Modern Devotion manifests an individualistic character. The devotee sees himself as a solitary individual, forsaken by God and man, burdened by his own guilt and responsibility. Here conversion is a killing of the flesh, not in the sense of sin – cf. Sunday 33 of the Heidelberg Catechism – but in that of the 'lower life', through murderous asceticism in fasting and self-chastisement. In order the better to 'suppress nature and kill beastly desire', the devotee had also to die to association with people, contact with family and even with pious company. Whoever thus in perfect solitude engaged 'incessantly with spiritual activities' could practice the 'art of living with Jesus' – and with himself.

> Yet with that the way to self-annihilation is not yet at an end. The devotee must also die to that which he perceives in solitude, to his experience of God, for 'maturity of the spiritual life consists not only in the possession of consolation but much rather in the patient bearing of the absence of consolation'. The ideal of the Modern Devotion is thus that of 'resigned desperation' (*getröste Verzweiflung*). Only one who feels his emptiness is worthy of meeting Jesus. That accounts for the immeasurable disregard for one's own life ... This ideal of piety is the Christianizing of the individualistic principle with regard to the indestructibility of the core of personality.[185]

Also in this circle we observe ever more far-reaching consequences, so that it cannot seem surprising that this mystical movement finally produced a purely humanistic temperament. The pious person in the end became the humanistic rational-ethical personality, and where there was once talk of people mystically following in the footsteps of Christ along the way of the cross, victory over hell, and resurrection – the imitation of Christ – there arose a kind of Sermon-on-the-Mount Christianity that saw in Christ a good example and nothing more. Erasmus was also strongly influenced by this circle. Erasmus, who did poke sharp fun at the failings of the church, in the end did not consider the church important enough to sacrifice his goods and blood for it. His single goal was after all the humanistic ideal of education, to form someone into a flawless and noble personality, and that could be accomplished inside the church as well. Erasmus opposed Luther precisely on the point of human free will, the cardinal point, of course, for these subjectivists.

Indeed, from this circle, which ultimately did regard the church as belonging to the lower sphere, since at bottom all that mattered was the higher side of humanity, their free, devout personality, from this circle reformation could not be expected. Besides, what was God's word? – a book suited perhaps for devout personal religious exercises, but beyond that . . . just a letter that could awaken no life.

c) The spirits of the two witnesses

But then God raised up the spirits of the two witnesses who had been silenced for more than two centuries by the violence of the Inquisition. The world looked up, astonished, for the idea that people might still hear this old voice after so many years was outrageous. In the persons of Luther and Calvin God called his church back to obedience to his word. Therein the Lord remembered his covenant with his church and he gave new life to dead bones. Now he does indeed give the Holy Spirit, not loose from the word, but in and through the word. Luther unmasked the falsehood of the thesis that people must be saved by their own works, but remained stuck at various points in the old division between the higher and lower spheres, which are now called the spiritual and legal spheres. Calvin had a keener insight and carried the work forward to reveal the full richness of the meaning of the covenant. How sharply he saw through the peril! And how he therefore fought against Castellio and others, kindred spirits of Erasmus, libertines, and all those who believed they had attained a 'higher stage of piety and spirituality' and who therefore could value everything except zeal for the truth against error. Later we will take a closer look at the renewal of the covenant and its importance even for today.

First we want to examine the consequences that the teachings of the Roman Church and of the individualistic and subjectivistic movements described above had in the area of culture. As far as the Roman Church is concerned we can say nothing other than that the criticism of its wealth, love of ostentation, immorality, lying, popular deception, ignorance, lack of love, superstition and worldliness as we may read about it in that splendid book, *Praise of Folly* by Erasmus, is indeed entirely correct. For in that way God's word was regarded as nothing – it was called a book for theologians and for pious musings – and as the 'lower', as nature, was separated from God and his word. Indeed, superstition, the putting of one's trust in all manner of relics in particular, had penetrated to the highest circles. Truly, the immorality was sometimes shocking: there were instances of bishops or monasteries drawing their income from bordellos, of a woman being brought before the Inquisition because she refused to give herself to a monk. And we will not expand upon the terrifying corruption of bribery and other dishonourable practices that the church applied in its power politics, which was piously justified as if it were a matter of maintaining the power of the church and religion over the sphere of the lower and nature. All who have steeped themselves in the story of Luther and devoted some attention to the machinations accompanying the various Diets [or Imperial Councils] as at Worms, where finally the infamous Edict of Worms was implemented – the signal for persecution – have seen something of a Mammon to which truly nothing Christian adheres except the pretension and the name. Happily, the Reformation had a good impact even on Roman practices, and in the course of the sixteenth century the most conspicuous failings were corrected. We will, however, at the end of our study return to the importance of Roman Catholicism for culture today.

Mystical movements. And the mystical movements? Will these perhaps, given their penchant to separate themselves from the world, have failed to affect culture? No, certainly not. Far from that. The history of the first half of the sixteenth century can teach us that in this period, as the Reformation undermined the power of the Roman Church, all kinds of mystical persuasions also had a chance to gain great influence with the general population. They preached the coming kingdom of God on earth, while state and society were seen as evil, mere lower powers; for should not everything be subject to Christ? Just as we saw earlier, in the case of Anthony, people now attempted to draw everything into the religious sphere – for only if everything was religious and only if everything worldly had been banned could there be peace with God. The cry of the Reformers for reformation becomes a call for revolution, for the overthrow of all worldly rule, of everything that is not religious. The kingdom of God must be established, Christ must reign – naturally not through obedience to his word, for what would that dead letter be able to teach the elect, the person in whose heart the Spirit of God dwells. Christ must reign. That meant: the elect must have the power and what the Spirit says in them, that will be law. Away with everything that is worldly, which did not mean away with sin but away with the government, with everything that was first called 'natural' and is separated from God and his word. The obvious conclusion was only seldom drawn, but the naked parading of the Anabaptists in Amsterdam, for example, an accompanying feature of these Anabaptist revolutionary movements, arose from a scorning of everything that in their opinion was not religious and hence was worldly. Thus they put off, so they believed, literally, what was of the world. Who can say how much immorality was committed in this period under the guise of piety: dying to oneself and the world, and self-willed 'tasting of the depths of Satan' so that the grace of God might abound? The old heresy of the Nicolaitans – to the pure all things are pure – evidently put down deep roots in the human heart, always ingenious in devising sins and perversities. We do not have to go into detail here about how these Anabaptists set about establishing a city of God at Münster under the leadership of the 'prophets' Jan van Leyden and Knipperdolling, or about how the most awful tyranny prevailed there and how it seemed more like a Sodom and Gomorrah than a heavenly Jerusalem, and we also do not need to recount how severe their judgment was after the city was retaken by its rightful Lord.

Later they withdrew again from the 'world' and in this country were usually absorbed into the Reformed Church, unless they followed Menno Simons. How the church had to struggle, however, with this old evil! – Marnix van St Aldegonde called it 'enthousiasm'[186] – allowing oneself to be led by the considerations of one's own heart under the pious guise of being guided by the Spirit.[187] And when apostasy appears in our churches, such heresies rear their heads again and again and the books of the 'enthousiasts' which were virtually entirely eliminated in the sixteenth century, are reprinted: Coornhert, Sebastiaan Franck – figures about whom one can read more in the fine book by Tunderman about Marnix van St Aldegonde – and they are read again zealously, just as is the immortal, alas, *Imitation of Christ* and other medieval mystical literature. In the circles of the governors especially, but not only there. And people looked down on the true old Reformed believers: intolerant characters who got excited about points of doctrine, hairsplitting, as one can find in the articles against the Remonstrants. People perceived themselves to be much more broadminded and did not dig in their heels so pharisaically in defence of their own opinion, as if they had a monopoly on truth. They looked down on those Reformed believers, who endeavoured to be pleasing to God in the 'natural' aspects of life. For in their quiet moments they perceived themselves to be much more pious, and much deeper, since they had the Spirit in their heart and not in a book, imprisoned in letters. No, they did not deify the Bible; they were not lackeys of dead letters.

Pietism. In the seventeenth century there arose then, fully in this line, a pietism that can be typified in brief with the words: 'Here then the inner and personal, the practical, expressing itself in brotherly love, are prominent; the believing heart and the grace-filled life stand at the centre of the considerations and the devotion.'[188] This movement spread from England through the Netherlands and Germany. In the last country especially it reached full bloom. Undoubtedly it sounds a great deal more scriptural than what we encountered earlier in the Anabaptists, and undoubtedly the wholesome influence of the Reformation continues to be felt in it, but the basic principles are not so different. It is then also not so surprising that many of the leading thinkers of the modern world came from pietistic backgrounds: names like Kierkegaard, Engels (the associate of Marx), Nietzsche and Kant speak volumes. Yes, especially German philosophy and the Romanticism of the period round about 1800 are unthinkable in isolation from pietism: this movement, which seeks the starting point of all science and other cultural work in the rational and ethical personality that stands free and unattached in the midst of this world, one may perhaps even call a secularization of pietism. What they both have in common is that the centre of attention is the deepest core of a person, from where all impulses must come, in the conviction that a better world is created when people rise above the lower aspects of life, above nature or the natural. That in and through all this Western culture increasingly loosened and emancipated itself from God and his word is clear. On the other hand, it can also be said that in this way many purely Christian ideas were incorporated into humanistic thought, so that far-reaching consequences were curbed and, in spite of all the evil that was done, still a great deal that was very good was also preserved. Yet the more keenly aware people become of their own basic principle and the more they dispense with these Christian vestiges, the more damaging the consequences are in the field of culture. Anyone who knows something about the work of the leaders of modern culture can attest to that.

d) The covenant and culture

We have focused our attention till now mainly on God's people in apostasy: we spoke of generations that fell away from the covenant and attempted to serve him in high-handed ways of their own, having demoted the Lord of lords to a God of religion. He was no longer the God of the covenant but the God that came to dwell in the devout heart, the God that viewed the devout on the basis of their good works and gave them experiences in their souls.

There was more at stake here than mere false teachings or doctrinal misconceptions, the kind of sins for which Christ has suffered and which can also be forgiven. Just think of the numbers of good Reformed believers who put their hope in going to heaven, where the soul is with Christ, and who therefore do not focus on the resurrection of the dead, a more glorious hope whereby both soul and body are delivered from the power of death. This misconception, undoubtedly not without some genetic connection to the Anabaptist undercurrent still always present in our Reformed lives, will surely not be charged to the faithful believer as a sin against the Holy Spirit – and that will also be the case with other opinions that, without one's being keenly aware if it, are of Anabaptist origin. No, at stake here was not simply some or other sinful opinion but apostasy from the Lord, while people started to live outside the covenant and outside forgiveness through the blood of Christ. Therefore God, after he had spoken to them through the prophets, handed them over to their own hearts, to walk in their own ways. He was with them, not benevolently but wrathfully, and handed them over to the spiritual wickedness in high places, against which they were powerless while they despised the sword of the Spirit – God's word – as a dead letter.

But as we said earlier, the Lord remembered his people, and he gave them reformation, which was not only a return to the word in the sense that pure doctrine was preached once again, but people rediscovered the covenant. People again knew themselves to be members of the covenant people. And that means that they are children of God, not exclusively, not even in the first place, in their religious moments, but always, even when they sleep, even when they are deathly ill and longing to lie down, even when they, God forbid, become mentally ill and behave like lunatics, even when they, anything but religiously, attentively and alertly, steer a middle course through traffic, and even when, equally anything but religiously, they treat themselves to a mouth-watering snack. God watches over his covenant people, is near us. The covenant is this in the first place, that he is near us, leads us, and preserves us in the presence of all dangers.

And what about religion? Yes, religion has its place as well. In distinction from self-willed religiosity it is limited to faith; or to put it the other way round, faith is the right religion as ordained by God. God has commanded us to praise him, to remember the Sabbath and to attend the worship service so that we may hear the word as delivered by an ordained minister. He has commanded us to read his word and to live by it, and he has enjoined us to pray to him and thank him not with a show of words, constantly and at length, but faithfully and uprightly. And we must not neglect all this, not only because that would be to the detriment of our souls, but also because we should fear him who has the power to destroy both body and soul in hell (Matthew 10:28).

But God, the Lord, the God of the covenant, has forbidden us to be always religious. Not only is that impossible – just think of what I observed earlier about Anthony – but it is not what he wants. Serving God is . . . no, not fasting and praying and singing psalms . . . but visiting widows and orphans, keeping your tongue and staying far away from sin. Again, do not understand this in the wrong way, as if James would preach something here that might even remotely resemble Anabaptist beliefs;

rather, we are taught here that God desires to be served in an obedient walk according to his commandments. And these commandments include: you shall not commit adultery – yes, God also concerns himself with what is lower and not religious – and he expressly forbids Jews to sacrifice animals religiously anywhere else than in the Temple in Jerusalem. Days of thanksgiving are pleasing to him, but the moment you celebrate longer than three days, your feast and your sacrifice become an abomination to me, he says (Leviticus 7:18).

All facets of life. The Lord is the God of the covenant, a God who as Creator and Lord over the entire creation also desires to be obeyed with respect to the facets of life that are not religious. This does not mean that those areas are therefore now to be numbered among the religious ones. If we do that, then we will always end up having to force the issue, and because there are areas that will not yield to such an operation the result will always be the development of an area that lies outside the terrain in which God is served: namely, that of the so-called natural matters. No, it is just as someone once so aptly put it: along with the baptism water the bath water enters the house. This means that God's covenant people, if they do indeed walk in his ways, will also devote attention to matters of hygiene, not because hygiene is religion but because hygiene is a good thing, something that belongs to the matters for which God demands consideration as well. Hygiene is not lower than religion; it is an extremely important matter that is worth taking to heart. In the same way they read in the laws of Moses, which are also very instructive for us, about the good treatment of animals, about safety measures such as the construction of railings around flat roofs, and about ever so many more matters which are all but religious, matters which do fall within the scope of God's attention as the God of the covenant. Yes, there is nothing that does not concern him. Indeed there is no terrain of his creation that he would be too high for or to which he would be indifferent.

Our fathers from the days of the Reformation understood this. And it is remarkable how the culture was utterly changed by it. It was not humanism, the secularization of the medieval individualistic mystical persuasions, but the Reformation that totally altered the culture in its broad scope. Public morals were healthy again. Around 1600 in Protestant countries it was impossible, for example, that there should be guilds of prostitutes – which actually still exist, albeit under other names, in various Catholic countries. The entire tone of public life changed. But in other areas a great deal changed as well. Thus in the field of science, for example, people began to take a real interest in the wonders of creation. Nature became a real object of investigation and not, as in the Middle Ages, a field that people did not need to study but about which they could reason and speculate smartly, in order to assign it its proper place in theology. This real science, which took an interest in everything that God has given in his creation, arose under the influence of the Reformation, even though in that period people never spoke, and perhaps rightly so, of Christian science. It simply was Christian science, as people investigated created things without scorning what the word of God had to say about them.

e) Liberation

Also in the field of art, yes, perhaps most clearly there, Calvinism brought tremendous liberation: liberation from the domination of the church, which did assign art to the realm of nature but which for that very reason wanted to subject it to the service of the church. There had been ecclesiastical art. Now, however, an entirely new art arose that knows that God's creation in all its diversity is worthy of depiction, an art that understood that there are other beautiful things besides the sacred Bible stories. Along with the lifestyle and the attitude towards life, art changed as well, starting now very soberly to capture the whole of reality, God's reality, in paintings. There is a break with the idealization and glorification of humanity as one finds it in the depiction of the lives of the saints, and people no longer look down on the lives of the lower folk who were once portrayed only as strange, uncultivated and wholly instinctual creatures, comical or criminal as the case might be. Indeed, Calvinistic art: art as we find it from the hand of van Ostade with his glimpses of peasant life, and van Ruysdael with his wonderful landscapes, or from the hand of Vermeer, this is real art, not ecclesiastical, not religious, but borne by a view of life that knows of both the pure perfection of the creation as God's work and of people as sinful, but not on that account less worthy, creatures.

This art reflects an entirely different style of life than one found, and finds, in Roman Catholic countries. Calvinists understand that when they possess or earn money, God has appointed them as stewards. They may not squander that money but must work with it to help their neighbour, to relieve need and to do something useful with that money. Thus one sees that in the Netherlands of the seventeenth century, for example, the wealthy indeed built solid houses and commissioned beautiful furniture, but one encounters no overabundance of luxury. People remained unpretentious. At the same time there are few if any beggars (cf. Deuteronomy 15:1-4). And – and in this we see how such an attitude towards life persists and carries over, even when people backslide from true belief – this still forms, even today, a remarkable difference between Protestant countries like the Netherlands or England and Roman Catholic countries. Here the contrast between the rich and the poor is much less sharp than in the southern countries of Europe, where people may observe overabundant luxury next to bitter poverty. In the Netherlands we find beautiful houses next to plain ones, in those countries palaces next to slums. It is remarkable that the impoverished population there feels so little compulsion to work their way up. Could that be because they ultimately regard money as nothing more than filthy lucre, in contrast to the Calvinists, who see it as a gift of God, not an end in itself and, when honestly earned, a blessing?

It is remarkable that a term like 'reliability' has no equivalent (e.g. in French) where people do not regard bribery and failure to fulfil one's obligations as serious sins against one's neighbour. Remarkable too is the difference in attitude towards governments: in Protestant countries people have learned to regard the government as the servant of God, which must be respected and obeyed. These too are things that still hold, despite the apostasy. Thus one does encounter tax evasion in the Netherlands – people are not perfect, certainly not – but in a Roman Catholic country like France, for example, it is hardly possible to levy direct taxes since virtually everyone cheats on a very large scale. This is possible because practically no one, including the civil servants, sees anything wrong with it but consigns it, instead, to the realm of cunning, as a schoolboy would, though wrongly, copy from his schoolmates.

To summarize, we see a considerable difference in lifestyle between Protestant and Roman Catholic countries, a difference that arose in the seventeenth century as Calvinism, here and elsewhere, put its mark on culture. It can only be regarded as a testimony to the strength of these principles that they have not been lost, even today, in spite of the fact that the basis, the underlying motive, has gone now that people deny God. This lifestyle can only be understood from the fact that people came to know God as the God of the covenant who desires to be obeyed in all things, who desires that we walk in his ways, also in being honest, also in being modest, also in our attitude towards the government he has placed over us. Precisely the fact that people have left to religion – that is, the right religion of the covenant – its own place, without detaching from God whatever is not religious, has had salutary consequences. Calvinist culture is not an ecclesiastical culture, far from it, and neither is everything drawn into the sphere of religion. No, politics is politics, and business is business, and art is art, and science is science and not theology – but that does not mean these areas have been secularized, that is, detached from God's commandments. That least of all!

Catholic vs. Calvinist. To end these reflections with a final contrast between Roman Catholic and Calvinist culture, notice the place worship and devotion hold in life. In Roman Catholic countries every crossroads is marked by a little chapel where people can offer their devout moments to God, while beyond and alongside that they lead their own lives. It is not a far-fetched and exaggerated example if we call to mind the example of King James of England, the Catholic king who prayed very much and sometimes even fined himself heavily but at the same time entertained mistresses, such that one of his ministers once observed that the king could only be moved to action by a woman or a priest, or perhaps by a combination of the two.

Consider also the matter of Sabbath day observance. For the Calvinists, in obedience to God's commandment, it is a day of rest in which worship receives their full attention, while the Roman Catholics attend mass early in the morning in order thereafter to devote themselves to entirely worldly pursuits. For the daily religious gatherings have undermined the difference between Sunday and the other days of the week. And during the week? We already discussed the Roman Catholics. And the Calvinists? Naturally there is daily prayer and the daily reading of the Scriptures, but not the devout minutes or half-hours. No secularized activity, but hard work, so that one earns one's living as a good worker and, at the place where one stands, does what the Lord would have one do, as a politician in one's politics, as a scholar in one's work, as – you name it – everyone in their own profession, with their own expert knowledge and their own responsibilities. Thus no secularization, no detachment from the God of the covenant in all those areas of life that do not belong to religion as such, but equally no 'elevating' of them into a pious or religious sphere. The butcher will go about butchering every day, but to butcher religiously . . .? It is Christianity that has made that a thing of the past. But undoubtedly also under the influence of the Calvinist lifestyle people now give consideration to animals and will attempt to shorten their suffering and to cause no unnecessary pain.

And the Anabaptist persuasions, are these still around? Certainly. We saw earlier how these eventuated in purely humanistic movements such as German Romanticism with its idealist philosophy. But in close contact with that, Anabaptist currents still exist amongst the Remonstrants, the Mennonites and other groups, all of which today are quite liberal. But alongside these groups that have a historical connection with the Anabaptists of the sixteenth century there are still other groups from our own era that evince similar characteristics but that seem to have rediscovered the old heresy independently, as it were – although closer scrutiny might also reveal historical connections and traditions. We have in mind in the first place the Jehovah's Witnesses. Have you ever had them at the door? And have you spoken with them for more than two minutes? Then it will have struck you that again and again one of their main arguments is that the church is nothing and has no importance. If in that case you cite the epistles of Paul, the answer inevitably follows: church people always hold on to the world, for the church is the world – do you recognize the old slogans? For it is written in the Bible, so they assure us, that there will be a spiritual kingdom, and that the believers will reign. But do we see this? Are the churches not fully secularized? If there truly were believers there, then the churches would not have supported the authorities in waging their wars in 1914 and 1940. Yes, the

Reformed respondent may then counter, governments are meant to be obeyed – apart from all other questions, what about Romans 13? Naturally, comes the JW reply, everyone should be subject to the powers placed over them, and it is clear that that is Christ, so everyone should obey Christ. For it is simply impossible that ordinary governments were intended here. For how can believers be subject to an unbelieving government? That cannot be the intention. And so on. One hears the same old tune, the disparagement of everything that does not belong to the field of religion and which is then called 'only the world'.

f) Faith and culture

But here we may also think of Karl Barth and his followers. Strictly speaking one can hardly call them Anabaptists, but the spiritual posture is so affinitive that we want to go into it briefly (we can of course make no pretence of completeness). Barth preaches the absolute separation between creatureliness and God, a separation so radical that it must be deemed impossible for anything like revelation to exist in this reality. It exists only with respect to the higher core of humanity where God grips people and, in religious moments, reveals himself to them, although ultimately that too can never become clear from any deeds done in the created realm, which is as such closed and alien to it. Revelation says nothing about this reality, and can say nothing about it. Anything of the sort that one finds in the Bible is derived from other sources and is surrendered entirely to modern biblical criticism. Barth accordingly completely condemns the idea of a Christian philosophy, and the very idea of a Christian culture, in general of any Christian activity in the 'natural' terrain, he condemns as a contradiction in itself. In this way the Bible itself is identified with the secular sphere. Yes, Barth contends that the moment the congregation or the preacher ascribes authority to the preaching and gives heed to it, as soon as the theologian believes he can speak with authority and works to form a school, as soon as the Bible is invested with authority and is held as the Bible to end all disputes, then orthodoxy has set in, a horrible caricature of true belief. And why? Because in this way divine freedom and freedom of belief are damaged. For ultimately the issue at stake is the free, subjectivistically and individualistically regarded human personality of the believing person, whose belief, however, is not susceptible to expression in articles of faith or restrictions on its freedom. The consequence of all this is that the whole of life, and given consistent reasoning that includes theology itself, is the world. Barth even defends a fundamentally a-Christian philosophy and science and culture. Here it is hardly possible to speak any longer of secularization, since everything is simply surrendered to the world (and I use the term 'world' in its biblical sense here).

Once again then, and finally: what about us? We do talk about Christian science, Christian politics, and although we often do not know what to do with it, about Christian art. Yes, we defend it with all our strength and write thick and thin books about the idea of a Christian culture. And just what does that entail? Are there no Anabaptist traces to be found in us? Is it not often the case that Christian science means science practised as religion, science by believers, by converted people, who investigate directly the connection with God and bring everything into a direct relation with him, people whose writings accordingly resemble confessions of faith or theological essays?

Is our political activity, which we often so stridently claim to be better at than the world because we are converted, always free of such alien contamination? A traffic regulation can be left to the secular specialists, can it not? Yet if such a regulation prohibits taking more than one child along as a passenger on one's bicycle, then we feel compelled to stand up for the strength of our principles and to say: 'Didn't we say it, these people have no understanding whatsoever of the fact that to have many children is an activity based in belief, yes, are believers not being repressed again by such a regulation?' So, our political activities often look more like theological exercises, and practical and sober insight into current problems is often scorned in comparison with knowledge of the principles in question.

Is this the reason why we always oppose the federation, for example, in the name of a few of our principles, without really working hard to think positively and constructively and to study with a view to finding solutions to the real and acute and concrete difficulties that it was hoped a federation could resolve? Let people examine themselves to see whether they have not indeed often, perhaps without formulating anything clearly, thought about it in this way. I only want to call attention to latent dangers. Perhaps it is already symptomatic that in our circles we seem to be interested almost exclusively in questions of political principles.

Culture is culture. What then is to be done? Are we no longer to speak of Christian politics or science or culture? Surely, but what we must mean by that is a walking in the ways of the Lord within the covenant. Politics is politics, the search for solutions to difficult political questions, problems of organization, planning, cooperation and lawful regulation, assistance and legislation, questions which a person who lives within the covenant does not want to solve, however, without the light that God has given him or her in his word. For God requires that in all these things believers must do what their hand finds to do, in the knowledge that their heavenly father is in it and not external to it. But again, politics is politics, and art is art, and science is science and, in general, culture is culture. Perhaps in the end it would simply be better not to talk of Christian culture. That is not to say that we want to view culture as a neutral terrain apart from the covenant. Certainly not. Yet we only want to say that the politics of the children of God must be good politics, sober and wise politics, indeed really politics and not, as is often the case with so-called unbelievers, a reasoning past and around politics in an otherworldly and unrealistic manner. For they proceed from a belief of their own, in humanity, for example, or in the attainability of a paradise on earth, or in the absolute correctness of the popular will. And because that belief is false and not in agreement with reality as it is – while they reject God's illuminating revelation – precisely for that reason they are often anything but realistic. Yes, their political actions too are often borne more by apostate prophecy than by real political wisdom and realism. No, not secularization, for that would involve following the gods of this age. Instead, obeying God in a realistic and practical manner, yes, also with an open Bible engaging in politics and culture. Wisdom resides in doing God's commandments, Moses once wrote. Let us focus on that, not because doing God's commandments would be religious and because we have to draw everything into the realm of faith distinguished from the realm of nature, but because God's commandments are words of life, and hygiene and justice and truth and correctness are good things while God's will is fulfilled in them. Everything has its place and time, including religion, and we must therefore not neglect church attendance and prayer and all the rest, but for the sake of God's will with respect to his covenant, we must not allow everything else to be absorbed into that.

Again, and finally: everyone must do what their hands find to do, soberly and concretely, practically or theoretically, in one terrain or another, and keep themselves far from the gods of this age, so that in this way we may be salt that salts in these times when apostasy slays its thousands and, with the decline of knowledge of God's word and the breaking with old Christian traditions, healthy insights become increasingly rare. For this may our God, the Lord of hosts, give us the strength, in grace, through his Son, our Saviour Jesus Christ.

• Christianity and culture: a reply[189]

I was not entirely happy with the reaction of Dr Aalders in the June issue of *In de Rechte Straat*. Like him, I have no exaggerated expectations of a Christian cultural mandate. I once gave a lecture on creativity in which I tried to take a new approach because I believed that the problem of Christianity and culture had never been satisfactorily resolved, which I took to be an indication that we have been on the wrong track. By 'creativity' I intended simply to propose an answer to the question of what the Christian life means, and I suggested that in order to answer this question we should ask, 'What do we make of it?' The 'of it' refers to the possibilities and talents that God has given us. If Christ truly sets us free, and through his saving work makes us truly human again, then we also have a better opportunity truly and creatively to bring to maturity in creation, which is the work of his hands, the possibilities that God has given us.

Christianity and culture – one can construe that negatively: what is the Christian to do, surrounded by an all too often not very Christian culture; or positively: what is the Christian's task. But in this way culture comes to be seen too much as an isolated, alien entity. If we pose the question more modestly as 'What shall we make of our lives?' or 'What shall we do with our talents?' the answer is likewise more modest and easier to draw directly from Scripture.

One of the difficulties lies in the term 'culture' itself, which during the last century and a half has acquired a very special colouration and significance. Culture has become something elevated, something to do with art (but then Art, with a capital A, something exceptional, detached from everyday life). It is therefore better that we no longer use the term culture in this connection.

I believe that Dr Aalders has also allowed himself to be led by this all too heavily charged sense of the word 'Art'. I do not believe that art is something so very special, something that stands outside or above life. Naturally we have no argument about the fact that Rembrandt and many others, in our own day Rouault, for example, have made many beautiful things, and we are thankful for that. Yet what did they do other than use their God-given talents in a good, positive, constructive way? Perhaps it is as a result of his somewhat Romantically tinted view of art that Dr Aalders arrives at his, what is to my mind strange, notion: that Christians should not develop themselves as artists. Does being a Christian not mean being human, attaining freedom in Christ – see the epistle to the Galatians – does it not mean liberation and openness? How can this be rhymed with such an inhibitive position? It is precisely the Christian who, as an artist, can arrive at the full deployment of his or her talents. Instead of freedom in the worldly sense of lawlessness, of having a fling, of taking one's frustrations out on others, a Christian attains real freedom and openness. What Christian freedom in art and artistry can mean is shown by Rembrandt, together with our seventeenth-century still-life painters, and our seventeenth-century landscape painters, and Rouault, and so many others who in their art have sung the beauty of God's creation.

I simply cannot accept – on the contrary, it strikes me as unscriptural – that when a person becomes a Christian she or he must be inhibited and lose her or his freedom. No, the Christian's portion is life – instead of death – and freedom, being truly human. That is so even if he or she is an artist, a person like anyone else, with his or her own gifts and talents. There are so many people who work in the artistic field: illustrators, typographers, decorators, interpreters of poetry or stories, musicians, composers, singers and songwriters. Not all their work is Art with a capital A, and we must not be fixated on just the greatest, like Rembrandt, any more than we should ignore the ordinary preacher in order to focus exclusively on people like Luther, Calvin, Kuyper, Groen van Prinsterer, etc. Everyone has their task, depending on their calling in relation to their God-given talents. Please let us not reinforce the negative attitude our people have towards art by regarding the artist first as someone special, in the Romantic sense, in order then to affirm that Christians cannot be like that.

It is a different matter that Christian artists perhaps more than other people must bear their cross as strangers in the world in these times. To be an artist is difficult today, if you are a Christian and must bear the reproach and must be confronted with all sorts of problems. Here, not different from but perhaps rather more than in any other profession, lies the difficulty.

• Affluence, the welfare state and culture[190]

Affluence not in the cultural sphere?

It would befit the style of our times to determine via a survey whether or not mainly people whose training and work lie in the social, economic and political spheres think about the questions pertaining to the affluent society. It is a simply observed fact that among those who are concerned with 'culture' – culture then in the stricter sense, and we will come back to that – affluence in the sense of health, happiness, and prosperity or wellbeing is seldom if ever a subject of discussion. The reasons for this are not difficult to find. Affluence has still not penetrated except very partially to the world of art and science (in the humanities). The situation there is different from that in the world of trade and industry, where 'work in affluence demands affluence in work,' as Zahn so aptly puts it.[191]

Indeed a trip taken by an academic is unlike a trip by a business executive. The quality of the hotels and meals is significantly lower for the academic; the luxury at scholarly congresses and the like cannot compare with what is considered appropriate for a good atmosphere at business negotiations. Not only is the pay in the so-called cultural sphere much lower, but people often work there with defective equipment, with scanty budgets in overcrowded spaces (expansion is always subject to long delays) and with too few personnel (because 'economically' the possibility of hiring more people does not exist). People are sometimes also confronted with a poor job market, but the reasons for this are different from those in industry.

This is not to say however that people in the cultural sphere will not experience the effects of greater affluence and increased free time. To the contrary. During the season (and that runs from early spring to late fall) one should visit the great museums of Florence, for example. Questionably qualified guides drag one 'horde' after another through them. Why do all these people go there? Probably for no other reason than that an earlier generation of travellers (usually prosperous culture-bearers) went to such places for such activities. We are compelled to note – and with that we are already suggesting something of the problem associated with our subject – that most of these travellers are totally unprepared for such encounters with culture and art and that those who design their itineraries for them can think of nothing better than to adopt the traditional itineraries, the cultural customs of earlier generations. One feels sorry for the poor people who, dead tired, must undergo the torment of so much art in so short a time with so little understanding. We always hope that a few may emerge really the richer for the experience, that a world will have opened for them in spite of the guides and the unfavourable atmosphere.

As a result of our current affluence and prosperity a large demand has arisen for 'cultural goods'. Partly as a result of this, prices in the antiques markets have risen dramatically.[192] A simple piece of old furniture, a painting by a master of some renown, is sold at auctions for prices that exceed all boundaries. And because the new rich who desire to have these things often do not have the education to pick out something beautiful for themselves, they depend on the tradition that honours this or that master or such and such a genre of furniture or ceramics as a high point. And in this way people restrict their field of choice to such a limited inventory that prices are pushed up even more. The tremendous increase in population in our century in comparison with earlier times, when the objects were made, contributes to a relative increase in demand and thereby to the rise in prices. And we will not here discuss the economic side of modern art lest we become bogged down in side issues.

Distribution of culture?

Because there is a great demand for culture from a part of the public – which in itself gladdens the heart – at a time when the number of workers in the cultural area is small, personnel are almost all over-extended. For very little remuneration they speak, they give courses, they write articles, make contributions and in short endeavour to fulfil a calling. Sometimes they do so, no doubt, without reflecting too deeply on the meaning and purpose of their work.

Their work could be called 'distribution of culture' (*cultuurspreiding*), which is to say, helping others to share in the riches of our culture. The question however is whether that provides a solution to the problem at hand: namely, to actually actively involve and connect with culture the many people who now have the time and the money to participate in it. This solution is too passive. People receive as it were an initiation into the world of culture, which now seems within their reach, by means of popularized knowledge, trivial facts and concepts. The existing culture is 'distributed' to a host of people who for the moment are still culturally immature.

Building a new culture

Does it make sense to keep on doing that? Should people not rather be put to work themselves? Should the concern not be cultural renewal, to build a new culture in which we not only use but also integrate the possibilities and means of the affluent society (I have in mind the new means of communication, the free time and the more ample finances), so that they acquire a new meaning and importance? Such a culture cannot be made by a few 'leaders', whoever they may be, but must grow through the work or at least the cooperation of all, leaders and co-workers alike. It means shaping intellectual and spiritual values, which can take shape gradually in the struggle for whatever is just, true, beautiful and good in a world in which so many new possibilities, materials and media are available.

The distribution of culture would mean the spreading of culture. But is the present culture worthy of being 'multiplied'? One could fill a large library with the books and articles on the crisis of culture in our [twentieth] century. Are we meant to distribute the crisis too? Will the crisis then end just like that? Or is this crisis just a figment of the imagination of professional prophets of doom, as Zahn suggests?[193]

The terms 'culture' and 'civilization'

It is time to say something about the word 'culture', which we used above in the common sense of the term. Culture in that case means an area of our society that corresponds approximately with the arts (including 'better entertainment') and sciences. The term can be used more broadly or more narrowly, but that is what people have in mind when they speak of distribution of culture. The question however is whether this usage really helps us, whether it does not point rather to where the shoe pinches in our . . . I almost said 'culture'. Here however we use the term 'culture' in the sense of civilization, as used e.g. in the expression 'Babylonian civilization'. In such a case we think of tools, institutions of government, law, even religion. It seems right to me to speak of civilization if we are dealing with the distinctive manner in which people in such a world gave form to the system of government, to law and jurisprudence, to societal relations, to the unique ways in which they practiced the arts and sciences, to the way in which they lived, felt, thought, to the things they did and left undone. In short, the whole of human life, individually and in all its various associations, is captured in a compilation of institutes, traditions, laws and norms through which people have given form to the possibilities and rules or requirements given them in the creation.

The term 'culture' I would prefer to reserve for the forming activity itself: in cultural activity (which thus may pertain to any area of life) a civilization is formed, or an existing civilization is modified and gradually superseded by another, formed in this way.

Our civilization

It is not a theory of civilization and culture that concerns us, however. What concerns us is the situation today including our task in it with a view to the world of tomorrow.

Since the eighteenth century, cultural work has involved a pre-eminent role for the natural sciences in close association with technology. People wanted to tame their environment and make it serviceable to them. The natural sciences were meant to provide not only the necessary insight and means; they were also assigned the goal of discovering the truth. Only natural laws were considered to convey absolute and indisputable truth, and people set out with all their strength to discover them. All the rest was at best subjective and thus at most an opinion, anything but certain, and of no importance where the purpose was to provide people with certainty. It was bound to happen that as a result of this attitude the natural sciences blossomed and technology made great advances. People spoke in those days of the great marvels of technology, and they believed that through it they would be able to harness the forces and powers surrounding them. And indeed people succeeded in many ways in gaining independence from natural circumstances. The medical sciences also blossomed as a result of these motives.

Soon however a great 'but' became attached to this culture driven by natural science. The Industrial Revolution in many respects ushered in more sorrow than blessing, more poverty than wealth, and instead of building culture up it seemed as if societally, ethically and socially everything was broken down. Beauty withered too, and many jeremiads were lifted against the ugliness of technical products.[194]

It seemed an obvious thing to do, and it was certainly entirely in line with the cultural ideals, to apply the natural scientific method to other areas of human life as well. First economists, and later sociologists, but by no means scientists from these disciplines alone, set about with the help of statistics and a knowledge of the natural laws in human and societal life, and an organization of society based on these insights, to save society from chaos, or to put it positively, to improve the world so that all people could enjoy the good life. Psychologists in particular played a substantial role in this; they could explain what people needed to do or not do in order to feel happy. What mattered, after all, was people's subjective wellbeing, their sense of being free from frustration and threats, and the point was to create circumstances in which people could stay mentally healthy.

This all culminated in the idea of the welfare state, which Thoenes defined as a form of society marked by a system of democratically based government care that, given the maintenance of a capitalist system of production, guarantees the collective wellbeing of its subjects.[195]

Many studies have been written about this society and its peculiar dangers. They all boil down to this, that with sophisticated means people are meant to be provided with mental happiness; invariably, however, human freedom and certainly people's 'higher aspirations' are regulated too and in fact taken from them in the process. Religion does not really fit into this natural-scientific view of humanity but, alas, people have their strange idiosyncrasies . . . So they are permitted to have them as some sort of metaphysical pill, a kind of religious aspirin to relieve them of their inner stress. The question of truth must never be posed, however, since it is alarming and opens up the possibility that the beautifully constructed purely human order, based on the laws of nature, might be disturbed.

In his overoptimistic book Zahn writes: 'It may be anticipated that the future will bring us an omnipresent mental comfort comparable to the soft, calming music that wafts from invisible sources in the halls of large American buildings.'[196] There is indeed a chance that the culture of the future will look like that of an actual 'Brave New World'.

In this civilization that is guided by natural science, which is viewed as revelation in the service of the god of 'human wellbeing', art too has a place. Art re-entered society after the intermezzo of nineteenth-century ugliness, so Zahn writes triumphantly.[197] Even apart from the question whether the positivistic culture (as one may call the attitude described here) may indeed take the credit here, it is unmistakable that a great deal of beauty may once again be found in our world. Just think of 'industrial design', the forming of technical products like cars, washing machines, irons and even light switches, furniture and so on. We can gratefully accept all that. It shows that it makes no sense to regard art and beauty as a field apart from human life, separated from the societal order. We encounter aesthetic design in the style of our times even in the smallest objects.

Thus one can say that there are today three kinds of art in our world. First, there is the art that we have just indicated. Second, there is art that lives on the past or simply (literally) brings the past into the present. This is art that exists at a variety of levels: antique furniture next to old-style imitation furniture, the classical music of our concert system next to the hit parade and popular tune, the museum piece next to the calendar print. All of this belongs to what in practice most people understand by art. And then, third, there is modern art, which for the vast majority is still strange and peculiar, monstrous and incomprehensible.

What then are the roots of that last type of art? The humanistic attitude that was the bearer of the positivistic culture was deeply interested in human freedom. And this threatened to go lost as a result of the development described. That is why resistance arose again and again to the positivistic attitude and its results – in the nineteenth century in Romanticism, in the twentieth century in modern art and philosophy (we use 'modern' here to indicate a cultural movement). Because humanistic humankind *believed* in the natural sciences as the means by which people can control nature, it was not really possible for them to oppose the politically and socially and economically planned and ordered reality. Yet they *believed* equally fervently in human freedom, and art and philosophy were the special areas where shape could be given to this, the areas thus where it was easiest to strike a different note.[198] In this way there arose in our world a dual culture of the positivistic and the modern. It was inevitable that, with the extreme refinement and advancement of the positivistic ordering of the world, the reaction from the counter-pole, human freedom, would be fierce and severe. Thus we can understand that in essence a great deal of modern art is grounded in an anarchism that, while it may perhaps speak out against the existing societal order, hardly dares to take action against it and so expresses itself all the more furiously in art. The course of development of modern art manifests an increasingly more consistent experience of human subjective freedom; subjectively people let themselves go, undisturbed by commandments or rules. The point, in fact, is to upset and overthrow commandments and rules and to proclaim that one regards them as of no value whatsoever.

One must not think that modern art can be viewed in just a small number of museums, in the collections of a few snobs and in the exhibitions of art dealers or that it has no influence on the public at large and lacks real cultural significance. That remains to be seen. For the vehement expression of human freedom and autonomy, severed from every tie including the most natural or the most primary ethical ones, is experienced by many (I mean onlookers) as emancipating. Or at least as an opportunity to get away for just one moment from the world of statistics and computers in which everything is regulated and the person is nothing more than a cog in the great machine. Modern art is much more than just a few paintings. There is literature, there is drama, there are radio plays and television programmes. Any onlooker can discover that morals and customs are often bluntly depicted as restricting people in their freedom and thus emptied of their meaning. It is worth noticing how existing values, and particularly relations of authority, are called into question again and again. This extends even into youth broadcasts, where the king is always portrayed as a half-wit and every bearer of authority as a buffoon. As someone wrote: 'There can be little doubt that radio drama and advertising art offer a very thinly disguised sort of teasing with middle class morals.'[199] As a matter of fact, calling it middle class morals already undermines that morality: it expresses a condescension that is pernicious.

In connection with all this we can also observe that the renewals occurring within the modern movement are in essence revolutionary acts. Those who are creatively engaged in it not only feel themselves to be an avant-garde, they actually are in many respects the vanguard of a new culture. We will return to that shortly. Yet this circumstance has a dual effect. On the one hand the leaps are so intense and so far removed from the ordinary person's experience of reality that people simply can no longer follow the development. As a consequence a great gap has appeared between the public and the artists. The artists have left the people behind. Hence the effect and impact of their work is relatively slight. In a certain sense that is good too, although it can hardly put us at ease. What is worse is the fact that as a result creations which are really new often remain unnoticed, particularly if they are not fierce and severely revolutionary enough in their attacks on established values, if indeed they are rather positive in wanting to assert something beautiful and good. In general the modern artist is doing reasonably well from an economic standpoint, but there will be many who remain unnoticed simply because they do not want to go along with the avant-garde and because they have something much more positive to say. Here lies a great loss, for it is precisely these individuals, who are not necessarily traditionalists, who could truly help us.

The crisis in our Western culture
In the situation sketched above lies the crisis in our culture. There is a grave disharmony, which we already alluded to above when we spoke of a gap. A sharp contradiction manifests itself between principles and practices in the area comprehended by the natural sciences, technology and the social and economic disciplines and the tendencies in the area of the arts and the so-called humanities. Two entirely opposed movements determine the current cultural activity: a generally positivistic movement and the anarchistic-modern movement. The latter of these is hostile to culture, glorifies the primitive, seeks freedom in dissoluteness, in lawlessness; the former desires to build a better world by calculating and regulating everything in an ever more far-reaching societal control and seeks its salvation in economic planning. It will not hesitate to regulate culture in the narrower sense, as is already happening to a certain extent through subsidy policies.

The crisis is heightened further by the fact that the positivistic current with its technology and its disposal over the mechanisms of power (including finances) in fact has the upper hand – a situation which is due in part to the fact that the modern stream is poorly understood and poorly followed by the public, while non-modern expressions of culture are often weak or remain unnoticed. It can thereby come about that people have magnificent machines that can turn out large quantities of beautiful prints in many colours in a short time, but no writers and journalists capable of making adequate use of them, so that what comes from the presses is often below standard (to put it mildly). Via television one can now reach many people on a night, but it takes a great deal of effort to put together a truly responsible programme that is culturally acceptable and accessible to everyone.

We are going into these problems in order to make clear that it is not possible to just speak, with unfounded optimism, about the distribution of culture in order next to launch into a discussion of the various ways and techniques for achieving that goal. We need to go much deeper and the solution is not simple. Especially because this crisis is gathering force and is only really becoming a crisis as a result of the falling away of the solid ground, the religious impetus and certainty. Present-day civilization is marked by a far-reaching neutralism that is at bottom an all-controlling relativism. Its genesis lies in part in the remarkable circumstance that at the end of the nineteenth century positivism rounded off its critique of every reality higher than the natural one, in the sense of the natural sciences including psychology (we think of Freud): thus values were 'unmasked' and all religion, art and love were interpreted as being no more than sublimation of essentially biological drives. Egoism and the 'struggle for life' were assigned as the core of human existence. At the same time, however, fierce criticism of the positivistic ideal of science emerged from a movement that would soon usher in modern art and philosophy (phenomenology and existentialism). In this way the ground was pulled from under both the poles of the Western humanistic culture – science and freedom – at the same time, so that nothing remained for people but to relativistically preach religious and ideological neutrality, to work on in one's own direction, but without any very deep-seated conviction.

The driving, essentially religious, motives behind the main cultural movements lost their force. Spiritual renewal is therefore a cultural desideratum; or civilization will need to be maintained by means of force in opposition to all the disintegrating, anti-cultural factors.

Something like that is going on in the communist world, which is essentially positivistic. Marxism is a product of the nineteenth century in Western Europe! In the communist world all modern art has been banned. There people oppose all religion in the Christian sense, and minds are moved by a belief in the communistic order, indoctrinated as they are by the new means of propaganda. There you have the compulsion that is meant to prevent all disintegration.

Relative health of our civilization

What could be so different between here and the other side of the Iron Curtain? Why have things not gone that far here? Is that only because here freedom has made neutralism a possible outcome? And how is it possible that in spite of this neutralism, which declares every religion culturally unfruitful and holds that human life is being exhausted in its human 'naturalness' – just read any modern novel for this – yes, how is it possible that despite all the criticism and outcry about a fundamental crisis one still feels like saying: be careful not to exaggerate, for there is still a great deal that is healthy and good, worthwhile and beautiful to be found in our world? Love and a sense of norms have not vanished entirely, no, not by a long shot. One reason lies, almost paradoxically, in the circumstance that talking about religion and the like is not regarded as meaningful, precisely as a result of the neutralism. Much need and difficulty, uncertainty and inner anxiety is being hidden; one does not hear about it unless one gets into a really deep and personal conversation. Many people live proper civil lives and keep up the appearances that everything is as it has always been, that there is no crisis, even if that is only on the surface. Yet however that may be, the fact is that norms are held high and our culture is anything but chaotic or coercive, a few excesses excepted. How then can this be?

Would the answer not lie in the fact that Christianity set an unmistakable stamp on our world, so that much that is good has been preserved, so that counter-forces proved to be present to oppose all revolutionary undermining, so that neither positivism nor anarchism has ever been deployed really consistently except in a few extreme circles, and society was in any case protected from this at least to a certain extent?

Christians were and are salt that salts. It was and is precisely the salt that salts that in its effect could and can preserve so much. This is the difference between here and behind the Iron Curtain. There we have an 'unsalted' society, which manifests bluntly, in an 'unsalted' manner, what the ultimate consequences are of those forces which also partly determine our own culture.

Our situation

To conclude what has been said up till now, let us summarize briefly the situation in which we live.

In essence culture has not changed so very much during the twentieth century. The movements have remained the same. But people have come a lot further in the realization of their ideas. Foremost among them is the positivistic current with its ideal of natural science and its technology. It is beyond dispute that people have come a long way and have made 'great advances'. In particular, a total civilization on this basis has been brought very close to realization, with all the dangers of a 'Brave New World'. In such a world everything is regulated through planning and people are made to experience wellbeing without stress through use of the new psychological methods. That is the 'welfare state'!

And then there is the other current, which finds its most distinctive expression in modern art. Here too one can speak of clear growth and consistency. Especially quantitatively people have come a lot further. When modern art found its first clear form with Picasso and Braque at the beginning of the century, this took place within a very small group.

After the First World War the Dada movement appeared, a little coterie of boisterous extremists, a group at which to shrug one's shoulders, some said at the time, and in part they were correct. But now in the art of the period since the last war what once lived only in the minds of a few has become a broad movement that is regarded by many, to a large extent correctly, as *the* art of the present day. In philosophy and literature too this new breadth is noticeable.

What has caused this growth? Is it perhaps a result of more Christians being won over to this neutralistic and essentially humanistic culture? Is 'dechristianization' not likewise a weakening of the salting power of the salt? And is the slackening within Christian circles perhaps even more responsible for this than the fact that many have broken completely with the church?

Could this not be the cause that the crisis in our civilization gradually gains in clarity? Mannheim claimed that the falling away of the Christian basis caused the crisis.[200] But has Christianity not been set aside already since the eighteenth century, since the inception of the present civilization? Let us not forget that it began with the Enlightenment, with that cultural movement in which people wanted to find the light themselves, by their own reason, accompanied by a rejection of all revelation. Could the crisis in our culture in essence be this: that people want a civilization that is the fruit of Christianity (for we all desire, do we not, whoever we may be, rather the Western than a communistic society) without Christianity itself as the basis? The more the Christian forces retreat, the clearer this situation comes to light: a civilization that is Christian in its most important elements (ethics, for example), while at the same time people repudiate Christianity itself. Let us not forget that the Enlightenment, yes, humanism as a whole, was and is in a large measure secularized Christianity. People often formulated Christian norms and ideals in a new way, without bringing Scripture or God to bear on them. They thought they could do so without penalty. What are they to do now, however, when that Christianity, which always was a positive source for them to draw on, dries up and loses its force? The crisis could therefore also be described in biblical terms, as in Deuteronomy 32:15: 'Jeshurun grew fat and kicked; filled with food, he became heavy and sleek. He abandoned the God who made him and rejected the Rock his Saviour.'

Through this situation people have landed up in difficulty. They often do not know what to do with the gains they have made. They have not been able to find the true meaning of 'welfare', leisure, wealth, freedom; they do not know what to do with the modern statements about life, even though they do regard them as a menace to our culture. People go on and on, outwardly optimistic but without a driving faith in the gods, natural science and freedom, in whose name so much was done. For many, that faith has by now lost its compelling force.

Meanwhile there is no longer a counterweight, no 'salt that salts', no robust biblical Christianity.

Christians in this situation

Hence there is no reason at all for us, Christians, to throw stones in an integral critique that reproves the world for being the world. We ourselves are partly to blame, for we were often absent; and where we were present we participated, perhaps grumbling a bit as we did so.

And we were certainly absent when it came to art and entertainment.[201] We have to realize that modern art became as avant-garde as it did and could proceed to live so clearly and consistently based in lawless freedom because Christianity was entirely absent from the arena. Under the influence of puritanical ideas, in essence mystical and Anabaptist, Christian people left the world for what it was, which in practice meant not only that they produced no art themselves but also that this area was left entirely to unchristian forces – we could also say to the spiritual powers in the air (Ephesians 6:12).

Hence today the situation for the Christian is anything but easy. Whether one is a worker or a middle-class merchant or a white-collar employee or an intellectual, the situation is in essence the same for all. The differences are at most gradual and the difficulties perhaps slightly different between the one and the other.

The efforts and difficulties of Christians with respect to 'culture'

We must now go on to discuss our real subject. In this last heading we again used the term 'culture' in the everyday sense. Yet we put it between quotation marks in order to make clear that we find the term an unhappy one. It is difficult, however, to find another one. Until now we have repeatedly restricted our discussion, no doubt as the result of a personal preference, to art. Yet 'culture' is not limited to that and nor do we wish to deal only with that. Thus in the continuation we shall understand by culture, unless otherwise indicated, all those matters with which people are associated either actively or passively outside work in the economic sector (as workers or as administrative personnel or as middle-class merchants) and also outside political and other societal activities; the lines are difficult to draw. Thus we have in mind art, but especially also entertainment (what the radio and television offer, literature at many levels). Furthermore, we do not by any means want to exclude various other meaningful leisure-time activities such as vacation travel and hobbies like collecting. Finally, non-professional activities involving study and the acquirement of knowledge should certainly also be included, even if the knowledge acquired can sometimes also be adapted to everyday professional work.

The Christian, often a child or grandchild of the 'little people' (*kleine luyden*) about whom Kuyper spoke, seems at times to have two left hands when it comes to these things. Yet that is also true of working people in general, and that is the point of departure for all the current discussions about the distribution of culture. As the result of a development that must be assessed without reservation as very positive, working people have come to dispose over free time and a certain measure of affluence. Thus many things have come within their horizon that they could not participate in before, including culture as we have just described it. How then are these people to be helped along? How can we see to it that they are not just left to be passive hearers who undergo 'culture'? How can we involve them in cultural activities, so that they can participate consciously and meaningfully and become culture bearers themselves in the real sense?

It is of no use to discuss these problems in merely general terms. That would not only mean capitulating to neutralism – as if the problems would be the same for all people regardless of their spiritual background – but also it would be unrealistic. The situation confronting the Christian, whether this person is a worker or an employee in some other sense or a middle-class entrepreneur, is different from that confronting people in general. There are also many things that we cannot meaningfully discuss with 'people in general', namely, things that we may not expect or ask of them. Today more may be expected and asked of Christians. The difficulties they face are often greater, because not only for the workman but for the Christian in general the ground is unfamiliar and undeveloped. In well-intentioned but essentially mysticistic Anabaptist world avoidance we have kept ourselves aloof (and I mean 'we', not just working people in the days when it was beyond their reach) from 'culture' as a sinful terrain. This naturally does not detract from the fact that today's typically Christian problems are directly interwoven with the more general questions concerning getting working people involved in civilization, in 'culture', yes, of involving them if possible in culturally formative activities themselves.

The Christian and the coming culture state

In the past, so people often say, there was first a constitutional state – everyone was equal before the law; after this came the affluent society – that is the situation we are in now, in which everybody participates in the affluence; and now we can anticipate the arrival of a culture state – in which everyone will have a part as a culture bearer in what used to be exclusively the privilege of a small elite. It may be clear that the latter will not just mean the distribution of 'cultural goods' but that it will be about the forming of a new civilization and a new world. Culture is forming, giving form to (given) structures and norms. And the spiritual struggle is part of that activity. Every neutralism is not only a surrender in this struggle but also a capitulating to the 'spirit of the age', which we should be all the less willing to do since the age itself is in crisis.

The choice for Christians then is the following: they may capitulate, secularize completely, allow themselves to be absorbed fully into a culture that no longer bears any Christian stamp at all, deny themselves as Christians in lifestyle and insight into life and become neutralistic people; or they may become people like Lot, dwelling in an unchristian world, therefore vexed but for the rest living quietly (cf. 2 Peter 2:7); or as Christians they may make a positive contribution to the evolving Western culture as it assumes a new form.

We may quite happily accept the affluence the present situation offers us as a blessing and gift from God. But it is at the same time a task, something with which we have to do something. And then we may not capitulate to positivism and expect all good things to flow from the natural sciences, or from the government that takes care of us and the leadership it will provide. Even less may we become materialists who are concerned only with increasing our wealth in order to spend it on pleasure. We may enjoy life, but the question is how we can do so meaningfully and responsibly. We may not capitulate to the preachers of freedom in our world. I have in mind here 2 Peter 2, in particular verse 19: 'They promise them freedom, while they themselves are slaves of depravity.' We may do well to be startled by this word of Scripture. Peter says it will be difficult to escape their allure (verse 18).

We do not yet need to surrender to the situation and sit down in vexation like Lot, as strangers in the midst of a corrupt world; a corruption that will rightfully only really assume its true proportions if we leave all the cultural work to neutralistic humanism. We can still get to work, as salt that salts, helping through our own positive activity to build the culture of the future. Yet there are a number of things that must be done to make that possible.

In the first place we must help each other to become mature with respect to 'culture'. Maturity means learning how to use our Christian freedom,[202] which involves self-discipline and keeping ourselves unspotted by sin. We must learn to be critical, to assess the quality of what is offered, to hold on to what is good and to reject and, where possible, oppose what is sinful. It will sometimes be necessary to abstain from something, which is not the same as surrendering an entire area of life to the world, to the spirit of the age.

We must learn to see that 'cultural products' are not neutral and that art and entertainment have a profound influence on our lives as a whole. Christians are often inconsistent. On the one hand people like to draw attention to bad phenomena, consequences of the proffered 'culture' – people love to cite the disastrous influence of the cinema on morals, even encouraging criminality – while at the same time acting as if cultural products have little to do with belief and morals. Art and entertainment shape our thinking, open our eyes to beauties, but they can also influence our minds negatively. Sometimes after having been engaged with anarchistic works of modern art people have difficulty in rediscovering and recognizing the legitimate lines of authority.

Yet we cannot avoid these cultural products. They are pervasive. They are like a constant advanced brainwashing by the neutralistic culture. This spirit of our age is everywhere, in the press, in literature at every level, on the radio even in the entertainment programmes, on television, in discussions with our neighbours, in the products advertised, yes, where does it not appear. Notice the undermining of civil morality referred to above; notice too how characters in radio plays and the like often live as if God and religion do not exist, even if for the rest they are ever such good people.[203] Again, to prevent misunderstandings, we do not say that everything that is offered corrupts morals or denies God; the point is that the mixture of good and evil and the mild form in which the spirit of the age is preached can be so dangerous.

We cannot avoid 'culture' and must therefore learn to discern sharply. Therein lies the great difficulty, because the Christian world has never really occupied itself with such matters. Therefore education for maturity is not simply a matter of transmitting established values to newcomers (the working people); rather, it will have to involve a learning to see together, an educating of one another for maturity. Learning to test the spirits, yes, that too, to be sure, but also learning to live with all these things that are offered to us again and again, things we simply cannot avoid.

We also cannot withdraw from 'culture' because by doing so we would become all the more vulnerable to contamination. We would not learn to recognize the dangers and we would have no weapons with which to resist when we happen to encounter them anyway in a variety of unexpected places. We cannot build little walls around our own estate and behave as if nothing is going on in the rest of the world. The world will soon be found inside anyway, having sneaked in in one disguise or another.

By withdrawing we could also not be salt that salts, and our guilt for the unchristian character of the emerging culture of the future would be all the greater. What it boils down to is that the problem facing Christian society is twice as great as the problem facing people in general: how to participate actively in the culture and at the same time shape our independence and maturity. The situation is comparable to that of Christian students: they must learn their discipline and at the same time master the foundations of Christian scholarship and develop a critical approach to the insights on offer.

Yet it makes equally little sense to develop something like a Christian version of cultural optimism. The danger is, and it is good to recognize it, that Christians will lose themselves in the cultural activity and will begin to identify their Christianity with it while forgetting the real basis, their bond with God through Jesus Christ. Christian culture is not just a matter of cultural work dressed up with pious words. We should not have great expectations. If it is true, as some say with some justification, that the world state of the Antichrist is taking shape and that we are very close to the Second Coming of Christ – that would be wonderful! – then we need not expect anything at all of our cultural efforts. Yet as long as there are possibilities, we must get to work. For the sake of our lives. For the sake of the preservation of ourselves and of our children. If the time should come that we perhaps must fight to escape by the skin of our teeth and to hold on to our faith as a small remnant of persecuted souls, bearing a seal and not the mark of the Beast, then that will be amply clear to us. In that case nothing will have been lost; our life is given us as a prey or spoil of war,[204] and we may truly look forward with joy to the coming of the Lord.

Education for maturity

The cultural maturity of which we spoke is thus an unavoidable demand. In the situation that exists it is impossible to call upon the available cultural workers whose profession lies in this area. They are all overworked. Moreover, the number in the (orthodox) Christian community is small; perhaps we even should say very small. Therefore it will be necessary to find a good mode, in which those who have something to say can provide leadership without having to play the *Führer* and without having to mark out every step of the path for others, the 'masses who do not know the law'. Not to teach, but to work together, to think things through together, not without leadership yet with respect for all Christian freedom as a given good that is anchored in the work of Christ and that is offered us in the Bible, that is the plan.

The matter at the moment is to prepare the ground for it. The first requirement is a mentality whereby everyone is filled with a sense of the great importance of these problems surrounding culture and committed to contributing to the solution. Perhaps the first task is to bring people, working people and many others, over the threshold in such a way that they dare: dare to participate, dare not to find it silly to study and get involved in doing something themselves, even to read a book, listen to a piece of music or take a thorough look at a painting, yes, even to set to work themselves. An atmosphere must emerge in which we are conscious of building something new together, a new Christian lifestyle, in which in maturity we learn to deal with our freedom and with the many possibilities. What is needed is enthusiasm for thinking things through together, for discussing and examining things together.

As long as people just come to listen to a lecture and afterwards say how interesting it was but then revert to the run of the mill, we are not yet there. As long as we just give courses to people whom we have gathered with great difficulty and warned of their precious duty (perhaps with pious words) or convinced of the utilitarian value (of a college degree, for example), there will be little effect. It must come from an inner need, from a doing of these things because one cannot do otherwise, because it is enjoyable and fascinating and because it really grips us. It may be play, but then in the real sense of joyful activity; think of Psalm 119:54: 'Your decrees are the theme of my song wherever I lodge;' and 119:27: 'Let me understand the teaching of your precepts; then I will meditate on your wonders.'

We shall have to get to know our civilization present and past. Naturally we have our limitations and we will not be able to fully comprehend everything, but that is also not necessary. Just being busy with these things is a great good, greater perhaps than knowing everything. We shall also have to investigate the cultural possibilities that God has given us – the world is rich; there is so much. In what we have called the cultural realm we may of course also include nature, countries and peoples, everything that meaningfully enters our horizon.

In dealing with all that we shall of course have to take into account our shortcomings and limitations. We may strive for perfection knowing that in this dispensation we will not attain it. Moreover, the moment we start we will discover how far behind we are in the cultural fields and just how little has been thought through from a Christian perspective. A direct gain from all this will be a keener eye and a better understanding of our weaknesses and our difficulties. Our criticism will become more conscious and precise and also milder. We have in mind here, for instance, the sharp criticism that is often levelled from the best Christian circles against the Christian broadcasting company NCRV, while people fail entirely to realize how difficult it is to define and implement a Christian policy, both because there is no general consensus about what it should be and also because it is so very difficult to find good personnel who are capable of mounting a genuinely positive Christian programme.

How we can be culturally active

Working together to attain maturity is activity too, to be sure. Yet correlated with that we must also work creatively in our culture ourselves, trying and testing, not fearing to make mistakes, stumbling and getting up again. Here it is especially necessary to dare to 'cross the threshold', as I have said above.

There is so much that is possible, even for working people, the middle class and all other newcomers to the field of culture. We could call that the meaningful use of leisure time. This must become an integrating component of life, a part of life that is just as filled and that is used just as actively as our hours spent professionally. This will involve mainly personal activity, often together with others, perhaps in new forms of association. But then we must not back out when called upon to cooperate. The renowned 'I have no time' is seldom really true.

What can we do? We can make music (how wonderful to be able to do that ourselves), garden, paint or draw or do ceramics, study in a field that particularly interests us, collect, stage a play together, sing, organize something together. There is so much.

Why, for example, should people not use their summer travel, their vacation, for something really fine and cultural? If people are planning to take a trip, why should they not prepare for it thoroughly, possibly during the course of a year, by reading about the history of the region, studying its monuments, the distinctive problems of the area (such as land consolidation), the geology of the countryside, in short, all the distinctive features that are to be found there? And if people are planning to go abroad, why should they not study the manners and customs and learn a bit of the language (even if only from a little book with a title like 'How to Learn French in Three Weeks')? They could take a close look at the churches to be found there and even try to prepare a French or an Italian meal, although this might better be left until after the trip. People will be amazed at how much more they will see and observe this way, at how much deeper their enjoyment will be, and how much more enriching as well. Do not be afraid to visit a library – we must overcome our fear of thresholds – the staff there enjoy nothing better than to help us with what we need.

Why should we not also include Bible groups amongst our activities, where together we can go deeper into the different facets of God's word? Nor must we overlook church history. Here too there is so much.

Let us not forget that the new possibilities (money and time) must make it possible for us to do a better job of what we have neglected until now. I think for example of typography and the editing of our church publications. Why should we not put our shoulders to this task, seek the advice of a professional, pay someone, and then get to work. We should do so in such a way that the little church newspaper is no longer a rag that cannot stand comparison with the beautifully printed advertising that is regularly stuffed into our mailboxes. Home furnishings: we might possibly make our own furniture as a hobby (there is information available that might help us here), study the problems of our own house, learn how to furnish it more efficiently and beautifully – doing so need not always cost a great deal of money.

Towards a new folk culture

If we were to set to work in this way a new folk culture (*volkscultuur*) could arise.[205] We could witness the appearance of a new folk music and a new folk art having deep roots in our own existence. That is possible! Indigent African-Americans created the Negro spirituals as religious songs and this genre has experienced tremendous development just in recent decades. It does not always have to be easy, but neither is beautiful music necessarily so difficult that only professionals can painstakingly produce it.

Art that is practised for relaxation by amateurs, accomplished amateurs, who produce their own art, their own creations, is a wonderful thing. And it is certainly something that is possible as the fruit of the work we discussed in the two previous sections. Naturally that must grow;

it cannot simply be made to appear at a snap of the fingers. Consumed – in the good sense of the word – by a real drive to create, we must set to work to make something new, something beautiful, something that is of ourselves and for ourselves. In that way we may be able to get away from all the tasteless entertainment music, the present-day surrogate for folk music. A new folklore could arise, rich and varied, and without the odd flavour of the 'living museum' that is so often attached to it today. Yet in that case are we not forgetting, some will say, what we said above about distinctively Christian activity? Not in the least. We never said that folk culture had to be something colourless and neutral. To the contrary. We do not have to be afraid to have our own (little) culture next to others. In every age various movements have existed side by side, different cultural worlds, in competition with each other and perhaps even engaged in a spiritual battle, yet each with its own distinctive spiritual or intellectual mark.

It would be wonderful if because we are self-aware and perceptive of our spiritual character we could form something. Perhaps others would be jealous of us. Perhaps in this way we could have some influence. That is to say: we could be salt that salts, and we could make our possibly small contribution to the culture of the future.

Such a Christian folk culture did exist in earlier times. I have in mind our seventeenth century. Sweelinck did not play at concerts for an elite. His art was for everyone. Bach's cantatas were for regular Sunday church services. Our seventeenth-century painters were supported by the 'little' Christian people (*kleine luyden*) of that day. Only when apostasy set in did this culture weaken and make way for the elite culture of such classicists as de Lairesse. That was no gain, and the names of these artists are usually forgotten. Our great painting evinced a folk character: everyone could understand it, although some undoubtedly saw more and further than others. Think for example of the well-known street scene by Vermeer. Next to the art of the great masters, not remote and elite and exalted but accessible to everyone, there were still thousands of others who painted for their own pleasure or for a small additional income. The number of names of our seventeenth-century painters fills large reference works!

Even though reluctantly, we shall have to overcome our inferiority complex as Christians, the notion that we mean nothing culturally and that we have to live from the cast-offs of others. We shall have to learn to live our own lives in our own style and to find our way ourselves. And we shall have to learn to recognize more perceptively what is distinctive and perhaps unchristian in others. It is only by being engaged with cultural problems ourselves that we may be able to see through and understand the solutions adopted by others.

Perhaps what we are formulating sounds like a utopia. It is not. Even without unfounded cultural optimism we shall have to set to work and see to it that we reach our ceiling. Quantitatively and qualitatively there are still enough Christians in our country to produce something, if only we have the desire to be positively and consciously engaged Christians. It is not a matter of rallying people to a new activism or of laying a new yoke on believers – that would be wrong – but something of all this could become reality if we set to work enthusiastically, if we simply aim to be ourselves, if we roll up our sleeves in an atmosphere of joyful activity based on our being children of God, with maturity and discernment as prerequisites. With the latter we must start and from there, as if driven by an inner need, we ourselves must begin to do the rest.

How we must begin: some practical needs and desires
Well then, what must we do? Could we set up a programme? I will not attempt to do that, but I do want to mention a number of points with which we could begin.

1. We need to begin to think seriously about educating cultural workers ourselves. Until now it has been the case that virtually all artistically talented individuals capable of contributing something in the cultural sector receive their training in so-called neutral institutes. Moreover, the mentality within the Reformed community (*Gereformeerde gezindte*) was such that these people were often regarded with great distrust. As a result many of them subsequently turned their back on the church and also on the Lord. Often we were to blame. Those who have remained have undertaken a life-long struggle to use their talent in the face of that distrust, without fixed guidelines about how to proceed and about how to be Christians in their own work, in a sometimes totally de-christianized environment.

   A Christian training institute, in whatever form, is no luxury. There people would have to be educated to make a positive contribution to culture via the mass media. We do not only need believing and positively formed actors, but also playwrights, writers of literature, painters (to produce meaningful designs for decorating our schools, for example), architects, musicians and composers. As soon as one starts to deal with these questions in practice, one feels as if one is entering a utopian vacuum. There are so few people who work in this direction, so few who can provide administrative leadership and teaching at such an institute. There is no general consensus about the path that must be taken, about what our attitude should be towards the current extremist directions in art, about what Christian work in this field might mean.

   Therefore we shall have to begin modestly. Perhaps we should begin by setting up an institute for reflection or a study centre, where in mutual discussions and cooperation the lines can become somewhat clear, so that a following generation (in five or ten years' time) can receive some guidance and be provided for. In this way we might fill a large gap, including ameliorating the needs of Christian institutions that run mass media for the Christian population, so that their work can be more positive and meaningful. Here people could receive their forming for providing leadership in what is usually called the distribution of culture, but which I prefer to call cultural forming. That brings us to the following point.

2. It will be necessary to establish some educational centres. This might be done in much the same way that the open university (*Volksuniversiteit*) does this, or the education centres of the Reformed (*Hervormde*) Church. Yet the work would have to be thought through and established more pointedly and consciously with a view to its specific task – and more broadly as well, in order to reach larger groups. The aim must be to help people conquer their fear of thresholds referred to earlier and to educate them for maturity and independence, in order that they may become co-workers and partners in discussion and, ultimately, people desiring to be formers of culture themselves. We must not be afraid to give this work a clearly Christian biblical stamp. Bible study, the deepening of the spiritual life and refinement of the Christian lifestyle should by no means be merely side affairs. For it is only through this that the cultural work proper in the narrower sense can acquire a basis and direction.

3. These matters also confront education in general. Our schools at all levels should not only prepare people for their professional work but also form them into a population capable of using their free time, without fear of thresholds, and having some insight into questions of culture and art. Art is no longer a luxury! Not only does it lie within our reach; it intrudes into our lives from all sides. The youth, the new generation, must be armed against the dangers and must learn to find their way positively and creatively.

4. With respect to cultural and artistic activities, people can join what is already there: orchestras, choirs, associations. But the work will have to be done with greater enthusiasm and in particular it must be broadened. We must dare to make things more difficult for ourselves in order that the fruits may be better, in a hopefully not too distant future. New associations having a varied range of activities should also be added.

5. With respect to youth work a new orientation will likewise be needed. Here people can join what is already available, the work of the youth groups and so many other projects that are already being implemented. Work will need to be done here, moreover, in the direction discussed in connection with schools and educational centres. Yet youth work is by no means identical to that of these institutes. It will have to find its own form.

6. A great deal of work can be done through Bible study groups and the like, at least if God's word and the history of the church are not approached exclusively from a theological standpoint; discussion should be centred instead on what God with his word has to say to us about all the cultural questions, including marriage, upbringing, mutual cooperation, etc. Perhaps through such groups the work of evangelism can also be given a new impulse. That in itself would mean a tremendous enrichment of Christian society as a whole.[206]

7. Radio and television may not remain unmentioned. We have already several times referred to the role they play in life and will not elaborate here on what can or must be expected of them. The task confronting the mass media is not easy and the personnel needed for an optimal result are difficult to find. Certainly we shall have to work in the same direction that was noted in connection with our other needs and desires. We can then hope that before long a greater number of eligible talents may be available.

I will remark only on one more thing. I sometimes have the feeling that radio and television aim too low. People want to reach the masses and therefore adapt their programmes to the minimum standards of their listeners and to the interests of the overwhelming majority. Yet the ideal should be to retain those audiences – and it is admittedly a difficult ideal to reach – while aiming, not lower than the dumbest, but instead higher at least than the middle. And even higher, so that these audiences are forced as it were to make an effort, to use their brains, their minds. It is said of the English second radio station, for example, that its listeners read the paper with greater attention and focus in order to be able to understand the jokes and avoid creating the impression of being 'out of it'. In this manner a gradual improvement in programming can be achieved without losing important groups of listeners.

The dailies and the weekly press also have a task here. Especially the list of priorities will need upgrading from time to time, for cultural matters nowadays are often virtually squeezed out. It should not be too much to ask that timely and extensive discussion be devoted to exhibitions and other cultural manifestations, sometimes even on the front page.

8. A general demand that we want to formulate is this: it is necessary that cultural institutions, libraries and museums, be open at times that people are free, in the first place on Saturdays but also evenings (or some evenings). Museums already are, to some extent, but seldom is that so in the case of the libraries. Staff shortages are often the difficulty; these people also have a right to a day off. Why not then, as abroad, close all the libraries and museums on Monday or Tuesday and open them on Saturday? It works for barbershops and the like.

Moreover, these institutions should not be shy when it comes to advertising. It is striking, for example, how often in brochures that sum up the public institutions of a place no mention is made of the smaller museums and especially of the libraries (with their opening and closing times). Here too greater interest and initiative on the part of the institutions themselves is certainly needed.

9. A sore point but one of great importance is the question of subsidies. If indeed we do not feel inclined towards the welfare state as defined above (see note 194), if indeed we really recognize the dangers of neutralism, if we really fear interference in cultural matters by an all-encompassing state, if indeed we are really gripped by the idea of Christian cultural activity, then we must oppose an all-embracing subsidy policy.[207] Subsidies lead to a loss of independence, to laxity, indifference, incompetence and obstinacy. Yet the need for subsidies often arose from precisely those characteristics. It is like a vicious circle that has to be broken. It has already proved paralyzing enough. Why must we support via taxes without any influence on our part all kinds of institutions for which we have no sympathy, while because we have to pay all those taxes it is impossible for us to contribute generously to causes that are dear to our hearts? Here we could take America as our example. Virtually all the museums there are private, but in spite of that they charge no admission fees, not even for special exhibitions. Think of it: the Metropolitan Museum in New York (comparable to our Rijksmuseum in Amsterdam) exists entirely on gifts. In spite of that it has a balanced budget from which it is still able to make very large acquisitions.

Subsidies arise from a lack of community spirit, from a dearth of interest. We must not oppose providing grants to artists for work trips abroad like those available through the Prins Bernhardfonds. Such grants, like those for students, are possible and useful nowadays. They have nothing in common with subsidies.[208] Such grants should be given by more or less private institutions. They can have a specifically focused character. We as people can support these funds or not, guided by our insight into their cultural interests.

It is however beyond dispute that one cannot demand the immediate abolition of every subsidy, for people from top to bottom must first learn to give. A gradual transition should occur, for otherwise numerous institutions would surely become victims. Maturity must also be nurtured: people must learn to be discerning in their judgments.

We should move things to the point they are in America, taking the Metropolitan Museum as an example. After the Museum purchased a Rembrandt for an exceptionally high price two years ago, they received many letters of congratulations that often contained small contributions of a few dollars. These letters came from working people, middle-class people, ordinary people. They did not come only from a so-called elite.

Ending subsidies would stimulate cultural interest and self-engagement. If we contribute to an orchestra, a museum, a scholarship fund, then we acquire an automatic interest, as it were, in the work it is doing.

Every neutrally slanted subsidy policy is lethally dangerous to cultural and intellectual freedom. In maturity we shall have to make our own little contributions to cultural activity. Even in our country this is not entirely unknown and unthinkable. Our broadcasting system is based on just such personal participation in the various broadcasting associations.

Closing remarks

Our goal cannot be to save our culture, our Western culture.[209] That is too abstract, too vague and too loosely formulated. What matters is to get to work, that everyone be culturally active in his or her own way. Negatively, that means opposing what we regard as evil; positively, it means making our own contribution. If in this way cultural life blossoms, then 'culture' will be saved, which is to say that there will be a renewal of culture. If Christians are then indeed active in their own way, we can await the outcome with serenity. If the neutralistic, uniform, totalitarian state of the Antichrist yet takes shape, we will not have to reproach ourselves for having failed to muster opposition to it or for having contributed to it.

Perhaps the reader will at times have thought that I am usurping the role of a clergyman. That was not the intention, yet it is impossible to speak about cultural matters today without taking the spiritual backgrounds, dangers and possibilities into account.

The thing that makes all the above doubtful for me is the question whether the current Christian generation will have the spiritual focus and stamina to set to work in such a way. Or has the apostasy advanced too far for that? Are we not already much too late? Everything that can be called Christian must be based on real Christian faith, a belief in God's word and his promises which are unconditional. Otherwise we attain at best a superficially Christian culture, saltless salt that pretends to be salt. Without real faith it makes no sense to talk about Christian cultural activity, for that can only be a fruit of faith.

Reformation is needed, renewal of our Christian life and certainly prayer, that the Lord may give us the people, the talents, whatever is necessary to will and to work. We need not, cannot and may not 'protect, preserve and maintain the church' (cf. Heidelberg Catechism Sunday 21); our Lord will do that. But we must use our talents, not deny him, be faithful and seek God's glory above all else, and this not as pious words but as a force for the preservation of all of life.

•Some comments on the culture state[210]

It is strange that we have to talk about culture. That already suggests that something is wrong. We call that a crisis nowadays. Isn't culture something that we just have, something that greatly influences what we do and what we leave undone and the form in which we do things? If things were healthy we would not be asking questions about culture, let alone about something as abstract as the 'culture state'. Rather, we would be addressing concrete problems such as how this or that can be brought about, an organization, an institute, a work of art, a building. People today like to say we are on the way, but posing the problem of culture suggests rather that we have lost our way. For people are not asking how we can overcome this or that difficulty; the question is instead one of where to go, and sometimes even of whether there is any meaning in going, in being on the move?

Every age had its culture, higher or lower, richer or poorer, flourishing or not. The state as such, the form of government, or if you prefer to put it more broadly, the societal structure and relationships, were not matters that stood above or alongside culture; rather, they were determined by culture. Every historian looks at the past in this way. But now there is a call for culture, and we call upon the state for help. Hans Zbinden in his eminently readable *De bedreigde mens* [threatened humanity] even talks about a 'flight into the state' as a defining characteristic of the present epoch.

Now, why do people pin their hopes on the state? The culture state, so they say, is the extension of the affluent society, which must inevitably evolve into it. Perhaps that is so. But let us notice that few things evolve by themselves and that behind all human work there are ideals, ideas or a vision. The affluent society as such is the expression of a culture and it is ruled by a vision, by a world view if one wants to put it more gravely, with all kinds of remarkable consequences and side-effects. I want to make some comments about this.

In the first place I want to state that affluence as such does not strike us as in any way negative. Bednarik entitled his book *Gevaarlijke welvaart* [dangerous affluence]. In it he does not speak like our Lord Jesus about the fact that wealth can make it difficult for a person to enter the kingdom of God; instead, he puts affluence and technical possibilities themselves into the dock. In this way he offers little that is constructive. But I do not see why we should need to complain about the fact that we have free time, a car, a washing machine and a well-illustrated book. However, the words of Prof. Baudet in his essay entitled 'Historisch perspectief' [historical perspective][211] do indeed seem to me to be worth heeding when he writes:

> Affluence is also a question of the relation between what people desire and what they are willing to do to attain it, between desire and effort. It is a question of norm, of psychology, of attitude towards life itself. Yet we do not

take the time to philosophize about it – not only because the political relations in the world do not allow us the time for it, but also because the modern Westerner does not regard philosophizing as a really meaningful and useful way of spending time. We play 'everything goes'. Philosophizing about the game would only keep us from playing it in ways in the effectiveness of which we want to believe.

Humanistic starting point

Notice that last word 'believe'. There is a belief involved. Von Martin says about it in his book *Orde en Vrijheid* ['Order and freedom'] – I like to cite various sources to show that one really does not have to be an adherent of the Philosophy of the Cosmonomic Idea in order to see such connections – that the starting point of nineteenth-century figures like Marx was the desire for humanistic freedom, to be sure, but that

> because this ... idea ... was implemented in a purely economic sense ... the means were elevated into a goal. The 'materialistic' – in combination with an intellectualistic-positivistic – mode of thought was elevated from a methodological orientation point into a world view. The view gained currency that with the implementation of a certain material and intellectual order of the 'social relationships', the objective 'conditions' would be created on the basis of which there would no longer be any conflict between the necessary demands of 'the collective' and the justifiable need for freedom of the 'individual'.

The difficult problems of society would be solved entirely automatically. And indeed, from this starting point a certain situation did evolve automatically, although it may be somewhat different from what people hoped for or expected. The number of 'independents' withered away significantly in the face of massification from below and bureaucratization from above. Von Martin discusses this development extensively in one of the most impressive chapters in his book, where he shows that the process is guided by an intelligentsia who attack the problems rationalistically, and in so doing consciously not only avoid religious considerations but actually lay them aside as being of no importance. He shows that modern rationalism has a humanistic starting point and that it believes it has no (more) need of God. We are confronted here with people who say as in the days of Zephaniah that 'the LORD will not do good, neither will he do evil' [Zephaniah 1:12].

This attitude fosters a far-reaching pragmatism in all kinds of political activities. And this attitude has slain its ten thousands. Where there used to be profound discussions grounded in various intellectual backgrounds, all problems today appear to be purely technical questions demanding a pragmatic approach. I say 'appear' because in fact it means only that people have agreed about their starting point, which they formulate in a characteristically humanistic way as 'concern for people'.

Crisis of conscience

The affluent society is thus a cultural product that has resulted from a broad movement of a humanistic nature that places concern for people at the centre and at the same time takes only economic and technical factors into consideration, or at least gives them priority. People driven by this spirit of the age now bow before the idol of economic security. And they are prepared to do an enormous lot for this. They are gripped by the fear that they may lose their affluence. Therefore it is a simple matter to put through a good many measures just by invoking the prospect of an economic crisis, even unpopular measures or measures that impinge upon human freedom to a significant degree. People are even prepared to hush the voice of their conscience a little.

People *believe* in a lovely, prospering world where everything is good. Naturally, far away, in any case not in one's own direct surroundings, there are people who get it wrong, who tread upon the rights of others – of other people, mind you, once again. Naturally, that does not happen in our own vicinity. In order to convince ourselves of this truth we must do two things. First we must lower our norms and standards significantly. What general opinion once deemed unacceptable because it was against the norm, is now fully accepted because we are afraid to apply a norm. And even when injustice and brutal crime stare us directly in the face we do not want to believe it. Then it is like a programme on television, 'fiction' and not reality. People refuse to accept it as such and are afraid to become involved, lest by doing so they forfeit their peace of mind. As in Brooklyn, where residents in a number of large apartment buildings watched quite happily for an hour while a girl was raped and then murdered, without even bothering to call the police. And it is certainly not only on the other side of the ocean that this is so. A similar case occurred recently in The Hague. Who still has the moral fortitude to put her or his life at risk for justice and truth? Is it really only the fear of the atomic bomb that enables us to swallow everything: the Moluccas, Hungary, Cyprus, and so forth, without taking recourse to action? Zbinden speaks in this context of a crisis of conscience; a psychologist would probably call it repression.

Homo economicus

There is constant talk by thinkers from all kinds of backgrounds about a crisis, growing normlessness, the revolt of the masses, and the like. It is certainly not the fault of the affluence or prosperity as such, but of a spirit that has taken control of people. It is a spirit that above all – and I consider this the worst part of it – has driven many to the following questions: what is the sense of working, of having aspirations? To what ideals should we aspire? To what end should we get involved? The idol of affluence seems in the end not to satisfy and to inspire, and natural scientific and economic thought have so damaged the image of being human that even humanism can no longer inspire people as it used to do. For it was humanism that brought forth that economic bias in the first place. The virtually theological justification of this feeling of meaninglessness we find in existentialism.

However that may be, the practically exclusive concern for economic factors in human life, for affluence in a rather restricted material sense, has had a withering effect on art and intellectual work. These are regarded as fields inhabited by unworldly dreamers who do not need to be taken seriously. But it is just at this point that we are confronted by a gargantuan problem. For now we have all kinds of wonderful appliances and machines and free time and money, but what are we to do with them? How do we fill our time? What shall we do with all the possibilities? And again many turn to the state. It has organized our affluence so well, they say, so why should it not now also organize our culture (in the narrower sense of that higher and in essence impractical aspect)? Culture in this sense has degenerated into a means of filling time, entertainment, something we discuss, diversion, albeit dressed up in fancy words of some sort and declared to be deeper or higher. Only snobs and visionaries still seem to take 'culture' seriously and devote some effort to it. 'Subsidy' is truly not an adequate answer to the material need that threatens culture in the sense described here. A state that cannot and may not dare to stand for a view of life can only subsidize those who already are established names, or those who do not stand out too conspicuously. In short, a state can only subsidize those who no longer really need subsidizing or those who belong to a middle group. The problem is all the more pressing because subsidies must be awarded by a group of functionaries, thus a *group* of people, which inevitably leads to acts of compromise and moderation, while many among them will be driven by the spirit of the age, which at bottom does not know what to do with culture and is not able to stand up for much in this area.

It is time we asked ourselves about the state of the culture we have been discussing. For a solution to the disharmony in our culture – material affluence and cultural poverty – is sometimes also sought in the direction of the distribution of culture. We should assist all those people who are now in a position 'to participate in culture' as a result of the newly acquired wealth, in the process of which we often first denigrate whatever real culture they already have as bourgeois and old-fashioned. We . . . that again is of course the intelligentsia, who created the affluent society and who, just like the ruling class of former times, commission the cultural work. That is clear in the field of art, for example. Present-day art is intellectual to a high degree, even where it is purported to be the brute expression of the subject. It seems a-religious, or is in any case presented as such. It is often antichristian, not surprisingly, as the intelligentsia have set out to clear away the last vestiges of ancient superstition. It is at the same time often an expression of anxiety and a feeling of meaninglessness. The tragedy of our times is that people would like so very much to grasp the fullness of humanity, but again and again encounter the dehumanized *homo economicus* or just some atoms or, better said, nuclear forces. It is a peculiar fact that the art that goes the furthest towards shattering values and breaking down all traditions could be defined as cultural anti-culture. By art people destroy art. Pop art can only exist as museum art; otherwise it is meaningless and nothing but a pile of old junk. Meanwhile, in contrast, the beauties produced by our times in industrial design, for example, are often passed over condescendingly as banal.

A-religious religion

This is a strange paradox. It can only be explained from the fact that the bearers of this culture, the ruling group (who are perhaps not even in the majority), are people who have wanted to ban religion and spirituality from their world picture only to find they cannot do without it. Thus a great deal of modern art is the real religion of our times, and many an abstract painting exudes a pretence as if it were an altarpiece in a nihilistic temple that will never be built. For this religion is there, to be sure, but it is at bottom never really believed. For the artistic is fundamentally not real, material enough to really matter and ultimately it is an unnecessary luxury.[212] And ultimately the revelation that art purports to give us is insufficiently real to live by; one cannot get much further than a vague religiosity. A snobbish attitude is often the result, or else a passionate but unsuccessful effort to surrender to this art-religion. Out of a profound need to obtain the revelation of deeper values and realities, people endeavour to this end to fathom and adopt whatever is newest and then, every time they are deceived, they cry out again for the next deception. A new work of art as a result of its shock does resemble something like a revelation, but in the face of prolonged observation it can seldom maintain this status. And at base people are only seldom really 'engaged'. In this way this religion almost acquires the character of a belief in crisis, in doubt, emptiness, unattainability, brokenness. This attitude too has slain its thousands. Art itself is thus transformed into a permanent prolonged iconoclasm.

A solution to the strange paradox of modern art, that it is an a-religious religion, may perhaps lie in this: that modern people regard both art and religion as necessary evils that accompany the unavoidable human structure. They often see both art and religion as a kind of aspirin tablet for getting rid of a peculiar cultural hangover.

No cultural unity

In any case, there are questions enough. Perhaps however you are not satisfied by what has been asserted thus far. I am not either. Just as I seldom read with total agreement a reflection on our times by a sociologist, economist or philosopher of culture. And that is not just because one person seldom fully agrees with another. It is because I miss something in these presentations. All too often there is too much generalization. What we have discussed so far is in fact no more than a tendency, a movement, a limited group, even if it has set the tone. Moreover, what I have asserted is in some respects an abstraction. Seldom will one encounter the matters I pointed out in all their clarity and sharpness in reality. Thus in reflections on culture today one reads again and again about the 'average person', a person who typically represents the general public. But have you ever met such an average person? Happily, human life is seldom consistent when it comes to evil, as it is alas also seldom consistent when it comes to good.

But the fact that we can talk about generalizing indicates that there are also other people and other movements. That we sometimes suppose every civilization is unambiguous and uniform is a result perhaps of the schematic oversimplifications of our childhood schoolbooks. In any case, solid historical research can make clear to us that in all periods there have been various groups and movements shaped by differences of an intellectual or spiritual nature. Every one of these contributed to the whole, to the general picture of that era, which I should like to call 'the mainstream'. It is precisely because of this common basis that a struggle of the spirits between the different groups is possible. A debate is impossible when one person speaks in Chinese and the other in Greek. For only when two people can understand each other can the differences between them come to light.

It is no different today. Our times are not unified. The positive and negative evaluations that appear in the reflections on culture referred to above arise from differences in starting point or attitude between the leaders of the various movements. The heated discussions about modern art demonstrate that in our civilization we are still far from being in the same line. For the sake of brevity I want to say that nowadays there are, besides the movement discussed above (and none of us are entirely free of it since it contributes so powerfully to the mainstream), three main cultural powers at work. There is actually still a living Christianity, more so and deeper than we perhaps suppose, even if we fear that Christians often do not speak out because of a kind of misplaced inferiority complex. There is still also a broad humanism; I even believe it is preparing to break through the current cultural crisis. And there is a neo-paganism, perhaps at its most palpable and powerful in the art world, that is preparing to construct an entirely new world that is neither Christian nor humanistic. Humanism, neo-paganism and Christianity are the three main powers that must and will compete for cultural supremacy in the period ahead.

The current ruling majority will certainly attempt to realize the culture state on the basis of their own position; the issues surrounding the culture state can only be understood in the light of their starting point. Yet creative minorities – I use Toynbee's theory of culture at this point – will also set to work. The positions are not yet clearly defined but they will become increasingly clear. We will leave that as it is now in order to take a closer look at our own task.

The task of the Christian

The question of today's cultural task cannot, as I see it, be posed in general terms. That's where sociological studies in that direction suffer. It would only be possible if articulated on the basis of a modern generality, which at its deepest would be relativism or, rather, a pipe dream in which the other subordinates his or her own particular opinions to the general, to the mainstream. I would like to cite Heinz Gerstinger is this regard, who in a lecture on Christian theatre stated that 'during a period when all regimes both East and West offer total ideologies that tend to force people into conformity, reflection on personal freedom of discernment remains an eminently Christian task.'

I do indeed believe that it is only by being very consciously and very radically Christian that we will best be able to fulfil our task. That is not only philosophically and sociologically true; much deeper, it is no more and no less than the mandate we received when we were called to be children of God. The path is narrow. If we stray to the one side we fall into spiritualism, such as that of the Pentecostal movement: there personal conversion is central, one's sole desire is for heaven and the Christian life is regarded as an individual matter. Scripture is devalued and doctrine is entirely secondary. This cannot offer much resistance to the spirit of the age and its distractions, since the sword of the Spirit of which Ephesians 6 speaks is missing.

If we stray to the other side we end up in dead orthodoxy. This will be wrapped in doctrine (confessionalism) and will pursue the Christian life via a strong legalism. Yet because here too the power of living out of the redemption by Jesus Christ is missing, the next step will be either cultural death, a becoming stuck in pure traditionalism, or secularization, virtually undetectable at first but gradually more conspicuous and pronounced. People have constructed strong legalistic walls for the defence of their own yard, to be sure, but they have no real weapons against the spiritual powers in the air. In any case, dead orthodoxy is always saltless Christianity.

Walking the narrow way means listening closely to God's word, out of love for God. Loving God and one's neighbour, of which Paul speaks in the famous passage in 1 Corinthians 13, is no over-spiritualized matter but a very concrete and actual, sober reality. Lovemaking without love is pure obscenity. And without love, cultural work degenerates as well: it becomes partisanship, formalistic insistence on sharply argued formulas, the application of rules and petty regulations. At bottom it becomes a desperate and bitter struggle to build and preserve something in one's own strength, a struggle for self-preservation that can only become more intense. And its sense of reality, the view it affords of the real relations and tasks, grows ever more obscure. In contrast, when love burns within us a sober sense of reality will be one of its first fruits. Then the fruits of the Spirit of which Paul speaks in the epistle to the Galatians will grow in us of themselves and Christian cultural work, in a certain sense the fruit of these fruits, will find its form without being forced.

We must not attempt out of a sort of snobbism or because of a kind of inferiority complex to go along with the world in many respects. On the contrary, we must be 'engaged', deepening our knowledge and venturing to say what is at stake. If we encounter cursing or if God's will is trodden under foot, if love is absent, if God is forgotten, then we must grieve for that. Out of love we must hunger and thirst for righteousness and desire to serve the truth in everything. Thus we must praise what is praiseworthy, regardless of the quarter from which it comes. We shall have to live close to Scripture once again. The world may fear the idea of losing the good life, but we must know that they who would save their life will lose it. We may also know that it will not always remain this way and that, even if God's judgment lingers, it will not be stayed forever. Anyone who does not believe that the Old Testament prophetic view of the acts of God does apply to our times as well, can learn something from the Revelation to John.

And if, living as new people out of the redemption in Jesus Christ, we fulfil our task in love and in Christian freedom we are active in all fields of life, then we will become a creative minority ourselves as a matter of course. The fear of the Lord is even today the principle of wisdom. Who knows how the Lord will bless our work and how he might perhaps make us again a head instead of the tail, which is often the most we are now in the all-encompassing cultural scene.[213] For myself, I do not believe that Christianity is a thing of the past, that it is over. I believe that a tremendous task is granted to every believer. There is so much to do, and we shall have to rebuild everything again from the ground up following the destructive period that is just behind us. If only we do not restore in the process lots of little old sacred houses that have long since been reduced to ruins! Reformation, revival, conversion, all this is needed. May love burn within us.

I have been reading the Minor Prophets again recently and their sometimes oppressive but sometimes also comforting actuality has gripped me anew. Permit me therefore to end with this citation from Micah, a word of comfort to us all, Christians in distress:

> I watch in hope for the LORD, I wait for God my Saviour'; my God will hear me. Do not gloat over me, my enemy! Though I have fallen, I will rise. Though I sit in darkness, the LORD will be my light. Because I have sinned against him, I will bear the LORD's wrath, until he pleads my case and establishes my right. He will bring me out into the light; I will see his righteousness. Then my enemy will see it and will be covered with shame, she who said to me, 'Where is the LORD your God?'.[214]

• Youth in revolt, youth in trouble: who's to blame? [215]

Young people are on the move – often quite literally: a generation of travellers and talkers. We are in the midst of a revolution, maybe the apex is already past. In the last five or ten years more has changed in the minds of young people than in the previous half century: their attitude to God, country, religion, morals, ideals, their way of life and their outlook on the future, on marriage and sex, on institutions and education, on the meaning of life, on war and peace, on politics, in short, on almost everything.

Are these symptoms of a new world which is growing? Are they the result of affluence, of new means of communication, of more spare time and greater social security? To a certain extent these things cannot be bypassed in thinking of the changes and their causes. Are they the result of the new nuclear weapons and their threat of a totally devastating war? This certainly has had and still has its effect, more today perhaps as a symptom of the problem. Are they due to of a feeling of lostness because of the population explosion? Or can they be explained by new ways of eating and drinking, by the polluted environment, or maybe even by the physical reaction to the increased radio-activity that assaults our bodies every day? All of these things may have their influence on the current youth scene.

If so, there would be only a technological problem to be dealt with on the level of nutrition, politics and sociology. Then there would be no need to ask who is to blame, whose responsibility it is, and who has to change. However, we feel that these questions may not be bypassed. Three answers are possible: the young people themselves, the world in which we live, or the church – the Christian community. We must try to avoid easy answers, one-sidedness and over-simplification. I will try to suggest some answers.

Who's to blame?

Is youth itself to be blamed? Certainly, young people often do not take their responsibility seriously, which leaves issues unsolved and may encourage them to look to unrealistic utopias. It is true that young people tend to look for the road of least resistance and try to avoid hardship and sacrifice. And no doubt there is a certain selfishness, a lack of care, a lack of respect for other people's views. We see escape through drugs alongside revolutionary activities, a certain hedonism alongside a wilful denial of the comfort earlier generations tried to realize. They are to blame in many respects, yet I hesitate to accuse them. Maybe these blemishes are the dirt they inherited. Maybe the problems have become too big for them to cope with. If so, we must look elsewhere.

Is the world to be blamed? Our Western culture as it has developed since the Age of Reason, the Enlightenment, has changed the world. It has accomplished many technological, social and economic feats which until recently have made people react in amazement, but in its very principles it already bore the seeds of disillusionment, decay and corruption. This culture was built on the premise of human autonomy: that people, out of themselves, with their brains and through their endeavour can accomplish a great new world, with happiness and comfort for everyone. They only had to define the natural laws that govern reality and manipulate them. Humanity is in the centre, and they are lord. Religion is at best something completely private, with no meaning for daily life and the organization of our world. It is in fact seen as a relic from a primitive past, when humankind were in their infancy. Now we have grown up!

In the box

How are morals viewed in this culture in which we live? They are seen as just a social contract, designed by people to make life better. Basically they are a human invention and can therefore be changed, if necessary. There are no absolutes; everything is relative. And who can say what is right or wrong. Sin is an outdated concept; after all, only circumstances and psychological problems are to be blamed for criminal actions.

Since the Age of Reason people have put great faith in science. Through science they hoped to find the basic laws of all reality, to explain the basic principles of our cosmos and gain insight into life, death, development and history. In this way they expected to be able to control economics, social change, in the future perhaps even war and peace. So that, if people just cooperate, we could expect a fine new world.

But the results look different. People have been caught 'in the box' of scientific naturalism: they themselves have become a part of the natural world, a product of evolution, maybe only a link in the chain. They have become a product of their sociological environment, their psychological make-up, governed by economic laws. They have lost their humanity and they have become only a complex molecule among the many molecules, or a different type of ape among the many types of apes. They have become a little cog in a big machine, a number in the computer. And they are more and more aware that they are open to manipulation by big powers, which are not always good and trustworthy.

In this way the great autonomous human has become less than human, living without freedom as a stranger in a world where only natural laws count. This has led to a feeling of meaninglessness and total senselessness in all of human life. As early as 1834 Carlyle already said: 'The universe is all void of life, purpose, volition, even of hostility. It is one huge, dead, immeasurable steam-engine, rolling on in its cold indifference to grind me limb from limb.'[216]

The existentialist philosophers have acknowledged these facts. They spoke of people being caught in meaninglessness with 'no exit' and of people being determined by their place in history, which they may try to transcend toward freedom in an existential leap, in a kind of nihilistic mysticism that reveals to them their humanity and their being unto death.

Many, also among the young generation, have understood these things and have cried in despair, knowing that they are human even if there is no place for the human. Knowing people ought to be free even if they are determined by natural laws, wanting to love and be loved even if there is no love, longing for the good even though good and bad are just questions of terminology. In the tradition of revolution that established itself since the French Revolution they look forward in their desperation, as a last straw of hope, to a total revolution that will change the world, give total freedom, and make them happy and good. It is not a hope based on reason; it is a wistful hope that they know to be wishful only. Who can fathom the despair behind these men and women?

Humanistic optimism

Of course there are many – 'the silent majority' – who live on as if the world were still 'normal', as if morals were still there, and human beings were still human. They continue to look in awe at humanity's great achievements, even while the young people sing: 'You may leave here for five days in space, but when you return, it's still the same old place.'[217] They are the optimistic humanists, who hope to achieve a great humanity even if they have no basis for it. And so their ethics have become legalism, and the final norm 'what will the neighbours say;' their smile has become a façade, their faith a hypocrisy and their lives a big lie. They are pragmatic and hope to make the best of it. They hope to find security in their money and their jobs, immortality in being well known and well thought of. They want to make life soft and easy, and the world safe through law and order.

These people belong to the previous generation: the generation born between the two world wars, still living on in the traditions dating from before World War I, with their eyes closed to the decay, the corruption, the insolvability of too many great problems. They dreamt their idealistic dreams, to be heavily shaken by World War II and the troubled times that followed it. But many still linger on in optimism, hoping a better, self-made future. They are the former generation who can say to the present one: 'Our generation was of a tougher moral fibre than yours. We were able to avoid facing reality without using drugs.'[218]

I feel that the present world with its multiplicity of unsolved problems is in many respects the legacy of the previous generation, for they left things unchanged out of fear for change. They bypassed problems that were too overwhelming and shut their eyes to reality, hoping for better times to come, just through the normal course of history. They not only left a world to our young generation in which all values, all institutions and accomplishments of the past are tumbling down, in short a dying culture with no strength to revive again, but they also showed this new generation the emptiness of their ideals, their secret lawlessness, their despair behind the façade, and their basic hypocrisy. The present generation is either tougher and ready to face the realities, even the despair, or they escape into drugs and cults and try to evade this world. In both cases the young people are more honest and more true in their evaluation of the situation we are in.

The church

And what about the church? Is it not true that young men and women in their honesty also flee from the church, leaving behind the faith of their parents while joining the ranks of this despairing generation? Statistics have shown that a much larger percentage than might be expected among the revolutionary youth and hippies come from Christian homes. There are indeed many disturbing questions to be answered.

The churches have, with few exceptions, accepted the separation of faith from life as conceived by the protagonists of the Age of Reason and the later humanists. Faith was seen as something above and apart from daily life. Therefore Christians followed humanistic teaching in almost all fields of reality, leading an almost double life, sometimes verging on the schizoid. Life was divided into religion, a kind of Christian mysticism directed towards being saved and getting to heaven, and daily life, in which the ways of the world were followed, even if morals were observed. In fact, too many of these Christians resembled the silent majority we just spoke of, even if their legalism was stronger because they could base it on biblical precepts.

As a result Christians were not really involved in the problems the world was facing. They sought escape through their faith as well as through the humanistic dream of a better world still to be built. Certainly this dualism was, and is, full of contradictions, but it had as its result that Christians have not built up a tradition of dealing with politics, science, economics, etc. – *as Christians.* The Bible, regarded as a holy book, remained closed when problems outside religion were discussed. Involvement in other fields often even resulted in guilt feelings, as basically only the work of a pastor or evangelist was considered Christian and really meaningful. This has also led to a certain anti-intellectualism.

Obsolete

Christians are often even more behind the times than their humanistic-optimistic friends, since they have not followed the new trends in ideas and ideals and do not know what is going on in the world. Christians often feel that the Bible is enough, that thinking is superfluous. Note that there has been a storm of protest against the Darwinian theories among Christians, but who among them has tried to check the evidence and build up new and better theories based on the given facts? Christians have not watched, and certainly not analysed, the new trends in art, and have completely failed to see that exactly the new forms of art were the strongest agents in promoting a new nihilistic antichristian world view.

So religion has become obsolete and far removed from all that matters in the world today. Our youth are trained in colleges and universities that often, even if they profess to be Christian, teach only from a humanistic, so called neutral, point of view. These Christian young men and women are confronted with a world in which there is no place for their kind of religion. And at home they are taught that indeed faith is outside of the world, so that they feel that God and the Bible give no answers to the problems they cannot bypass. How many of our church youth have lost the track in this way and have put Christianity to the side as a cult without meaning?

And what about Christianity itself, its theology and its understanding of the world? Christianity and theology itself were undermined, and Bible-believing orthodoxy often faltered because too often the humanistic theories were believed to be facts and the unchristian character of many modern ideas was not clearly seen. Even theologians were often not trained to understand the trends of modern philosophy, so that they fell for ideas that were incompatible with biblical teaching. As a result, modern theology has undermined our faith in the Bible and its trustworthiness. Many chapters in the Bible were declared myth. Should it surprise us that the young generation translated this into 'fairy tales' with no real meaning? Christians, also orthodox Christians, have failed to see that the battle is not between science and faith, but between two different faiths: the biblical faith in God, his Son, humanity and the world as creation versus faith in reason, starting from an autonomous humanity who have laid down the rule never to accept anything their reason cannot understand or their scientific observation cannot prove.[219]

Christianity itself is in a crisis. It has no answers to the problems of the world today, and its faith and attitudes are open to doubt and criticism, and often rightfully considered to be mere traditionalism. Or, where the compromise with modern thought has gone so far in modern theology that it ends up with a slogan like 'God is dead', its Christian character has been lost, and certainly the gospel and its timeless message of salvation, freedom and renewal is not heard anymore. No legalism, no attempt to shut out the world and to make the church a closed fortress can ever help Christianity. Either it becomes a strange sect, a kind of museum piece, or it is wiped out, having failed to fight against the 'spiritual forces of wickedness in heavenly places' (Ephesians 6:12).

No wonder that Christianity has lost its meaning for many of the younger generation. Indeed we can only thank God that there are still so many left who, in spite of all the confusion, see the glory and the power of being a child of God. But I feel that we must be honest and say that the church has failed, has failed to fight the spirit of our world, its science and its faith in humanity. Or maybe it has fought on the wrong frontier and has therefore become either a part of the world itself or a weak and old-fashioned institution with no strength to handle the problems of today.

Reformation

Maybe I have simplified and overstressed my picture of the church today, yet I hope to have pointed to the heart of the problem. Is there no hope for the future then? No hope to reach the young? Yes, but something has to be done. Happily – thank God – there are still many Christians who believe in our Lord Jesus Christ and his word, and deeper still, thank God that he truly lives and can never be a victim of our failures. So there is hope, if we start again in faith in this living God!

A reformation is needed in which we rethink the biblical teaching and renew our lives, practising the things we believe in. We must see that we need more than only good theology. Christianity can only become a force again if we listen to men like C.S. Lewis, who once wrote:

> What we want is not more little books about Christianity, but more little books by Christians on other subjects, with their Christianity latent. It is not the books written in direct defence of materialism that make modern man a materialist; it is the materialistic assumption in all the other books. In the same way it is not books on Christianity that will really trouble him. But he would be troubled if, whenever he wanted a cheap introduction to some scientific subject, the best work on the market was always by a Christian. The first step to the reconversion of (our) countries is a series, produced by Christians, which can beat the Penguin and the Thinker's Library on their own ground.[220]

We must study the real problems of today and work towards their solution, showing something of Christ's concern for this world. We must understand the all-encompassing breadth of redemption as well as the curse. We must have the courage as Christians to be different, not left-wing, not right-wing, not part of any faction of our confused world.

We must stop thinking that it is enough to say that God is love and all that is needed is to 'be saved'. To be saved is always the beginning of a Christian life, never an end in itself. And as evangelists we are not speaking to heathen people. It is more appropriate to compare our evangelists to the prophets, calling out: 'Repent, for the wrath of God is at hand.' Do we not see that the mess in which our world is, is a sign of God's judgment over our Western world, which calls itself Christian but denies its very Lord and Saviour?

Will there be a future for Christianity before the Lord comes back? Nobody knows. Maybe the last days are at hand, while we are witnessing Satan, delivered from his chains, at work. If so, let our faith in God be true and real, and let us prepare our young people for hardship and maybe even martyrdom. For there is hope, and a great future awaits us. But as long as we can, let us work and pray for reformation, pray that the Holy Spirit will renew our hearts and souls and minds. And let us work to be prophets with a message that is relevant to our time.

Faith and Lifestyle

• Art and lifestyle[221]

It has become virtually commonplace to claim that Western culture is in a crisis, a crisis in which all values, achievements and insights are at risk, challenged, overthrown or trampled upon. The optimists think the matter is one of clearing away antiquated principles and breaking through stultified traditions with the expectation that out of the chaos a new life, a new culture with new values will arise. There is not yet much of that to be detected, however, and one can say that the cultural activity of this [twentieth] century remains to this day an ever newly begun, a permanently prolonged revolution: our century majors in the negative, in tearing down, in revolting yet again, time after time. One could practically say that our era has established a new tradition, one of continually attacking and breaking down what has been built up and established. This may have a paradoxical ring to it, but a new traditionalism has appeared, namely, that of being revolutionary.

Leaving the nineteenth-century prelude to our times aside, we could say that this spirit began in art, then affected philosophy and nowadays increasingly determines people's lifestyle. Aggressive teddy-boy attitudes are found not only amongst the real jacks in the streets, the asphalt youth who out of great inner emptiness smash everything to pieces, oppose all authority and desire to be tied by nothing. This posture is characteristic of many, many more people, even if they behave somewhat more respectably. Does the scant real interest in political questions not flow from a feeling that to build anything today is meaningless and without perspective? Is the steadily declining motivation to work not a consequence of the oppressive awareness that all work serves no purpose after all? Is the ever louder call for leisure time, more money, more fun and more entertainment not an expression of a lifestyle that has as its adage: let us eat, drink and be merry for tomorrow we die? Inner boredom, a feeling of emptiness, lack of a firm foundation in life surface all too often once one pierces the thin crust of outward accommodation of socially acceptable forms of behaviour.

This is all the more remarkable since people have never before been so well off – I refer to the West. Electric light, refrigerators, vacuum cleaners, canned food, a hundred-and-one aids for our everyday convenience, all in unprecedented supply, make life better; and hygiene, medical assistance, and security measures make life less dangerous and vulnerable than ever before. Moreover, not only is prosperity at an all-time high; it extends to a greater percentage of the population than in any previous time.

Technology and medicine and prosperity and security are undoubtedly gifts of the Lord, blessings that he has bestowed upon the West as a fruit of their listening to his laws for life – we think of Deuteronomy 28. Yet the West is well on the way to forfeiting this blessing, in the first place by saying: 'My power and the strength of my hands have produced this wealth for me' (Deuteronomy 8:17). Because of their having exalted their 'imaginations' – in violation of the Second Commandment – instead of listening to him, the Lord has sent them the curse described in the second part of Deuteronomy 28.

Thus it is possible, when we want to understand our times, to turn to the Scriptures: the people of Romans 1:32, of 2 Timothy 3 and 2 Thessalonians 2 (we assume the reader has a Bible in hand) are modern people. And when we want to understand something of the current crisis we do well to turn to that book in the Bible that gives us a profound and eye-opening commentary on history, its importance, and the significance of the great events to which we are witnesses. Let us read Revelation 16; then we will understand better the meaning of lawlessness and rebellion and pervasive negativism.

Modern art

Nowhere does all this come more clearly to light than in modern art. Perhaps that is because such a mentality is more easily implemented in art than in everyday life. There can be something heroic about the struggle for a new culture determined in its meaning by humanity alone; thus one of its forerunners stated: 'I begin to destroy . . . this unfit world and to make it over again in my own image.' And this man, John Davidson, was in turn described in the following words, which at the same time provide an outstanding definition of modern cultural activity: 'The courage and honesty of a mind valiantly beating itself to destruction against the locked and barred door of an unknown and perhaps non-existent reality.'[222]

Modern people, who blaspheme God, who regard his creation as unworthy and bad, who want to violate every norm and law and want to have no ties, seek freedom. The impossibility of realizing such freedom fully is perhaps the direct reason for their feeling of malaise, of 'thrown-ness' (*Geworfen-sein*) of meaninglessness and defeat (*échec*). For the word of that prophet of modern times, Carlyle, is true: '(Even) the Shoeblack . . . would require, if you consider it, for his permanent satisfaction and saturation, simply this allotment, no more, no less: God's infinite Universe altogether to himself, therein to enjoy infinitely, and fill every wish as fast as it rose.'[223]

Now, this freedom, which is at the same time the source of the misgivings about reality, is the ground upon which all modern art and philosophy is built. Gauguin, shortly before his death in 1902, wrote the manifesto of twentieth-century art, defined its task and pointed its way – and seldom has a will been so faithfully executed to the letter as this:

While taking into account the efforts and the investigations, even those of science, it was, necessary to think of a complete liberation, to break the windowpanes at the risk of cutting one's finger, to leave it to the next generation, henceforth independent, free from any shackles, to solve the problem completely. I do not say definitively, for it exactly means an art without strict boundaries, rich in all kinds of technique, fit to translate all the emotions of nature and man. For this purpose it was necessary to risk body and soul in the struggle, a struggle against all the schools, all of them without any distinction, not by disparaging them, but by something else, by offending not only the officials but also the Impressionists, the Neo-Impressionists, the older and the newer kind of public ... And as to the work, a method of contradiction, if you like, venturing into the strongest abstractions, doing all that was forbidden, and reconstructing more or less happily, without any fear of exaggeration, even with exaggeration. Learning anew, and then, once having learnt, learn again. Conquer any timidity however much ridicule it may occasion. In front of his easel the painter is no slave, either of the past or of the present, either of nature or of his neighbour. He is himself, again himself, always himself.[224]

Do you doubt that this lies behind modern art? Read in that case what the artists themselves or their closest spiritual kin have to say. There is so much literature about recent modern art that it cannot be difficult for someone interested in the subject to discover the deep-seated antichristian religious hostility to the creation and reality of this world and the exigency and anxiety that modern art expresses. Naturally there is an easier and less time-consuming way: simply go and look. Yet there are many who think that, where something is said in pictorial language rather than in the language of words, nothing is said and certainly not something antichristian. Yet the words of the painters themselves must open these people's eyes to the fact that there is more happening here than a new concept of beauty, which would be religiously indifferent. Is modern jazz – serious modern jazz – just a matter of new stylistic characteristics, of new harmonies and melodies? Reading the pertinent sections in the good book by Stearns,[225] a man who experienced the history and put a positive value on it, can cure us of that misconception. No, serious modern jazz does express a view of life.[226]

'And all being is flaming suffering,' wrote a modern painter on the back of one of his canvases around 1912.[227] And anyone who has even just a little understanding of modern irrational literary language will need no further commentary to the following words from an invitation to the exhibition of a young female artist:

We live in a strange world, Ans Wortel, with strange names, bewildered gestures, and vanished phenomena. We eat purple, laugh at pink, go in and out with blond, the sun burns all surfaces ochre, white we die, and black is our new Book of Blissful expectations. A photo is no longer a photo if we take the scissors to it, paintings no longer leap to the side but also to the fore, out of their frames, our mono-type ink is as fat as fertilized earth, but our Blissful Book is black. You are 30, you stand at a boundary. Behind Appel: red. Armando ahead: black. A good belief is no belief, support is not support, paint is not blood but paint, just tear it, split it, go ahead, and when you are there there are all, horizontal, and what we sought we did not find.

And do the following last bitter words not testify to the awareness of existential emptiness and hopeless desperation?: 'Becoming, we are always becoming, again and again, but we never become something; we are always en route but we never arrive, for to arrive is death, and we prefer to attend to the meaningless meaning-giving of life.'[228]

Indeed, the latest painting is not just aesthetic experimentation. Rather, 'we see that it concerns adopting a truly existentialist position after a fundamental conflict of conscience. Refusing with finality to copy reality is to offer a solution not previously given to what some call the conflict between man and nature.'[229] We see that with all this non-figurative art there is something more going on than playing with paint on a canvas. Lambert says so matter-of-factly; Sandberg, the champion of the informal painters (or whatever one may call them) puts it more sharply: 'The period of oppression and counterfeiting in which we live does not demand our answer but screams for protest – that protest, harsh and piercing in music, gripping and often dark in book and play, breaks loose cursing and raging in painting, depicting in images destruction next to newly burgeoning life.'[230]

Such passages accompany the works of the moderns again and again. Do you suppose that these writers could read all that into the work of their friends if it were not there? Just read Jaguer's typification of the present generation that is being pushed forward.[231] There you will find in a multiplicity of variations what Volboudt wrote about Jean Dubuffet: 'This art that mocks the creature does no longer have respect for the Creation.'[232] Behind the abstraction, with all its aestheticism, its play with artistic possibilities, there lies more than a neutral search for new possibilities. Mondrian, who felt himself the prophet of a new world, a builder of a new natureless reality, said: 'The life of the present-day, cultivated person turns slowly away from the natural: it becomes more and more an abstract life.'[233]

These abstract painters endeavour to eliminate all 'literary' qualities – or subject matter – from the canvas. Thus it may seem to be a remarkable coincidence that a writer conceived the first abstract painting! Edgar Allen Poe lets the gruesome main character in *The Fall of the House of Usher* create one: 'There arose out of the pure abstractions which the hypochondriac contrived to throw upon the canvas, an intensity of intolerable awe, no shadow of which felt I ever yet in the contemplation of the certainly glowing yet too concrete reveries of Fuseli.' Thus it is clear that one need not look just amongst the most recent generation. The whole of modern painting is permeated by this crisis. How otherwise could the work of half a century ago still be called modern today if that were not the name given to a movement, to the art of a particular intellectual current? Finally, by way of illustration, consider just one more citation from Kandinsky's *Über das Geistige in die Kunst* written in 1912: 'The clash of tones, the lost balance, falling "principles", unexpected drumbeat, great questions, seemingly purposeless ambition, seemingly torn inner urge and longing, shattered ties and bonds, making plurality one, opposites and contradictions – that is our harmony.' And is Kandinsky not after Mondrian the most harmonious of the abstract artists? Even then, still . . .

Is there anything that is different?

Yet is all this true? Certainly there may be a group of people who act crazily and feign nausea in an ivory tower – pardon, in a plastic 'prefab mast' – but surely there are others too, different, and better? Yes, but then do not turn to the present-day film, which in its three-dimensional colour and sound naturalism is stylistically the extreme counter-pole to Appelian art. For there is much truth in the statement of another modern painter: 'The critics of modern art, the timid curators, the politicians who are under pressure, and a great many simple but honest people concur with the content of modern art but not with its form. They want to pour the new wine into old vessels.'[234] Of course the commercial producers of present-day popular entertainment know that people want extreme naturalism in the presentation but also want to have a reality served up in which – perhaps in an even rawer manner than in painting and sculpture – norms, respect for values, love and beauty are damaged at their core. Tough guys and easy girls form the themes; we are reminded of Romans 1:32. Naturally, there are better films, but do they offer much else? Does the resolution of conflicts lie in bowing before God's law or in conforming to passion and so-called 'facts'? Where in the film world is God still taken into account? Is it not much rather a completely secularized world picture that is projected to us? And if religion is brought into it, usually in a rather sentimental way, is it then not often the case that 2 Timothy 3:4–5 correctly comes to mind? I am thinking of the 'biblical' films.

Modern novels, are they really different and better? Is there not often a shameless exhibitionism, a desire for a lawless life, in full awareness of the inner emptiness that this evokes? Materialism, eroticism, crime and punishment but no repentance, is that not often the picture that looms before us? Or, if a deeper level is attained, existential anxiety, meaninglessness, emptiness, nihilism, casting about for an ideal without having one? Crisis, judgment, lawlessness, anxiety, a world in which the second part of Deuteronomy 28 seems to be true in its full force, more than we perhaps have ever realized.

But is there nothing else? Yes, there is. The past, cultural treasures, values and attainments are challenged again and again in the prolonged revolution, but they persist. I do not primarily have in mind here our passion to preserve things, despite the 'museological taboo' that attaches itself to old things: for are we not confronted by things that manifestly no longer have any value for today? The world that leaps from modern paintings is often a hell – anyone who does not yet understand the mode of expression through forms alone should take a good look at the Surrealists, Matta, Ernst, Delvaux – but happily the reality of hell cannot be fully realized. And there is still resistance, often with a lament for the loss and the demise on the lips (Revelation 18:16–18). There is still much warm personal humanism, still much normalcy, still much of value, still much capacity for work, skill, knowledge, love and positive attitude. Only, it is as if the drive is gone and all that is possible only by living in the past. Note also this: anyone who reads Revelation and other prophecies concerning the last days as if they evoke the sensational picture of a super-cruel dictator, dark henchmen, organized crime and perpetual rape, has not understood; for our Lord says that in those days it will be as in the days of Noah: they eat and drink, marry and give in marriage, in short, they live ordinary little lives, as always.

Yet there is still much of value. But let us not take on something of an inferiority complex, for being out of touch with our times, as it were. 'Be careful not to think that the most recent work is ugly,' people tell us. 'Just remember how wrong people were about van Gogh less than a century ago.' And we may be tempted to bow our heads, fearful that posterity will ridicule us if we fail to find Appel less than the sum total of humanity and beauty.

But posterity is our posterity too. Future culture will be in part a fruit of our work. We must not forget that. If we neglect the struggle for the sake of a scarcely concealed inferiority complex, then there is indeed a good chance that the future will be entirely 'Appeled'. But then we will be partly responsible for that. Therefore let us support, build and assist the good and beautiful that there is, even if it does not arise directly from Christian circles. It may be true that the existentialist is more consistent and honest than the humanist, but the latter still has some knowledge of meaning and norms, morality and humanity. We may oppose Appel and those around him with a clear conscience. Not because they mess about with paint and do this differently from painters in the past, but because they are, and evoke, forces of destruction. Did Appel himself not say: 'I do not paint, I hit. Painting is destruction.'?[235] It will have to be a spiritual struggle and not one in which, in the manner of Prange with his god Hai-Hai, we declare the adversary to be a charlatan lacking skill. It will have to be a fair struggle in which we must learn to know and understand the other thoroughly. Otherwise we have perhaps already lost. Otherwise we certainly cannot help, for this struggle means helping in love.

Fighting is not in the first place being tremendously active, polemicizing, debating, although that may at times be a part of it. It does not mean scheming and skilfully manoeuvring. God's kingdom is never served in unfairness or in taking the wind out of another's sails. Fighting the good fight of faith is described in Ephesians 6:10–20; and it is summed up in the word of the Lord: be salt that salts.

Christian lifestyle

And so we come round again to ourselves, to present-day Christians. There are many. Perhaps there was never an age as Christian as our own, if we consider the numbers and all the activity. But the problem is that we are not salt that salts because we have no style of our own and just hobble along after the world with an inferiority complex. In the sixteenth century there was much unbelief, but it had hardly found the forms to express itself, and the unbelievers of that time knew no better than that the Bible was true.[236] But the series of great thinkers from Descartes to the Encyclopedists and further to Heidegger sketched and perfected the unbelieving world picture, and now the roles are reversed. We have all undergone a rationalistic brainwashing, more horrifying and more effective than what has been achieved by any totalitarian regime. And if the Lord had not protected us[237] we would not even have been here any longer. A humanistic-rationalistic brainwashing, whereby it is often difficult for twentieth-century Christians to believe that their Father in heaven even can work wonders and hear prayers, here and now, and difficult to believe that he did this in the days of the writers of the Scriptures. Also our concept of truth has been rationalized, so that even though perhaps we do not confess it with the mouth, we nevertheless believe de facto that only what can be seen, measured or determined scientifically can be true. Is this not the source of many of the debates about Genesis 1? Is this not why we are of so little faith that we do not dare to depend on God's promises that he will hear our prayers but think that we primarily have to do it ourselves? Do it ourselves, and rely on our own strength. That often determines our actions. And this is why we often surround ourselves and our circle with a series of commandments and prohibitions and prescriptions and endeavours by which to build a wall around ourselves. We try to keep the world out, almost in the manner of the ostrich: look, but not at modern art, which is after all the work of charlatans; read, but not modern writings, which will not make you any the wiser; live, but just within the walls we have erected. Yet it could very well be that without knowing it we have lived and worked inside these walls in nearly the same way as people on the outside, and that what is modern has slipped in unnoticed. After all, is there not a great deal of materialism in our circle – living for money and an insured future – and could the fact that we often have so little awareness of the content of modern art and music not also be a symptom of this?

No, we should not do it ourselves but should live rather as branches abiding in the true vine, drawing strength from the finished work of our Saviour. That is where we should begin. Having a Christian lifestyle is a fruit of faith, that is righteousness, peace and joy in the Holy Spirit (Romans 14:17). A Christian lifestyle is not a conforming to rules of the touch-not-taste-not-handle-not variety, even less is it an imposing of such rules on others, for true freedom is the freedom for which Christ has set us free (Galatians 5:1). This is the major emphasis of the gospel message: that there is unity, love, faithfulness, and obedience in freedom: freedom that does full justice to our individuality without any need to speak of 'individualism'.

Therefore it is also not possible, in this article about the Christian life in relation to art and entertainment, to provide a catalogue of advice or to formulate guidelines to which Christians would need to adhere. Colossians 2:20–23 forbids me to do that. We must live from the freedom Christ won for us. What does that mean? It means that the one reads a book but another lays it aside. Why does one lay it aside? Because it may give them impure thoughts and drive them to sin. That can be inherent in the book in question – there are also norms for art, I am not advocating irrationalism – but that may also be a reaction connected with the character, the upbringing, the past, in short, with the personal identity of the reader. And why does another person read the same book all the way through to the end? Possibly because they have not understood it, so that the evil in the book does not touch them. Or perhaps they have understood it but want to see how the writer resolves the issue. It may be that the reader has a friend troubled by questions on which the book can shed some light. In short, there are a thousand-and-one reasons why some people may decide subjectively that they have to lay a book aside, while others who in principle share the same judgment of the work may equally justifiably continue reading it, yet both may come openly and honestly before the Lord when it is time to pray, saying that they have walked in his paths through his strength.

We must be on our guard against sin, which is a concrete power. Certainly. Thus the Bible gives us a great deal of good advice: avoid bad company and do not follow in the path of evil. We must come to God as his children, bearing fruit, walking in the light, trusting him and listening to him. Only in doing so do we come to understand what sin is, and only then, too, does the Lord forgive us our sins (1 John 1). Yet what that means for the one or the other of us concretely with respect to art, modern art, entertainment, and ever so much more cannot be stated in general. There is freedom. There is the incredibly rich diversity of people, in their possibilities, calling, character, weaknesses and strong points.

Indeed, it may very well be that you walk away from an exhibition of modern art because it upsets you and makes you rebellious, because you cannot bear to see such cursing, or because at the moment you would rather avoid dealing with the problems posed because you have other things on your mind. Meanwhile, your good friend and brother or sister in Christ continues to look, and tells you later that it was there that he or she first apprehended what nihilism means, and as a result was able to discover and eliminate a particular sin, the nature of which had gone previously unrecognized, from his or her life.

The person who claims to be a child of the Lord and walks in darkness lies. It is impossible that someone who loves God will seek sin. That is also why there can be freedom. But does such freedom not call forth lawlessness? Those who understand at all what we have said so far will know better. It only makes sense to speak of freedom, which is freedom in Christ, if there is faith. For what is the work of Christ for us? We can read about this in the verses introducing the passage in Colossians 2:16–23 in which Paul enjoins us to let no one judge us or impose ordinances upon us after the doctrines and commandments of people. In this pericope, verses 10–15 of the same chapter, we can read that Christ overcame evil, that he forgives our trespasses, but also that with him and in him we have gained a new life, that our hearts are circumcised and that we have become new people. If we live close to him, as his children, as new people, then and only then, but also definitely then, there is freedom, there must be freedom. Paul therefore continues directly after this short and powerful summary of the importance of Christ's work for us with the words: 'Therefore do not let anyone judge you by what you eat or drink, or with regard to a religious festival, a New Moon celebration or a Sabbath day.' In other words, he tells us not to let anyone impose rules upon us. That would be foolish, since the reality is found in Christ! (verse 17).

Freedom

This article is threatening to turn into a sermon. Still, if we cannot say all this it makes little sense to talk about a Christian way of life. For where there is no faith we cannot expect its fruits. If we ask about a Christian lifestyle, also in matters of present-day art and entertainment, then that discussion can only begin when we build together on the firm foundation that is Christ and when we refrain from snatching away from one another the freedom that we have gained in him. What, then, of sin? This is a force in our lives that sometimes makes us sigh with Paul for deliverance; but then the knowledge breaks through again that it has been given and attained in him (Romans 7:25). Yet this sin, which persists despite our walking in the light – to say it is not there is to deceive oneself (1 John 1:8) – or better said, the sin we only come to see and know when we walk in the light, means each of us must watch our step. As long as we live in this dispensation, and sin rules the world, and many who are filthy make themselves filthier still (Revelation 22:11), the problem of 'Christian involvement with art and entertainment' will remain unresolved. For sin makes all logical or singular reasoning unreal and impossible.

Yet it is our task to walk more and more righteously (Revelation 22:11) and to use our freedom to help build a Christian lifestyle, which Paul describes in Colossians 3:5–17. This is not uniform, as if dictated by current rules about how things should be, but there is unity in Christ through mutual love, even if the one person does things which another prefers to leave undone. Thus we can find a lifestyle that bears our own mark, as a fruit of the Holy Spirit (Galatians 5:22–24). And then we are also salt that salts. By our way of life we then show what the truth is, because we do the truth – to this end we are even called to be children (John 17:21) – in order to withstand the spirit of the age, which initially reduced us to an inferiority complex.

Reformation is necessary. Then perhaps another art can arise and in our culture we can perhaps be made by the Lord into a head again and not a tail (Deuteronomy 28:13). But only in this way, seeking the Lord and building in freedom on the foundation laid by him, does it make sense to talk about a Christian lifestyle, also in connection with art and entertainment. But even if it should become darker in our world, the raging of Satan even more ferocious, and even if God's people should become very small and as nothing, faith will bear its fruit and we shall save up for ourselves treasures in heaven. If we do not build like this we are saltless salt, worth only to be thrown out. Do we take this threat seriously, do we fear it? May God preserve us from assuming an indifferent attitude – just read Deuteronomy 29:19–20! Yet if we do not dare to live in freedom according to the Spirit, if faith is not there as a force in all our works and words, then yes, we have to bind one another by rules and laws. Or there will be chaos. Then even the attainments of the past will be lost.

We have still written nothing about the norms for art. We may be brief about that. We believe we may find these in Philippians 4:8: 'Whatever is true, whatever is noble, whatever is right, whatever is pure, whatever is lovely, whatever is admirable – if anything is excellent or praiseworthy – think about such things.' This certainly applies to the artist as well. What it means concretely we shall not work out further now. People will discover it for themselves if they become more intensely engaged with art. Or with entertainment. Then they will discover that art and entertainment are formidable powers, more formidable than is often supposed. The fact that people are inclined to blame the moving pictures at least in part for the rise in criminality may speak for itself. Yet this same art can also help us to understand our times better and thus help us to be of better service to our neighbour. The truth of this cannot be proven by words but must be shown in practice. If only we are salt that salts, walking in freedom, abiding in Christ, then we need not be worried about all these things. He will call us to work, to be sure, and show us our task. And also show us where we can find our relaxation, and in what art we may find diversion.

• Art and entertainment on radio and television[238]

It is the tragic story of the cultural crusader in a mass society that he cannot win but that we would be lost without him.[239]

Inventions never just happen by accident and without a deeper background. Thus books were only printed for the first time in the fifteenth century despite the fact that textiles were already printed in Europe during the fourteenth century and woodcuts since around 1400. From a technical standpoint the 'invention' could have happened earlier than it did. Where the need is born, inventions follow so that things may be done as efficiently as possible. That also helps to explain the rapid spread and general application of this new means of communication during that period. It is worth reflecting more extensively on this in order to gain a better insight into the importance of the invention of radio and television in our own time.

We will not here explore the circumstances that led to the printed book but it will be useful to notice the effects. It affected our Western civilization profoundly. The first thing we notice is that large groups of people were introduced to matters into which they previously had no entry. Their horizons were broadened and they read extensively about matters they previously perhaps would only have heard rumours about. Their horizons were broadened, perhaps much more so by this invention than by the discovery of America. The importance of the discovery of 1492, in contrast to that made much earlier by the Vikings, can be largely attributed to the printing press, which made it possible for knowledge to become common property in that part of the world. It was accordingly also named after one of the first people to write about it in a book, Amerigo Vespucci.

But the book brought about more than that. It became the means par excellence for propagating thoughts and ideas. The influence of the live speech of the master became less important than the publication of a book whereby many could be informed in a short time about new developments. But gradually the book also became a means of diversion, at various levels. Cats's *Sinne- en Minnebeelden* [or 'amorous sketches'] were certainly not written as a textbook, but for entertainment, as light literature. We need not doubt that alongside the many good books that appeared a great deal that was dubious also came from the presses. Pornography, for example, is not an invention of our [twentieth] century.

The book was of formidable importance in the fierce and profound spiritual conflict of the sixteenth century. Neither humanism nor the Reformation would have gained the prominence they did if they had arisen two centuries earlier. Perhaps we may even conjecture that the Reformation would not have become the broad and deep popular movement that it did without the book! Nevertheless, we can imagine a debate that might have taken place in about AD 1500 in which the printed book would not necessarily have been judged positively only. The inquisitor might perhaps as the first speaker have called attention to the danger of the spreading of heretical ideas, from his point of view rightly so. As a result, an index of forbidden books was soon initiated. But the book as such could also be subjected to criticism. Let us listen to the reservations of the (fictive) cultural critic of those times: 'The book makes people passive, brings them everything without their having to do anything for it and creates a situation in which they simply swallow uncritically everything that comes along. The book turns people inward upon themselves, thus endangering family life! Family members just sit in their own little corners clutching their own little books. Communal bonds will break down as a result. And then of course there is the risk of levelling down; to exploit the book economically people have to look to the larger markets and hence lower the level. The popularization of science is a menace to science itself. The book will undoubtedly have a morally corrupting effect: it passes forward all the sins of all the ages, and who will stem the flood? Will democratization not precipitate the revolt of the hordes? And finally, what is printed acquires authority, which leads to the vitiation of judgment: are readers really in a position to read critically and to understand that not everything that is printed is also true?' That this last argument is partially justifiable but also incorrect will be clear to us if we think of the [Dutch] expression: 'You are lying as if it were printed!'

The cultural divide

I have mentioned this little piece of cultural history not only to make clear that there is nothing new under the sun.[240] But also to show that if there is talk, and rightly so, about the danger of levelling down and that if criticism is voiced, and rightly so, against the level of entertainment broadcast via radio and television, this is not due to these media but the cause must be sought much deeper. It must be sought in the structure of our culture itself. Moreover, it can already be stated that the sombre expectations have proven to be only partly correct and that people have actually begun to read more rather than less since TV came along – and probably even more since the advent of radio. Television will have to win a legitimate place in our culture in the same way that the book and the radio did.

This is all part of the history of civilization or will soon become so. It is therefore incorrect to speak of culture and then of radio and television as if these were two entirely different things. Culture, the actual forming activity, and civilization, the result of that cultural work, are not separate fields nor can they be restricted to Art with a capital A (that difficult, elevated, deep and serious business that 'goes over the head' of the ordinary person) and science (in which 'people' cannot even be educated but only exposed to some of the popularized results). Arts and sciences are distinct fields within our civilization, no doubt, but if a small, esoteric group takes it into their heads that these fields alone constitute culture and that their coterie alone participate in it – condescending to the hosts of people who know nothing of this law even while desiring to initiate them into it by the distribution of culture – then something is wrong in civilization. In that case, paradoxically, art (and to some extent science) is set outside reality and as a consequence loses its place in culture. Its place is then just with an 'avant-garde,' reinforced perhaps by a group of snobs seeking to use art as a status symbol. 'Culture' is then only for an upper crust of intellectuals and financiers. If that is so, however, then a division has opened up in our culture that is damaging to all.

It is worth noting that shows staged for the masses – and this is what people often think of nowadays in connection with TV entertainment – are not unique to our time. There have been spectacular public showpieces in every age. We find traces of their history in books from the 'Cultural History' shelf. Also in earlier times ordinary people were treated to visual diversions. They saw plays at their annual markets (somewhat comparable to our fairs, the final vestige of these events). Perhaps the performances were rude and rather shallow at times; certainly they were seldom of high quality. But today we call such things folklore! And of course all things human were appreciated by these ancestral generations. For example, they liked to watch executions, which were carried out in public. 'Sensationalism' we would call that today. Yet there was more. A ruler's solemn entry into a city called for constructing ceremonial gates and staging processions. The 'pageants' in London in the sixteenth century celebrating the annual entry of the mayor ('the Maire') were renowned. And when Ferdinand staged his entry into Antwerp in 1635 after his great triumph at Nördlingen during the Thirty Years War, triumphal gates and carriages were constructed and a magnificent spectacle was mounted that we would unreservedly call Baroque today, a first-rate cultural manifestation. Rubens actively worked on the whole event, designing the triumphal gates and much more. In fact, we constantly encounter the names of great artists in connection with such occasions. Art, 'culture', had not yet elevated itself to great heights away from the common folk. In those days fireworks were a powerful spectacle worked on by the best artists and organized on every occasion people could devise. This art too is languishing in our time, partly because artists are too 'cultural' to bother about it.

Furthermore, funerals of rulers and the great of this world were 'staged' with the greatest possible splendour. I would also like to say a few words about music. Naturally, there was court music and there was intimate chamber music for the more refined nobility, but besides that, in Germany for example in the seventeenth and eighteenth centuries, music was literally blown from the tower every day and musicians were hired to play at every festive occasion. This sort of music was neither low nor poor. To the contrary. A municipal musician saw to it, an artist who was appointed to look after public music. If we perform this type of music today it would be taken up in a 'classical' programme. Yet even Bach's music was not 'culture' (understood as the opposite of 'popular'). A great deal of his music was church music and it was performed during church services. In all these cases the norm was undoubtedly upheld that the music should fit the occasion and that its function had to be kept in mind. These examples show that in earlier times the public was offered a great deal to see and hear that was by no means 'cultureless' or less worthy in quality.

Radio and television were born in part out of a need that people have had in all ages for such entertainment. Today we use technology to make this kind of enjoyment available to everyone. The scale of our cities, the demise of pompous displays of princely power and the increased tempo of everyday life made it impossible to continue to do things in the seventeenth-century way, i.e. directly, publicly, and in our presence. Our times offer us radio and television instead. Another aspect that the invention of radio and television has stimulated and made culturally possible is the tendency for quick news coverage and information. The public, once they were involved by the book in the political and spiritual struggle, wanted to be kept up to date about the most recent developments. Thus the pamphlet, the little occasional brochure with the latest news and comment, and the polemical tract, designed to influence public opinion, also soon appeared on the scene. In the course of time these evolved into periodicals and newspapers. In the nineteenth century, partly out of a need for an exact and direct representation, people invented photography. A bit later the gramophone appeared, which made sound reproducible in a way similar to what photography did for the image and the book for the word. Finally, movies appeared as a dynamic kind of photography. By thinking in this line and perfecting one thing after another, people arrived first at the radio and then, much later (because the difficulties that had to be overcome were much greater) at television. Radio and television did not just happen. Their roots lie deep in our culture.

That there are problems and worries and even very real dangers need not be denied. Not only are they there; in fact, it could not be otherwise in our dispensation, between the Fall and the Day of the Lord. That does not mean we should simply sit down and accept the situation as it is, especially with respect to the peculiar problem of our time, namely, that the gap between 'culture' and entertainment has become so wide that it is difficult to realize quality in the latter and comprehensibility in the former. The narrowing of the meaning of the term 'culture' is already indicative of the problem.

Well then, what does radio mean as a cultural factor? Much, very much. With respect to music, to choose an example, radio has brought thousands into contact with music and genres of music that they seldom if ever otherwise experienced. Who heard the best orchestras in about 1920? Small groups in the largest cities. Who today? Everyone who will turn on the radio. That may truly be called a positive development; it has fulfilled a long cherished desire borne out of love for one's neighbour, namely the wish: 'If only others could have experienced it too.' But there is more. This development has also stirred the musical world. Competition arose between orchestras and soloists in a way that had never been possible before and their achievements thereby grew steadily. Radio stimulated the study of music and (with the gramophone) broadened our musical horizon. We can now hear stylistically pure renditions of seventeenth-century and even older music, and our knowledge of exotic musical genres has exploded from virtually nothing into something that is by now quite extensive. By 'we' I mean in the first place those who are simply interested in music and for whom it has become attainable, but I also mean professional musicians who now have a chance to be active in areas where previously they seldom had any opportunity.

Naturally there are also some negative aspects to be considered. More than in earlier times a 'star' system has developed, together with a spoiled public who want to listen only to the music of established great interpreters. As a consequence less value can be attached to amateur performances, and that is a pity not only for the amateurs but also for the listeners. Do not forget the saying: 'One who cannot appreciate what is small is not worthy of what is great.' The worst of it however is that as a result of this situation 'people' engage much less today than they used to in actively making music themselves. Certainly contemporary music, which is often very difficult to perform, has moved beyond the scope of the many musicians who play or perform mainly for their own enjoyment.

That last observation brings us to a very difficult problem that has much deeper roots than the ones we have mentioned thus far; the implications reach well beyond the world of active non-professional musicians. Nowadays just listening to contemporary music is a pleasure for a small group of the initiated only. Moreover, a similar phenomenon is discernible in virtually all fields of art. Who for example can read James Joyce's *Work in Progress* with understanding and pleasure? And modern poetry? The problem stated here is not new. It is a legacy of the nineteenth century. It was then that the division in civilization mentioned above began: artists became bohemians, estranged from reality, dwelling high upon a pedestal, alone and not understood. That they built an ivory tower around themselves did little to change this situation except cosmetically.

Besides this, a second break occurred in the nineteenth century, this time in the social structure of society. The divisions are connected but it is not an easy matter to show their relation to each other. The causes of these divisions, gaping wounds in our culture, must be sought in the Industrial Revolution, in Romanticism and in positivism. The Industrial Revolution that began towards the end of the eighteenth century created a proletariat of masses in wage slavery to whom every cultural activity and also all art and artistry were foreign. Without idealizing the period that preceded this era – certainly not in pre-Revolutionary France – we can nevertheless say that the guilds, the many feast days (which were public holidays) and in general the artisanship, whereby there was a direct link between maker and end product, prevented massification of the workforce. The artisan who participated in creating beautiful things – furniture, pottery and porcelain, parts of buildings, etc. – was not spiritually and intellectually detached from the fruits of his or her labour: one knew what one was doing and could appreciate its value. Anyone who looks at the quality of even the smallest ornament in a German Baroque church building, for example, knows what we are talking about. For all its grandeur and courtliness there is still something of a folk character in this art. Besides, churches and palaces were not only for the ruler but were certainly meant also to impress ordinary people. Socially speaking, the guilds too were institutions which protected the artisans and guaranteed them a meaningful place in the greater societal whole.

That changed with the coming of factories with their machines and modern capitalism. Impoverishment followed – labour had to be cheap in order to be 'economical' – and the link became minimal between a worker and his or her work and the larger whole. Poverty held the trump card not only in an economic but also in a cultural sense. These factory workers knew virtually no beauty or joy anymore. Since the end of the nineteenth century a tremendous amount has been done about the economic emancipation of factory workers, yet their societal and cultural elevation has only recently started. Here lie many of the difficulties of our time, the fruits of misgovernment in the past. Work will have to be done towards a solution. It is therefore better and more modest not to speak of 'the masses' and the 'mass person who is incorrigible and cultureless'. For in the nature of the case that is both incorrect and uncharitable. Equally superficial is the notion that the solution is to distribute culture by handing out 'our' culture, that of an elite, to these indigent souls of yesterday.

Nature vs. freedom

The first of the divisions in our culture as mentioned above has been described from many standpoints in numerous studies of the crisis in our culture. It is likewise a fruit of the nineteenth century and then of Romanticism and positivism alike. We shall not set about analysing this complex segment of cultural history here, but we do want to refer to its results. An inner contradiction inherent in seventeenth- and eighteenth-century philosophy developed into a reality, a crack in the cultural edifice. It can be characterized with the words 'nature' and 'freedom'. 'Freedom' was orientated towards the free human personality, in response to which Romanticism in particular developed. Its ideal was the ingenious artistic creation. By 'nature' we mean the natural scientific attitude that in close association with technology works towards controlling reality. Here people make use of the fixed laws of nature, 'applying' them ever more widely. Impressive results have been booked but at the same time human freedom has come under pressure. For through such sciences as economics people have undertaken to control their own fields of society and economic life in the manner of the natural sciences. This is the core of positivism. All of this has undoubtedly been done with the best of intentions. Yet it is feasible only if people are willing to behave like little cogs in a machine, like numbers in a computer.

Human freedom, following in the footsteps of Romanticism, seeks refuge in the arts. Art becomes virtually a kind of religion, the place where 'people' – not numbers in a computer – can manifest themselves. In the life of society they must assume their regular places, to be sure, but in the area of art they can proclaim with freedom that in the deepest sense they do not submit to being dominated by these law-like regularities and that they find this world bad, rotten and intolerable precisely because everything truly human is alien to it. This posture of protest explains a great deal about modern art and its constant complaint, expressed in many ways, that our world is dark and menacing to humanity, a hell here and now. To all intents and purposes technology and the 'social' sciences – sciences practised in a positivistic way – offer people affluence, leisure and control over nature; but they are unable to give any real meaning to it all. People do not know what to do with it and experience it as menacing, yet they do not want to part with it.

These ruptures, these inner contradictions in our culture, stand out clearly when we consider a modern rotary press. In a minimum of time these machines can turn out a tremendous number of beautifully printed periodicals containing multi-coloured reproductions. In short, they are technically out of the top drawer. Yet who is going to make meaningful use of these possibilities, who is going to write articles of a high standard or make illustrations befitting the medium, such that the greater public for whom all this is intended can indeed enjoy it, recognize the sense of it and actually be served by it? As a result of the two divisions, the inner contradictions within our culture, what people achieve with this press can sometimes only be described as pitiful. It is virtually impossible to identify a solution that can lead to optimum use of these almost perfect machines with their splendid possibilities. What rolls from the presses is usually 'mass pulp' of questionable content or the occasional magazine slanted towards a more intellectually elite public, but then often wry and far from elevating in content. This is the case with a few positive – but then also expensive – exceptions. In these exceptional cases, however, one often still feels like a guest in a group of snobs. In short, there is trouble and 'crisis' enough.

An incidental difficulty is that these contradictions, the two poles between which the fault lines run, have a tendency to reinforce themselves. Is there not talk today of the danger that the masses will truly become the masses through television, something made all the more likely by programming aimed exclusively at what 'cultureless people' demand? And does positivistically-oriented science not steadily draw more areas into its sphere, thus strengthening its power through new 'triumphs of science and technology' so that it begins to look as if everything must eventually end after all in the world described by Orwell or by Huxley in his *Brave New World*? And in the face of all this is modern art not increasingly esoteric and are its posture of protest, its flight from the world and its sense of meaninglessness not increasingly transparent, and is it not drifting ever further away from 'people' as a result? From this perspective the last great manifestation held in the Stedelijk Museum of Modern Art in Amsterdam, entitled 'Nul Negentienzesenvijftig' ('Zero 1965'), is a handwriting on the wall.

Yet there is no reason for us to resign ourselves fatalistically and to do nothing. For in cultural life nothing happens automatically. Moreover, people do not control the structure of this world, the given character of the creation. There are other forces and powers at work in our world. Our Western society and culture are shaped by more factors than just the humanism in crisis and the social divisions to which we have referred. Though we are not able to be optimistic either, we should take proper notice of the fact that the state of affairs that we have described is clearly determined in part by an ever deepening and broadening apostasy, a forgetting of the blessings and abundance bestowed on us by the Lord. One can already discern something of God's judgment in the confused cultural situation, in the anxiety, the despair, the loneliness, in short, in the crisis of our civilization. We may fear that he will strike our Western world even more sharply. Upon reading the Old Testament prophets one is struck by how applicable they are to our times, which is anything but reassuring; and that is only underscored again by the Revelation of John.

Into this world came radio and television. They were new factors in our civilization. As media they must inevitably reflect our civilization.

Radio and television cannot be wiser or deeper or more beautiful but neither can they be worse or more negative than our complex times. Naturally, they can have an accelerating effect, both for better or for worse. What remains is the responsibility of those who have acquired positions of responsibility in the industry. Television in particular, which is a more complete medium than radio – combining word and image – is a cultural medium of importance, and what radio has meant and still means will apply to a greater extent to television as well.

What can television – to restrict our attention to that – accomplish and what is it in fact accomplishing? In the first place there is the tremendous broadening of our field of vision, of our horizon of experience. Just as radio touched the musical life of our time in ever so many ways, so television is doing with respect to film and theatre. It is to be anticipated, for example, that in the course of the years we will be able to experience a further disclosure of the dramatic repertoire, that from the past not just Shakespeare but a great deal more will be brought into our current cultural domain. Whatever of importance is to be found there is known at the moment only to a handful of experts, and even then only very sketchily. Through this broadening of the cultural horizon people are informed about many matters of which they previously had little notion. Ballet is often mentioned as an example of this.

In many respects television – in this regard like speeches or lectures – will be able to do no more than convey people to the threshold. It can offer people a taste of the world of the visual arts, for example; but one only becomes an art lover by actively going to explore in museums oneself. One can inform viewers about the latest movements in literature or even science, but they have to think along actively for themselves if they want to be culturally 'with it'. That television has already had such an effect to some extent is revealed by the fact, as reported above, that more and better books are being sold.

We will not discuss here the direct importance of television for political and societal life as this was again illustrated by the decisive appearance on television recently of Claus von Amsberg [at that time the German fiancé of Beatrix, later Queen of the Netherlands] and its immediate impact on Dutch public opinion. Television brings us into direct contact with the questions of the day. In the fields of spiritual and intellectual life and the arts, however, we may soon find ourselves drowning in a sea of current events. The task of television for these areas must therefore be to illuminate backgrounds, provide surveys and report on developments. In this respect television can better be compared with a periodical than with a daily newspaper. That is also because there are many matters today that people call 'cultural' but to which they can only devote limited time. Television must provide material for discussion, enhance our competence to form opinions, strengthen if possible our sense of norm, and in this way contribute to the healing of one of the divisions in our culture, namely, the one between the 'cultureless masses' and the 'culture-bearing elite'. Radio offers essentially the same possibilities, although some areas may be more suited to one medium than the other.

Change of mentality

That 'culture' might once again be a common good, shared by everyone, and that we might all participate once again in cultural life, and that our civilization might once again be unified in this respect, will not happen by itself. 'The distribution of culture' is not the solution either, because it is too simplistic and too one-directional and because those on the receiving end are exaggeratedly perceived as immature. In contrast to this, I believe two things are needed. First, 'culture' must get down, off its pedestal. As long as much modern music makes listeners sit on pins and needles confronted by a high-cultural, extremely complicated whole from which rhythm and melody have virtually vanished and in which the harmony is abrasive, and as long as in and through art people are confronted with nausea, with a throw-the-bone-into-the-bourgeois-chicken-coop mentality, and as long as art is intended to undermine norms and values – modern art sometimes brings 2 Thessalonians 2 to mind – and as long as art is art for fellow artists, in short, as long as art refuses to serve one's fellow human beings with what is beautiful, true and good, we cannot expect people (outside a small circle of highbrow initiates) to show much real interest in it. That 'the public' definitely is interested however and that not everything has to be 'easy' is shown by the success, also in terms of numbers, of the exhibitions of the works by van Gogh and Rembrandt and performances of Bach's *St Matthew Passion* and the like, and by the fact that in London, for example, Shakespeare still always draws sell-out audiences. Implicit in all this is a critique of what is being produced today, although this is often overlooked. In short, even with respect to artistic activity the commandment to love one's neighbour applies. All this is possible but it requires a change in mentality. Something like this has happened before in history. The intellectualism and courtly aestheticism of the Mannerist art of the sixteenth century – which in spite of its restoration to a place of respect in professional circles is today still considered strange and is therefore unknown to the wider public – was followed by the Baroque, an art undeniably popular in character yet without any concessions in quality and artistry. This Baroque is the fruit of the work of a dedicated group, a movement of people who were not satisfied with the state of affairs.

Two things are necessary, we said. Not only must those who are culturally active get off their pedestal; the 'people' too must lay aside their prejudices. These prejudices are partly a consequence of the dizzying heights upon which art had ensconced itself, as if art is not something 'ordinary'. In this connection I am reminded for example of the remarkable phenomenon that classical music – by which we shall mean for the moment all music from before 1900, with the exception of folk music – has a reputation for being serious, heavy, difficult and practically indigestible, in short, the opposite of cheerful. We are thus surprised again and again by the remarkable fact that when the radio wants to broadcast a subdued programme on an occasion of national mourning, for example, it treats us to our surprise with a great many cheerful tunes: music from Telemann, Vivaldi, Bach, Mozart, and so on. Such misunderstandings exist, also in other fields. How many do not avoid museums for similar reasons?

If the division in our culture is to be healed, then art must be freed of its fishy 'cultural' taste. No longer may it serve as a class symbol. It will have to lose its aura of exclusivity and loftiness. For radio and television this is undoubtedly a tough assignment. The human and/or societal meaning and significance of what is offered will constantly have to be made implicitly clear. Perhaps in this way the other division in our culture can also gradually be healed, so that 'culture' is no longer the refuge of those intent on realizing their freedom in the face of technology and positivistic science. By the same token, technology truly will have to be made human again by being given a place of service in human life without reducing people to little cogs in a machine. To this end it can be useful to make clear to the public as well how beauty and artistry must be sought not only in the 'higher', the 'difficult' and the 'strange', but also in things near us, in industrial design, in furniture, in automobiles, in posters, and much more. We must show for example how typographers design the jackets for gramophone records. What is distinctive of art and everything that is artistic is not that it is high and far from us, but that it is beautiful. That 'beautiful' is not synonymous with 'old', with the past, speaks for itself.

Radio and television have already contributed a great deal in this sense, even if they have seldom done so intentionally. They can still do much more if they work consciously in this direction, even if the problem can or should seldom be posed explicitly. In a certain sense the solution must be shown in practise. This is probably easiest where radio and television are able to work out their own style and develop their own forms or 'language', as it were. It is more difficult to break through old prejudices, even where they are completely unfounded, than it is to convince people of the distinctive meaning, language and beauty of new forms of art. One does so not by talking about them but by doing them. That people in radio have already done some things in this direction is clear; as an example I mention the radio drama. In television people are also busy discovering the distinctive possibilities of the new medium. In the long run that will certainly lead to a new artistic language, a distinctive form. It is already apparent that the distinctive character of television is different from that of film, although there are many points of contact. Here however the word must be left to the experts, of whom I am not one.

Already now, after a decade of television, it has become clear that television by no means needs to make people passive. It can foster a critical spirit and stimulate wider interest. How lovely it would be if television eventually resulted in the active participation in culture of many. There was a time, in the nineteenth century, when workers worked and that was that. They worked themselves sometimes literally to death. A period followed when people had the time they needed for diversion, in the psychological and physical sense. Now, however, we increasingly find ourselves in a situation that affords many people an overabundance of free time.

Only a portion of this time needs to be devoted to relaxation in the strict sense. For the sake of the public mental health it is good and perhaps even necessary that this time be used for creative activity. Of course not everyone can take up art in one form or another, and that is also not necessary. For culture is more than art. In this way the work might be spread so that the burden of those engaged in 'culture' could be lightened. That would come about in part because some of the work would no longer be needed and in part because people could obtain help and support. It is still too early to say how this can all be worked out in practise. For the time being it may be a pipe dream. Yet it is good to think about it now. We must move away from the present situation where a very small circle 'gives' and countless hordes just take and consume.

It strikes me then as a good idea to establish contacts between 'consumers' and 'producers,' not in the spirit of a few meetings but directly and more actively, through television clubs, by actively engaging people in particular broadcasts, even if only behind the scenes with the preparations, the documentation, etc. In this way a direct exchange of ideas can be facilitated and people can build something up together instead of the one party having to wait to see what the other party has to offer. Briefly formulated, we must not only educate people so that they can recognize or understand what is best; we must also bring them along to the point that they are willing to participate.

We spoke, in passing, about diversion. We have already argued that what was offered visually in the form of pageants, fireworks and much more had a place of great importance in earlier times. It can have that now too. The demand for quality remains. And therefore it would be lovely if artists were to become active in the entertainment field once again. That fits in directly with the argument made above. For entertainment is not something that is not cultural; it is culture itself.

In the case of background music too – more the task of radio – we should not just think of something negative. There has been background music, in every age. Think of the ensemble in the restaurant. When we recall Haydn's *Surprise Symphony* – a striking drum stroke was worked into it just to call people's attention to the music – we are reminded that in those days even such symphonies were in many respects background music to be played at gatherings that we today might call 'parties', music meant to add colour to the life of 'high society'.

Quality must always be a primary goal, perhaps even more for 'light' than for 'heavy' programmes. Cabaret is also art, as is dance music or the work of an elocutionist or a stand-up comedian. One must not be satisfied here with anything that is not up to standard and fully responsible, lest one underestimate and even insult one's public. The norm is that what in the seventeenth century was called decorum should be taken into account, which is to say one should be mindful of the time, the place and the circumstances. At a parade one should play a fanfare and not Bach; at a party one should have a cabaret and not a 'heavy' play, and so forth. The distinction between light and heavy is really based on a misunderstanding, and one that has sometimes had fatal consequences, as I have already mentioned. There must be discrimination in the kind of art presented, keeping in mind the place, time and occasion: in deciding the length of the piece, the problem presented, the language used, the topicality, and more. Thus the difference lies not in the quality but in the genre.

A good entertainment programme is much more difficult to realize today than a good 'cultural' programme, if only because talented artists tend to shy away from it. To suggest a comparable example from the visual arts: many artists consider the field of illustration less worthy; it is work they do just to stay alive. In fact, illustration is a difficult assignment that calls upon all an artist's gifts and that should actually be considered particularly important. A good cartoonist is no less worthy than a person who turns out oil paintings for an exposition. Everyone must recognize his or her own gifts and talents in these matters.

Radio and television can play a role of great importance in our culture. Naturally they will remain an influence alongside others. We may not expect that the world can or will suddenly be changed by these media. They certainly exert an influence, even if it is often not measurable. For television to be truly integrated into our culture it is needful that people really learn to see. In practise this actually turns out to be quite difficult, perhaps precisely because it seems to be so easy, learning to see, just as people must 'learn' to see films and paintings. It involves learning to recognize the means used by presenters, how they apply them, what effects they achieve. Here is a task for education. In instructional music programmes people compare different renditions of the same composition. In the same way it is possible to show how different television producers do the lighting differently for the same subject, what the importance is of the camera person, etc. A great interest in the medium itself may be assumed, and knowledge of its possibilities and limitations is certainly neither undesirable nor superfluous. In this way people learn to watch critically and an awareness of norms is awakened in them. For then people become aware of the work of the television producer as such and assess it against norms such as truth (or objectivity or correctness if you prefer), purity, clarity in execution, and much more.

Perhaps this is all a pipe dream. Yet this too can be creative in its effect in much the same way that once, long ago, people dreamed of remotely transmitting pictures with the result that now, many years later, we have television. My dream can also only be realized in the long run, and perhaps never fully. Yet here, as in everything, the best is hardly good enough, and we may not allow ourselves to be satisfied too easily.

Christian broadcasting

What I have said until now I have framed in general terms. That is partly because radio and television more than any other medium are impossible to discuss with exclusive reference to one's own closed circle. Everyone can watch or listen to what they want and no one who broadcasts a programme can direct it exclusively to a small, selected group. Yet we want to turn our attention now to questions connected with Christian broadcasting. Let us get right into it by asserting that our group is by no means prepared for its task. Our puritanism, our never flagging seriousness and resolute seclusion, or rather our distrust of everything that could be called art or diversion, has meant that in our circle many areas were left to lie fallow. A great deal of talent was nipped in the bud. As a result we hardly had a tradition and certainly no common consensus about questions of form, style, themes, and normativity in these areas. We scarcely thought about it, let alone got involved in it. We were often negative only. It does not seem necessary to elaborate, and we will not try to trace the causes. Everyone who is not a stranger in Jerusalem knows these things. That is why the work the NCRV has taken upon itself is so courageous and so exceptionally difficult. Thus we must certainly not deny praise to those who have done pioneering work here, who are in essence still pioneers.

These matters are all the more difficult and all the more important because in constantly increasing measure it is precisely in the fields of art and diversion, which people call 'culture', that the spiritual struggle will be waged in the future. That is inevitable. The possibilities for actively deploying oneself 'culturally' will increase with every expansion of our free time. Precisely because the struggle will be about the face of our culture in the future, with the spiritual movements presenting themselves and exercising influence via radio and television – where performances of all sorts more than thetical explanations of principles and ideas will be important – it is in this field that the battle about the spirit of the age will be fought, a battle that is about cultural power, at bottom with people's souls at stake. What the world of the future will be, neo-humanistic, neo-paganistic or essentially Christian, will in an important measure be decided here.

Given our negative past this unavoidable situation confronts us as Christians with dreadful dangers that are not theoretical. The negativism could persist. One sees this happening. The remarkable thing about it is that precisely because people are unarmed and want to stay so, they swallow and accept everything indiscriminately. Often they have built a wall around their own group, a wall of commandments and prohibitions having a strongly legalistic character, intended for self-protection. The wall works effectively only, however, in keeping people out. The legalistic character of the prevalent morality in the orthodox Protestant churches does great damage to the outreaching character of the congregation. Yet this wall is not effective against spiritual dangers, against what Paul called spiritual powers in the air. People swallow everything, virtually uncritically, because in a certain sense they have placed it beyond the reach of criticism (while at the same time when anyone from their own circle does or says something that seems to slightly overstep the correct or supposed boundaries they are immediately ready to offer a fierce critique).

People often also fail to grasp the spiritual thrust of what is offered. For they have their commandments, their rules and regulations, to be sure, but they have never learned to apply them to the 'cultural' matters that now confront them. Only seldom do their commandments have any bearing on these, since in this regard the only rule was really the negative one of abstinence. This attitude is very difficult to fathom and definitely far from consistent. Certainly it is dangerous. Various writers have called attention to the fact, and rightly so, that modern means of mass communication, given their frequency and usually unstated spiritual bias, mean a kind of brainwashing. Surely this has already slain its thousands, and the deepening de-christianization and depopulation of the churches are unquestionably partly attributable to it.

The negativism mentioned above has never been creative in the fields of art and entertainment. There is no way that it could be. Therefore those who desire to be active in one way or another in these areas that are so important for our times naturally can no longer support that negativism in their lives. In that case another danger threatens that we could call 'culturism': a surrendering of oneself with hide and hair to the latest trend and a hurling of oneself with uncritical abandon into what the world offers as current and 'important'. This position can only be maintained if people have no clear norms of their own and if they close their eyes to the ideological content of many of the products of modern culture. Culturism goes hand in hand with neutralism, which means that in a certain sense people throw themselves away, while also misjudging the artists and their brainchild and failing to recognize their value. The danger is not inconceivable that they will fall into a sort of snobbery, which is always false and without a proper style of its own. Because those who become caught up in culturism often have a strongly negative view of everything their own background has to offer them, they adopt a strongly emotional posture and proceed to judge harshly everyone who prefers not to share their culturism, criticizing them in terms that even by worldly standards of civility would be considered discourteous, uncharitable and unfair. In short, it is an attitude that may be understandable, but that can be dangerous and unedifying particularly for those who have worked themselves into this reactionary frame of mind. It is the consequence of a cultural short circuit. Thus they cannot be expected to manifest cultural creativity in the Christian sense.

For those who do truly want to participate in a Christian work in these cultural areas and who believe they have a calling to fulfil in radio and television, the work is like sailing between Scylla and Charybdis. Either one falls into a rigid orthodoxy that is harsh and sometimes tactless, which serves no one and which is experienced by 'the world' as uncharitable or unreal, or – and that is an even greater danger – one forfeits one's own identity by neglecting to show one's true colours. In essence those who do this deny their Saviour. They are afraid to uphold a fixed norm out of a (justifiable) fear of the first attitude. But our work will be judged in the light of our claim to be Christians. The viewer or listener is often very finely attuned to such matters. They will not mind if occasionally we miss the mark, but they will mind if we either just go along with 'the world' or else adopt a legalistic attitude that manifests a lack of love. We must never forget that, particularly in the Netherlands, 'the world' is made up for a large part of people who only just recently became estranged from the church and nevertheless still often maintain direct contacts with it. Hence they understand exactly what is going on and they watch it closely.

We must have a stance of our own, a Christian one. That we are Christians will have to be made clear, however, not so much from the criticism we have of the work of others as from the positive work that we do ourselves. Certainly the criticism in question is necessary and will have to be expressed from time to time, if only it is positively stated, fair, founded and not levelled without love. Yet we shall have to demonstrate that our being Christians does not mean we subscribe to an outdated cultural pattern, that we cannot cope with the problems of our time, and that we are creatively sterile.

So our being Christians also goes into the crucible. What is just external show, outdated, all that is merely manners and customs and that is not fully biblically founded, in short, all that is not directly from the root of the Christian life, the relationship with Jesus Christ (cf. John 15:4), may not be permitted to determine our own stance. All must be tested anew and nothing may be kept if unfounded. In this day and age, when the world around us is on the move and we are confronted with entirely new challenges, we may certainly not just cling to traditions. Yet our times also preclude every synthesis, every accommodation to the spirit of the age.

Only a radical Christianity can render Christian work, including cultural work, meaningful. Such work can only exist as a fruit of faith, a trusting in the Lord and listening reverently to his word, a life in which the realities found in the gospels and the epistles of the New Testament are really taken into account – a living belief that saturates everything, that works as leaven and that in love and out of a sense of calling places itself in the service of the Master. This is more than having a world view. Non-Christians also have theirs, and in this respect we are alike. One who is wise will glory in knowing the Lord (Jeremiah 9:23, 24). That may not be taken as just so many pious words; it must essentially and really determine our work, not as a little 'extra' or as a Christian flavouring, but as something implicitly (and where necessary also explicitly) visible in our activities. Then we can also be genuinely creative in a Christian sense.

In our thinking about these matters and in our creative work there is however often still another legacy from the past that hinders us, namely, a theology or cultural theory that splits life in two. A very old and decisive notion, which surfaced soon after the Reformation, is that a realm of faith, of grace, of piety is separated from a natural realm where ethical norms obtain which are not essentially determined by our relationship with God. Just how strong the effects of this legacy may be is made clear again and again when people talk about Bible reading, psalm singing, theology and church history as Christian programming, while continuing to regard an 'ordinary' music programme as something neutral where the most we can demand is quality. Precisely because of this strong tradition a virtually endless debate is raging about 'what can be called Christian art and entertainment'. In the process people quickly forget that non-cultic matters too belong to a part of creation over which Christ as our God and Lord reigns, so that it cannot be considered apart from him without dishonouring him and his glory. Elsewhere[241] I have tried to elaborate this, partly by showing how the norm, also for art and entertainment, is to be found in Philippians 4:8: 'Whatever is true, whatever is honourable, whatever is right, whatever is pure, whatever is lovely, whatever is of good repute; if there is any virtue and if anything worthy of praise, let your mind dwell on these things.'

Some of these terms may perhaps bring with them old-fashioned and in a certain sense loaded connotations, whereby this scriptural passage could be misunderstood; yet in our opinion, if the passage is well thought through, it provides a guideline for our work in the artistic sector. If we work in this way, then what we form creatively ourselves or what we retrieve from the rich treasures of art past and present, with a capital A or a small one, can decidedly not be separated from our being children of God. In these matters too we must bring forth the fruit of faith, which will be characterized by 'love, joy, peace, patience, kindness, goodness, faithfulness, and self-control' (Galatians 5:22). If we hunger and thirst after righteousness in this way, we are truly active in a

Christian way, even if that is with a radio detective story, a work of instrumental music, a cabaret programme or a news documentary.

Radio and television belong to the technical kit of our times. We have to use them. Naturally we may not expect everything of this work alone – it is no panacea. The problems are extremely complex. But we must do what our hands find to do. Living in faith, bringing forth the fruits of faith, stumbling and rising we shall have to show what our being Christians is worth. In this way we can be salt that salts and make our little contribution to the new culture that is under construction. If the Lord desires to bless this difficult work, then perhaps it can even be decisive. Everyone who is active in this field must be able to justify her or his own work and strive for optimal quality.

Not only the workers in these fields, but also those who want to support and help them in their work must pray for wisdom and insight, for talents and gifts, for the gift of the Holy Spirit and for renewal, awakening and reformation, for it is only from a living Christianity that this work can really be meaningfully done. If even in the Protestant world there are much uncertainty and crisis, unbelief and a lack of faith, unresolved problems and a lack of unity of spirit, then that will cripple the work and make it all the more difficult. Moreover, the work cannot succeed without competent personnel and pertinent insight into the matters at hand. Therefore there is a great deal of work to be done in our Protestant world. Study is indispensable, study of the possibilities and techniques. A search must be made for the treasures of the past and the present with which we can meaningfully fill our programmes, accompanied by evaluating, sifting, judging and deciding. A contribution will have to be made to educating listeners for maturity, beginning in our own circle. Perhaps first of all by appealing to their maturity. Perhaps in this way the negativism referred to above can gradually be overcome and there can be a breakthrough. Yet we must also not lose sight of the other listeners.

We shall have to reflect upon such issues as Christian freedom and questions concerning the importance and distinctiveness of Christian cultural work. In short, despite our rich past we still stand in many respects at the beginning. Certainly that is also because the challenge before us is new in many respects. It is good to know that these things are being worked on in NCRV circles. We may be grateful for what they are doing and for what they have already accomplished. We must remember that a Christian broadcasting company cannot be perfect, but that it is defined in the first place by the spirit in which its people work. Perfectionism, the demand for perfection, is often linked to legalism instead of Christian virtue. Thus we are free to have our criticisms as long as these are meek, long-suffering and edifying.

The task confronting Christian broadcasting is immensely difficult and demanding. At stake is the face of Christianity in our century, in connection with which the use of the new media can be decisive in many respects. Perhaps this work has even more far-reaching perspectives. 'Ora et labora!'

• On Art and Entertainment: a response letter[242]

In response to the series of six articles that appeared in *De Sleutel* about prof. Dr H.R. Rookmaaker's book *Art and Entertainment*, the author wrote an extensive letter in which he addresses the various questions and comments. We ask your full consideration for this reaction. For the sake of good order, we would note that the six articles were published in *De Sleutel* in September, October and December 1964 and January, March and April 1965.

To The Editors, De Sleutel

Dear Mr Molenaar,

In what follows I would like to discuss a number of the points that you have raised. But above all else I want to thank you for the congenial and correct way in which you have reviewed my book. I wish that all discussions in the church press – to limit ourselves to that – were conducted in such a way. I shall accordingly respond only to a few points where you have raised a question or where I have the impression that you have not understood me entirely correctly.

In the first place, in the January number you expressed some reservations about the fact that I treat art and entertainment in principle as being equivalent. Thus I would like to offer some comments here that will hopefully serve to clarify my position. It is obvious that I was not talking about football, camping and comparable forms of leisure time activity. To my mind these were never regarded as forms of entertainment. I did include what is offered to us via the radio and television. And then it is unmistakable that the greater part of that is 'artful': drama, music or performance. By entertainment I also meant light novels, stories and illustrations, and also cartoons and the like. I meant to assert that in principle there is no difference between a drawing made as an illustration and a painting in a museum, no difference between a play by Shakespeare and a performance for young people, no difference between a television drama loaded with weighty problems and a little skit presented as part of a children's programme. Structurally they are the same. Music is music, whether we are talking about Bach or Beethoven, Hindemith or Duke Ellington, Badings or the Beatles. In taking this approach it was not my intention to elevate entertainment, but rather to make clear that truly good entertainment cannot be cheap or inferior, so that the norm that applies for it may be all the clearer. It is also not the case that art alone presents a view of reality or that art alone proceeds from a view of reality. On the contrary, the same is true for entertainment. For many people, entertainment is in fact the only art with which they will ever come into contact.

What I meant to underscore is that art is really entertainment. The difficulty is that in our times the term 'entertainment' has acquired ugly connotations because so much that is on offer is below standard. People play a concert by Bach because of the enjoyment or pleasure it gives them. I do have my reservations using the term 'pleasure' here – as if people like myself who deal professionally with art would be 'pleasure-seekers' – but I know of no better term. Yet I wrote that the difference between art and entertainment lies not in the structure but in the function; this is a matter of time and occasion, for whom and when, as you so ably summarized in one of the first parts of your study. Bach and Mozart also composed music to be enjoyed on special occasions – and not for concerts as we now know them, with a museum-like quality about them. And in visual art there is also a difference in function between a cartoon, an illustration, a painting to hang on the wall (where even the intended room makes a difference), a mural in a public building, or the decoration of an exhibition hall. Every specific function confronts the artist with the problem: how do I satisfy the demands of the assigned situation. Thus there may be differences in the point of departure, depending on the function for which the commission is intended, but not between art and entertainment.

Ultimately it is thus not a question of elevating entertainment but rather of soberly assigning art its place. Without a pedestal, without an aureole, without all that 'extra', art is already important enough. The point is to give art once again its proper place in life, to remove it from the museum atmosphere, in short to let art be what it once actually was. This misplacement of art goes together with an almost religious role that people assign to art today. Art is revelation, an interpreter of the times; the artist is a prophet. I discussed this extensively in my inaugural address.[243] Precisely because the artist today no longer wants to or no longer is allowed to simply be an artist but is regarded instead as some kind of a priest or prophet, a great deal of trouble arises. Artists no longer want to lovingly serve their neighbour with art, but they want to interpret the times, which often means browbeating people with the 'rottenness' of their 'bourgeois existence'. They want to display the chaos, now that God no longer exists (in their subjective view).

Here lies the difficulty that you have with the last part of my book. I asserted that we ought not to concern ourselves with the subjective intentions of the artist but that we should simply enjoy what we are able to enjoy. It is clear that when cursing appears in a work of art – I took as an example a particular Picasso work – precious little pleasure will be gained from it. I believe that we may indeed enjoy art, in much the same way as the Scriptures enjoin us to rejoice with the wife of our youth [Proverbs 5:18]. To do that is not to put her on a pedestal. We may also speak of riches concerning art without giving it an aureole. For we are rich when we use the good gifts of God in a good way. Here centuries of education in which art was glorified deceive us. To repeat, what I desire of art is nothing more and nothing less than that art be what art is, namely an important facet of life, indispensable but in its proper place and in the proper time and way.

But let me return to the question of why we must not concern ourselves with the artist's own intentions. In the first place, the artists have their own responsibility before God. Perhaps they made a particular work out of pure self-interest, for glory or profit. I am not sure that I can see that, or hear it, or infer it from the words of a writer's book. That is also not necessary. It would distract us from the work before us. Moreover, we must be mindful that there are horrible works by extremely devout people and magnificent pieces by godless characters – there are some truly lovely Picassos. How that is possible is a question in itself. I personally do not believe that the theory of common grace provides a good answer. Whatever answer one gives, one has to be mindful that it is also proof of the brokenness of our world. Because of sin. We may not detach art from its background – my book shows that I do not want to do that – but the background seldom makes itself felt radically and consistently. And that is a good thing with respect to the works of the godless, and lamentable with respect to the works of believers. Let us not always be concerned with the artist. Often he or she is long dead and gone and it will be extremely difficult to learn anything meaningful about his or her inner life.

And if all that concerns us is the dialogue with the artist, then perhaps it would be better to go and have coffee with him or her. But the discussion or dialogue to which I referred is that with the work of art. It surprises us, opens our eyes to one facet or another – intended or not intended by the artist – and it offers us something beautiful. It can also offer us something repulsive, something expressing hatred. In that case we can only be sad or 'hunger and thirst after righteousness'.

What it boils down to is that we must oppose the subjectivistic way of criticizing, which always focuses on the artist, and instead concentrate on the artistic phenomenon. That will prevent us from falling into subjectivism and making judgments ungoverned by norms. I am convinced that judging the artist does lead to that. Naturally we must always interpret a work of art, and in doing that we are fallible people. There is simply no way out of that. But let us not forget that when we want to judge artists and engage them in discussion via their works we have to take an extra leap, because after interpreting the works we have to then go on and also interpret the intentions of their makers, or at least distil these from what we suppose we have observed.

I believe it is incorrect to think that in interpreting a work we project our own wisdom onto it. If a work of art allows that, then it falls short because it does not present its meaning clearly. We – Calvinists with an exceptionally verbal culture – are often fearful that we cannot see or hear a painting or music well. I believe that a work of art, once we have learned to 'read' it, is as clear as words, and sometimes even clearer. It is not necessary to regard visual images askance. Words are just as difficult to interpret.

Your example, finally, of the image of the idol is correct. It is evidence of the brokenness of our reality. When Nebuchadnezzar pronounced Babylon beautiful [cf. Isaiah 13:19], he was really right – but the city was full of idols. It is even so that the more artistic and beautiful an idol is, the more terrible it is. Think also of Greek sculpture, virtually all of which was in the service of the gods of the Greeks. Yet the *Venus* of *Milo* is unmistakably beautiful. Our association with the statue is quite subtle though, and not unequivocal. We detect in it something of an exaggerated glorification of humanity. In saying that, I am saying something about Greek culture. I know nothing at all about the artist who made the sculpture.

I have tried not to give the impression that these are simple problems. But let everyone set to work with the wisdom with which they have been endowed, without fear or reticence. As children of God – you represented me very well on that point – we will find the way, stumbling and picking ourselves up again from time to time, of course. But that is the case in everyone's life. Looking at art can be no exception. Arriving at a responsible and refined judgment without short-circuits – 'it is an idol and therefore it is "ugly"' – is something we really very much need to achieve in our times if we are to test the spirits and be salt that salts in the midst of our fellow human beings. I hope that these comments may serve to further the debate. Again, my heartfelt thanks for your contribution.

H.R.R.

The Westminster Discussions: Faith, Art, Culture and Lifestyle

Seven tapes of question-and-answer sessions were recorded at Westminster Theological Seminary in January 1976. In this edited version of the transcription the questions are concisely stated at the beginning of each discussion. Answers touching on the same topic have been grouped together.

What is art?

Question: What is art?

I would like to counter this question with another question: what is a tree? Do its many functions define a tree? I would say no, in the first place a tree is a tree because God made it to be a tree. It is a given, total entity that asks for no justification because the only justification for the tree is that God made it. And so we stand in front of the tree and say: 'Thank you Lord that you made the tree.'

Why is there marriage and love? People have said in the past that marriage is there because people need to produce children. What about a marriage without children? Is that not a marriage, or is it a bad marriage? Marriage defies definition in this way because that makes it utilitarian. People do not marry in order to produce children. And couples who do, don't understand what marriage and love mean. They make marriage too superficial because it is something much deeper. I can talk for hours about the importance of marriage and the family as social structures, for the deepening of the personality, and so on. But that is not what marriage is there for, just some of its many outcomes. What is marriage? There is only one way to approach it: God made it and therefore it does not need any justification. We cannot justify it by saying it is there for this or that. Then I would always say beware, because now we start making reality smaller than it is.

In the same way art can only be accepted from the hands of God, and we can only say thank you. Even so, art does many things in our world. For instance, it helps us to understand reality and it deepens our knowledge of reality. If you dare (because it is very hard work) to visit a museum in the way I try to do it then, when you get outside again after you've sat in front of a painting for two hours, you will say: 'Wow, I've never seen that the sky is so blue. Now only I begin to see the sky.' Because the painter has shown it to you – he or she has opened your eyes.

Let me give an example. One of the most intriguing things I have experienced in my life is that when I take people on a museum visit, especially women, their first remark when they come to fifteenth-century paintings of Mary and the Christchild is this: 'These babies are just like little old men. These painters didn't understand.' And then we walk on and come to Rubens and they say: 'These are like real babies.' I must say I think they have been brainwashed, or 'eyewashed', because their own babies are not like the little Hercules Rubens painted. Their babies are rather more akin to those of the fifteenth-century artists, who were much nearer to reality. But these women have learned to look at reality through the eyes of Rubens. In the same way literature gives us metaphors about reality, it deepens our understanding of reality and it enhances our grasp of the world. That is why Calvin Seerveld recently said that it is so important to tell fairytales to our children. They deepen a child's understanding and knowledge of reality. But this in itself does not justify literature and art. We cannot say that art is there to epistemologically make us understand reality better. That is too narrow. Sometimes it does that, but not always.

Art is also a means of embellishing our surroundings which is a very human thing to do. From the very beginning of history, people have built houses and decorated them with colours and shapes. People beautify things. Women wear earrings. Why? There is no answer to that. But these things do not need any justification because they belong to the aesthetic side of life. People always try to beautify their surroundings; it is the most natural thing to do, 'natural' because it is God-given.

Recently in Vancouver I became aware of another thing. What does one find hanging on the wall when one comes into a Vancouver home? A little painting of a waterfall from some twenty miles away. Or one comes into a farmer's home and finds he has a picture of a cow hanging on the wall, the very cow that is grazing outside the house. Or one comes into the home of a married couple and there is a photograph of their wedding in a very conspicuous place. Why? Is it silly? No it's not silly, for it helps people grasp reality. It opens our eyes and makes the things close to us more dear to us. As a teenager I went to England and from the moment I touched English soil felt very much at home. I often wondered why, and I think the answer is that as a younster I was very fond of English literature. I read many English novels and poems, so in a way I understood England better than my own country because I never read Dutch literature like that. Why did I want to go to America? Because I know the music of America so well. And in a way when I meet black people I feel at home with them because their music has taught me so much about them.

Art also opens our eyes to the beauty of nature. I don't know whether anybody in the Middle Ages was able to see the beauty of, say, a sunset or anything outside, for that matter, because they never painted it. It is interesting that around 1300, when the study of anatomy began, female sculptures for the first time began to show breasts. Before that time breasts were represented in a very subdued manner or not at all.

But at the moment when people began to be interested in the body, they started to depict these things in paintings and describe them in poems. Going back in history, how would a man have looked at a woman in the year 1000? Obviously he looked at her, because otherwise we wouldn't be here. But what did he look at? Well, there's no way of telling because we don't know. We don't see it in their art and we don't read it in their poems. Nobody talked about it. And it may be that because of that it had little reality for them. One of the functions of poetry is to name things, and by naming things they become important to us. Poetry deepens our understanding of reality; it makes it real for us. That is exactly what poems are there for or paintings, which are 'visual' poems.

Now, if we don't have a name for something, does it exist? In my surroundings, at L'Abri for instance, when a young couple plans to get married, I always have a little talk with them. And I tell them that in the man-woman relationship communication is very important and that this also means you have to give names to whatever is involved in the sexual side of the relationship. Of course there are the little definitions you find in medical textbooks, but that is not the type of language you use when talking to your wife or husband. You have to give names to these things because if there are no names for them, in a way they don't exist. The first few years you wouldn't find pain in that, but at a certain moment problems begin and then you have no way of communicating about them, because you have no words for these things. There are women who have become a mother many times over but who have never in their lives had a sexual experience. Of course they had sexual experiences in the sense that they had to undergo something. But they never integrated them into their lives; in a way they never lived them. Maybe we get too much information these days, which may kill some of the joy for us because it takes the discovery away. The joy of discovering, of giving names and of communicating are so important. And that is what poems and paintings help us do. Here I have a little criticism of modern art, which deals with all kinds of intellectual problems but tells us very little about reality; it closes reality to us. Consequently reality is brought to us through all kinds of very cheap information. That is one of the poverties of our time.

I would like to add a little story about seeing the beauty of the landscape around us. In the seventeenth century and before then, no one ever looked at mountains. Rather, when people had to travel from northern Europe to southern Europe they would draw the curtains when going over the High Alps because the mountains were too horrible to look at. One of the mistresses of Louis XIV was given a big palace somewhere in France. She became famous for her diaries and letters. In a letter to a friend she describes the gift of the king to her and she says:

> It's a beautiful, beautiful palace. When I open the windows to the west I see rolling hills and a lake. When I open the windows to the north I see orchards.

When I open the windows to the south I see more beautiful things. But I never open the windows to the east, because they look out on the Alps.

It was obvious to them that one does not look at the Alps. However, in the eighteenth century a new category was invented, or rather discovered because it meant a widening of experience. A new aesthetic quality was uncovered, namely the 'sublime', referring to the things that we stand in awe of. And precisely in 1803 for the first time in history people went to the Alps in order to experience them as a positive thing. If one looks in the guestbook from 1803 in the cabin on top of Mount Rigi, one finds the names of Goethe, Shelley, Coleridge, Turner and such people. They all rushed there to look at the mountains, fantastic! This was tied up with their thinking about the sublime.

Thinking, looking, art, philosophy and discussion: these all go together. Of course the change in reaction to the mountains was tied in with the Romantic movement. Today people stand before mountains and say: 'Look, how beautiful.' But I'm bound to say: 'Your eyes are closed, for you don't see anything or you wouldn't call them beautiful; you would say they are sublime! They are not in the same category as the nice dangling earring of that beautiful girl beside you.' We lose something when we lose awe.

Maybe there is a bit of romanticism and sentimentality in the typically Christian predilection for sunsets. However, the opening of our eyes to the beauties of nature is something we can be thankful for. The beauty of nature should matter to us. We try to grasp the meaning of the outside world, and if we do it in the right way we should hate pollution and the destruction of that beauty. I heard a horror story about a Christian college somewhere in this country, based in a building reached by a winding path through some woods. One day someone said: 'Isn't it awful that we have to drive all that way through the woods. Why don't we cut down the trees and make a straight path?' I would have answered that, yes, there is freedom to take away the trees. People are not the slave of nature; people are the master of nature. But neither is nature the slave of people, and one cannot kill trees just like that for utilitarian purposes, they are too beautiful. I think Christians have often been very insensitive in this. And if these people who are so insensitive then watch the setting sun and say it's so beautiful, I would ask whether that is not a bit sentimental? Because it's not part of their total experience.

I started out by saying that a tree is a tree and asks for no justification. A tree being a tree is loaded with meaning, and in history we, being human, try to grasp that meaning. In a way there is so much meaning that it is infinite and we will never be able to grasp it fully. I used the example of a tree because a tree fulfils many functions and has many ties to reality. It is the same with art. Art needs no justification. I cannot say art becomes good art only when it is useful for evangelism or education, or when it plays a role in the epistemological sense we have been discussing. Yet art also fulfils many functions and is tied with a thousand ties to reality.

In the eighteenth century people began to make art with a capital A: they tried to make art autonomous, 'art for art's sake', with no ties to reality. Art became a kind of idol, for itself, to itself, and this has impoverished art tremendously while in this way it falls short of its potential reality, the fullness of what art is and can be. It caused art to end up in museums and become far removed from everyday reality. The fact that art ends up in a gallery is so desperate, to begin with for the artists themselves. They try to say something, and what happens? I'm an exceptional man because I talk about the content of art but most art critics and art historians don't speak about that. So a person is shown around a museum of modern art and told that these artworks are telling one the same things that old art has said before, and one ends up brainwashed out of any understanding of what one is seeing.

What is our answer? That we should stop viewing art as something autonomous. That has caused so many splits in our culture, between high culture and popular culture, between fine art and the art we can buy in supermarkets (which is a kind of imitation of the fine arts), and then there is ceramics, etc. The same applies to music. No self-respecting musician would make popular music today, and because of that popular music has become of a very low standard. But if you are a black person you probably have little chance of making it into the better type of music, and so you have to make popular music. That is why black popular music is so fantastically strong, because the good people are working there.

So there are many strange problems in our culture. We have to think and work to solve these problems. They are not just Christian problems but problems of our culture in general; many people are working on them, and no one has yet been able to find a solution. Now, the solution is never just a little book or a little definition or a little plan, and it will certainly take one or two generations to accomplish. The answer is not another kind of utilitarian art, Christian utilitarian art, because we shouldn't be prostituting art to become something it was never made to be. Art was not made for evangelism. We should start a new development that bridges the gaps and solves the problem of the unreality of art in the museum. But first we have to pose the right questions. However, we are only just beginning to see those questions.

Learning to see

Question: How can we become more knowledgeable about art?

In order to learn more about art it is very important to go to museums. When you go to a museum, this is the way to do it: enter the museum and take a quick tour round, say for a quarter of an hour or maximum half an hour. Just walk through the various rooms and look. You may pause here or there just for a second, but then go on. After you have done that round, go back to the room where you thought 'Here is something I want to go into more deeply.' And then take your time, It's better to spend two hours in front of one painting than to see a whole museum. It's a great misunderstanding that we should be able to see a picture immediately. We have such strange, superficial ideas about seeing: that when we look, we see. But that's not true; we don't see. My experience is that when you sit down and look at a painting, after five minutes you will probably start asking yourself what you are doing there. Are you there because that man on the course had said there was so much to see? But you don't see it at all, and after five minutes you feel cheated and you want to go away. Just wait one second more and then you will find that, oh, there is something you didn't see before. You will soon find it becomes very exciting because you begin to discover more and more things that you did not see before.

Let me tell you a lovely little story about that. One of my friends went to the Rijksmuseum in Amsterdam a couple of months ago. He was looking at the *Nightwatch* and there was an elderly lady next to him, so they began to talk. She told him that she was American and that each summer for the last twenty years she had come to Amsterdam to go to the Rijksmuseum and look at the *Nightwatch* because it is so fantastic. So he remarked, 'Yes it's a fantastic painting and look at that girl there that's so fascinating.' And she said: 'Which girl?' For twenty years she had come to look at the painting and she had never seen that girl, who is very difficult to see.

I once had a big debate with a professor of communication sciences and he said: 'Visual communication is unclear.' The next morning I said to him: 'I don't understand why you make that point, because it's silly, and you are too intelligent to say silly things.' And he said: 'Yes, but every time I go and look at a painting, let's say the *Nightwatch*, I see new things.' And I said: 'Of course you see new things, because you never yet have looked at it in the right way. Looking at an artwork like the *Nightwatch* is like reading a thick book, it takes hours.' You don't read a novel by Jane Austen in ten minutes. If you look at any paining that is more complex than just a portrait or flower, it takes hours. You need to take that time for it to become fascinating. Therefore it's better to look at one or two pictures than at many. Of course, after a while you will begin to make shortcuts and it will go quicker. Just go to museums and occasionally to exhibitions. When you are at an exhibition, buy a catalogue. That is how you build up a nice little private library. At home you can then browse through these books again and after a while you will begin to understand something. It's also good to buy other books with reproductions, just to look at them – though you must understand that reproductions are not works of art. That's one of the things I have against for instance Janson's book, because people think that that book is full of works of art, but there is not one work of art in it. If I had made that book, I would have put no reproductions in it at all, because then people would have had to try and see the originals.

If you want to go into art, music or literature just pick up some books that look sensible. There are many good books, though very seldom written from a Christian perspective. Preferably go to the more specialist books, but not too specialist. A book of 500 pages on the first half of the third scene in *Macbeth* is, of course, fantastic but usually not something you read as an introduction to Shakespeare. On the other hand, don't take books that are too superficial. There is no field in the world, except perhaps theology, where there is so much nonsense being written. If a book is very popular, forget it.

There is one thing you should try to avoid and at the same time not avoid, and that is textbooks. A textbook is always an excerpt of an excerpt of an excerpt, which means it is neither scholarship nor science, so the best way to not learn anything about art is to read twenty textbooks – then you really miss the point. But you need some general knowledge, and some general dates and so on. There are two textbooks that I can recommend: the first one is Janson's *History of Art*, a very well produced and popular textbook, which is used almost all over the world. Never believe what he says, but that's true, of course, for every book. The second book I would recommend if you want to go into modern art is Arnason's *History of Modern Art: Painting, Sculpture, Architecture.* These books are rather expensive but they give you a good survey; you can also just go into a library and look for them there. Another book that I recommend highly is a booklet by Gombrich, the greatest living art historian today. Many years ago he wrote an art history book for children called *The Story of Art* and it's one of the best introductions to the history of art. He does not give many facts and names, but he gives a good survey of art history, written with much insight. Further, anything that Gombrich has written is always valuable, even though I do not always agree with what he says. Another man that is good to know the name of, at least, is Panofsky, who worked in Princeton for the last twenty years of his life. He is of the German school, just like Gombrich. Gombrich works in England but is originally from Vienna.

Recently there has been much more emphasis on the interrelation of art and social context written within a Marxist framework. There are some Marxists around who have done this in a very intelligent way. One of them is Baxandall, who in my opinion has written one of the best introductions to the Florentine art of the Renaissance. It's called *Art and Experience in Fifteenth Century Italy* and is an excellent discussion of what this art meant, why it was made, who the people were who ordered these paintings, what the relationship with religion was, and so on. It is also one of the very best writings on Giotto and the beginnings of the Renaissance.

Judging works of art

Question: How do we judge art?

I could answer this question by saying that it's not difficult, while stating with the same breath that it's very difficult. Of course it's difficult. All human things are difficult. We can compare a work of art with a human being. How do we judge a person and find out who this person is? Is he or she a good or bad person? We will make a judgment at first sight and then we will have to readjust that. In a way we never get to know another person really deeply. The same is true of art. When we try to judge a work of art we make a first judgment, and after looking more closely we may have to come to the conclusion that we were wrong. It is very human that as we grow, our insights grow. So in a way it's just like living with these artworks.

There are norms and structures outside of us. Without them we would not even know whether we are looking at a painting or a human being. They are simply given to us, so in a way there is nothing mysterious about them. They are there though we may not always be able to verbalize them. But not being able to verbalize them does not mean that they are not there. The verbalization, the explanation why we feel about a painting as we do, tends to be very difficult. We usually say 'That's a very fine painting.' And someone else will ask 'Why?' or 'How do you know?' Then we say: 'Maybe we can try to analyse it.' But in the end it often eludes us, just as we may not be able to put into words why we say something about someone else. Discussion is very important. In a way every work of art is there to be discussed and our dialogue becomes a trialogue with the artwork. It's very important to go to a concert together with other people, because in the intermission you can talk about it. Culturally speaking human beings are just like cows. We eat and later we ruminate, and this ruminating is done together. We talk and discuss and in this way the concert becomes part of our experience. In other words, it's not directly experienced but takes shape by way of discussion. It's good to listen to records together and then lift up the gramophone needle and say: 'Let's listen what happens in that passage again and then talk about it.' Our understanding of art does not come by itself; it needs discussion. Through discussion art becomes part of our life and reality.

The question of how we judge art is not one that comes up naturally. We have all been brainwashed by the Cartesian tradition. Descartes said that only those things are true which are clear and distinct, which can be analysed and understood by our reason, which can be affirmed and asserted by experiment. Take two apples and another two apples and count them. There are four apples. That is clear and distinct. These are the eternal laws that Descartes talked about. It means that everything that does not fit into the definitions of Descartes is vague and probably not true. In the eighteenth century Baumgarten wrote an aesthetic – it is often said that he wrote the first aesthetic, which is just sheer Cartesian pride. People have been writing about art ever since the beginning of humankind. Adam probably wrote the first book on art. However, Baumgarten wrote the first Cartesian aesthetic and that means he wrote that art is part of all those things which are vague and unclear, too subjective because one cannot prove them in the Cartesian framework. But I disagree completely, for painting is just as true as mathematics.

To illustrate this, many years ago I attended a series of meetings of a Dutch society of scientists. They had invited me to speak about art and in the discussion I said the same thing I just said in the previous paragraph. All these scientists raised their voices in protest, for they had been talking about atoms and such things, which are certainly true, and I was talking about pictures, which are as vague as anything can be. So I said: 'No, and I will prove it to you.' So the next week I gave a lecture on Dutch landscape art. When I had finished they said, 'You were right, you are just as clear and precise as we are and you prove your points just as precisely as we do in our field. There is no difference.'

I once met a professor who was working in nuclear physics at MIT. We had lunch together. He is a Christian and we were discussing Christianity as it applied to his work. I said, 'I know very little about nuclear physics, but I can explain my problems as a Christian art historian.' After I had talked for half an hour he said 'I recognize all you say. Our problems are the same.' We should not make a Cartesian distinction between certain and uncertain, objective and subjective. We need to get past that. Theologians too need to get past that because it simply doesn't work. That's why I talk about truth in a completely different way; we have to, otherwise we will never get anywhere. Things are, they exist outside of us. Of course we make mistakes and deepen our understanding the more we study. And of course we have to start by looking at what is there. (That's why I urge people not to start with theory or studying but with looking.) At first one's judgment will not be of very much value. But after twenty years one's judgment will be more valuable. That is obvious in any field. There is of course always visual communication implied in art and when one looks at old art one needs to be aware that they did things differently. But what I have tried to do is to look at paintings in a very commonsense way, to get away from all the mysterious talk and the myths that are built up around art. Then it starts to become very clear.

Certainty

What are the basic problems we as scholars face and need to work on?

In order to answer this question, I have over the years developed the following four theses:

1. Nothing is certain. It's very foolish for people to think that in any way whatsoever they can ever make an assertion that is certain. No scholarship will ever be final. It is a human endeavour and therefore not only open to sin but also finite and open to mistakes. Basically what we do is to discuss. Your professor may say that the final book on the interpretation of Matthew 12 has arrived. But then someone writes a critique and says the book is totally wrong, and that's the end of that 'final' book. A discussion follows and fifteen years later we might have moved one little inch further in our understanding of Matthew 12. Nothing is certain. Nothing is final. It is foolish to expect certainty. And the worst place to look for it is in anything made or done by people, including scholarship.

This assertion is a rather violent statement that goes against all popular belief today, because everybody is looking to science for the final answers. That is today's revelation. If someone says 'Science has proved . . . ', everyone stops talking and responds with 'Yes, amen!' People accept what is said by science.

Science makes tentative statements that have to be proved to be true. I have found that the most dangerous statement people make is that 'Of course it is true.' Then we should be very critical, because it means most people agree. However, if most people agree it may just be the superstition of our age. For example, today everyone says that 'Of course we have a subconscious.' But do we? It's just a little invention of Mr Freud. This idea is not even a hundred years old. It has a little pre-history in the pre-Romantic era, that's true, for there was a man around fifty years before Freud who began to talk about it. But it may be that they invented the subconscious to fill up the hole created by the absence of God. So, this is something to think about, a question to start a discussion with. Questions are crucial. It is only when you have a good question that you can expect to find a good answer or at least the beginning of an answer, or that you can move an inch forward towards an answer.

So, nothing is certain. Never expect anything from human endeavour. There is only one thing certain: God. God is not a question mark; we are the question mark. God is the Creator; we are the creatures. Everything is relative, everything we do has meaning only in relationship to God. We can never get out of this relatedness (not relativism), because we are meant to be in relationship with God. That's what Dooyeweerd means with 'meaning'. That is what Seerveld talks about. God is certain, and everything we do is uncertain.

2. There are many many things which are totally certain! I am very certain that I am sitting on this chair, speaking into the microphone in front of me to a bunch of Americans. Anyone who would say that this is a foolish statement and uncertain may need to go the hospital. There is no problem in my mind that at this very moment we are in a suburb of Philadelphia, Pennsylvania, United States. These chairs are blue. It is winter and it is daytime. We could go on and on. Even if you were driving with a friend through the mountains in thick fog, and your friend would tell you that normally there is a very lovely view which you cannot see at the moment, most of us would not say 'How do you know? Can you prove it? I don't believe you.' No, we would say: 'I am very sorry that it's not more clear.' We take things for granted. We cannot live without doing that. Life would be completely unbearable without these certainties. When driving, for example, one takes it for granted that the road will not disappear into a big hole. I wouldn't dare to go to New York if I thought it might not exist. In the philosophical life everything is a problem, but not in real life. Many things are certain. This is human experience. We draw a very clear line between reality and fantasy. In the book by Tolkien there is a fantasy map. The map you buy at the gas station is a reality map. Both are maps, but nobody will confuse them.

The most Christian thing in the world is to say 'Thank you Lord, thank you that you gave me this world, my existence in the midst of this reality, and the certainties that you made and gave me.' That's the basis of our certainty. We want to know, we want to investigate, we want to understand. And nobody can stop us because that's one of the things we are called to do. God tells us to go ahead and investigate, and so we investigate physics, macrophysics, microphysics, psychology etc., and we try to understand what is given, what is certain.

We stand before a painting. It is there, that is certain, and then someone comes and asks: 'Why is it beautiful and what does it mean?' and so on, and suddenly we get into all sorts of uncertainties. There is a painting, but how do we interpret it? Many questions, approaches, discussion, that's human. But it is a very Christian truth that we don't start out from our thinking; we start from the reality outside of us. Never follow those people who say that these things are only our thought forms, that they are only in the mind.

Also evil things are really there. In Uganda I once heard about a witch. He called the pastor and said that he wanted to be a Christian and wanted to get rid of his witchcraft materials which he had buried in the back of his garden. Then the pastor said: 'I will ask some of my friends to dig them up.' They came to do that, but after two hours they couldn't dig any more because their hands couldn't move. Why were their hands lame? Because those fellows didn't believe that there was real power in that garden and so they didn't pray before they started their work. They didn't go in the belief that God is more powerful than the evil powers. No, they thought they were just digging up some old stuff belonging to some deluded foolish old person. They had to learn that these powers are real. Whoever wants to believe in God must also believe in the reality of evil. This goes against the grain of current popular thinking.

3. *All our experience is coloured by our starting point.* If you are a Christian you look at the world through Christian-tinted glasses. I

believe that Christian glasses are clear and that they don't disfigure reality. But that's my faith, and it is very hard to prove. So what is the difference between my view and that of a humanist or a Marxist, and how can we communicate with each other? The difference is like this: imagine tea, coffee, Coke, 7-up, wine and sherry. What is the difference between them? Very little indeed. They smell and taste differently, they have a different meaning when you offer one or the other to a particular person at a particular time. But basically they really differ only in about 5 per cent of their substance, for they all consist of 95 per cent water. But that 5 per cent is very important. It's the same with faith. The Marxist, the humanist and the Christian are all the same for 95 per cent in that they are all human and experience the same world. They differ only in the remaining 5 per cent. The point is that communication is possible because as humans we have so much in common.

Though we live in the same world, all of our experience is coloured by our starting point. This exposes the superstition of modern scholarship that we can have 'objective truth'. People ask me for objective truth, and I answer them that they are fools because that is humanly impossible. What I can give them is personal knowledge. One can never go beyond personal knowledge and one should never try to. For as soon as one goes beyond that it becomes 'inhuman' knowledge. We see today that more and more historians republish old manuscripts, so that we may end up with a complete library of republished works. But no one ever tries to assess what these works mean because then one has to become personal and subjective. Of course that is the case, but only then it becomes worthwhile to talk about things. Republication is just an escape; and we call it scholarly. It is just phoney! It illustrates the superstition of our age. As a Christian I say no to that. We cannot escape being human, and why should we even try to? As humans we can say things, starting from reality, taking a beautiful painting by Rubens for example, and then going on and discussing how to interpret it, and no one else will do it in quite the same way as I do it. That doesn't mean that I should then say 'Look how great I am.' It's just that I cannot avoid talking personally. All I say is coloured by my personality. No experience is without that colouring. The reality that we start with is certain, but our talking about it is always coloured.

4. *We can communicate.* This is the real mystery. I must say that I don't understand it. If I could explain it, I would be the greatest philosopher of all time. Much has been said on this topic but still not enough. Although we see the world only through our own coloured glasses we can nevertheless communicate. One reason for that is that we are creatures in creation – the 95 per cent water. The inexplicable part, however, is this: Mr A, an existentialist, writes a play and it is performed. Mr B, a humanist, sees the play and writes a criticism that expresses his opinion. Then Mr C, one of your nice Christian friends, reads the criticism of Mr B and talks to you, Mr D, about it. By listening to him it's

not very difficult for you to reconstruct the play of Mr A because you know your Christian friend misunderstood Mr B completely, and you understand the colour of Mr B and why he said what he did about the play of Mr A. So you can discover what Mr A was about, not only his specific outlook on reality, but even the reality he was referring to. It's complex and it's a great mystery. It's the basis of hermeneutics. Even though the Bible is one big sermon about the supreme Creator God, yet we can read and understand it. The colour of our glasses can present us with problems and questions, but more as a result of our specific social environment than of a particular spiritual problem. For example, in my church the Law is read every Sunday and every Sunday we hear the very important statement that we should not covet the ass of our neighbour. Of course nobody in my congregation in Amsterdam even thinks about having an ass, so it seems to be a silly statement. But the reason why it's not foolish to hear this every Sunday is that everyone understands it is really about something more, and that's why we have communication. Very simple. No, actually, very complex; communication is very complex.

All the theories I could develop about communication would fall under category 1 above – they are all uncertain, a matter of interpretation. Where does the Bible fit in? It belongs in category 2 – with the certainties that are not up for discussion. That we should not covet the ass of our neighbour, that God created the world, these things do not belong to human uncertainties, which is where the modern theologians place them because they think that these statements are human creations. But the miracle is exactly this, that though the knowledge of Moses, Isaiah, Jeremiah and Paul was personal, it was nevertheless universal, i.e. certain, in the same category as the statement I make when I say that we are sitting in this room and that the light is turned on.

There is one great difficulty that surfaces when a person asks a question, namely that this question comes out of the framework in which that person is thinking and working. For example, in L'Abri, people often ask the question: 'How do you know that God exists?' And for years I have given my answer, and I know the answer, otherwise I wouldn't be a Christian. But at some point I completely stopped answering that question, because I understood that my answer was not the answer. That question always comes out of a Cartesian framework of thinking. In such a framework I cannot answer that question because the Cartesian framework was constructed to get God out of the picture. In the Cartesion framework my answer is a useless answer. So since that time my answer has been this: 'Your question is a good question, but your framework is wrong.' And then I try to analyse the framework and show what a better one would look like.

Sometimes I may be answering your questions in a different framework from the one you think the answer is being given in. This is a problem that results from the combined effects of categories 1 and 3:

the uncertainty of all human knowledge and the fact that we always look through coloured glasses. Many of your questions arise from this problem. You may ask: 'What do you mean when you say that nothing is certain except God?' And I would answer that it is not God who needs to be proved. In a way the question whether God exists is a silly question because the better question would be to ask whether we exist. God is prior to everything and we are the works of his making, so it is we who have to be proved, not God. God is completely certain. If everything falls away, then there is still one thing that is certain, namely that God exists. I know this is not the language of Cartesian epistemology, which starts from humanity, which is a point of uncertainty, and wants to build up certainties from there. Then of course God becomes a big question mark. Therefore I would answer people who think in this framework as follows: 'Of course you will never know, because you start from the human. But the Bible begins with "In the beginning God". That is certain and everything else follows. The whole world proves that it is so. Read your Bible, read history, look at the world around you. It is one big living proof, because everything is relative and exists in relationship to God. Otherwise it would not exist. Otherwise it would have no meaning.'

This four-point system has been devised precisely to stand up against the Cartesian framework. And I think it's in this very area that we have an important Christian battle to fight.

Another question we need to ask ourselves is how the tension that results from uncertainty affect our view of preaching? Can we still preach authoritatively? And if the answer is yes, how far does that authority go?

If you are a preacher, you must preach out of the certainties. Otherwise you shouldn't preach. That doesn't mean that you should know and understand everything. You don't need to turn yourself into God. There is also much uncertainty built into your work, and you must be honest about that. As far as your being a theologian, everything you say is uncertain. Theology, being a human endeavour, is full of uncertainties and coloured by personal presuppositions and starting points as our human brains try to grasp something bigger than our minds. So of course we fail. Theology therefore should be left out of preaching. Theology does not belong on the pulpit but should be taught in a college. Preaching is talking about the certainties of the gospel. What is the gospel? That God created the world and is interested in it. And preaching is talking out of the certainties of the realities in which we live, expressed in a personal way, using personal words, seen through a particular colour of glasses. That is not theology, not a little theory about what Genesis 1 or any other text mean. Do you think Jeremiah or Isaiah would have said: 'I am not sure what to say'? I am certain they said: 'So says the Lord.' We sometimes think they were very holy people who always had an angel whispering in their ears. But they were people like us, talking in the same way we do when we stand on the pulpit. Let's hope that in three centuries' time people will still read our words because they were so full of the holy Spirit and so true. The words of the prophets were: 'Turn back to the Lord and repent, because I see all the iniquities in the land.' These were not uncertainties or vague assertions that applied only to those who happened to believe.

What is belief? A person may say: 'If we do this or that, we will solve such and such a problem.' And someone else may respond: 'And I think you are wrong.' Now we get close to what belief means. Belief is conviction. A conviction is based on knowledge, even though it talks about things we don't know. Take for instance the following statement: if all black girls would marry white men and the other way around, the whole race problem would be solved in America. That is a belief. Someone else could say: 'But that's not the solution. I believe . . .' Both people may have a valid argument, otherwise they would be foolish statements. But who is right? We can discuss it. We look at something we don't know and then we come to a conviction about it. No one will call it just his or her own subjective opinion. No one talks like that. The Bible says that faith is the certainty of the hope that is in you. I can pound my fist and say that God exists and that he cannot stand the iniquities of our Western culture and that he is coming with his curse. These are things we can preach about. And preaching is in the realm of the second category, the things we can be certain about: the word of God, and the world around us. Our preaching may be coloured by our views, but that is not a problem because the certainties exist. Even if it is sometimes difficult, communication is possible. People can understand it when we say something, they can understand the reality we are referring to. Even though all our glasses are a little bit differently tinted, nevertheless there can be certainties. But we should not preach theologies, theories and philosophies for then we get into the uncertainties. Are there no questions here? There are billions of questions. These matters have not been thought through for three or four centuries, possibly not even since the scholastics, despite all their confusion about thought patterns and so on.

But be careful. We need to be able to talk with authority. My personal life has been like this: I was raised in a world where there was no church and no Christianity. So as a young boy I went out to dance and I have been dancing all through my youth. Later in a prisoner-of-war camp I became a Christian and still later I came into the church. That was a big surprise. I have never yet recovered from that surprise. I am speaking out of that surprise. For instance, I heard a pastor say that we should not dance, and then he gave an explanation that was completely beside the point. Of course there are some brothels in the world where there is dancing, for a very specific purpose. But kids who go to a dance do not usually go there as a sort of sexual indulgence. Dancing is a way of socializing and has nothing to do with sex, at least not in any specific sense. So when a pastor says that dancing is a kind of adultery, it is just like saying that swimming will make you dry – completely removed from reality. So be very careful that you know what you are talking about.

Every preacher or pastor should study things like television, rock music, film, the things of the day, things young people are interested in. Statistics have shown that very few people working with young people have ever studied rock music. That means that in nine out of ten catechism classes nonsense is being said about this music. Better to ask the young people to bring in some of their records and let them tell you about them. Keep your ears open to grasp what they say and then start a discussion. Maybe you learn something and teach the kids that these are things are to be thought about, that they are important. Because the records we have in our homes are part of us. They are an expression of who we are. They are our lifestyle. It's not neutral what we choose to listen to – it's part of us. That does not mean it has to be 100 per cent Christian, because we cannot be 100 per cent Christian – we are part of this world. But at least we have the antidote.

We have to be with it and know what is going on because that is what communication with the people we love asks for. We have to be a Greek to the Greeks. Sit as a student among the students and listen to their crazy records. If we don't know the names and songs, we can never say anything about them or get into any good discussion. We have to do these things. But if we don't do them, then we should also not talk about them with certainty. We are not doing them just to show that we are so with it. That's phoney. To know what's going on, to be contemporary, to help people answer their questions, to anticipate their needs, that is the task. Don't preach against Bob Dylan if you have barely heard any Bob Dylan. And don't quote hearsay, like a story from a little book on rock music that states with complete seriousness that a lady played rock music to her plants and they all died within two weeks. That is foolish. The book goes on to say: 'Get rid of your rock records and buy classical records: Bach, Mozart, Beethoven, Brahms and even Bartok and more modern composers.' And I would respond that I can't see the difference, because many of these composers also make unchristian statements. Beethoven is worse than Bob Dylan. I always look at the records people have. And if I feel there's something wrong I ask them to play me a favourite bit so that we can discuss it. Above all, be honest with yourself. Don't just listen to your pastor. In the end you have to stand before one person only, and that is God himself, the great God Almighty who is interested even in your record collection.

Can we use modern and abstract art forms?

Question: Can we as Christians use modern art forms?

Before we can answer this question we have to know what exactly we are talking about. Are we talking about twentieth-century art forms or modern ones? I would say it is impossible for a Christian to be modern because that means following a very deeply anti-Christian stream. But we can be contemporary. Actually, it's impossible not to use twentieth-century forms. It's like asking: may we speak English? If a Christian comes up to me and asks 'Can I be an existentialist?' I would say 'No, that's impossible.' But if he or she asks 'Can I be a philosopher?' I would answer: 'Of course you can. You cannot avoid being a philosopher if you think.'

Styles and forms are not neutral; they are vehicles for content. Some can be used and some can't. We must be very careful, not only as to the art forms but also as to the other cultural forms we use. Certain forms that people around us use we may not want to use, or if we use them we may want to change them. As Christians living in the twentieth century we cannot avoid living in the cultural forms and the framework of our time. We use the same cars, the same food, the same language, we read the same papers, we look at the same television, we have the same kinds of holidays. Nevertheless, there are many things we don't like. And I think precisely that is the most important point: we can be different and try to change some things, get rid of what we don't like and add what we miss. That little difference is exactly what we are fighting for because it makes all the difference. A good friend of mine once taught a course in an American college. He told me: 'I taught about Augustine and the students were so interested in my lecture and found it so different because I talked about the greatness of Augustine.' In that theological college they were always taught that Augustine was wrong. But what he was wrong about belongs to the category of the mistakes of his time. If you really want to talk about Augustine, you have to talk about all the points on which he differed [from his culture]. Because that's Augustine's great achievement. It is the difference that counts. People in his time knew the difference and they do so in our time.

Some ten years ago the miniskirt was invented. The miniskirt can be beautiful, at least when the girl who wears it is beautiful enough. But to my amazement and displeasure Christian girls immediately followed suit. And I think they followed too quickly. The miniskirt was an expression of a certain way of life. The people who were behind it even said so: 'The miniskirt stands as symbol for the fact that a woman is more easily available.' Christians should have been aware of this. I do not mean it in a moralistic or legalistic sense, but I think that Christian girls should have their skirts just one half inch longer. That's exactly the difference. In a world where everybody wears miniskirts we of course cannot expect girls to wear long skirts and to be out of the world.

We cannot be out of the world, because then we would have no contact with the world and we would not be able to work in the world. And we do have a task in this world: we are called to be in this world and to be salting salt. But the half inch, metaphorically speaking, makes all the difference.

A filmstar once visited L'Abri and accepted the Lord. Though she did not change her dresses then, her appearance nevertheless changed. It's also the way you wear your clothes that counts. When Christian girls are just like the world, there's something wrong. It is simply too easy; it is secularization. But we cannot take them to task for wanting to be part of their own time. So, we should be aware and do things just a little bit different. My sons have very long hair and my wife has always said to them: 'Go ahead, I love it, but there is one little rule and that is that it should be clean.' As long as it is clean and well kept it's okay, but don't walk around like a hippie who doesn't care, who doesn't bath and so on. Because that's not the way to behave as a Christian or a human being. This does not mean that Christians must always try to be different and walk around like idiots but it means we have to try and do the good things. And if we see that something around us is not good, we should try and change it.

We cannot be otherwise than contemporary. And when we start to paint, we have to start with the art forms of today. If we should try to imitate the past we will never succeed because we can never fully understand the things of the past. Even in that we cannot avoid being contemporary. As an art historian I would immediately notice it if a twentieth-century artist should try to work in a seventeenth-century style. So don't try to paint in an 'old' style but simply be yourself. In a way there is no choice. Yet we also have to understand that things are loaded with meaning and that we sometimes need to take away from or add to the contemporary art forms.

Sometimes I get asked 'What kind of style should I choose?'

This is a typically American question. I remember one day I walked in downtown Manhattan, New York, and happened to meet Willem de Kooning, the American modern painter. We had a very nice Chinese meal together and he told me a little joke. He said: 'This is America: the newest kind of architecture in Madison Avenue is a building with some buttons somewhere in the basement, and if you push one of the buttons you get a nice façade for the winter; and in spring if you push another button, you get another façade; and if a new fashion comes along, like art nouveau, you get an art nouveau façade; and then the next week you may get a modernist façade or a classical façade, or whatever you want . . .' If there is such a thing as an American style, maybe it's stylelessness. The other day I showed an American painting that incorporated three different styles. It's a very difficult and involved problem: how is it possible that people can make stylelessness their style?

At this moment a very funny story comes to my mind. In 1961 I had a wonderful time in America. I spent four months there and I happened to drop in at Wheaton College. I was invited to speak there and I gave about seven lectures within 24 hours. I arrived at twenty past ten in the morning. Half past ten was chapel time. So when I arrived I was immediately hurried to the platform of Wheaton College chapel. When I had finished speaking, people said to me: 'What do you think of our chapel?' Well, I'm a very kind man, as you all know, very sweet and softspoken, so I said: 'It's beautiful.' What else could I say? And then they said to me: 'Yes, we made it three years ago.' Then I said: 'Wow, it's awful!' I couldn't imagine anyone in 1960 wanting to make a neo-classical, colonial-style chapel. We shouldn't make new buildings in the colonial style because we can't make proper colonial buildings anymore. We don't have the same feeling for form, scale and relationships. And what should light switches look like in a colonial-style building? One gets into all kinds of crazy problems. But it does communicate. For every time a boy or a girl goes into Wheaton chapel it communicates this: Christianity is of another age, it's something of the past. So then they asked me: 'Should we have built a modern building?' And I said: 'No, not if you mean by modern something that expresses the modern movement. Because you are not modern, not in your theology and not in your general thinking. But you should have made something contemporary. There is beautiful contemporary architecture and so you should have chosen a good architect who could have made you a beautiful building.' That would have been possible, just like this building in which we are here [at Westminster Seminary], which is not the most fantastic kind of architecture but is of our time. At least it communicates this: these Christians are not behind the times; they know how to make things and they care.

So the answer to the question above is that you cannot choose a style; you are a style. The things you do are an expression of your self. You set to work and you find the forms that suit you. I can understand that a young artist in art school experiments with different ways of doing things. There's nothing wrong with that. But when the artist becomes more mature, there are no choices anymore. You cannot ask 'Can I make a piece of music in the twelve-tone system?' For you are your own person and you have something to say, and if you should try to use the twelve-tone system you would very soon find yourself trying to change it, because it was invented in order to avoid harmony and to blot every difference out of reality. In its own way the twelve-tone system illustrates that old saying of Diderot: 'There is no difference. Everything is the same.' But as a Christian one does see differences. So even if a person started with the twelve-tone system, one would very soon find one had to change it into something else if one really cared about what one communicates. In a way we cannot be different from what we are. And we shouldn't try to be; we should just be ourselves. Where do we start?

Well, perhaps we experiment and find it doesn't work and then we say 'This was a mistake.' We should not be afraid to make mistakes, because without them we would never learn anything and culture would stop.

I mentioned earlier that there is contemporary art and modern art. There is also non-figurative art, which is not necessarily modern in the specific sense. Can we use it for Christian expression?

It just depends what exactly you are talking about. When you are choosing fabrics for your curtains, of course the designs will often be non-figurative. When you design a cover for a book, it would probably be non-figurative too. But can we make a painting that is non-figurative? My answer would be 'Why not? But I've never seen a good one because I ask for much more reality in a painting than what can be conveyed by non-figurative means.' I once talked with someone who represented the art department of a Christian school here in the USA and she showed me the work of the staff. All of it was abstract art. Later on we had a discussion, which turned out to be rather violent because I think we should explore reality and these paintings were all escapism – they avoided talking about anything serious in the world. They were not only escapist but also mystical. These paintings showed the spirituality of people whose souls were saved but who were way 'out of the world'. They were not fighting racism or the decay of Western society or caring about television or anything else. Just because they tried to shun the world and therefore were not aware of what they were actually doing, their works were worldlier than anything I have seen Christians do. Their work was similar to what you would find in any art school in America. They were making the same trite, nonsensical no-statements young students make when they first try to grapple with these things. I'm not talking here about the real, serious and great non-figurative art one also finds in America but about the average paintings of this kind. They are just nice little decorative things without much meaning. And if that's Christian, then I don't want to be a Christian.

That's why I think we should avoid the question of whether we can make abstract art. I actually did already answer the question when I said that one does not choose a style. One does not think 'Shall I make a non-figurative painting?' One makes a painting, one says something, and if it is appropriate one says it with non-figurative means. And then we may debate whether that was the right choice: yes or no. But I have never seen any abstract works by Christians that were not lower than the level at which I want art to communicate. I could mention Le Corbusier here, who is a Roman Catholic mystic. Chagall is a Jewish mystic, just as Rothko, one of the most strong and extraordinary non-figurative artists that the American 1950s have produced. Abstraction and mysticism go together, and mysticism is very near to gnosticism. It's not exactly the same, but very near it.

Christian art

Question: What do you mean by 'Christian' art, 'Christian' film, 'Christian' literature?

I do not mean art with Christian subject matter in the narrow sense. To make Christian art or literature is not identical with portraying biblical subjects or writing stories of missionaries. I think that most of all Christian artists must try to get back into reality, because our century has lost reality. As examples I showed two paintings by the English painter Peter Smith: one of a bird in a cage and the other of a highway. These paintings talk about our present world; they show it in its ambiguity, which means that they show the good and the bad. A highway is fascinating and beautiful; nevertheless it pollutes the countryside. We have a kind of love-hate relationship with these things, and when the artist begins to paint a visual poem about them, then he or she talks about the present age. It means that the artist is engaging with the reality outside, that he or she is trying to go into that reality and not to avoid it as art for art's sake does. Even though art needs no justification, nevertheless it has a million ties to reality and precisely those ties to reality make art valuable.

We all lead a 'thin' life: we are 'thin' people. I want us to be thick, strong people again. I think that our conception of God is too small and therefore our conception of ourselves is too small. Or we can reverse that. Perhaps it is because we think so thin and small about ourselves that God is dragged down to the same size. At L'Abri I often get asked 'What does it mean to feel the Lord?' Many of us have been taught repeatedly that we can call Jesus our friend, but I do not think that's the right level at which to talk about him. If we do not understand that we should stand in awe before the Lord of lords, the great God Almighty, that we are too small to even look at his footstool, then [our God is small and] we become very small ourselves. In the end we wane and become the same as the animals and plants and things, and there is no difference anymore. We have to fight to regain reality.

Artists like Peter Smith are fighting for just that. The interesting thing is that it does communicate, that people do notice. And when we have made this kind of art for some time and we really know what we are talking about – it will take at least a generation – then we can try to take the next step and talk about the realities that we find in the Bible. That will create new problems again: when dealing with a historical subject, should one for example paint Isaiah as a man living so many hundred years before Christ or should one paint him as a contemporary person? I have no answer to that and I'm not ready to even try and give an answer to that because I think we have to do something else first, we have to try and understand what reality is. Only when we have answered that question will we perhaps get to this one.

We are all thin people – not just the world outside of us – and we have all been brainwashed and need to relearn and rediscover. By being aware of and concerned about all the cheapness and corruption of life around us, we may begin to enter into reality and rediscover its beauties. As I say to my friends, 'Christianity is joy, but when it becomes a Pepsodent [a brand of toothpaste] smile, forget about it.' We can never have joy if there are not also tears because beautiful things are being destroyed or are threatened with destruction. We cannot say we love people if we are not weeping when we see how some of our students are being destroyed by drugs, or whatever. The tears and the laughter go together. The amazing beauty of Christianity is that we can still laugh, even in the midst of all this negativity, sin, death, corruption, violence, rape etc., because we know that finally it is not those things that are victorious but Christ who is! If we cut the Last Judgment out of Christianity, as some people do, then I would say forget about all that laughter. And one sees that people who hold to modern theology are often very tense, because they think they have to change the world by themselves. I would say yes, we have a calling, but salvation is the Lord's. Thank God I don't have to do it myself. So that's what I'm trying to teach artists: just try to make something good and don't try to be 'Christian', because we barely know what spirituality is.

Maybe it's good to tie this in with another question I've been asked, namely why I often state that Christ did not come to make us Christians?

Well, read the Bible. One barely finds the word 'Christians' there. In the New Testament it's never said: be Christians. Christ didn't come to make us Christians. That wasn't the point. He came in order to take away sin, in order to be the centre of history, to renew humankind. What did he do? You can read that in the Gospels and in Revelation 5 and 6. You can read about the reality of the Cross, so real you could put your hand on it and get splinters in your fingers: real agony, real suffering, real dying. The Lamb slain, and the Lamb given the book of Life, which was sealed with seals. They are opened, and that's history. Christ who is the centre of history, why did he die on the cross? Why is he doing all the things we read about in Revelation? What are all these curses and trumpets about? Why are they happening? They are there because God wants to clean up the world, because in the beginning of history, people fell, and in falling they lost their humanity. People threw away their freedom, became less than human. But God said: I do not accept that. We mostly think much too lightly of the Fall. And that's why I understand that non-Christians sometimes ask 'What's all the fuss about? A little eating of a little fruit?' And I say: 'I'm sorry, I can't explain it to you, it's too much. I can talk about it but I can't really grasp it.' But God knew that when the Fall happened, something so deep was destroyed that in order to restore the fullness of life, Christ himself would have to come and do it.

So why did Jesus come? To restore humanity, that we may be human again and free. To make the resurrection of the body possible, and a new earth. We are redeemed not just of our little sins and sicknesses, we are saved not just in order that we might become spiritual ghosts in heaven. No, Christ came in order to make us human in the fullest sense, to renew our lives at all levels, from the physical to the highly spiritual, from our thoughts, feelings, sex and artworks to our marriages, holidays and the food we eat. Christ made us free in order that we may be human. Nothing is human unless there is love. And in this world love means also tears for the destruction one sees when beautiful things are torn down. Christ looked at Jerusalem and said: 'I loved you and I tried to help you but what do I see?' And he wept. If we take away tears our faith becomes sentimental, 'out of the world'.

Christ came to bring us back to the fullness of humanity. That's what the Epistle to the Romans talks about. And the righteous shall live by faith. We shall live. We need faith in order to be human. Faith affects everything we do. Do we act in love? Do we protest when we see something wrong? Can we stand by while someone is being mistreated? That's what Christ came for, to renew the world and to bring about a new earth, the earth as God had originally designed it. People in their foolishness chose the long way of suffering. God had chosen a long way in any case, the long way of cultural development. He filled the earth with possibilities. Adam and Eve never sung a hymn in paradise, because singing was not yet discovered. It only came a bit later, in the time of Lamech. So, they didn't sing. But God gave them the possibility and one day someone began to grasp that. God told them to open up these possibilities, to take care of the garden he gave them, to make it a beautiful place. But people chose another way. God, however, said: 'I keep you to it. You have to do that work anyway, open up the possibilities, turn this world into a liveable place.' But now it has become a long road of suffering. Yet in the centre of history is Christ himself, who will bring about the new earth.

Revelation does not talk about souls. It talks about people. When a person becomes a Christian, one moves from death to life. That hippie who cried out about ten years ago 'Is there life before death?' understood this. I would say yes, there is life before death. Just like there is life after death. It begins here and now. That's what Christ died for. And the people who say yes to that great God who came down in order to suffer for us, they are the ones who are called Christians. But we should see that it means becoming truly human, renewed people, new men and women in the sense of Romans 6 and 7. Christians are people whose lives have been renewed. They have not been 'christianized'. God created us as human beings and we have to try and realize the fullness of what that means. Without Christ life simply does not work. That's why he came. The totality of life is at stake. Christ does not want just a little sect that follows him. He wants the whole world. He does not want just a person's religious feelings. He wants the whole person. He makes it possible for the totality of a person to be renewed. That's humanity. That's Christianity.

On portraying God and Christ

Question: How should we view the Second Commandment in relationship to art?

It's very interesting that in the early days of Christianity people thought very much about this question, whether we are allowed to make visual images, but not so today. The first answer that was given was: no, we cannot make any visual art. I think that they were right to say so because they were living in a culture where there were idols all around them. They saw that they could not make their Jesus in the way that other people made their Apollo. So, they refrained. They refrained for about 200 hundred years and then, at the moment that people realized that they were made in the image of God, that began to change. What does it mean to be made in the image of God? Their answer was this: has anybody seen God? No? Yes, of course we have seen him: Jesus was God, so we are made in the image of Jesus. Adam resembled Jesus because he was made in the image of God, which is a very interesting and challenging thought. And Jesus resembled Adam because he came to earth as a man. And so people said: but then we can make images of Christ and of people. And very slowly and reluctantly they started to make them.

A number of centuries later the answer that came out of a rather mystical stream (which means that I'm suspicious) was this: no, we are made in the image of God only in a spiritual sense, as to our character. And then we enter the art of the early Romanesque and Romanesque period which was spiritualistic and tried to avoid portraying the world around us.

I personally feel that it is a wrong question to ask whether we can make visual images, because what the Bible says is that we should not make images in order to adore them. That is the biblical emphasis, just as the whole Bible emphasizes that we should not follow idols or false gods. If this is not so, I can no longer understand the Bible because on the very porch of the temple of Solomon was the Sea, supported by twelve bulls, and inside were the sculptures of the seraphs, and so on. There was figurative art in Israel and there was a portrayal of plants and beasts. But their art went wrong when they made a calf and said 'That's our God.'

Thinking about European art I would say all the sculptures of saints that people pray to are against the Second Commandment. I can understand very well why the Reformers destroyed these images, because people had been deceived by them. They were idols and they had to be destroyed, according to the Scriptures. But the Second Commandment is not against sculptures and paintings in general.

Question: Can we portray God or Christ? If so, how?

Yes, we can. I did it at the very beginning of this lecture when I portrayed the great God Almighty, the Trinity, with a little triangle, a little symbol. That's the only way one can portray God. Artists sometimes do it with a little beam of light. It's interesting that many Christians accept almost without discussion Michelangelo's picture of *Creation,* in which one sees God Almighty reaching out his hand to Adam. It is a beautiful picture, but theologically, Christianly, I have some questions here. Big questions. It's a very powerful painting, but it falls far short of the reality of God. And I think the Second Commandment is against that. God says no. And we should keep it no.

What then about Christ? We can portray Christ in his humanity. There is all the freedom to do so. But we should not make Christ into an icon, a little God-image, to be revered. Here we have to be very careful. And if you ask me 'Can we portray Christ now, at this moment in history?' then I have big questions. For our image of Christ is so weak that we better not try. What I've seen makes me sick. Think of the kind of Christ pictures you see here in America, for example that awful picture of Christ knocking at the United Nations building. Or of *St John of the cross* by Dali which you find in many Christian homes and which is a totally non-Christian picture, mystical but not of a Christian mysticism. On the other hand, Crucifixions and many Bible stories have been portrayed, and there is nothing wrong with that. But let it be done in a way that is really honouring to God. Some of these illustrations are below standard. So we can portray Christ, but let's be careful.

If one wants to portray Christ it must be loaded with meaning. At an exhibition I recently saw a painting of three people in a room. The painting was made in order to portray that where two or three are gathered in Christ's name, he is present. The picture shows three people very intensely together, but where is Christ? I could not see him. So the woman who painted it came up to me and said: 'Have you seen my painting?' I said: 'Yes, I have seen it, but where is Jesus?' She said: 'Don't you see him on the wall?' On the wall was a shadow and in the shadow was Christ's face. I told her: 'Yes, I see it but, to be honest, I didn't see it before.' I wondered what to say, because she had worked so hard on it and I did not want to be unkind. But because I wanted to help her along, I said: 'Your picture is a beautiful picture but it does not portray the presence of Christ. Christ in our midst is a reality that is so strong that you should have made a granite block in the middle of the room, and then those gathered together would have seemed like the shadows.' Christ's being spiritual doesn't mean he becomes ghostlike; he is spiritual yet very concrete. But how can one portray that? I must say, I don't know. So I would rather wait with tackling a theme like that until I felt sure that I could really do it justice. There's not an easy answer when one thinks about the how and what of Christian art. One should not try to do it too quickly. And one should look for it in the direction of one's understanding of reality rather than in trite depictions of things that are too big for human understanding.

Question: What do you think about crucifixes?

Let me answer it in this way. I was a student of a professor of art history who was a great connoisseur. And just after the War there was the greatest forgery case in all history, of a Vermeer. When they showed this professor the new picture that had just turned up, he said: 'That's a forgery, and it's made by the same man who made the other one, and his name is this.' The forger stood trial and was convicted. Later on I asked my professor what he thought about it all. And he said: 'It's awful. It has taken away all my joy in looking at paintings. When I walk through a museum I don't believe any picture anymore.' I sometimes feel that the same thing happens with a crucifix. Why shouldn't we display one in our home? There is no reason why we shouldn't, because it is the centre of our understanding of the gospel. Of course we do not display a crucifix in order to pray before it. Then we better throw it away. But we may have it as a reminder that we live out of our salvation. However, the crucifix has been used and misused and has become more or less a symbol of Roman Catholicism. There are so many associations attached to it that we do not feel free to use it anymore, and because of that we have lost something. But we cannot just jump over our emotions and understanding. By the same token I personally don't like a cross in a church. Which is perhaps going a bit too far, but that is how I feel. So these things are difficult for we have lost so much. But to fill up the loss with that cheap Christ you see around which is really blasphemous, that's worse.

Rembrandt did some portraits of Christ and there are a few others that seem to come close to something that Christ could have been, but they usually fall below the standard. But it may be right and good to portray biblical stories, if they are done with real understanding. I am so sick of that little picture I saw in Boston the other day, showing Christ sitting down, a very effeminate Christ with very long hair (it's very interesting that people who hate men with long hair love a Christ with long hair), with a nice well-dressed little girl on his knee, a little wealthy American, who looks at Christ and asks: 'Why do you have this little wound?' That is so cheap. Even the fantasy is cheap. I'd rather have a strong Crucifixion. And in this type of picture people always evade the central issues and sentimentalize them. Sentimentality to me is emotion that is not backed up by reality. If a person has no true understanding, things become emotional. One can be emotional in one of two ways.

Many songs are emotional, by which I mean that they are sung as if they are filled with something while nothing real backs them up. They evoke something without the reality being there. Sometimes they use the sweet strains of a violin, slow and soft, and so on. But there is also another kind of emotionality, as one finds in a blues concert at the end of the evening when the music just lets go: very strong rhythms are blared out and everybody jumps around. That is sheer emotionality, not soft and sweet but strong and wild, though equally much not backed up by anything real. So we must be careful; we shouldn't be sentimental.

Sentimentality became fashionable in the eighteenth century, at a time when people began to repress sex and call lust something animal-like and sinful, and at the same time it became fashionable to weep. Women of high society were supposed to faint three times in an evening to show how weak and fragile they were. They had to prove this socially, and weep when just the smallest sad thing was mentioned. And they were never to have sunburn, so they walked around with parasols. Sheer sentimentality. And in the literature of that time people would go into a graveyard at night when the moon was shining to sit on a grave and weep. About what? Well, just read it, they wept about nothing. There was nothing to weep about, for they didn't know the people who were buried there. Later on they made gardens with epitaphs in them so that they could sit there at night and mourn a long-lost friend. All of this began in the eighteenth century; sentimentality is a modern phenomenon.

Art and mission

Question: What do you think about art and mission?

Missionaries made great mistakes in the past in the area of the arts. Of course they did, because the problems are awfully difficult. If you come in a country and you teach these people Christianity, what are you going to do on the cultural level? Do you introduce your hymns? Do you introduce your little Jesus pictures? Or don't you? I think the worst way of handling these problems was exemplified by a story I was told. Around 1880 there was a missionary in West Africa and a friend of his wrote to him: 'What kind of music do these people have?' He answered: 'These people have no music, they only make noise.' That means he never tried to understand their music and did not care about what these people did. If one does not care, one is not interested in them as people. How can one bring the gospel to people in whom you are not interested? Now I know that this missionary was interested in their souls. But how can one reach souls without bodies? Then one reaches no-bodies! In the end one gets no-bodies; and there are too many no-bodies around in the mission field.

So we need to really think about what we are doing. My answer, which is probably an impossible answer, my ideal of what ought to have happened is something like this, and sometimes it has been done. First it was done by Paul and later by some missionaries in China. There's a little book about it that was written around 1950 and it was called *The Jesus Family in Communist China*. What I think we ought to have done was to go to these people, preach the gospel to them and as soon as they had accepted the gospel to say 'Praise the Lord! Here, have a Bible, and goodbye. God bless you.' But in most cases we began to coax them as if they were little children and to send more missionaries (because they were considered so stupid and bad at organization, and so on, mainly because we expected them to jump straight into twentieth-century Western culture). But why should we even think and dream of these people becoming culturally westernized when our culture today is in such a crisis? Why should we want to export the crisis of our Western culture? Much better to let these people start anew. Of course that's a dream, that's past. We have brought our music, which means that we have killed their music, and brought our art, which means we have killed their art. Where do we start now? At this point I should really stop, because I don't know the answers. I have a very intelligent student, and I try to lure him into writing a thesis on this problem – mission and art. He thought about it and then he said no, because a) there is no literature on the subject and b) there is almost no practice of the subject, so there is nothing with which to start. That means if we should start now, perhaps in 25 years' time that thesis can be written – and let's hope it will be written in 25 years' time. How should Christians teach art history in Africa? Should we teach these people about Rembrandt and Raphael? Or should we refrain from that? We should work on these things so that an answer can begin to be formulated. The tragedy is that I wish we could have said to these people that we have something wonderful to offer them. But what we really bring them is crisis, ugliness, and apart from that we destroy what they have and we take away their own initiative.

When you go to China or India, what you see in the missionary office or in the homes of the Christians or in the books they publish are the most awful and cheapest kind of images imaginable. But when you go into the non-Christian world you see the same thing. I read an Indian magazine some time ago in which there was a long discussion on 'Why do we Indians who have produced so many good things in the past, nowadays have such a low taste that we buy all this trash?' This trash is not coming from Europe; it's produced in India. How much of it is due to the introduction of Christianity, how much of it is the result of the overwhelming influence of Western culture, and how much of it is due to the decay inside these countries themselves? That's very difficult to answer.

Of course it's true that a culture is shaped by the introduction of the Bible into that culture. But look at Europe. If it would be true to say that the high point of Christian art is to be found in the seventeenth century

– Schütz, Rembrandt, Sweelinck, some writers like John Donne – then that means that this was achieved around seventeen hundred years after Jesus Christ. Sixteen hundred years after the Crucifixion and the Resurrection something was finally happening. Maybe we should not overlook the Gothic period, but even that was twelve hundred years after Christ. It takes hundreds of years before something is realized. One may read about early Christian art, but when was that? Roughly four hundred years after Christ. That is the same distance in time from the time of Christ as 1975 is from 1575, which was just after the Reformation.

There was of course carpentry and other crafts made by Christians during the first centuries after Christ. But if I look at the works of these people from the first century, I see no difference between their work and what was produced by the surrounding cultures. There is only one difference: they didn't make idols. They began with a 'negative' and then slowly, after three or four hundred years, there emerged something that could be called Christian art. It takes time. Of course things happened in the meantime or we wouldn't have had the art that emerged after the three or four hundred years. But it doesn't come in one day; it comes with hard work over many generations. Don't expect it tomorrow but realize that hard work needs to be done in order that our great-grandchildren may have it.

I'm not just talking about painting, music, literature, poetry and theatre here, but also about sermons and theology and many other things. When did Christian thinking manifest itself? We may point to Augustine as an early Christian, but when did he live? Four hundred years after Christ, not twenty years after Christ. When did Calvin live? Fifteen hundred years after Christ. We shouldn't think that it will come so easily. If we had gone to Africa and just given them the gospel and left, we could have said to them 'We will come back in five hundred years to see a Christian culture here.' But then it would have been a truly Christian culture and not the bad thing we see now, which is not the fault of the Africans but our fault. I don't know whether it could have been avoided, but I think we should now set things right.

Christianity and culture

Question: How can art and beauty become more integrated into the lives of Christians?

My answer is that I don't know the answer, but I know it is something valuable to fight for. Let's take fifty years or one or two generations to try and find an answer. Nobody knows the answer because we have simply not yet asked the very first question. Some things have been done, but if I should present some of them here they would only create misunderstandings because people are not yet ready to understand what we are aiming at. I'm just beginning to see the beginnings of a development in the right direction. It will take time, because due to the neglect of the previous generations it has come to be like this. So what are we to do? Think, work, fight, show the world that we are aiming for something that is worthwhile. Beauty and art, of course, are not ends in themselves. We are not people who live for art, we live for life, we live for Christ because he is the Giver of life. Art is just an expression of that. So we have to change our lives. Without a reformation – a real and deep change in our spiritual understanding, our biblical grasp of things – this will never come about.

A French artist was once sent to me by a Belgian Bible college. He was an accomplished artist and came to interview me. The first question was 'Is there any need in the Christian life for art?' The second question was 'What do we do with modern art?' And so he went on. I got very angry and said to him: 'What are you doing? You are in a Bible college and you are asking me whether art has any meaning for the Christian life. But don't you see that the question of art is the most relevant question to ask if you are in a Bible college to become an evangelist? Because the next thing you will do is to set up a big tent, and what do you do in it? You play music! And you send out leaflets. And it's all art! But because you refuse to ever think about it you end up with stuff that is so third-class and bad. And that communicates that you don't care. And if you don't care, who will care to listen to you? If you as an evangelist want to use music, you have to think about what's good to play.'

When people ask me what kind of music they should play in their coffee bar, then that's a very deep and important question, one that's basic for every Bible college and not to be answered in half an hour but in a full course, which examines all the complexities and difficulties. What should we do? What should we not do? What does this particular kind of music communicate? We cannot play Bach or the Velvet Underground in the coffee bar. We have to play something that's appropriate. What do we play? I'm not going to answer that. The point is that these things are very important.

Twenty years ago one of my students became a Christian. He lived in another city and I visited him. Very angrily he threw something down before me and said: 'I am now a member of a church, but look what they produce.' It was a church newspaper and it was so tasteless. He said: 'This dirty thing, that's what they dare to send me each week. They do not honour my person with this, they insult me.' This paper is blasphemous in a way. It insults God. If you love your neighbour, you will send him or her something good. Of course we cannot spend ten thousand dollars each week to have artists make new paintings for our newspaper. That would be out of balance. But ask people who have some knowledge about it to do it, and pay them for that. Don't ask them to do it for free just because it's for God. The preacher does not preach for free. He or she is paid for the work. Why not the artist?

I am not asking for phoney snobbishness but for a beautiful reality. And if you make something that's solid and beautiful, it's good for the most uncultured person as well as for the most highly cultured person. At least that's what we should aim for, even though there are these divides in our social culture that make it difficult to produce something that is good for everybody. And perhaps we won't succeed, but we have to try – instead of doing it as cheaply as possible and giving the job to the first person we can think of or ordering materials from a company that makes sweet but meaningless things. In 25 years' time let's be making something that's really worthy of God.

Question: What do you think about the hymnals we use?

I became a Christian during the last war. And after that war was over I came into the church. I had never before been to church. I must say that becoming a member of the church was the hardest thing in my life, much harder than becoming a Christian. When I came into church, I felt very unhappy about the singing. And I have been in that church for 30 years and have never become used to it. How do we solve that problem? I wish that I was a musician and I could get to work on it, but I'm not and so I have left it. I think that the main problem is not the words – of course the words should not be trite or too sentimental or sweet – but we cannot always sing psalms. I do agree there is a place for hymns. But even when we sing the best psalms, with the best words and melodies, sometimes it's still no good because they just lack life. And they lack life because of the way we sing them. We can have the most beautiful words, written in the most positive way, but our singing turns them into little pious songs that lack life and reality. That's where we should begin with change, have a little more guts, put a little more rhythm into our songs. When the rhymed psalms were first made and Calvin brought the *Genevan Psalter* to the world, the Reformation was spreading all over Europe. People said 'These songs are wonderful; they speak of life and reality.' Queen Elizabeth I called them 'Geneva jigs' because they were so joyful and real. And now we have turned them into pious little songs, because of our way of singing them and our attitude to the songs. Don't ask me to give you an example because I'm not a good singer. I can't show you how to do it. But I think that we should think first of the way in which we sing rather than of the songs we sing. But of course, form and content have to be one. If the words are trite we cannot expect the song to be good.

The answer is not in rock music. If we use rock music in church, we communicate to the world that we have nothing to say and that we can only follow what they do. We cannot just adapt rock music because we have barely understood the content and meaning of that sort of music, what it expresses and stands for, and it is too alien to us for use in a knowledgeable way. That doesn't mean that in other ages people couldn't pick up the songs and forms of their time; and it doesn't mean that this would be completely impossible even now. But we have grown too far away from anything like this. It is a shortcut to jump into rock music; it's a short circuit.

I was about to weep a few days ago when I was in Boston to speak to a graduate group in a church. Before I went I asked what kind of people I would be speaking to. I was told it was a group of people between 25 and 35 years of age, highly professional, educated intellectuals. When I arrived they started the meeting with a hymn. And they sang: 'I'm gonna lay down my burden down by the riverside, down by the riverside.' And I thought to myself that these people were above this. It's not a bad song, it's maybe even better than some others. But these people needed something more solid. One does not give milk to spiritual adults, to quote Paul. And this was milk. It would be a nice song for singing in the children's classes; it would be wonderful to sing in Sunday school. But here professional intellectuals were singing it. What's the solution? Can we wait until the attitude towards these things has changed and assume that then the outer forms will change as well? No, we can't wait for that. Let's listen to what people like James Ward are doing and assess it. We must begin to work and experiment.

Question: Should we not have it as our priority to serve and love God?

Yes, of course, but that does not mean that we should be out of touch with our culture. That would be the wrong answer, because we cannot avoid being involved in our culture. If we say evangelism first and the rest is nonsense, our presentation of the gospel will be nonsense, because the music we play will be nonsense, and the music communicates as much as our words do. What we do on stage and what the stage looks like communicates even more than our words. An evangelist's words, or any Christian's words, are always measured by other people as to their truthfulness. If one says: 'Christ is the Life!' but people don't see any life, one's words are in vain for they are not backed up by reality. If one says: 'We are concerned for your soul,' but one never looks at a poor person, people will get angry. I know too many evangelists who meet a person and at a certain moment one can almost hear the 'click', and from then on they give their message like a tape recorder, a message they have learned by heart, and when they have finished it 'clicks' again and they become a normal human being once again. But the other person has sharp ears. That person knows that the 'evangelist' was not interested in him or her but was just interested in the message. And that person will not listen but simply be turned off. Our care for people means that we should come with good music and with a presentation that can stand the test – not in a worldly sense, being the finest of the finest and most expensive, because then it becomes plush and phoney, and there are too many phoney Christians around (that's not what I say, that's what the world says). We have to be real. If we don't live the gospel, we speak out of emptiness.

What is our priority? Christ said, 'I am not taking you out of the world, but I pray that you may be guarded against the Evil one.' We cannot be out of the world; we simply can't. We have to communicate and we have to understand. How can one preach the gospel and proclaim that God is the Lord of everything when one has no interested in biology or geology? As Christians we have to live in the world and show that we are concerned and interested, and that we want to fight evil in politics and everywhere. We want to fight alongside those people who fight the good fight for otherwise we will be fighting against them. And they will listen because then our message counts. Otherwise our words are in vain.

God says in Isaiah 1:

> I hate you (God is speaking to Israel, to the church of that time), you go to church and you do your offerings and you do all those things, but I hate it! It is a stench in my nose! Why? Because you don't care for the poor, you don't care for the world, you don't care about what is presented on television, the bad programmes people see, the way people's understanding of values is torn down, their lives are impoverished and the world is being abused and polluted. You stand aside and you don't even weep!

We cannot separate these things from our so-called Christian activities for they are all interrelated. Yes there is a list of priorities to be made, but it never puts preaching versus culture.

We should care what churches we build but they don't need to be expensive; they can be tasteful but simple. There is something good in the protest of the hippies who say they do not want our luxurious lifestyles. We must be concerned about all the poverty in the world. There are many things we don't need. How may we help others? We should be on the front line of thinking about this. Christians have done great works in the past. All over the world one finds hospitals and schools that have been founded by Christians. But are we still concerned today? We cannot separate our faith from these things, they belong together. The Bible says that if we walk in the ways of the Lord, then it means that we will care for the orphans and the widows. That's the way to show it. James says 'You say you have great faith? You're a great preacher? I'm telling you, if you don't show the works, forget about it.' This is not a strange commandment. We should love the world because it's God's world. It is cynical, in a Greek philosophical way, to say 'Out with the world.' Rather, God says 'Out with what? I gave it to you!' Of course there is a right time for everything under the sun. We should not sit at home sipping coffee when it's time to stand up and say 'This is what the Lord says', even if we know that it means we may be put in jail or worse. That's putting our priorities right, because the kingdom of God is first. But if the kingdom of God is first, then all the other things will follow, not fall away. We shouldn't despise them or we may not be following the kingdom of God anymore.

When I was in the South, I asked many people about race relationships. Someone told me this story. It's a horror story, a small horror story for there are others, much worse than this. In a church in the South a lady bought new hymnals. So the church had a whole set of beautiful new hymnbooks. Three weeks later some very well-known, prominent theologian came and said that it was an unscriptural, bad hymnal. The church discussed it and decided to buy a new set of hymnals, because these were no good. So far this is an excellent story. But then the problem came: what to do with the old hymnals that had just been bought for thousands of dollars? Someone suggested 'Why don't we give them to the black church in town?' I think if any of us were present at that moment, we would have had to stand up and say 'If you do that, I'm not staying here any longer.' I often ask why these Christians are so racistic and then am told that there are many people who are not, but that they dare not stand up because people would just turn away from them and the churches would run empty. But might it then no be better for the churches to run empty? We should protest the moment something happens that cries out for a protest.

Christ never talked softly about things like that. He said: 'Woe unto you, you who go around the world and make many converts, and turn them into people who are more dead than alive.' He was protesting against the kind of evangelism the Pharisees were doing. That's the kind of talk we should imitate a little bit. Of course, we have to do it with tact. We should not turn people away because we are so hard-headed and unloving. We must protest in love. The other person should know that we do it because we love him or her. And that's not easy. I have no little recipes for that. It is life, and it involves weeping and sometimes sheer frustration. But we should not accept the evil and the wrong things. The Christian's life includes acceptance and non-acceptance. We accept that people are sinful. When a young man in L'Abri tells me that he has been to a prostitute, I do not say: 'Get out, go away.' I accept it. He is a sinful man. But maybe there's a problem, and then I have to help him solve it, because I also don't accept that and want to try and find a better way for him. So we always live in this tension of acceptance and non-acceptance, in protest yet knowing that the world will never be perfect. When to act, when to protest? I do not have the answer. But we certainly cannot accept everything. Some people feel sick about one thing and others about something else. Let's help one another and build one another up.

Question: How as Christian leaders can we take part in cultural things that might offend the very people we are responsible for, whether those things are wrong or not?

This is a great problem, for which there is no theoretical solution. Paul faced that problem with Timothy. Although Paul did not think it was necessary, he circumcised Timothy. But when he was asked to go to the Temple he said no, for the Temple was old-fashioned, its time was past. Later he gave in. It's a matter of wisdom and insight, and it's also a matter of teaching. I know that I sometimes shock people. I hope that I have shocked some people, but I hope that I have shocked them out of complacency and wrong prejudices into a better understanding. Maybe it's good to show our young people some pornographical material, to let them see it and then to say 'Don't you think that's awful? Don't you see what it leads to?' That may be a better sermon than to preach from the Bible text only – about not committing adultery – which puts it at a safe distance, bearing no relation to the world around us. Sometimes we must speak out strongly because our young people and the congregation live out there in the world, much more so than we perhaps may think. Talk about the movies. Sometimes it's good to go to a film together and to talk about it, and at the end to pray and ask God to make us clean again if the movie has defiled us. I know that there are dangers. I know that we must try to avoid the dangers, but we cannot avoid the dangers of living. We have to be careful that we don't put away too many things. What can a person take? And what not? That's a matter for each one to decide.

One text that you should never allow to be misused in your face is the wonderful words in Romans that says 'Don't do these things if you offend your brothers.' It is spoken to the 'strong' people in order that they may be careful not to offend the 'weak' ones. But this text is often used in the following way: some young people walk into a church and they look different, and then the church says 'You've got to conform, you've got to dress nicely, don't give offense.' But if a group of young, immature Christians come to church and they think they have to worship on bare feet, well just get out of your shoes and go on bare feet too because you should not want to give offense to them. You are the strong ones and they are the weak! We always need to be careful in the application of that verse. It tends to be people who have been Christians for a long time, the strong ones, who make the others conform, but Paul says exactly the opposite. The strong must conform to the weak.

I'm not saying it's easy to draw the lines. It's always dangerous, but it's much more dangerous to live with do's and don'ts because God forbade that. It was the heart of the lifework of Paul to fight for freedom. Just read Colossians 2. We all make mistakes. I have made mistakes, I moved ahead too quickly and some people were perhaps offended, but other people were liberated from their cages. How can we live without making mistakes?

Question: How far should we go, possibly even adapting to the kitschy quality of our culture, in order to make the Bible understandable?

I tend to say to all my students: never compromise. But that doesn't mean to be foolish, hard-hearted and without concern. One cannot compromise the principles of translation, so one's Bible translation must be accurate and clear. But one has to accept that certain words and language constructions are no longer widely understood and that one may need to use a lesser translation than before in order to be understood. That's not a compromise, that's an act of love and concern and understanding. When our language has lost in quality we may weep, but we must accept it because not only the culture around us contributed to that but we too. Yet let the Bible be just a little bit better than where the people are, so that they may gain something, even if just from its language. Some of the modern translations do this well; some are better than others. I leave it up to the theologians to assess the quality of each translation but I understand the problem. I suggest that we should not compromise the meaning and the content, because then we lose something. That's what the modern theologians do: oh, you don't accept the virgin birth? Then we won't talk about it, just forget about it, after all, it doesn't matter. But God says it matters, it means something, it's not in there for nothing but it's perhaps not the most important point in the Bible. A modern theologian once said to me: 'Do you really think it's necessary to believe that Christ walked on the water – is your faith built on that?' The implication was that one can happily take away that text from the Bible. I said: 'Of course my faith is not built on Christ's walking on the water. It's built on the finished work of Christ. But if I accept that Christ is the God who came to this world to redeem us, why should I not also accept that he who was there at Creation can walk on water? It's silly to deny it.'

So we should be careful not to compromise on the content but, at the same time, we should be lenient, just because we don't want to be out of the world.

Question: Should a Christian spend ten dollars on a concert while one's brothers and sisters in Africa are starving to death? Or should we build a fabulous church for half a million dollars?

This is a matter of priorities. Christ was very careful when he said that you should love your neighbour as yourself. I don't think that Christianity asks of one to go around naked so that someone else can have clothes. It doesn't ask one to be poor and to refrain from all things in order to help in other places. But even if I send my ten dollars to Africa, it will not really help, because the problem is not money but something else. Money is a Western answer. Europe was poor after the last war; America sent money and Europe recovered, but that was within a Western cultural system. In the Third World it doesn't work like that.

We also have to think through the implications. If we don't spend the ten dollars on the concert, then the implication is that others shouldn't, and then the musicians are going to starve and culture will decay. Every time you will have to weigh the specific situation. One may spend a lot in one place because one thinks that's important, but at another time one may say 'No, I cannot even spend half of that, because I have another priority.'

The building of a church is a much bigger issue. I must say I have been very worried about that. In the last months we have had many Christians in L'Abri asking questions about how a church should invest its money, and whether a church should get rich. In my opinion a church should never invest its money in order to become rich. We laid down some rules together, and of course they are not absolute rules but, for example, one rule was that a church should never have more money in reserve than one year's budget. Everything beyond that is too much. Regarding church buildings, on the one hand there is no real need to build a church. There are so many halls and schools and existing church buildings – why not just rent space as the church needs it? On the other hand it is not a sin to build a church building, but how should it be done? It should be done well, in good taste; it should be beautiful but not lavish or elaborate. If it is a ten-million-dollar structure, then something has gone wrong.

Eight years ago I flew to the west of Canada to give a course there. I landed in Vancouver with my family, someone picked us up and we drove through Vancouver. My children became really angry and said: 'This is impossible! These cars are too big, these houses are too big, it's too wealthy!' Now perhaps if you come from India or Africa into Holland you would say the same thing.

Personally I was very angry when the following happened: before the War, I had a discussion with some friends about television. At that time none of us doubted that television was a possibility. No problem. But we all agreed that it would be so expensive that it would never become common. Very soon after the War it appeared everywhere. Around 1960 Holland was in a difficult economic position. And at that particular time colour TV was introduced! I found that sinful, a shame! Everyone suddenly had to buy new TV sets. Why not spend that money in a better way? Were there no more important values than colour television? Every time I see a colour TV I still get that feeling in my body. That's not just a question of a concert of ten dollars but something much more basic.

Should we have a church building? God tells us that we should come together as a congregation and if we need a building for that, then the function follows the form and the need can be met. But if a church can avoid constructing a new building they ought not to have one. If a congregation builds a church, do it in good taste, let it be an expression of the values you stand for. Economics is a matter of weighing up values.

The Lord is always coming with his judgment on those things people do when they don't walk in his ways. If we make a decision on the basis of wrong values, especially in the area of economics, we can expect to see the consequences. Isaiah and Jeremiah called the Israelites to turn back to the Lord and to use their money in a better way, because they mistreated the poor. And that applies to us as well. But the answer is not to be extremely poor ourselves. That has never worked. That answer has been given over and over again. St Francis of Assisi had a very rich father but chose to be poor. Maybe it was needed in those days. But less than one generation later in the Franciscan movement this attitude had gone completely. Some people tried to live by these principles but they are too extreme and do not work in the end. We need to have a balance. The balance is difficult and everyone will make mistakes. One day I might spend ten dollars on a concert and later on think 'What have I done? I shouldn't have gone. That was silly and sinful.' Another time I might say 'Why didn't I go and spend the ten dollars? That was silly and sinful. I should have been there.'

Nudity

Question: If art has an ethical side, that implies certain limitations. What are the limitations we need to consider and how far does our freedom go? For instance, in depicting nudity?

As a rule, as a kind of yardstick, we can say that we should always be careful to judge art by what it wants to say and not by what it portrays. Is it a sinful thing to portray the breast of a woman? I would say that's a silly question. Because an obscenity or something wrong in this respect are not defined by square inches of flesh but are defined by what the portrayal wants to express. Many years ago I had a long discussion about this and I came up with the following thought: why are Christians always talking about nudity, because what is really unhealthy, what is really wrong, the thing we should really be fighting is precisely all the clothed women. I had in mind the cover images of the magazines around us which mostly use women as a kind of attraction feature. Of course these women are nicely clothed – this was twenty years ago and they were all nicely clothed then because one could not show more at that time, but of course they were all very tempting and seductive, in a way they were adulterous persons. So what matters is not the clothing or the absence of clothing but the intention.

There is a great difference, and that's where the confusion begins, between something that's social and something that's in art. When you make a painting of a nude woman, that has nothing to do with nudity in the social reality. Even if there is a relationship it is not a direct one. Winckelmann, the great classicistic theoretician from the middle of the eighteenth century, said: 'Why is Greek art so beautiful? That is because the artists were able to see nude figures around them in daily life. And these people were all doing sports and that's why they were so beautiful.' I would say that this is a naturalistic fallacy, because that was never true. The classical world was not such a fantastically ideal world where everybody walked around as if in a nudist camp. No, the [Greek] artists were painting and sculpting their ideas about humanity. Art is a metaphor, a symbol. I wish I could show you Jan van Eyck's *Eve* [from the *Ghent altarpiece*] at this moment, one of the most beautiful nudes ever painted and one of the most chaste pictures in the world. Even though it is more precisely painted than most nudes are, in that it shows pubic hair and so on, nevertheless it is so pure. If people viewing such a picture have bad sexual thoughts, the source of such thoughts is inside them and not in the painting. But pictures with completely clothed figures can be very obscene and negative and bad. So we should judge on the basis of the meaning of things and of what is communicated, and not on the basis of a set of rules because that is legalistic.

Nudity is used as a metaphor and in the sixteenth and seventeenth centuries people did not have the prudishness that came later. And of course they did look back to the Greeks. But why did I use nudes as examples in my lectures? Because they communicate easily, directly, strongly. To explain the same things without the nudes would have meant lectures three times as long – and probably less clear.

Question: But was it not because of their own nakedness that Adam was unable to look at Eve without shame, so that God had to make clothes for them?

I don't think that shame in this case should be understood in the sense of never showing any nudity. If in our culture it were a social custom that we bathe in the nude on the beaches, then there would be a difference on the beach between some women and others. Some women would be very sexy and would go beyond the limits of shame, and other would not. Just as at this moment some women with bathing suits are very unchaste, and very seductive, and sexually very provocative, and some are not. That has nothing to do with their clothes. It all depends on how a person uses one's body. Let me tell you a little story. A very, very sexy woman came to L'Abri. This happened about fifteen years ago. She was a filmstar. She became a Christian after three weeks. And Dr Schaeffer said to me later: 'I wish I had some photographs: three weeks before and three weeks after.' Because three weeks afterwards she was not sexy anymore. What had happened? What happened was that her attitude to life and values had changed. But she had certainly not gone out and bought new clothes. She was wearing the same dresses. It is not the dressing or the undressing that makes people chaste but the way we wear our clothes, the way we move, the way we express our corporality.

In art there are two types of nudity. Kenneth Clark, who wrote a book on this, says that there is nudity in the sense of shame, as in medieval art, and heroic nudes, as you find for instance with Michelangelo. I would say that we find the least shame of all in Michelangelo's *David*. It's a shameless sculpture. I say that not because he happens to be nude but because of his attitude. He stands there and radiates: 'Here I am. I'm not afraid. Look how beautiful I am!' But *Adam* [from the *Ghent altarpiece*] of Jan van Eyck stands in shame before the Lord. He says: 'I am weak.' Just like the Bible says that every person will stand naked before the Lord – that means with nothing to cover oneself. One's weakness will be exposed; one will stand before the Lord knowing that one has failed. That is what shame means in Genesis 3.

There's another, related point to be made about shame. When God does something in the Bible, it always has a double edge to it. I mean this: when God comes with the curse he also brings grace. To be more precise, when God said: 'From this moment on death will be a reality' no one said 'Hurrah, now we are going to die.' Nevertheless there is one reason for saying 'Hurrah, people die.' Just imagine for one moment that after the Fall people were not to die. That would mean having all the worst tyrants and criminals of all of history around us. Happily these people have finished their lives. In that there's grace. People are also afraid of dying and that puts a check on their wickedness, but the gangster who can live without fear of death will quickly become a really nasty menace.

Now the same is true of shame. If God had not given shame to people (and I think it is a gift) then there wouldn't be boundaries. Now when men and women approach each other there are always barriers to overcome, little thresholds to cross, little doors to open. A man never just jumps on a woman unless he rapes her and then we call it rape and that is wrong. But if a man comes to a woman, he starts by touching her softly, and she accepts or answers his touch. And so they go on meeting each other, and every time a little barrier has to be overcome. When there are strong barriers we talk about shame. So there is a difference between bathing together in the nude, as is done in some places in the world (and I don't think there is anything wrong in that), and jumping into bed with one of the women. There are boundaries because there is shame.

Shame is very much tied up with our most intimate parts. If you look at paintings, you will find that there is a limit. The most intimate parts of a woman are never shown. A woman can stand without clothes without her intimate parts being visible. They are hidden. That's maybe why it is easy to portray a woman in the nude, because one can depict her completely in all her beauty and she can become a symbol for humanity in its manifold aspects while evading the real tough point. And you may see many pictures of nude men, but rarely will you see an erection. If you do, it is usually very strong in a wrong sense. You will normally not see that, because that's the moment of shame. It's a gift of God that he put restraints on our sexual relationships. So we don't have free love, thanks to the Lord, because God gave us shame. But we shouldn't say one has to be ashamed whenever one sees a person in the nude. That's a little bit over the top and not how it was meant to be. That's a nineteenth-century interpretation that comes out of Victorian sensibilities. I think we should strive for the right barriers and the right forms, and of course our own feelings are also involved here. We should strive for more freedom, more openness at this point, even though that is very difficult. If parents are not able to deal with their children on this level, they should try to get their children to go further; maybe in two or three generations' time we will have more openness. We shouldn't be idealistic, though, for never in history was the man-woman relationship completely right. We live in an imperfect world as sinful beings.

Question: But how can you be positive about a painting like Rubens's 'Rape of the daughters of King Leucippus', which in my opinion depicts sin?

I put Rubens's painting [see Plate 5] on the screen next to a horrible picture by Corinth that shows rape in a very cheap way. We need to understand what exactly Rubens is doing here. His painting deals with a subject that is not just rare in art but totally unique. He uses a classical story that talks about rape. The interesting thing is that Rubens depicts these men, who were guards, as good guards with nothing rough about them. And the story goes on, for it says that afterwards they immediately married these women, which means it was not rape for rape's sake in the bad sense of misusing a woman and then leaving her in the road while getting away. You might say yes, it's not the worst kind of rape but nevertheless it is not according to the laws that God gave for the man-woman relationship. I agree, but I don't think that's the point. Because Rubens was searching for a very strong visual image and he used the story to provide him with a motif: the motif of woman being the inspiration for man. The real content of that picture is woman inspiring man to great deeds. There is nothing against the Scriptures in that. The beauty of Rubens's picture is exactly in its not telling about sex in the sense that twentieth-century people talk about sex, but that it tells about the erotic in a very fully human sense. This to me is very beautiful and something we have little understanding of today because sex has been brought down to the animal level. It is precisely the man-woman relationship, a love relationship, which is exalted by this picture. So, don't look at the little story in too narrow, too myopic, a way because Rubens was only using the story as a metaphor for something great he wanted to say, namely that woman, including her bodily presence, yet not only by the sexual impulse but through the fullness of her womanhood, inspires man in the fullness of his manhood to great deeds.

Question: How do we determine what is beautiful, not only as to form but also as to content?

You ask for something that one knows. You ask for definitions, and definitions are so difficult. There is a relationship between truth and beauty, a very narrow relationship. The one painting of the nude woman is ugly, not because the painter was a bad painter in the technical sense, or was below standard, because in his own class he was a very good one. But it is ugly because alienation was built into the work. It lacks in its grasp of reality. Because of that, because of this 'objectivity' the woman becomes pornographic. Pornography always implies alienation. It's something that is presented to us in a cold way, devoid of meaning, and we can then add our thoughts to it. We cannot add our thoughts to the Rubens painting because the picture gives us our thoughts. And there is true knowledge, an opening of our eyes so that we begin to see and know women in a new way. We wouldn't know women unless they were drawn for us. That's why the pin-up is an eternal thing. But to have portraits of women around us is important for us in order that we may grasp more and more of reality and humanity. These portraits work as metaphors.

The truth of a painting is certainly not divorced from its beauty. I have a record at home. Suppose that you do not understand the language in which the song is being sung and you would say to me: 'That's a beautiful song.' And suppose I was a magician who could snap my fingers and say: 'Now you can understand the language.' And then I play the record again and you can hear that from beginning to end it's one big curse. Then, when the record finishes, you will no longer say it's a beautiful song. For when you grasp the meaning of the song you will say: 'Well, it's very strange but in a way I now understand that that melody, which I perhaps found intriguing, just makes the curse more powerful.' Because there is a unity in every good work of art, just as in every good human thing there is unity. All the parts work together.

A work of art gives us more than just beauty. It is a trite remark to make when standing in front of a painting to say that it is beautiful. Rather, one tries to assess more of it, to determine what it means, what it expresses, what its relationship is to reality. That is very complex. I cannot give a simple definition and, to be honest, if I knew it I wouldn't give it to you. I'm always asked: 'Can't you give us a nice way to understand what beauty is and how you judge art?' I always tend to say: 'I know it exactly. It's written on a little piece of paper and I have it in my pocket but I won't tell you. Because if I tell you, the danger is that you might believe me. And if you believe me, I would become the pope in art. And I don't want to be the pope in art.' There are no easy definitions. Just as there are no easy definitions of faith and love. But that doesn't mean judging art is random. No, it's very precise. However, the difficulty is that you ask me a question that is universal, while I'm convinced that the universal can only come to us in the specific. If at this moment we were standing in front of a specific painting, I could have told you what is beautiful and what is ugly. With that there is always a measure of reality and truth implied. If a lie is presented in a beautiful form, the lie becomes more ugly and that makes the lie more of a lie. It is very interesting how that works in fairy tales: the bad woman, the stepmother, is usually ugly because her form is in relation to her content. But sometimes there is a very beautiful evil woman, the enchanting witch. Then she becomes even more ugly, just because she is so beautiful. Her beauty enhances her ugliness. If a person is tortured in a beautiful palace, in a beautiful room with a lovely shape, the torture becomes more horrible. That's why tortures normally take place in dungeons, ugly places, more in conformity with the ugliness of the deed.

Question: Can we depict the negative?

Yes, we can portray corruption, murder and all the bad things in the world around us. We can protest in our art and show how ugly and bad these things are. But we must be very careful because the artists around us, the modern artists, also depict these things, though in a very different way. In the way of gnosticism they say that this whole world is bad. But if one paints rape as rape in order to say it's rape and therefore it's bad, one has made a beautiful picture. At least, possibly so. In literature, in theatre or film it is possible to have very strong moments that talk about things that are very ugly. If they are shown in their ugliness, they are true. A film that I found wanting, just to give an example, is Barbara Streisand's *The Way We Were*. It begins: leftwing girl, rightwing boy, meet each other, fall in love, but things are difficult, they have such different understandings and lifestyles. He's a writer, she becomes his conscience, as it were, and they marry. Well, people who marry leftwing-rightwing, they find it difficult. And the film shows us the difficulties. And it works, and it's fine, it's fantastic! They go to Hollywood and he becomes a very famous filmmaker and so on. Up until that point the film is fine and beautiful. But at a certain moment the man compromises. And that can happen – that's wrong, that's ugly, he shouldn't have compromised but he did, that's human. But then, how do they solve it? Well, in the film they could find only this trite solution that the marriage has to break up, and so there is a divorce. On the very day the baby is born, the man leaves. In the next shot you see the woman ten years later, still a leftwing girl walking around with a 'Ban the Bomb' protest march, and you see the man going into the Hilton with a beautiful woman for a fantastic dinner: a leftwing versus a rightwing attitude to life. I would say that at the moment of the divorce that film became a total lie! And it's bad propaganda, because it makes people think that they can have a divorce that easily. But I know from experience with people who come to L'Abri that it doesn't work that way. The man would never have written another book in his life and the woman would have come, let's say, to L'Abri and we would have had a long and hard time just to help her live a normal human life again. It doesn't work like that, it's a lie. It's a lie because it goes against reality, and the wrongness of the film is that it doesn't show that. It has a very sweet, sentimental ending where it could have had a strong and real one.

We always have to do two things, namely to show ugliness as ugly and to hold up beauty as beautiful. If we don't do both at the same time the result will always be found wanting. Because then beauty becomes sentimental or we become gnostic in saying the world is bad. There is always a tension between accepting that we live in a sinful and broken world and at the same time not accepting it. Both acceptance and non-acceptance need to be shown, and they need to be shown together in their inner tension.

Question: But isn't Rubens's painting a lie as well? Does it not suggest rape?

No, it doesn't suggest rape. The picture talks about strong marriage relationships. It uses rape as a metaphor but it's not a story about rape. The other picture shows rape in the bad sense, but this one is not about a real rape – Rubens never said: 'If you rape a woman it's beautiful.' He would have said: 'That's ugly. But the married situation is fantastic, because then woman becomes an inspiration to the man.' And if anyone in the world could say that, it was Rubens himself. He was married twice and both times very happily. He has depicted his wives, also in the nude, because they were his inspiration, in a physical way but in a much deeper way as well.

So you misunderstand the word 'rape' in the title of the painting, because the work brings us into deep realities. Seventeenth-century pictures always stress the strong relationship between man and woman. Rape in the sense of real rape you find in the etching by Rubens of the wife of Potiphar. There you have sheer sex in all its ugliness. Rubens and Rembrandt always show a very high regard for women – not as sex objects (that is twentieth-century) but in the fullness of their humanity. The woman is shown as an inspiration to the man, and not only in relation to her body, because then we get into the Playboy kind of thing. It is not the playgirl that inspires the playboy to be horny! But it is the woman in the fullness of her womanhood that inspires the man to be a real man and to do great deeds in the world. And it can only be done if they live together in a very close relationship, because the strongest unit in the world is a marriage in which the partners are fully man and fully woman. And that's what Rubens is telling us about. This is clear in all of his other pictures and it's so clear when you read seventeenth-century literature. They had a much better and healthier view of marriage than many people around us today, even in Christian circles. Their ideals were much better than ours, and much less sentimental.

Question: Do we then need to have knowledge of all that is implicit in these artworks in order to be able to understand what they are saying?

No. I did start off by saying that you see what you know, and of course your knowledge is implied. But it's not true that one can only understand a painting when one has a lot of art-historical knowledge.

That is drawing a wrong conclusion out of a right definition. What we chance upon here is exactly the greatness of seventeenth-century art. I'm not saying that there is no criticism to be made of Rubens, but I think we should begin with giving honour where honour is due. Rubens is one of the greatest artists in the world. He was a man who at least at this point had a very deep understanding, which he was able to express very beautifully. So, let's not begin with criticism but end with it, very softly in the case of this painting. Rubens's art, as well as Dutch and other seventeenth-century art, works in layers. So, if you're walking in a palace with Rubens's *Rape of the daughters of King Leucippus* [see Plate 5] hanging on the wall, what you see is a very beautiful ornament. Fantastic colours. You can pass it by like that. But when you stop and you look at it, what you see is this: movement, magnificently painted women and men. That is the next layer. Then you begin to ask about the story. What does it tell me? Next you reflect on the implications of the story. Why was it used? I tried to clarify the meaning of subject matter in seventeenth-century art with my scheme of motifs and themes. The painting is not just telling a little story but the story is used to depict a motif. Once you have understood the motif, you can go deeper and deeper until you end with the universal: that love is so important. And then you begin to see that this is one of the greatest works of art. Now when you come to Munich for the first time and you stand in front of that painting, you are not able to talk about it like I am doing now. That's obvious, because I am a professor in the history of art and you are not. But that does not mean that I see things that you do not see. Because the moment I start seeing things that you do not see there is something wrong.

Maybe there *is* something wrong here. Maybe you were raised in the wrong framework. Let me try to clarify this with a story. I gave this same lecture with the Rubens painting half a year ago in Calgary. During the lecture some people left the room. And the next day many people came up to me and said: 'Are these nudes not obscene? Is that not pornography?' Well, when one person comes to you like that, you think to yourself: 'Maybe I overrated my audience, maybe I made a mistake, maybe I didn't make myself clear, of course these people are not accustomed to this type of thing, after all they live in Calgary.' But when people kept on asking me the same thing, I became very worried. Two evenings ago I gave a lecture about God's salvation and our calling. When I had finished, someone said to me: 'I have a question: if a Christian is an artist and he goes to an art school, is that a good thing, for he has to paint nudes and so on?' What is happening here? Are you not living people? You can compare it with this: say you are going to start a new bank. You need to have money, a building, personnel, and to have an understanding of banking and money problems. But if you would then come to me and tell me that you are worrying all the time about where you are going to buy the paper for your office, I would say that maybe you shouldn't start a bank, because your mind is too fixed on insignificant things. Well, if you talk about art, you don't talk about nudity. It's such a little thing in relation to the big things!

Of course nudity is a loaded thing. Why? Not because the nude is so loaded, but because humanity is so loaded and reality is so loaded. And it's good to think about it, but we shouldn't make it too strong. I get really worried when people in America always talk about it. I think it's completely out of context. It's a little thing, not a big thing. It's so beautiful. And if anybody wants to drag the Rubens down and say that it is pornography, I really get angry because they don't know what they are talking about and they are debasing the world. They say that something that is beautiful is ugly. That's rape, rape of the beauty of that woman in that painting. I'm worried about America, I'm worried about Christianity. Why are we talking about it? Is it small legalism? Is it sentimentality? Is reality in which men are men and women are women too strong for us? Having bodies? I'm worried that we may end up as people who don't have bodies, who don't live, who are dead people! This reminds me of the question of a hippie, and I think it is one of the most forceful questions we have to answer. And we as Christians have the answer, and we have to live the answer. The question is: Is there life before death?

So maybe you were raised in a wrong framework and I'm challenging that framework, the legalistic fundamentalism. The answer to fundamentalism is not to jump into the world and become worldly, but the right response is to get back to the Scriptures because the Scriptures do embrace life in all its fullness. People in the past said it is impossible that the Song of Songs could be about the relationship between men and women, it has to be a kind of metaphor for Christ and the church. Well, of course, the Bible is full of this: the relationship between Christ and the Christian community is that of the bride and the groom. Therefore the Song of Songs is also talking about Christ and the church. But in the first place it's talking about the relationship between a man and a woman. We barely dare to read it at table to our children because it's so strong, strong with all the beauties of life. God says in Ezekiel: 'I found you lying naked in the wilderness. And you were bathing in your blood, you were a newborn baby. And I bathed you and I raised you, and then you became beautiful and your breasts were like towers . . .' And so on. That's the way God speaks about it in the Bible, not as a shameful thing but as something beautiful. Why do we try to rape the Bible and take these things out of it?

Question: Why are evangelical or fundamentalistic people in America so very tight about nudity in art?

Somebody gave me a very interesting answer recently: 'It is because they have always used that little tag to avoid talking about art.' As a result, when anyone begins to talk about art, the very first thing they respond with is: 'O yes, but then you have to go to college and draw nudes and that's no good.' Then they don't need to think about it any further. So they cling to this little question to avoid the big questions. Even so the interest in art is growing and there are many young Christian artists, which is a very new situation and one I'm very happy about. It's so important that artists are there, for there will never be a real reformation without the arts, because the arts bring it to us.

Nevertheless there are questions, and I am not denying that. We need to look at these things from a historical perspective, with an understanding of history and culture, but twentieth-century people tend to be weak in this respect. I remember some years ago saying to an audience of nice American girls from some university: 'You must understand as you're all sitting here very nicely dressed that if we happened to be in Bali, of course, you would all be considered very immoral. For in Bali women walk around with the upper part of their body uncovered but for a woman to show her ankles is considered obscene.' Cultural customs do play a big role. And we should be very careful to judge other cultures. When people, let's say in Japan, bathe together in the nude that doesn't mean that they are immoral people; it only means that they have a different way of doing things.

In Europe since the beginning of Christianity the attitude to nudity has always been ambiguous. Sometimes people said yes, sometimes they said no. Some of the things they did we may find strange, but it's our own time that I find very strange indeed. When I go on an excursion with my students it's impossible for boys to sleep in the same room as girls. And everybody would think it very strange if that should happen. But at the same time these same boys and girls read things and look at things that everyone in a previous age (and that is perhaps just ten years ago) would have considered wrong. There's a strange tension in our world in that things which are not acceptable are considered acceptable while acceptable things are considered unacceptable.

In the sixteenth and seventeenth centuries there was on the whole a much more healthy approach to these things than there is today. People were not prudish. There is a very interesting story I want to mention: during the time of Cromwell there was an Englishman who travelled in Holland and kept a diary. He tells us about his experiences when he visited Delft. What he talks about was not anything extraordinary but something very normal. He went to stay at an inn. As he came in he asked: 'Do you have a bed for me?' And they said: 'Yes.' He ate and drank something and then the guests were ushered to the sleeping hall. There were no small rooms, just one or two big rooms with many beds. And in these beds women, men or couples would sleep. And as they all slept naked in those days (they didn't have any pyjamas) everybody would undress, because that is how one would go to bed. And nobody thought anything about it; it was the most natural thing. So this Englishman describes how he woke up in the morning and saw a lovely lady wake up and rise. He says: 'And I looked as she dressed, because this Dutch fashion is such an interesting thing. It's so different and wonderful.' Later on he mentions how he didn't dare to kiss the hand of that lady because that was something one just did not touch. So they were not prudish, but at the same time they had strong morals.

In the homes of those days the beds were in the living-room. In Holland they were built into the walls, and one found that in many European countries. So, let's say you were having a gathering in the evening and the daughter of the house said: 'It's time for me to go to bed, for tomorrow I have to wake up early. You gentlemen, you just talk on.' Then she would go to bed, and that would happen in the room. All this changed in the middle of the eighteenth century, one of those very difficult passages in history. Somewhere around 1730 or 1740 there was a medical doctor in Lausanne who published a little book about masturbation saying that masturbation causes sicknesses. He had made it all up, but everyone believed him. And people started to consider lust as something sinful or bad or ugly. Someone in Holland recently made a very extensive study of this. And this man, who is not a Christian, came to the conclusion that the change occurred first of all in humanistic circles. Humanism brought in the change and about ten to fifteen years later the Christians followed suit – which to me is a tragic moment in history. Why did the humanists have such a negative attitude towards lust and the body? Well, just imagine a duke reading in his library. He's reading the latest thing: Diderot and the *Encyclopaedia* from France. He's very well educated and he reads French. And so he reads: 'What is a man?' The answer is basically this: 'There is no difference between people and animals and plants and things.' There is no difference, people are just like the animals. Who said that people were so different? Of course this was meant to be a very violent antichristian statement. It was also something completely unproven. Suppose the duke who was reading that book then says: 'Wonderful what this man is saying, it's great, fantastic, convincing.' An hour later his wife, the duchess, comes in. As he has just been reading that there is no difference between people and animals, when the duchess comes in, basically, she is equivalent to a female rabbit. And he is a rabbit, and they produce children. But it's a little bit difficult to look at the duchess, who is a very cultured person, as a kind of rabbit. So, what should one do? Well, in order to accept Diderot and the *Encyclopaedia* and all that went with it, one had to save one's humanity. And in order to save one's humanity one had to push human carnality right out of the picture, which people certainly did. That's my explanation of why people became so prudish.

In the nineteenth century people even went so far that little girls could have an operation to take away a little piece of their body in order that they would never enjoy sex, because sex was so lustful and sinful. It went that far, I'm not inventing this. But as a Christian I would say that if God gave women that little part, even if it is there only for sexual arousal and enjoyment, then we're not going to say it's wrong. We have to accept it from God's hand and say thank you. It was really wrong that the Christians followed the humanists. It's very interesting that nowadays the humanists violently reject the repression of sex and have turned around to an overindulgence in sex. But Christians, being afraid of the overindulgence – and it's good not to go along with it – cling to the repression instead of raising their own voice and saying clearly what is good. I am not saying that it is easy to have a right balance, but we do need to rethink these things.

Even if we do gain a new perspective on sex and nudity and our bodies, this doesn't mean that we can change everything . . . by tomorrow. There's too much emotion involved, because these things are so very deep and important. Also, the way we were raised and the things that have been brought to us from our own background go very deep and it's very difficult to just jump out of them. So, when a young artist comes to me and he says: 'I'm in the academy, but I have difficulties in going to the life-drawing class' my first reaction would be: 'Why don't you try it, because you will find out in five minutes that it's not as you think. It has nothing to do with sex. But if you continue to have difficulties, you know there's Christian freedom and there's no one who's going to force you.' Just as Paul said: if you cannot eat meat because for you the meat is contaminated, then don't eat it because you cannot go against your conscience. Though there is a very interesting passage in the Bible, in one of the letters of John, where it's written: if your conscience goes against you, but God says you can do it, God knows better, so don't be afraid. However, if someone comes to me and says: 'I really can't do that, it's against my conscience,' I would say: 'Never force yourself.' Because whatever we do we must do to the honour of God. Even if there's freedom to draw nude figures, this should never be forced upon anyone. But I would also like to stress that we should think these issues through carefully. If personally we cannot do certain things, we should not do them. But that does not mean others who can do those things are sinful and wrong.

Television and film

Question: What should our stance and involvement be as to television and film?

A while ago someone said to me something that made me really angry: 'I never look at television, I don't really care what is being shown.' And I said: 'Does it not matter to you that every day millions of people in this area of the world look at the cheapening of values? Do you just sit down and say: "It's no business of mine"?' I think it is our concern that what is shown on television should be wholesome and good, even if we do not own a television or never watch it. Because that is how people are taught and brought their values. Just as you cannot see someone you love being assaulted, you cannot see this. That's what love means. Sometimes you have these very nice idealistic people and they are so pacifistic and they talk about love, love, love. I would say love is fine, but if you walk with your girlfriend and some guys come up and start raping her and you stand aside and look at it and say 'love', what do you think your girlfriend will say to you later? She will say: 'I didn't see any love, because if you love me you should have been fighting for me.' In the same way we need to fight in the area of television and film. These things are not neutral. They may not concern our Christian world directly, but even so it's something we have to go into.

This leads me to a very difficult question, the question not just of morality but of censorship. I am on the board of film censors in the Netherlands. How much do we accept and how much do we censor? This is a real problem today. In a way I think that there ought to be censorship, just because you love people and not everything goes. On the other hand you're not to be some sort of authoritarian person who is wiser than everybody else. And of course, other people are mature but, we must add, they are mature to a certain extent. There are things that are not good for us to look at. I watch things and sometimes I wish I hadn't seen them, and then I say no to it. To give an example, there was German film on group sex and the film was apparently very thorough and serious, and based on scientific investigation. So it began with a discussion about what group sex is and what it means and what the legal aspects of it are and so on. But of course it was just a sex film, which had a nice framework so that you could look at it and think that you were very learned and deep while you were just enjoying something else. That was the first lie of the film. But the whole movie was one big lie, because all the girls were young and beautiful. What if a girl is not beautiful? What happens when these people get a little bit older? Should the men discard those women and get new young ones? But these problems were never discussed. If somebody comes in and says: 'I advocate group sex' and then he talks about it in a serious way, I would answer him seriously. But this film was just propaganda. So the film was bad not because it showed some nude girls and nude men, because that was not the issue. The issue was that a lie was presented to people, and it was put forth so persuasively that people might believe it and begin to act on it. I could not support a film that is advertising this type of lifestyle in such a superficial way that people could walk into the greatest disaster of their lives without thinking about it. It could take years and years of psychiatric visits and care in places like L'Abri to bring some people back to normalcy again.

There are other films I did fight against, but later on I wondered whether I should not have accepted them. For instance a film that presents a hippie view of life. It is not my view of life but it is good that it can be presented freely, so that the people who watch the film can think about it and make up their own minds. We are not free to silence someone else. Take for example *Blow-Up* by Antonioni, which is a philosophical statement. Today I would say: 'Go ahead and have it shown, and the next day I'll write my negative criticism, because there is freedom to discuss.' I'm not going to accept it, but I accept it as a statement. I have to live with people who hold to different philosophies.

The worst type of films are those of the *Partridge Family* kind. This was a TV series a couple of years ago about a very nice family, living very nicely, and of course very terrible things happen but everything always ends well. And everybody looks at it as very pleasant entertainment. But I'd like to take exception to that. I would like to warn Christians. As a censor I have no freedom to say no to a series like that, because I think it's too nice and sweet. What this kind of film communicates is that you can have a very nice life without any religion or Christianity. Religion is never discussed, as it is an impossible option for television to portray a nice Christian family that prays, and so on. The result is secularization; it means a lifestyle that excludes Christianity yet uses all the fruits of Christianity but without saying so. And that is false, because you cannot have the fruits without the roots; you would get something very ugly in the end. And so it is very important to also analyse the light entertainment films. Take your children to films. Someone recently told me of a new film about a family in the wilderness that she went to see with her children, and she said: 'I was so angry, because it was so false and totally out of reality.' The children will have learnt more from the anger of their mother, who said it was so phoney, than they would ever have learnt from a thousand sermons about morality and reality.

There is a very important point to make at this moment. I always say I'm very proud to be a Calvinist. Being a Dutch Calvinist means that we fought eighty years against the Spanish Roman Catholic oppression. What were we fighting for? We were fighting for freedom. What kind of freedom? Not just freedom for the Calvinists but freedom for everyone. In practice this meant that in seventeenth-century Holland there were more books printed than in the rest of Europe together. Every second day an illustrated book came off the press. Why? Because in Holland things could be printed that could not be printed anywhere else. If you have followed my course, you know that my greatest enemy is Descartes. But Descartes was able to work in Holland only. And all his books were published in Holland. And I'm very proud that he could work there, because it means that there was freedom. So, if some philosophical statement comes out in the form of art like *Blow-Up*, then I'm not going to fight that, just like I'm not going to censor any book by Jean Paul Sartre or Beckett or Wittgenstein, or anybody else. Where do we draw the line? Wittgenstein is after all more dangerous than Sartre, so should Wittgenstein be out? I believe we should get beyond that sort of censorship because we fight for freedom. On the other hand we do care for public spiritual health. The practice of this is not always easy. But, as I have repeated over and over again: to live and to be a Christian is a mentality; it is not to follow a number of little do's and don'ts. And one works out of that mentality. The questions put before us are very difficult and there are no simple rules. Only when you ask: 'What should I do in this specific case?' can I begin to think about it and discuss it and finally say: 'I would probably do this.' My answer will come out of my mentality and I may make mistakes. I may be right; I may be wrong; I may be somewhere in between, because it's seldom a black-or-white option.

At this moment they are in fact passing a law to abolish all censorship in Holland. The only thing that we can still do is to give an age restriction: films for over 14s or 18s, but that's all. Everyone can see everything. I think that's a loss and I'm afraid that as a result we may see films that censorship in the past would have stopped. The German early Nazi films for instance, which were designed to make people anti-Semitic. They were so cleverly made that nobody saw through them in those days and I'm afraid that people won't see through them today. It would be fine if it was shown in the right framework, with an explanation that this is an early Nazi film and this is how they did it, so let's discuss it. But if it is shown as just a little nostalgic piece, then it becomes dangerous and we should be careful.

What I also have been saying no to were films of violence. When the action films from Hong Kong with a lot of fighting came to Holland for the first time, there was quite a bit of discussion in the board of censorship whether we should accept them or not. What happened is that we did accept the first one. After that there was no stopping any of the next ones. And the director of the board of censorship said: 'I'm so sorry that we did accept the first one. That was a mistake.' All we can do now is to cut out little bits of violence here and there. What we cut out of the films is usually the violence and not the sex, as violence is actually more obscene than sex. The Italian 'spaghetti westerns' (as we call them) tend to be worse than the American westerns because the latter are sentimental, but the former are really violent. So, we are not just talking about sex. We need to understand what the big issues are and we need to fight for freedom. That's our Christian calling.

Question: What do you think about a movie like Clockwork Orange? It's very violent and it has a certain philosophy.

I would not say no to that film as a censor, which doesn't mean that I would not write a criticism of it. That is a different matter. I'm standing for the freedom of the press as well as freedom for films. Maybe I would take some of the excessive violence out of the film. In a way I would be doing something wrong then, because in taking out the violence I'm making the film more acceptable. In a way I'm cheating because the bad thing is not shown in all its badness. But in our culture certain things have been taken to such extremes that anything I do will be wrong, and then I must choose for the lesser evil or the better of the possibilities. It's a living situation and we must understand that we live in a culture that is very far removed from Christianity. Of course what we really want to see is films made by Christians which have a much more positive message without skirting the real issues. Not these very nice little films where you see Christian people go about their lives in a fine way without any religion involved, because that's a lie too.

Suppose that the greatest of all things would happen, that tomorrow there is a reformation and all Christianity in this country and the rest of the world comes alive. And soon we come to power and the government is ours. The president of the United States of America, all the ministers and all the members of Congress are fine Christians. Well, I would be very sorry if the next day we should have to say that America has become a dictatorship and that anyone who does not behave exactly as the Christians want them to behave, is put in jail. Then something would have gone wrong, because we're not fighting for tyranny, we're fighting for freedom. And that means that we need to take chances.

I will try to make this clear with a little story. I invented this story about twenty years ago when I was talking with a pastor of my church. I had been speaking at a conference where I had said to the kids: 'You have to go and watch films. You have to get a little exposure in order to build up a kind of antiserum in order to live in this world. You need to know what's happening and where you stand.' The next day the minister, who was the chairman of the conference, was very worried and he said to me: 'What are you saying?' And I tried to defend myself. I said it's like this: say you have twenty young people, fine young Christian kids. And then you give them all your do's and don'ts. What do you find after ten years? Most of these kids, say fifteen, will still be there, but there will be no joy in their lives for you have put them in a gilded cage. Now I come. I know that I'm doing something that is dangerous. But it is more biblical because I'm doing what God told me to do and that is never to take away freedom where God has not clearly said no. And as God didn't say 'Don't go to the movies!' I'm not going to make that into a law. But of course I'm going to discuss the films with these young people. I'm going to try and open their eyes, to make them understand. Nevertheless, I know that after ten years there will only be ten left. I will certainly have lost more. I'm taking chances. But God took chances when he gave Adam and Eve freedom in the Garden of Eden, and we all know what the result was. So if God can take chances, who are we to try and make things safe? That kind of safety cannot be guarded by us. So, after ten years there may be only ten left, but they will all be full of joy and know what it is to be alive! And the amazing thing is that there will probably be another five or ten who weren't there before.

Faith and Scholarship

- **Gird your minds for action and keep sober in the Spirit**[244]

The task and place of the believing scientist
In speaking today about the task and place of Christian science, or better, of the Bible-believing confessing Christian who is a scientist,[245] it is not our intention to present a scientific argument. We are not concerned here with establishing a theory of science or a theory of knowledge, or with a theological or philosophical discussion of the relation between natural and revealed knowledge. Neither is it our intention to develop a Christian cultural theory, in the context of which we would then proceed to determine the place of science.

No, we are concerned with that which must precede all theoretical engagement. For when as believers we go to work in the field of the sciences, then we ought to know what the task is that God has given us, we need to know what we want to accomplish through our work, what responsibility and mandate we have with respect for example to our brothers and sisters, fellow servants of Christ, and also with respect to the rest of humanity, apostates, unbelievers and heathen.

I formulated the question as broadly as possible. During the argument that follows the answers to the various parts will become clear. At the outset, however, let us take note of this: the answers to these questions, which as such are not of a theoretical-scientific character themselves – they precede every scientific question – can and may not be framed in a theoretical-scientific way. The Scriptures must teach us here. For these are questions relating to the Christian life rather than questions of Christian science. For scientific work is about life and activity and is not a scientific abstraction.

Therefore when we discuss a subject of this sort we must take care not to land up in scientific problem-solving and theories. We do that all too easily, for science has acquired such a prevalent role in the lives of people in Western Europe that we are sometimes hardly aware of being theoretically engaged. We certainly cannot claim that Reformed people have remained free of this. That is not only because we too are children of our times but also because amongst us science is often overestimated and assigned too high a place.

That is why I already interrupted myself at the beginning of my argument to say that the matter is not one of establishing the task of Christian science but of establishing the task of the Christian who is a scientist. For 'Christian science' as such does not exist; it is an abstract entity about which we can talk without any reference to a particular person or even ourselves and our closest friends. No, the matter is one of the task that we have as confessing believers who desire to walk in the ways of the Lord even when we are engaged in scientific work. If we state the question in this way it is direct and concrete and we will not be so quick to assign 'Christian science' too high a task, since we know all too well our own modest capabilities, our failings and our weaknesses. We will first ask what God wants us to do, now. For in this way we will focus on today: we are talking about scientists now and in this world.

In contrast, a scientific argument about the place and task of Christian science would be couched in abstract terms, and it would probably suggest various theoretical possibilities without taking into account – and in that context it would also not be necessary – the particular circumstances of today. Such a discussion might even take place amongst martyrs in their cells during times of persecution.

I have just said that our talking and reasoning often takes a theoretical turn without our realizing it. That can already be seen from our choice of terminology. I want to comment on this in order to avoid any misunderstanding. When for example we speak about the church and the differences that may exist in our ideas about it, then we have to distinguish clearly between our confession concerning the church and our idea of the church. In our confession we express what we believe about the church and the substance of it we seek in the Scriptures. Other people may have other beliefs and confessions concerning the church, and in the best cases will also desire to base theirs on the Scriptures; however, those will surely very often arise from their own human insights. Science has thus far played no role in any of this. What we have here, opposite one another, are different beliefs and different attitudes towards life. The situation is quite different when we are talking about the idea of the church instead of our confession concerning it. It is quite possible that people who share the same confession concerning the church will have in reality, not just on paper, different concepts of the church, of its structure and of its theoretical definition. These differing insights are theoretical and scientific in character. We distinguish these matters far too little, which helps to explain our far too casual use of terminology: we often seem to be talking about a concept of the church when in fact we are talking about our confession concerning the church.

We find this same casual use of terminology in other areas as well. Thus people talk about a psychological disposition when they should really say psychic, and about a sociological connection that should really be called social. One must keep in mind that psychology is the science of the psychic and that sociology is the science of the social, and so forth. Let us be alert to such casual usage because sometimes, without our realizing it, it can put us on the wrong track and it will always dull our capacity to discriminate and make us lose sight of the difference between scientific theory and the actual matter in reality. But enough about that.

Given this introduction we will now proceed with our actual theme, the believing scientist's task and place. We will approach it from two angles. First we will discuss the place and task of believers in general as they live amongst apostates and unbelievers. This discussion will include the task of the Christian who is a scientist outside the congregation and the people of the covenant. Then in the second place we will turn our attention to the task of the scientist within the congregation, within the community of the saints.

Thus we want to begin by asking ourselves what our place is, as Bible-believing children of the covenant, in this world of 1952 where unbelief and apostasy hold sway.[246] Our Lord describes this task for us in his word: it is to seek his kingdom before all else. To seek his kingdom means to acknowledge him as our Lord and King in all our life and to keep his commandments. It means walking and acting as befits true subjects of their Lord and King, in distinction from all those other subjects who do not love their King, who do not keep his laws and commandments, who, in a word, are rebellious, revolutionary lawbreakers within his kingdom.

In fact, all people, whoever they are, whatever they think or desire, are subjects of the Lord Jesus Christ, who has been given dominion and who already reigns day by day over the whole of creation, sitting on the throne at the right hand of God, who will do so until he has put all his enemies under his feet – when, according to 1 Corinthians 15, he will hand back his kingdom to his Father. He already was King when he stood before Pilate, according to his own testimony, not a king of the world but very concretely in the whole world.

Therefore if, as Kuyper put it, there is no terrain of which the Lord does not say 'mine', then that is not meant to be understood as a battle cry of one who is already sure of the victory, or an ultimatum, or a wish that will certainly be fulfilled. On the contrary, it is, now already, the simple reality, from day to day during the year 1952: now already it is all his; he is King of all. There is only this distinction: that he has faithful, believing subjects, who call his yoke easy and his burden light; and rebellious, unbelieving subjects, who blaspheme his name and over whom he rules with a rod of iron.[247]

He rules them with a rod of iron, yes, but does not yet destroy them. He will accomplish that in his own time. That is why his faithful followers currently live in the midst of those who hate him, waiting patiently, knowing that victory is sure. They know the injustices done to them will be avenged for the sake of his good name and that they will rule over the new Jerusalem, which the Lord had prepared for them.

In their exile they do not need to be afraid, for the Lord looks after his people. He protects and maintains them in a place 'prepared by God' in the wilderness, out of view of the serpent, according to Revelation 12. The wilderness: that is the place where the congregation, the people of the Lord now dwell, where they are assigned a safe abode until Satan, the old deceiver and antagonist, shall be cast into the lake of fire [Revelation 20:10–15].

The wilderness: that is the area that lies outside the great culture of this world, a place without theatres and cinemas, where one may perhaps just very occasionally find a school that can offer secondary or further education and where the central meeting place is often nothing more than a sports hall or a school building. Yet in this hiding place provided by God it is safe; there the Lord feeds his people with the 'bread of heaven'; they live by the word of God and are refreshed at 'fountains of living water' [Revelation 7:17]. There is no shortage there, just as the children of Israel were not in need when they were in the wilderness.[248] The Lord knows very well what his people need.

Thus God has shown his people their place, and nowhere has he given them a mandate to go and conquer the culture; why should he, since he already rules it, albeit with a rod of iron. He tells them only to be patient, to keep the lamps burning, to do what he has told them clearly and plainly in his word it is their duty to do. For it is by that word that we shall be judged. Let us therefore also not yield to temptation, the temptation to go and live in the culture of this world with all its pomp and splendour or to ape that culture and follow its path, if perhaps only in a somewhat provincial style. If we live according to God's word the world will see us as strangers anyway and not accept us fully. The 'antithesis' will become manifest by itself, we surely do not need to 'proclaim' it! This divide is there and it can only be bridged by conversion.

It is our task to live in the wilderness in the manner the Lord requires of us. But the Lord has not assigned us heavy and difficult tasks, tasks so difficult we would almost collapse under them. 'For my yoke is easy, and my burden is light,' he says, and what in the end could be more ordinary and normal than to walk in his paths according to his commandments and creation ordinances?[249] He asks of us that we follow him as our Good Shepherd and Teacher.

What then is our task in this world? It is not, as we have already said, to go out and conquer the culture for our Lord. What then could it be? Surely we are not meant to withdraw peacefully and do nothing? Yes, sometimes that can be our task – and then that 'doing nothing', that waiting, can be awfully difficult, more difficult than all the activity. Indeed there are times when God the Father says to his children that they should stay quietly out of range and wait calmly. Thus in Isaiah 26:20 he says to his faithful people: 'Come, my people, enter into your rooms, and close your doors behind you; hide for a little while, until indignation runs its course.' And in Zephaniah 2 and 3 he promises to provide a hiding place to those who truly fear him and are meek and upright in the day when he comes with war and violence to visit the earth with his judgments.[250] But these indeed refer to exceptional times of persecution and judgment.[251]

In general we can express our task with the word of the Lord Jesus Christ: 'You are the salt of the earth.' That is not something that in one way or another we have to become. It is simply what we are when we are his faithful followers, his people. Being the salt of the earth means preserving, resisting putrefaction and making food appetizing. This is not an extra task or an exceptionally difficult assignment, but just this, that you 'let your light shine before men, that they may see your good deeds.' Being salt that salts does not mean solving with our Calvinistic wisdom the difficult problems of the world or knowing the right answer to every difficult question. Being salt that salts does not mean condescending to the world out of a sense that we, after all, have a monopoly on wisdom since we possess the right rudiments and principles. That is not the way it is, for very often the difficult problems the world has to wrestle with are a tangle of not only sin, sorrows and the effects of sin but also good efforts and things that are indispensable. These problems cannot be solved just like that, not even with our 'principles', because they arise from an often incomprehensible combination of forces and powers; they are there because we live on an earth that is cursed, where sin and judgment pull things awry.

Let us therefore harbour no lofty pretensions. That is also not necessary. We are salt that salts when we are faithful and keep the Lord's commandments. Does Peter not write, 'For it is God's will that by doing good you should silence the ignorant talk of foolish men'?[252] And does Paul not say, 'Be wise in the way you act towards outsiders . . . Let your conversation be always full of grace, seasoned with salt'?[253] We are salt that salts indeed when we just seek his kingdom. To be salt that salts is to be steadfast, unmovable: 'Always give yourselves fully to the work of the Lord, because you know that your labour in the Lord is not in vain.'[254]

Now, when we begin to see our place in this way, we are freed from the compulsion and weariness of many activities that were not assigned to us by the Lord but by our own conceit and that far exceed our capacities in both scope and gravity. Especially in times like ours, when God has sent a delusion into the world, when the Devil with his two myrmidons, the beasts of Revelation 13, are preparing to establish his kingdom, in times like these when apostasy and unfaithfulness are found on such a large and constantly growing scale and we see how true it is that as lawlessness increases the love of many will grow cold,[255] in such times it can be tremendously comforting to know that the LORD does not require great things of us but that he has appointed us a place in the wilderness. In times like these when the Lord visits his judgments upon the earth, we turn to the word spoken to Baruch in Jeremiah 45:5: 'Should you then seek great things for yourself? Seek them not. For I will bring disaster on all people, declares the Lord, but wherever you go I will let you escape with your life.' God desires obedience, not voluntary, self-willed sacrifices. If we just do that, if we just obey him, then he will be near us and will keep us. In his word he has also provided many wonderful words of comfort for us to read and believe. I am reminded, for example, of the Sermon on the Mount, and of not being afraid because the very hairs of our head are numbered, etc.

It may appear that this is all self-evident, and indeed my deepest wish is that everything I am saying may be superfluous. Yet I believe that it is precisely at this point that we can discern just how far we have strayed from the Lord our God during the course of the last several decades. How many nowadays do not find political activity in the world more important than living soberly according to God's commandments and working in his church to fight there for justice and righteousness? How many do not rank the science of the Christian so highly that a scientific argument is more convincing to them than a word spoken simply according to Scripture? Science, politics and the like are often more highly regarded among us than simple obedience to the 'everyday', 'ordinary' commandments in the Scriptures. Are we not often so steeped in all kinds of work that the Lord has not commissioned us to do that we neglect to speak edifying, exhorting and comforting words and to do the work that we have been called to do in the first place?[256]

If we ask what our task is as believers in this world, the only answer is this, that we keep his word, walk in his ways, trust in the Lord our God as our Father in the covenant, turn away from all self-willed activity, and lead our lives like people in the wilderness who may expect to have a very difficult time remaining untainted by the spirit of this age. If we wait on the Lord in this way, then he can bless our work and make us a head and not a tail.[257] In this way he can make us a blessing, if he wills it, to the entire nation or indeed to all nations. Yet this is the only manner in which God's congregation, God's church can be a blessing to the unbelieving world: namely, by doing our task well, in the first place in the church.

It is perhaps no longer necessary to expand at this point on the question concerning what this means for our scientific work. To 'conquer the culture' or, more modestly, to influence it through our scientific work may not and must not be our goal. Our only task is to walk faithfully in the ways of God and, if we are scientists, also in our scientific work not put the light of Scripture under a bushel – we shall come back to that. We must also be ready always to give account of the hope that is in us: even in our scientific work we must not be afraid to be known as children of the covenant. Groen van Prinsterer shows this clearly in the introduction to his *Handboek der Vaderlandse Geschiedenis* ('Handbook of the History of our Fatherland') where he says among other things: 'I have not misused history to present my view of religion . . . But by the same token I have considered it equally unacceptable in a science called above all to bear witness to the whole truth to set the highest truth aside.' And further on, 'To testify, not persuade, is the duty the responsibility of which is imposed upon us.' Let us keep this last point firmly in mind. To make scientifically acceptable or to endeavour to show in a scientific way how correct the scriptural view of reality is, is vain labour that will never attain its goal. We must not try to convince people, no, our task is only to testify to the highest truth. And we can do that in part by modestly, meekly and faithfully doing our work, including our scientific work and fulfilling our duty in the place where we have been put, as labourers who are 'worthy of their hire'. And then, if the Lord desires to build, if the Lord desires to use our work and gives it his blessing, then a good influence can proceed from it and it can be salt that salts![258]

The task of the Christian as scientist in the community of God's people

We come now to our second point, the task of the Christian who is a scientist within the community of the people of God. Here too it is not our intention to present a scientific theory about what science really is or, more specifically, what 'Christian science' really is.[259]

The first question to be posed is what the firm foundation must be upon which science should be constructed. If we know that it will show us at the same time what is not the task of science.

Science – there is no discussion about this – ought to investigate reality, the world as it is in its structures and/or as it has developed in the course of the ages, all the great works of God. It must endeavour to account for it and to explain patterns and nexuses, distinguish what can be distinguished, and go into the thousand-and-one problems that confront the scientist. Scientists must proceed from their experience of reality, from the data it affords them. That is self-evident, for without this pre-scientific experience and knowledge of reality they would not even be able to begin their work, the work that according to the word of the Preacher is to explore by wisdom, 'all things that is done under heaven. What a heavy burden God has laid on men!' (Ecclesiastes 1:13)

Christians as scientists can as people of the covenant have a knowledge of reality – with which I mean a pre-scientific knowledge of the world, norms and history – that is different, better and more complete, from that of the worldling, simply because they know and accept God's revelation, which allows them access to a knowledge of the truth that the apostate suppresses in unrighteousness. The insight of Christians, even before they commence their scientific work, can in that case already be deeper, wider, broader and, above all, more sober and faithful to reality. They can thereby be preserved from pseudo-problems and incorrectly framed questions. For example, a believer who investigates our sixteenth and seventeenth centuries will know that the Lord wrought the Reformation; he or she will know the Reformers were weak, sinful people whom the Lord our God called as his servants to lead his people out of the house of bondage of the Roman hierarchy. And he or she will also know that the great blossoming that followed was God's blessing, a fruit of the working of the regenerating word. Now, from the outset all of that will give a different colour to a scientific historical investigation and perhaps lead to entirely different insights from what one finds in the current handbooks. In the same way, the history of the eighteenth century culminating in the French Revolution can never be studied satisfactorily if a person does not take into account the apostasy that manifested itself in all kinds of theories of unbelief and in the ready reception these enjoyed.

All this clearly shows how tremendously important the word of the Lord is for all scientific work. Scripture reveals not just a 'ground motive', a life and world view, it gives not only eternal, ever valid 'principles', no, it lights our path, even our scientific path, every step we take.

Holy Scripture is perspicuous and clear. That also makes it possible for a confession to arise. A confession states what the word has revealed to us as a fruit of the struggle against heresies and deviations in the course of the generations. The developed, written confessions that we have are in truth formulas of unity, for in them is laid down what is surely and certainly revealed in the Scriptures about God, people, salvation and the works of the covenant. In them is laid down what we confess as truth, in agreement with God's word, together with all Bible believers of all times. That we in that confession confess the same as what all the others confess calls into life a community that is beautifully expressed by the term 'communion of saints' [a phrase from the Apostles' Creed]. Here we find edifying and very comforting literature, and we can never thank the Lord enough that he has given his church these writings, which express so faithfully what is written in his word.

As the gift of God the Creed may not be disdained, yet it is never sufficient and conclusive because it can never replace Scripture itself. The Bible is so rich, so full of instruction, comfort and edification that all the confessions and later formulations of men will never contain and exhaust it completely.

Well then, we have spoken till now about the certainties that we possess, namely, those that we have from our experience of reality, our knowledge of the world around us and of history – again, I am not speaking here about knowing scientifically – and then about the certainties that Scripture offers us in wisdom and insight, and finally we also said a few words about the never to be disdained certainty that our confession gives us. These are all certainties with which we may never tamper. Thus we must also proceed from them in our scientific thinking; yes, we are called to build on these certainties to account for the given states of affairs.

It is certain – what follows is just a selection from the many certainties we possess as believers in the Scriptures – it is certain that the walls of Jericho fell on the seventh day, that God spoke with Moses on

Sinai, that Jeroboam made the people sin, that Sunday 1 of the Heidelberg Catechism is correct when it states that our only comfort is in the saving suffering of our Lord Jesus Christ, that the Lord gathers, defends and preserves his church [Sunday 21], that the Reformation of the sixteenth century was wrought by God who visited his people in it for the good, that unbelief brought forth its fruits in the French Revolution, that everyone born here has a father and a mother, that 2 x 2 = 4, that there are many stars in the sky at night, that the Krakatau lies on the Strait of Sumba, that Russia has a large army, that in the South it is sunnier and warmer than it is here [in the Netherlands] – there are so many certainties, and there are infinitely more, as great a number as God's creation is great, which people cannot tamper with without holding the truth in unrighteousness. Undoubtedly the certainty of the matters we enumerated varies in character, but it is from such certainties that science must proceed and it is such certainties that science can ignore only to its own detriment – they are certain because God's covenant with Noah and Abraham is solid and sure.

Science, by contrast, is uncertain. In science nothing is sure. This is the realm of the problematical. And is it not the case that when we have solved one problem a dozen new ones appear, begging for resolution? By advancing science we attain not a reduction but an increase in the number of problems. But that is not what we want to emphasize at the moment. Science is uncertain because it possesses only a historically relative theoretical certainty. In science we are children of our time who wrestle with particular problems and advance particular solutions until our successors come along and show that our framing of the problems was incorrect, that our solutions were really quite relative, and that a thorough revision is necessary – just as we once came along and dealt with the problems and solutions of our predecessors.[260]

Scientific works quickly become outdated and unusable, good only for the historian whose focus in his or her own science is on what people used to think and say and believe. 'All is vanity', all our scientific work. Who will remember the scientists with all their insight and perspicacity once they have passed away? What remains of all the wisdom of a Moses, a Daniel, of their studies in the science of their century? What is left of all the knowledge of the people of the Middle Ages, of the great scholars of the Renaissance, of . . . all that work done by serious researchers throughout the ages? They are now yellowed and thickly covered by dust and of no other use than to pose problems for the historian, whose own insights are likewise transient in character.

This is all as true for Christian as it is for non-Christian science. Our scientific thought is fallible too. We too sometimes miss the mark by a wide margin. Our work too is constantly susceptible to review, just as we must often strongly revise the work of our predecessors and sometimes reject their framing of the problem as simply wrong.

Therefore let us all realize one thing very well. Our science and all its results are uncertain, fallible, and offers no sure foundation on which to build. Uncertain is Einstein's theory, our view of the Renaissance or economic laws, Toynbee's historical theories, the insights of modern psychology, our ideas about the relation between classicism and Romanticism, the science of prehistoric humanity, our knowledge of the composition of the atom, our understanding of the way in which hereditary characteristics are transmitted from a couple to a child, our theories about the relation of religion and belief to culture and art, our opinions about the influence of the economic system on culture . . . well, every scientific opinion is provisional and even the apparently most certain and best founded theory may be challenged today or tomorrow on good grounds. We have in mind here for example the theories of common grace, which once appeared so self-evident. Let us therefore leave science in its place and above all never overestimate it by supposing that it must provide the rule for our conduct and the guide for our way, that it should be the captain and pilot in the life of God's people. We do not find our rule and steadfastness in science, however fruitful and flourishing that may be, no, we find it in Scripture and in understanding and acknowledging the reality encompassing us in the light of Scripture.

We must in the first place desire to be wise so that we can glory in knowing God.[261] We must be sober and watchful, mindful of the signs of the times – that is, we must regard and weigh the events of the day in the light of the word of the Lord. We must know ourselves and the situation in which we find ourselves: if there is sin amongst us, then that is truly not only a matter of theory, and repentance and turning to the Lord is certainly not just a matter of adopting another perspective or view?

There is no science that can teach us, for example, that there is apostasy in the church, that reformation is necessary, that a certain church is a false church – for that we need to submit ourselves to the discipline of God's word, as it is written, 'do not be foolish, but understand what the Lord's will is.'[262] The requirement stated here is not that we should in the first place read complicated books or construct complicated theories, although doing so may very well be part of what a scientist does.

If we think that in order to grow in wisdom and insight into the situation of the day and God's will respecting it we have to construct better theories and broaden the scope of our scientific research, and that answers will be forthcoming primarily from our activities in this area, then we are deceiving ourselves. The outcome will be that we receive stones instead of bread and that we know ever less and have ever fewer certainties. For in that case we will have sought our salvation and our certainty in the uncertain, in science.

This holds for all science and all theory. That includes theology. A knowledge of the Scriptures and a believing understanding of God's word is the basis of every sound theology, as of every other sound science. For if we suppose that the reverse is so, and that we can only understand the Scriptures if our theology is sound, then we deceive ourselves and have turned matters upside down. In that case we are trying to found the certain upon the uncertain. We are making the uncertain the touchstone for the certain. We are calling upon human wisdom and insight to shed light on matters with respect to which God has stated plainly and clearly how things are and what he requires of us.

I do not need to warn here against underestimating science. If there was ever a danger that does not threaten us, that is it! Developing theories and scientific arguments seems to have become our meat and drink to the point that we sometimes are hardly aware of our preoccupation with it – that we work with theories instead of certainties, that we talk about abstractions instead of concrete realities. Yet how could it be otherwise after so many years during which science set the tone especially amongst the 'intelligentsia', and people had such great confidence in science that they sought all their wisdom in it.

In case you may still think otherwise, let us listen to the following citation from one of the early issues of *De Reformatie* from the year 1920:

> It cannot be denied that in part as a result of the triumphs of science ... the horizon of revelation was widened to a much broader depth ... I want to say that natural science sheds more light on the history of creation, that epistemological philosophy gives us material for deeper insight into the nature of belief, and the discoveries of psychology can help us approach the concept of inspiration better.

And then follows the assertion that is so dangerous to the life of the church: 'The church is called to develop its confession in agreement with this science.' Here, if anywhere, one can see what I mean by 'making the uncertain the foundation of the certain'.[263]

If we allow science to hold sway in this way and then carry it over into a full-blown practise of life, the consequences will be disastrous. For then, instead of the certainties of the Scriptures and of reality viewed in their light, one gives the people theoretical uncertainties, problems and conceptions, stones instead of bread. And that can only stir up many controversies in the life of the congregation, of God's people. For if scientific controversies spill over beyond the university, where they belong, then the word applies: 'Avoid godless chatter, because those who indulge in it will become more and more ungodly. Their teaching will spread like gangrene.' Moreover, 'See to it that no one takes you captive through hollow and deceptive philosophy, which depends on human tradition and the basic principles of this world.'[264] Remember that when science is introduced without qualification into practical life, academic questions become vital questions and the contest between professors becomes a real-life struggle.

Who among the children of God sitting in church and listening to the words: 'We believe with our hearts and confess with our mouths' [Belgic Confession, Article 1] will not know what 'believe' means? A good student of the catechism will even be able to formulate the answer clearly and directly with the answer to Question 21 of the Heidelberg Catechism ['What is true faith?']. Pose this question to a group of Christian philosophers and theologians, however, and see what happens. One will quickly say, 'We do not yet really know what belief really is, we shall have to think deeply about this and discuss it for a long time.' It would attest to precious little wisdom, however, if we were to say to a young catechumen: 'But young man, we are still a long way from knowing what faith really is. Now, choose for yourself, idea A or idea B?' For in that case controversies and hair-splitting would arise that would not strengthen the congregation but only undermine established certainties and real belief. After all, many may say: 'We do not even know yet what faith really is.' Just how devastating the introduction of theological controversies into the life of the congregation can be we all experienced just a few years ago. Hopefully we have all learned some lessons from that experience.

Let us especially see sharply to ourselves in this matter. The science ideal – a Christian science ideal, of course, that gives priority to a Christian science that is true to the Scriptures – has overly preoccupied us and has had us much too firmly in its grip, and this leaven has not yet worked itself out. Far from it. Often we are virtually unaware of its influence. But that is all the more reason to take a long, hard look at the problem.

Is it not the case that in practice we often applied our own schemes, according to our own often no more than surmised Scriptural theories, and then tried to solve the problems that resulted by appealing to the Scriptures? Far too often we pose questions for the Scriptures rather than letting the Scriptures pose questions to us. Sometimes we posed dilemmas that are foreign to the Scriptures and neglected to consider dilemmas known to the Scripture. Our basic attitude often was (and is) so theoreticized that we turned the most ordinary, everyday difficulties and questions into complicated theoretical problems.

Consider for example our approach to the so-called problem of the movies. We set out to solve the tricky problem of how the Christian view of life in general related to the new possibility that technology has disclosed, moving pictures, and in that connection we talked about film as such, we dragged in theories of culture, views of life and everything else we could think of in order, in a word, to pose the question in a general, theoretical and scientific way. And in the process we often neglected to say how an ordinary member of the congregation should regard the cinema around the corner. Indeed, sometimes we did not even know how to deal with that question because we wanted to see the general problem resolved first, in order to be able to deduce the scriptural answer from the scriptural theory. And when someone occasionally interjects a simple word of Scripture into our discussions, that often does not satisfy us and we want to add another line of reasoning – and that line of reasoning with its arguments sometimes has a firmer hold on us than the simple word from Scripture. We allow ourselves to be convinced by the arguments rather than by the Scriptures alone.[265]

The task of the believing scientist

Our argument has perhaps been rather negative until now in the sense that we have said more about what science is not meant to do than about what its task is. Well then, what is the task of the believing scientist who is a member of the Christian community, the church of the Lord? In the first place as members of the congregation scientists have the same task as every other child of the covenant, that is, to 'be ready always to give an answer to everyone who asks you the reason for the hope that is in you,' to be a good member of the church who does not neglect their duty, and to fulfil what is traditionally called the general office of believers. One might add that given their position, in which people may look up to them, they must be even more careful to fulfil their duties well. A believer who is a teacher or professor has no more right than any other person to skip a church service, for instance, but should always give a good example in such matters.

The believer's proper task in the congregation and thus the believing scientist's task too is best defined from the answer to Heidelberg Catechism question 55: 'that everyone must know himself bound to employ his gifts readily and cheerfully for the benefit and salvation of other members.'

In the first place, we have in mind here the warning against and unmasking of intellectual or spiritual movements that are dangerous for the church and its members: 'Have nothing to do with the fruitless deeds of darkness, but rather expose them;'[266] and 'See to it that no one takes you captive through hollow and deceptive philosophy, which depends on human tradition and the basic principles of this world rather than on Christ.'[267] That is what Groen van Prinsterer did, for example, when he awakened the people of the Lord and opened their eyes to the humanistic principles that were the mainspring for politics, beginning with the French Revolution; and, later, that is what the leaders in our own churches did in warning against the danger of a Karl Barth. And that is what every scientist does who on a larger or smaller scale investigates critically the teachings of this world and then uses the knowledge gained through such study to warn and inform the non-scientific members of the congregation or fellow believers who study other disciplines.

If we take this approach, then our task will be determined by the time and place in which we find ourselves. God always calls us to do what our hands find to do according to the time and circumstances. Our calling as scientists is never timeless and general.

In all this our task is not primarily one of transmitting scientific knowledge, of constructing better theories, but of helping others through the results of our study. In general, where that is necessary and useful, we must keep the Lord's people informed about the facts, warn them, and so keep them from apostasy and from going off in ways that are not the Lord's. And we must seriously guard against raising controversial questions that can lead only to uncalled-for arguments and divisions.[268] Especially here we must be sober and exercise all possible wisdom, discriminating between what is useful and what is not, what is of timely and important interest and what is not an item for discussion now.

More often than not our task will indeed be negative in the first place or, if one prefers, preservative: recognizing and opposing things that are wrong and dangerous to the Lord's church.[269] That should not surprise us. Has it not been so since the days of Adam that believers have always been 'negatively' active, which is to say, in less humanistic language, that believers have had to battle constantly against sin and apostasy, the powers in the air, the corrupted heart and its propensities – the old struggle of the antithesis that was already there in Paradise. I used the phrase 'in less humanistic language' because it is worth noting that when people who call themselves believers begin to say that 'this or that is so negative, we are always so negative in our approach,' then that is often a vague sign of the beginning of apostasy. Are the Ten Commandments not also 'so negative' with their 'You shall not'?

Let us well remember in what situation we as believers have been since the Fall into sin: a tiny flock under assault from all sides and heavily burdened to remain unspotted by the world and to keep hold of the good thing entrusted to us and to endure unto the end. If there were ever times when this was not so, they were exceptions. And in our own times especially it seems as if the church is small and has come to nought, particularly when we consider the entire world. Let us accordingly fulfil our task with great modesty, not seeking great things.[270]

After all, there is a great deal that we do not have to do. The scientific world of the unbelievers is also at work, even hard at work – and what is amassed there is certainly not all totally useless philosophy or unprofitable or senseless knowledge. Let us not forget that, and let us also show modesty with respect to it. How would our physicians, our economists, our statesmen, our historians, our this and our that, yes how would we all be able to work if we did not have all the manuals and encyclopedias and the special studies that provide a wealth of data, that contain tremendous stores of science and knowledge that we too may make use of and virtually all of which have been written by unbelievers?

That vast terrain – 'all things that are done under heaven' – is not one that we have to investigate all by ourselves, from the ground up, on the basis of correct principles. No, that task has also been given to the children of Cain. The cultural mandate given in Eden still holds for all people. And it is also written: 'to the sinner he gives the task of gathering and storing up wealth to hand it over to the one who pleases God.'[271]

Our task as the children of Seth is in the first place and primarily to keep the word of God, to live by it and witness to it, and to keep ourselves unspotted by the world. That is why we have such a grave battle to wage against the wicked powers in the air, not to mention our own corrupted hearts.

In this battle as people of science we have our own extremely responsible and also difficult task. However, if we approach our work as believers and modestly assign science its proper place, which is to serve and not to reign, then we will be able to carry out our work to the edification of the congregation and make our little contribution to building God's church. In this way we fulfil our task within the fellowship of the saints, teaching, admonishing and instructing one another according to the Scriptures, in meekness forbearing one another.

We shall have to free ourselves of the notion, which like old leaven has not yet been purified from our midst, that reformation consists of studying harder, attacking more difficult problems, and being theologically more pure. For reformation means being converted from sin and walking anew in the ways of the Lord.[272] On the other hand, it cannot be denied that theological purity and study will often be a result of reformation. For although reformation is not grounded in science, a true reformation of thought may be the result of real reformation, of conversion. A scientist can fulfil his function of service well in times of reformation by testing the 'opinions of the day' against God's word and investigating history, so that we can understand what the prophets and predecessors from earlier times (whose gravestones we beautify but whose words we fail to heed[273]) have to tell us that applies also to our own times and difficulties.

We come to the end of our argument and would therefore like to summarize concretely what the confessing scientist's place and task is. In the first place he or she should know the Scriptures well and not adopt a stance proudly aloof from the fellowship of the saints. Scientists should walk according to God's commandments like all other church members, and not only that, but should fulfil the responsibility that their place in the fellowship of the saints imposes upon them. Every office bearer – and a scientist is such a person too: he or she stands in the general office of believers! – needs to have a profound sense of responsibility, a responsibility that is the greater in proportion to whether more or less depends on his or her being faithful or unfaithful. 'From everyone who has been given much, much will be demanded; and from the one who has been entrusted with much, much more will be asked.'[274]

For us as students this means that we are not finished when we have prepared for all our tests and examinations, although it is certainly our task to do that well and on time. No, one must delve into the problems confronting Christians in today's world and become thoroughly familiar with what is going on, with what is current and alive and happening. Furthermore, one must not neglect to consider deeply the questions of principle pertaining to a truly Christian scientific practice directed by God's word. Thus one may neither neglect out of laxness what an earlier generation has attained and done in this respect nor haughtily dismiss it out of a sense that one detail or another of it may be open to justifiable criticism.[275] As students preparing for our exceptionally responsible task we should study twice as hard as our unbelieving colleagues, for we ought to be at home in the area of Christian scientific practice and its history and also its direct connection with the history of the church – I want to call special attention to this since it is so often neglected – and at the same time be good, yes better than all the others in the mastery of our own discipline.

We must never neglect that last point. For academics, intellectuals, must also be worthy of their hire. In all humility they must devote their powers to the work to which they have been called, to the work to which they were commissioned, whether as teacher or professor, as preacher, physician, economist, jurist or whatever else.

Finally, if an academic has received the special gifts and possibilities needed to do so, then he or she will be able to produce truly independent work. To this end one must do what one's hand finds to do, not seeking remote problems but as a matter of priority putting one's talents in the service of one's brothers and sisters in the Lord. An academic's task thus stands in a direct connection with the needs of the community of saints in which he or she has been placed. In that regard we have in mind in particular the difficulties and problems of his or her brothers and sisters who are also called to do scientific work. One must help them to the best of one's ability to solve the problems with which they are wrestling.[276] If anywhere at all, then certainly here the emphasis should be placed on the believing community of thought. In mutual discussion and debate, inquiring, criticizing, studying, all of us who are engaged in science must work together.

I want to stress for a moment the point I just made implicitly, namely, that we are not all called to do independent scientific work. No one needs to feel the lesser for not having such a calling. To the contrary, the task of those, who certainly include the majority of us, may actually be much broader and more responsible in scope. I have in mind for example the many preachers and physicians. If only we will be faithful in everything, making the best use of the talents and possibilities given us, then we will not have to goad one another into doing things we were probably not called to do – if only we do not lose the bond that binds us to the believing community of thought and continue to support those doing scientific work by posing questions, offering honest criticism and, at the very least, showing interest.

Let us think seriously about all this and be responsible about it, so that when we come before our Lord and Master saying 'Lord, Lord' we might not be sent away with an 'I never knew you' even though we thought we had been working in his name – so that it will not have to be said of us that we had a zeal for God but lacked understanding.[277]

'Wherefore gird up the loins of your mind, be sober, and hope to the end for the grace that is to be brought unto you at the revelation of Jesus Christ. Love one another with a pure heart fervently, for all flesh is as grass' – even science too is only fleeting – 'but the word of the Lord endureth forever' (1 Peter 1:13–25, KJV).

• Book review: Kalsbeek, Faith and Science[278]

This nicely published pocketbook addresses very difficult problems. Basically, it is not difficult at all, since it is about not leaving the Bible closed and not denying the Lord in scientific work as a believer. It becomes difficult because we live in a world in which much scientific work is driven by a spirit that is not from God, so that our scientific activity to a great extent takes on the character of a struggle against the spiritual forces of evil in the sense of Ephesians 6:10 ff. We therefore have to test the spirits. This is not always easy, because the scientist, also the unbeliever, will be busy investigating what has been given in reality, either in creation or that which is formed by people, and it will often be difficult to draw the line between observation, correct diagnosis and possibly incorrect interpretation. Insight in the facts can be incorrect simply because a scientist failed or because, from a religious point of view, he or she had laid the wrong foundation for their work, but sometimes it can also be correct in spite of an unbelieving starting point.

In short, it is not simple, and this also explains why even among believing Christians profound differences exist in scientific insight. But we must maintain that science is not a neutral activity, and that philosophy in particular, as the science which is concerned with the totality and the mutual coherence between the structures that are given in human experience and the concrete facts, is more often a 'theology of unbelief' than that it is a 'pure science'. The author of this book did not keep this fact sufficiently in mind.

The book is a remarkable product of our time in that for the author science does not actually include much more than the natural sciences – he does not elaborate on history, language, ethics or art. And this one-sided interest causes him sometimes all too quickly, nearly naïvely we would say, to lapse into statements which are inherent to a (natural) scientific approach to problems which in essence do not have a (natural) scientific nature. This is simply because we are dealing with matters that are not part of the physical, biotic, or mathematical spheres. The author is not conscious enough of the fact that since the seventeenth century the Western natural sciences have been imprinted with an outspoken humanism, in which an attempt is made to control all of reality through science. This humanistic ideal of science, which also determines thought in the areas outside of the natural sciences, has become his flesh and blood. Yet the author is a believing Christian, which sometimes leads him to a weak protest or an effort to modify the results of humanistic thought in a Christian sense.

This rather naïve and uncritical attitude is also apparent in his eclecticism: the author follows one philosopher and then another, and does not realize that the opinions presented are sometimes total opposites since they are based on totally different religious viewpoints. In particular, it is not possible for a Christian to adopt Kant's epistemology or to claim that in mathematics complete certainty can be obtained, because here we are dealing with creations of the human spirit. The triangle and the straight line, etc. are creations of God and are not products of human thought, even though they are far-reaching abstractions. The theorems of Euclidean geometry are correct or incorrect, insofar as they correlate with God's created laws, insofar as they do justice to that which is given in creation. But here we are not talking about thought products which for that reason are true. And even if they were true, is the human mind not a creation of God, and would not the truth of a mathematical theorem also in that case remain anchored in the will of God as Creator?

That the author can be Kantian in relation to the epistemological questions and can also be very sympathetic towards existentialism proves once more his eclecticism. An existentialist like Merleau-Ponty has made – justifiably from his point of view – a scathing judgment about Kant.

His [Kalsbeek's] lack of radical Christian thought about the problems is evident as well. The chapters at the end of the book are – especially for the uninitiated – frequently confusing, because the author tries to Christianize existentialist thoughts. When he says, for example, that 'existing' means to be oneself and that that would mean to obey the First and the Second Commandments, he really does injustice to the existentialists who mean something quite different with the term 'existing'. It becomes even more difficult because, in his effort to accommodate existentialist thoughts to Christian truths, he does not always adhere to the Bible. On page 180 for example he quotes, without any comment, a pure Aristotelian-Thomistic thought about God as if it would do justice to God's revelation about himself. It becomes especially frightening when, without critique, he relates Kierkegaard's opinion about truth (and faith) as an objective uncertainty that could only be truth through our subjective acknowledgment; Hebrews 11:1 tells us quite differently. Even the quotes from the direction of the Philosophy of the Cosmonomic Idea lose their impact through this eclecticism. It is a pity that the author has understood so little of this; especially the views of Dooyeweerd relating to humanism and to Kant could have helped the author to be more critical.

We have dealt with this rather extensively because we think that the book will probably be read by many, and because various problems are discussed in it which may not be neglected by anybody, including us. For example, think of the problems of evolution and exegesis. His chapter entitled 'Why was Galileo condemned?' is particularly valuable and already justifies the price of the book; it also shows us to what extent we are all determined in our thoughts by various 'current' concepts and how difficult it can sometimes be to judge the true intent of new insights. If with this the author wants to warn us against a simplistic fight against the ideas of evolution which are currently popular and wants to help us to distinguish facts from interpretations in order to make a correct judgment, then we would like to support him wholeheartedly.

The subsequent discussion of the state of affairs in today's scientific research relating to evolution is, as far as I can judge, very reasonable. But the author does not see sufficiently that all this research is limited to the area of the natural sciences, and that even if biological, or rather biologistic, evolution would be a fact – which, by the way, would be more miraculous to believe than that God created species (which as such are variable) – nothing would have been 'explained' with regard to the typical human spheres, such as cultural activity, language, economics, art, law and ethics, as well as faith. At most, evolutionism can determine in which order living beings were created, and which elements of biochemical nature were involved. As soon as evolution is explained, we are in the territory of unprovable hypotheses. And with all of this, nothing has yet been said about what makes a person truly human.

Perhaps the crux of this point of view is located in the reasoning given in passing at the bottom of page 49, namely that (natural) science allows only purely (natural) scientific explanations and views the rest as (natural) philosophy, which is determined by one's world view and must therefore be left out of consideration. However, we have to clearly observe that this idea in itself is already determined by a philosophy and world view, especially humanism, and therefore will totally determine the observation and direction of research.

As Bible-believing Christians we should not be afraid of the real results of research, and we certainly do not have to close our eyes to them. If we really believe God, we know that God's revelation cannot be contradicted. However, we may have to revise our insights concerning certain passages of Scripture – in particular I am afraid that the first chapters of Genesis have too often been read through scientifically coloured glasses. But in this area we have to test the spirits and see what the given facts are and where an interpretation starts that is undoubtedly prejudiced.[279]

We will have to leave things here. In short, this is an interesting book from orthodox Reformed circles, interesting if we read it as an expression of the difficulty that many Christians in our time have in dealing with the problems that face them, as a sign also of the confusion which reigns among us. Yes, let us say 'us', because if we claim to be isolated from this, then we have truly buried our heads in the sand. If we want to read it to obtain insight, then we should be very careful and critical.

• The method of art history[280]

It is a curious and striking phenomenon that in the course of the years relatively little has been written about the method of art history. 'Theoretical art history' is only seldom practised. To many it does not seem a very useful discipline. Of course it is nice to theorize from time to time, but one does not emerge much the wiser for it, so people say. As a result this science threatens to end dead in a more or less positivistic activity: people devote themselves to dating and attributing works of art to artists, or to investigating the lives and the oeuvre of the various artists. If one ventures to speak in that context of the method of art history, then the question is simply one of where the emphasis should be placed in such investigations. One's own method in that case is not presented as an absolute but is instead simply put alongside other approaches as a complement to them. Thus one can highlight the iconological method, which pays attention especially to the rise and development of the visual material. Here it is not so much the 'what' as the 'how' of the depicted material that is the centre of attention.

Another way of approaching the problems of art history is the genetic method. Here one endeavours to discover how the artist arrived at his or her conception, what influences had a bearing on a particular work, and what reminiscences must have been alive in the artist's mind to bring about the execution of such a work in such a way. One can also proceed from the stylistic forms themselves and investigate how they changed in the course of time. Focillon entitled this the *vie des formes* ('the life of the forms'). Others today prefer a more social-historical method. They investigate how changing social circumstances and historical events alter taste and how older conceptions disappear and new conceptions arise with respect to both content and visualization. Of course all of this work is neither useless nor meaningless. Indeed, in the reality of the development of art we see constantly how artists connect with the past, both stylistically and in terms of visualization, while under the influence of recent events certain representations come into vogue and enter into the sphere of interest of both the artist and the public. But ultimately the true requirements of a science, namely to account for reality, have not been met in this way. Why do entirely new mindsets arise in art? Why do new genres appear? Why does a new paradigm or *Kunstwollen* appear, as the Germans, and Dvorak in particular, call it? Dvorak is one of the few to have addressed these issues. Yet he too does not undertake to offer a theoretical account of it. In his book *Kunstgeschichte als Geistesgeschichte* ('Art History as Intellectual History') he discusses a number of periods in order to show that the intellectual history is reflected in the art history, but the 'how' and the 'why' he leaves unaddressed. Even aesthetics, which seeks to answer the question concerning what art is, usually lies outside the interest of the art historian even though only this science would be able to provide the basis for an encyclopedia of art history. On the other hand it is somewhat understandable when one considers that aesthetics, which is often intimately connected with philosophy, has so detached itself from everyday reality that it indeed has little 'practical' value for actual scientific practice.

I would now like to distinguish three successive steps in art-historical activity. In the first place, in the nature of the case the monuments must be found, gathered, catalogued, dated and attributed to the various masters. That of course forms the material upon which the art historian must draw. It is a necessary precondition for every art-historical activity and moreover also offers the advantage of keeping scientists in constant contact with real works of art: without the disclosed, naïve experience of seeing, undergoing and knowing the monuments, every art-historical activity is doomed to sterility. It can also keep us from empty speculations that have no connection with the real states of affairs.

Inconceivable apart from this, and automatically emerging from it, is the second step: the seeking of connections, the distinguishing of various schools, movements, etc., the investigation of influences, the detection of how styles change, the establishment of the distinctive characteristics of the work of particular masters, movements and periods, etc. Here we are already engaged in abstraction. Our focus is no longer on the investigation of the works of art in their full structural reality, as was the case in the first stage, but on the style aspect, on the aesthetic aspect singled out from the total coherence of all the aspects of the concrete monuments. Here one investigates the development of styles, and which historical shapers of styles created new forms, and which new styles arose or, in other words, how in the various periods form and a positive shape were given to the aesthetic norms.

Naturally iconography must furnish important auxiliary services to the investigation. Iconography investigates the meaning of what is depicted: the symbolism, the story told, the matter illustrated. The history of religions and church history, economic history, social history and political history must be brought in as well. These form the auxiliary sciences par excellence, which is immediately understandable when we consider that the development of styles is directly founded upon the developments in these different areas.

The 'accepted' art history restricts itself to these two points. Yet because people carry on without an agenda or plan, without providing an explanation of the goal and task of the science of art history, they often steep themselves in all kinds of details the significance of which is questionable. They attack ever pettier subjects and the discussion sometimes concerns differences in attribution or dating that no longer have any real importance for insight into the history of art. Such activity runs aground in a sometimes erudite game.

However, to my mind the first two steps form just the preparatory study for the following: the investigation into and the attempt to explain why a style changed in a certain way, or why a particular new paradigm appeared and gave occasion for the forming of an entirely new style, or why people sought their inspiration in new and until that moment entirely unexploited fields. In a word, the third step is the investigation into the direction and disclosure of artistic activity.

An immediate key to this can be to take account of the pistical anticipation of the aesthetic function, whereby one starts to see that the new ideals of art are dependent upon a new conviction of faith, a new positivizing of the norms of belief. Religion too must not be overlooked as a source that drives all art activity. Moreover, one must take into account the disclosure of belief in the process and development of apostasy. Then one can begin to grasp why an entirely new stylistic direction arises and why the old is set aside as no longer consonant with the attitude towards life. And in this way one can also offer a meaningful explanation for the connection between the development of art and the development of the other fields of the intellect.

All of this contributes, furthermore, to our understanding of the place of art as a historical power and to our taking that more fully into account in our science. As a result we may better understand and grasp the tremendous historically formative power that art has had in some periods.

I hope to illustrate that shortly in *Philosophia Reformata* with a concrete example.[281]

• Depth and breadth of art history[282]

I want to make a preliminary observation about the term 'art history': I assume that there is a history of art; there is something that happened in the past and there is something we call art. There is a great deal to debate about. Does art include only large paintings or also small ones or perhaps even things that are not paintings at all? Would it not be quite meaningful to write a history of the frames around the paintings and that sort of thing? I will not deal with such questions here.

Thus there is art and there is a history of it; there is a science that endeavours to study this history and to say something about it, and we call this science art history. Yet we should really call it 'the science of the history of art'. Thus we speak of art history by way of abbreviation when we mean this science. But actually we do not mean only this science but also the actual practice of it. We also have in mind the work that is done in museums, in programmes for preserving historical buildings and monuments, in education and even in tourism, where an art historian does and should have a task.

Certainly we should not make an idol of any science, and thus also not of the science of art history. In our tradition that has happened rather often; the Western tradition is one that shows great respect for science. I would like to formulate the science of art history very simply as 'with concentrated attention, with our entire understanding, with our entire humanity, being engaged with the art from the past and present and trying to say something sensible about it'. This science is autonomous in the sense of being free from politics, free from powers, free from fashion, free from any coercion to do something because we ought to do it that way, because it is 'in'.

I believe that science must be autonomous and independent of such powers – at least that is a norm; whether science is actually always so is another question. Science is not a function of something else. Science has its own proper function, and it is not necessary to find a justification for it outside art history. Yet when I say 'autonomous' I must add at the same time that art history is not autonomous in the sense that it has to be detached from reality, so that we should practice science for the sake of science. For then we would end up in some sort of scholasticism, which by definition is dry and arid and barren. For science, if it is good and especially if it is independent of the powers external to it, is connected by thousands of virtually indistinguishable links to cultural life, contemporary movements, practical questions, practical projects (exhibitions) and artistic life, both the artistic ideals of the past and those of the present. At any given moment there are on the one hand thousands of links with science, while on the other hand science is autonomous. If one tries to sever these links, one ends up in a world-avoiding scholasticism; if one talks exclusively about these links, one ends up in functionalism. I would like to leave them for what they are.

An open art history

Now, if we proceed to think about how art history should be practised, I am reminded of a method that is adopted particularly in some American universities, and perhaps more widely as well, that looks at things from the past abstractly and in detachment from history. Artworks from the past are viewed as if they were modern works: only the compositions are analysed. Justice is not done in this way to works of art, and the unhistorical manner of approaching them leads to a loss of culture. In a certain sense people have landed themselves in a vicious circle. Malraux was of course the one who promoted this view of art from the past.

We always look at art through the eyes of our time. Yet I believe we easily fall into a *Malraux ad absurdum*: present-day art determines our view of art (also of the art of the past) and art from the past, in turn, conditions present-day art, so that we are trapped in a vicious circle and entirely lose our critical distance. I think we are meant to view art on its own merits and in its own context precisely for the sake of this critical distance. This afternoon we have heard a beautiful disquisition about connoisseurship and about the history of styles, and we can all be grateful for what is achieved with the methods involved; yet if that is all that happens it is one-sided, even if deepened iconologically.

We need to consider the work of art in a broader cultural context. For – and that is the thesis I wish to assert – the issue is one of the total meaning of the work of art, of its *Aussage*, of what it has to say, what it expresses, its total meaning. And this total meaning pertains not only to a great work of art, a famous Michelangelo, but also to a minor work of art that has more than historical importance even if it was just a devotional item that someone carried about: what is its meaning? Secondary art too, comic strips and posters, must be considered; for that belongs to an understanding of what such things meant in the first place, in their own time. A prerequisite to that is a stylistic analysis connected with a history of style, which we undertake to reconstruct. Iconography is also essential, iconography that goes as deep as possible. Even more essential than all of this, however, is consideration of art in the rich relation in which it stands with the many things in life.

Like the history of art, which as I said requires no justification, art itself also requires no justification. Art is a given. Yet that given is not a static given but a dynamic one, a possibility, a created possibility. We must get to work with it. Love, a tree, these are all givens, and as such they form a task. In this way it was the task of art to make things beautiful, all manner of things and not just those unique little things on little panels. It requires no justification. It is not necessary to say of any art that it is so good because people will then learn to look, or because people will then see more deeply, or because it strengthens piety. That is so even if the art in question can accomplish that at a certain moment. For art too, just like art history, is not autonomous but is always connected to reality by a thousand ties. In short, we must be on guard against functionalism, but also against art for art's sake, an aestheticism, an ivory tower, an abstraction.

Therefore I would like to advocate an open art history. Besides style and iconography there is also the question concerning function, both societal and religious. Even a piece intended for worship has an economic background and social backgrounds. And all these things are sometimes more and sometimes less important for understanding what an item meant in its situation. For understanding why a piece was hung just there or was even made at all, or why something was made that is simply not important. Why do we call one thing decorative and something else an icon that is loaded with meaning? You enter a church and see mosaics on the wall. What do they mean? Were they intended to beautify the space? Was their meaning deep, and how deep? And how did people apprehend that in their own day? All these questions must be examined: the relation to reality, the relation to nature and cultural reality, including economic, social and political life.

If we begin in this way then one of the first questions, naturally, is that of visual communication. What does it say and how does it say it? But as you proceed you quickly encounter additional questions, the underlying questions, questions that have to do with art history or with aesthetics, with how people thought about art in their own day, with why they did what they did. And yesterday's reflections on yesterday's art naturally had an influence on that art, but in order to understand it we too must have our relation with it. We must ask ourselves what we desire of art, what we think of it. In that dialogue with the past we hope in any case at some point to have something sensible to say.

In this connection I want to say by way of an aside that I consider it extremely sensible to concentrate on component problems. In our discussions during recent months I have noticed that there is a tendency among some art historians to say: 'Oh, that fellow is only busy with a small, marginal area.' What is the societal relevance of devoting time or perhaps your entire life to such a small field, say Irish miniatures? I would say that if someone wants to devote time to Irish miniatures then I do not have the right to say that that is not good, that that may not be done. Perhaps that person for all his or her possible limitations is exceptionally talented in that area. What I do have the right to do is to criticize his or her work and to ask, 'Are you asking the right questions?' and 'Are you perhaps not really quite restricted in your approach?'

The restrictions however are not inherent in the field with which one is engaged but in one's way of tackling it. I find that in this respect some Marxists force the issue – to put it cautiously – and I do want to express some disapproval of that. For in a certain sense they want to deprive people of their freedom. Everyone must proceed like them, and if anyone proceeds differently then that is not good. And there is a great danger that we must envisage, namely, that this will become a fashionable tendency. They do concentrate on extremely important problems, yet I regard these problems as component ones. They investigate the economic and social relations. I cite a few titles of recent works from the Frankfurt school. A book has been written entitled *Autonomie der Kunst: Zur Genese und Kritik einer bürgerlichen Kategorie* ('autonomy of art: on the genesis and the critique of a bourgeois category'). I believe it is very useful indeed to raise these questions, and perhaps the older art history devoted insufficient attention to them. They are certainly an important complement to the range of questions addressed in the discipline. Another title is *Funktionen der bildenden Kunst in Spätkapitalismus, untersucht anhand der avantgardistischen Kunst der sechziger Jahre* ('the functions of visual art in recent capitalism, researched on the basis of the avant-garde art of the sixties'). And in America there has been an exhibition about nineteenth-century art with the subtitle, 'Monuments of the Middle Class'. Such a title would not have been given to an exhibition fifteen years ago. Yet I believe this illuminates an important aspect of this art. In this connection I would also like to relativize the word 'ideology' and warn that while it can in itself be a valuable and important term, it should never be de-natured into something derogatory. For to politicize and say 'that is an ideology' – and that, I think, is what the Marxists do – is all too easy, for in this way one politicizes one's own ideology (it is easy to say someone else has an ideology without realizing that you also have one yourself). Politicizing from the standpoint of an ideology can lead to impoverishment. I think that we have a tremendous example of that in the history of French academic art, which in the seventeenth century was harnessed to the service of absolutism, the consequences of which remained palpable deep into the nineteenth century and perhaps even into our own times. And if you then read Boime's book about French academicism in the nineteenth century and see the difficulties in which French art landed up, and at the same time the impoverishment of this art, then I think we should all be warned that politicizing can lead, or perhaps inevitably leads, to impoverishment.

Again, we must not reject this approach in itself for it can be a complement, but it must then be viewed as a component of what I would like to call 'an open art history'.

The unfinished past and the present

And I think that we have to begin by being honest. We must be honest towards the artwork before us. We must let the past be the past and judge it fairly. Perhaps you disagree with it, perhaps you think it should have been done differently, but consider the achievement in its own context, relatively. We must discern its value, and in doing so acknowledge the quality or perhaps criticize it. Thus we endeavour to establish the connection with the present, and the societal relevance of what Romein called 'an unfinished past'.

Our questions are always new questions. And our task is to keep the artwork of the past open and accessible for today. We must open eyes to values that are there. We must make the meaning clear, even if we perhaps reject it, in which case we must explain why we reject it and account for what was going on there. And if I just referred critically to French academicism, then that is because one must always be critical, for that is how one is engaged in establishing connections with the present. We must – and I believe it is a fundamental law of our humanity that we see what we know, and what we do not know we do not see – open our eyes because we know. And I think that this is the task of science, and certainly of our science. For other sciences it may often be a metaphor, but for our science it is very direct. It is preserving values, critically assessing them and transmitting them for the future. That may happen critically, but it must happen and it must be constructive.

Thus I think, proceeding from the position that art history is engaged with an unfinished past, that art history stands in the service of the present – and that is being realized especially when a work of art is considered in its own context first. And I think that with Malraux's view as I described it at the outset we lose the work of art altogether and it has no more meaning. Yet it is precisely the task of the present to point out all possible shortcomings, merits and relationships in the art of the past. And so I arrive, almost ineluctably, at our own art, as we must pose these questions to the art of our own times as well, as a proper part of our work.

The unfinished past ended yesterday, or five minutes ago. How did our own art arise? What does it mean, positively and negatively? In order to understand that we shall have to delve into the past. We shall have to examine the 'grand tradition' and learn how it has its roots in the Middle Ages, how Christianity and humanism conditioned it. And we must ask: 'What did an artwork mean in the tradition from Raphael to David? What was the *Aussage*? And we witness in the eighteenth century, and that is an extremely important and difficult point to analyse, a discontinuity that leads to the present. We witness an aestheticizing – just think of the concept 'the picturesque'. We witness an abstracting and a loss of functionality; the work of art becomes an object for the collector. It is hung in collections, whether of the state or of individuals. It has become art for the connoisseur. There is a loss of societal relevance. For this a new word is introduced, the word 'disinterestedness'. According to Kant's definition art is that which serves no purpose. And at the same time as this change in the relation to art is taking place, we witness new foundations being laid, new foundations which lead to naturalism and abstraction, in the same sense in which Kandinsky too saw these as two extreme poles of the same thing. And so we come to the analysis of the problems peculiar to the nineteenth and twentieth centuries, asking what art ought to do and what it can do. We shall have to think about that, and then we shall have to recognize that art is not something that stands on its own, not a separate little universe. It is autonomous, yet for all that it manifests thousands of ties with reality. Starting from this point of view we automatically arrive at a critique of culture.

I would therefore like to take a closer look at this, because I believe it can shed some light on our own situation. Out of the changes that took place in the eighteenth-century situation a new concept of culture arose. Today we have two concepts of culture side by side. One is old, very old, which you will find in a book such as *The culture of the Babylonians*. There you expect to read something about kitchen inventories, the kinds of food they ate, about their form of government and, finally, something about science and religion. All of that falls under culture. But since the eighteenth century a new concept of culture has arisen that is more in line with what Kant says: 'Everything that is not useful, the things that are beautiful, art in its various forms, that is culture.' Alongside that are technology and socio-economic matters, which are real, true and essential. There is thus a sort of division in the world in which culture and technology are played off against each other and in which the technologists have the say since they are in the majority. And not only that, they control the purse-strings and are therefore powerful. And art may live, together with culture and museums and us as art historians, by the grace of the money earned by the technologists. Therefore they are powerful and they say: 'What are you really? You are just hobbyists!' (I will return to this later.)

Yet the question is: 'What is the role of modern art in all of this? Is it the fruit of this problem? Has it contributed to it? What is the influence of modern art? Has it perhaps helped to confirm the division in question or does it work to heal this fracture in our Western culture? What is the influence of this art on our lifestyle and manner of living? Has it contributed to a solution? I think that these questions in themselves lead to action; in a certain sense you can say that just being engaged with the problem is action, for in this way we endeavour to get a grip on things and by doing so we are already working (because we are engaged in discussion – and it begins with a discussion) on the construction.

Here I want to say again: be careful not to politicize, for that just narrows and falsifies matters. But such a discussion undoubtedly has an influence on culture. For art history is a part – and that is perhaps the thesis that underlies this entire lecture – of the cultural life of this culture in the broad sense, namely, of embracing all of life. In this sense art history is a part of cultural life and we must not concur with the opinion that we are only marginal, only a luxury, a fringe, as the real problems belong to the technocrats, the politicians, the socio-economists. Naturally things will not just develop for the better by themselves; to the contrary. That is why I say that we must pose questions and that questioning is action; and it definitely means engagement. We shall have to delve into these problems and be part of the total cultural construction. And then again, that entire problem of our being a fringe or a luxury is one that we must reject out of hand because it is based on a mistaken standpoint, namely that life can be divided into culture and technology, or however you may prefer to formulate the division.

Therefore the idea that art is only a luxury or a decoration in the worst sense of the word is a concept I reject, and therefore I can also say with conviction that, of course, art should be a hobby. I hope that everyone who works, even the technician, the engineer or the natural scientist, all of whom are engaged with things that are perhaps even more abstract and fringe-like than the things we deal with – atoms and that sort of thing or infinitely distant stars – can practice their discipline as a hobby. For I think that is what we are working for, that societally it is desirable that everyone's work might be her or his hobby. This is a goal we are all committed to.

Accordingly the next question is: 'Is being engaged with art not a one-sided interest?' And then I say yes, naturally it is one-sided, we are one-sided in the sense of being busy with a component problem of the whole of reality, just as another is with natural scientific problems or yet another with economic problems and another with theological problems. For it is precisely through concentration that we can discover things. Yet it is not science for the sake of science, art history for the sake of art history, it is a matter of the whole, a matter of today, a matter of gaining real insight into the present cultural situation, and that demands concentration. Here all kinds of questions arise, such as ones addressing the fragmentation of science that is inherent in our present cultural situation. We shall have to be mindful of this, we shall have to be engaged with this, and we shall have to work towards a solution.

Therefore I do not believe that if you practice art history as a hobby you are some kind of a professional idiot. But again, I believe it is only possible given an open art history that also focuses on preventing the loss of culture and that seeks to keep the past open for the present.

That 'keeping the past open' – referred to also by the previous speakers, I would say, as something virtually self-evident – means keeping the past accessible. The moment we no longer talk and think about Raphael, Raphael is dead. Therefore we must keep that lost cultural good alive, at least if we find it worthwhile, and that is our critical mind, and we shall perhaps have to dig out and consider anew things that earlier generations discarded and even discover that these were valuable after all.

In short, we must undertake to preserve cultural values. That means participating actively and directly in the cultural struggle being waged today, addressing the problem of our times but also the question of what the real value is of the past. And if we wish to fight for freedom and humanity – and I think we all do, albeit that our definitions may differ – then that means we must put ourselves at risk in the arena and engage in the cultural struggle of today. Is art history a hobby in that case, to pose the question again? I say yes. All science, as Plato said long ago, is born of curiosity, of a desire to know, and that desire to know leads to discovery. But curiosity and discovery lead automatically to responsibility. It even goes further and deeper – it is, I think, a calling.

Sometimes I even wonder – but that is a mischievous little footnote from a professor – given such extensive discussion about the meaning of art history, whether some people are really called to it after all and whether the feeling of calling and responsibility has perhaps not dissipated too much? Perhaps it has evaporated because we have been brainwashed by the technocrats who claim that we are just a fringe.

What is our task?

What is our goal? Are we engaged in the struggle, with our feet planted in reality? What is our goal?

I think our goal is simple to state but difficult to attain. Our goal is the truth: what is it? What does it mean? We shall have to analyse, we shall have to discover, we shall have to open our eyes so that, knowing, we may see.

And about this truth – I could talk long about it but have no time for that now – I should like to say this: this truth is not something static, something on the outside. About this truth – and it is a word from which I have learned a tremendous amount, and it is a word that I have thought about a great deal, and it is not a simple word – the Bible says that we shall have to do the truth. The moment you say that truth must be done it means that truth is an action, an activity, edifying, helping, assisting one's neighbour.

And if I now refer to one's neighbour, then I think for example of tourists. I do not believe that art historians from their scientific heights must debate with their scientific colleagues about scientific matters in order to pursue scientific objectives and in that way to mean something scientifically in order eventually to be awarded a scientific ribbon. I think that our task lies squarely in the midst of reality. When I walk through museums and see all those tourists – I have just been in Florence and that is perhaps the most hateful example of it; what goes on there is simply an indecent assault on the city – then one asks: is it wrong that so many people are walking around here? The answer, of course, is no. It is great that so many people are able to do that, but is it not a shame that no one is told anything, that those people are not prepared – and that already starts in education – that their eyes are not opened, that they walk right past the most beautiful things and just look in their little books and see three little stars and then look up and discover that it is really rather boring after all. Of course it is boring, because they know nothing and see nothing. Then they get home and say: we have seen all the Michelangelos, but art is unnecessary and boring. And that closes them to whatever else there may be.

I think the fault lies with us, since we perhaps do not write popular books. We severely criticize popular books, but let us rather write popular books ourselves and improve on them. When we talk in that way about doing the truth in the midst of today's reality, about being engaged, then the goal is of course subjectively formulated. It is subjective and, I think, cannot be otherwise. How as human beings can we ever be anything but subjective?

If I say 'subjective' then I do not have in mind some form of relativism but the recognition of multiformity, and openness; it also means engagement and vision. Being subjective is opposed to objectivity. And I must add that I do not believe in objectivity in science. Indeed, I will go even further: objectivity leads automatically to attenuation, to weakening; if we want to restrict ourselves to the facts, the demonstrable facts, then we have a great deal to tell but nothing to say. It is fine to put all the data into a computer and then wait for the computer to provide the solution, but then I still only have facts, which still are of no significance. The significance comes only with our interpretation. We need the facts in order to discuss the meaning. Therefore discussion is necessary for the sake of truth.

Here and precisely at this point I want to call special attention to the Marxist debate. I am glad that the Marxist scholars have come, also here in the Netherlands, because they have unmasked the pretensions of objectivism and have said: no, this is not objectivity, but ideology. Here at this university we have always said that there are ideologies involved. And it is good to say these things. It compels us to reflect upon them and to explain our own starting point, for things and our viewpoints are not neutral. It compels us to consider where we stand, to see that there are also other opinions and to realize that we can benefit from listening.

Therefore I feel no need at all to say: you may not be a Marxist. For there is freedom, and we must not deprive others of their freedom. And again: let us guard against it degenerating into a fashion. Marxism is critical, and I believe it is a plus when we are encouraged to be critical.

It is quite stupid, inhuman and wrong, it is a sort of self-blinding to think that we cannot be critical, that we just have to go along. We always have a point, and it is good that we know we must be critical, that we must raise our questions, that we must not accept things simply because they are there.

We must add that the Marxists have no monopoly in this. This university in particular, where you are now guests, was founded on a critical attitude. People said: that things are as they are in science today is not good, there are shortcomings, there is one-sidedness, to say the least – and they said it more harshly than that. We have our task. I would like to highlight here the fact that this university is founded on ideas that were first formulated by Groen van Prinsterer in his *Ongeloof en Revolutie*.[283] This book is from the time of Marx. Both the author and Marx were critics of their time, contemporaries in a very profound sense. I believe they never engaged each other directly, and I am sorry about that, but I believe that the discussion can still be beneficial today for both sides.

So, is art history a hobby? Certainly it is, and a very subjective and very personal one at that, and I believe we cannot and may not eliminate that personal and subjective element. I am very happy with what colleague Gerson said this afternoon, for he expressed that subjective element and that personal element and that is a tremendously important thing. Yet perhaps I go even further when I say that I see art history as a task and a calling in the midst of today's reality, with openness and the acceptance of one's own talents and attitude and the acceptance of the talents and attitudes of others. I want to end with a citation from a book by John Berger, from his collection of essays entitled *Permanent Red*. And it is very interesting that I agree completely with him when he says: 'Ours is a period of mannerism and decadence. Historical and social explanations are not hard to find. It may be unpopular, but it is not stupid to condemn works as bourgeois, formalist and escapist.' I said that sort of thing some ten years ago; Berger said it even earlier, but I have sometimes been criticized for that. Berger continues: 'And the question I ask is: does this work help or encourage people to know and claim their social rights?' I believe, by the way, that this is too narrow a definition, and Berger bails out of it himself, for he goes on to say, 'but what I do mean is this, the artist's way of looking at the world.'

What do artists have to say and how do they elevate the humanity of those who consider their work? That is their engagement. And I believe that we encounter them in that engagement and that this is where our task lies as well, in exactly the same way. That asks for a view of what reality is, of what truth is. And with such questions in the midst of our times we have our place as art historians; therein we are relevant; therein we have a cultural task and calling. And 'cultural' also embraces the societal, unless we want to slide back again into a dichotomy of culture and technology, or society and culture, or however you choose to formulate it. We are relevant and we have our task, at least if we are willing to work. So is art history a hobby? Yes, but one charged with meaning and significance.

• Art history at the Free University of Amsterdam[284]

Now that the writer has been appointed to the faculty of the Free University [of Amsterdam] and people have asked me to write something, I think it will be a good idea to present a short *oratio pro domo* to give you some insight into what is to happen next – or rather, into what the meaning of this discipline is for our circle.

There are many misunderstandings, and not in our circle alone, about the discipline of art history. These are connected, at least in part, with a (wholly outdated) conception of art as the utterly individual expression of purely individual emotion in a manner not rational and hence inexplicable. If art were indeed that, then the discipline of art history would be little more than frivolous. It would be no more than the assertion of private opinions in the absence of any possible evidence or possible criteria. I do not believe I should have wanted to become an art historian in such circumstances, for in that case I would be asking others to listen to my opinions, nothing more, to the expression of my feelings alongside the feelings of others, which seems to me to be asking too much, and to be rather pretentious as well. One also sometimes hears it claimed that art history as a discipline is a 'luxury'. What that means is not entirely clear to me, but we may begin by saying that no one will find a life of riches in this discipline and that it is also hard work. In general, art historians carry a heavy load, and a large dose of idealism is expected of them to give time and energy, often for minimum compensation. There are too few people to do all the work, and cultural work – which is called uneconomical – is simply poorly paid. But for the sake of the good and so highly important cause, people do it anyway.

It is truly not the case that the discipline is important because art historians have to make the delightful field they have chosen – 'looking at nice pictures all day long' – seem weighty in order to be able to preserve a semblance of self-respect and convince others of the usefulness of their work, under the motto that 'after all, there has to be bread on the table as well'. Its importance is much more sober and down-to-earth than that, and also far more essential. I will try to say something about this.

1. It is an undeniable fact that people today have much more frequent and intense contact with art than they did in the past. Our affluent society is certainly the first reason for this. In addition to the mass media and the many publications in this area, people also travel a great deal today, visiting churches and museums during their vacations and, in short, places that previously were frequented by just a select group. Thus it can be nothing other than useful to teach people to see, so that they are in a position to recognize the essential features of what they have before them. Someone standing before a Gothic cathedral with no knowledge of the system of construction – flying buttresses, great windows, vaulting structures – does not understand what he or she is looking at, does not apprehend its structure, and is therefore hardly in a position to gain more than a superficial impression of it. And someone who walks through a museum without knowing the first principles of art history and the structures of the old paintings – we will discuss modern art later – sees little. A museum visit is then not only largely fruitless but basically tiring and rather boring in the end, as all those paintings and images seem more or less the same unless one has learned to see the differences.

   I want to make two observations by way of an aside. First, one must know that art history is not aesthetics, thus theoretical reflection on art, but a science that seeks to approach and study the works of art themselves. The many works that have come down to us are ordered – catalogued – and the mutual interconnections, their style and its development, the themes, the causes of changes, etc. are closely investigated. Art history is a relatively young science – it is nearly two centuries old now, and it has been a university subject for a little less than a century – and the unfolding of events has led to its dealing exclusively with visual art, architecture and applied art. Music, drama, literature and the like do not fall within its competence, although some art historians may take an interest in these things from time to time.

Secondly, it must be emphasized that experience teaches that seeing is really very difficult. Nothing may seem simpler than just seeing what is in front of us, a building, a sculpture, a painting. The reality is quite otherwise. You should hear young students flounder when asked to say what they are seeing. You would discover that they see very little, sometimes literally overlooking even the most elementary things. Thus it strikes me as quite important, to return to our argument, that in our day and age students learn to see and to approach monuments of art and architecture with a modicum of understanding. That will make travelling more meaningful and open the mind to many experiences that one would otherwise have literally overlooked.

2. We live in an age in which the natural sciences, technology and economics demand all our attention and fascinate many people. That is not just a practical matter but one that goes very deep. People have given their hearts to these things, and they colour our entire view of life. As a result, our culture is not just on the way of becoming somewhat one-sided; it is on the verge of a fundamental disharmony. Thus we know how to make ever more beautiful television sets, for example in many colours and so on, but are hardly able to find those who can put together a responsible programme for broadcasting.

People can develop the most magnificent printing techniques, but there too something needs to be done with the possibilities. The twentieth century is charmed by the means but loses sight of the fact that all those beautiful machines have to be used for something, that something adequate must be done with them. Art and culture in the narrower sense demand a great deal of attention in order for our culture, in the wider sense, not to be thrown off balance. And the small number of cultural workers who are available are doing everything they can to restore the balance, if possible or, as it seems at times, to save what they can before it is completely lost. Art is no luxury but a bitter necessity if we want to keep our culture from withering, and prevent intellectual bankruptcy and chilling ugliness. The joy of life, human warmth and depth are at stake.

3. Well then, the art historian has a task and a calling in all of this. It is remarkable that in recent years more and more people have opened

their eyes to these questions. Thus the growth in the number of students entering these sectors have been striking, as has been the fact that it is also often the very good students who choose this direction. Until recently the natural sciences drew the best students. So there are some encouraging signs. Art history is a scientific activity that is practised in the first instance for its own sake, like every other science. So the fruits of such concentrated work must come later. For instance, every museum where one finds the works arranged in a comprehensibly structured and clear way, every exhibition, every simple little book about art and its history is based on such work. Unknown areas are opened up, understanding and insight into various movements are developed, and the fruits of this benefit all later exhibitions.

4. In our own circle art has been a neglected terrain for many years now, for a variety of reasons that I shall discuss here. We have accumulated a great deficit. Much confusion, much uncertainty, many conflicts (as between parents and children) are a result of this, or at least in part a result of it. That is all the more so now that Reformed people too (of whatever signature) are often strongly confronted with art and culture (in the stricter sense), as the affluent society inevitably evolves into the culture state and people simply cannot close their eyes to what they see around them every day. For this reason especially, reflection and study in our own circle into the problems in the field of art are by no means a luxury but on the contrary a bitter necessity. If we want to be able to evaluate what is put on offer, then we need to be able to look at it with understanding, simply so that we can comprehend what it is. And again, looking at art is not something everyone can do just as a matter of course, without study or instruction. One can only form a real critical judgment when one knows what one is talking about.

5. Modern art confronts us with some extra problems. Modern art itself is highly problematical, a genuine product of crisis. That is attributable in part to its being art in a technical-scientific age which threatens its very existence, and in part to deeper reasons of a religious and philosophical nature. Also in this respect we shall have to learn as a group and segment of the nation to define our own position sensibly and meaningfully. We shall have to do so if for no other reason than that we may otherwise simply not even see what is going on, in which case our speaking could be doomed to fruitlessness. Certainly this applies to the whole of our Christian testimony.

6. Art history deals with art from the past. It differs from other historical sciences in that here an as it were solidified little portion of the past has been retained, which art historians see in front of them when they look at a work of art. That makes it possible for this science to provide auxiliary services to other branches of historical research: frameworks of

thought can be clarified, as in art we can see opinions and conceptions objectively before us; what people saw with their eyes in the past (with all its possible distortions) is literally visible to us.

7. People today are often very distrustful of visual images. That is by nature even more so in our circle. People regard things that are stated verbally as clear and unambiguous. Images however seem 'poly-interpretable': one can at best express an opinion about them which, however, is not provable, for one expects proofs only in connection with verbally communicated sources. It needs to be stated emphatically, however, that once one has learned how to 'see', an image is as unambiguous and clear as a text. A text can be difficult to interpret, and a painting can be difficult to interpret too. In this they do not differ. An image is in this respect not inferior. An image can unquestionably make many things comprehensible that can hardly be expressed in words; by the same token, an image cannot take the place of language when it comes to other matters. The one is not necessarily secondary to the other. It is not true that language goes deep and that an image just touches the surface any more than the reverse would be so. They are simply different human modes of expression, each with its own possibilities and limitations.

8. Art is an expression and reflection of the life of the spirit and the intellect. Art is therefore as rich and variegated as life itself. All that we are, all that is human, we rediscover in art. Religious aspects are by no means excluded. Art is not neutral, for human being is not neutral. From this it follows that the practice of art history has a great deal to do with one's own starting point. Yet we shall not go into that more deeply here, since this publication often addresses the issue of the direct relation between science and religion, between human utterance and the heart's deepest yearnings.

9. Finally, there is another task that art history in our time and in our circle simply cannot ignore. Strictly speaking, it is not part of its task. It is to seek, from the experience gained through the study of past and present-day art and from reflection on our own starting point, an answer to the question concerning a Christian theory or conception of art. Not only the questions as to the principles of art criticism – concerning the interaction with the art confronting us – but also the problems with which the Christian artist wrestles today in order to arrive at a distinctive, responsible artistic expression, demand our attention. Here we touch upon one of the most fascinating but at the same time most difficult aspects of our work. We hope to speak more concretely about that in the future.

I have here spoken briefly – and more practically than theoretically – about what art history involves. Yet I have said little about precisely what I shall be doing. Naturally, I will lecture about past art and modern art and conduct seminars where problems are discussed with students. I will especially also lead excursions to the local museums, for example, where in confrontation with the works themselves we will discuss their structure and content. And we will travel abroad to study monuments intensively (not to engage in sightseeing).

In closing I would like to mention the following request in order to build up an apparatus that will benefit the Free University and our department and at the same time be an asset to the entire world of art history: we want to work hard on a project that has already for several years now enjoyed a modest beginning, namely, a collection of reproductions arranged iconographically (which is to say by subject). Thus may I ask you, if you own reproductions of works of art, regardless of the period, era or genre, that you no longer use and never look at, to think of us. They could be a useful addition to our collection. We shall also have to build up a reference library virtually from scratch. I hope that here too the sympathetic reader will need no more than this hint.

• Interview by art history students from the Free University[285]

WvL: How do you prefer to see yourself, as a member of L'Abri Fellowship, as a Professor of the History of Visual Art at the Free University, or as the author of 'Modern Art and the Death of a Culture'?

That is a strange question, since those things are inseparable. Someone who is active in this world as an art historian and who thinks about art and contemporary art will also publish something from time to time. I am one person. I publish, and that is not in conflict with what I teach to my students. L'Abri is a much older matter chronologically; I have been involved with that much longer, and that is also a part of my life that is not in conflict with the things I do here. What I do there is good for what I do here and what I do here is good for what I do there. These are two sides of a single life which I endeavour to use to do my work as a person and a Christian who sees his task as being broader than just being engaged with little works of art. One can indeed keep busy with little facts and little subjects, but I try to obtain a larger view. I have a theoretical bent, call it philosophical if you will, and I also take a tremendous interest in cultural problems. I do not see art as isolated but as something connected with a much larger whole, with what we call culture or modern culture. I want to analyse the problems we face today, I want to see where we are going, but for the rest I cannot say I am in the first place this or in the first place that. I devote far less time to L'Abri than to my art-historical work. That is just a little portion of my time, leisure activity if you will. But I do not have a twofold life in the way that people have a hobby like philately that has nothing to do with their work. For me it is not like that.

WvL: You say that L'Abri is chronologically the first. Perhaps you have adapted your professorship to the ideas you already had at L'Abri?

No, that is certainly not the case. I started with art history as a young student just after the Second World War. After that I got to know the people who later started L'Abri. I had some influence in shaping the ideas of L'Abri, and I have always been closely associated with it. I have also always been engaged in teaching art history, initially for a while in a secondary school, then in Leiden and finally here. My thinking took shape through the years, and L'Abri made it possible for me to have a great deal of contact with young people, sometimes with extreme ideas, sometimes in the protest movement, and to be in close contact with that and perhaps even to play a role in it.

I made a specific choice for the Free University. I had my work in Leiden and all at once in 1964 a great many positions were offered to me, some of them in America. It was very difficult to choose and finally I decided to come here. I will not go into the reason why, but it was at least in part because I felt that I would be able to realize something of my own work here and because I like to be scientifically engaged and to have the opportunity for that. Actually, the opportunity has turned out to be less in practise than in my dream, because a tremendous amount of my time is co-opted for administrative and governing matters.

I believe that one does not achieve a great deal in art history when one restricts oneself. If I must be categorized as an art historian, then that would be roughly as one of the Panofsky school – precisely because I believe one must set the buoys very wide and that art history must be open, with many elements facing outwards. That is a matter of my attitude towards my discipline and not of my finding art history too narrow a field; no, I just find art history as some practise it too narrow.

DB: How do you see the future of our faculty? As you know, there have been reports of its being dismantled and absorbed into the University of Amsterdam. This would be to achieve greater efficiency.

I lend no credence to these ideas. I believe that it was just a trial balloon put up in an incorrect manner. It reflects a wrong-headed notion of efficiency. Every university should have a department devoted to art history, or at least offer a minor in it – and you cannot really offer a good minor unless you also offer a major; it is just a part of the total package of a university. I could imagine them saying: we want to concentrate art history in one place where we will set up a large institute, and keep it small in other places. Abstractly speaking, I can agree with that.

DB: Art history at the Free University aims at something different from other universities. To what extent would you find it detrimental if there were to be a concentration of art history students in Utrecht, for example?

I would say that there should please be more than a one-way traffic and that as many different people as possible should work there and above all be free to go their own way. I believe that we all have our own cachet. Groningen is different from Leiden, and Leiden from the University of Amsterdam, and the University of Amsterdam from Utrecht, and we are different yet again from each of them. I believe there is nothing illegitimate in that. It has nothing to do with the special character of this university; we all have our own specialties, our hobbies, and our personalities – to try to eliminate that would be impossible or you would have to gag everybody.

DB: Do you want to send your students off committed to a particular direction that distinguishes them from the graduates of other universities?

I have a little theory about that, namely that every professor anywhere divides his students into three categories. You have people who study with you and finish at a certain moment, having of course learned what is necessary. I am talking about what is referred to nowadays as the 'normal' student, the average, solid student, not the quitter.

Then you have the second type of student, which I suppose includes most of the students here, and the dream that I have about them is that when they have finished they will say: I have studied at this university for a number of years under these people and I have learned a great deal. The ideal that I have for these students is that because they have been confronted with Christianity they will have been compelled to think seriously about who they are. Thus I do not see this second category being sent off as Christians; I do not even see them departing thinking along the same lines as I do. But they are certainly people who because of the confrontation with Christianity say: I have learned a great deal there and am departing the richer for it, I have learned to find my way, I learned to think things through, I am perhaps not of that school but I have certainly been formed in part by that school.

To give an example, I see in Vollemans such a student of the second category. That is a student of my school and he is an extreme Marcusian or whatever you might want to call it. We have engaged in endless discussions with each other. I believe he is a better Marcusian for having studied with me, and when I read his articles I again recognize regularly things about which I say: well, he learned that from me. I do not find that at all lamentable. I am a student of the second category myself with respect to Professor Van Regteren Altena. I learned a great deal from him. I do not experience it as a problem to be called one of his students, but no one can say that I have carried on in his direction. As a student I was always engaged in sparring with him, precisely because again and again I was freshly challenged by his approach, which I considered unsatisfactory but which was very good in itself.

And then there is a final category, and that is a category of which you dream as a person, as an instructor and as a scientist, that you would have students who think things through in your direction and follow you in it. These are of course not parrots. Thus they can think entirely independently – and the more independently, the better. Birtwistle is such a student, I believe, and there may be a few more. But if you have two or three students of that sort in a lifetime – and they are given you, you cannot make them – then you have had a good life as a professor.

WvL: To mention a term, you have sometimes spoken of 'evangelizing'.

Have I spoken of that? No, I do not understand the place the word has here. The Free University has never been like that, and I have never understood it that way nor would I ever want to regard it as an institute for evangelizing. Yes, if people become Christians because of their contact with the work here, then I can of course only be thankful for that.

DB: You do not even see it as a subsidiary activity?

Not even a subsidiary activity. Perhaps that lies in the difference between the second and third categories of students. But it is not just friendliness, a nice gesture and a sort of compromise if I say that the second and third categories of student are equally dear to me. I would almost say that if anyone really wants to be my pupil, I am inclined to make all the heavier demands on him or her. Students of the first category are of course given all the attention they seek, but they usually demand less attention because they pose fewer critical questions, are less persistent and simply do their work and bring it to a good end. The second and third categories can be extremely inconvenient students who pepper you constantly with all kinds of questions.

WvL: Do you see a clear difference between the foreigners (in particular those from Anglo-Saxon countries) who have come to the Free University especially for your lectures and ideas and the Dutch students?

That is a difficult question, for one can never say without qualification that they are exactly the same. The foreigners are in the first place people who are a little older and who as such generally fall into the category of postgraduate (*doctoraal*) students. Naturally and unavoidably you have the most contact with your postgraduate students; you are more directly engaged with them scientifically, you have seminars together, they write research papers. That is also the phase, I believe, during which a solid foundation is laid for exchanging ideas with one another at an appropriately high level. If one looks at the graduate echelon, I doubt that you will detect much difference between the foreign and the Dutch students. The reason why I find it a matter of common hospitality to devote some extra attention to the foreign students is because they face extra difficulties. In the first place, it turns out time and again that the level of study with us is far higher than what they have been accustomed to. They require auxiliary schooling – which I do not see as my task – but you have to give them something extra through conversations and discussions in order to help them on their way. These people have often sacrificed a great deal to come and study here, and we must not disparage that. Thus in principle they come as students of the third category and they have made a deliberate choice to come to me. I make no distinction, I do not seek people out, but if they come to me I do not say: you have to go away because someone else thinks he has just as much right. Such a person should exercise that right and come along too. Thus I have indeed set up a special seminar, especially with a view to these people, because I have observed that during the first year and sometimes longer they experience such difficulty with the language that they walk around rather lost. Lectures are useless to them; they sit there politely, really more in order to learn the language than to gain anything else. Moreover, they come to the Free University for a special subject (Christianity and art) which ideally has a place here as I see it but which I in practice seldom get to, given the way things have grown here with so many non-Christian students. Thus I devote special time to that in an English-language seminar on Christianity and art. It is of course also open to Dutch students. I can imagine the situation arising that we switch into Dutch. I know that there are also other departments here at the university that have large numbers of foreign students, and it always surprises me that they do not do something of the same sort – not because these are special people but simply because they have come from far away and you need to take care of them.

I think it would be sad and stupid, both, if students here were to regard these foreigners as undesired aliens. We must view them as an enrichment of the community and a broadening of our circle. This is not just because you can make friends for life and thereby have contacts abroad with colleagues which may, even from a purely egotistical standpoint, benefit you later in your life; no, it is also simply a pleasure. And yes, we have a South African here, and we have a few Americans. Most recently I received a letter from a Japanese person who may want to come here. I must say, I have no idea why that Japanese student would want to come, or why to me in particular. So perhaps he will come, and then there is also a Korean.

WvL: We have heard that your book 'Modern Art' may be translated into Japanese.

My book, yes. But that has nothing to do with the Japanese student. That book is not out yet, and I have no idea why he would come to me, certainly not for the Free University or its special character. I last wrote to him in answer to his questions, and since then I have heard nothing. Perhaps he is looking for the money to come.

WvL: Do you have any explanation for the fact that you so strongly attract foreigners?

Well, that is not so difficult to understand. That is at least in part a result of my book, which is read widely abroad or at least has attracted widespread attention. There are some who simply transfer from other universities. Our Australian first attended the University of Amsterdam, but she was received with greater friendliness here than there, where they seem to give every new arrival dirty looks. Because I am a somewhat friendlier and hospitable person I think it is fine that she has come here, but she did not come for me at all, as she had never even heard of me.

I am also very internationally oriented because of L'Abri. Last summer I made an extensive trip through America to give lectures. In England I am fairly well known; yet we do not attract more English students, mainly because of difficulties in the financial area. The Americans can do it more easily, but the English really have no scholarships available, which is a pity. I would like the Netherlands to give more grants. I am not at all sorry that I am married, but I have often thought: I wish I had married somewhat later, or better said, met my wife somewhat later. When I finished my first degree (*kandidaats*) I had really planned to study further at the Courtauld, and nothing came of that then. I really think that in this day and age we should all travel abroad – and everyone can do that more easily nowadays. What I always greatly encourage is that before completing their second degree (*doctoraal*) everyone should spend some time abroad, like Loes Rotshuizen-van Sitteren, who studied at the Sorbonne. We still think too small in the Netherlands. The chauvinism in art history is an international problem. In France you will not get a foot on the ground as a Dutch person if you ever want to have a job there.

Well then, those foreigners – one must help them over the threshold as well. Maybe they are more inclined to come and have discussions with me. After my Monday afternoon lecture I almost always have a discussion with people. Then they come and say 'What you said today, I do not believe that and I do not see that point.' And afterwards I think about it and ask myself 'Why did they not see it?'

Notes to Volume 3

Part I: Art and Entertainment

1 Part I was originally published in Dutch as *Kunst en Amusement* (Kampen: J.H. Kok N.V., 1962)

2 These were French philosophers, including Diderot and d'Alembert, who contributed to the *Encyclopédie* that began to appear in 1750. This, some say, was the real Revolution that made 1789 inevitable. See, e.g. Groen van Prinsterer, *Ongeloof en Revolutie*, esp. chs 8, 9 and 11.

3 Emile Doumergue, *L'Art en le sentiment dans l'oeuvre de Calvin* (Geneva, 1902); Leon Wencelius, *L'aesthétique de Calvin* (Paris, 1938).

4 Platschek's book appeared in a Dutch translation: *Nieuwe figuratieve kunst* (1960). See p.88.

5 Ibid., p.107, 104.

6 *Kroniek van Kunst en Kultuur*, p.47.

7 E. Jaguer, in *Museumjournaal* 3, no. 1, 1957.

8 'Salon' refers to the great annual (official) exhibitions held in Paris during the nineteenth century.

9 See Matthew 7:9; Luke 11:11.

10 2 Corinthians 3:6: 'for the letter kills, but the Spirit gives life.'

11 Hebrews 10:15–16: 'The Holy Spirit also testifies to us about this, for ... I will put my laws in their hearts, and I will write them on their minds.'

12 Cf. 2 Timothy 1:12.

13 2 Corinthians 12:9.

14 Cf. Galatians 1:5.

15 'human commands and teachings'.

16 Cf. for the above: E. Panofsky, 'Poussin and the Elegiac Tradition', reprinted in his collection *Meaning in the Visual Arts* (Garden City, NY, 1955) pp.223–254.

17 See for a more extensive discussion of this point my *Synthetist Art Theories* (1959) reproduced in the *Complete Works* 1, pp.162 ff.

18 I have discussed extensively the connection between life and world view and cultural activity, and between the work of the individual artist and that of his or her contemporaries and associates, in my article: 'The Constituent Factors of a Historical Deed'. See part III of this volume.

19 Cf. *Sartor Resartus* (London, 1898) p.222.

20 Holbrook Jackson, *The Eighteen Nineties* (Penguin, 1950, 6th edn.) pp.191–193.

21 P. Gauguin, *Avant et Après* (1923) p.5.

22 *Racontars d'un rapin* (Paris, 1951) p.75.

23 J.C. Lambert, *Corneille* (Paris, 1960) p.27.

24 *Museumjournaal* V, 5 (1955) p.95.

25 P. Selz, *New Images of Man* (New York, 1959) prefatory note.

26 Editorial note: Here H.R.R. echoes Groen van Prinsterer's *Ongeloof en Revolutie*, ch. 11.

27 *El dos de Mayo y los Fusilamientos* (Barcelona, 1946).
28 In his *Ueber das Geistige in die Kunst* (1912).
29 *Kroniek voor Kunst en Kultuur*, pp.46–50 and 82–87.
30 You will have noticed that this is an allusion to the Beatitudes (see Matthew 5:1–12).
31 L.P.J. Braat in *Kroniek van Kunst en Kultuur* (1946) p.129.
32 Read the wonderful little book by A. Janse, *Eva's Dochteren* [Eve's daughters] (Kampen, 1922).
33 I recommend here for further study: F. Würtemberger, *Weltbild und Bilderwelt* (Vienna, 1958); W. Hofmann, *Das irdische Paradies: Kunst im 19. Jahrhundert* (Munich, 1960); W. Haftmann, *Malerei im 20. Jahrhundert* (Munich, 1954); and for a different angle of approach to the nexus of problems sketched in the section above, much can also be found in J.H. v.d. Berg, *Het menselijk lichaam* (Vol 1: Nijkerk, 1959; Vol 2: Nijkerk, 1961).
34 See John 3:21: 'But whoever lives by the truth comes into the light, so that it may be seen plainly that what he has done has been through God.'
35 See in this regard the illuminating book by W. Schöne, *Über das Licht in der Malerei* (Berlin, 1954).
36 See for example *Ontmoeting* 15, April/May 1962, a special issue of this magazine devoted to the new sacred song.
37 *Gereformeerde Zede* (1955) pp.65 ff.
38 See L. Corinth, *Frauenraub*; Berlin-Schönenberg; figure in R. Waldmann, *Kunst des Realismus und Impressionismus* (Propyläen-Kunstgeschichte), p. 329.
39 See above, p.58.
40 See above, pp.12 f.
41 See above, pp.69 f.
42 Originally published in 1864. Reprinted by Christian Focus Publications (Geanies House, Ross-shire, 1999); see p.7.
43 See Colossians 2:15; cf. John 16:11, Matthew 12:28, Revelations 9:4, etc.
44 Which we find summed up in Galatians 5:22; cf. Romans 8:9–10.
45 Cf. 1 Peter 1:17; Psalm 39:12.
46 Cf. Matthew 25:37 ff. and James 1:27.
47 Cf. James 4:2: 'You do not have, because you do not ask God.'
48 John 13:35 and 17:31; Romans 15:5.

Part II: The Creative Gift

49 Part II was originally published as *The Creative Gift: Essays on Art and the Christian Life* (Westchester Il: Cornerstone Books, 1981) and as *The Creative Gift: the Arts and the Christian Life* (Leicester: Inter-Varsity Press, 1981). *The Creative Gift* has been republished here as in its 1982 Inter-Varsity Press (UK) edition with minor editorial changes, mainly for gender neutrality.
50 See further on, chapter 3 of this part, 'Creativity in Love and Freedom'.
51 Thomas Carlyle, *Sartor Resartus* (St Clair Shores, Mich.: Scholarly, 1977).

52 See chapter 5 in Os Guinness, *The Dust of Death* (Downers Grove, Ill.: InterVarsity Press, 1973).

53 Popma, *Philosophia Reformata* 38(1973) pp.103, 104.

54 Ibid., p.110.

55 Allen Ginsberg, 'Howl,' from *Howl and Other Poems* (San Francisco: City Lights, 1956).

56 [In M.C. Smit, *Toward a Christian Conception of History*. Edited and translated by Herbert Donald Morton and Harry Van Dyke. Christian Perspectives Today (Lanham, New York and Oxford: Institute for Christian Studies and University Press of America, 2000) p.278.]

57 John Cage, *Silence: Lectures and Writings by John Cage* (New York: Wesleyan University Press, 1961) p.195.

58 Martin Esslin, *The Theatre of the Absurd* (Garden City, N.Y.: Doubleday, 1961) p. 316.

59 The Heidelberg Catechism, question 54.

60 R.E.D. Clark, *Christian Belief and Science* (London: English Universities Press, 1960) pp.27 ff.

61 Charles Darwin, *Autobiography and Selected Letters*, edited by Francis Darwin (New York: Dover, 1892).

62 [Probably referring to the hippie-beatnik-velvet underground of the sixties – making the point that given the loss of norms and standards the behaviours of the cultural Underground are ever less distinguishable from those of the criminal underworld.]

63 Fyodor Dostoyevsky, *The Brothers Karamazov* (New York: W. W. Norton, 1976) ch. 35.

64 Jean-Paul Sartre, *Huis Clos* (Englewood Cliffs, N.J.: Prentice-Hall, 1962).

65 Henry Miller, *Tropic of Cancer* (New York: Grove, 1961) pp.56, 257.

66 Ibid.

67 See chapter 3 above, 'Creativity in Love and Freedom'.

68 Although some of the following ideas about artistic freedom appear elsewhere in this book, I include them here as well because of their relevance to our discussion of Buñuel and modern art.

69 Max Klinger, *Graphic Works of Max Klinger* (Magnolia, Mass.: Peter Smith) plate 72.

70 Revelation 4:11.

71 Martin Esslin, *The Theatre of the Absurd*, p.316.

72 Peter Gay, *The Enlightenment: The Rise of Modern Pragmatism* I (New York: Knopf, 1966) p.159.

73 Micah 6:6–8.

74 See also Walter L. Strauss, *The Complete Drawings of Albrecht Dürer* 4 (1520–1528) (New York: Abaris Books, 1974) pp.1993–1995.

Part III: Articles on History, Faith and Culture, Lifestyle, and Scholarship

75 This article was originally published in three parts as follows: Part 1: *Philosophia Reformata* 19, 1 (1954); Part 2: *Philosophia Reformata* 19, 2/3 (1954), starting with 'Judging Historical Deeds'; Part 3: *Philosophia Reformata* 19, 4 (1954), starting with '4. World View'.

76 This quotation is the beginning of I. Stone, *Lust for Life* (Pocket Book, 1946).

77 Dr H. Faber, *De geschiedenis als theologisch probleem* (Arnhem, 1933) p.42.

78 Cf. Prof. H. Dooyeweerd, *Wijsbegeerte der Wetsidee* II (Amsterdam, 1935/6), hereafter W.d.W. II – pp.143 ff. (In English: *A New Critique of Theoretical Thought* II (Philadelphia, 1969), hereafter NCTT II – pp.181 ff.)

79 As e.g. Rickert wants to do. Cf. Prof. Dr J.P.A. Mekkes: 'De Betekenis van het subject in de moderne waarde-philosophie onder het licht van de Wetsidee' (Leiden, 1949, lecture) p.13; E. Troeltsch, *Der Historismus und seine Probleme: Ges. Schriften* III (Tübingen, 1922) pp.150 ff. We shall refer to the latter as Troeltsch, *H.u.s.P.*

80 C.f. W.d.W. II, p.139 ff.(NCTT II, p.192 ff).

81 Cf. Mekkes, 'De Betekenis van het subject', pp.64 ff.

82 W.d.W. II, p.181, 185, 189 ff. (NCTT II, pp.241, 246, 257 ff. respectively)

83 H. Butterfield, *Christianity and History* (London, 1949) pp.63, 106.

84 Cf. J.H. Plumb, *England in the 18th Century* (Pelican Book, 1950) p.23.

85 For the concept of disclosure see W.d.W. II, pp.126 ff. (NCTT II, p.181).

86 We will return to some of these in the final part of this article.

87 Cf. W.d.W. II, p.143; cf. NCTT II, pp.197–199.

88 Cf. for example, my article in *Philosophia Reformata* 14 (1949) pp.63 ff.

89 Cited in Waetzold, *Deutsche Kunsthistoriker* I (Leipzig, 1921) p.202.

90 W.d.W. II, pp. 81/2; cf. NCTT II, pp.241–242.

91 Cf. my article in *Philosophia Reformata* 14 (1949) p.68.

92 Cf. Troeltsch: *H.u.s.P.*, pp.370 ff.

93 The word 'historically' here and in other places is used as indicating a modal specificity, i.e. concerning the formative aspect. It does not mean therefore: according to an insight from the past.

94 This refers to a movement in art and literature at the end of the nineteenth century in England that rebelled against rationalism and naturalism. They were looking for a new kind of romanticism that would elevate 'life' above reason, whereby a kind of aesthetic Epicureanism was preached. Especially with respect to the latter they claimed to have heard a kindred voice in this famous postscript in Pater's book, which was first published in 1873. Pater omitted the postscript in the second edition of 1877, as he feared that his words were misunderstood. And yet, Pater can justly be charged with a certain aestheticism – witness his writings about Renaissance art, written in such a sublime style in this little book, which are more fiction than art history. Cf. Holbrook Jackson, *The Eighteen Nineties* (Pelican Book, 1950) pp.58–59.

95 W.d.W. II, p.182; cf. NCTT II, p.243.

96 We think here for example of the simultaneous appearance of Expressionism in Germany and in France in the years around 1905.

97 See my article in *Philosophia Reformata* 14 (1949) p.65.

98 This would indicate that the aesthetic assessment cannot really be kept out of consideration when studying art history. For the historical deed in artistic life implies a positivization of the aesthetic norm.

99 Cf. H. Sedlmayr, *Verlust der Mitte: Die Bildende Kunst des 19. und 20. Jahrhunderts als Symptom und Symbol der Zeit* (Salzburg, 1951, 5th ed.) and Prof. S.U. Zuidema, 'De dood bij Heidegger', *Philosophia Reformata* 12 (1947) p.49. We need not refer to further literature regarding existentialism and related movements.

100 See Butterfield, *Christianity and History* pp.68 ff., p.100, pp.54–55. The informed reader will note that I have not used the theory of common grace. We are of the opinion that the way the problem is posed in this theory is already incorrect in its origin. We are trying to approach the status quo that was really the cause for all these discussions, in a historical-theoretical way by proposing a solution. See also the final part of this article. For a critique on the theory of common grace we refer you to Prof. Dr. K. Schilder, *Heidelbergse Catechismus* (Goes, 1947) I, pp.158 ff., pp.429 ff., pp.491 ff., III, pp.235 ff. and especially IV, pp.15 ff.

101 Cf. *W.d.W.* II, p. 188; cf. *NCTT* II, pp.251–262. The general question of how people can obtain scientific knowledge of the norms belongs to the realm of the theory of knowledge, with which we cannot concern ourselves here. See also *W.d.W.* II, especially pp.399 ff,; cf.*NCTT*, especially pp.466 ff. Just take note here that in our experience of reality we do certainly know these norms, even if we do not want to recognize them theoretically. In general, the sources for our knowledge of the norms are the Scriptures and reality itself, both of them are totally adapted to each other and complement each other. In reality the norms are manifest, revealed in the Scriptures. Cf. N.G.B. (Belgic Confession) article 2.

102 G. Jedlicka, *Manet* (Zürich, 1941) p.133; J. Rewald, *History of Impressionism* (New York, 1946) pp.151–152.

103 Cf. *W.d.W.* II, pp.174–175; cf. *NCTT* II, pp.289–290).

104 Cf. *W.d.W.* II, pp.180 ff.; cf. *NCTT* II, pp.241–243)

105 T. Craven, *Modern Art* (New York, 1940) pp.225–226.

106 See my article in *Philosophia Reformata* 14 (1949) pp.63–64.

107 Craven, *Modern Art*, p.70.

108 The view of life expressed in this movement can already be found in Munch, in his woodcut *Angst* of 1895 (see my article in *Stijl*, Febr. 1952). We will return to the role that art played in the formation of the modern cultural ideal in the final part of this article, see p.304.

109 We see something similar in the history of the Anabaptists in the sixteenth century. Cf. A. Janse, *De verhouding van de christelijke politiek tot de wereldse* (1933), especially pp.19 ff.

110 Cf. also H. Read, *Philosophy of Modern Art* (1952) p.22.

111 We refer here to historicism in the sense of Dilthey, Troeltsch and Simmel, which has entangled itself in 'the antinomy between the requirement of every world and life view to be universally valid, and historical consciousness' – Dilthey, *Gesammelte Schriften* [collected works] VIII: *Weltanschauungslehre* [doctrine of world view] p.1. See also Troeltsch, *Historismus und seine Probleme* (1922) p.76; Dr M.C. Smit, *Historicisme en Anti-Historicisme: Wetenschappelijke Bijdragen door leerlingen van Prof. Dr*

D.H.Th. *Vollenhoven* (Franeker, 1951) pp.153 ff. and *W.d.W.* II, pp.146–147; cf. *NCTT* II, pp.205–207).

112 Troeltsch, *H.u.s.P.*, pp.164 ff.

113 With respect to this issue see also: M. Mandelbaum, *The Problem of Historical Knowledge: An Answer to Relativism* (New York, 1938).

114 Cf. Dr M.C. Smit, *Historicisme en Anti-Historicisme*; also Troeltsch, *H.u.s.P.*, p.75 and pp.221 ff.

115 As is the opinion of Troeltsch, *H.u.s.P.*, pp.703 ff.

116 See inter alia K. Breysig, *Die Meister des entwickelnden Geschichtsforschung* (Breslau, 1936); *W.d.W.* II, pp.191 ff. and pp.218 ff.; cf. *NCTT* II, pp. 259 ff. and pp.290 ff.

117 Troeltsch, *H.u.s.P.*, p.226.

118 Cf. Denis Mahon, *Studies in Science, Art and Theory* (London, 1949) pp.213–214.

119 Cf. also Rewald, *History of Impressionism*, p.26. More about Marinetti, the leader of the Futurists, in S. Cheney, *The Story of Modern Art* (New York, 1945) pp.467–468, where he cites the Futuristic Manifest of 1911: 'We wish to glorify war, the only health-giver of the world, militarism, patriotism, the destructive arm of the anarchist, and the beautiful Ideas that Kill; we glorify contempt for women. We wish to destroy the museums and libraries, to fight morals, feminism and all opportunist meannesses.' Hilla Rebay, Director of the Museum of Non-Figurative Art in New York recently wrote a letter to Germany about the usefulness of the destruction of old artistic treasures.

120 In Toynbee's sense.

121 Cf. Butterfield, *History and Christianity*, pp.93 ff.

122 For example Ezekiel 14:21–23.

123 For example also Deuteronomy 32 and Revelation 5 ff.

124 We cannot develop an extensive Christian philosophy of history here. Apart from the works cited in this context, see also K.J. Popma, *Calvinistische Geschiedbeschouwing* (Franeker, 1945); K. Schilder, *Christus en Cultuur* (Franeker, 1948).

125 Cf. also Troeltsch, *H.u.s.P.*, p.657.

126 Cf. Butterfield, *History and Christianity*, p.106.

127 Cf. my article in *Calvinistisch Jongelingsblad* (16 November 1951). The repeated apostasy of this race, resulting in a failure to fulfil its task, makes reformation a constant necessity.

128 See Revelation 11 and 17.

129 Butterfield, *History and Christianity*, pp.26 ff.

130 Prof. Dr D.H.Th. Vollenhoven, *Geschiedenis van de Wijsbegeerte* I (Franeker, 1950) pp.18 ff.

131 Cf. H. Sedlmayr, *Verlust der Mitte*. In another context I hope to elaborate on this matter.

132 See Windelband-Heimsoeth, *Lehrbuch der Geschichte der Philosophie* (1948, 14th ed.) p.413.

133 Troeltsch, *H.u.s.P.*, pp.117, 119.

134 Prof. K. Schilder, *Christus en Cultuur*, p. 75.

135 See A. Janse, *Eva's Dochteren* (Kampen, 1922).
136 Cf. J. Huizinga, *Herfsttij der Middeleeuwen* (Haarlem, 1947, 6th ed.) pp.152–153; *The Waning of the Middle Ages* (London: E. Arnold, 1924).
137 Heron applied his inventions exclusively to the temple at Alexandria.
138 Troeltsch, *H.u.s.P.*, p.166, pp.181 ff.
139 See my article in *Philosophia Reformata* 14 (1949) pp.68, 69, 70.
140 Quotation from 'Notes' of 1903, cited by C. Morice, *Gauguin* (Paris, 1920) p. 244.
141 According to A. Springer in 1887, cited by Waetzold, *Deutsche Kunsthistoriker* II, p.127.
142 F. Hoffet, *L'Impérialisme protestante, Considérations sur le destin inégal des peoples protestants et catholiques dans le monde actuel* (Paris, 1948).
143 Ibid., p.253.
144 *H.u.s.P.*, p.414; so also Windelband-Heimsoeth, *Lehrbuch*, p.552, where he writes correctly about Comte's 'Aufforderung eines positivistischen Papsttum'.
145 'Christianity' is indeed the correct term here, and not faith, or confession and suchlike, precisely because Christianity is a broad and undelineated concept. Cf. K. Schilder, *Christus en Cultuur*, pp.17 ff.
146 Cited in C. Morice, *Gauguin*.
147 C.f. Butterfield, *History and Christianity*, p.45, also pp.26 ff.
148 Dilthey, *Gesammelte Schriften* VIII, p.82.
149 Ibid., p.82.
150 We cannot expend on this question here. See *W.d.W.* the Prolegomena; Prof. Dr H. Dooyeweerd, 'Inleiding op de encyclopaedie der rechtswetenschappen' (stencil), pp.1–16 and Dr F.H. von Meyenfeldt, *Het 'hart' in het Oude Testament* (Leiden, 1950).
151 In the English literature 'world and life view' is now designated as simply 'world view', which is what will be used in what follows. The observation concerning religion and world view that follows, relates especially to humanists. The Greek and other religious ground motives are different in structure. They could give rise to similar observations, but this writer does not feel competent to deal with them. Cf. Dooyeweerd, *Reformatie en Scholastiek in de Wijsbegeerte* I (Franeker, 1949) pp.41 ff. and, regarding the Greek view of life, pp.20 ff.
152 So also, approximately, the 'naturalism' of Dilthey, *Gesammelte Schriften* VIII, p.100.
153 Dilthey's 'Idealismus der Freiheit', ibid., p.109. With Troeltsch we come across it in the following: 'The goal of ethical action is to gain and maintain a free and unified personality based in one's own self.' *Historismus und seine Ueberwindung* (Berlin, 1924) p.8.
154 Cf. *W.d.W.* I, pp.152 ff.; cf. *NCTT* I, pp.188 ff. In the literature we often come across these polar opposites in all sorts of shapes, as in: intellectualism – voluntarism; natural sciences – humanities; rationalism – irrationalism; positivism – idealism; determination – contingency; theoretical – practical; masses – individual, etc.
155 C.f. also C. van der Waal, *Antithese of Synthese* (Enschede, 1951) pp.73 ff. and passim.

156 Dilthey, *Gesammelte Schriften* VIII, p.79.
157 Holbrook Jackson, *The Eighteen Nineties* (Pelican Book, 1950) p.193.
158 Cf. H. Sedlmayr, *Verlust der Mitte* (1951) pp.129 ff., pp.145 ff.
159 Windelband-Heimsoeth, *Lehrbuch*, pp.560 ff., p.437 and elsewhere.
160 H. Redeker, 'Balans van een puberteit', in *Het Woord* (1946) p.424.
161 Sedlmayr, *Verlust der Mitte*, p.160 passim.
162 Ibid., pp.157–158.
163 Ibid., pp.118 and 139.
164 The world view preached by him is not, after all, a norm itself, but a strictly subjective attitude to life, subjected to a norm.
165 In our opinion this represents an anticipation of the formative modality on the modality of faith.
166 K. Marx, F. Engels, *Het Communistisch Manifest* (Amsterdam, 1948) Introduction pp.10–11.
167 Ibid. II, pp.75–76.
168 Ibid., the introduction, p.24.
169 Ibid., p.74.
170 In this connection, see *W.d.W.* II, pp.76–177, p.219, p.238 passim. (*NCTT* II, pp.238–239, pp.291–292, pp.310–311 passim)
171 H. Redeker, *De dagen der artistieke vertwijfeling* (Amsterdam,1950) p.118.
172 Ibid., p.143.
173 Ibid., p. 160.
174 Ibid., p. 161.
175 Sedlmayr, *Verlust der Mitte*, comes to approximately the same conclusions, by a different route. Moreover, he sees precisely in the purely artistic character of this movement, that wants to make 'absolute' art, also a symptom of the above-mentioned crisis. Cf. p.171, pp.80 ff.
176 L. Woolf, *After the Deluge: a Study of Communal Psychology* (Pelican Book, 1937) p.142.
177 See Sedlmayr, *Verlust der Mitte*, p.15, pp.102–103 and passim.
178 See Prof. H. Dooyeweerd, *De Reformatie en de Scholastiek in de Wijsbegeerte* I (1949) pp.42 ff.
179 We do not wish to deny that this 'understanding' would involve a scholarly problem, but consider this to be a question for epistemology rather than history. Cf. also *W.d.W.* II, pp.356–364; cf. *NCTT* II, pp.426–433.
180 This writer would like to express his special thanks to Prof. Dr H. Dooyeweerd for his interest and the many edifying comments regarding this study.
181 This English summary appeared at the end of Part Three in *Philosophia Reformata* 19, 4 (1954). It was compiled by Mr H. de Jongste.
182 *Calvinistisch Jongelingsblad* 6, 29 (1951) pp.231–232'
183 Rookmaaker alludes here to the secession (or Liberation) in 1944 of the Reformed Churches in the Netherlands (Liberated) from the Reformed Churches in the Netherlands. He was a member of the Liberated Churches.
184 *Calvinistisch Jongelingsblad* 10, 39 (1956) pp.332, 333; 10, 40, (1956) pp.337, 338; 10, 41 (1956) pp.345, 346; 10, 42 (1956) pp.354–356; 11, 1, 19 (1956)

pp.1, 2; 11, 2 (1956) pp.9, 10.

185 From J. W. Tunderman, *Marnix van St Aldegonde en de subjectivistische stromingen in de 16e eeuw*, pp. 36–37.

186 For the Dutch term *geestdrijverij*.

187 For an account of Mennonite beliefs in sixteenth and early seventeenth century Dutch history based on contemporary sources, see A. Th. van Deursen, *Plain Lives in a Golden Age: Popular Culture, Religion and Society in Seventeenth-Century Holland* (Cambridge: CUP, 1991) pp.255–259 and pp.304–318.

188 Bakhuizen v.d. Brink – Lindeboom, *Handboek der Kerkgeschiedenis* 2, p.220.

189 *In de Rechte Straat*, 13, 9 (1970) pp.18–20, originally published under the title 'Rookmaaker's View'.

190 *Evangelie en Maatschappij*, 17, 4 (1964) pp.105–126.

191 E. Zahn, *Leven met de welvaart* (Amsterdam, 1962) p.164.

192 Cf. G. Reitlinger, *The Economics of Taste* 1 and 2 (London, 1961 and 1963).

193 Zahn, *Leven met de welvaart*, p.148.

194 See for example F. D. Klingender, *Art and the Industrial Revolution* (London, 1947).

195 W. Banning, 'Moderne élites en politiek', *Wending* (February 1963) p.784.

196 Zahn, *Leven met de welvaart*, p.149.

197 Ibid., p.101.

198 'This ... then was the true nature of the modern: naturalistic lack of freedom, and compensation for this by the sovereign play of the aesthetic fantasy.' Simmel's characterization, cited in E. Troeltsch, *Historismus und seine Probleme* (1922) p.581.

199 E. B. Feldman, 'The Artist and Mass Culture', *College Art Journal* 18 (1959), p.343.

200 Cf. F. L. Polak in F. Boerwinkel et al., *De Nederlandse Cultuur, haar geestesmerk en toekomst*, The Hague, 1950, p.17; cf. also K. J. Popma, 'Diagnose van onze tijd', *Antirevolutionaire Staatkunde* 9, 1949, p.129 ff., a critical reflection on Mannheim's *Diagnosis of Our Time*.

201 Entertainment is meant here in a broad and not derogatory sense. Cf. my *Kunst en amusement*, Kampen 1962 [English translation in Part I of this volume.]

202 See chapter 5 of my book *Kunst en amusement*, referred to above.

203 Cf. my article 'Kunst en levensstijl' in the anthology *Vier Glazen, gedenkboek 1886–1961 van S. S. R.*, 1961, p. 325. In this collection there are also some other contributions that are of importance for the subject now under discussion. For the translation of 'Kunst en levensstijl', see 'Art and Lifestyle' in this volume.

204 Jeremiah 45:5 [cf. Jeremiah 21:9 and 38:18 – the NIV does not include the image, to which HRR referred, in its translation].

205 Cf. P. J. Bouman, *In de laagvlakten der cultuur*, Groningen, 1960; the contribution by F. L. Polak in *Crisis der Cultuur, uitdaging en antwoord*, The Hague, 1951, p.36.

206 Cf. my articles in *Opbouw* dated July 1, 1960 and May 10, 1963; see *Complete Works* 4: 'Bible Study Groups'.

207 We are not talking about subsidies in other fields, where we do not feel

qualified to judge. See in this connection: *Antwoord aan deze tijd, studie voor een nieuw sociaal program van Patrimonium* (Franeker, 1963) pp.205 ff.; *Welvaart en Welvaartsdenken, een studie samengesteld door de commissie voorsociale zaken van de Oecumenische Raad van Kerken in Nederland* (Amsterdam, 1960) p.27; cf. also F. L. Polak in *Crisis der Cultuur* (The Hague, 1951) p.35; G. van der Leeuw, *Nationale Cultuurtaak* (The Hague, 1947) p.135 – both for subsidies.

208 This against *Antwoord aan deze tijd*, p. 205.

209 This against F. L. Polak in *Crisis der Cultuur*.

210 *Regelrecht* 2, 4, 1965, pp.126–136; also delivered as a speech on November 11 1964 at the public meeting to announce the award contest of Stichting Prosper.

211 In the compilation *Wij en de welvaart*, 1964.

212 See also in this connection M. Mierendorff, H. Tost: *Einführung in die Kunstsoziologie*, Cologne, 1957, p.9.

213 I refer to Deuteronomy 28:13 here.

214 Micah 7:7–10.

215 Address delivered at the European Congress on Evangelism. Published in: *Evangelism Alert*. European Congress on Evangelism, 28 August – 4 September 1971, Amsterdam, the Netherlands. Edited by G.W. Kirby (London: World Wide Publications).

216 Thomas Carlyle, *Sartor Resartus* (1834).

217 P.F. Sloan, 'Eve of destruction'.

218 Cartoon text, *Playboy* (June, 1971).

219 Hutton's law of uniformity: 'No powers are to be employed that are not natural to the globe, no action to be admitted except those of which we know the principle, and no extra-ordinary events to be alleged in order to explain a common experience.' From: *Theory of the Earth* (1785); Lyell summarized it as "the exclusion of all causes not supposed to belong to the present order of Nature', in R.T. Clark and J.D. Bales, *Why Scientists Accept Evolution* (Philadelphia, 1966), pp.11–12.

220 C.S. Lewis, *God in the Dock: Essays on Theology and Ethics*.

221 *Vier glazen: Gedenkboek 1886–1961 van de Societas Studiosorum Reformatorum* (1961) pp.325–338.

222 Holbrook Jackson: *The Eighteen Nineties* (Penguin, 1950, 6th printing) pp.191–193.

223 *Sartor Resartus* (London, 1898) p.222.

224 *Racontars d'un rapin* (Paris, 1951) p.75. For the French text, see Volume 1, note 512.

225 *The Story of Jazz* (1957).

226 See also my *Jazz, Blues and Spirituals*, reproduced in *Complete Works* 2.

227 F. Marc, *Tierschicksale* in Museum Basle.

228 Simon Vinkenoog.

229 J-C. Lambert, *Corneille* (Paris, 1960) p.27.

230 *Museumjournaal* V, 5 (1955) p.95.

231 *Museumjournaal* III, 1 (1957) pp.3 ff.

232 'XXe Siècle', *N.S.* XX, 11 (1958) p.30.

233 Stedelijk Museum of Modern Art, Cat. 81, *De Stijl*, p.48.
234 Stedelijk Museum of Modern Art, Cat. 170 (1957) Duncan.
235 *Museumjournaal*, V, 10 (1960).
236 See the instructive book by L. Febvre, *Le problème de l'incroyance au XVI-ième siècle: La religion de Rabelais* (Paris, 1942).
237 See the Heidelberg Catechism, Sunday 21, answer 54.
238 *NCRV* (1964) pp.59–83; the NCRV is a Dutch Protestant Christian broadcasting company.
239 N. Jacobs (ed.), *Culture for the Millions* (Princeton, 1961) p.xxiv.
240 We have briefly summarized the discussion surrounding the printed book and dealt with it at the very beginning of this article in order to avoid complications. Cf. L. Lowenthal, *Literature, Popular Culture and Society* (New York: Englewood Cliffs, 1961).
241 See my book *Art and Entertainment*, to be found in Part I of this volume.
242 *De Sleutel* 20, 8 (1965) pp.223–226
243 See 'The Artist as a Prophet?' in *Complete Works* 5.
244 *De Reformatie* 27, 49 (1952) pp.390–391; 27, 50 (1952) pp.395–397; 28, 2 (1952) pp.13–15. The title is taken from 1 Peter 1:13.
245 This paper was presented to the Congress for Reformed Students (Liberated, i.e. *Vrijgemaakt*) in Kampen on 8 January 1952. I have made several minor editorial changes for this publication, none drastic in character, and added notes here and there where the discussion that followed the presentation indicated there could be some misunderstanding.
246 What follows I discussed more extensively in the *Calvinistisch Jongelingsblad* of 19 October 1951. See 'We and the Kingdom of God' in *Complete Works* 4.
247 Revelation 12:5.
248 Cf. Deuteronomy 29:5–6.
249 1 John 5:3–4.
250 Cf. also Amos 5:13.
251 Cf. Matthew 10:23.
252 1 Peter 2:15.
253 Colossians 4:5,6.
254 1 Corinthians 15:58.
255 Matthew 24:12.
256 I have in mind here, for example, witnessing to unbelievers about the salvation that may be found in our Lord Jesus Christ through deliverance by his blood, to say no more
257 Deuteronomy 28:13 ['The LORD willl make you the head, not the tail.']. For a good understanding of the Scriptures this chapter is as fundamental as the first chapter of Genesis.
258 Some say that in order to exercise any influence for the better we must possess a certain power, that we must form a cultural power lobby. The question however must be raised whether God asks us to strive for such power and to devote all our resources to that end. In the Scriptures as I see it one finds nowhere a demand that we launch offensive 'cultural' activities directed at the 'unchurched'. The Lord asks of us that we be faithful, which is to say that we walk according to the First and Second great

Commandments, in which all of the Ten Commandments are contained. And then he can make us a head, in part by giving us cultural power – as for example in the time of the Reformation, when scriptural norms such as honesty, reasonableness and the like acquired general validity to the salvation of the entire nation, also the non-Calvinistic part. No 'strategy' thus – let God be the 'strategist', for we can make no far-reaching plans; he holds the future in his hand. Did the Reformers know what the consequences would be of their acts of obedience? Naturally, that is not to say that we must not use our common sense if situations arise in which he gives us opportunities: we must use our talents economically and not waste them. That is, at most, tactics – if people prefer to use military terminology – which Scripture does use almost exclusively defensively and never offensively (cf. Ephesians 6:10–18, for example).

259 What concerns us is after all what the scriptural presuppositions and norms are for working scientifically. It was not our intention to write a prolegomena to science itself here. Thus we shall not address the questions in that area that are being discussed at this moment in our circles – such as the relation of scriptural revelation to the 'phenomenological' knowledge of reality, the question of the 'ground motive', the relation of the various sciences to each other, etc., although we certainly believe that the guidelines for scientific practice we develop here are fraught with consequences for those discussions.

260 To prevent any misunderstanding I want say the following. In the totality of what generally is called science one must distinguish two things. First there is the activity of investigating still unknown facts and sources of knowledge; and second there is science – in the proper sense, as I see it – that aims to investigate relationships, explain patterns, and provide a theoretical account of the 'facts' discovered and thus known as a result of the first activity just mentioned. The first activity 'discloses' our experience, enlarges the scope of our knowledge and aims, with the aid of instruments where appropriate, to bring new areas of reality within the range of our vision (microscopic plants and animals, stars) so that we can then go on to make observations (e.g. as to the reproduction of single-celled organisms, the measuring of the speed of light, etc.). If an expedition visits a particular part of Africa it may return with a tremendous amount of material – meteorological observations, knowledge of flora and fauna, ethnographic artifacts – that must then not only be catalogued but that also pose problems for countless branches of science. It needs no argument that such research is not conducted in an undisciplined manner but that it is conditioned rather by the questions and problems posed; in scientific work the two activities just distinguished are closely interconnected.

For us it is important to notice that the kind of activity that is aimed at disclosing our horizon of experience can offer certainties – e.g., that plankton exists, that the speed of light is thus or so, that the Donation of Constantine was a forgery, that one thing or another happened here or there – but that these are not scientific certainties in the proper sense of the word. Rather, they are certainties, as we called them above, of our experience of reality. Moreover, even in science it is useful to maintain a certain reserve towards the facts 'discovered' in this way – to err is human!

In our argument we have more in mind however the theoretical activity that endeavours to solve the problems with which the data of reality confront the scientist.

261 Jeremiah 9:24.

262 Ephesians 5:17.

263 See *De Reformatie* (Jubileum issue, October 1950). Cf. the statement by a Neo-Kantian like Goedewaagen: 'The artistic experience and the religious experience have no meaning were it not for the fact that the psychology of artistic and religious experience shows what such experience really is' (as cited in H. Fabius, *De geschiedenis als theologisch probleem* (1933) p.45).

264 2 Timothy 2:16; cf. Colossians 2:8.

265 In the matter of the Christian and the movies, one should reflect for example on 1 John 2:15 ff.

266 Ephesians 5:11.

267 Colossians 2:8.

268 Philippians 1:9–10. Especially important here is what we referred to in an earlier note as the disclosure of the horizon of knowledge. Through the study of the past, for example, one can point to important events that shed their light on today's facts, etc. To make little-known or virtually inaccessible data known can be of extraordinary importance.

269 We would not deny that in this regard it can be necessary to seek solutions of our own to certain problems – to the problem of defining value in economics, for example – or to develop insights of our own into various states of affairs. It goes without saying that great professional knowledge is a prerequisite. That was already implicit in the demand that we should do our work as well as possible wherever we find ourselves, including in secular employment.

270 Some are quick to label such a train of thought with the odium 'Anabaptist'. It is an easy but dangerous thing to go about opposing each other by assigning labels. It is better to engage in argumentation with the Scriptures in hand and to refute in a frank way the arguments advanced. After all, this has little to do with the so-called 'old Reformed' (*Oud-Gereformeerde*) movements as these may still be found in some parts of the Netherlands that have a direct historical connection with the sixteenth-century Anabaptists. Cf. the different essays about this in A. Janse: *Leven in het Verbond* (Kampen: Kok). On the other hand one must not forget that the Anabaptists waged the 'struggle for the kingdom of God on this earth' (Münster!) with full consistency. One might therefore perhaps with greater justification pin the label 'Anabaptist' on the offensive (as distinct from defensive) Kuyperian cultural ideal. There is a better way than that of Anabaptist culture avoidance or an equally Anabaptist conquer-the-kingdom-of-God-on-earth-here-and-now approach, namely, the scriptural approach.

271 Ecclesiastes 2:26.

272 Cf. my article in the *Calvinistisch Jongelingsblad*, 25 May and 16 November 1951; see in this volume: 'On Being Salt that Salts' and in *Complete Works* 4: 'Seventeenth-century Dutch Art: Christian Art?'. See further Ezekiel 18:30–32 and Deuteronomy 30:1–10.

273 Matthew 23:29–30.

274 Luke 12:48.

275 I have in mind here the Philosophy of the Cosmonomic Idea. It is therefore good that questions connected with this are to be raised at the next student congress.

276 Thus a Christian academic's choice of the field or problem to be studied should be directly connected with the current circumstances in which the people of God find themselves. Indeed, for a sympathetic church member this is obvious and goes without saying.

277 Romans 10:2.

278 *Opbouw* 6, 29 (1962) pp.231–232, with reference to A. Kalsbeek, G*eloof en Wetenschap.*

279 That in this field something certainly can be said from our side is proved by the 14 September 1962 edition of the well-known American orthodox Protestant journal *Christianity Today.*

280 *Correspondentiebladen van de Vereniging voor Calvinistische Wijsbegeerte* 13, 2 (1949) pp.11–13.

281 See 'The Art of the Fourteenth Century in France' in *Complete Works* 4.

282 Report of the twentieth congress of Ikon on 'Art history between hobby and society: meaning and methods of a science', held at Amsterdam Free University on 2–3 May 1974, pp.25–34.

283 1847; the text of a series of lectures on history delivered in 1845–1846; cf. Harry Van Dyke, *Groen van Prinsterer's Lectures on Unbelief and Revolution* (Jordan Station, Ontario: Wedge Publishing Foundation, 1989; diss, Free University Amsterdam). It contains an abridged translation of *Ongeloof en Revolutie.*

284 *Mededelingen van de Vereniging voor Calvinistische Wijsbegeerte* (1964) pp.9–11.

285 Interview with Prof. Rookmaaker by Wilfred van Leeuwen and Dick Borsje, in the *Newspaper of the Art History Faculty of the Free University*, pp.3–9. Date unknown.

The editor and publishers thank the following institutions for permission to reproduce the b/w plates in this volume:

Copyright Alinari / Art Resource, NY: Plates 4,6,7

Copyright Erich Lessing / Art Resource, NY: Plate 5

Copyright Rijksmuseum, Amsterdam: Plate 2

Copyright A.J. Veldhoen, used with the artist's permission: Plate 8

Copyright Sylvester Jacobs, used with permission: photograph facing title page of Hans Rookmaaker leading a lecture/discussion in the 1970s.

Every effort has been made to trace the sources of all copyright materials used. In the event of an inadvertent omission please contact the publishers to rectify this in subsequent editions.

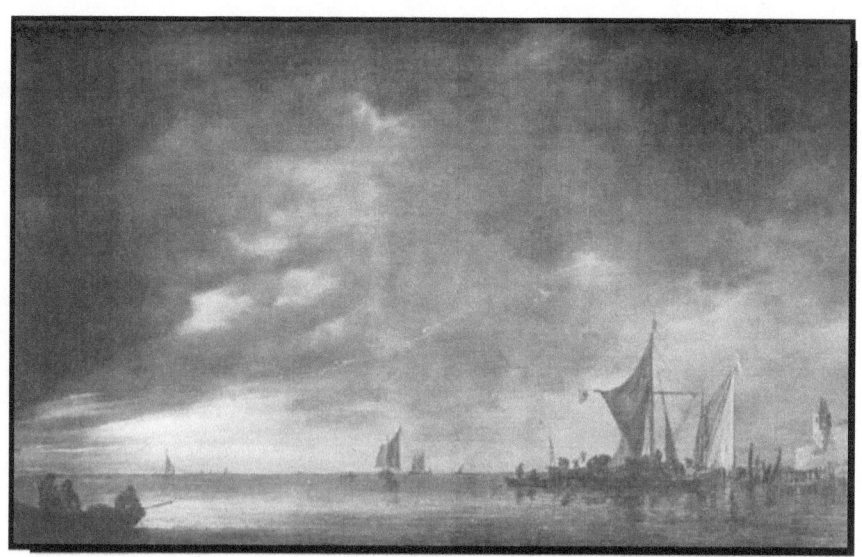

1. Jan van Goyen, *Approaching storm* (1646)

2. Jan Steen, *St Nicholas morning* (c. 1670)

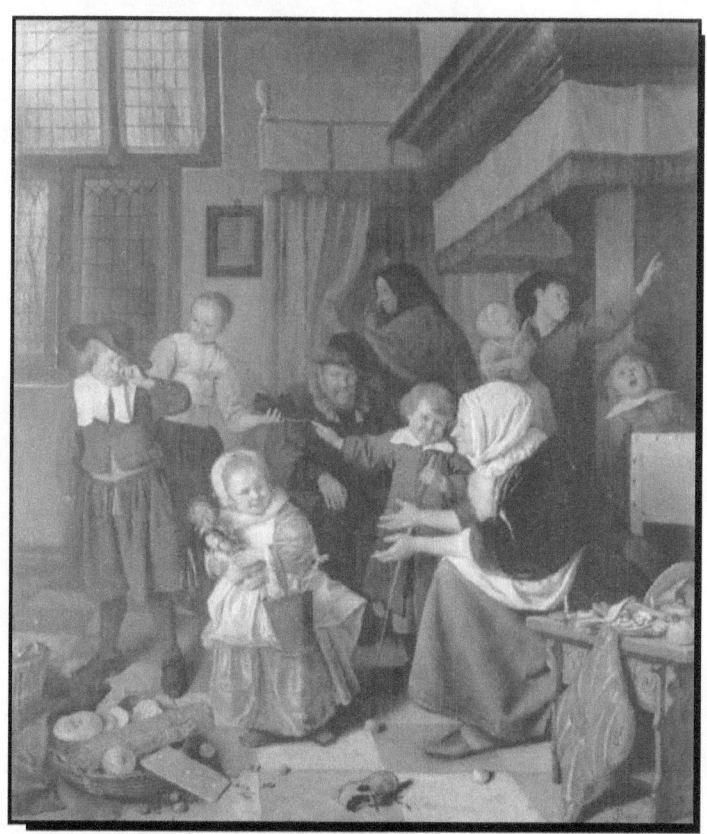

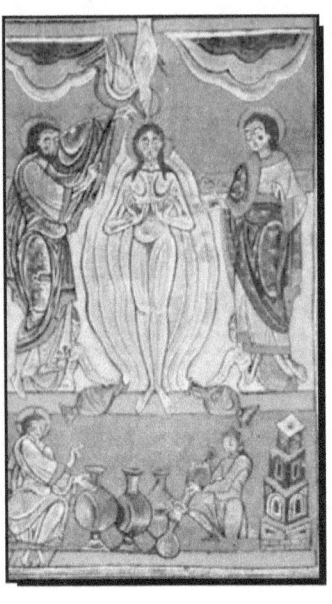

3. *Baptism of Christ*. Miniature (c. 1100)

4. Piero della Francesca, *The baptism of Christ* (c. 1450)

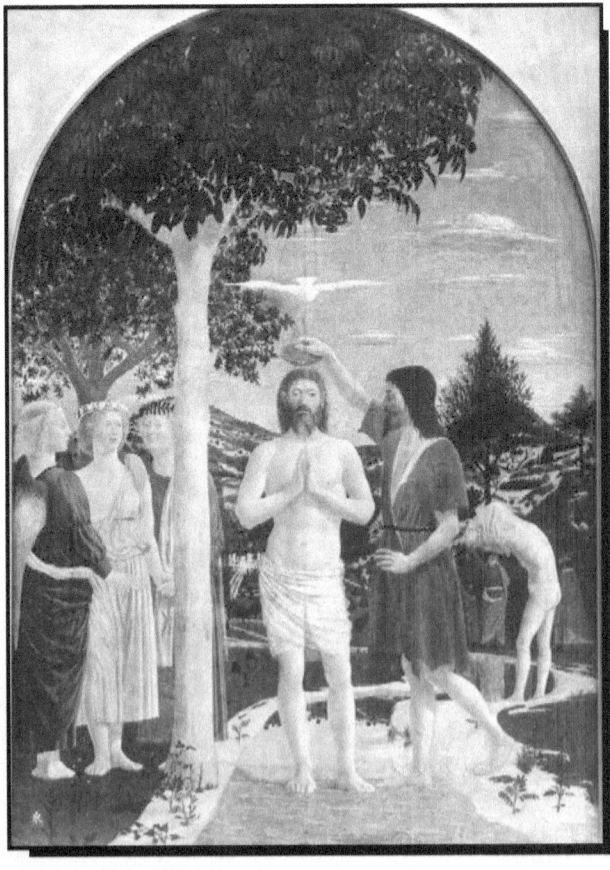

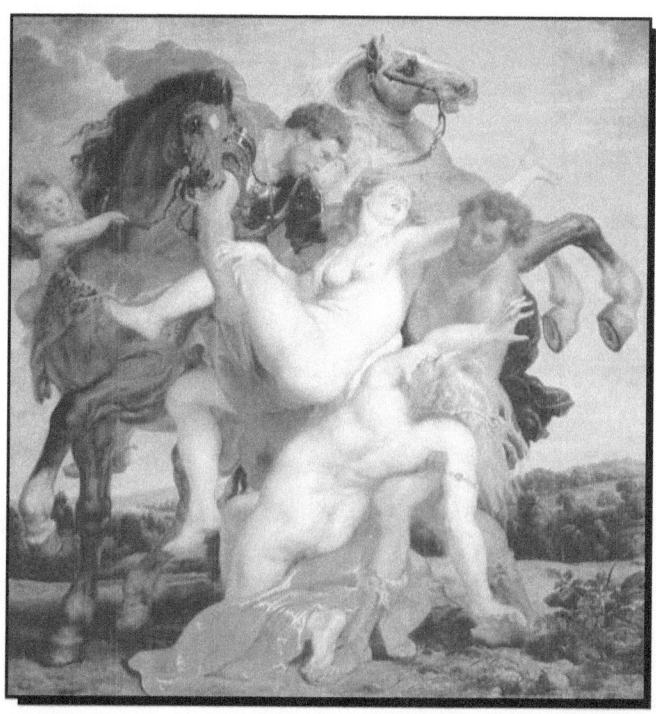

5. P.P. Rubens, *The abduction (rape) of the daughters of Leucippus* (c. 1618)

6. Rembrandt van Rijn, *Bathsheba at her bath* (1654)

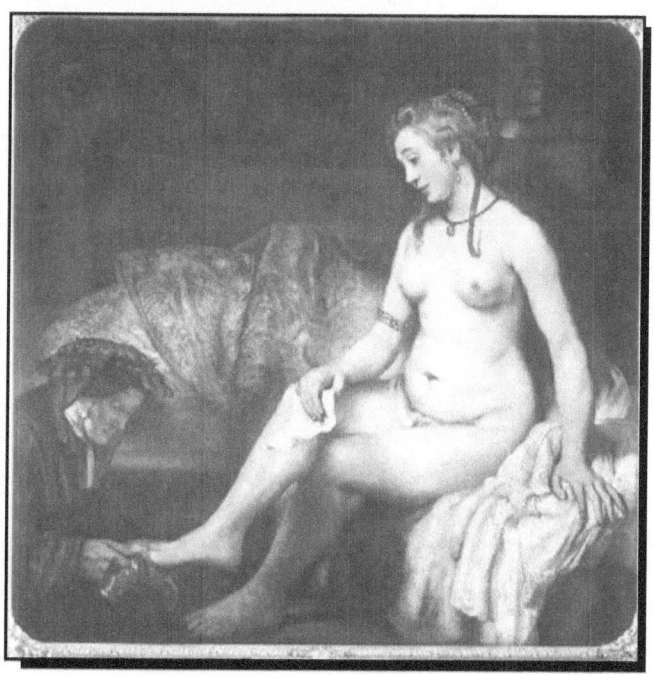

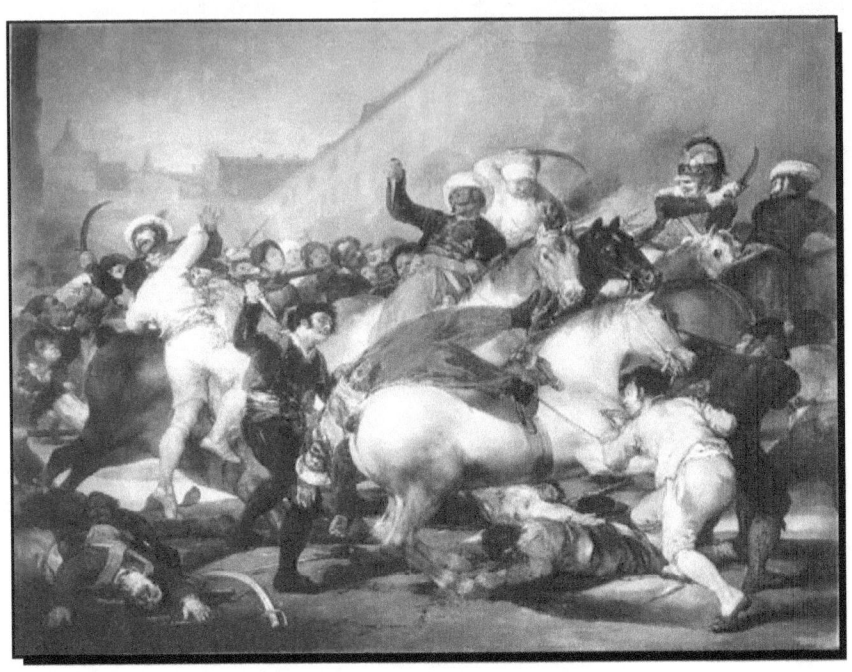

7. Francisco de Goya, *Battle of second of May, 1808* (1814)

8. A.J. Veldhoen, *Fighter pilot* (1654)

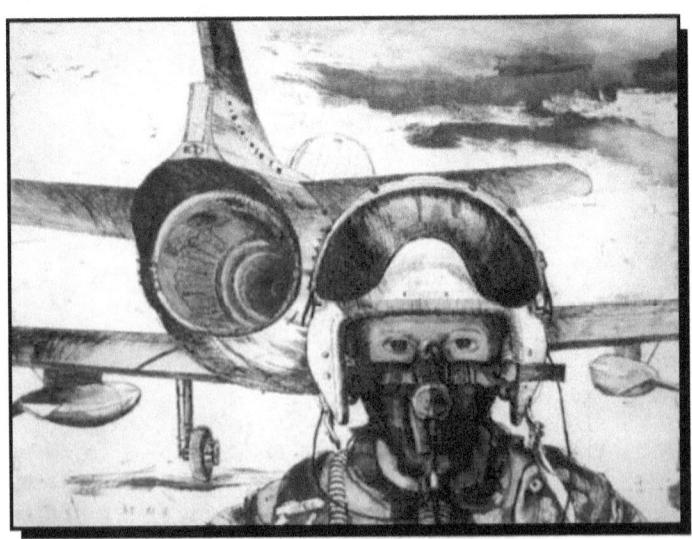

www.ingramcontent.com/pod-product-compliance
Lightning Source LLC
Chambersburg PA
CBHW031602210526
45464CB00004B/1394